WITHDRAWN
UTSA Libraries

WATS 458-4574

BY THE SAME AUTHOR

History
THE NORMANS IN THE SOUTH
THE KINGDOM IN THE SUN, 1120–94
Reissued in one volume:
THE NORMANS IN SICILY

A HISTORY OF VENICE

BYZANTIUM: THE EARLY CENTURIES
BYZANTIUM: THE APOGEE

Travel
MOUNT ATHOS (with Reresby Sitwell)
SAHARA
A TASTE FOR TRAVEL: AN ANTHOLOGY
VENICE: A TRAVELLER'S COMPANION

Miscellaneous
THE ARCHITECTURE OF SOUTHERN ENGLAND
FIFTY YEARS OF GLYNDEBOURNE
CHRISTMAS CRACKERS, 1970–79
MORE CHRISTMAS CRACKERS, 1980–89

BYZANTIUM

The Decline and Fall

JOHN JULIUS NORWICH

Alfred A. Knopf   NEW YORK   1996

University of Texas
El Paso Library

THIS IS A BORZOI BOOK
PUBLISHED BY ALFRED A. KNOPF, INC.

Copyright © 1995 by John Julius Norwich

All rights reserved under International and Pan-American Copyright
Conventions. Published in the United States by Alfred A. Knopf, Inc.,
New York. Distributed by Random House, Inc., New York.
Originally published in Great Britain by Viking, London.

ISBN 0-679-41650-1
LC 95-81164

Manufactured in the United States of America
FIRST AMERICAN EDITION

Library
University of Texas
at San Antonio

Contents

CONTENTS

List of Illustrations

The Virgin and child, flanked by John II Comnenus and the Empress Irene (1118–43), in the south gallery of St Sospia, Istanbul [*e.t. archive*]

Manuel I Comnenus and the Empress Mary of Antioch [*Giraudon*]

A mosiac portrait of Theodore Metochites, presenting the Church to Christ, *c.* 1320, from the Church of St Saviour in Chora (Kariye Camii), Istanbul [*e.t. archive*]

A Byzantine mosiac of Christ Pantocrator, *c.* 1150 Cefalù Cathederal, Sicily [*Scala*]

A Crusader castle, Krak des Chevaliers, Syria *c.* 1140 [*Sonia Halliday Photographs*]

The monastery of the Peribleptos, Mistra, late fourteenth century [*Sonia Halliday Photographs*]

Seljuk architecture: the bridge at Batman, Anatolia, thirteenth century [*Sonia Halliday photographs*]

John VI Cantacuzenus, portrayed as both Emperor and monk [*Bibliotèque Nationale, Paris/Giraudon*]

Marshal de Boucicaut, with St Catherine, from the Boucicaut Hours [*Musée Jacquemart André, Paris/Giraudon*]

The Emperor Frederick Barbarossa [*Vatican Library/Sonia Halliday Photographs*]

The Emperor Manuel II Palaeologus (1391–1425) [*Bibliotèque National/Giraudon*]

John VIII Palaeologus, a medal by Pisanello, 1438 [*Bargello, Florence/Scala*]

The Emperor Andronicus II (?) Palaeologus [*Byzantine Museum, Athens/ Giraudon*]

A Turkish Janissary, by Gentile Bellini, late fourteenth century [*British Museum*]

The Fortress of Rumeli Hisar on the Bosphorus, built by the Sultan Mehmet II in 1452, photographed *c.* 1914 [*AKG London*]

The Land Walls of Constantinople, with the ruins of the Imperial Palace of Blachernae (Tekfur Saray) [*Ancient Art & Architecture Collection*]

St Leonard's Church, Landulph, Cornwall: an inscribed plaque in memory of Theodore Palaeologus, decendant of the last Emperor of Byzantium, 1636 [*Sonia Halliday Photographs*]

Second section of colour plates

The Green Tomb (Yesil Türbe), the mausoleum of Sultan Mehmet I, d. 1421, in Bursa [*Sonia Halliday Photographs*]

The Baptism of Christ, the monastery of the Peribleptos, Mistra, late fourteenth century [*Sonia Halliday photographs*]

Maps

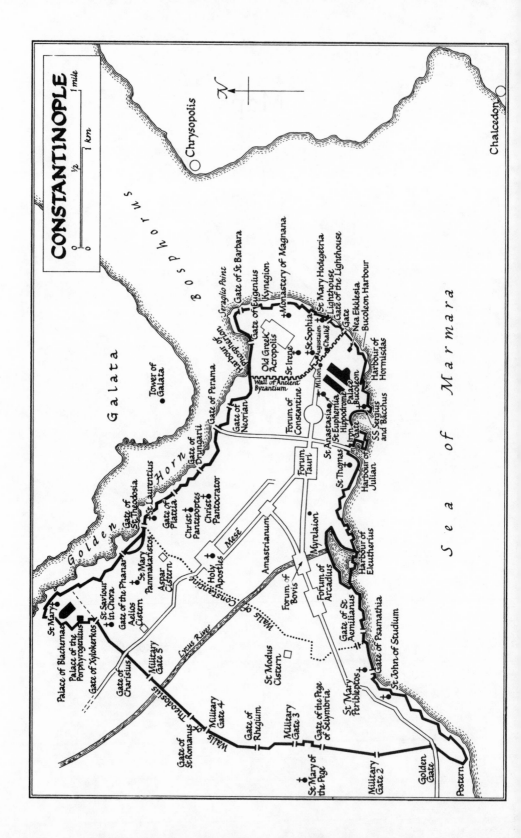

CONSTANTINOPLE

1 mile

½   1 km

0   0

Chrysopolis

Chalcedon

Bosphorus

Galata

Tower of Galata

Golden Horn

Seraglio Point

Gate of St Barbara

Gate of Eugenius
Kynegion

Monastery of Magnana

St Mary Hodegetria

Lighthouse
Gate of the Lighthouse

Gate of Perama

Harbour of Prosphorion

Old Greek Acropolis

St Irene

St Sophia

Chalke

Augusteum

Million

Nea Ekklesia

Bucoleon Harbour

Gate of Neorian

Wall of Ancient Byzantium

Gate of Drungarii

Gate of St Theodosia

St Laurentius

Gate of Plataia

Christ Pantepoptes

Christ Pantocrator

Forum of Constantine

St Anastasia

St Euphemia

Hippodrome

Palace Bucoleon

Harbour of Hormisdas

SS Sergius and Bacchus

Iron Gate

St Thomas

Forum Tauri

Mesé

Amastrianum

Myrelaion

Harbour of Julian

Holy Apostles

Aspar Cistern

St Mary Pammakaristos

St Saviour in Chora

Gate of the Phanari

Aetios Cistern

Walls of Constantine

Lycus River

Forum of Bovis

Forum of Arcadius

Harbour of Eleutherius

Gate of St Aemilianus

Gate of Psamathia

Palace of Blachernae
Palace of the Porphyrogenitus

St Mary
Gate of Xylokerkos

Gate of Charisius

Military Gate 5

Walls of Theodosius

St Modus Cistern

St Mary Periblentos

St John of Studium

Gate of St Romanus

Military Gate 4

Gate of Rhegium

Military Gate 3

Gate of the Page of Selymbria

St Mary of the Page

Military Gate 2

Golden Gate

Postern

Sea of Marmara

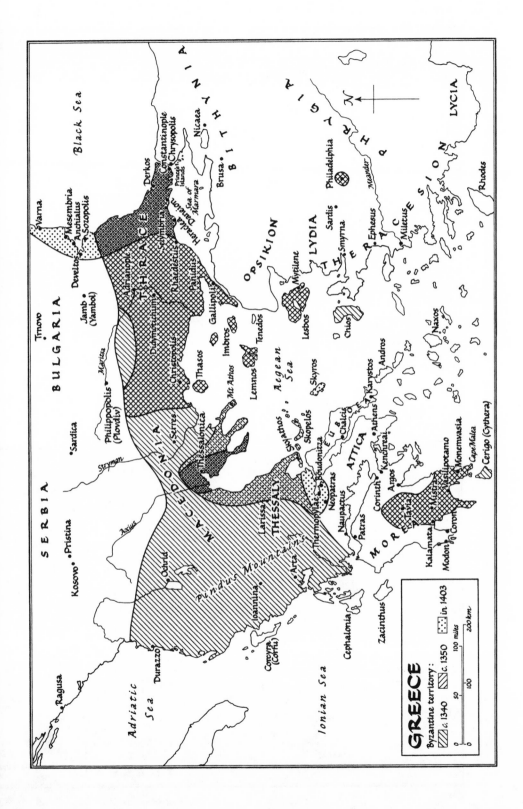

GREECE

Byzantine territory:

c. 1340 | c. 1350 | in 1403

0 50 100 miles

0 100 200 km.

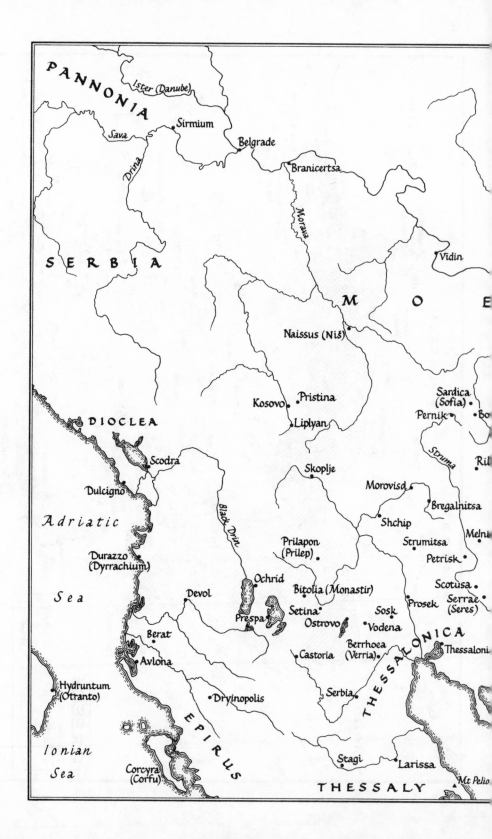

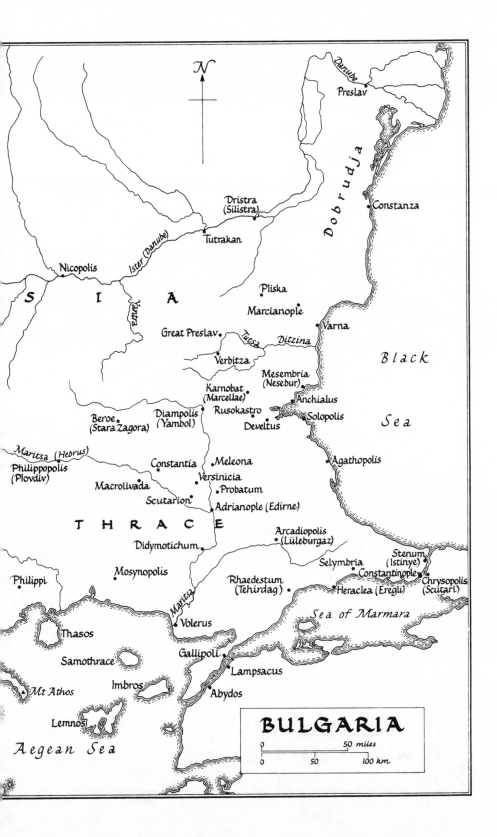

NORICUM PANNONIA

Verona
Aquileia
Padua Tergeste
Venice (Trieste)
Bologna
Ravenna

Florence
Pisa

Perugia

Ostia Rome

Adriatic Sea

Siscia
(Sisak)

Sirmium

Naissus (Niš)

SERBIA

Sigidunum
(Belgrade)

Ister (Danube)

Sava

Sardi
(Sofi

Durazzo
(Dyrrachium)

Ochrid

Thessalonica
of

*Tyrrhenian
Sea*

Naples

Taranto

Avlona

Hydruntum
(Otranto)

Crotone

Coreyra
(Corfu)

DESPOTATE OF EPIRUS

KINGDOM OF

Neopatras
Thermopy
Naupactus D. or

Palermo

SICILY Catania

Syracuse

*Ionian
Sea*

Zacynthus

Elis PR. OF
Corin
Naupli
ACHAIA
Mistra
Pylos Monen
Methoni
Maina

Mediterranea

THE MEDITERRANEAN
WORLD *c.* 1214—1254

Family Trees

THE COMNENI

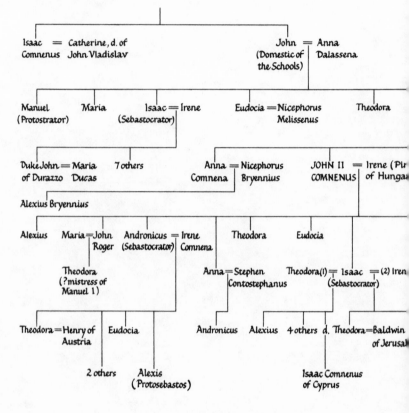

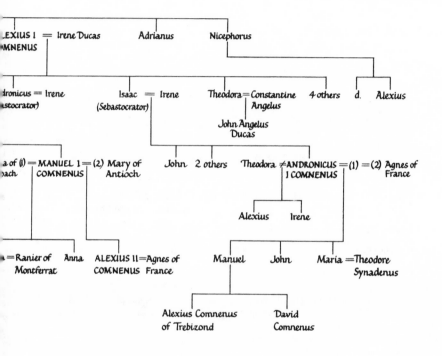

LEXIUS I = Irene Ducas   Adrianus   Nicephorus
MNENUS

dronicus = Irene   Isaac = Irene   Theodora = Constantine   4 others   d.   Alexius
stocrator)   (Sebastocrator)   Angelus

John Angelus
Ducas

a of (1) = MANUEL 1 = (2) Mary of   John   2 others   Theodora ≠ ANDRONICUS = (1) = (2) Agnes of
ach   COMNENUS   Antioch   I COMNENUS   France

Alexius   Irene

= Ranier of   Anna   ALEXIUS II = Agnes of   Manuel   John   Maria = Theodore
Montferrat   COMNENUS France   Synadenus

Alexius Comnenus   David
of Trebizond   Comnenus

THE DYNASTY OF ANGELUS AND THE DESPOTATE OF EPIRUS

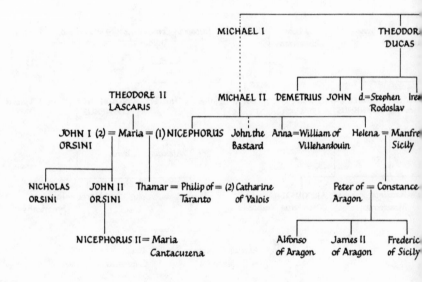

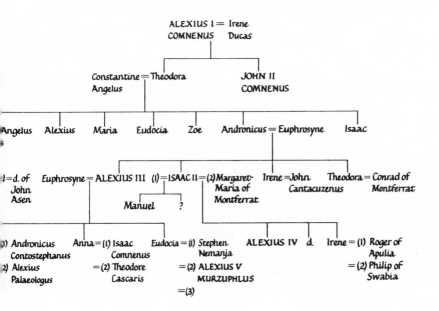

ALEXIUS I = Irene
COMNENUS   Ducas

Constantine = Theodora   JOHN II
Angelus   COMNENUS

Angelus   Alexius   Maria   Eudocia   Zoe   Andronicus = Euphrosyne   Isaac

...l = d. of   Euphrosyne = ALEXIUS III   (1) = ISAAC II = (2) Margaret-   Irene = John   Theodora = Conrad of
John   Maria of   Cantacuzenus   Montferrat
Asen   Manuel   ?   Montferrat

...1) Andronicus   Anna = (1) Isaac   Eudocia = (1) Stephen   ALEXIUS IV   d.   Irene = (1) Roger of
   Contostephanus   Comnenus   Nemanja   Apulia
...2) Alexius   = (2) Theodore   = (2) ALEXIUS V   = (2) Philip of
   Palaeologus   Lascaris   MURZUPHLUS   Swabia
                                               = (3)

THE PRINCES OF ANTIOCH AND KINGS OF SICILY

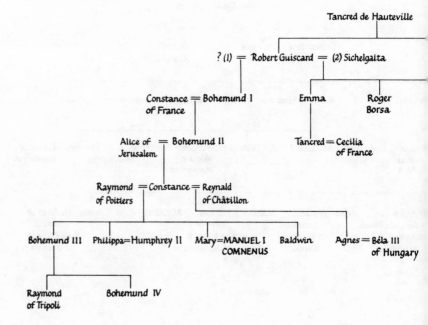

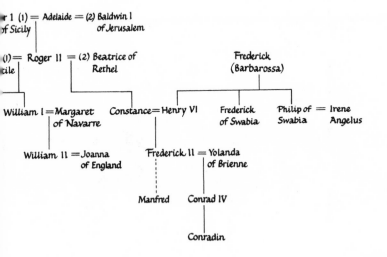

r 1 (1) = Adelaide = (2) Baldwin I
f Sicily   of Jerusalem

(1)= Roger II = (2) Beatrice of   Frederick
tile   Rethel   (Barbarossa)

William I = Margaret   Constance = Henry VI   Frederick   Philip of = Irene
              of Navarre   of Swabia   Swabia   Angelus

    William II = Joanna   Frederick II = Yolanda
                 of England   of Brienne

              Manfred   Conrad IV

                           Conradin

THE LASCARIS DYNASTY OF NICAEA

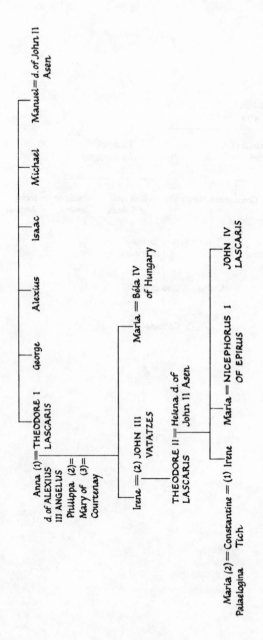

THE LATIN EMPERORS AT CONSTANTINOPLE

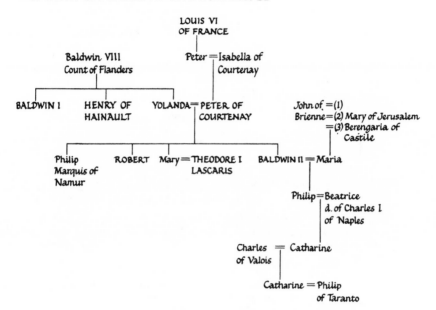

LOUIS VI
OF FRANCE

Baldwin VIII
Count of Flanders

Peter = Isabella of
Courtenay

BALDWIN I   HENRY OF   YOLANDA = PETER OF   John of = (1)
             HAINAULT   COURTENAY   Brienne = (2) Mary of Jerusalem
                                                                = (3) Berengaria of
                                                                       Castile

        Philip   ROBERT   Mary = THEODORE I   BALDWIN II = Maria
        Marquis of   LASCARIS
        Namur

                                                      Philip = Beatrice
                                                               d. of Charles I
                                                               of Naples

                              Charles = Catharine
                              of Valois

                                     Catharine = Philip
                                                 of Taranto

THE CANTACUZENI

JOHN VI = Irene
CANTACUZENUS Asen

Matthew I = Irene   Manuel   Andronicus   Maria = NICEPHORUS II   Helena = JOHN V
           Palaeologina Despot of   OF EPIRUS   PALAEOLOGUS
                         the Morea
                                                             Theodora = Orhan

THE PALAEOLOGI

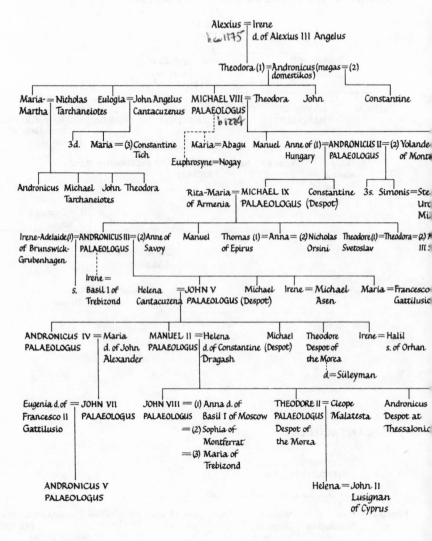

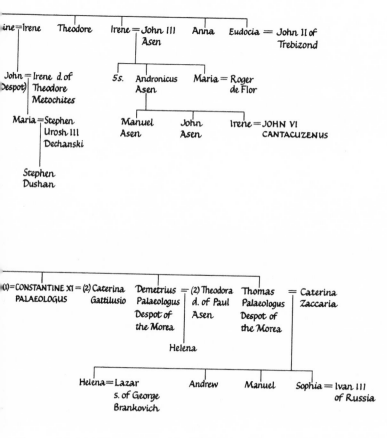

...ine=Irene   Theodore   Irene=John III   Anna   Eudocia = John II of
                                  Asen   Trebizond

John = Irene d. of   5s.   Andronicus   Maria = Roger
Despot)   Theodore   Asen   de Flor
         Metochites

Maria = Stephen   Manuel   John   Irene = JOHN VI
       Urosh III   Asen   Asen   CANTACUZENUS
       Dechanski

Stephen
Dushan

...(1) = CONSTANTINE XI = (2) Caterina   Demetrius = (2) Theodora   Thomas   = Caterina
   PALAEOLOGUS   Gattilusio   Palaeologus   d. of Paul   Palaeologus   Zaccaria
                                     Despot of   Asen   Despot of
                                     the Morea   the Morea

                                         Helena

Helena = Lazar   Andrew   Manuel   Sophia = Ivan III
      s. of George   of Russia
      Brankovich

Acknowledgements

My thanks, as always, to the staff of the London Library, without whose unfailing help and sympathy this book and its two predecessors could never have been written. I also owe a particular debt of gratitude to Judith Flanders, for her eagle eye, computer memory and flawless ear for the rhythm of language; and to Douglas Matthews, for compiling yet another immaculate index.

Introduction

It was on the day or rather the night of the 27th of June 1787, between the hours of eleven and twelve that I wrote the last lines of the last page in a summerhouse in my garden. After laying down my pen, I took several turns in a *berceau* or covered walk of Acacias which commands a prospect of the country, the lake and the mountains. The air was temperate, the sky was serene; the silver orb of the moon was reflected from the waters, and all Nature was silent. I will not dissemble the first emotions of joy on the recovery of my freedom and perhaps the establishment of my fame. But my pride was soon humbled, and a sober melancholy was spread over my mind by the idea that I had taken my everlasting leave of an old and agreeable companion, and that, whatsoever might be the future date of my history, the life of the historian must be short and precarious.

So wrote Edward Gibbon, describing the moment when he finally completed *The History of the Decline and Fall of the Roman Empire*. Let no one think that I should dream of comparing my own modest attempt to tell the story of Byzantium with the greatest historical masterpiece of English literature; but it happens that after I typed the final full stop to this trilogy, at precisely 11.30 on a sultry July evening, I too walked out alone into a moonlit garden. And though I cannot pretend that my view was as spectacular as Gibbon's – or that I ever contemplated the establishment of my fame – I found that I could share at least one of the emotions that he describes. Now that my work is done I too feel that I am saying goodbye to an old and valued friend.

The first part of this trilogy told the story of the Empire of Byzantium from its foundation by the Emperor Constantine the Great on Monday, 12 May 330 A D, to the establishment of its imperial Christian rival, the Holy Roman Empire, with the coronation of Charlemagne on Christmas Day, 800. The second followed its fortunes through the dazzling dynasty of the Macedonians to the apogee of its power under the terrible Basil II *Bulgaroctonus*, the Bulgar-Slayer, but ended on a note of ill omen: the first of the three great defeats of Byzantine history, suffered at the hands of the Seljuk Turks at Manzikert in 1071. This third and last volume shows just how fateful that defeat was to be, robbing the Empire of most of Asia Minor – the principal source of its manpower – weakening it and impoverishing it to the point where, rather more than a century later, it was powerless to resist the onslaught of the Fourth Crusade. The fifty-six years of Latin rule that followed, ending with the triumphant return of Michael VIII Palaeologus, seem at first sight to have been little more than an unedifying interlude; in fact they proved to be the second blow from which Byzantium never recovered. The story of the Empire's last two centuries, seen against the background of the growing power of the Turkish House of Othman, is one of helpless decline and makes, I fear, occasionally painful reading. Only the final chapter, tragic as it is, once again lifts the spirit – as all tales of heroism must inevitably do.

In the Introduction to the first of these volumes I mentioned how forcibly I had been struck by the difference, from the point of view of a writer, between the history of the Byzantine Empire and that of the previous object of my attention, the Republic of Venice. As the centuries pass, these two histories become ever more intertwined, both before and after the tragedy of 1204–5, with the Serenissima becoming guilty of what might almost be described as a second betrayal – this time by apathy – in the final years of the Empire's existence; and it consequently seems worth while to press the comparison a little further. At first glance, the two have much in common. Venice was after all the child of Byzantium, and spent her formative years as a Byzantine colony, with all her early cultural influences coming directly from Constantinople. Both mother and daughter were of such beauty and opulence as to become legends – fabled across the world as cities of marble and malachite and porphyry, reputations so near the truth that many, seeing them for the first time, declared in amazement that the half had not been told them. Both endured for well over a thousand years – a period comfortably longer than that which separates us from William the Conqueror. Both, on occasion, wielded immense political power, and gained for themselves sinister reputations – deserved or not – for cruelty, duplicity and intrigue. Finally, both lasted too long and were obliged to suffer a slow and humiliating decline.

But there the similarities end. Venice was a republic, and although technically an oligarchy was in fact a good deal more democratic than any other nation – with the arguable exception of Switzerland – in the world; God-fearing in her way, she was throughout her history resolutely opposed to any interference of the Church in her internal affairs, braving more than one papal interdict in consequence. Byzantium was somewhere between an autocracy and a theocracy, absolute power being vested in an Emperor who was himself the representative of the godhead on earth – *isapostolos*, the Equal of the Apostles. Venice was materialistic, hard-faced, down-to-earth; Byzantium was the most spiritually-orientated temporal state the Christian world has ever known, the Holy See not excluded. Venice, set amid the still, shallow waters of her lagoon, enjoyed a physical security unique in continental Europe; Constantinople lived under almost perpetual threat of attack. In her last, sad centuries, Venice gave herself over to the pursuit of pleasure and a degree of mild debauchery, finally surrendering to the young Napoleon in the most humiliating circumstances conceivable, firing not a single shot in her own defence. Byzantium, on the other hand, kept her soul intact. Three times in the last two hundred years, her Emperors sought to buy security by submitting her Church to Rome; but the people of Constantinople never wavered from their ancient and traditional faith. And when their time came they fought to the end for fifty-five desperate days, ten thousand against a quarter of a million, their last Emperor dying heroically on the battlements as the city's defences, so long believed impregnable, finally collapsed around him.

Readers of the first two volumes of this history will not need to be reminded that it is in no sense a scholarly work. The four years of ancient Greek that constituted an important part of my public-school education have not enabled me to read the simplest of Greek texts without a lexicon at my elbow; I have consequently been forced to rely almost entirely on those authorities of whose work there exist either translations or summaries in secondary sources. This has in fact been less of a hindrance than I expected; particularly for the centuries covered by this present volume, these secondary sources are so copious that the difficulty has been less one of obtaining information than of selecting it. Besides, the need to cover a period of nearly twelve hundred years – since for the sake of clarity the curtain must rise some time before the Empire really begins and for that of tidiness it must fall a few years after it ends – in roughly as many pages means that at all costs the story has to be kept moving, and I make no pretence of doing anything more than skating over the surface of my subject – an activity which is, by its very definition, the negation of scholarship.

But I am unrepentant. My aim has never been to cast new light on history. Since the day I put pen to paper, I have had two purposes only in mind. The first has been to make some small amends for that centuries-old conspiracy of silence that I remarked upon in the Introduction to the first volume: a conspiracy thanks to which countless generations of Western Europeans have passed through our various educational systems with virtually no knowledge of the longest-lived – and, perhaps, the most continuously inspired – Christian Empire in the history of the world. The second has been quite simply to tell a good story, as interestingly and as accurately as I can, to the non-specialized reader. I cannot hope that that reader, having reached the end of this final volume, will lay it down with the same regret that I feel on the completion of a long yet wholly enjoyable task; but he will, I trust, at least agree with me that the tale was worth the telling.

John Julius Norwich
Castle Combe, July 1994

A Note on Names and Transliteration

Consistency has always seemed to me a greatly overrated virtue, and I have made little or no effort to preserve it where the spelling of proper names is concerned. In general I have preferred the Latin versions to the Greek – Thessalonica for Thessaloniki, Palaeologus for Palaiologos, etc. – on the grounds that they will probably be more familiar to English readers. Where the Greek spelling has seemed more suitable, however, I have not hesitated to use it.

I have found the Turkish undotted i (ı) beyond me – not only because I speak no Turkish, but also because English readers almost invariably blame the publishers for defective type. I hope my Turkish friends will also forgive me for referring to Constantinople throughout, rather than Istanbul. As Sir Steven Runciman once wrote in a similar context, it would have been pedantic to do otherwise.

A Note on Names and Transliteration

I

The Rise of Alexius

[1081]

We have prepared a very fine dish, not without a rich, savoury sauce. If you would like to share in our feast, come as soon as you can and sit with us at this supreme banquet.

Alexius and Isaac Comnenus to the Caesar John Ducas, February 1081.
The Alexiad, II, 6

On Easter Sunday, 4 April 1081, in the Great Church of St Sophia at Constantinople, the twenty-four-year-old general Alexius Comnenus formally ascended the throne of a sad and shattered Empire. It was now ten years since that Empire had suffered at the hands of the Seljuk Turks, just outside the little garrison town of Manzikert a few miles to the north of Lake Van, the most disastrous defeat in all its history: a defeat which had resulted in the capture of the Emperor Romanus IV Diogenes, the ignominious flight of the once-invincible Byzantine army and the gradual spread of the conquerors across Anatolia until some 30,000 square miles of the imperial heartland had been overrun by Turkoman tribesmen. At a stroke, Byzantium had lost the source of much of its food supply and most of its manpower. Its very survival was now in doubt.

Had Romanus been allowed to continue as *basileus* once his liberty had been restored, he might have done much to redeem the situation. The Seljuk Sultan Alp Arslan, preoccupied as he was by the far greater threat to his people presented by the Fatimid Caliph of Egypt, had no real quarrel with the Empire. He and Romanus had got on surprisingly well together, and the treaty which they had concluded as the price of the latter's freedom made no extensive territorial demands. But Romanus was overthrown by a palace revolution in Constantinople and, after a brief and unsuccessful attempt to regain his throne by force, was blinded so brutally that he died soon afterwards; the treaty was abrogated by his pathetic successor Michael VII – cultivated and intelligent, but utterly unfit for the throne – and by Michael's two *éminences grises*, his uncle the Caesar John Ducas and the scholar Michael Psellus; and the way was open for the Seljuks to do as they liked.

In the West, the horizon was equally black. On 16 April 1071 – just four months before Manzikert, but after a siege of nearly three years – the Normans of South Italy under their brilliant brigand of a leader Robert Guiscard had captured Bari. For over five centuries – since the time of Justinian – Bari had been an imperial city. Formerly the capital of a rich and prosperous province, in recent years it had become the Empire's only remaining outpost in the peninsula, the centre of a tiny enclave from which the banners of Byzantium fluttered alone in a turbulent and hostile land. On that day, the Saturday before Palm Sunday, those banners were struck – effectively for the last time. Henceforth, the phrase 'Byzantine Italy' would be a contradiction in terms. The following year had seen a dangerous uprising in Bulgaria, in the course of which a certain Constantine Bodin, son of Prince Michael of Zeta,[1] had been crowned Tsar in the city of Prizren; order had finally been restored – at considerable cost – but revolution was in the air and no one doubted that there would be more trouble before long.

Finally there was the problem of Rome. The Emperor Michael, in another sublime demonstration of political misjudgement, had appealed to Pope Gregory VII after the fall of Bari for help against the Norman menace; he was consequently in a poor position to object when Gregory began openly extending his influence over the eastern shores of the Adriatic – crowning a vassal named Demetrius Zvonimir King of Croatia in 1075 and bestowing a second – papal – crown on Michael of Zeta two years later. Meanwhile both the Hungarians and the barbarian Pechenegs had gone back to their old tricks, throwing the whole Balkan peninsula back into chaos.

With disasters like these occurring on every side, it was little wonder that various sections of the army should have broken out, not once but several times, in open revolt. The first insurrection had been led by a Norman soldier of fortune named Roussel of Bailleul, who had attempted to set up an independent Norman state in central Anatolia, much as his compatriots had recently done in South Italy. Roussel had been finally brought to heel by Alexius Comnenus, and after a brief spell in prison had subsequently fought at Alexius's side against two more claimants:

---

1 Zeta (formerly known as Dioclea, and a semi-independent principality within the Empire) had rebelled in about 1035 and had since refused to recognize Byzantine suzerainty.

Nicephorus Bryennius, *dux* of Durazzo – one of the few officers to have distinguished himself at Manzikert – and an elderly member of the Anatolian military aristocracy named Nicephorus Botaneiates. In November 1077 Bryennius actually reached the walls of Constantinople before being driven back into Thrace; Botaneiates too made preparations for a direct attack on the capital, but in the event it was to prove unnecessary. In March 1078 riots broke out; Michael, totally unable to deal with them, fled for his life and sought refuge in the monastery of the Studium; and on the 24th of the month Botaneiates entered Constantinople in triumph. Faced as he was with a *fait accompli*, Alexius had no choice but to submit to the new Emperor, who granted him the personal rank of *nobilissimus* and the office of Domestic of the Schools, or commander-in-chief, in which capacity he was immediately sent off to deal with Bryennius. A few months later he brought back his second insurgent general captive to Constantinople; but instead of being received with gratitude as he expected, he was barely allowed to enter the city and was immediately ordered back to Anatolia, where another insurrection was already brewing. As for Bryennius, he was thrown into the palace dungeons where, shortly afterwards, his eyes were put out.

Alexius, while obeying his orders, made no secret of his displeasure at the coldness of his reception, the reason for which he perfectly understood. Nicephorus Botaneiates was afraid, as well he might be. The old man – he was already well into his seventies – had already lost control. Over the next two years the Empire slipped further and further into chaos. Revolt followed insurrection; insurrection followed revolt. The Turks advanced relentlessly, until by 1080 Alp Arslan's son Malik-Shah had extended the Seljuk Sultanate of Rum till it covered all Asia Minor from Cilicia to the Hellespont. Meanwhile Nicephorus grew daily more unpopular. Previous usurpers – Nicephorus Phocas for example, or John Tzimisces, or Romanus Diogenes – had all claimed to be the guardians of such of their predecessors' children as they found to be their titular co-Emperors, thus giving themselves some slight semblance of legality; Botaneiates on the other hand had made no attempt to associate Michael VII's four-year-old son Constantine with him on the throne and so remained, in the eyes of all right-thinking Byzantines, morally beyond the pale. Even more insensitively, on the death of his second wife soon after his accession, he had married the ravishing Empress Mary of Alania[1] – more beautiful even, writes Anna Comnena,

---

1 She was the daughter of Bagrat IV of Georgia, and had married Michael Ducas in 1065.

than the statues of Pheidias – despite the fact that her husband Michael was still alive. True, she had of necessity been cast off when her husband had entered his monastery; but such alliances were understandably frowned on by the clergy, while third marriages of any kind had been condemned by St Basil himself as 'moderated fornication' and carried the penalty for both parties of no less than four years' denial of the Sacrament.[1] In his vain attempts to buy back the support that he had so unnecessarily lost, Nicephorus had virtually emptied the imperial treasury; and inflation, which had already begun under Michael VII,[2] spiralled more dizzily than ever. Without a stronger hand at the helm, there could be no hope for Byzantium.

Meanwhile, as the popularity of Nicephorus declined, so that of Alexius Comnenus steadily grew, until he was generally looked upon in Constantinople and beyond as the only possible saviour of the Empire. He had first seen action under his elder brother Manuel during the expedition against the Seljuk Turks in 1070, when he was fourteen;[3] since then, whether fighting against the Turks or against Byzantine rebels, he had never lost a battle. He had proved himself a superb general, and because he had led them again and again to victory his soldiers loved and trusted him. But Alexius had other qualifications too, just as important in Byzantine eyes. He came from imperial stock, his uncle Isaac Comnenus having briefly occupied the throne some twenty years before; his mother, the immensely ambitious Anna Dalassena, was known to have brought up each of her five sons – of whom Alexius was the third – in the belief that he might one day become Emperor. Moreover his marriage to Irene, granddaughter of the Caesar John Ducas and daughter of that Andronicus Ducas who had so shamefully betrayed Romanus Diogenes at Manzikert,[4] assured him the support not only of the richest and most

---

1 For more about plural marriages, and in particular the *four* marriages of the Emperor Leo the Wise, see *Byzantium: The Apogee*, Chapter 8.

2 He was popularly known as *Parapinaces*, or 'Minus-a-quarter', since the gold *nomisma*, after having remained stable for more than five hundred years, was said to have lost a quarter of its value during his reign. (See *Byzantium: The Apogee*, p. 359.)

3 According, that is, to his daughter Anna Comnena (*The Alexiad*, I, i), whose biography of her father is the fullest – and by far the most entertaining – contemporary record that we possess. Zonaras, on the other hand, claims that when Alexius died in 1118 he was seventy; if so, he would have been born in 1048, and by 1070 would already have been twenty-two. Anna's testimony is not always to be trusted, but such early baptisms of fire were not unusual in the Middle Ages and in this case we can probably accept her word. She was, after all, in a far better position to know.

4 See *Byzantium: The Apogee*, pp. 352–3.

4

influential family in the Empire but of the clergy (whose Patriarch until his death in 1075 was John Xiphilinus, a Ducas protégé) and most of the aristocracy as well.

For these very reasons, however, Alexius had enemies at court; it was here above all that he needed a champion, and he found one in the Empress herself. Mary had no love for her new husband, who was after all old enough to be her grandfather. As the former wife of Michael VII, her first loyalty was to the Ducas family, of which Alexius was a member by marriage. Perhaps she knew that (as the contemporary chronicler John Zonaras reports) two of her husband's cronies, a sinister pair of barbarian origin named Borilus and Germanus, were plotting to destroy the young general, and felt it her duty to protect him; possibly too, aware that her husband was considering naming a distant relation as his successor, she was trying to safeguard the interests of her son Constantine. It may even be – and subsequent events were to lend the theory additional weight – that she had fallen in love with Alexius, and saw herself in the role of Theophano to his Tzimisces.[1] Any of these hypotheses may be true, or none of them; we have no means of telling. All we know is that, some time in 1080, Mary of Alania adopted Alexius Comnenus as her son.

Botaneiates seems to have made no protest. A weak man, utterly dominated by his wife, he seems by now to have been quietly sinking into senility. Far from raising any objections, towards the end of the year he rather surprisingly appointed his adoptive son-in-law to lead a new campaign against the Turks, who had recently captured Cyzicus. This was just the opportunity Alexius needed. For some time already he had been convinced that the doddering old Emperor must be removed before it was too late, preferably – since he was reluctant to contemplate assassination – by straightforward military means. The problem had been to rally the necessary troops without arousing suspicions. Now, at a stroke, that problem had been swept away. He immediately gave orders that the army should be summoned to the little village of Tsouroulos, some distance outside the capital on the Adrianople road.

For Borilus and Germanus, Mary's adoption of Alexius and his new appointment could hardly have been more unwelcome. They saw their old enemy in a stronger position than ever, able as a member of the imperial family to go in and out of the palace as he pleased, in daily contact with the Emperor and – more dangerous still – the Empress, whose spies were everywhere and who could keep him informed of all

1 Op. cit., pp. 207–10.

that went on. When they heard of the mobilization of the army they realized that their only chance was to act at once. But Alexius, forewarned, was too quick for them. In the early hours of Quinquagesima Sunday, 14 February 1081, he and his brother Isaac silently made their way to the Palace of Blachernae, where the great Land Walls at their northern end slope down to the Golden Horn, and forced their way into the imperial stables. There they took the horses they needed, hamstrung the rest to prevent their being used for pursuit, and galloped away at top speed. Their first destination was the so-called Cosmidion, the monastery of SS. Cosmas and Damian at the northern end of the Golden Horn, where they alerted Alexius's mother-in-law Maria Traiana Ducas, and, chancing to meet the rich and powerful George Palaeologus, husband of Irene's sister Anna, enlisted his help also.[1] They then hurried on to Tsouroulos, where mobilization was almost complete, and dispatched an appeal to the Caesar John to come to their aid.

The Caesar was now living in retirement on his estate at Moroboundos, some miles away. He was taking his afternoon siesta when the messenger arrived, but was roused by his little grandson with the news of the revolt. At first he refused to believe it and boxed the boy's ears; then the message was handed to him. According to Anna Comnena, it contained the thinly veiled invitation quoted at the head of this chapter; and that, for John Ducas, was enough. He called for his horse and set off at once for Tsouroulos. Before long he met an imperial tax collector, on his way back to Constantinople with a considerable quantity of gold for the Treasury, whom he somehow persuaded to accompany him. Later he encountered a group of Turks; they too agreed, in return for the promise of large rewards, to join the rebellion. Not surprisingly, the full party received a jubilant welcome when it reached the waiting army.

After two or three more days – during which several other important adherents rallied to the cause – Alexius and Isaac gave the order to march. Up to this moment, surprisingly enough, there seems to have been no suggestion of acclaiming a new Emperor; only when they

---

1 Chalandon (*Essai sur le règne d'Alexis Ier Comnène*) refuses to accept that this meeting was an accident. If so, he argues, why – as Anna Comnena specifically reports (*The Alexiad*, Book II) – did George Palaeologus, by his own admission, have all his movable wealth with him? Is it not more likely that the whole thing had been carefully planned in advance, and that George was in fact an accomplice from the beginning? What Anna actually reports, however, is that this wealth had been deposited with the monastery. She does not seem to see anything surprising in this and nor, I think, should we. She adds that Palaeologus was at first most reluctant to give the Comneni his support, and that he finally did so only at the insistence of his mother-in-law. Why, at such a moment, should he have feigned opposition if it were not genuine?

stopped for the night at the little village of Schiza was the question put to the army, and even then in the form of a choice: whom would they prefer as *basileus*, Alexius or Isaac? It was not altogether the foregone conclusion that might have been imagined: Isaac – who was after all the elder, and whose military successes in the East had already earned him the Dukedom of Antioch – had plenty of champions among the soldiers. But he himself seemed happy to defer to his brother, and the influence of the Ducas family finally carried the day. Alexius was enthusiastically acclaimed with the imperial titles and, there and then, formally shod with the purple buskins, embroidered in gold with the double-headed eagles of Byzantium, which were reserved for the Emperor – and which, we can only assume, he had prudently abstracted from the palace before leaving.

The new claimant and his brother were not the only members of their family in revolt against Botaneiates. On the very day of the ceremony at Schiza, their brother-in-law Nicephorus Melissenus – husband of their sister Eudocia – had drawn up his own rebel army at Chrysopolis,[1] immediately opposite Constantinople on the Asiatic shore of the Bosphorus. Having just arrived from distant Anatolia, Nicephorus had till then heard nothing of their activities; when he did, he at once sent a letter to Alexius suggesting that they should divide the Empire between them, one taking the East, the other the West. Alexius had no intention of sharing his Empire with anyone; fearing, however, that a categorical refusal might induce his brother-in-law to make common cause with Botaneiates against him, he deliberately prevaricated with a non-committal reply. Meanwhile he pressed on with all speed to the capital.

He was still uncertain of his next step. There could obviously be no question of a siege: having himself defended Constantinople against the forces of Bryennius three and a half years before, he knew that those great triple ramparts could withstand forces far greater than any that he might fling against them. A day or two's careful reconnaissance with the Caesar, however, suggested to him that although certain of the regiments defending the various sections of the walls (the Varangian Guard, for example, or the so-called 'Immortals') could be trusted to fight to the death for the reigning Emperor, others might prove susceptible to blandishments of one kind or another – most notably the regiment made

---

1 The modern Üsküdar – the Turkish form of the Greek Scutari, to which the city's name was changed in the twelfth century after the construction of the imperial palace of Scutarion.

up of Germanic tribesmen who guarded the Adrianople Gate. Somehow George Palaeologus managed to make contact with their leader, and the matter was soon settled. One evening, just as darkness had begun to fall, he and a few followers put ladders against one of the German-held towers and slipped over the bastion; then, under cover of night, Alexius concentrated his entire force at the foot of the tower. By daybreak all was ready. Palaeologus, standing high on the wall, gave the signal; his men opened the gates from within; and the rebel army poured into Constantinople.

It met with little resistance. The citizens had scant love or respect for their old Emperor. A good many of them must have known that he was bound to be deposed sooner or later, and were probably only too happy to see him replaced by an energetic and popular young general. What they did not expect was to be treated like a conquered enemy; but the barbarian element in Alexius's army was too strong, and quickly infected the rest. No sooner were the soldiers inside the walls than they scattered in all directions, looting, pillaging and raping; before long they were joined by the local riff-raff, and confusion quickly spread throughout the city, to the point where the success of the whole operation seemed in doubt and those who had remained loyal to the legitimate Emperor began to wonder whether the insurgents might not after all be defeated. One of these was Nicephorus, father of George Palaeologus, who had been horrified by his son's defection; another was Alexius's old enemy Borilus, who seems to have possessed some kind of military command and who now drew up the Varangian Guard, with such other units as could be implicitly relied on, in close order between the Forum of Constantine and the Milion.[1]

Botaneiates himself, on the other hand, knew that he was beaten. An attempt to enlist the services of Melissenus and his men had been frustrated by the imperial fleet, which had been won over by George Palaeologus and now blocked the straits, and he no longer possessed the will to resist. The aged and much-respected Patriarch Cosmas was imploring him to abdicate in order to avoid the shedding of any more Christian blood; in fact, he needed little persuasion. His first offer, brought to the Comneni by Nicephorus Palaeologus, was that he should adopt Alexius as his son, make him his co-Emperor and surrender to

---

1 The 'First Milestone' – in fact a set of four triumphal arches forming a square – from which all the distances in the Empire were measured. It stood some hundred yards south-west of St Sophia. See *Byzantium: The Early Centuries*, p. 65.

him all effective authority, retaining only his imperial title and privileges; but when this was scornfully rejected by the Caesar John he did not argue. Covering his imperial robes in a loose cloak, he crossed the square to the church of St Sophia, where he declared his formal abdication. Later he was sent on to the monastery of the Peribleptos, the huge and hideous building on the Seventh Hill endowed by his distant predecessor Romanus Argyrus half a century before,[1] where he embraced – somewhat reluctantly, it must be said – the monastic life. Anna Comnena tells of how, some time afterwards, a friend came to visit him and asked how he was getting on. 'Abstinence from meat,' the old man answered, 'is the only thing that worries me; the other matters give me little concern.'[2]

The young man who now found himself the seventy-sixth Emperor of Byzantium was short and stocky, with broad shoulders and a deep chest. His eyes, deep-set beneath arched, heavy eyebrows, were gentle but curiously penetrating. His beard was thick and full. Even his daughter Anna admits that when standing he did not strike people as particularly impressive; once seated on the throne, however, it was a different matter: 'he reminded one of a fiery whirlwind . . . radiating beauty and grace and dignity and an unapproachable majesty'.[3] Particularly when she writes of her father, Anna's testimony must obviously be treated with caution; at the same time there can have been little doubt among those with whom Alexius came in contact that he would prove the ablest ruler since Basil II and that, for the first time in over half a century, the Empire was again in strong and capable hands.

On his arrival at the Great Palace he went immediately to work. The overriding need was to reimpose discipline over his soldiers; not only because he would rightly be held responsible for their recent behaviour, but because if they were not properly controlled there was always the possibility that they might break out into open mutiny. The task was not easy, since by now they had permeated every district and thoroughfare in the capital; but after twenty-four hours they had been rounded up and confined to their barracks to cool off. Constantinople was again at peace. But Alexius was a Byzantine, and his conscience still troubled him. It

---

1 See *Byzantium: The Apogee*, pp. 274–5.

2 *The Alexiad*, III, 1. All quotations from *The Alexiad* are based on the translation by E. R. A. Sewter.

3 Ibid., III, 3.

was he, after all, who had brought these barbarians into the city; was he not as guilty – perhaps guiltier – than they? On his mother's advice he confessed his anxieties to the Patriarch, who set up an ecclesiastical tribunal to settle the matter. There was, the tribunal concluded, evidence of guilt: the Emperor, his family and all who had participated in the *coup* – together with their wives – were sentenced to an appropriate period of fasting and to various other acts of penance. He himself, according to his daughter, went even further: for a further forty days and nights he wore a coat of sackcloth beneath the imperial purple, sleeping on the ground with only a stone for a pillow.

Meanwhile, however, there were serious affairs of state to be dealt with – and, in particular, the breach which was already appearing between his own followers and the family of Ducas. Its point of departure was the relationship between himself and the Empress Mary of Alania. As the wife of the deposed *basileus*, she might have been expected to leave the palace on his arrival; in fact she did nothing of the kind. True, she was also the new Emperor's adoptive mother; but even that did little to explain Alexius's decision to settle his fifteen-year-old wife Irene Ducas in another, smaller palace on lower ground, together with her mother, her sisters and her paternal grandfather the Caesar, while he himself remained with the fabulously beautiful Mary at the Boucoleon.[1] The reaction of the Ducas family to this arrangement can well be imagined; they had supported the Comneni not for any reasons of special affection, but simply because Alexius was married to one of their own clan. George Palaeologus – Irene's brother-in-law – had actually admitted as much when a party of Comnenus supporters had refused to couple her name with her husband's in their acclamations. 'It was not for your sakes,' he had told them, 'that I won so great a victory, but because of that Irene that you speak of'; and after winning over the fleet he had insisted that all the sailors should cheer for both Irene and Alexius – in that order.

But the indignation was not confined to George and his family. Rumours spread quickly through the city. Some whispered that Alexius was planning to divorce his child wife to become the Empress's third husband; others, that the real force behind these sinister developments

---

1 The Great Palace of Constantinople was not a single building. Instead – not unlike the Palace of Topkapi, its Ottoman successor on the same site – it was a collection of small palaces and pavilions, occupying the entire hillside that slopes downward between St Sophia and the Sea of Marmara. The Boucoleon was one of the more important of these palaces, with its own small harbour below it.

was his mother, the formidable Anna Dalassena, who had always hated the Ducas and was determined – now that her son was safely on the throne – to remove the family once and for all from power and influence. The first of these rumours may well have been true; the second certainly was. A few days later on Easter Sunday, still more dangerously inflammable fuel was added to the flames when Alexius refused to allow his wife to share his coronation.

To the Ducas, and indeed to all respectable Byzantines, this was a gratuitous insult. By long tradition, an Empress was not simply an Emperor's wife; once crowned she was the holder of a recognized rank, which carried considerable power. She had a court of her own and enjoyed absolute control over her own immense revenues; and she played an indispensable part in many of the chief ceremonies of the Empire. There is evidence to suggest that Alexius himself was far from happy at excluding his wife from the coronation that they should have shared. He may have cherished no great love for the Ducas, but he unquestionably owed them an enormous debt; besides, was it really sensible to antagonize, almost before his reign had begun, the most powerful family of the entire Byzantine nobility? For the moment, he allowed his mother to persuade him; but it was not long before he realized that this time she – and consequently he – had seriously overstepped the mark.

Matters were finally brought to a head not by any of the chief protagonists but by the Patriarch. Old Cosmas had reluctantly performed the single coronation, but his conscience continued to trouble him; and when, a few days later, he was approached by representatives of Anna Dalassena with strong suggestions that it might be in his best interests to retire in favour of her own nominee – a eunuch named Eustratius Garidas – he exploded in wrath. 'By Cosmas,' he shouted – to swear an oath by one's own name was, in Byzantium, to give it particular solemnity – 'By Cosmas, if Irene is not crowned by my own hands, I will never resign this patriarchal throne.' Whether he openly committed himself to the obvious corollary of this vow is not recorded; suffice it to say that, on the seventh day after the public proclamation of her husband's accession, the young Empress was duly crowned in St Sophia; and that on 8 May of the same year Cosmas withdrew to the monastery of Callias – to be succeeded, predictably, by the eunuch Garidas.

With this second coronation in a week, the Ducas family knew that it had won; and Alexius had learnt his first lesson. If there had been any emotional ties between himself and his adoptive mother, these were now broken: the Empress Mary agreed to leave the Boucoleon, firstly on condition that she should be given a written guarantee of security, 'inscribed in letters of scarlet and sealed with a golden seal', for herself and Constantine, her son by Michael VII; and secondly that Constantine himself should be made co-Emperor with Alexius. Both these requests were immediately granted; whereupon she and her son retired to the sumptuous mansion adjoining the monastery of the Mangana, built by Constantine IX for his mistress some thirty-five years before.[1] They were accompanied by Isaac Comnenus, to whom – the title of Caesar having already been promised to Nicephorus Melissenus – Alexius had awarded the newly-invented rank of *sebastocrator*, second only to the two co-Emperors themselves. He himself at once brought his wife back to the Boucoleon, where their married life proved a good deal happier than anyone had expected, ultimately resulting in no fewer than nine children.

But however brightly the sun might shine on the new Emperor's domestic life, on the political horizon the clouds were gathering fast. Within a month of Alexius's coronation, the Norman Robert Guiscard, Duke of Apulia, launched his grand offensive against the Roman Empire.

1 See *Byzantium: The Apogee*, pp. 308–10.

2

The Normans

[1081-91]

This Robert was a Norman by birth, of obscure origin, with an overbearing character and a thoroughly villainous mind; he was a brave fighter, very cunning in his assaults on the wealth and power of great men; in achieving his aims absolutely inexorable, diverting criticism by incontrovertible argument. He was a man of immense stature, surpassing even the biggest men; he had a ruddy complexion, fair hair, broad shoulders, eyes that all but shot out sparks of fire ... Homer remarked of Achilles that when he shouted his hearers had the impression of a multitude in uproar, but Robert's bellow, so they say, put tens of thousands to flight.

The Alexiad, I, 11

The story of the Normans in South Italy begins around 1015, with a group of some forty young pilgrims in the cave-shrine of the Archangel Michael on Monte Gargano in northern Apulia. Seeing in this underpopulated, unruly land both an opportunity and a challenge, they were easily persuaded by certain Lombard leaders to serve as mercenaries against the Byzantines. Word soon got back to Normandy, and the initial trickle of footloose younger sons in search of wealth and adventure rapidly grew to the point where it became a steady immigration. Fighting now indiscriminately for Lombard and Greek alike, the Normans soon began to exact payment for their services not in gold but in land. In 1030 Duke Sergius of Naples, in gratitude for their support, invested their leader Rainulf with the County of Aversa; thereafter their progress was fast, and in 1053, at Civitate in Apulia, they defeated a vastly superior army, raised and led against them by Pope Leo IX in person.

By this time supremacy among the Norman chiefs had been assumed by the family of one Tancred de Hauteville, a somewhat dim knight in the service of the Duke of Normandy. Of his twelve sons, eight had settled in Italy, five were to become leaders of the front rank and one – Robert, nicknamed Guiscard ('the crafty') – possessed something very like genius. After Civitate papal policy changed: and in 1059 Robert was invested by Pope Nicholas II with the previously non-existent Dukedoms of Apulia, Calabria and Sicily. Of these territories much of the first two remained subject to Byzantium, while Sicily was still in the hands of the Saracens; but Robert, strengthened by his new legitimacy, could not be checked for long. Two years later he and his youngest brother Roger invaded Sicily, and for the next decade they were able simultaneously to keep up the pressure both there and on the mainland. Bari, as we have seen, had fallen in 1071, and with it the last remnants of Byzantine power in Italy; early the next year Palermo had followed, and the Saracen hold on Sicily was broken for ever. In 1075 it was the turn of Salerno, the last independent Lombard principality. In all Italy south of the Garigliano river the Normans under Robert Guiscard now reigned supreme.

For many centuries already this land had been known as Magna Graecia, and at the time of which we are speaking it was still in spirit far more Greek than Italian. The vast majority of its inhabitants spoke Greek as their native language – as, in one or two remote villages, a few still do today; the Greek rite prevailed in almost all the churches and in most of the monasteries. Apulia and Calabria continued to be known as themes, as they had been in Byzantine days, and many of the more important communities were still headed by officials who retained the old Byzantine titles – *strategos*, *exarch* or *catapan*. No wonder that the Guiscard, finding himself already successor to the Roman Emperor where his Italian dominions were concerned, should begin to harbour designs on the imperial throne – designs which were unwittingly encouraged by the Byzantines themselves. Already in 1073, he had received two letters from Michael VII suggesting, in return for a military alliance, the marriage of the Emperor's brother, born in the purple[1] and 'so handsome, if one must talk of such qualities, that he might be a statue of the Empire itself', to one – the most beautiful, he was careful to specify – of Robert's daughters. When both these letters went unanswered Michael had written a third, improving his proposal: he now suggested his own newly-born son Constantine as the prospective bridegroom, and went on to offer Robert no fewer than forty-four high Byzantine honours for distribution among his family and friends, carrying with them a total annual grant of two hundred pounds of gold.

---

[1] i.e., born to an Emperor during his reign. To be *porphyrogenitus* was considered a far greater distinction than that of primogeniture.

The Guiscard had hesitated no longer. There was always an element of uncertainty in the imperial succession; but a son of a ruling Emperor certainly stood a better chance than anyone else, and the opportunity of seeing his own daughter as Empress of Byzantium was not one that he was prepared to miss. The offer of the honours, which would effectively put all his principal lieutenants in receipt of open bribes from Michael, was probably less attractive; but it was a risk worth taking. He had accepted the proposal, and shortly afterwards had bundled off the bride-to-be to Constantinople, there to pursue her studies in the imperial *gynaeceum* until her infant fiancé should be of marriageable age. Anna Comnena, writing some years later, rather bitchily implies[1] that young Helena – she had been re-baptized with the Greek name on being received into the Orthodox Church soon after her arrival – proved, despite the Emperor's stipulation, to be a good deal less well-favoured than had been expected, and that her intended husband was as terrified at the prospect of the marriage 'as a baby is of a bogeyman'; but since Anna was herself later betrothed to young Constantine, with whom she was to fall passionately in love, she can hardly be considered an impartial judge.

The overthrow of Michael VII by Nicephorus Botaneiates in 1078 put paid to all Helena's chances of attaining the imperial throne. The ex-Emperor himself, as we have seen, was allowed to retire to a monastery – a welcome translation from his point of view, since the cloister suited his bookish temperament far better than the palace had ever done. The hapless princess, on the other hand, found herself immured in a convent of her own with which she was, we may confidently assume, rather less well pleased. Her father received the news with mixed feelings. His immediate hopes of an imperial son-in-law had been dashed; on the other hand the treatment accorded to his daughter gave him the perfect pretext for intervention. A rebellion in South Italy prevented his taking any immediate action, but by the summer of 1080 he was able to begin preparations in earnest. He had in fact lost nothing by the delay: with every day that passed, the Empire was slipping deeper and deeper into chaos. In its present condition, a well-planned Norman offensive would seem to have every chance of success.

Not being satisfied with the men who had served in his army from the beginning and had experience in battle, he formed a new army, made up of

---

1 *The Alexiad*, I, 12.

recruits without any consideration of age. From all over Lombardy and Apulia he gathered them, old and young, pitiable wretches who had never, even in their dreams, seen a weapon; but were now clad in breastplates and carrying shields, drawing bows (to which they were completely unaccustomed) awkwardly and clumsily and, when ordered to march, usually falling flat on their faces.

Thus Anna Comnena describes Robert's preparations for his new campaign; and all through the autumn and winter the work went on. The fleet was refitted, the army increased in size – though not as dramatically as Anna suggests – and re-equipped. In a mighty effort to stir up enthusiasm among his Greek subjects, the Guiscard had even managed to produce a disreputable and transparently bogus Orthodox monk, who appeared in Salerno at the height of the preparations and gave himself out to be none other than the Emperor Michael in person, escaped from his monastery and trusting in his gallant Norman allies to replace him on his rightful throne. Nobody believed him much; but Robert, professing to be entirely convinced by his claims, persisted in treating him with exaggerated deference throughout the months that followed.

Then, in December, he decided to send an ambassador to Constantinople, with the triple purpose of demanding satisfaction from Botaneiates for the treatment accorded to Helena, gaining the adherence of the considerable number of Normans who were at that time in the imperial service, and winning over the Domestic of the Schools, Alexius Comnenus. He chose a certain Count Radulf of Pontoise – whose mission, however, was not a success. How he fared with the Emperor and his Norman followers is not recorded; but he had immediately fallen under the spell of the Domestic, and at some point on his homeward journey he had heard the news – not, probably, unexpected – of Alexius's *coup*. Finding his master at Brindisi, he innocently tried to persuade him to cancel his expedition altogether. The new Emperor, he assured him, wanted nothing but friendship with the Normans. He had been a good friend of Michael VII and had in fact served as the official guardian of young Constantine – Robert's prospective son-in-law – to whom, despite the latter's youth (he was now seven), he had even offered a share in the government. As for Helena, she was as safe with him as she would have been with her own father. Moreover, continued Radulf, he had with his own eyes seen the ex-Emperor Michael in his monastery; there could consequently be no doubt that the pretender whom Robert kept at his side and by whose claims he set so much store was an arrant impostor.

He should be sent packing at once, and an embassy dispatched to Alexius with offers of peace and friendship. Then Helena might still marry Constantine, or return to the bosom of her family; much bloodshed might be averted; and the army and navy could disperse to their homes.

Robert Guiscard was famous for the violence of his rages; and his fury with the luckless Radulf was fearful to behold. The last thing he wanted was peace with Constantinople. His expeditionary force was lying at Brindisi and Otranto, magnificently equipped and ready to sail; the grandest prize in Europe lay within his grasp. He had lost all interest in the imperial marriage – which, if it were to take place, would no longer be all that imperial anyway. Even less did he want his daughter back at home; he had six others, and she was serving a far more useful purpose where she was. So far as he was concerned the disreputable pretender was still the Emperor Michael – though it was a pity he was not a better actor – and Michael was still the legitimate Emperor. The only important thing now was to embark before Alexius cut the ground yet further from under his feet by returning Helena to him. Fortunately he had already sent his eldest son Bohemund – a magnificent blond giant of twenty-seven – with an advance party across the Adriatic. The sooner he could join him the better.

The great fleet sailed towards the end of May 1081. It carried some thirteen hundred Norman knights, supported by a large body of Saracens, some rather dubious Greeks and several thousand heterogeneous foot-soldiers. At Avlona[1] it was joined by a few Ragusan vessels – the Ragusans, like so many Balkan peoples, were always ready for a crack at the Byzantines – and then moved slowly down the coast to Corfu, where the imperial garrison surrendered at once. Having thus assured a bridge-head, and with it the free passage of reinforcements from Italy, Robert Guiscard could begin fighting in earnest. His first target was Durazzo,[2] capital and chief port of Illyria, from which the eight-hundred-year-old Via Egnatia ran east across the Balkan peninsula through Macedonia and Thrace to Constantinople. Soon, however, it became clear that progress was not going to be so easy. Heading northward round the Acrocerau-nian cape – respectfully avoided by the ancients as the seat from which Jupiter Fulminans was wont to launch his thunderbolts – Robert's ships were overtaken by a sudden tempest. Several of them were lost, and no

1 Valona, or Vlon, in what is now Albania.
2 The classical Dyrrachium, now Durrës, in Albania.

sooner had the battered remainder hove to in the roadstead off Durazzo than they saw a Venetian fleet on the north-western horizon.

The moment he heard of the Guiscard's landing on imperial territory, Alexius had sent Doge Domenico Selvo an urgent appeal for assistance. It was probably unnecessary; the threat to Venice implied by Norman control of the straits of Otranto was every bit as serious as that to the Empire. In any case Selvo had not hesitated. Taking personal command of the war fleet, he had sailed at once; and as night was falling he bore down on the Norman ships. Robert's men fought tenaciously, but their inexperience of sea warfare betrayed them. The Venetians adopted the old Byzantine trick, used by Belisarius at Palermo five and a half centuries before, of hoisting manned dinghies to the yard-arms, from which the soldiers could shoot down on to the enemy below;[1] it seems, too, that they had learnt the secret of Greek fire, since a Norman chronicler, Geoffrey Malaterra, writes of how 'they blew that fire, which is called Greek and is not extinguished by water, through submerged pipes, and thus cunningly burnt one of our ships under the very waves of the sea'. Against such tactics and such weapons the Normans were powerless; their line was shattered, while the Venetians were able to beat their way to safety in the harbour of Durazzo.

But it took more than this to discourage the Duke of Apulia, whose army (which he had prudently disembarked before the battle) was still unimpaired and who now settled down to besiege the city. Alexius had sent his old ally George Palaeologus to command the local troops, with orders to hold the enemy at all costs while he himself raised an army against the invaders; and the garrison, knowing that relief was on the way, fought stoutly. All summer long the siege continued, enlivened by frequent sorties on the part of the defenders – in one of which Palaeologus fought magnificently throughout a sweltering day with a Norman arrow-head embedded in his skull. Then on 15 October Alexius's army appeared, with the Emperor himself riding at its head. Three days later he attacked. By this time Robert had moved a little to the north of the city and had drawn up his line of battle. He himself had assumed command of the centre, with his son Bohemund on his left, inland, flank and on his right his wife, the Lombard princess Sichelgaita of Salerno.

Sichelgaita needs some explanation. She was cast in a Wagnerian mould: in her we come face to face with the closest approximation in history to a Valkyrie. A woman of immense build and herculean physical

1 See *Byzantium: The Early Centuries*, p. 215n.

strength, she hardly ever left her husband's side – least of all in battle, one of her favourite occupations. At such moments, charging magnificently into the fray, her long blond hair streaming out from beneath her helmet, deafening friend and foe alike with huge shouts of encouragement or imprecation, she must have looked – even if she did not altogether sound – worthy to take her place among the daughters of Wotan: beside Waltraute, or Grimgerda, or even Brünnhilde herself.

As was the invariable rule when the Emperor took the field in person, his Varangian Guard was present in strength. At this time it consisted largely of Englishmen, Anglo-Saxons who had left their country in disgust after Hastings and had taken service with Byzantium. Many of them had been waiting fifteen years to avenge themselves on the detested Normans, and they attacked with all the vigour of which they were capable. Swinging their huge two-handed battle-axes round their heads and then slamming them into horses and riders alike, they struck terror in the hearts of the Apulian knights, few of whom had ever come across a line of foot-soldiers that did not immediately break in the face of a charge of cavalry. The horses too began to panic, and before long the Norman right had turned in confusion, many galloping straight into the sea to escape certain massacre.

But now, if contemporary reports are to be believed, the day was saved by Sichelgaita. The story is best told by Anna Comnena:

Directly Gaita, Robert's wife (who was riding at his side and was a second Pallas, if not an Athene) saw these soldiers running away, she looked fiercely after them and in a very powerful voice called out to them in her own language an equivalent to Homer's words: 'How far will ye flee? Stand, and acquit yourselves like men!' And when she saw that they continued to run, she grasped a long spear and at full gallop rushed after the fugitives; and on seeing this they recovered themselves and returned to the fight.

Now, too, Bohemund's left flank had wheeled to the rescue, with a detachment of crossbowmen against whom the Varangians, unable to approach within axe-range, in their turn found themselves defenceless. Having advanced too far beyond the main body of the Greek army, their retreat was cut off; they could only fight where they stood. At last the few exhausted Englishmen remaining alive turned and sought refuge in a nearby chapel of the Archangel Michael; but the Normans immediately set it on fire – they were a long way now from Monte Gargano – and most of the Varangians perished in the flames.

Meanwhile, in the centre, the Emperor was still fighting bravely; but the cream of the Byzantine army had been destroyed at Manzikert, and the motley collection of barbarian mercenaries on whom he now had to rely possessed neither the discipline nor the devotion to prevail against the Normans of Apulia. A sortie from Durazzo under George Palaeologus had failed to save the situation, and to make matters worse Alexius suddenly saw that he had been betrayed by his vassal, King Constantine Bodin of Zeta, and by a whole regiment of seven thousand Turkish auxiliaries, lent to him by the Seljuk Sultan Süleyman, of whom he had had high hopes. His last chance of victory was gone. Cut off from his men, saddened by the loss on the battlefield of George's father Nicephorus Palaeologus and Michael VII's brother Constantius, weak from exhaustion and loss of blood and in considerable pain from a wound in his forehead, he rode slowly and without escort back over the mountains to Ochrid, there to recover and regroup what he could of his shattered forces.

Somehow, Durazzo was to hold out for another four months; not till February 1082 were the Normans able to burst open the gates, and even then only through the treachery of a Venetian resident (who, according to Malaterra, demanded as his reward the hand of one of Robert's nieces in marriage). From Durazzo on, however, the pace of conquest quickened; the local populations, aware of their Emperor's defeat, offered no resistance to the advancing invaders; and within a few weeks the whole of Illyria was in the Guiscard's hands. He then marched east to Kastoria, which also surrendered instantly – despite the fact that its garrison was found to consist of three hundred more of the Varangian Guard. This discovery had a further tonic effect on the Normans' already high morale. If not even the crack troops of the Empire were any longer prepared to oppose their advance, then surely Constantinople was as good as won.

Alas for Robert: it was nothing of the kind. The following April, while he was still at Kastoria, messengers arrived from Italy. Apulia and Calabria, they reported, were up in arms, and much of Campania as well. They also brought a letter from Pope Gregory VII. His arch-enemy Henry IV, King of the Romans,[1] was at the gates of Rome, demanding to be crowned Emperor of the West. The Duke's presence was urgently required at home. Leaving the command of the expedition to Bohemund, and swearing by the soul of his father Tancred to remain unshaven until

---

1 A purely honorary title, normally adopted by the elected Emperor of the West until he could be properly crowned by the Pope in Rome.

he could return to Greece, Robert hurried back to the coast and took ship across the Adriatic.

The Venetians were not the only people whom Alexius had approached for help against Robert Guiscard. Already at the time of his accession he had been fully aware of the preparations being made against him, and he had lost no time in seeking out potential allies. The nearest at hand was one of Robert's own nephews: Abelard, son of his elder brother Humphrey, who had been dispossessed by his uncle and had later sought refuge in Constantinople, where he needed little persuading to return secretly to Italy and, with the aid of his brother Herman and a quantity of Byzantine gold, to raise the revolt. Meanwhile the Emperor had sent an embassy to Henry IV, pointing out the dangers of allowing the Duke of Apulia to continue unchecked; subsequent exchanges had ended in an agreement by which, in return for an oath of alliance, Alexius sent Henry no less than 360,000 gold pieces, the salaries of twenty high court offices, a gold pectoral cross set with pearls, a crystal goblet, a sardonyx cup, and 'a reliquary inlaid with gold containing fragments of various saints, identified in each case by a small label'. It was, by any standards, an expensive contract; but when in the spring of 1082 the Emperor received reports of Robert's sudden departure, he must have felt that his recent diplomatic activities had been well worth while.

He himself had spent the winter in Thessalonica, trying to raise troops for the following summer's campaign. Bohemund and his army were steadily extending their power through the Empire's western provinces, and his father would probably be back in person before long, ready to march on the capital. A strong and adequately-trained defence force was essential if the Normans were to be resisted; but mercenaries by definition cost money, the imperial treasury was bare, and to have asked any more from the hard-pressed Byzantine taxpayer would have been a virtual invitation to rebellion. Alexius appealed to his mother, his brother and his wife, all of whom provided what they could, paring their living expenses to the bone; but the proceeds were nowhere near enough for his purposes. Finally his brother Isaac the *sebastocrator* summoned a synod at St Sophia and, invoking ancient canons which allowed ecclesiastical gold and silver to be melted down and sold for the redemption of Byzantine prisoners of war, announced the confiscation of all church treasures. Byzantine history recorded only one near precedent: when, at the time of the invasion of the Persian King Chosroes in 618, the Patriarch Sergius had voluntarily put the entire wealth of every church and monastery at the disposal of the State and the Emperor Heraclius had gratefully accepted his offer.[1] On this occasion the initiative came from the other side. The hierarchy showed itself distinctly less public-spirited and made little attempt to conceal its displeasure. It had no choice, however, but to submit, and in doing so enabled Alexius to raise his army.

Yet even that army, in the first year of its existence, proved powerless to halt Bohemund's advance. After two more major victories, at Yanina and Arta, he had slowly pressed the Byzantines back until all Macedonia and much of Thessaly lay under his control. Not until the spring of 1083, at Larissa, did Alexius succeed in turning the tide. His plan was simple enough. When he saw that battle was imminent, he handed over the main body of the army, together with all the imperial standards, to his brother-in-law George Melissenus and another distinguished general, Basil Curticius, with orders first to advance against the enemy but then, when the two lines were face to face, suddenly to turn and run as if in headlong flight. He meanwhile, with a body of carefully picked troops, crept round under cover of darkness to a place behind the Norman camp and lay there in hiding. At daybreak Bohemund saw the army and the standards and immediately launched his attack. Melissenus and Curticius did as they had been instructed, and before long the Byzantine army was galloping away in the opposite direction, with the Normans in pell-mell pursuit. Meanwhile Alexius and his men overran the enemy camp, killing all its occupants and taking substantial plunder. On his return Bohemund was obliged to raise the siege of Larissa and to withdraw to Kastoria. From that moment on he was lost. Dispirited, homesick, its pay long overdue and now still further demoralized by the huge rewards which Alexius was offering to all deserters, the Norman army fell away. Bohemund took ship for Italy to raise more money, and his principal lieutenants surrendered as soon as his back was turned; next, a Venetian fleet recaptured Durazzo and Corfu; and by the end of 1083 Norman-held territory in the Balkans was once again confined to one or two offshore islands and a short strip of the coast.

Across the Adriatic, on the other hand, Robert Guiscard was doing splendidly. The insurrection in Apulia had admittedly taken him longer to deal with than he had expected, largely owing to the generous subsidies that the rebels had been receiving from Constantinople; but by mid-summer the last pockets of resistance had been satisfactorily

---

1 See *Byzantium: The Early Centuries*, p. 288.

eliminated. He had then set about raising a new army with which to rescue Pope Gregory – who had barricaded himself into the Castel Sant' Angelo – and to send Henry packing. Early the following summer he marched; and on 24 May 1084, roughly on the site of the present Porta Capena, he pitched his camp beneath the walls of Rome. The Emperor, however – who had deposed Gregory and had had himself crowned by a puppet anti-Pope on Palm Sunday – had not waited for him. Three days before the Duke of Apulia appeared at the gates of the city he had retired, with the greater part of his army, to Lombardy.

Had the Romans not been foolish enough to surrender to Henry the previous March, the Normans would have entered the city as deliverers; instead, they came as a conquering enemy. On the night of 27 May, Robert silently moved his men round to the north of the city; then at dawn he attacked, and within minutes the first of his shock-troops had burst through the Flaminian Gate. They met with a stiff resistance: the whole area of the Campus Martius – that quarter which lies immediately across the Tiber from the Castel Sant' Angelo – became a blazing inferno. But it was not long before the Normans had beaten the defenders back across the bridge, released the Pope from his fortress and borne him back in triumph through the smoking ruins to the Lateran.

Then, and only then, came the real tragedy. Despite all the depredations it had suffered, Rome still offered the Guiscard's men possibilities of plunder on a scale such as few of them had ever before experienced; and the entire city now fell victim to an orgy of rapine and pillage. For three days this continued unabated – until the inhabitants, able to bear it no longer, rose against their oppressors. Robert, for once taken by surprise, found himself surrounded. He was saved in the nick of time by his son Roger Borsa, who in an uncharacteristic burst of activity smashed his way through the furious crowds with a thousand men-at-arms to his father's rescue – but not before the Normans, now fighting for their lives, had set fire to the city. The Capitol and the Palatine were gutted; churches, palaces and ancient temples left empty shells. In the whole area between the Colosseum and the Lateran hardly a single building escaped the flames. When at last the smoke cleared away and such Roman leaders as remained alive had prostrated themselves before the Duke of Apulia with naked swords roped round their necks in token of surrender, their city lay empty, a picture of desolation and despair.

A few weeks later, Robert Guiscard returned to Greece. As Anna Comnena has occasion to point out, he was nothing if not tenacious. Though now sixty-eight, he seems to have been in no way discouraged at the prospect of starting his campaign all over again; and in the autumn of 1084 he was back, with Bohemund, his two other sons Roger and Guy, and a new fleet of 150 ships. At the outset, things could hardly have gone worse: bad weather delayed the vessels for two months at Butrinto, and when at last they were able to cross the straits to Corfu, they were set upon by a Venetian fleet and soundly beaten in pitched battle twice in three days. So severe were their losses that the Venetians sent back their pinnaces to the lagoon with news of the victory; but they had underestimated the Guiscard. Few of his ships were in fit condition to venture a third battle; but seeing the pinnaces disappear over the horizon and recognizing the opportunity of taking the enemy by surprise, he quickly summoned all those vessels that were somehow still afloat and flung them forward in a last onslaught.

He had calculated it perfectly. Not only were the Venetians unprepared; their heavier galleys, already emptied of ballast, stood so high in the water that when, in the heat of the battle, their entire complements of soldiers and crew dashed to the same side of the deck, many of them capsized. (So, at least, writes Anna Comnena; though her story is hard indeed to reconcile with what we know of Venetian seamanship.) Anna reports 13,000 Venetian dead, together with 2,500 prisoners – on whose subsequent mutilations at the hands of their captors she dwells with that morbid pleasure that is one of her least attractive characteristics.[1] Corfu fell; and it was a generally happier and more hopeful army that settled down into its winter quarters on the mainland.

But in the course of the winter a new enemy appeared – one more deadly to the Guiscard's men than the Venetians and the Byzantines together. It was a raging epidemic – probably typhoid – and it struck without mercy. By spring five hundred Norman knights were dead, and a large proportion of the army effectively incapacitated. Yet even now Robert remained cheerful and confident. Of his immediate family only Bohemund had succumbed, and had been sent back to Bari to recuperate; and in the early summer, determined to get his men once again on the move, he dispatched Roger Borsa with an advance force to occupy Cephalonia. A few weeks later, he himself set off to join his son; but now, as he sailed southward, he felt the dreaded sickness upon him. By

---

1 Anna goes on to describe a fourth battle, in which she claims that the Venetians had their revenge; but there is no trace of such an engagement in the Venetian records, and since we know that Doge Selvo was deposed as a result of the Corfu catastrophe, it looks as though she is guilty of a particularly unscrupulous piece of wishful thinking.

the time his ship reached Cape Ather, the northernmost tip of the island, he was desperately ill. The vessel put in at the first safe anchorage, a little sheltered bay still called, in his memory, by the name of Phiscardo. Here, on 17 July 1085, he died, his faithful Sichelgaita beside him.

The past four years had seen the two greatest potentates of Europe – the Eastern and Western Emperors – fleeing at his approach, and one of the most redoubtable of medieval Popes rescued and restored by his hand. Had he lived another few months, he might well have achieved his ambitions; and Alexius Comnenus might have proved one of the more transitory – possibly even the last – of the Greek Emperors of Byzantium. With the Guiscard's death, the Empire was delivered from immediate danger. Immediately and inevitably, his sons and nephews plunged into quarrels over the inheritance and soon lost sight of the grand design that had dominated his last years. But they did not altogether ignore the new horizons that he had opened up to them. Henceforth we find the Normans of the South looking with increasingly envious eyes towards the East; and in only twelve years' time we shall find Robert's son Bohemund carving out for himself, at the Emperor's expense, the first Crusader principality of Outremer.

'The Empire was delivered from immediate danger': for anyone attempting to write its history, these are brave words. Byzantium was never safe for long. Her western neighbours were at the best of times unreliable, betraying her as they did time and time again; those to the east were almost invariably hostile – and were destined, one day, to deliver her death blow. More continually troublesome than either, however, over the centuries, were those who came from the north: the barbarian hordes – Goths and Huns, Avars and Slavs, Gepids and Bulgars, Magyars and Uzz – who descended in wave after wave from the steppes of Central Asia and who, if they never succeeded in capturing Constantinople, continued by their very existence to threaten it and seldom left the Emperors and their subjects altogether free from anxiety.

Now, with the temporary disappearance of the Normans from the scene, it was the turn of the Pechenegs. They were by no means new arrivals. For more than two hundred years they had been a force to be reckoned with; over that time they had proved themselves the most grasping (as well as the cruellest) of the tribes, and readers of the previous volume may remember how, in the middle of the ninth century, Constantine VII Porphyrogenitus had warned his son Romanus to keep them happy at all costs with pacts, alliances, treaties of friendship and an endless stream of expensive gifts.[1] Recent Emperors, however, had ignored this advice, and the Pecheneg menace, aided and abetted by Bogomil[2] heretics in the eastern Balkans, had steadily increased. In the spring of 1087 a huge barbarian army, estimated by Anna at eighty thousand, invaded the Empire; three years later, after several desperate battles in which victories were scored on both sides, it stood within reach of Constantinople.

Nor were the Pechenegs and the Bogomils the only enemies with whom Alexius had to contend. The Turkish Emir of Smyrna, Chaka by name, had over the previous decade extended his power along the entire Aegean coast. He had lived for a year or more in Constantinople, where Nicephorus Botaneiates had finally granted him the title of *protonobilissimus*; but his ambitions, like those of Robert Guiscard before him, were directed at nothing less than the Byzantine throne. The Pecheneg invasion gave him just the opportunity he had been awaiting. For some time he had been preparing a fleet, and in the late autumn of 1090 he had little difficulty in capturing the key Byzantine islands of Lesbos, Chios, Samos and Rhodes. Fortunately for Byzantium, Alexius too had been building up his navy; and early the following year an imperial squadron under the command of his kinsman Constantine Dalassenus drove back the Emir from the entrance to the Marmara. But Chaka was by no means beaten, and there is little doubt that he would have renewed his attempt had he not been murdered by his Sultan, Kilij Arslan, at a banquet in 1092.

Meanwhile the Pechenegs kept up the pressure on Constantinople. Alexius fought hard: he could hold them at bay, but with his chronic shortage of manpower it was impossible to drive them back to the lands from which they had come. And so, in desperation, he resorted to one of the oldest of Byzantine diplomatic tricks: to enlist the help of one tribe against another. It was a dangerous ploy, since there was always a risk that the two would join forces, and that the Empire would consequently find itself with two barbarian enemies instead of one; but his principal source of manpower had been lost at Manzikert and he had little choice. And so, just as Leo the Wise had called in the Magyars against Symeon of Bulgaria almost exactly two centuries before,[3] Alexius Comnenus now appealed to the Cumans.

---

1 See *Byzantium: The Apogee*, p. 164n.

2 The Bogomils were a neo-Manichaean, puritan sect who believed the material world to be the creation and dominion of the Devil. Originating in tenth-century Bulgaria, they had spread rapidly through the Balkans and parts of Asia Minor and were later to give rise to the Albigensians (Cathars) of south-west France.

3 See *Byzantium: The Apogee*, p. 108.

The Cumans have already appeared in these pages under the name of Scythians, by which in former times they were more usually known.[1] A race of nomad warriors and cattle-breeders of Turkic origin, they had appeared from the East in the eleventh century and had settled in what is today the Ukraine. They had no fundamental quarrel with the Pechenegs – the two tribes had plundered Thrace together in 1087 and seem to have enjoyed it thoroughly – but Alexius made them an offer they could not refuse and they willingly answered his call. They arrived in the late spring; and on Monday, 28 April 1091 the two armies faced each other under a hill known as Levunium, near the mouth of the Maritsa river.

That evening the Emperor called his soldiers to prayer. 'At the moment', writes Anna,

when the sun set below the horizon, one could see the heavens lit up, not with the light of one sun, but with the gleam of many other stars, for everyone lit torches (or wax tapers, according to their means) and fixed them on the points of their spears. The prayers offered up by the army no doubt reached the very vault of heaven, or shall I say that they were borne aloft to the Lord God Himself?

They certainly seem to have been; for in the battle that was fought the next day the Pechenegs – whose women and children, as was the barbarian custom, had followed them to war – suffered a defeat so crushing that they were almost wiped out as a race. Anna goes further and states that they were totally annihilated; she exaggerates, but only a little. Some of the prisoners survived and were taken into imperial service; the vast majority – they are still said to have outnumbered their captors by thirty to one – perished in a general massacre.

Neither the imperial army nor Alexius Comnenus as its commander[2] emerges with much credit from the bloodbath of Levunium; the fact remains, however, that it was by far the most decisive victory to have been won by the Byzantine army in the field since the days of Basil II. Not only did it deliver the Empire for the next thirty years from the Pecheneg menace; it provided a healthy example for other tribes, together with a vitally necessary tonic for Byzantine morale. More important still,

1 A still more familiar appellation to many people might be that of Polovtsi, who captured – and danced for – Prince Igor of Kiev in the old Russian folk tale and Borodin's opera.

2 Anna exonerates her father from any involvement in the massacre; but then she would, wouldn't she?

it secured the Emperor's own position. He had, it must be remembered, seized the throne by force. Many an ambitious young commander from any one of a dozen noble Byzantine families could have boasted as good a claim to it, and Alexius's obvious ability had in the past offered him small protection against the intrigues of jealous rivals. Now at last he had proved himself capable of restoring to Byzantium at least part of her former greatness. The *basileus* who, a few days after the battle, rode proudly through the Golden Gate of Constantinople and down the decorated streets to the Great Church of St Sophia – his subjects meanwhile cheering him to the echo – could look to the future, as never before in the ten years since his accession, with confidence and hope.

3
The First Crusade

[1091–1108]

They assembled from all sides, one after another, with arms and horses and all the panoply of war. Full of ardour and enthusiasm, they thronged every highway; and with these warriors came a host of civilians, outnumbering the grains of sand on the sea shore or the stars in the heavens, carrying palms in their hands and bearing crosses on their shoulders. There were women and children too, who had left their own countries. Like tributaries joining a river, they streamed from all directions towards us.

The Alexiad, X, 5

Some time towards the end of 1094, Alexius Comnenus received an embassy from Rome. Urban II had now been seven years on the pontifical throne, years during which he had worked hard to improve relations between Constantinople and the Holy See. Some efforts had already been made on both sides to re-establish contact after the ridiculous and quite unnecessary schism of 1054,[1] notably on the part of the Emperor Michael and Pope Gregory VII; but on hearing of Michael's deposition Gregory had summarily excommunicated the usurper Nicephorus Botaneiates, and in 1081 he had extended the sentence to Alexius. It is doubtful whether the ban of the Church caused the *basileus* much concern – although he was a deeply religious man, he had scant respect for the Pope's authority in matters spiritual – but such a gesture hardly made for good relations, and his esteem for Gregory had sunk still further when he heard of his alliance with the hated Duke of Apulia. The Pope, meanwhile, had been similarly appalled to learn that Henry IV was in the pay of Alexius, and by the time of his death in 1085 relations between Rome and Constantinople were as bad as they had ever been.

When Urban had succeeded to the papal throne three years later he

---

1 See *Byzantium: The Apogee*, pp. 316–22.

had been at first too preoccupied with his own affairs to bother overmuch with the Empire of the East. As a result of the struggle between Pope Gregory and Henry IV, Rome was still in the hands of an anti-Pope; it was five years before Urban succeeded, by patient diplomacy, in installing himself at the Lateran. Already in 1089, however, he had started the reconciliation by lifting the excommunication on Alexius; the Emperor, who had previously closed all the Latin churches in Constantinople, had responded by opening them again and by calling a synod which decreed that the Pope's name had been omitted from the diptychs[1] 'not by any canonical decision but, as it were, from carelessness' – an assurance that can have deceived nobody but at least showed a measure of goodwill. Letters were exchanged; theological and liturgical differences were discussed with a mildness almost unparalleled in Byzantine Church history; and thus the breach was gradually healed, until by the time the papal embassy reached Constantinople Emperor and Pope were once again on genuinely friendly terms.

The legates carried with them an invitation to send representatives to a great council of the Western Church, to be held in Piacenza the following March; and Alexius accepted at once. Most of the proceedings, he knew, would be concerned with domestic matters – simony, the adultery of King Philip of France, clerical marriage and the like – which would interest him only insofar as the views expressed might differ from those held by the Orthodox; but the council might also provide him with the opportunity he had long sought, to appeal for Western aid against the Turks. The situation in Anatolia was in fact a good deal more promising than it had been at any time since Manzikert: the Seljuk Sultanate of Rum had largely disintegrated, and the various Emirs who now held effective power were far more occupied with their own internecine squabbles – many of them carefully engineered by Byzantine agents – than with a united stand against the Empire. For the first time, the reconquest of Asia Minor seemed a distinct possibility. But until that should happen the Emperor remained desperately short of manpower, dependent on foreign mercenaries – most of them barbarians of varying degrees of reliability – on his largely Anglo-Saxon Varangian Guard, and on the occasional Western soldiers of fortune who took temporary service in his army. All these together were just capable of guarding his long frontiers to the west and north, and for keeping watch against

1 These were lists of names – read aloud during the Eucharist – of those dignitaries, living and dead, upon whom the divine blessing was particularly sought.

further Norman incursions from South Italy; but for a concerted campaign against the Seljuks they remained hopelessly inadequate. What he needed was military assistance from the West, on a considerable scale; and Piacenza promised to be just the place to say so.

The Byzantine spokesmen did their work well. Sensibly, in view of the circumstances, they laid their emphasis less on the prizes to be won – though we can be sure that these did not go unmentioned – than on the religious aspects of the appeal: the sufferings of the Christian communities of the East, the submergence of Asia Minor beneath the Turkish tide, the presence of the infidel armies at the very gates of Constantinople and the appalling danger they represented, not only to the Empire of the East but to all Christendom. The listening delegates were impressed – none more, perhaps, than Pope Urban himself. From Piacenza he travelled to Cremona to receive the homage of Conrad, Henry IV's rebellious son, and thence across the Alps to his native France; and, as his long and arduous journey progressed, a scheme gradually took shape in his mind – a scheme far more ambitious than any that Alexius Comnenus had ever dreamed of: for nothing less than a Holy War, in which the combined forces of Europe would march against the Saracen.

Piacenza, he had decided, was only a prelude. When he arrived in France he called another council, larger and far more important, to meet at Clermont[1] on 18 November. It would last for ten days, most of which would be taken up with routine Church business; on Tuesday, 27 November, however, there would be a public session open to everyone, at which, it was announced, the Pope would make a statement of immense significance to all Christendom. This promise had precisely the effect that Urban had intended. So great were the crowds that poured into the little town to hear the Pontiff speak that the cathedral was abandoned, and the papal throne was erected instead on a high platform set in an open field outside the eastern gate.[2]

The text of Urban's speech has not come down to us, and the four contemporary reports that have are different enough to make it clear that none of them has any serious claims to accuracy. The Pope seems to have begun by repeating the points made by Alexius's delegates at

---

1 Clermont – which merged with its neighbour Montferrand in 1650 and has been known ever since as Clermont-Ferrand – appears at first sight to be depressingly industrialized and is consequently ignored by most tourists. This is a pity, since it boasts a magnificent thirteenth-century cathedral of the local black lava (the whole town is built over an extinct volcano) and a superb romanesque church, Notre-Dame-du-Port, two hundred years older still.

2 The site is now occupied by the Place Delille.

Piacenza, developing their arguments and endorsing their appeal; unlike the Byzantines, however, he then turned to the plight of Jerusalem,[1] where Christian pilgrims were being regularly robbed and persecuted by the city's Turkish overlords. Such a state of affairs, he declared, could no longer continue; it was the duty of Western Christendom to march to the rescue of the Christian East. All those who agreed to do so 'from devotion only, not from advantage of honour or gain', would die absolved, their sins remitted. There must be the minimum of delay: the great Crusading army must be ready to march by the Feast of the Assumption, 15 August 1096.

The response to his impassioned appeal was more enthusiastic than Urban can have dared to hope. Led by Bishop Adhemar of Le Puy, several hundred people – priests and monks, noblemen and peasants together – knelt before his throne and pledged themselves to take the Cross. The First Crusade was under way.

Alexius Comnenus on the other hand, when he heard of the proceedings at Clermont, was appalled. A crusade such as Urban had preached was the last thing he had had in mind. To him as to his subjects, there was nothing new or exciting about a war with the infidel; Byzantium had been waging one, on and off, for the best part of five hundred years. As for Jerusalem, it had formerly been part of his Empire – to which, so far as he was concerned, it still properly belonged – and he fully intended to win it back if he could; but that was a task for his imperial army, not an obligation on Christendom in general. Now at last the Anatolian horizons were brightening and there seemed to be a real chance of regaining his lost territory; but instead of being allowed to do so in his own way, and in his own time, he was faced with the prospect of perhaps hundreds of thousands of undisciplined Western brigands pouring across his borders, constantly demanding food while almost certainly refusing to recognize any authority but their own. He needed mercenaries, not Crusaders.

Meanwhile, he did everything he could to limit the potential damage. In the hopes of preventing the rabble armies from ravaging the country-side and plundering the local inhabitants he ordered huge stocks of provisions to be accumulated at Durazzo and regular points along the Via

---

1 Jerusalem had been in Muslim hands since its first capture by the Caliph Omar in 638, but for most of the intervening period Christian pilgrims had been freely admitted and allowed to worship as and where they wished, without let or hindrance. The city had been taken by the Seljuk Turks in 1077.

Egnatia, while each party on arrival was to be met by a detachment of Pecheneg military police – presumably survivors from Levunium – and escorted to the capital. These precautions taken, he could only sit back and await the coming invasion; and the arrival of the first wave – preceded by a voracious swarm of locusts, from which the soothsayers of Constantinople drew their own conclusions – confirmed his direst fears.

Peter the Hermit was not in truth a hermit at all; he was a fanatical itinerant monk from the neighbourhood of Amiens, ragged and malodorous, and yet possessed of a personal magnetism that was both curious and compelling. Preaching the Crusade throughout northern France and Germany, he had quickly attracted a following of some forty thousand. It included large numbers of women and children, many of whom – confusing the Old Jerusalem with the New – believed that he would literally be leading them into that land flowing with milk and honey of which their priests had told them; but whereas the expeditions that were to follow were to be led and largely financed by the nobility, Peter's army was – apart from a few minor German knights – composed essentially of French and German peasants and their families. Somehow, this straggling and unwieldy company made its way across Europe, without serious mishap as far as the Hungarian town of Semlin – the modern Zemun – which faces Belgrade across the Sava river. There, however, the troubles began. A dispute said to have arisen over a pair of shoes led to a riot, in the course of which Peter's men – though almost certainly against his wishes – stormed the citadel and killed four thousand Hungarians. Crossing the river to Belgrade, they pillaged and set fire to the city. At Nish they attempted the same thing again; but this time Nicetas, the Byzantine governor of Bulgaria, sent in his own mounted troops. Against a trained and disciplined force, the Crusaders were powerless. Many of them were killed, many more taken prisoner. Of the forty thousand who had started out, a good quarter were lost by the time the party reached Sardica (Sofia).[1]

Thereafter there were no more incidents; nor – surprisingly – were there recriminations. The expedition, it was felt, had suffered enough for its misdoings – of which its leader himself and the vast majority of his followers had been in any case totally innocent – and was received graciously at Constantinople when it arrived on 1 August, Peter being

---

1 Numbers are notoriously uncertain in medieval history. The chroniclers invariably exaggerate; never, under any circumstances, do they agree. The above figures are taken from Albert of Aix (I, 9–12), who is probably more reliable than most.

even summoned to an audience with the Emperor. A single conversation with him, and a glance at his followers, was however enough to convince Alexius that, once in Anatolia and confronted by the Seljuks, this so-called army would not stand a chance. In other circumstances he might have forbidden Peter to continue so suicidal a journey; but from the outer suburbs in which the Crusaders were encamped – the rank and file were allowed through the gates only in small, strictly-controlled parties of sightseers – complaints were already pouring in of robberies, rapes and lootings. Clearly the army could not be allowed to remain; and since it refused to return whence it had come it must continue on its way. On 6 August the whole force was ferried across the Bosphorus under heavy escort and left to look after itself.

The end of the story can be quickly told. At Nicomedia – now Izmit – a mere fifty miles from the straits, the French and the German sections quarrelled and separated, a smaller Italian contingent siding with the Germans. Both sections then continued around the Gulf of Nicomedia to the village of Cibotus, a few miles east of the modern Yalova. With this as their base, they settled down to ravage the local countryside, the French penetrating as far as the walls of Nicaea itself – by now the Seljuk capital – killing, raping and occasionally torturing[1] the local inhabitants, all of whom were Christian Greeks. Their success aroused the jealousy of the Germans, who pushed well beyond Nicaea – confining their bestiality, however, to the Muslim communities – and captured a castle known as Xerigordon. It proved to be their downfall. Xerigordon was set high on a hill, its only water supplies outside the walls; so that when at the end of September the Seljuk army laid siege to the castle the defenders were doomed. For a week they held out; on the eighth day, by which time they were drinking not just the blood of their horses and donkeys but even each other's urine, they surrendered. Those who apostatized had their lives spared and were sent off into captivity; the rest were massacred.

When the news reached Cibotus it caused something approaching panic; and morale was not improved by reports arriving soon afterwards that the Turks were advancing on the camp. Some advised that no action could be taken till the return of Peter, who had gone to Constantinople for discussions; but he gave no sign of coming, and as the enemy continued to approach it became clear that a pitched battle was inevitable.

---

1 The story that they roasted Christian babies on spits can probably be discounted, though it was widely believed at the time.

On 21 October, the entire Crusading army of some twenty thousand men marched out of Cibotus – straight into a Turkish ambush. A sudden hail of arrows stopped it in its tracks; the cavalry was flung back on to the infantry, and within a few minutes the whole host was in headlong flight back to the camp, the Seljuks in pursuit. For those who had remained at Cibotus – the old men, the women and children and the sick – there was little chance. A few lucky ones managed to take refuge in an old castle on the seashore, where they barricaded themselves in and somehow survived, as did a number of young girls and boys whom the Turks appropriated for their own purposes. The rest were slaughtered. The People's Crusade was over.

The rabble army that had followed Peter the Hermit across Europe in the summer of 1096, only to be annihilated on the plains of western Asia Minor a few months later, was in no way typical of the armies of the First Crusade. Over the next nine months Alexius Comnenus was to find himself the unwilling host to perhaps another seventy or eighty thousand men, and a fair number of women, led by some of the richest and most powerful feudal princes of the West. The challenges presented by this horde – economic, logistic and military, but above all diplomatic – were unparalleled in Byzantine history; the Empire was fortunate indeed in having at its head during this most critical period a man possessed of sufficient tact and intelligence to meet them, with what proved to be a quite extraordinary measure of success.

The basic problem was one of trust – or rather the lack of it. Alexius simply did not believe in the high Christian motives professed by most of the leaders of the Crusade. His unhappy experience of Roussel of Bailleul and later of Robert Guiscard had convinced him that the Normans at least were out for what they could get – ideally the Empire itself but, failing that, their own independent principalities in the East. This latter objective did not worry him unduly: a few Christian buffer-states between himself and the Saracen might prove to be no bad thing. The important points so far as he was concerned were, first, that such principalities should not be founded on territory that properly belonged to the Empire and, second, that their princes should acknowledge him as their suzerain. Feudalism in Western Europe was, he knew, based on solemn oaths of fealty; he therefore resolved to demand such an oath from all the leaders who should pass through Constantinople in respect of any conquests that they might make in the future.

The first of these leaders, Hugh of Vermandois, was the younger brother of King Philip I of France. He appeared in Constantinople in early November 1096, severely shaken by a disastrous shipwreck in the Adriatic; and after Alexius had loaded him with rich presents, willingly swore the oath required of him. The next two, however, proved somewhat less tractable. They were Godfrey of Bouillon, Duke of Lower Lorraine, and his brother Baldwin of Boulogne – who, as a younger son without a patrimony, had brought his wife and children with him and was determined to carve out a kingdom for himself in the East. With them were many prominent knights from northern France and the Low Countries, together with a large and well-trained army. They travelled via Hungary, with no serious mishap until they reached Selymbria[1] on the Marmara where, for reasons unclear, morale suddenly broke down and the army ravaged the surrounding countryside for a week; but the brothers were finally able to reassert their authority and arrived two days before Christmas near the present Eyüp on the upper reaches of the Golden Horn, where they were required by the imperial authorities to pitch their camp.

A day or two later, Hugh of Vermandois arrived as a special emissary from Alexius, with an invitation to an audience at the Palace of Blachernae to take the necessary oath. Godfrey categorically refused, pointing out that in return for his Dukedom he had already sworn fealty to the Western Emperor Henry IV; besides, he had by this time heard of the catastrophe that had befallen Peter's army, which the few survivors were openly attributing to Byzantine treachery. Alexius, now seriously concerned, reduced the provisions that he had made available to the Crusaders' camp; but when Baldwin began raiding the neighbouring suburbs he was obliged to give in, and so the stalemate continued for three long months until the Emperor, learning that new Crusading armies were on their way, decided to cut off supplies altogether. He thus provoked his unwelcome guests into open aggression – which was almost certainly just what he had intended. He himself could not have initiated violence on a Christian army that had arrived – ostensibly at least – under the flag of friendship; but if he excused the brothers the oath of allegiance, how could he hope to impose it on those who would follow? Clearly the time had come for a showdown, and this was the best way to ensure it.

Godfrey and Baldwin – whom he had allowed to move their camp to the hill of Galata opposite Constantinople – now crossed the Golden

1 Now Silivri.

Horn and drew up their men at its junction with the northern end of the
city walls, immediately outside Blachernae. Alexius, horrified by their
lack of regard for religious proprieties – it was the Thursday of Holy
Week – and convinced that they were making a bid for the Empire
itself, brought out his own troops (though not before giving them strict
and secret orders not to engage) and commanded his archers to fire from
the walls over the enemy's heads. At first these tactics seemed to work:
the Crusaders withdrew, having killed only seven of the imperial soldiers.
But when they suddenly returned to the assault, the Emperor decided
that he had had enough and sent in his crack regiments to do battle.
Bewildered and demoralized, the Frankish troops turned and fled. The
brothers had no choice but to capitulate. On Easter Sunday they and
their leading knights swore their oaths at last. Immediately, amicable
relations were restored. Alexius showered them with presents and entertained them all to a banquet. The next day he shipped the lot of them
over the Bosphorus.

Of all the leaders of the First Crusade, there was one whom Alexius
Comnenus mistrusted more than any other. Bohemund, now Prince of
Taranto – who arrived in Constantinople on 9 April 1097, at the head of
an army which included no fewer than four other grandsons and two
great-grandsons of old Tancred de Hauteville – was the eldest son of
Robert Guiscard who, had he not succumbed to that most fortunate
epidemic twelve years before, might well have displaced Alexius on the
Byzantine throne. The fact that Robert had divorced his first wife –
Bohemund's mother – to marry the formidable Sichelgaita, and that he
had subsequently left his Italian dominions to the latter's son Roger
Borsa, made Bohemund arguably more dangerous than ever: having
nothing to hope for in Italy, he could be expected to wreak still greater
havoc in the East. Moreover, his military reputation – based as much on
his brilliant leadership and the care with which he trained his men as on
his own outstanding personal courage on the battlefield – was unmatched
in Europe. As to his looks, even Anna Comnena finds it hard to
withhold her admiration:

Bohemund's appearance was, to put it briefly, unlike that of any other man
seen in those days in the Roman world, whether Greek or barbarian ... His
stature was such that he towered almost a full cubit over the tallest men. He
was slender of waist and flanks, with broad shoulders and chest, strong in the
arms; in general he was neither too slim nor heavily-built and fleshy, but of
perfect proportions ... To the acute observer he appeared to stoop slightly ...

The skin all over his body was very white, except for his face which was both white and red. His hair was lightish-brown and not as long as that of other barbarians – it did not hang on his shoulders but was cut short, to the ears. Whether his beard was red or any other colour I cannot say, for the razor had attacked it, leaving his chin smoother than any marble; yet it gave an impression of redness. His eyes were light blue and gave some hint of the man's spirit and dignity. He breathed freely through broad nostrils ... He had about him a certain charm, but it was somewhat dimmed by the alarm inspired by his person as a whole; there was a hard, savage quality in his aspect – owing, I suppose, to his great stature and to his eyes: even his laugh sounded like a threat to others.

The Emperor received him the day after his arrival and, according to Anna, politely reminded him of his former hostility. Bohemund cheerfully admitted it, pointing out, however, that this time he had come of his own free will, as a friend. When asked to take the oath of allegiance, he agreed at once. Alexius's relief was admittedly somewhat mitigated when his guest then asked point-blank to be named Grand Domestic of the East – effectively commander-in-chief of the entire imperial army in Asia; but when he in turn suggested that such an appointment was not for the time being appropriate – although it might well in due course become so – the Prince of Taranto seemed to accept this obvious piece of prevarication philosophically enough. Bohemund was in fact playing his cards beautifully. A southerner himself, he knew and understood the Greeks and spoke their language; and, unlike the other Crusaders who preceded and followed him, he was well aware that success in his great enterprise – which, however it might turn out, must certainly begin by his being accepted as leader of the whole expedition – would largely depend on having the *basileus* on his side. To antagonize him at this stage would be folly. With this thought in mind he had specifically forbidden his soldiers, on pain of instant execution, any marauding or other misbehaviour on their way to Constantinople. So far they had shown themselves to be in every respect model Crusaders, and he was determined – at least for the time being – that they should remain so. A fortnight later he and his army were conveyed in their turn across the Bosphorus, while Alexius struggled to come to terms with the next arrival.

Raymond IV of Saint-Gilles, Count of Toulouse and Marquis of Provence, was the oldest, richest and most distinguished of the Crusaders. He was also the most experienced: as the husband of Princess Elvira of Aragon he had fought many a battle against the Moors in

Spain. Finally, from the point of view of Alexius Comnenus, he was by far the most difficult. Though already in his late fifties, he had been the first nobleman to take the cross at Clermont and had publicly vowed never to return to the West; his wife and his son Alfonso had accompanied him. His was almost certainly the largest of the properly-organized Crusading armies – perhaps some ten thousand strong. He travelled with his friend Bishop Adhemar of Le Puy, to whom Pope Urban had entrusted the spiritual well-being of the Crusade; and there can be little doubt that, like Bohemund, he coveted the military leadership for himself.

Unlike the Prince of Taranto, however, Raymond seems to have made little attempt to control his men, whose taste for indiscriminate rape and pillage brought them into repeated confrontation with their imperial Pecheneg escort. Within a few days of their arrival on Byzantine territory two Provençal knights had been killed. Soon afterwards the Bishop of Le Puy inadvertently strayed from the road; he too was attacked – and quite badly wounded – by the Pechenegs before they realized their mistake and returned him to his flock. Raymond himself narrowly escaped a similar fate as he passed Edessa, while at Roussa in Thrace his army actually forced its way into the town and plundered it. A day or two after this outrage, messengers arrived from Alexius urging him to come at once to Constantinople, in advance of the rest; in his absence the situation grew rapidly worse, until the Pecheneg escort decided that things had gone far enough. Supported by several Byzantine regiments stationed in the region, they attacked the Crusaders and defeated them in pitched battle, taking possession of their baggage and equipment.

News of the débâcle was brought to Raymond just as he was preparing for his first audience with the Emperor. It did not improve his temper. At the outset, he made it clear to all concerned that he had no intention of taking the oath. To do so would not only have meant surrendering the special authority that he believed he had received from the Pope; it would also have risked his being subordinated to Bohemund if, as rumour in Constantinople had it, the latter was to be appointed by the Emperor to a senior imperial post. Raymond is unlikely to have made this last point directly to Alexius; he did however say that if the *basileus* himself were to assume personal command of the Crusading army, then he, Raymond, would be happy to serve under him. To this Alexius could only reply that much as he might wish to do so, in present conditions he could not leave the Empire. So the stalemate continued for the better part of a fortnight, while one Western leader after another pleaded with the Count of Toulouse to change his mind rather than imperil the success of the whole expedition. Finally, a compromise was reached: the Count agreed to swear a type of oath common in the Languedoc, promising to respect the life and honour of the Emperor and to see that nothing should be done to his detriment; and Alexius, realizing that this was the best he could hope for, very sensibly accepted.

And so we come to the fourth and last expedition of the Crusade – that of Robert, Duke of Normandy, eldest son of William the Conqueror, who set out in September 1096. With him rode his brother-in-law Count Stephen of Blois and his cousin Count Robert II of Flanders, the three of them sharing the command of an army which included Bishop Odo of Bayeux and many distinguished noblemen and knights from Normandy, Brittany and England. Travelling by way of Italy through Lucca (where Pope Urban granted them an audience), Rome and Monte Cassino, they finally reached the Norman Duchy of Apulia, where Duke Roger Borsa gave them a warm welcome. Thence Robert of Flanders – despite the fact that Roger was his brother-in-law – pressed on almost at once, taking ship from Bari to Epirus in the first week of December. For the Duke of Normandy and the Count of Blois, however, the delights of South Italy proved irresistible: it was April 1097 before they set sail across the Adriatic. Alas, the first ship to leave Brindisi almost immediately capsized and went, with some four hundred passengers and their horses and mules – to say nothing of many coffers stuffed with gold and silver – to the bottom: a disaster which sent a good many of the less enthusiastic Crusaders straight back to their homes.[1]

Those who persisted were rewarded by an agreeable and uneventful journey – apart from a flash flood in the Pindus mountains, which swept away a pilgrim or two. They reached Constantinople in early May. All their predecessors were by now safely in Asia Minor, and the leaders – none of whom made any difficulties over the oath of allegiance – were enchanted by the Emperor's generosity, as well as by the quality of the food, horses and silken robes that he pressed on them. 'Your father, my love,' wrote Stephen of Blois somewhat tactlessly to his wife Adela, the Conqueror's daughter, 'made many great gifts, but compared with this man he was almost nothing.'[2] The rank and file were less lavishly

---

1 The discovery that every corpse washed up on the shore bore a cross miraculously inscribed on its shoulder-blade doubtless impressed them, but failed to make them change their minds.

2 Sir Steven Runciman, *A History of the Crusades*, Vol. I, p. 168.

indulged; as usual, however, all those who wished to do so were allowed to enter in groups of half a dozen at a time to see the sights and worship at the principal shrines. There were no complaints. After a fortnight they followed the other armies over the Bosphorus – no worse, wrote Stephen, than crossing the Seine or the Marne – and joined them at Nicaea.

The relief of Alexius Comnenus, as he watched the last of the Crusaders embark on the vessel that was to carry them over to Asia, may well be imagined. He himself can have had little idea of just how many men, women and children had crossed his territory in the course of the past nine months; the total – ranging from Peter the Hermit's rabble to the great feudal lords like Raymond of Saint-Gilles – cannot have been far short of a hundred thousand. Inevitably, there had been a degree of desultory marauding and a few unfortunate incidents; on the whole, however, thanks to his preparations and precautions – in particular the regular food supplies which he had arranged and the admirable policing by his own troops – the armies had caused remarkably little trouble. Whether willingly or not, all the commanders except Raymond – with whom he had come to a private understanding – had sworn him their allegiance; even if they were later to break their oaths his own moral position would be immeasurably strengthened.

On this last score he had no delusions. The Crusaders were still within his Empire, and although they were at present engaged against his Turkish enemies there was no telling what long-term ambitions they might cherish. As they had already made all too clear, they had no love for the Byzantines. In the Balkans and Thrace, where they had expected to be welcomed as saviours, they had been received with suspicion and mistrust. In Constantinople itself, the small and carefully-shepherded groups of sightseers had been thoroughly shaken by what they had seen. For a French peasant or the burgher of a small medieval German town the first sight of the richest and most luxurious city in the world, of its markets of silks and spices redolent of all the exoticism of the East, of its extravagantly dressed noblemen with their retinues of slaves and eunuchs, of its great ladies borne along on gilded palanquins, their faces brilliant with paint and enamel beneath coiffures of astonishing elaboration, must have appeared first incredible and then profoundly shocking; while such religious services as they attended would have seemed unfamiliar, incomprehensible and deeply heretical into the bargain.

The Byzantines felt no more warmly disposed to the Crusaders.

Foreign armies, however friendly they might be in theory, were never welcome guests; but these dirty and ill-mannered barbarians were surely worse than most. They had ravaged their lands, ravished their women, plundered their towns and villages; yet they seemed to take all this as their right, unaccountably expecting to be treated as heroes and deliverers rather than as the ruffians they were. Their departure had occasioned much rejoicing; and when they returned they would, it was devoutly hoped, be considerably fewer in number than on the outward journey. Fellow-Christians they might be; but there must have been quite a number of the Emperor's subjects who secretly hoped for the success of Saracen arms in the encounters that were to come.

Alexius Comnenus did not share such hopes. He had not summoned the Crusade – he did not even approve of it – but now that it was there he was determined to give it all the help he could, provided only that it kept to its original purpose to deliver the Holy Places from the Infidel. Up to that point, the interests of Christendom and of his Empire went hand in hand. They would cease to do so only if the Crusaders began to forget the Cross that they bore on their shoulders and to act on their own initiative; as Alexius well knew, though it was an easy matter to allow foreign armies to enter one's territory, it was a good deal harder to get them out again.

Contrary to the expectations of many, the First Crusade turned out to be a resounding, if undeserved, success. In June 1097 Nicaea was besieged and captured, with the consequent restoration of Byzantine sovereignty in western Asia Minor; on 1 July the Seljuk Turks were smashed at Dorylaeum in Anatolia; on 3 June 1098 Antioch fell to Crusader arms; and finally on 15 July 1099, amid scenes of hideous carnage, the soldiers of Christ battered their way into Jerusalem, where they slaughtered all the Muslims in the city and burnt all the Jews alive in the main synagogue before, in the Church of the Holy Sepulchre, clasping their bloodstained hands together in prayer and thanksgiving. Two of their former leaders were not, however, by then among them: Baldwin of Boulogne had made himself Count of Edessa on the Middle Euphrates, while Bohemund – after a bitter quarrel with Raymond of Toulouse – had established himself as Prince of Antioch.

In Jerusalem itself, an election was held to decide upon its future ruler. The obvious candidate was Raymond: he was the oldest of the leading Crusaders, the richest and by far the most experienced. But, to everyone's surprise, he refused. His arrogance and his overbearing manner had made him unpopular with his colleagues: he would never be able to count on their obedience or support, and he knew it. The choice eventually fell upon Godfrey of Lower Lorraine. He had not shown any particular military or diplomatic ability during the Crusade, though he had fought bravely enough. A more important consideration was his genuine piety and – in marked contrast to most of his fellows – his irreproachable private life. He too made a show of reluctance; but he eventually agreed provided that, in the city where Christ had worn the crown of thorns, he was not obliged to bear the title of King. Instead, he would take the title of *Advocatus Sancti Sepulchri*, Defender of the Holy Sepulchre.

To Alexius Comnenus, devout Christian that he was, the news of the recovery of Jerusalem could not have been anything but welcome. It was not that he trusted the Crusaders; but the city had been in infidel hands for the best part of four centuries, and was anyway too far distant from Constantinople to be of major strategic importance. The situation in Antioch, on the other hand, caused him grave anxiety. This ancient city and patriarchate had also had a chequered history: it had been sacked by the Persians in the sixth century and occupied by them for nearly twenty years in the early seventh, before falling to the Arabs in 637; but in 969 it had been reconquered by the Empire, of which it had thereafter remained an integral part until 1078. Its inhabitants were overwhelmingly Greek-speaking and Orthodox; and in the eyes of Alexius and all his right-thinking subjects it was a Byzantine city through and through. Now it had been seized by a Norman adventurer who, despite his oath, clearly had no intention of surrendering it and was no longer making any secret of his hostility. He had even gone so far as to expel the Greek Patriarch and replace him with a Latin, Bernard of Valence, formerly Bishop Adhemar's chaplain.

There was, however, one source of comfort: Bohemund was every bit as unwelcome to his neighbours to the north, the Danishmend Turks;[1] and Alexius's satisfaction can well be imagined when he heard, in the summer of 1100, that the Prince of Antioch was their prisoner and had been carried off in chains to the castle of Niksar – the Greek Neocaesarea – far away in the mountains of Pontus. There he was to remain for three

---

1 A Turkoman dynasty whose founder, the Emir Danishmend, had appeared in Asia Minor some fifteen years before and ruled in Cappadocia and the regions around Sebasteia (now Sivas) and Melitene. Over the next century, as we shall see, the Danishmends were to play a significant part in Byzantine history; but after the Seljuk capture of Melitene in 1178 they were to vanish as suddenly as they had appeared.

long years until he was finally ransomed by Baldwin, who had become King of Jerusalem – unlike his brother Godfrey, he had had no qualms about the title – on Godfrey's death in July 1100.

During these first years following the Crusaders' triumph, it became ever more clear that Bohemund was not alone in his attitude to Byzantium. After the capture of Jerusalem, the genuine pilgrims – many of them sickened by the atrocities they had seen committed in Christ's name – had begun to trickle home; the Franks who remained in Outremer (as the Crusader lands in the Middle East had come to be called) were the military adventurers who, having recaptured the Holy City, were now out for what they could get. Of all the leaders of the First Crusade, only Raymond of Toulouse – who, ironically, had alone refused to swear the oath at Constantinople – had acted in good faith and had returned to the Emperor certain conquests of what had formerly been imperial territory. The rest were proving little better than the Saracens they had supplanted.

None of this came as any surprise to Alexius; indeed, it confirmed what he had always known. But it could not have improved his temper when he saw, in 1101, no fewer than four more expeditions arriving at his capital on their way to the East: a Lombard army of some twenty thousand under Archbishop Anselm of Milan; a large group of French knights – including poor Stephen of Blois, who had taken flight during the siege of Antioch and was now returning at the insistence of his formidable wife Adela – she was not the Conqueror's daughter for nothing – to redeem his reputation; another French army led by Count William of Nevers; and an immense Franco-German force under the joint command of William, Duke of Aquitaine and Welf, Duke of Bavaria – which also included Hugh of Vermandois, who had retired from the First Crusade after the capture of Antioch and was determined to fulfil his vow to reach Jerusalem. What would have been the consequences for Byzantium if these armies had met with the success of their predecessors is a question on which one would rather not speculate; in fact, all met with disaster. The Lombards – who, soon after their arrival, had forced an entry into the Palace of Blachernae and killed one of the Emperor's pet lions – joined up with Stephen and his knights and set off under the command of Raymond of Toulouse, who had been paying a visit to Alexius; they captured Ancyra (now Ankara) and duly returned it to the Empire, but shortly afterwards were ambushed by the Danishmends and their allies at Mersivan, near Amasea (the modern Amasya). Four-fifths of the army perished; the women and children –

for once again many of the Crusaders were travelling with their families – were carried off as slaves; Raymond, his Provençal bodyguard and his Byzantine escort fled the field under cover of darkness and made their way back to Constantinople.

The other two armies fared no better. William of Nevers crossed the Bosphorus towards the end of June and led his men via Ancyra to Iconium (Konya), which he tried to capture without success. He then moved on to Heraclea Cybistra (Ereğli), which the enemy had recently abandoned, having poisoned all the wells. The summer was now at its height; the Nivernais army, half-mad with thirst, searched desperately for some alternative water supply, but in vain. The Turks, under the joint command of the Seljuk Sultan Kilij Arslan and the Danishmend Malik Ghazi, allowed them a few days to exhaust themselves; then they struck. The Christian cavalry broke and fled, the infantry and non-combatants were slain or captured. William, his brother and a small company of knights managed to escape, and hired some local Turcopoles[1] to take them to Antioch; but their guides betrayed them, stole their horses and all their possessions and left them to fend for themselves, naked in the wilderness. At last they reached the city, where Bohemund's nephew Tancred took pity on them and gave them shelter for the winter. The following spring they rode on, sad and dispirited, to Jerusalem.

The Crusaders from Aquitaine and Bavaria seem to have suffered much the same fate. They too encountered poisoned wells and the torments of thirst but, unlike the Nivernais, they found a river near Heraclea. Unfortunately, this was just what they were intended to do. No sooner had they flung themselves into the water than the Turks loosed a hail of arrows and charged out from their ambush. As usual it was the leaders, with their faster horses, who survived: William of Aquitaine escaped to Tarsus and thence to Antioch, while Welf of Bavaria threw away all his arms and armour and slipped off incognito through the mountains. Hugh of Vermandois was less fortunate. Badly wounded in the knee by an arrow, he too somehow reached Tarsus; but the effort was too much for him and he died there on 18 October, his vow unfulfilled.

The release of Bohemund of Antioch in 1103 was the signal for a renewed burst of activity on the part of those Crusaders who had now settled in Outremer. By this time they were fighting Arabs, Turks and Byzantines more or less indiscriminately, with occasional brief truces;

---

1 Turkish horsemen serving in the imperial army.

but they were not outstandingly successful, and in the early summer of 1104 they suffered a crushing defeat by the Turks beneath the walls of Harran, some twenty-five miles south-east of Edessa on the Balikh river. Bohemund's army managed to escape without serious losses – though Patriarch Bernard was so frightened that he cut off his horse's tail as he fled, lest some Turk should seize hold of it and catch him – but the forces of Edessa were massacred almost to a man. Both Baldwin and his cousin, Joscelin of Courtenay, were captured.

The catastrophe at Harran, together with the failures of the expeditions of 1101, dealt the military reputation of the early Crusaders a blow from which it never recovered. Together they virtually closed the overland supply line from the West, which was of considerable value to Antioch and essential to Edessa for its very survival. They also made it possible for Alexius Comnenus to recapture several vital fortresses, including Adana, Mopsuestia[1] and Tarsus, and coastal cities from Laodicea (Lattakieh) as far south as Tripoli. Bohemund now felt dangerously threatened. Leaving Tancred to look after his principality and taking with him the *Gesta Francorum* – an account of the First Crusade written by a Norman and heavily biased in favour of his countrymen – he set sail in the late autumn for Europe, to raise reinforcements.[2]

Arriving in Apulia early in 1105, he stayed there eight months; after an absence of nearly a decade, there was much work to be done on his long-neglected estates; meanwhile he took every opportunity to encourage groups of young Normans to follow his example and seek their own fortunes in the East. Then, in September, he moved on to Rome to see Pope Paschal II, whom he effortlessly convinced that the arch-enemy of the Crusader states of Outremer was neither the Arab nor the Turk, but Alexius Comnenus himself. So enthusiastically did Paschal accept his arguments that when the time came for Bohemund to go on to France he found himself accompanied by a papal legate with instructions to preach a Holy War against Byzantium.

The Prince of Antioch had spent much of his life fighting the Eastern Empire, and would soon be doing so again; yet never, before or since, did he do the Empire – or indeed, the whole Christian cause – so much harm as in those conversations with Pope Paschal. Henceforth the

---

1 This was its classical name; it later became Misis, then Mamistra. Now it is Yakapinar.

2 Anna Comnena ludicrously claims that in order to avoid capture Bohemund feigned death and he was put on board his ship in a carefully ventilated coffin, together with a dead cockerel to provide the necessary smell of putrefaction. One sometimes thinks that she would believe anything.

narrow, predatory policy that had been pursued by his father and himself became the official policy of Christendom. Those Crusaders – and they constituted the vast majority – who disliked the Byzantines, whether for reasons of jealousy or resentment, puritanical disapproval or sheer incomprehension, now found their prejudices endorsed by the highest authority and given official sanction. As for Alexius and his subjects, they saw their worst suspicions confirmed. The entire Crusade was now revealed as having been nothing more than a monstrous exercise in hypocrisy, in which the religious motive had been used merely as the thinnest of disguises for what was in fact unashamed imperialism. Not even Cardinal Humbert and the Patriarch Michael Cerularius, half a century before, had struck a more telling blow against the unity of the Churches of East and West.[1]

In Paris, King Philip I gave Bohemund a warm welcome and granted him permission to raise recruits throughout his Kingdom; then, as a further sign of his benevolence, he bestowed on him the hand of his daughter Constance in marriage,[2] simultaneously offering his younger, illegitimate daughter Cecilia to Tancred. Bohemund stayed in France throughout 1106 – at Easter he met the English King Henry I in Normandy – collecting men and materials; then at the end of the year he returned with Constance to Apulia. Cecilia had already sailed off to Antioch, but he was in no particular hurry to follow her, and it was not till the autumn of 1107 that his new army was ready to sail. His plan was basically the same as that of Robert Guiscard a quarter of a century before: to land on the coast of Epirus in what is now Albania, to ensure a bridgehead by capturing the mighty fortress of Durazzo and then to march eastward on Constantinople.

This time, however, the fates were against him. The Apulians landed successfully enough near Valona; but Alexius had reinforced Durazzo, and the mercenaries he had hired from the Seljuk Sultan stoutly resisted every attempt to take it by storm. Bohemund, not greatly perturbed, settled down to a siege; but almost immediately he found himself blockaded by a Byzantine fleet, cutting off his communications with Italy throughout the winter. Then, as spring approached, so did Alexius with the main body of his army. The invaders, now surrounded by land

1 See *Byzantium: The Apogee*, pp. 315-22.

2 Although such distinguished alliances obviously did much to enhance the prestige of the House of Antioch, it must in fairness be admitted that Constance's slightly chequered past – she had previously been married to the Count of Champagne, from whom she was divorced – made her a slightly less desirable *parti* than she might otherwise have been.

and sea, slowly fell prey to famine and malaria, and by September the Prince of Antioch had no choice but to surrender. Brought before Alexius in his camp on the bank of the Devol river, he was obliged to put his name to a treaty of peace, in which he expressed regret at having broken his former oath, swore fealty to the Emperor and recognized him as his suzerain for the Principality of Antioch, the borders of which were meticulously defined. Finally he agreed that the Latin Patriarch of the city should be replaced by a Greek.

The Treaty of Devol marked the end of Bohemund's career. Such was his humiliation that he returned at once to Apulia, leaving Antioch in the hands of Tancred, with his two sons by Constance to inherit after him. He had been a fine soldier and a charismatic leader of men; but his ambition had betrayed him and brought him low. He died three years later in relative obscurity, never again having dared to show his face in Outremer. He was buried at Canosa in Apulia, where visitors to the cathedral can still see, huddled against the outside of the south wall, his curiously oriental-looking mausoleum – the earliest Norman tomb extant in South Italy. Its beautiful bronze doors, engraved with Arabic designs and a eulogistic inscription, open to reveal an interior bare but for two little columns and the tombstone itself – on which is carved, roughly yet somehow magnificently, one word only: BOAMVNDVS.

4
Alexius – The Last Years

[1108–18]

Listening to them, you would think that my roads were covered with cheese, that my mountains ran with rivers of milk, that I was immeasurably rich, that I lived like a satrap, that the luxury of Media was as nothing in comparison with mine, and that the palaces of Susa and Ecbatana were hovels compared to my own dwellings.

Theophylact, Archbishop of Ochrid,
on the imperial tax-collectors, Letter No. xli

Alexius Comnenus returned to Constantinople during the last weeks of 1108, well satisfied with what he had achieved. His Empire was, for the moment, at peace. It was true that Tancred of Antioch had already disavowed the Treaty of Devol, thus making it effectively a dead letter; but the treaty, having broken Bohemund, had served its purpose well enough and Tancred, together with his fellow-Crusaders, was temporarily too occupied with his Saracen enemies to cause any serious trouble to Byzantium. Thus, for the next two years, the Emperor was able to concentrate on domestic matters; and since the pressure of events in the international sphere has allowed little opportunity to consider these during the last two chapters, it might be as well for us, briefly, to do the same.

The first decade of Alexius's reign had been hard indeed. As a brilliant and apparently invincible young general during the reign of Nicephorus Botaneiates, he had appeared to many of his subjects as the only hope of survival that remained to a beleaguered Empire; but once the supreme power was in his hands, his magic had quickly faded. In the very year of his coronation, he had suffered at Durazzo the most shattering defeat of his career. Admittedly he had had his revenge at Larissa eighteen months later; but the Normans had been back again in 1084, and but for the sudden death of Robert Guiscard they might easily have advanced to Constantinople. Meanwhile, apart from one relatively unimportant and indecisive campaign against the Emir Chaka of Smyrna, he had made no serious attempt to dislodge the Turks from Asia Minor. By Easter 1091, after ten years on the throne and with virtually no major achievements to his credit, Alexius was generally accounted a failure; and people were beginning to wonder whether Byzantine Europe, under almost constant pressure from Normans, Pechenegs or Bogomils, was not going the same way as Byzantine Asia. Would there, they asked themselves, within a very few more years, be any Empire worthy of the name outside the walls of Constantinople itself?

The Patriarch of Antioch, John the Oxite, went further and, in the course of two bitter diatribes against the Emperor which were published at about this time, referred to this whittling away of the Empire as a *fait accompli*. The people, he continued, were depressed and disillusioned. In the past they had believed that defeats and reversals of fortune were God's punishment for their sins; now they increasingly felt that God was no longer concerned with them at all. The rich were becoming poor, and the poor – particularly those of Macedonia, Thrace and the northern Balkans – were facing starvation and death from exposure as they fled from the barbarian invaders. The only exceptions to the general misery were the members of the imperial family, 'who have become the greatest scourge upon the Empire and upon us all'.

The Patriarch may have been exaggerating a little; since Antioch was a good six hundred miles from the capital and still in Saracen hands, he was not in any case particularly well qualified to pronounce on the situation in the European provinces. But there was much truth in what he said. What is less certain is how justified he was in holding the Emperor responsible. It was not Alexius's fault that first the Normans and then the Pechenegs had devastated an immense area of the Balkan peninsula, burning towns and villages, killing thousands of their inhabitants and rendering many more thousands homeless. He had fought back fiercely and, only a few weeks after the Patriarch had launched his attack, had decisively defeated the Pechenegs at Levunium. The Normans, admittedly, were to take him a little longer, but it is hard to see how he could have done more than he did.

The accusations of nepotism are more difficult to answer; nor was the Patriarch of Antioch by any means the only man to make them. The chronicler John Zonaras bears him out:

He provided his relatives and some of his retainers with cartloads of public money and made them generous allowances, so that they abounded in wealth and kept retinues more appropriate for Emperors than for private citizens. Their dwellings were comparable to cities in size, and not unlike imperial palaces in the luxury of their appointments.[1]

It could of course be argued that all reigning families, in all countries and periods, have enjoyed special privileges of one kind or another. We must also remember that, at least in the early years of his reign, Alexius had few people that he could trust outside his immediate family. Given the chaotic conditions prevailing in Byzantium during the middle decades of the eleventh century, the circumstances of his accession and the number of enemies he had in Constantinople, some degree of nepotism was surely permissible; without the support of a powerful family around him, he would not have remained *basileus* for long. Was he not to some extent justified, therefore, in raising his mother Anna Dalassena, his brother Isaac, his brother-in-law Nicephorus Melissenus, his son John, his son-in-law Nicephorus Bryennius and several other of his close relations to key positions, and rewarding them accordingly?

Perhaps he was; unfortunately, he did not content himself with loading the members of his family with highly remunerative offices and specially minted new titles; he gave them regional power as well. In former times, public lands – those, that is, which belonged to the state rather than forming part of the Emperor's personal demesne – were the direct responsibility of the imperial government; Alexius now granted to his relatives the administration of large tracts of such lands, together with their revenues. These grants, technically known as *pronoia*, were admittedly only temporary: he could take them back whenever he liked, and they anyway reverted to him on the death of the holder. But they were nevertheless a dangerous precedent, and a further drain on his hard-pressed treasury.

Already for a good half-century before his accession, the Byzantine economy had been in steady decline. We have already seen[2] how, twenty years before, the value of the gold *nomisma* had already fallen by 25 per cent; under both Botaneiates and Alexius this debasement had continued, to the point where six different *nomismata*, of six different baser metals, were in circulation – though the imperial exchequer, which had minted them, at first insisted that all payments to itself should be made in the original gold. The resulting confusion caused economic chaos through-

1 Zonaras, Book III.
2 See p. 4, note 2.

out the Empire. In 1092 Alexius introduced the gold *hyperpyron* ('highly refined') which became the standard Byzantine coin for the next two centuries; but it was not until 1109 that he finally managed to restore some sort of order by establishing a proper rate for the whole coinage. The situation was still far from satisfactory; but at least it allowed an effective operation of the fiscal system – and that, for Alexius Comnenus, was the most important consideration.

It had to be. Through most of his reign, the Empire was facing attack either from the East or from the West, and quite often from both. He had inherited from his predecessors only a poorly-equipped and hetero-geneous army and a small and long-neglected fleet – so ineffectual that when Robert Guiscard had sailed against him in 1081 he had had to seek aid from Venice. If Byzantium were to survive, the former had to be reorganized and strengthened, the latter rebuilt virtually from scratch; and neither of these objectives could be achieved without considerable cost. Alexius had set to work at once, seeking the money wherever it could be found; and ten years later, as we have seen, he scored important victories on both land and sea. For him, it had been a labour of love. He had always been, first and foremost, a soldier. The art of warfare fascinated him. As *The Alexiad* makes clear time and time again, he was never happier than when taking part in military exercises, transforming his soldiers from ill-disciplined barbarians into trained fighting men. And once he had moulded his army as he wanted it, he was determined to keep it to himself. He knew – no one better – how easy it was for a brilliant and successful commander to win the support of his soldiers and then, at the first sign of weakness in the government, to stage a *coup d'état*; and he had no intention of allowing any of his own gen-erals to topple him as he had toppled his predecessor. It was for this reason as much as for his genuine love of battle that he would assume personal command whenever possible, placing himself at the head of his troops and, incidentally, proving himself the greatest military commander that Byzantium had seen since Basil II nearly a century before.

Given the huge expenditure necessary for adequate imperial defence, it is understandable that Alexius's fiscal policy should have been harsh and, at times, none too scrupulous. He never repeated his action of early 1082, when he – or, more accurately, his brother Isaac – had seized the treasures of the Church to pay for the campaign against Bohemund; but the aristocracy (excepting, of course, members of his own family and other close adherents), the senatorial families (whom he hated) and the richer monasteries suffered greatly from his extortions. With the economy in such confusion it was easy to claim that previous payments had been insufficient or paid in the wrong coin – or even that they had not been paid at all – and then to impose swingeing surcharges.

For the Emperor's more humble subjects, too, times were hard. This had been one of the themes of the Patriarch of Antioch in 1091; twenty years later, the situation was very little better. Archbishop Theophylact of Ochrid – whose remarks about the imperial tax collectors, quoted at the head of this chapter, will arouse the instant sympathy of all those who have ever been subjected to a wealth tax – writes to the Emperor's nephew, Duke John of Durazzo, of the conditions in one of his dioceses that had been trampled over time and time again by Normans and Greeks, Pechenegs and Crusaders:

> I could not hold back my tears. In the church the people no longer sing, the candles remain unlit; the bishop and clergy have been forced to flee, and the townsfolk have left their houses to live hidden in the woods and forests. And in addition to all these evils, which are the results of war, the peasants have had their land seized by the great landowners, both lay and ecclesiastical, and are as heavily oppressed by the demands of military service as by taxation.

True, the Archbishop was writing only of one particular diocese; but the conditions he described could have been found throughout the European provinces of the Empire. He was right, too, about the compulsory military service, which was bitterly resented wherever it was enforced. The peasantry, even more than the dwellers in cities and towns, lived under constant dread of the imperial recruiting sergeants, who were for ever scouring the Empire for able-bodied young men. Their fears were well justified – and not only because they desperately needed the labour in their efforts to restore their ravaged fields; there was also the very real danger that those same young men, when their period of service was over, would settle in Constantinople or elsewhere and never return to their old homes.[1] It was all very well to say – as Alexius himself would have said – that any sensible family would prefer to provide a soldier for the Empire than to have its house destroyed, its sons slaughtered and its daughters violated by foreign invaders; hungry and frightened peasants are little impressed by such logical

---

1 In the Theme of Pelagonia, writes the Archbishop, the population has declined to such a point that the Theme ought to be renamed Mykonos – in his day (though not in ours) one of the smallest, poorest and emptiest of the Cyclades.

arguments. The truth was that the Emperor, held responsible for all these tribulations, was hated by the vast majority of his people. And he knew it.

What steps, if any, did Alexius Comnenus take to brighten his image in the eyes of his subjects? From the outset of his reign he had struggled hard to win, if not their love, then at least their respect. In the fifty-six years between the death of Basil II in 1025 and his own accession in 1081, the Empire had acknowledged no fewer than thirteen rulers; his first task, therefore, had been to show that he had no intention of being just such another. His message was clear. His pathetic predecessors had been the products of a system that was rotten through and through: depraved, decadent and corrupt. He would reform that system, and restore the Empire to its former greatness.

Before it could be restored, however, it must be cleansed and purified. While his mother tackled the alleged Augean stables of the *gynaeceum* in the imperial palace,[1] he himself launched a campaign to free the Empire of heresy. His first victim, a pupil of Michael Psellus named John Italus, whom he believed had gone too far in his advocacy of the works of Plato and Aristotle at the expense of those of the early Christian Fathers, was found guilty at an elaborate show trial and condemned to lifelong seclusion in a monastery. Similar investigations continued throughout his reign, including one which took place in its very last year and which resulted in the principal representative of the Bogomils – known to us only by his Christian name of Basil – being burnt at the stake in the Hippodrome: a penalty hitherto almost unknown in Constantinople.

Although all these proceedings obviously contained a strong element of propaganda, there can be no doubt of Alexius's profound religious faith. However involved he might be with other, more immediately urgent preoccupations – on campaign against Robert Guiscard or Bohemund, defending the Empire against the Pechenegs, or striving to control the flood tide of the Crusading armies as it swept across his frontiers – he never for a moment forgot his religious responsibilities as *basileus*, Equal of the Apostles. Nor were these confined to questions of

---

1 'The women's quarters in the palace had been the scene of utter depravity ever since the infamous Constantine Monomachus had ascended the throne ... but Anna [Dalassena] effected a reformation; a commendable decorum was restored and the palace now enjoyed a most praiseworthy discipline. She instituted set times for the singing of sacred hymns, and fixed hours for breakfast ... the palace assumed the appearance rather of a monastery' (*The Alexiad*, III, viii). There must, one feels, have been many around the place who dreamed nostalgically of the good old days.

doctrine; he was also deeply concerned with Church affairs, and early in his reign instituted a radical reform in the long-established practice of what was known as *charisticum*, by which the administration of monasteries and monastic property was handed over to lay patrons. This practice, which had increased dramatically during the eleventh century, was aimed principally at the economic development of such properties and usually worked well enough; but the inevitable element of secularization had its dangers. The patron could introduce lay brothers, who lived off the monastery while making no contribution to its spiritual life; he could put pressure on the abbot – and even on the monks – to involve themselves in business; he might even, if he chose, milk the monastery dry.

As the founder of several generously-endowed monasteries himself, Alexius was determined to prevent such abuses. He did not abolish the system, which he had found extremely useful during his first months on the throne when he had wished to recompense his supporters and endow members of his family. He decreed, however, that all transactions in monastic property must be registered with the appropriate patriarchate, thereby increasing the degree of patriarchal control over the monasteries and monastic life. In 1107 he went still further, with a general reform of the clergy and, in particular, the foundation of a special order of preachers, each of them working within his own 'parish' and serving also as a one-man vice squad and guardian of public morals. How effective these preachers proved in practice is uncertain: later chroniclers scarcely mention them. A good deal more effective was the vast 'orphanage' – really more of a hospital and refuge – which he established next to the church of St Paul on the acropolis of Constantinople, on the site of the present Topkapi Palace. His daughter describes it as 'a city within a city':

All around it in a circle were innumerable buildings, houses for the poor and – even greater proof of his humanity – dwellings for the disabled. Seeing it full of those who were maimed or completely incapacitated, you would have said it was Solomon's Porch. The buildings were in a double circle and were two-storeyed ... So large was the circle that if you wished to visit these people and started early in the morning, it would be evening before you were done. They had no land or vineyards, but each lived in his appointed house and all their needs of food and clothing were provided by the Emperor's generosity ... The number of persons catered for in this way was incalculable.[1]

Alexius's motives were not, however, entirely altruistic. One of the

1 *The Alexiad*, XV, vii.

symptoms of the breakdown of morale under his predecessors was the enormous number of professional beggars in the city. Any minister or senior civil servant, on promotion to higher rank or office, was expected to make generous dispensations to the poor and would on occasion find himself literally besieged in his house by those laying claim to his generosity; and the almost incredible number of promotions with which Nicephorus Botaneiates had sought to boost his waning popularity had still further increased the number of claimants. Strangely enough, they were not always unpopular with those whom they pestered; social standing in Constantinople at this time was largely governed not only by rank but also by patronage and charitable donations, and many a rich man asked nothing better than to be given the opportunity of publicly demonstrating the extent of his largesse. Certainly, the opening of St Paul's enabled Alexius to control the beggars of the city; but it also tended to diminish the prestige of his senior officials, thereby correspondingly increasing his own.

Consummate diplomatist that he was, it would have been surprising indeed if the Emperor had not worked hard during his reign to heal the breach between the Eastern and Western Churches. Unfortunately, he was too devoutly — some might say narrowly — Orthodox in his beliefs to show much flexibility in negotiations: when in 1089 Pope Urban sent the Abbot of Grottaferrata to Constantinople with an urgent appeal to permit services in the Latin rite, Alexius's only reply had been to suggest a joint council to discuss matters. The findings of this assembly have not come down to us; it seems however to have had at least a measure of success, since at its conclusion the Pope is known to have lifted the ban of excommunication that lay over the Empire of the East. Only two years later, though the breach was by no means entirely healed, relations were friendly enough for Alexius to have appealed to him for help against the Pechenegs. Further talks were held at intervals: in 1108 a papal legate was present to witness the signing of the Treaty of Devol, and in 1112 – if we are to believe the Chronicle of Monte Cassino – Alexius went so far as to suggest the union of the two Churches in exchange for the crown of the Western Empire, actually planning a visit to Rome in the summer of that year.

The accuracy of this report has been challenged, and probably with good reason. First of all, the Western Empire was not for sale. The Emperor Henry V was admittedly a bitter enemy of Pope Paschal — whom he had actually imprisoned, with sixteen of his cardinals, for two months in 1111. But Paschal had bought his freedom by performing

Henry's coronation on 13 April, and he could hardly crown a rival Emperor little more than a year later. What is a good deal more probable is that Alexius had his eye on South Italy, which had been without a master since the deaths of Bohemund and his half-brother Roger Borsa within a week of each other in that same year of 1111 and which he would have dearly loved to regain for Byzantium. Even so, though his position was by now a good deal more secure than it had been in the past, it is unlikely that in the circumstances then prevailing he could ever have contemplated so long an absence from Constantinople.

Such plans that he might have had would anyway have been in vain, for in the summer of 1112 Alexius fell gravely ill and seems to have been incapacitated for several weeks. Correspondence with Rome continued intermittently; but the Pope insisted as firmly as ever on his supremacy, Byzantium refused to compromise its independence and nothing was settled. In any case, the Emperor soon found his attention taken up with other, more immediate problems.

The peace that had begun at the end of 1108 with the Treaty of Devol continued for three years; then, in 1111, the wars began again and continued for the rest of the reign. That autumn, indeed, Alexius narrowly avoided having to fight simultaneously on two fronts, when a new outbreak of hostilities against the Turks coincided with the arrival of a fleet of Genoese and Pisan ships which threatened to ravage the Ionian coast. Fortunately he was able to buy them off by concluding a treaty with the Pisans, by which he undertook not to impede them in their Crusading activities, to make an annual present of gold and silk to their cathedral and – most important of all – to allow them to maintain a permanent trading colony in Constantinople, the most prominent members of which would enjoy reserved seats both for services in St Sophia and for games in the Hippodrome.[1]

The Turks were less easily dealt with. Fortunately for Alexius, they were not yet out for conquest; they still had more than enough territory to absorb and consolidate in Asia Minor. Their invasions across the imperial border were more in the nature of carefully planned raids than anything else: they avoided pitched battles wherever possible, attacking

---

1 This was not the first treaty between the Empire and the Italian trading republics: Basil II had concluded one with Venice as early as 992. (See *Byzantium: The Apogee*, p. 257.) Strangely, perhaps, the Genoese did not insist on similar privileges – which they were not to receive until 1155, from Manuel I.

on a wide front at several points simultaneously – thus obliging the Byzantines to spread their forces – and then making a quick getaway with as much plunder and as many prisoners as they could. In 1111 they had crossed the Hellespont into Thrace, where Anna reports that her father was campaigning against them early the following year. In 1113 another Turkish army, estimated this time at fifty-four thousand, laid siege to Nicaea; but it failed in its attempt, was surprised by Alexius near Dorylaeum and soundly defeated. The next year saw the *basileus* back in Thrace to defend the northern frontier against a new invasion by the Cumans; and scarcely had they been successfully repulsed than, in 1115, the Turks were once again on the march, this time beneath the banners of Malik-Shah, Seljuk Sultan of Iconium.

But the Emperor was slowing down. By now nearly sixty – sixty-eight if we are to believe Zonaras[1] – and already prey to the disease that was to destroy him, he delayed his reaction until the following year: only in the autumn of 1116 did he set off with his army to attack the Sultan in his own Anatolian heartland. He advanced as far as the city of Philomelion, meeting with little of the resistance that he had expected; his progress was, however, appreciably delayed by the appearance at every halt of vast numbers of homeless Greeks – families who had fled the Turkish invaders and who now emerged from their various places of refuge, attaching themselves to the army for protection. At this point, for reasons unclear, he decided to retire; and it was only after he had started on his homeward road that Malik-Shah decided to attack. This, according to Anna,[2] proved a serious mistake. The Sultan's army was, she reports, so destroyed by the Byzantines that he was forced to sue for peace, abandoning his recent conquests and recognizing the imperial frontiers that had existed immediately before Manzikert, in the reign of Romanus Diogenes.

Here, she continues, was a historic victory indeed. Alas, she seems to have been indulging in more of her favourite wishful thinking. Romanus's old frontiers stretched eastward to Armenia – which, quite apart from other considerations, were not the Sultan's to restore. Subsequent events, in any case, strongly suggest that no such surrender of territory was made. Malik-Shah may well have closed down his advance outposts in western Anatolia; but he remained in Iconium and it is unlikely that the Emperor returned with any major territorial conces-

1 See p 4, note 3.
2 *The Alexiad, XV, vi.*

sions. Thanks to the hopeless confusion of Anna's account – as well as her obvious bias – and to the paucity of our other sources,[1] we shall never know the truth about Philomelion; all that can be said is that, whether the Emperor's victory was decisive or negligible, it was his last. He returned to the capital a sick man, to find himself in the centre of bitter domestic strife.

Admittedly this was no new experience for him. Ever since his accession, his family had been divided. In the early days the fault had been very largely his own; we have seen how much power he gave to his mother, Anna Dalassena, and how he had rejected his fifteen-year-old wife Irene Ducas – even trying to prevent her coronation – in his infatuation with Mary of Alania. Mary, it is true, had soon faded out of the picture and Irene had returned to her husband's side; but Anna had continued for several years as the principal power behind the throne – more formidable even than her second son, the *sebastocrator* Isaac, with whom she theoretically shared the regency while Alexius was away on his numerous campaigns. She thus became more and more unpopular in Constantinople, to the point where the Emperor began to see her as a serious liability. Some time around 1090, therefore, she had retired – ostensibly of her own accord – to the monastery of the Pantepoptes where she had died, not altogether in disgrace, a few years later.

With the disappearance of Anna Dalassena, the Empress Irene finally comes into her own. Her daughter Anna – in whom the virtue of filial respect almost becomes a vice – describes her thus:

Her natural inclination would have been to shun public life altogether. Most of her time was devoted to household duties and her own pursuits – reading the books of the saints, or turning her mind to good works and acts of charity . . . Whenever she was obliged to appear as Empress at some important ceremony, she was overcome with shyness and blushes. The story is told of how when the woman philosopher Theano[2] once inadvertently bared her elbow, someone lightly remarked 'What a beautiful elbow!' 'But not,' Theano replied, 'for public show.' Thus it was with the Empress my mother . . . So far from being pleased to reveal to the common gaze an elbow or her eyes, she was unwilling that even her voice should be heard by strangers . . . But since not even the gods, as the poet says, fight against necessity, she was forced to accompany the

---

1 Our only other valuable authority is Zonaras, who attaches no particular importance to the campaign.

2 The pupil, and possibly the wife, of Pythagoras.

Emperor on his frequent expeditions. Her innate modesty would have kept her inside the palace; on the other hand, her devotion to him and burning love for him compelled her, however unwillingly, to leave her home ... The disease which attacked his feet required the most careful attention; he suffered excruciating pain from gout, and my mother's touch was what he most valued, for she understood him perfectly and by gentle massage could relieve him to some extent of his agony.[1]

Now all this may be perfectly true so far as it goes; but it seems likely that there was another consideration, apart from his gout, which caused Alexius to insist so firmly on Irene's accompanying him on campaign. He did not trust her an inch. It was not for his own safety that he feared; but he knew that she and her daughter had conceived a bitter hatred for her eldest son John Comnenus, heir apparent to the throne, and were for ever intriguing to disgrace or eliminate him so that Anna's husband, the Caesar Nicephorus Bryennius, might succeed instead. Gradually these two scheming women had become the focus for a number of other malcontents, among them the Emperor's second son Andronicus.

Irene never let slip an opportunity to blacken John in his father's eyes, representing him as a drunkard and debauchee hopelessly unfit to govern. Alexius, however, always refused to listen. He loved and trusted John, and – rightly, as it turned out – retained complete confidence in his abilities. Besides, he was determined to found a dynasty. One of the chief causes of Byzantine decline in the previous century had, he believed, been the fundamental instability of the throne itself, either passing to one or another of the Empress Zoe's feckless husbands or being looked upon as little more than a toy, to be shuttled backwards and forwards between the richest and most powerful families of the Empire. He himself had acquired it in just this way; but he would be the last to do so. If his own considerable achievements were to endure, the crown must be handed down in orderly succession to his first-born son and, God willing, to his son after him.

After his return to Constantinople his health steadily declined, until by the summer of 1118 it was clear that death could not be far away. By this time he was in constant pain and suffering serious respiratory difficulties; soon he was obliged to sit upright in order to breathe at all. Then his stomach and feet began to swell, while his mouth, tongue and throat became so inflamed that he could no longer swallow. Irene had him carried to her own palace of the Mangana, spending hours a day by

1 *The Alexiad*, XII, iii.

his bedside and ordering prayers said throughout the Empire for his recovery; but she could bring him no relief, and saw, with everyone else, that he was sinking fast.

Some time in the afternoon of 15 August the news was brought to John Comnenus that his father had only a few hours to live and urgently wished to see him. He hastened to the Mangana, where the dying Alexius gave him his imperial ring and ordered him to lose no time in having himself proclaimed *basileus*. John did so, then ran across to St Sophia where, in the briefest of ceremonies, the Patriarch crowned him. Returning to the palace, he was at first – presumably on Irene's orders – denied admittance by the Varangian Guard; only when he showed them the ring and told them of his father's imminent death did they stand back and let him through.

What, meanwhile, of Irene herself? Still determined to secure the succession of Bryennius, she would not willingly have absented herself from her husband's last conversation with his son; and yet, although she seldom left his bedside, he had somehow contrived to remove her at this crucial moment for her plans. By the time she returned it was too late. Even now she made one last attempt to force him to recognize the rights of his son-in-law; but he only smiled and – by now too feeble to speak – raised his hands as if in thanksgiving. That evening he died, and was buried the next day with the minimum of ceremony in the monastery of Christ Philanthropos, founded by Irene some fifteen years before.

He deserved a more elaborate farewell; for his subjects owed Alexius Comnenus far more than they knew. First of all, he had achieved his principal object: to halt the political and moral decline that had begun after the death of Basil II in 1025 and to give the Empire a new stability. After fifty-six years during which it had been misgoverned by thirteen different monarchs, he alone had reigned for thirty-seven; his son was to continue for another twenty-five before his accidental death, his grandson for another thirty-seven. Next there was his military record: no Emperor had defended his people more courageously, or with greater determination, or against a greater number of enemies; nor had any done more to build up the imperial forces by land and sea. Thirdly, there was his brilliant handling of the Crusade, organizing the passage of perhaps a hundred thousand men, women and children of all ranks and classes of society, feeding them and so far as possible protecting them from one end of his Empire to the other. Had those Crusading armies marched a quarter of a century earlier than they in fact did, the consequences for them – and for Byzantium – might have been grave indeed.

Thus, in three different ways and in three different capacities – as statesman, general and diplomatist – Alexius Comnenus may be said to have saved the Empire. Inevitably, he had had his failures: the restoration of the economy, the healing of the rift with Rome, the recovery of South Italy. But of these only the first was serious; the other two were little more than dreams, never to be realized by Alexius or any of his successors. He had his failings, too – among them his shameless nepotism and his susceptibility to women: Mary of Alania, Anna Dalassena and his wife Irene all exerted far more power over him than he should have allowed. Even over the supremely important question of the succession he had not trusted himself to impose his will upon Irene, preferring to achieve his ends by trickery rather than by firm imperial command.

Did he regret that – except among his soldiers, by whom he was idolized – personal popularity should always have remained beyond his grasp? Not, probably, very much. He never courted it, and certainly never compromised his principles to win the plaudits of the crowd. From the outset of his reign he had ruled conscientiously, energetically and to the very best of his ability; and he left his son an Empire incomparably stronger and better organized than it had been for a century. He died content – as well he might.

5
John the Beautiful

[1118-43]

Should I not be considered mad if, having acquired the crown in a manner that was scarcely legitimate, and indeed scarcely Christian, I were to place it upon the head of a stranger, rather than upon that of my own son?

Alexius Comnenus to his wife, quoted by
Nicetas Choniates, 'John Comnenus', I

The account of the death of Alexius Comnenus as given in the previous chapter, which is principally based on the testimony of John Zonaras and Nicetas Choniates,[1] bears little resemblance to that with which Anna Comnena ends *The Alexiad*. Anna paints an affecting picture of the distinguished doctors bickering round the bedside; of the increasing horror of the Emperor's sufferings; of the selflessness of his wife Irene, weeping 'tears more copious than the waters of the Nile' as she tended him through the long, agonizing days and nights; of the devoted ministrations of their daughters – Maria, Eudocia and of course Anna herself; of the candles that were lit and the hymns that were chanted; and, at the moment of death, of the widowed Empress kicking off her imperial purple slippers, tearing aside her veil, seizing a knife and slashing away at her beautiful hair. Anna gives, however, no hint of her father's last, not entirely creditable *coup*, when he prevented the succession of herself and her husband in favour of John, the rightful heir – whom, in her entire chapter, she mentions only once, and then does not even deign to call by his name.

Anna's hatred for John, which lasted all her life, was a simple matter of jealousy. As Alexius's eldest child, she had been betrothed in her infancy to the young Prince Constantine – son of Michael VII – and thus,

---

1 Nicetas began his career as an imperial secretary at the court, and ended as Grand Logothete under the Angeli. His *History*, which begins with the death of Alexius and continues until 1206, is the most descriptive and colourful that has come down to us since the days of Psellus and will, I hope, do much to enliven the following chapters.

for the first five years of her life, had been heiress-presumptive to the throne of Byzantium. Then, on 13 September 1087, the Empress Irene had given birth to a son, John; and Anna's dreams of the imperial diadem were shattered. But not for long. On the premature death of Constantine she had married in 1097 Nicephorus Bryennius, son[1] of that general of the same name who, having made a bid for the throne in 1077, had been captured and blinded by Botaneiates. Nicephorus too had proved himself a fine soldier and leader of men, to the point where, in 1111 or thereabouts – the precise date is uncertain – Alexius had conferred upon him the title of Caesar; and immediately all his wife's ambitions were resurrected. The story of her recruitment of her mother Irene and her brother Andronicus to her cause has already been told, as has that of their ultimate failure; but even now Anna did not give up. She was almost certainly behind a plot to murder John at their father's funeral – from which her brother, having received advance warning, wisely stayed away; and a few months after John's accession she organized a conspiracy – to be led by her husband Bryennius – to murder him in the Philopation, a country palace just outside the Golden Gate. Unfortunately, Bryennius's courage failed him at the last moment and he never turned up at the rendezvous. Meanwhile his fellow-conspirators, whom he had failed to inform of his defection, were caught wandering about in the palace and immediately arrested.

The new Emperor showed himself surprisingly merciful. There were no blindings, no mutilations. The guilty were sentenced to nothing worse than the confiscation of their possessions – which most of them were later able to recover. Nicephorus Bryennius escaped scot-free and served the Emperor loyally in the field for another twenty years until his death, occupying his idle hours in the composition of a remarkably boring history. His wife was not so lucky. On hearing of what had happened at the Philopation, she had flown into a hysterical rage and had cursed Providence in the crudest possible terms for having endowed her husband with certain attributes of virility which, she claimed, had far better been given to her. She too suffered the temporary confiscation of her property; worse, she was barred in perpetuity from the imperial court. Abandoned and humiliated, she settled in the convent of the Theotokos Kecharitomene,[2] where she lived for the next thirty-five

---

1 Not, I think, the grandson as is often claimed; see *The Alexiad*, VII, ii.

2 i.e., the Virgin Full of Grace. This convent adjoined the monastery of Christ Philanthropos (see p. 61n.) and was also founded by the Empress Irene; the two buildings were separated by a wall,

years, writing the life of her father and endlessly lamenting her injuries, nearly all of which – had she had the honesty to admit it – were self-inflicted.

At the time of his accession, John Comnenus was a month short of his thirtieth birthday. Thanks to his sister's reticence on the subject, we know disappointingly little of his early years, although she does give us a brief description of his appearance at birth:

The child was of a swarthy complexion, with a broad forehead, rather thin cheeks, a nose that was neither flat nor aquiline but something between the two, and darkish eyes which, as far as one can divine from the look of a new-born baby, gave evidence of a lively spirit.

For once, Anna was letting her brother off lightly: even so great an admirer of John Comnenus as William of Tyre[1] admits that he was small and unusually ugly, with eyes, hair and complexion so dark that he was known as 'the Moor'. He had, however, another nickname too: *Kaloiannis*, 'John the Beautiful'. It has been suggested that this was intended ironically, but even a cursory reading of the chroniclers shows that it was nothing of the kind. The description referred not to his body, but to his soul. Both his parents – whatever their failings in other respects – had been unusually devout, even by the standards of the time; John carried their example further still. Levity and ribaldry he hated: members of the court were expected to restrict their conversation to serious subjects, or otherwise to hold their peace. Luxury, too, was frowned upon. The food served at the imperial table was frugal in the extreme; wealthy noblemen and their ladies, seeking to impress the Emperor by the opulence of their palaces or the sumptuousness of their robes, would receive instead a stern lecture on the vanity of such adornments – which, in his eyes, could lead only to decadence and depravity.

Today, more likely than not, most of us would find the Emperor John Comnenus an insufferable companion; in twelfth-century Byzantium he was loved. He was, first of all, no hypocrite. His principles may have been strict, but they were sincerely held; his piety was

---

but shared a single water system. The forty nuns of the Kecharitomene lived a strictly coenobitic life, sleeping in a common dormitory; Irene had, however, considerately added one or two rather more comfortable apartments for the benefit of female members of the imperial family.

1 William of Tyre (c.1130–86), Chancellor of the Kingdom of Jerusalem and Archbishop of Tyre, whose *History* (see Bibliography) is the most important source we possess for Byzantine relations with the Crusader states of Outremer.

genuine, his integrity complete. Second, there was a gentle, merciful side to his nature that was in his day rare indeed. Nicetas Choniates's testimony that he never condemned anyone to death or mutilation may seem to us faint praise; but John's treatment of his sister Anna and her fellow-conspirators certainly seems in retrospect to have been almost dangerously lenient. He was generous, too: despite the austerity of his own life, no Emperor ever dispensed charity with a more lavish hand. Never was he accused, as his father had been, of favouring his family at the expense of his subjects; on the contrary, he deliberately kept his brothers and sisters, as well as his more distant relations, at arm's length, often choosing his ministers and closest advisers from men of relatively humble origins. Most trusted of all was a certain John Axuch, a Turk who had been captured in infancy by the Crusaders at Nicaea, given as a present to Alexius Comnenus and brought up in the imperial household, where he soon became the young prince's boon companion. On his accession John at once took Axuch into his service, after which his promotion was swift. Before long he had been appointed Grand Domestic, or commander-in-chief of the armies.

It was a sensible appointment for a man whom the Emperor wished to keep at his side; for John Comnenus was, like his father, a soldier through and through. He believed, as Alexius had believed before him, that the Empire had been bestowed on him by the Almighty as a sacred trust, together with the responsibility for its protection; but whereas Alexius had been largely content to defend it against its manifold enemies, John saw his duty in more positive terms – to liberate all those imperial territories now occupied by the infidel, and to restore to Byzantium the glory and power that it had known in the days of Basil the Great, or even Justinian. Here was an enterprise indeed; but he embarked on it with determination and energy, continuing his father's programme of military reorganization, improving still further his methods of training, constantly setting his soldiers an example of courage and endurance that few of them could hope to follow. To his subjects it seemed as though his life were one long campaign; and though he seems to have loved his Empress – the Hungarian princess Piriska, who had adopted the more euphonious but distressingly unoriginal Byzantine name of Irene – and remained faithful to her all his life, he certainly spent far more of his time in the field than in his palace at Constantinople, as did his four sons as soon as they were old enough to accompany him.

In one important respect John Comnenus was more fortunate than his father: the situation in the West was, in Alexius's day, seldom settled enough to enable him to concentrate on the Muslim threat in Asia. At the time of John's accession, however, and for several years afterwards, Europe presented comparatively few immediate problems. Across the Danube, the Cumans and the Pechenegs were quiet; in the Balkan peninsula, the Serbs acknowledged Byzantine suzerainty and were anyway too divided to make trouble, while the Hungarians were fully occupied in consolidating their position on the Dalmatian coast – a region which, though remaining technically an imperial province, had in fact long been abandoned to the Venetians. Further west again, Pope and Holy Roman Emperor were still locked in their long struggle for supremacy. As for the Normans of Apulia – who had caused poor Alexius more anxiety than all his other European enemies combined – Robert Guiscard's pathetic son Roger Borsa and, after Roger's death in 1111, his equally feckless son William had failed utterly to assert their authority over the local barons, and their Dukedom was little by little subsiding into chaos. True, their cousin Count Roger of Sicily was rapidly making a name for himself and by 1130, as King Roger II, would have gathered all the Norman lands of the south under his sceptre; but that was twelve years away in the future and John, as we shall see, was far too good a diplomatist to allow the King of Sicily to become an immediate threat to Byzantium.

He could thus focus his attention on Asia Minor – where, nearly half a century after Manzikert, the situation was still hopelessly confused. Roughly, it could be said that the Empire controlled the northern, western and southern coasts and all the land to the north-west of a rather wavy line drawn from the mouth of the Meander a few miles south of Ephesus to the south-eastern corner of the Black Sea a little beyond Trebizond – which was an imperial fief under its own Duke, Constantine Gabras. To the south-east of that line were the Turks, most of them subject to the Seljuk Sultan of Iconium, Mas'ud; but recent years had seen a diminution of the Sultan's effective power due to the rise of another Turkish tribe, the Danishmends, whose Emir Ghazi II now ruled from the Halys river[1] to the Euphrates and was steadily pressing westward into Paphlagonia. There were also large numbers of armed Turcoman tribesmen who may have paid lip-service to one or the other of these potentates, but who effectively did as they wished. Throughout the second half of the reign of Alexius, these nomads had

---

1 Now known as the Kizil Irmak.

been infiltrating the fertile valleys of Phrygia and Pisidia, where the climate was more gentle and the pasture for their flocks incomparably richer than that of the scrubby plateau of central Anatolia. They had thus succeeded in virtually cutting off the Byzantine port of Attaleia (Antalya), which was now accessible only by sea. It was they, as much as the Seljuks themselves, who were the target of John's first campaign.

He set out in the spring of 1119, and made straight for the old Phrygian capital, Laodicea on the Lycus, some four miles to the north of the modern city of Denizli.[1] Captured by the Seljuks in 1071, Laodicea had been briefly recovered by Alexius Comnenus twenty-five years later; but like so many other towns and villages along that all too flexible frontier, it had since fallen away again. John had sent Axuch and a party of men out in advance to prepare the siege, and his Grand Domestic had done his work well. Resistance collapsed at the first assault; the local Emir Abu-Shara fled; and John surrounded it with a line of new walls to ensure that he did not return.

At this point the Emperor, for reasons unknown, returned hurriedly to Constantinople. It has been suggested[2] that the intrigues of his sister may have had something to do with his decision. Obviously her unsuccessful plot was not to blame, since that must have been timed for when John was already in the capital; but there were very likely other intriguers besides Anna, and during the first possibly insecure years of his reign he seems to have been reluctant to leave it for too long. At all events he was back again a few weeks later for the fall of Sozopolis – some thirty miles north of Attaleia – and for the capture of a whole string of castles and strong points commanding the road leading from the Meander up to the central plateau. By late autumn the vital land links with Attaleia had been re-established; John and Axuch returned to the Bosphorus well satisfied with what they had done.

It is unclear whether they were back in Asia Minor in 1120; our principal chroniclers,[3] admirable as they are in many respects, show maddeningly little interest in precise chronology. In the following year, however, the Emperor's attention was brought back forcibly to Europe, where there was a dangerous irruption of Pechenegs across the Danube.

1 There is not much to see of Laodicea today. Formerly an important Hellenistic city, famous for its wool and cloth production and one of the Seven Churches of Asia, its ruins are nowadays deserted and rather sad. Few tourists stop there at all, and even those that do pass on hurriedly to the petrified waterfalls of Pamukkale, a dozen miles further on.

2 F. Chalandon, Les Comnène, Vol. II, p. 47.

3 Nicetas Choniates, John Cinnamus and Michael the Syrian.

Since its defeat by Alexius at Levunium in 1091, this restless people had given little trouble; but thirty years had now passed, a new generation had grown up, and in the summer of 1121 tens of thousands of barbarian tribesmen overran Thrace, causing the usual havoc. As an invasion, it was nowhere near on the scale of its predecessor; on the other hand, John's ambitious programme in Asia depended absolutely on peace in Europe, and it was essential that he should deal with the invaders firmly and expeditiously. While preparing his army and bringing it into position he attempted to buy time by sowing discord among the various Pecheneg tribes – fortunately they had no supreme leader – and by offering them rich presents, as recommended by Constantine Porphyrogenitus nearly three centuries before;[1] but the Pechenegs had learnt a lot since Constantine's day and remained unimpressed.

It hardly mattered. Once the army was ready, the Emperor saw no reason to delay the action any longer. The first phase of the battle proved indecisive. John himself was slightly wounded, and though a fair number of the enemy were captured, the large majority managed to regain their camp, where they drew up their chariots to form a great circular rampart and dug themselves in. Several times the Byzantine cavalry attacked, but the chariots stood firm. At last the Emperor – who, whenever not actually engaged in battle, had been on his knees before an icon of the Virgin – gave the general order to dismount and, flanked by his Varangian Guard with their long shields and huge battle-axes, led the way forward on foot. The battle-axes made short work of the chariots, and the Pechenegs' morale disintegrated. Some of them managed to escape; the rest were taken prisoner. Many of the captives were however later released and given lands within the Empire on which to settle, in return for joining the imperial army on the spot or giving an undertaking of future military service. The Emperor doubtless remembered how invaluable the Pecheneg regiments had been to his father in policing the Crusader route across the Balkans; he must devoutly have hoped that they would not be necessary again in such a capacity, but they would certainly have their uses during the years to come. Meanwhile, to celebrate his victory, he instituted an annual 'Pecheneg holiday', which was still being celebrated when the century ended.

With the Pechenegs effectively subdued – so effectively, indeed, that

---

1 See *Byzantium: The Apogee*, p. 164n.

they never troubled Byzantium again – John Comnenus would have liked to return as soon as possible to Asia Minor; but his work in Europe was not yet over. The Venetians were on the war-path; and both the Hungarians and the Serbs, so quiet and well-behaved during the first years of his reign, were now in similar mood.

In Alexius's day, Venice had been the Empire's closest ally; she had had to be, because her fleet was of vital importance against the Normans of South Italy – first Robert Guiscard and later Bohemund. To keep the Venetians well-disposed, the Emperor had not hesitated in 1082 to grant them trading privileges enjoyed by no other foreign merchants, including the complete remission of all customs dues. Thus their colony on the Golden Horn had grown both in size and in wealth to the point where it had aroused the intense resentment of the Byzantines, many of whom had appalling stories to tell of Venetian arrogance and *hauteur*. By the time of John's accession, however, the Norman menace had faded; and when Doge Domenico Michiel, elected in the same year, sent ambassadors asking for the renewal of the current arrangements and the confirmation of all the old privileges, the new Emperor refused point-blank. From now on, he told them, they would enjoy only the same treatment as was accorded to their competitors. The Venetians were furious, and on 8 August 1122 the Doge's flagship sailed out of the lagoon with seventy-one men-of-war in its wake.

Their objective was Corfu, an important Byzantine outpost, defended by a strong and determined garrison. They besieged it for six months, and would probably have continued longer had they not received, in the spring of 1123, a desperate appeal from Palestine: King Baldwin had been taken prisoner, and their help was essential if the Latin East were to survive. So the siege was raised and Corfu enjoyed a brief period of tranquillity; but over the next three years the Venetians continued to be active in the eastern Mediterranean, capturing Rhodes, Chios, Samos, Lesbos and Andros. When, early in 1126, they sent troops to occupy Cephalonia, John Comnenus had had enough. His own fleet was powerless to stop the aggression, which was costing him far more than the commercial privileges he had withheld. In August that same year he swallowed his pride and restored them. Even taking account of the inevitable loss of Byzantine face, it was a small enough price to pay.

Where Hungary was concerned the Empire's problems had begun in 1095, when the newly-enthroned King Coloman had dispossessed his brother Almus, whom he had later ordered to be blinded, together with the latter's son Béla. Shortly before John's accession, Almus had sought refuge with his kinswoman – the future Empress Irene – in Constantinople, where he had been warmly received; he had even been granted an estate in Macedonia, which had rapidly become a centre for his many compatriots in exile, voluntary or otherwise. Coloman seems to have made no objection; but his brother and successor, Stephen II, growing increasingly concerned over the activities of these discontents, had made a formal protest to the Byzantine court – simultaneously demanding that Almus should be expelled from the Empire. John, predictably enough, had refused; and in the summer of 1128 Stephen attacked. Crossing the Danube, he captured Belgrade and Nish; then, continuing into what is now Bulgaria, he ravaged as far as Sardica (Sofia) and Philippopolis (Plovdiv) before retiring again to the north.

But the Emperor was also on the march. Reaching Philippopolis shortly after the Hungarian army had left it, he advanced northward – almost certainly up the valley of the Iskur[1] – to a rendezvous on the Danube with a flotilla from the imperial navy. Stephen had by now withdrawn to the north bank; he had fallen ill, but had given strict orders from his sickbed that his troops were on no account to follow him across the river. As it happened, they had no opportunity to do so. John found them encamped beneath the fortress of Haram – near the confluence of the Danube with its little tributary, the Nera – and used his ships to make his own secret crossing a mile or two downstream. He then fell on them from behind, pinning them against the bank. Of the survivors, some managed to escape but many more were taken prisoner. All the captured towns were recovered.

At some moment either shortly before or shortly after these events, John Comnenus fought a similarly successful campaign against the Serbs under their leader Bolkan, the Zhupan of Rascia, settling many of them in Asia Minor as he had the Pechenegs. Our knowledge of this episode – as indeed of all Serbian affairs at this time – is lamentably slight; but it seems clear enough that although the Serbs continued to resent imperial domination and to make periodical attempts – often supported by the Hungarians – to shake it off, they were never again to cause John any serious anxiety. By 1130 he was ready to leave Europe to look after itself, and to turn his attention once again to the East.

*

1 Some historians have suggested the Morava valley; but this would have involved a long and pointless detour to the west for both armies. Nicetas Choniates shifts the whole scene further north still, to the wooded hills between the Sava and the Danube nowadays known as the Frushka Gora; but again the balance of probability is against him.

In the decade that he had been away, the situation in Anatolia had changed considerably for the worse. The Danishmends had continued to spread at the expense of the Sultanate of Iconium, which had been virtually incapacitated by internal dissension; and their ruler, the Emir Ghazi – who had annexed Melitene in 1124 and had gone on to acquire Caesarea, Ankyra, Kastamon and Gangra[1] three years later – was now the most formidable power in all Asia Minor. Three years later, in February 1130 on the banks of the river Pyramus (now the Ceyhan) in Cilicia, his army had destroyed that of young Bohemund II of Antioch in a total massacre. Bohemund's head was brought to Ghazi, who had it embalmed and sent it as a gift to the Caliph in Baghdad.

John Comnenus shed few tears for the Prince of Antioch, whose principality he saw – with good reason – as rightly belonging to his Empire; but it was clear to him that Ghazi must be dealt with while there was still time. Between 1130 and 1135 he led no fewer than five separate expeditions against the Danishmends. For the first three years he was seriously hampered by the intrigues of Alexius's third son, the *sebastocrator* Isaac, who was doing his best to form a league of all the enemies of the Empire with the object of supplanting his brother on the imperial throne; but in 1132 Isaac left for the Holy Land – whether for reasons of piety or for more unworthy motives we cannot tell – and thereafter John's progress was swift. During the remainder of that year and the beginning of 1133 he went from one success to the next, marching through Bithynia and Paphlagonia, capturing the important stronghold of Kastamon and advancing to well beyond the Halys river. As he advanced, Christians and Muslims alike from the towns and villages flocked to his banner, while several of the local Emirs surrendered at his approach.

On his return to the capital, he made a triumphal entry in the traditional manner – the first that Constantinople had seen since that of John Tzimisces in 972.[2] As befitted the troubled times, the ceremonial chariot that waited for him at the Golden Gate with its four snow-white horses was trimmed with silver rather than with gold; but the streets were decorated, as always on such occasions, with damasks and brocades, and rich carpets hung from the windows of the houses. The whole route from the Land Walls to St Sophia was lined with specially erected stands, where virtually the entire population of the city stood cheering

---

1 The modern Kayseri, Ankara, Kastamonu and Chankiri.
2 See *Byzantium: The Apogee*, p. 224.

as the procession passed by: first the prisoners, next the fighting regiments, then the generals and finally the Emperor himself, on foot and carrying a cross. Like Tzimisces before him, he had refused to mount the chariot, preferring to give pride of place to the icon of the Virgin that had accompanied him throughout his campaigns.

But his work was not over: the following year saw him back in the field. The campaign was tragically interrupted by the sudden death in Bithynia of his wife Irene; he and his sons left the army at once in order to escort her body back to Constantinople. They returned, however, immediately after the funeral and rejoined the army on the road to Gangra where, towards the end of the summer, there came news of another, more welcome, death – that of the Emir Ghazi himself. The Emir's last hours must have been somewhat brightened by the arrival of an embassy from the Caliph, to inform him that he and his descendants had been awarded the title of *Malik*, or King, and to present him with 'four black flags, drums to be beaten before him whenever he appeared in public, a golden chain to wear about his neck and a golden sceptre with which the ambassadors were to tap him on the shoulder in recognition of his new rank and title'; but none of these were of much use to him. He expired almost at once, and the title passed to his son Mohammed.

The confusion which almost invariably followed the demise of a Muslim ruler ensured that the Byzantines could expect little opposition from the Danishmend army in the immediate future. Individual garrisons, on the other hand, could still give trouble. Gangra for example, although the Governor had recently died and left the command to his wife, put up so spirited a resistance that John decided to pass on to Kastamon, which Ghazi had recaptured in the previous year. It surrendered quickly enough – on one or two conditions that he was happy to accept – and he returned at once to Gangra, this time to besiege the city in earnest. The garrison held out for a little while, in the hopes that certain Turkish troops rumoured to be in the neighbourhood might come to their aid; but by this time the country was in the grip of an unusually hard winter and provisions were short. After a week or two, there being still no sign of a relief force, the Governor's widow sued for terms – among them permission to leave the city for any who wished to do so, and the return of some of the prisoners taken on the previous occasion. Once again John willingly agreed – though Cinnamus tells us that few of the inhabitants took advantage of his offer, many of them preferring to enlist in the ranks of his army.

*

Leaving a Byzantine garrison of two thousand men in Gangra, early in 1135 the Emperor returned once again to his capital. During the last five years he had achieved much. For Ghazi's death he could hardly take the credit; nevertheless he had succeeded in everything that he had set out to do, restoring to the Empire extensive lands that had been lost to it for over half a century. The Turks were not beaten; but they had sustained several crippling blows and it would be some time before they could return to the offensive. He himself was now almost free to work towards the realization of his greatest ambition of all and to march, not against a Muslim army but against the two Christian states at that time occupying what he considered to be imperial territory: the Armenian Kingdom of Cilicia and its close ally, the Norman Principality of Antioch.

Almost, but not quite. He had one other potential enemy to deal with before that ambition could be achieved. Roger of Sicily had worn his crown for little more than four years; since that time, however, he had gained steadily in power and influence, and he too dreamed of foreign conquest. The Apulian sea-ports were only some sixty miles from the imperial lands across the Adriatic, and the rich cities of Dalmatia constituted a permanent temptation to a little gentle freebooting which, in recent years, Sicilian sea captains had not always managed to resist. Other raids, on the North African coast, had indicated that the King of Sicily would not long be content to remain within his present frontiers and, if not checked, might soon be in a position to close the central Mediterranean at will. He was known, too, to have his eye on the Crusader states. As the cousin of Bohemund II he had a strong claim to Antioch; while the marriage of his mother Adelaide to Baldwin I as his third wife in 1113 had been solemnized with the clear understanding that if it proved childless – which, given the ages of the parties concerned, it almost certainly would – the Crown of Jerusalem was to pass to her son. Baldwin's subsequent behaviour, by which he first spent all Adelaide's immense dowry, then had the marriage annulled and packed her off unceremoniously home to Sicily, was an insult that Roger never forgave; at least in his eyes, it in no way weakened his case. Admittedly he had no similar claim to Constantinople, but such considerations had inhibited neither his uncle Robert Guiscard nor his cousin Bohemund; and even if he were to confine his energies to the conquest of Crusader Outremer the long-term prospects for Byzantium would be grave indeed.

And so, early in 1135, ambassadors set out from the Bosphorus bound for Germany and the court of the Western Emperor Lothair; and by autumn agreement had been reached. In return for generous financial support from Byzantium, Lothair would launch a major campaign in the spring of 1137 to crush the King of Sicily. John welcomed his envoys warmly on their return. With his rear now satisfactorily protected, he could at last set off for the East.

The story of the Armenian settlement of Cilicia – the region extending between the southern coast of Anatolia and the Taurus mountains, from near Alanya to the Gulf of Alexandretta – goes back to the early eleventh century when Basil II, during his surprisingly peaceful incorporation of most of Armenia into the Empire, offered in return to the Princes of Vaspurakan extensive territories running from Sebasteia to the Euphrates.[1] Similar grants were made by his successors, so that by 1070 or so there was a steady trickle of emigration from the harsh Armenian uplands to the warmer and more luxuriant country to the south. After Manzikert the trickle became a flood, gradually giving rise to a number of semi-independent principalities, for ever squabbling among themselves; and this was essentially the situation in Cilicia when the Crusaders passed through on their way to Palestine.

It did not last. Once the Frankish Crusader states had established some order in their own affairs, they decided to do the same in Cilicia – which, as their principal link with the West, they naturally wished to have under their control. Most of the Armenian princelings were liquidated; one family only was strong enough, or cunning enough, to survive – that of a certain Ruben, who claimed kinship with Gagik II, last of the Bagratid Kings of Armenia,[2] and had established himself in the Taurus in 1071. His grandson, Leo, had succeeded to the throne of what was by now known as Lesser Armenia in 1129, and three years later had embarked on an ambitious programme of conquest, capturing Tarsus, Adana and Mopsuestia – although whether he took them from the Byzantines or the Crusaders is, oddly enough, uncertain.[3] Before long, however, Leo overstretched himself: late in 1136, a vendetta with the new Prince of Antioch, Raymond of Poitiers, led to his capture and

---

1 See *Byzantium: The Apogee*, p. 264.

2 'More likely a henchman than a kinsman' – *Oxford Dictionary of Byzantium*.

3 Chalandon (*Jean Comnène et Manuel Comnène*) devotes two whole pages (108–9) to this knotty problem; the three cities had been taken and retaken again and again and it is hard to say exactly where the frontier lay. He finally concludes that Leo more probably captured them from the Byzantines – but it remains an open question.

a brief period of imprisonment, from which he was released only after surrendering to his captor both Adana and Mopsuestia – though not, apparently, Tarsus – together with sixty thousand pieces of gold. Hardly had he regained his liberty when, in the early spring of 1137, messengers arrived with the worst news he could possibly have received: John Comnenus was marching against him.

The Emperor was taking no chances. He had brought with him not only his old army, tried and trusted, case-hardened after nearly twenty years' hard campaigning; he had also added several new regiments, including one composed of his Pecheneg prisoners and others recruited from the Turkish populations who had rallied so enthusiastically to his standards over the past few years. There may even have been substantial numbers of Armenians; for the Rubenids were no more popular among the majority of their countrymen than were the Frankish Crusaders, and many were the refugees from both regimes who had found their way to Constantinople. From the moment that this tremendous force appeared in Cilicia it carried all before it. The three great cities referred to above changed hands yet again; so too did Seleucia (Selifke), and – after a siege of thirty-seven days – the near-impregnable fortress of Anazarbus (Anavarza) on its 500-foot escarpment above the river Pyramus. Even now Leo did not surrender, but withdrew with his two sons deep into the Taurus. John, anxious not to lose time, did not bother to pursue him. Pausing only to mop up a few more Armenian strong points, he pressed on via Issus and Alexandretta, and on 29 August drew up his army before Antioch.

The city had been passing through a time of crisis. Young Bohemund II, arriving from Apulia at the age of eighteen in 1126, had been killed by Ghazi less than four years later, leaving a two-year-old daughter, Constance. His widow Alice, daughter of King Baldwin of Jerusalem, should properly have waited for her father – as her nominal suzerain – to appoint a successor. Instead, she had assumed the regency herself; and on hearing that the furious Baldwin was on his way to Antioch to settle matters as he thought fit she had gone so far as to send an envoy to Imad ed-Din Zengi, Atabeg of Mosul and effective master of all northern Syria, offering him a magnificently caparisoned horse and the promise of homage in return for his recognition of her right to rule over Antioch as its Princess.

But the envoy never arrived. Intercepted by Baldwin's men, he was brought before their master and executed. The King had then continued his journey to Antioch, only to find the gates shut in his face. It was several days before two of his supporters inside the city were able to open them again under cover of darkness to admit him and his troops; and even then Alice had barricaded herself in a tower, emerging only after guarantees had been given for her safety. Her father forgave her, but exiled her to her property at Laodicea and himself assumed the regency – which, after his death in 1131, passed to his son-in-law and successor, Fulk of Anjou, who had married his eldest daughter, Alice's sister Mélisende. For four years Alice had bided her time; then in 1135 Mélisende had persuaded Fulk to allow her sister to return, and Alice had immediately sent another envoy – to Constantinople this time, with a proposal of marriage between her daughter Constance (now aged seven) and the Emperor's youngest son Manuel.

In the circumstances prevailing, such an alliance would have been no bad thing for Antioch; but the Franks in the city were outraged at the thought of Constance's marriage to a Greek – even an imperial one – and King Fulk, when he heard the news, had reacted in much the same way. Obviously an alternative husband for Constance must be found, and Fulk did not take long to make up his mind. His choice fell on Raymond of Poitiers, younger son of Duke William IX of Aquitaine, who chanced at that time to be in England at the court of King Henry I. Fulk secretly sent off one of his knights to fetch him, and in April 1136 – narrowly escaping capture by King Roger of Sicily, who as we have seen claimed the principality for himself – Raymond had duly arrived in Antioch. The problem of obtaining Alice's consent was neatly avoided by the Patriarch, Radulf, who told her that this handsome young prince had come to ask for her own hand in marriage. Alice, who was still under thirty and longed for a new husband, was predictably delighted and withdrew to her palace to prepare for his arrival. Meanwhile Constance was carried off to the cathedral, where the Patriarch married her to Raymond on the spot. Faced with a *fait accompli*, her mother knew that she was beaten. She returned disconsolately to Laodicea where she died shortly afterwards.

When the Byzantine siege engines started their bombardment of the walls of Antioch and the Byzantine sappers began tunnelling beneath them, many of those within the city must have reflected that if only Alice had had her way and Constance had married Manuel Comnenus, they would not be in their present predicament. How much better, they must have thought, if their new Prince had remained in England. Raymond of Poitiers probably felt much the same. After scarcely more than a year in the East, what was Antioch to him, or he to Antioch? He had little love for his new principality, which possessed none of the sophistication that he was accustomed to in Europe. He was bored and lonely, and his child wife had nothing to offer a husband almost thirty years her senior. He knew, too, that against the forces of John Comnenus there was no possibility of holding out for long; nor was there the slightest chance of a Crusader army coming to his relief. For a few days he made a show of resistance; then he sent a message to the enemy camp. If he were to recognize the Emperor as his overlord, would John in return allow him to remain as his Imperial Vicar, or Viceroy?

But John Comnenus was in no mood for bargaining. He demanded one thing only: unconditional surrender. To this Raymond replied that he was not empowered to make such an offer without first consulting the King of Jerusalem. Fulk's answer was careful. Zengi was growing stronger every day and was by now posing a serious threat to the survival of the Crusader states; it would have been folly to antagonize the only Christian power capable of holding him in check. Besides, just how far into Syria and Palestine did the Emperor intend to go? If the sacrifice of Antioch would prevent his further advance to the south, should Antioch not be sacrificed? In any event, his reaction was better than Raymond – or John – can have dared to hope:

We are all aware, as we have learnt from our elders before us, that Antioch was part of the Empire of Constantinople until it was taken away by the Turks, who held it for fourteen years, and that the claims made by the Emperor concerning the treaties made by our forebears are correct. Should we then deny the truth and oppose what we know to be right?[1]

And so Antioch capitulated, and John for his part showed his usual generosity. Raymond must come on foot to his camp and swear allegiance to him, giving him free access to the city and the citadel. He must also undertake that, if the *basileus* were successful in his coming campaign and were to return to him Aleppo, Shaizar,[2] Emessa (Homs) and Hama in perpetual fief, he would surrender to him Antioch in exchange.[3] The imperial standard was then hoisted over the city, the Emperor bestowed

1 Ordericus Vitalis, XIII, 34.

2 In classical times known as Larissa (not to be confused with the city in Thessaly), and today as Saijar: an important fortress on the Orontes, some twenty miles north-west of Hama.

3 Chalandon (op. cit., p. 132-3) is wrong when he suggests that the Emperor also insisted, '*sans doute*', on the appointment of an Orthodox Patriarch. In March 1138 Pope Innocent II forbade any member of the Western Church to remain with the Byzantine army should John take any action against the Latin authorities in Antioch. See Runciman, *A History of the Crusades*, Vol. II, p. 218.

rich presents on Raymond and all the local Latin nobility, and some time in the first half of September the victorious army struck camp. It being by now too late in the year to start a major campaign, John decided to complete his unfinished business with the Armenians and set off for the high Taurus, where Leo and his family had entrenched themselves. A few weeks later their resistance was at an end: all the Rubenid princes were safely in imperial hands, and were sent off to prison in Constantinople.

With the Armenians crushed and his position at Antioch assured, the Emperor was free to embark on the next stage of his plan: to join forces with his Crusader vassals against the Arabs of Syria. Towards the end of March 1138 he was back with his army in Antioch, where he and Raymond were joined by a regiment of Knights Templar and an additional force commanded by Joscelin II of Courtenay, Count of Edessa.[1] Joscelin, now twenty-four, inspired neither liking nor trust. From his Armenian mother – the sister of Leo, whose three sons had actually sought refuge with him a few months before – he had inherited his unusually dark complexion, the effect of which was not improved by a huge nose and deeply pock-marked face. Devious and deceitful, lazy and lascivious, he was in every way the antithesis of the popular image of a Crusader. To John Comnenus, a soldier to his fingertips, he appeared even less impressive than the Prince of Antioch.

It was thus with two most unsatisfactory allies that the Emperor settled down to plan the coming campaign. His first objective was Aleppo. A month before his departure he ordered the arrest of all merchants and travellers from that city and its neighbourhood, to prevent any word of his preparations reaching the inhabitants; then he set out eastward. He managed to take one or two small castles along the route; but a quick reconnaissance of Aleppo itself, its garrison reinforced in the nick of time by Zengi, showed that it would put up a formidable resistance. Rather than waste time and energy on a long siege, he pressed on to the south until on 28 April he reached Shaizar. In comparison with Aleppo it was a small and commercially unimportant town, the property of an equally insignificant local Emir; but it controlled the valley of the middle Orontes and promised to be invaluable in blocking

---

1 Joscelin was the son of Joscelin I, who had received the County of Edessa from Baldwin II of Jerusalem as a reward for recommending him for the throne after the death of the childless Baldwin I.

any further advance by Zengi into Syria. The army surrounded it and dug itself in; its eighteen huge mangonels were manoeuvred into position at strategic points along the walls; and the siege began.

All the sources, Christian and Muslim alike, agree on John's energy and courage. Conspicuous in his gilded helmet, he seemed to be everywhere at once, encouraging the faint-hearted, berating the idle, consoling the wounded, instructing the siege engineers, infusing all his soldiers – Greek, Varangian, Pecheneg or Turk – with his own indomitable spirit. If his Latin allies had only proved worthy of him, Shaizar might have been theirs. But neither Raymond of Antioch nor Joscelin of Edessa had stomach for the fight. For Raymond, there was always the danger that if the Emperor made too many conquests he would, by the terms of the recent agreement, exchange them for Antioch; and he dreaded having to move into the front line. Joscelin for his part, who hated Raymond almost as much as he hated the Emperor himself and had no wish to see him extending his territory to the south or east, lost no opportunity of stirring up his suspicions and mistrust. The result was, according to William of Tyre, that the two took virtually no part in the siege and spent most of their time back in the camp, playing endless games of dice.

Meanwhile Zengi was approaching, his army swelled by a strong contingent from the Caliph in Baghdad. Left to himself, John Comnenus could almost certainly have defeated him; but he could not leave his siege engines undefended, nor could he trust the Franks. He was still debating the matter with his sons when a message arrived from the Emir of Shaizar, offering recognition of the Emperor as his overlord, an annual tribute, a large indemnity and presents which included his two most treasured possessions: a table inlaid with precious stones, and a cross set with rubies that had formerly belonged to the Emperor Romanus Diogenes and had been taken from him at Manzikert. Had John succeeded in actually storming the town, he could hardly have asked for more. He accepted the Emir's terms at once. On 21 May he raised the siege and headed back towards Antioch.

On his arrival, he exercised for the first time his rights as its suzerain by making a solemn entry into the city together with his sons, his court and a representative detachment of his army. Received at the gates by the Patriarch, he proceeded on horseback through the decorated streets, while the distinctly surly-looking Prince of Antioch and Count of Edessa escorted him on foot as his grooms. After Mass in the cathedral he passed on to the palace, where he took up his residence. Then, after a few days' rest, he sent for Raymond, Joscelin and the leading Latin barons. The war, he told them, was not ended; Aleppo remained in infidel hands; he could not yet make over to Raymond the territories he had promised him. Future campaigns, however, must be planned in Antioch; furthermore he needed a safe place in which to store his war equipment and his treasure. He must therefore require Raymond, according to the treaty of the previous year, to surrender the citadel forthwith.

Silence followed. Hitherto the Emperor had treated Antioch as an honoured ally; now he was dictating terms as to a conquered enemy. Faced with the prospect of the long-term occupation of their city, the Franks were momentarily speechless. At last Joscelin spoke, requesting time for Raymond and his advisers to consider what they had just heard. Then, slipping out of the palace unobserved, he told his men to go through the streets telling all the Latin population that the Emperor had ordered their immediate expulsion and encouraging them to attack their Greek fellow-citizens. Within the hour the rioting had begun; Joscelin then rode back at full gallop to the palace, where he flung himself breathlessly at John's feet. He had, he claimed, narrowly escaped death at the hands of a furious mob, which had broken down the doors of his house, accused him of betraying the city to the Greeks and threatened to kill him.

After over two months in the company of the Count of Edessa, the Emperor was well aware of the duplicity of his nature; but by this time the tumult outside was clearly audible to those in the palace. He was anxious at all costs to prevent a massacre of Greeks by Latins and vice versa; he was also conscious that his entire army – apart from a few members of his personal guard – was encamped a mile or more away across the Orontes, leaving him dangerously exposed in an increasingly hostile city. In these radically changed circumstances there could clearly be no question of any early resumption of the Syrian campaign. He told Raymond and Joscelin that for the moment he would be satisfied with the renewal of their oaths; he had decided to return to Constantinople. Then he rejoined his army, and a day or two later left for home.

Good news awaited him on his arrival. His brother Isaac and Isaac's son John, who had been intriguing for the past eight years with the Muslim princes, had given themselves up. Whether they had genuinely repented of their past behaviour, or whether the Emperor's recent successes in the East and the consequent increase in his popularity had simply convinced them that their ambitions were doomed to failure, we can only guess; but they received a full pardon – which was a good deal more than they expected or deserved.

The story of John's last campaigns can be quickly told. In 1139 and 1140 he was fully occupied with the son of his old enemy Ghazi, the Danishmend Emir Mohammed. His task was complicated by the fact that Constantine Gabras, Duke of Trebizond, had rebelled against his authority and formed an alliance with the Danishmends. In 1139 all went well: the Emperor marched his army eastwards through Bithynia and Paphlagonia and along the southern coast of the Black Sea, his enemies steadily retreating before him. Before the end of the year the treacherous Duke had made his submission, after which John turned southward against the Danishmend stronghold of Neocaesarea. Here for the first time his good fortune failed him. A natural fortress magnificently defended by Mohammed's garrison, it proved effectively impregnable; the savage and mountainous terrain made communications difficult, and Byzantine casualties were high. For the Emperor, the greatest humiliation of all came when his own nephew and namesake, the son of his brother Isaac who had so recently sought his forgiveness for past disloyalty, defected to the enemy, embracing simultaneously the creed of Islam and the daughter of the Seljuk Sultan Mas'ud.[1] Towards the end of 1140 he raised the siege – during which, incidentally, his youngest son Manuel showed great heroism in dealing with a sudden sortie by the defenders[2] – and returned to Constantinople, intending to resume operations the following year; by then, however, Mohammed was dead; and the usual squabble between his heirs enabled John to change his plans and concentrate his energies once again on the situation in Syria.

In the three years since his departure, during which Zengi had been fully occupied in his attempt to capture Damascus, the Latin princes could have achieved much. Instead, they had missed every opportunity. Not only had they made no further progress against the Saracens; they had failed even to preserve John's earlier conquests, nearly all of which had been retaken and were back in Muslim hands. This did not imply that a further Syrian expedition would be useless; what it did mean was that no trust could be placed in the rulers of Antioch or Edessa. The

---

1 Much later, the Ottoman Sultans were to claim descent from this couple.

2 There is some doubt over Manuel's precise age at this time. In Book I of the *Epitome* of John Cinnamus, it is given as eighteen; in Book III – quoting his mother – as 'barely sixteen'. But mothers have been known to miscalculate, or Irene may even have been recalling an earlier skirmish.

Emperor made his preparations; and in the spring of 1142 he set off, once again with his four sons, on his last journey to the East.

They took the road to Attaleia on the south coast, whose land communications were once again under threat. The first weeks were spent driving back the Turkoman nomads and their Seljuk masters and strengthening the frontier defences where necessary; it was high summer by the time they reached Attaleia – and there tragedy struck. John's eldest son Alexius, the recognized heir to the Empire, fell ill; within a few days he was dead. The Emperor, who had loved him dearly, ordered his second and third sons, Andronicus and Isaac, to escort their brother's body by sea back to Constantinople; and on the voyage Andronicus – infected, presumably, by the same virus – died in his turn. This double blow left John heartbroken; but he pressed on by forced marches through Cilicia and then on yet further east, until in mid-September he arrived unexpectedly at Turbessel – now Tell el-Bashir – the second capital of the county of Edessa where Joscelin, taken by surprise, immediately offered him his little daughter Isabella as hostage. The 25th of the month found him at the immense Templar castle of Baghras, from which he sent a message to Raymond demanding the immediate surrender of the city of Antioch – repeating his earlier promise to compensate him from his future conquests.

This was the moment that Raymond had long dreaded. He was incapable of stirring up an immediate riot as Joscelin had done four years before, his incompetence having made him so unpopular that the majority of his native Christian subjects would have been only too happy to welcome the Emperor in his stead. His one chance was to play for time. He replied with elaborate courtesy that he must consult his vassals, which he immediately did; and the vassals refused. Raymond, they pointed out, ruled only as the husband of the city's heiress. He had no right to dispose of her property, and even if she were to signify her consent it would be invalid without their own, which they would in no circumstances give. Any attempt to surrender Antioch would result in the immediate dethronement of both Raymond and his wife.

When this reply was brought to the Emperor at Baghras, he saw that it meant war. But winter was coming, the army was tired and he decided to postpone the offensive until the spring. He allowed his men a week or two to pillage the Frankish estates in the neighbourhood – just to give Raymond and his friends a taste of what was coming to them – and then returned to Cilicia, where there were still a few Danishmend outposts to be dealt with and where he could spend the winter making proper preparations for a campaign that promised to be the most decisive of his life.

Alas, those preparations were in vain. In March 1143, when all was ready, the Emperor set off on a brief hunting expedition in the Taurus, in the course of which an arrow accidentally wounded him in the hand. The wound seemed slight, and at first he ignored it; but it soon became seriously infected, and septicaemia set in. Before long it was clear to him that he was dying. He had faced death too often in his life to fear it now: quietly competent as ever, he began to make provision for the succession. Of his two surviving sons the elder, Isaac, was still in Constantinople; the younger, Manuel, was at his side. Both had their partisans, to whose arguments he listened with close attention; but the final decision, he reminded them all, was his alone.

On Easter Sunday, 4 April, the dying Emperor received holy communion. Next he gave orders that the doors of his chamber should be opened to all in the camp, and that anyone with a request should be allowed to speak to him freely; he was determined that there should be no unfinished business left behind when he died. The following day – during which the whole camp was flooded by driving rain – the doors were opened again, and he distributed his last presents – including food from the imperial table – to those who had served him most faithfully. Then and only then did he call a council to announce his successor. Both his sons, he said, were fine young men – strong, intelligent, full of spirit. Isaac, however, was prone to anger, while Manuel possessed, with all the qualities of his brother, a singular gentleness which enabled him to listen carefully to advice and follow the dictates of reason. It was therefore Manuel – the youngest of his children – who should succeed him. Turning to his son, who knelt at his bedside, he somehow summoned up the strength first to take the imperial diadem and lower it on to the young man's head, then to drape the purple robe across his shoulders.

The Emperor lived on, growing progressively weaker, for three more days. Then, on 8 April 1143, he sent for a holy monk from Pamphylia to hear his confession and perform the last rites. His death, which followed almost at once, was pious, efficient and well-ordered, just as his life had been; and indeed no Emperor had ever worked harder, or sacrificed himself more consistently, for the good of his Empire. To be sure, he died a disappointed man: had just a few more years of life been granted to him, he would almost certainly have extended Byzantine power deep into Syria – perhaps even into Palestine – and might indeed have gone a long way towards undoing the fearful damage sustained at Manzikert. Dying as he did at only fifty-three, John Comnenus was obliged to leave his work in the East unfinished; yet he could take comfort in the knowledge that the Empire he was passing on to his son Manuel was stronger, more extensive and infinitely more respected than it had been at any time in the seventy-two years since the great defeat. And there was another consolation too: Manuel himself – who would, he was convinced, prove a worthy successor.

6

The Second Crusade

[1143-9]

You have commanded, and I have obeyed ... I have declared and spoken; and now they [the Crusaders] are multiplied, beyond number. Cities and castles are deserted, and seven women together may scarcely find one man to lay hold on, so many widows are there whose husbands are still living.

St Bernard of Clairvaux
to Pope Eugenius III, 1146

Manuel Comnenus had been proclaimed *basileus* by his father, before any number of witnesses; but his succession was by no means assured. Emperors, he was well aware, were made in Constantinople: he was still in the wilds of Cilicia, impossibly placed to deal with any rival claimants to the throne. Clearly there could be no question of pursuing the war against Antioch; he must get back to the capital as soon as possible to consolidate his position. On the other hand, he had his filial duties to perform. First there was the funeral service to be arranged, and a monastery to be founded on the spot where John had died; the body must then be carried overland to Mopsuestia, and thence down the river Pyramus to the open sea, whence it would be taken by ship to the Bosphorus for burial in his own foundation of the Pantocrator. Manuel therefore decided to send Axuch ahead of him to Constantinople, with the title of Regent and instructions to put under immediate arrest the most dangerous of possible contenders: his elder brother Isaac, passed over by his father but already installed in the Great Palace and thus with instant access to the treasure and the imperial regalia.

Axuch id his work well, travelling so fast that he reached the capital even before the news of the Emperor's death. He seized the protesting Isaac and locked him up in the Pantocrator; for good measure, he also ordered the arrest of that other Isaac, John's brother, exiled at the Pontic Heraclea. The only other possible source of trouble was the Patriarchate, on which Manuel had to rely for his coronation. As it happened, the chair was vacant – the previous incumbent of the office having died a short time before and his successor having not yet been appointed. In order to ensure that his master would have the support of every possible candidate, the Grand Domestic therefore summoned all the senior churchmen to the palace and presented them with an impressive diploma, its silken ribbons sealed in scarlet wax, by which the new *basileus* undertook to pay annually to the clergy of St Sophia two hundred pieces of silver. They accepted it with every show of gratitude, assuring him that there would be no difficulties over the coronation. Little did they know how cheap they were selling themselves; concealed in his robe Axuch had another, similar document for use as necessary, offering two hundred pieces not of silver but of gold.

Thanks to his speed and efficiency there were no disturbances in the capital – and only one conspiracy. Its leader was the Caesar John Roger, a son-in-law of the late Emperor who had been given his title in recognition of his marriage to Manuel's sister Maria. He seems to have been a Norman, one of the number of barons from South Italy who, having unsuccessfully rebelled against the King of Sicily in the years following his accession in 1130, had been expelled from their lands and had sought refuge in Constantinople; and it was from them, not surprisingly, that he drew his support. Fortunately Axuch was informed of the plot at an early stage, by the Princess Maria herself; and within hours her husband too was under arrest.

It was only after several weeks that Manuel was able to leave Cilicia for the capital. Before doing so he had an acrimonious exchange of letters with Raymond of Antioch who, saved by the unexpected turn of events from almost certain catastrophe, was showing all his old arrogance and bluster; but with the imperial succession at stake, the situation in the East would have to wait. The moment therefore that he had properly fulfilled the obligations resulting from his father's death, Manuel set off with his army; and once on the road nothing could stop him. Not even when he heard that Raymond, having invaded Cilicia the moment he had left it, had regained several of the castles taken from him by John – not even when his cousin Andronicus, the latter's son-in-law and a group of noblemen wandered off into the countryside on a quick hunting expedition and were captured by Seljuk soldiers – would he agree to call a halt. They had, after all, no one to blame but themselves; he was certainly not prepared to risk his throne to rescue them.

When he arrived in Constantinople – it was probably around the middle of August – his first priority was to appoint a new Patriarch, a certain Michael Curcuas; and the first task of the new Patriarch after his installation was to crown the Emperor. Immediately after the ceremony, Manuel laid two hundred pounds of gold on the high altar of St Sophia, over and above his promised annual subsidy, and decreed that in celebration of the occasion two golden pieces should be presented to every householder in the city. A few days later he ordered the release of his brother from captivity and lifted the sentence of exile on his uncle, the *sebastocrator* Isaac: there was nothing more to fear from either of them. He had been nominated by his father, crowned by his Patriarch and acclaimed by his subjects. At last his position was secure.

The first thing people noticed about Manuel Comnenus was his height. The chroniclers all remark upon it; and though it would probably seem fairly normal today, by the standards of the twelfth century it was certainly exceptional. But for the fact that he walked – despite his youth[1] – with a slight stoop, he might have looked taller still. Nicetas describes his complexion as being dark, but not unduly so; later, however, he tells us how, during the siege of Corfu in 1149, the Venetians mocked him by dressing up an Ethiopian slave in imperial robes – a story which suggests that he had inherited all the swarthiness of his father. But in two respects at least he differed from him dramatically. First, he was outstandingly handsome; secondly, his charm of manner, his love of pleasure and his sheer enjoyment of life stood out in refreshing contrast to John's humourless and high-principled austerity – to which, indeed, they may have been a very natural reaction. For Manuel, whether in his Palace of Blachernae, a hunting-lodge or one of the several villas on the Bosphorus in which he was to spend so much of his time, any excuse was good enough for a celebration.

Yet there was nothing shallow about him. When he was on campaign all his apparent frivolity fell away to reveal a fine soldier and superb horseman. He was, perhaps, too much in love with adventure for its own sake to be quite the brilliant general that his father had been – few of his campaigns were outstandingly successful – but there could be no doubting his energy and enthusiasm. He was indifferent alike to the extremes of heat and cold, his powers of endurance were legendary, his only weakness a propensity for riding off alone into enemy territory and exposing himself unnecessarily to danger. 'In war,' wrote Gibbon, 'he

---

1 See p. 82 note 2. If we were to put Manuel's age at twenty-one at the time of his coronation we should not be far wrong.

seemed ignorant of peace, in peace he appeared incapable of war.' A skilful diplomat, he was to show again and again during the coming years the imagination and sureness of touch of a born statesman. And somehow, through it all, he remained the typical Byzantine intellectual, cultivated and well-read in both the arts and the sciences, a man who liked nothing better than to debate for hours with monkish theologians and to immerse himself in doctrinal issues of the most speculative kind. Some of his more outrageous suggestions would often horrify his interlocutors; but Manuel made no pretence of being deeply religious, as his father had been. He debated not so much for the sake of winning an argument or arriving at the truth as for the love of the debate itself. No wonder, as his reign went on, that he became increasingly unpopular with the Church – which mistrusted his continued attempts to achieve a reunion with Rome, disapproved of his frequent tactical alliances with the Saracen and was scandalized when he not only invited the Sultan of Iconium to Constantinople but actually proposed to include him in a solemn procession to St Sophia.

Most of all, perhaps, it deplored his private life. Manuel's appetite for women was prodigious, his way with them irresistible. His infidelity to his first wife was to begin almost immediately after his marriage; on his deathbed thirty-four years later he was still confidently expecting an early resumption of his infidelity to his second. As to the identities of the other ladies concerned, our sources are irritatingly discreet: the only one to whom we can give a name is his niece Theodora,[1] who bore him a son and whom he set up as a *maîtresse en titre*, with her own palace, retinue and personal guard. She behaved in every respect like an Empress, and a Byzantine Empress at that: on one occasion, scenting a potential rival to her position, she is known to have had the girl eliminated. Future members of the imperial harem took due warning.

Manuel would always have been an unfaithful husband; but his natural proclivities were doubtless given additional impetus by the appearance and character of his first wife. As early as 1142 John Comnenus had suggested a dynastic marriage, with Manuel as bridegroom, to seal his alliance with the Western Emperor-elect Conrad[2] against King Roger of Sicily; Conrad, delighted with the idea, had

1 Even her precise identity is doubtful, since Manuel had at least three nieces and one great-niece of this all-too-frequent name. The most likely candidate is the daughter of his sister Maria and the Norman John Roger, but we cannot be sure.

2 Though effectively Holy Roman Emperor, Conrad was never crowned by the Pope in Rome and consequently had no right to any title higher than that of King of the Romans. See p. 20n.

proposed his sister-in-law, the German princess Bertha of Sulzbach, and had sent her off on approval to Constantinople. Manuel – who at that time had three elder brothers living and virtually no prospect of the succession – had been distinctly lukewarm about the whole idea, and his first sight of his intended bride had done little to inflame his ardour; but towards the end of 1144 he began to have second thoughts, and after more discussions with Conrad – which culminated with a treaty of alliance – the arrangements were made. Bertha, who had been living for the past four years in the obscurity of the imperial *gynaeceum*, now re-emerged into public view, shed her barbarous Frankish name for the more euphonious if sadly unoriginal Greek one of Irene, and in January 1146 duly married the Emperor.

According to Basil of Ochrid, Archbishop of Thessalonica, who preached Bertha's funeral oration in 1160, the Empress 'by her form and figure, the rhythmic beauty of her movements and her fine and flower-like complexion, gave a sense of pleasure even to inanimate objects'. No man, however, is on oath in a funeral oration, and it can only be said that other more objective authorities paint a rather different picture. Nicetas Choniates tells us that

she was less concerned with the embellishment of her body than with that of her spirit; rejecting powder and paint, and leaving to vain women all those adornments which are owed to artifice, she sought only that solid beauty which proceeds from the splendour of virtue. This was the reason why the Emperor, who was of extreme youth, had little inclination for her and did not maintain towards her that fidelity which was her due; although he bestowed great honours upon her, a most exalted throne, a numerous retinue and all else that makes for magnificence and induces the respect and veneration of the people.[1]

By the time of her death, she was not enjoying much respect or veneration either. However hard she tried – which was not, one suspects, very hard – Bertha never endeared herself to the Byzantines, for whom she remained too stiff, too inelegant: frankly, as they put it, too German. Her meanness, too, was legendary. Only in the diplomatic field did she conclusively prove her worth, coming several times to the rescue when relations between her husband and brother-in-law became strained and playing a valuable part in the political alliance concluded between Manuel and Conrad on the latter's visit to Constantinople in 1148. For the rest, she spent her life quietly in the palace, occupying herself with

1 Choniates, 'Manuel Comnenus', I, ii.

Battle between Crusaders and Saracens (Paris, Bibliothèque Nationale)

The Crusader assault on Jerusalem, 1099 (Paris, Bibliothèque Nationale)

Ani, Armenia: the Cathedral (989–1010)

Budapest: the Crown of St Stephen, which contains
inset portrait medallions of the Byzantine Emperors

The First Crusade: the army of Peter the Hermit is massacred by the Seljuk Turks
(Paris, Bibliothèque Nationale)

Doge Enrico Dandolo crowns Baldwin of Flanders
Emperor of Byzantium, 1204. From a faïence plate
(Venice, Museo Civico Correr)

Seljuk Architecture, Konya: (*above*) the Mevlana Tekke, 1274,
with the green turret added in 1397 by the Karaman Emir Alaeddin Ali
(*below*) the Ince Minare Mosque, 1251

John VI Cantacuzenus at the Church Council in the Palace of Blachernae, 1351
(Paris, Bibliothèque Nationale)

Istanbul, The Church of St Saviour in Chora (Kariye Camii):
the Anastasis (The Harrowing of Hell), apse fresco in the south paracclesion

Sultan Bayezit I, Turkish miniature from the Genealogy of the Ottoman Sultans
(Istanbul, Topkapi Museum)

pious works and the education of her two daughters, one of whom died in infancy. Her death occasioned little regret – to her husband none at all.

Manuel Comnenus had ascended the throne of Byzantium with anger in his heart. He could not forget the insults he had received from the Prince of Antioch at the time of his departure from Cilicia, nor could he forgive the alacrity with which Raymond had moved to reconquer the captured castles the moment his back was turned, doing all the damage he could to Byzantine cities, towns and country estates. It was as inglorious a beginning to his reign as could have possibly been imagined, and he was determined that it should not go unpunished. Unfortunately he could not lead a campaign himself, much as he would have liked to do so; to leave his capital so soon after his coronation would have been to invite upheavals. Early in 1144, however, he dispatched a major amphibious expedition to the south-east, the fleet being entrusted to a certain Demetrius Branas and the army to the joint command of the brothers John and Andronicus Contostephanus and a converted Turk named Bursuk. The lost castles were regained and – to give Raymond a dose of his own medicine – the land around Antioch devastated. Branas, meanwhile, swept the entire coastline of the principality, destroying all the ships he found beached on the sand and taking many of the local inhabitants into captivity, including a tax collector with his money-bags.

Whether or not the Prince of Antioch planned revenge we do not know, for before the year was out the whole situation in Outremer had changed: on Christmas Eve, after a siege of twenty-five days and amid scenes of terrible butchery, Imad ed-Din Zengi captured the Crusader principality of Edessa. Antioch, it seemed to many, would be next on the list. For Raymond, one course only was open: to swallow his pride, travel to Constantinople and seek help from Manuel. At first the Emperor refused to receive him; only after the Prince of Antioch had made his way to the monastery of the Pantocrator and knelt in silent contrition at John's tomb was he granted an audience. Manuel then treated him with surprising consideration, promising him a regular subsidy – though stopping short at direct military assistance; and Raymond returned to the East moderately satisfied with what he had achieved. He would have been more so had he known that news of his visit – but not of its results – had been brought to Zengi, who had consequently decided to postpone the new attacks on the Franks that he

91

was already preparing. The following year the great Atabeg was murdered by a drunken eunuch, and the Crusader states were rid of the most formidable enemy that they had yet confronted.

The news of the fall of Edessa, however, had an effect that went far beyond Antioch. It horrified the whole of Christendom. To the peoples of Western Europe, who had seen the initial success of the First Crusade as a sign of divine favour, it called in question all their comfortably-held opinions. How, after less than half a century, had Cross once again given way to Crescent? Travellers to the East had for some time been returning with reports of a widespread degeneracy among the Franks of Outremer. Could it be, perhaps, that they were no longer worthy in the eyes of the Almighty to guard the Holy Places under the banner of their Redeemer?

As for the Franks themselves, long familiarity with these shrines had made possible a more rational approach. They knew well enough why Edessa had been captured. It was because of their own military weakness. The first great wave of Crusading enthusiasm, culminating in the jubilant capture of Jerusalem in 1099, was now spent. Immigration from the West had slowed to a trickle; of the pilgrims, many still arrived unarmed according to ancient tradition, and even for those who came prepared to wield a sword a single summer campaign usually proved more than enough. The only permanent standing army – if such it could be called – was formed by the two military orders of the Hospitallers and the Templars; but they alone could not hope to hold out against a concerted offensive. Reinforcements were desperately needed. And so from Jerusalem an embassy under Hugh, Bishop of Jabala, was sent to the Pope to give him official notification of the disaster and to ask, with all possible urgency, for a Crusade.

Pope Eugenius III was in none too strong a position himself: in the usual turmoil of medieval Rome he had been obliged to flee the city three days after his election and had taken refuge in Viterbo. He was thus unable to assume the leadership of the new Crusade as Pope Urban had tried to do; and when he came to consider the princes of the West, he could see only one possible candidate. King Conrad, to whom the honour should properly have been given, was still beset with difficulties in Germany; King Stephen of England had a civil war on his hands; Roger of Sicily, for any number of reasons, was out of the question. That left King Louis VII of France. Though still only twenty-four, Louis had about him an aura of lugubrious piety which made him look older – and irritated to distraction his beautiful and high-spirited young wife, Eleanor of Aquitaine. He was one of Nature's pilgrims; the Crusade was his duty as a Christian – and there were family reasons too, for was not Eleanor the niece of the Prince of Antioch? At Christmas 1145 he announced his intention of taking the Cross and formally notified the Pope; then, in order that the hearts of all his subjects should be filled, like his, with Crusading fire, he sent for Bernard, Abbot of Clairvaux.

St Bernard, now fifty-five, was far and away the most powerful spiritual force in Europe. To the twentieth-century observer, safely out of range of that astonishing personal magnetism with which he effort-lessly dominated all those with whom he came in contact, he is not an attractive figure. Tall and haggard, his features clouded by the constant pain that resulted from a lifetime of exaggerated physical austerities, he was consumed by a blazing religious zeal that left no room for tolerance or moderation. His public life had begun in 1115 when the Abbot of Cîteaux, the Englishman Stephen Harding, had effectively released him from monastic discipline by sending him off to found a daughter-house at Clairvaux in Champagne. From that moment on his influence spread; and for the last twenty-five years of his life he was constantly on the move, preaching, persuading, arguing, debating, writing innumerable letters and compulsively plunging into the thick of every controversy in which he believed the basic principles of Christianity to be involved. The proposed Crusade was a venture after his own heart. Willingly he agreed to launch it – at the assembly that the King had summoned for the following Palm Sunday at Vézelay in Burgundy.

At once the magic of Bernard's name began to do its work; and as the appointed day approached men and women from every corner of France began to pour into the little town. Since there were far too many to be packed into the basilica, a great wooden platform was hastily erected on the hillside; and here, on 31 March 1146, Bernard made one of the most fateful speeches of his life, with King Louis – already displaying on his breast the cross which the Pope had sent him in token of his decision – standing beside him. The text of what he said has not come down to us; but with Bernard it was the manner of his delivery rather than the words themselves that made the real impact on his audience. As he spoke the crowd, silent at first, began to cry out for crosses of their own. Bundles of these, cut in rough cloth, had already been prepared for distribution; when the supply was exhausted, the Abbot flung off his own robe and began to tear it into strips to make more. Others followed his example, and he and his helpers were still stitching as night fell.

It was an astonishing achievement. No one else in Europe could have done it. And yet, as events were soon to tell, it were better had it not been done.

Some time during the summer of 1146 Manuel Comnenus received a letter from Louis VII, attempting to enlist his sympathies for the coming Crusade. Manuel was fonder of Westerners and the Western way of life than any previous *basileus*; nevertheless, he found the prospect of another full-scale incursion into his Empire by undisciplined French and German armies – for St Bernard had gone on from France to Germany, where his message had been received with equal enthusiasm – unpalatable in the extreme. He fully understood the extent of the nightmare that the First Crusade had caused his grandfather half a century before, and had no wish to see it repeated. Admittedly he was having a good deal of trouble with the Sultan of Iconium, against whom he was at that moment involved in the second of two fairly indecisive campaigns; it was just conceivable that the new wave of Crusaders might be better behaved than their predecessors and even turn out to be a long-term blessing; but he doubted it. His reply to Louis was as lukewarm as it could be made without actually giving offence. He would provide food and supplies for the armies, but everything would have to be paid for. And all the leaders would be required once again to take an oath of fealty to the Emperor as they passed through his dominions.

Any faint hopes that Manuel might have entertained about the quality of the new champions of Christendom were soon dashed. The German army of about twenty thousand that set off from Ratisbon in May 1147 seems to have included more than its fair share of undesirables, ranging from the occasional religious fanatic to the usual collection of footloose ne'er-do-wells and fugitives from justice, attracted as always by the promise of plenary absolution offered to all who took the Cross. Hardly had they entered Byzantine territory than they began pillaging, ravaging, raping and even murdering as the mood took them. Often the leaders set a poor example to their followers. Conrad himself – who had at first refused to have anything to do with the Crusade but had repented the previous Christmas after public castigation by Bernard – behaved with his usual dignity; but at Adrianople (Edirne) his nephew and second-in-command, the young Duke Frederick of Swabia (better known to history by his subsequent nickname of Barbarossa), burnt down an entire monastery in reprisal for an attack by local brigands, massacring all the perfectly innocent monks. Fighting became ever more frequent between the Crusaders and the Byzantine military escort which Manuel had sent out to keep an eye on them, and when in mid-September the army at last drew up outside the walls of Constantinople – Conrad having indignantly refused the Emperor's request to cross into Asia over the Hellespont (now the Dardanelles), avoiding the capital altogether – relations between German and Greek could hardly have been worse.

And now, even before the populations along the route had recovered from the shock, the French army appeared in its turn on the western horizon. It was smaller than the German, and on the whole more seemly. Discipline was better, and the presence of many distinguished ladies – including Queen Eleanor herself – accompanying their husbands doubtless exercised a further moderating influence. Progress, however, was not altogether smooth. Not surprisingly, the Balkan peasantry was by now frankly hostile, and asked ridiculous prices for what little food it had left to sell. Mistrust soon became mutual, and led to sharp practices on both sides. Thus, long before they reached Constantinople, the French had begun to feel considerable resentment against Germans and Greeks alike; and when they finally arrived on 4 October they were scandalized to hear that the Emperor had chosen that moment to conclude a truce with the Turkish enemy.

Although King Louis could not have been expected to appreciate the fact, it was a sensible precaution for Manuel to take. The presence of the French and German armies at the very gates of his capital constituted a far more serious immediate danger than the Turks in Asia. The Emperor knew that in both camps there were extreme elements pressing for a combined Western attack on Constantinople; just a few days later, indeed, St Bernard's cousin Geoffrey, Bishop of Langres, was formally to propose such a course to the King. Only by deliberately spreading reports of a huge Turkish army massing in Anatolia, and implying that if the Franks did not make haste to pass through the hostile territory they might never manage to do so at all, did Manuel succeed in saving the situation. Meanwhile he flattered Louis – and kept him occupied – with his usual round of lavish entertainments and banquets, while arranging passage over the Bosphorus for the King and his army at the earliest possible moment.

As he bade farewell to his unwelcome guests and watched the ferry-boats shuttling across the straits, laden to the gunwales with men and animals, Manuel foresaw better than anyone the dangers that awaited the Franks on the second stage of their journey. He himself had only recently returned from an Anatolian campaign; though his stories of gathering Turkish hordes had been exaggerated, he had now seen the

Crusaders for himself and must have known that their shambling forces, already as lacking in morale as in discipline, would stand little chance of survival if suddenly attacked by the Seljuk cavalry. He had furnished them with provisions and guides; he had warned them about the scarcity of water; and he had advised them not to take the direct route through the hinterland but to keep to the coast, which was still under Byzantine control. He could do no more. If, after all these precautions, the Crusaders insisted on getting themselves slaughtered, they would have only themselves to blame. He for his part would be sorry – but not, perhaps, inconsolable.

It cannot have been more than a few days after bidding them farewell that the Emperor received two reports, from two very different quarters. The first, brought by swift messengers from Asia Minor, informed him that the German army had been taken by surprise by the Turks near Dorylaeum and virtually annihilated. Conrad himself and the Duke of Swabia had escaped, and had returned to join the French at Nicaea; but nine-tenths of their men now lay dead and dying amid the wreckage of their camp.

The second report brought him less welcome news: the fleet of King Roger of Sicily was at that very moment sailing against his Empire.

The Sicilian fleet was commanded by George of Antioch, a renegade Greek who had risen by his own brilliance to the proudest title his adopted country had to offer: Emir of Emirs, High Admiral and Chief Minister of the realm.[1] It had sailed in the autumn of 1147 from Otranto and had headed straight across the Adriatic to Corfu. The island fell without a struggle; Nicetas tells us that the inhabitants, oppressed by the weight of Byzantine taxation and charmed by the honeyed words of the admiral, welcomed the Normans as deliverers and willingly accepted a garrison of a thousand men.

Turning southward, the fleet then rounded the Peloponnese, leaving further detachments at strategic positions, and sailed up the eastern coast of Greece as far as Euboea. Here George seems to have decided that he had gone far enough. He turned about, made a quick raid on Athens and then, on reaching the Ionian islands, headed eastward again up the Gulf of Corinth, ravaging the coastal towns as he went. His progress,

---

1 It is perhaps worth mentioning here that the word *admiral*, found with minor variations in so many European languages, is derived through Norman Sicily from the Arabic word *emir*; and in particular from its compound *emir-al-bahr*, Ruler of the Sea.

Nicetas tells us, was 'like a sea monster, swallowing everything in its path'. One of his raiding parties penetrated inland as far as Thebes, centre of the Byzantine silk manufacture. Together with innumerable bales of rich damasks and brocades, George also seized a large number of women workers, expert alike in the cultivation and exploitation of the silkworm, the spinning of the silk and its subsequent weaving, and brought them back triumphantly to Palermo.

The news of the Sicilian depredations stung Manuel to a fury. Whatever he might have thought about the Crusade, the fact that a so-called Christian country should have taken deliberate advantage of it to launch an attack on his Empire disgusted him; and the knowledge that the admiral concerned was a Greek can hardly have assuaged his wrath. A century before, Apulia had been a rich province of the Byzantine Empire; now it was little better than a nest of pirates. Here was a situation that could not be tolerated. Roger, 'that dragon, threatening to shoot the flames of his anger higher than the crater of Etna ... that common enemy of all Christians and illegal occupier of the land of Sicily',[1] must be driven for ever from the Mediterranean. The West had tried to do so, and failed; now it was the turn of Byzantium. Given adequate help and freedom from other commitments, Manuel believed that he could succeed. The Crusading armies had passed on. He himself had already concluded a truce with the Turks, and this he now confirmed and extended. It was essential that every soldier and sailor in the Empire should be free for the grand design that he was planning, a design that might well prove to be the crowning achievement of his life: the restoration of all South Italy and Sicily to the Byzantine fold.

The problem was to find suitable allies. With France and Germany out of the running, Manuel's thoughts turned to Venice. Her people, as he well knew, had long been worried about the growth of Sicilian sea power. No longer could they control the Mediterranean as once they had done; and while the bazaars of Palermo, Catania and Syracuse grew ever busier, so affairs on the Rialto had begun to slacken. Moreover, if Roger were to consolidate his hold on Corfu and the coast of Epirus he would be in a position to seal off the Adriatic; and Venice might at any moment find herself under a Sicilian blockade. The Venetians bargained a little, of course – they never gave anything away for nothing – but in March 1148, in return for increased trading privileges in Cyprus, Rhodes and Constantinople, Manuel got what he wanted: the full support of

1 Imperial Edict of February 1148.

their fleet for the six months following. He himself was meanwhile working feverishly to bring his own navy to readiness; John Cinnamus, by now his chief secretary, estimates its strength at five hundred galleys and a thousand transports – a worthy complement to an army of perhaps twenty or thirty thousand men. The army he entrusted as usual to the Grand Domestic, Axuch; the navy to his brother-in-law, Duke Stephen Contostephanus, husband of his sister Anna. He himself would be in overall command.

By April this huge expeditionary force was ready to leave. The ships, refitted and provisioned, lay at anchor in the Marmara; the army waited for the order to march. Then, suddenly, everything went wrong. The Cumans swept down over the Danube and into Byzantine territory; the Venetian fleet was held up by the sudden death of the Doge; and a succession of freak summer storms disrupted shipping in the eastern Mediterranean. It was autumn before the two navies met in the southern Adriatic and began a joint sea blockade of Corfu. The land attack, meanwhile, was still further delayed. By the time he had dealt with the Cumans it was plain to Manuel that the Pindus mountains would be blocked by snow long before he could get his army across them. Settling in in winter quarters in Macedonia he rode on to Thessalonica, where an important guest was awaiting him. Conrad of Hohenstaufen had just returned from the Holy Land.

The Second Crusade had been a fiasco. Conrad, with the few of his subjects that had survived Dorylaeum, had continued in the company of the French as far as Ephesus, where at Christmas he had fallen gravely ill. Manuel and his wife, on hearing the news, had immediately sailed down from Constantinople, picked him up and brought him safely back to the palace, where the Emperor, who prided himself on his medical skills, had personally nursed him back to health. The King of the Romans had remained in the capital till March 1148, when Manuel had put ships at his disposal to carry him to Palestine. The French, meanwhile, had had an agonizing passage through Anatolia, where they had suffered heavily at Turkish hands. Although this was entirely the fault of Louis himself, who had ignored the Emperor's warnings to keep to the coast, he persisted in attributing every encounter with the enemy to Byzantine carelessness or treachery or both, and rapidly developed an almost psychopathic resentment against the Greeks. At last in despair he, his household and as much of his cavalry as could be accommodated had taken ship from Attaleia, leaving the rest of the army and the pilgrims to struggle on as best they might. It had been late in the spring of 1148 before the remnant of the great host that had set out so confidently the previous year dragged itself into Antioch.

And that was only the beginning. The mighty Zengi was dead, but his mantle had passed to his still greater son Nur ed-Din, whose stronghold at Aleppo had now become the focus of Muslim opposition to the Franks. Aleppo should thus have been the Crusaders' first objective, and within days of his arrival in Antioch Louis found himself under considerable pressure from Raymond to mount an immediate attack on the city. He had refused on the grounds that he must first pray at the Holy Sepulchre; whereat Queen Eleanor, whose affection for her husband had not been increased by the dangers and discomforts of the journey – and whose relations with Raymond were already suspected of going somewhat beyond those normally recommended between uncle and niece – had announced her intention of remaining at Antioch and suing for divorce. She and her husband were distant cousins; the question of consanguinity had been conveniently overlooked at the time of their marriage, but if resurrected could still prove troublesome – and Eleanor knew it.

Louis, for all his moroseness, was not without spirit in moments of crisis. He had ignored his wife's protests and dragged her off to Jerusalem; had antagonized Raymond to the point where he refused to play any further part in the Crusade; and had arrived, his tight-lipped queen in tow, in the Holy City in May, soon after Conrad. There they remained until, on 24 June, a meeting of all the Crusaders was held at Acre to decide on a plan of campaign. It did not take long to reach a decision: every man and beast available must be immediately mobilized for a concerted attack on Damascus.

Why Damascus was chosen as the first objective remains a mystery. The only major Arab state to continue hostile to Nur ed-Din, it could – and should – have been an invaluable ally to the Franks. By attacking it, they drove it against its will into the Emir's Muslim confederation – and in doing so made their own destruction sure. They arrived to find the walls of Damascus strong, its defenders determined. On the second day, by yet another of those disastrous decisions that characterized the whole Crusade, they moved their camp to an area along the south-eastern section of the walls, devoid alike of shade or water. The Palestinian barons, already at loggerheads over the future of the city when captured, suddenly lost their nerve and began to urge retreat. There were dark rumours of bribery and treason. Louis and Conrad were shocked and disgusted, but soon they too were made to understand the facts of the situation. To continue the siege would mean not only driving Damascus into the arms of Nur ed-Din but also, given the universal breakdown of morale, the almost certain destruction of their whole army. On 28 July, just five days after the opening of the campaign, they ordered withdrawal.

There is no part of the Syrian desert more shattering to the spirit than that dark-grey, featureless expanse of sand and basalt that lies between Damascus and Tiberias. Retreating across it in the height of the Arabian summer, the remorseless sun and scorching desert wind full in their faces, harried incessantly by mounted Arab archers and leaving a stinking trail of dead men and horses in their wake, the Crusaders must have felt despair heavy upon them. For this, they knew, was the end. Their losses, both in human life and material, had been immense. They had neither the will nor the wherewithal to continue. Worst of all was the shame. Having travelled for the best part of a year, often in conditions of mortal danger; having suffered agonies of thirst, hunger and sickness and the bitterest extremes of heat and cold, their once-glorious army that had purported to enshrine every ideal of the Christian West had given up the whole enterprise after four days' fighting, having regained not one inch of Muslim territory. Here was the ultimate humiliation – which neither they nor their enemies would forget.

Louis was in no hurry to return to France. His wife was now determined on divorce, and he dreaded the difficulties and embarrassments that this would involve. Besides, he wanted to spend Easter in Jerusalem. Conrad, on the other hand, could not leave quickly enough. On 8 September he left Acre with his household on a ship bound for Thessalonica, where the Emperor met him and, for the second time, bore him back to Constantinople. The pair were by now close friends. Despite the recent débâcle, Manuel remained fascinated by Western culture and customs, while Conrad for his part had totally succumbed to Manuel's kindness and charm – to say nothing of the unaccustomed luxuries of the imperial palace, which made a refreshing contrast to the draughty halls of his homeland.

That Christmas was marked by a further union of the two imperial houses when Manuel's niece Theodora – the daughter of his late brother Andronicus – was married to Conrad's brother, Duke Henry of Austria.[1]

---

1 A slight gloom may have been cast over the proceedings by the horror felt by many Byzantines at the fate of a Greek princess being delivered into the hands of Frankish barbarians; a poem by Prodromus in honour of the occasion describes poor Theodora as being 'sacrificed to the beast of the West'.

Before the King of the Romans left for Germany in early February, the two rulers had cemented a further alliance against Roger of Sicily and agreed on a joint South Italian campaign later in the year. They had even reached agreement on the fate of Apulia and Calabria after the King's downfall. Both territories were to go to Conrad – who would, however, immediately make them over to Manuel as the belated dowry of his sister Bertha, now the Empress Irene.

This alliance was in fact to achieve little: it certainly failed to topple the King of Sicily, and when a few years later Manuel was to find himself briefly master of much of Apulia this was the result more of his own efforts than of any generosity on the part of the Western Empire. It remained, however – for what it was worth – the only positive result of the Second Crusade, which in all other respects had proved a disgrace to Christendom. With the single personal exception of Conrad himself, it had sown dangerous dissension between Frenchman and German, Frank and Byzantine, and even between the newly-arrived Crusaders and their own brethren who had long been resident in Outremer. It had afforded untold encouragement to the forces of Islam, giving them new solidarity and strength; and it had utterly destroyed the military reputation of the West.

Many centuries were to pass before that reputation was restored.

7
Realignments

[1149-58]

The Emperor Manuel often held that it was an easy matter for him to win over the peoples of the East by gifts of money or by force of arms, but that over those of the West he could never count on gaining a similar advantage; for they are formidable in numbers, indomitable in pride, cruel in character, rich in possessions and inspired by an inveterate hatred of the Empire.

Nicetas Choniates,
'Manuel Comnenus', VII, i

Considerate host that he was, Manuel Comnenus showed no sign of impatience while Conrad lingered in Constantinople, nor any desire to speed the parting guest; the moment he had bidden his friend goodbye but, he set off to rejoin his forces at Corfu, where the siege had continued throughout the winter. Recent reports of its progress had not been encouraging. The Sicilian-held citadel rose apparently impregnable from its high crest above the old town, almost out of range of Byzantine projectiles. The Greeks, wrote Nicetas, seemed to be aiming at the very sky itself, while the defenders could release downpours of arrows and hailstorms of rocks on to the besiegers below. (People wondered, he adds disarmingly, how the Sicilians had captured the place so effortlessly the previous year.) By now it seemed clear that the only hope of victory would be to starve out the garrison; but they had had a full year in which to provision themselves, and even then the Byzantine blockade might at any moment be broken by a Sicilian fleet arriving with supplies.

A long siege could impose just as great a strain on the attackers as on those within; and by spring the Greek sailors and their Venetian allies were barely on speaking terms. The climax came when the Venetians occupied a neighbouring islet and set fire to a number of Byzantine merchantmen anchored offshore. By some mischance they also managed to gain possession of the imperial flagship, on which they even went so far as to stage the elaborate charade mentioned in the previous chapter,[1] dressing up an Ethiopian slave in the imperial vestments and staging a mock coronation on the deck, in full view of the Greeks. Whether the Emperor arrived in time to witness this insult we do not know. He certainly heard about it afterwards, and never forgave the Venetians their behaviour; but he needed them too much to protest. Patience, tact and his celebrated charm soon restored tolerably good relations. Meanwhile the siege continued, with himself now in personal command. There would be time enough, later, for revenge.

Within months he was rewarded: in the late summer Corfu fell – probably through treachery, since Nicetas tells us that the garrison commander subsequently entered the imperial service. The Emperor sailed at once to the Dalmatian port of Avlona, whence he proposed to cross the Adriatic to keep his rendezvous with Conrad in Italy; but he was delayed by storms and was still waiting for the weather to improve when reports were brought to him of a major insurrection by the Serbs, to whom the neighbouring Kingdom of Hungary was giving active military assistance. He also heard to his fury that George of Antioch had profited by his absence to take a fleet of forty ships right up the Hellespont and through the Marmara to the very walls of Constantinople. Thence, after an unsuccessful attempt to disembark, the Sicilians had sailed some distance up the Bosphorus, pillaging several rich villas along the Asiatic shore, and before departing had even fired a few impudent arrows into the grounds of the imperial palace.

Here was another unpardonable insult that the Emperor would not forget; but the Serbian uprising was a good deal more serious – particularly if, as seemed more than likely, the King of Sicily were behind it. The Serbs and the Hungarians were certainly hand in glove, and Roger – whose cousin Busilla had married King Coloman – had always maintained close ties of friendship with the Hungarian throne. What Manuel did not know was that, in his determination to sabotage the projected expedition against him, Roger had engineered a similar diplomatic *coup* against the King of the Romans by financing a league of German princes under the leadership of Count Welf of Bavaria, Conrad's still-hopeful rival for the imperial throne. Thus it was that the King of Sicily, facing the most formidable military alliance that could be conceived in the Middle Ages, that of the Eastern and the Western Empires acting – as they rarely acted in the six and a half centuries of their joint

1 See p. 88.

history – in complete concert one with the other, had succeeded in the space of a few months in immobilizing both of them. He may have been, in Manuel's eyes, a usurper of imperial lands and an unprincipled adventurer to boot; but he was at least a worthy adversary.

On 29 July 1149, King Louis VII and Queen Eleanor landed in Calabria on their way from Palestine and rode inland to the little town of Potenza, where Roger of Sicily was waiting to greet them. Louis was not in a good mood; he had rather misguidedly entrusted himself and his household to Sicilian ships – dangerous craft in which to brave Byzantine waters – and somewhere in the Aegean had encountered a Greek squadron (presumably on its way to or from Corfu) which had turned at once to the attack. He himself had managed to escape by running up the French flag, and Eleanor – whose relations with her husband were now such that she was travelling on a separate vessel – was rescued by Sicilian warships just in time; but one of the escorts, containing several members of the royal household and nearly all the baggage, had been captured by the Greeks and borne off to Constantinople. For Louis, who had already persuaded himself that Manuel Comnenus had been solely responsible for the failure of the Crusade, this incident had been the last straw; and he was only too ready to listen to the proposal now made to him by the King of Sicily.

Briefly, it was for a European league against the Byzantine Empire. Roger explained, clearly and convincingly, how in his hatred of the Christian cause Manuel had allied himself with the Turks, whom he had doubtless kept fully informed about the progress of the Crusading army: the locations of its camps, the state of its preparedness, the routes it proposed to follow. With such a viper in its nest, he continued, the Crusade had been doomed before it started. The first priority, therefore, was to eliminate the *basileus* altogether, together with the depraved and schismatic Empire over which he ruled. Then and only then could the allies launch a victorious Third Crusade to wipe out the humiliations of the Second.

The whole proposal could hardly have been more disingenuous. The King of Sicily was no Crusader, either by temperament or conviction. For the fate of the Christians of Outremer he cared not a rap; as far as he was concerned, they deserved all they got. He himself infinitely preferred the Arabs, who made up a considerable portion of his Sicilian population, who ran much of his civil service, and whose language he spoke perfectly. On the other hand, there were his claims on Antioch and

Jerusalem to be considered, together with the fact that if he did not take the offensive against Manuel, the Emperor would unquestionably do so against him. Was opposition not the best defence? And if so would there ever be a better time than the present, when he – alone among the major princes of Europe – had emerged from the Crusade with his reputation unscathed, while Manuel Comnenus was the most hated man in Western Europe?

The irony of the situation, though clear enough to Roger, was lost on Louis. Delighted with their discussion, he travelled on to Tivoli to sound out the Pope. Eugenius was lukewarm; he was all for putting an end to the alliance between the two Empires, but he had no wish to see Roger in a position any more powerful than in already enjoyed. The other leading churchmen, on the other hand – including St Bernard – were enthusiastic; and so, after the King returned to Paris, was the highly influential Suger, Abbot of Saint-Denis, who became the leading champion of the projected new Crusade.

The plan foundered because of Conrad. The King of the Romans could now add to his many reasons for detesting Roger yet another, perhaps the strongest of all. He knew that his reputation had been dealt a severe blow by the failure of the Crusade; Roger's, on the other hand, had never been higher. But it was the German Emperor, crowned or not, who remained historically and by divine right the sword and shield of Western Christendom; and Conrad bitterly resented this new usurpation of his imperial prerogatives, as unpardonable in its own way as the seizure of South Italy itself. He strongly suspected, too, that Roger was financing the league led by Welf of Bavaria. St Bernard tried hard to change his attitude, but to no avail. The Abbot of Clairvaux was a Frenchman, and in Conrad's book the French were almost as bad as the Sicilians; besides, he had painful memories of the last time he had taken Bernard's advice against his better judgement. The man was known to be rabidly anti-Byzantine; responsible more than anyone else for the whole ill-fated Crusade, he was obviously only too anxious to shuffle as much of the blame as possible off his own shoulders and on to those of the Eastern Emperor. Manuel on the other hand was Conrad's friend, in whom he had put his trust. Moreover the two were bound by a solemn alliance, which he had no intention of breaking.

So the great anti-Byzantine league came to nothing, and if Conrad and Manuel were obliged to postpone their joint expedition against the Sicilian Kingdom, this was only because of King Roger's brilliant diplomacy. Before long, however, the obstacles that he had put in their path had been effectively surmounted. At Flochberg in 1150 Count Welf and his friends suffered a defeat from which they never recovered, while after a punitive expedition led by Manuel himself the following year, the Serbs and the Hungarians had, for the moment, no more fight left in them. At last the forces of the two Empires were free to march into South Italy. The much-delayed campaign was confidently planned for the autumn of 1152. Venice had pledged her support. Even Pope Eugenius had finally been won over. For Roger, the future had never looked blacker.

Then, on 15 February 1152, Conrad died at Bamberg at the age of fifty-nine. In the two centuries since the restoration of the Western Empire by Otto the Great, he had been the first Emperor-elect not to have been crowned at Rome – a failure which somehow seems to symbolize his whole reign. 'A Seneca in council, a Paris in appearance, a Hector in battle', in his youth he had shown high promise; but he died with that promise unfulfilled – never an Emperor, just a sad, unlucky King. The presence at his bedside of several Italian doctors – probably from the famous medical school of Salerno – gave rise to inevitable mutterings about Sicilian poison; but although King Roger must have welcomed this timely removal of his arch-enemy there is no reason to suspect that he was in any way responsible.

Conrad's mind remained unclouded to the end, and his last injunction to his nephew and successor, Frederick of Swabia, was to continue the struggle which he had begun. So far as the King of Sicily was concerned, Frederick asked nothing better. Encouraged by the Apulian exiles at the German court, he even hoped at one moment to improve on his uncle's original schedule and to march against Roger immediately, picking up the imperial crown on the way as he passed through Rome. As always, however, the succession brought its own problems, and he soon had to accept an indefinite postponement. Where he parted company with Conrad was on the matter of Byzantium. Temperamentally he was quite unable to accept any arrangement which might diminish the power and prestige of his Empire. The very thought of a rival Emperor in the East was bad enough; the idea of sharing, let alone making over, the disputed South Italian provinces was anathema to him. If Manuel Comnenus wished to join him in fighting the King of Sicily, well and good; but any victory would have to be its own reward. Barely a year after his accession he had signed a treaty with the Pope at Constance, by the terms of which it was agreed that Byzantium would be allowed no concessions on Italian territory; if its Emperor were to attempt to seize any by force, he would be expelled. The brief honeymoon between the two Empires was at an end.

The death of King Conrad, on the other hand, was only the beginning. On 8 July 1153 Pope Eugenius died suddenly at Tivoli. He had not wished to be Pope – till the day of his death he continued to wear, under his pontifical robes, the coarse habit of a Cistercian monk – and he had shown little talent for the role that had been thrust upon him; but his gentleness and unassuming ways had earned him the love and respect of his flock and he was deeply mourned. The same cannot be said of Bernard of Clairvaux, who only six weeks later followed him to his grave. All his life Bernard had exemplified that fortunately rare phenomenon, the genuine ascetic who feels himself compelled to intervene in the political field; and since he saw the world with the eye of a fanatic, his interventions were almost invariably disastrous. His launching of the Second Crusade had certainly led to the most shameful Christian humiliation of the Middle Ages. Many might have believed him to be a great man; few would have called him a lovable one.

Next, on 26 February 1154, King Roger died at Palermo. His son and successor – generally known as William the Bad – did not altogether deserve his nickname, which was largely due to his alarming appearance[1] and herculean physical strength; but he was lazy and pleasure-loving, with little of his father's intelligence and diplomatic finesse. We cannot imagine Roger, for example, writing as William did to the Byzantine Emperor within weeks of his coronation, offering him in return for a treaty of peace the restitution of all his Greek prisoners and all the spoils of George of Antioch's Theban expedition. Manuel Comnenus rejected the offer outright. To him, it could only mean that the new King was afraid of an imperial invasion. If he was afraid, he was weak; if he was weak, he would be defeated.

The last in the series of deaths that brought a whole new cast of characters on to the Western European political stage was that of Pope Eugenius's successor, the old and ineffectual Anastasius IV. His seventeen-month reign had been concerned chiefly with his own self-glorification; but when, in the last days of 1154, his body was laid to rest in the gigantic porphyry sarcophagus that had previously held the remains of the Empress Helena – transferred, on his orders, to a modest

---

1 He was a huge ogre of a man, 'whose thick black beard lent him a savage and terrible aspect and filled many people with fear' (*Chronica S. Mariae de Ferraria*).

urn in the Ara Coeli a few weeks before – he was succeeded by a man of a very different calibre: Adrian (or Hadrian) IV, the only Englishman ever to wear the Triple Crown. Nicholas Breakspear had been born around 1115 at Abbot's Langley in Hertfordshire. While still a student he had moved first to France and then to Rome, where his eloquence, ability and outstanding good looks had caught the attention of Pope Eugenius – who was, fortunately for Nicholas, an enthusiastic Anglophile.[1] Thereafter his rise had been swift; and a mission to Norway in 1152 with the purpose of reorganizing the Church throughout Scandinavia had been accomplished with such distinction that on Pope Anastasius's death two years later he was unanimously elected in his place. His election came, as it turned out, not a moment too soon: within six months he was called upon to face a major crisis, which would have utterly defeated either of his two predecessors. Frederick Barbarossa had arrived in Italy and demanded his imperial coronation.

Frederick, now thirty-two, seemed to his German contemporaries the very nonpareil of Teutonic chivalry. Tall and broad-shouldered, attractive rather than handsome, he had eyes that twinkled so brightly under his thick mop of reddish-brown hair that, according to one chronicler who knew him well,[2] he always seemed on the point of laughter. But beneath this breezy, light-hearted exterior there lurked a will of steel, dedicated to a single objective: to restore his Empire to its ancient greatness and splendour. In pursuit of this ambition no concessions would be made, no quarter given – to the Pope, the Eastern Emperor or anyone else. Arriving in North Italy in the first weeks of 1155, he had been surprised and infuriated by the intensity of republican feeling in the cities and towns, and had immediately decided upon a show of strength. Milan, that perennial focus of revolt, had proved too strong for him; but he had made an example of her ally Tortona, which he had captured after a two-month siege and then razed until not one stone was left on another.

After celebrating Easter at Pavia – where he had received the traditional Iron Crown of Lombardy – Frederick had descended through Tuscany at such a speed as to cause the Roman Curia serious alarm. Several of the older cardinals could still remember how, in 1111, his forebear Henry V had laid hands on Paschal II in St Peter's itself, and

---

1 He once told the English scholar and diplomat John of Salisbury that he found his countrymen admirably fitted to perform any task they attempted, and thus to be preferred to all other races – except, he added, when frivolity got the better of them.

2 Acerbus Morena, *podestà* of Lodi, one of the first lay historians of North Italy.

had held him prisoner for two months until he capitulated; and they had heard nothing of the new King of the Romans to suggest that he would not be fully capable of doing the same. Adrian therefore decided to ride up to meet him; and on 9 June the two met at Campo Grasso, near Sutri. The encounter was not a success. According to custom, at the approach of the Pope the King should have advanced towards him on foot and led his horse the last few yards by the bridle, finally holding the stirrup while the Pope dismounted; but he did not do so, and Adrian in return refused to bestow on him the traditional kiss of peace.

Frederick objected that it was no part of his duty to act as papal groom; but Adrian held firm. This was not a minor point of protocol; it was a public act of defiance that struck at the very root of the relationship between Empire and Papacy. It was Frederick who finally gave in. He ordered his camp to be moved a little to the south; and on the morning of 11 June, near the little town of Monterosi, the ceremony was restaged. This time the King advanced on foot to meet the Pope, took his horse by the bridle and led it the distance, we are told, of a stone's throw; then, holding the stirrup, he helped him dismount. Adrian settled himself on the waiting throne; Frederick knelt and kissed his feet; the kiss of peace was duly bestowed; and conversations began.

There seemed no longer any reason to delay the coronation; on the other hand, since the ceremony had last been performed the Roman people had established a Commune and revived their Senate; and the delegation of senators which appeared a few days later at the imperial camp adopted an attitude at once bombastic and patronizing, insisting that before receiving his crown Frederick should make a sworn guarantee of the city's future liberty, together with an *ex gratia* payment of five thousand pounds of gold. Frederick replied calmly that he was claiming only what was rightfully his. There could be no question of any guarantees; as for gifts of money, he would bestow these when and where he pleased. The senators withdrew in discomfiture; but they left the Pope – who had previous experience of the Commune – in no doubt that serious trouble was to be expected. If they were to avoid it, both he and Frederick would have to move swiftly.

At dawn the following morning – it was Saturday, 17 June – the King of the Romans entered Rome by the Golden Gate and went straight to St Peter's where the Pope, who had arrived an hour or two before, was awaiting him on the steps of the basilica. A quick Mass was celebrated, after which, standing directly above the tomb of the Apostle, Adrian hurriedly girded the sword of St Peter to Frederick's side and laid the imperial crown on his head. As soon as the brief ceremony was over the Emperor, still wearing the crown, rode back to his camp outside the walls, while the Pope took refuge in the Vatican to await developments.

It was not yet nine o'clock in the morning; and the senators were assembling on the Capitol to decide how best to prevent the coronation when the news reached them that it had already taken place. Furious to find that they had been outmanoeuvred, they gave the call to arms. Soon a huge mob was pressing across the Ponte S. Angelo, while another advanced northward through Trastevere. Back in their camp above the city, the German soldiers received the order to prepare at once for battle. Had not their Emperor sworn before them all, just a few hours ago, to defend the Church of Christ? Already, it seemed, it was under threat. For the second time that day Frederick entered Rome, but he wore his coronation robes no longer. This time he had his armour on.

All that afternoon and evening the battle raged between the Emperor of the Romans and his subjects; night had fallen before the imperial troops had driven the last of the insurgents back across the bridges. Losses had been heavy on both sides. For the Germans we have no reliable figures; but among the Romans almost a thousand are said to have been slain or drowned in the Tiber, and another six hundred taken captive. The Senate had paid a high price for its arrogance; but the Emperor too had bought his crown dearly. His victory had not even gained him entrance into the city, for the sun rose next morning to show all the Tiber bridges blocked and the gates barricaded. Neither he nor his army were prepared for a siege; the heat of the Roman summer was once again beginning to take its toll, with outbreaks of malaria and dysentery among his men. The only sensible course was to withdraw, and – since the Vatican was obviously no longer safe for the Papacy – to take Pope and Curia with him. On 19 June he struck camp and led his army up into the Sabine Hills. A month later he was heading back towards Germany, leaving Adrian, isolated and powerless, at Tivoli.

For Manuel Comnenus, following these events from Constantinople, the whole situation was now changed. Since Conrad's death he could no longer expect any help from the Western Empire. True, he was unaware of the precise terms of the Treaty of Constance and may still have believed in the possibility of some sort of Italian partition; but it was clear from Frederick's attitude that from now on he would have to fight for it. If – as seemed likely sooner or later – the Germans did march against William of Sicily, it was essential that a strong Byzantine force should be present, ready to defend the legitimate rights of Constantinople; if they did not, he would have to take the initiative on his own.

The good news was that the Norman barons in Apulia were once again on the point of open revolt. They had always resented the house of Hauteville, whose origins were after all no more distinguished than their own and who had established their supremacy as much by intrigue and low cunning as by any conspicuous courage in the field; and they had rebelled more than once in the past, not only against King Roger but against Robert Guiscard before him. Roger's death, and the comparative weakness of William as his successor, had encouraged them to make yet another effort to shake off their Sicilian shackles; as always, however, they needed support. They had first put their trust in Frederick, and had been much disappointed by his hasty departure; but they felt no special ties of loyalty to him. Now that he had let them down, they were perfectly ready to accept help from Manuel instead.

And Manuel was ready to give it. He could not offer a full-scale expedition: the war with Hungary had flared up again and he needed his army along the Danube. But in the summer of 1155, as a first step, he sent two of his senior generals, Michael Palaeologus – a former Governor of Thessalonica – and John Ducas, across to Italy. Their brief was, essentially, to make contact with the principal centres of resistance among the Norman barons and to coordinate a general rising throughout the province, which would be supported by a small Byzantine army and any other mercenary forces that could be recruited locally; if, however, Frederick was still in Italy and there was any chance of intercepting him on his way back from Rome, they were to make one last effort to persuade him to join forces. As an eventuality, it seemed improbable enough; but on their arrival in Italy a few inquiries soon revealed the Emperor to be in the imperial city of Ancona, where he willingly received them.

Frederick had marched northward with a heavy heart. The Pope had already implored him to keep to his original plan and lead his army without further delay against King William of Sicily, and for his own part he would have been delighted to do so. But his ailing German barons would not hear of it. They had had enough of the remorseless sun, the unaccustomed food and the clouds of insects that whined incessantly round their heads; and they longed only for the day when they would see a firm mountain barrier rising between themselves and the scene of their sufferings. After this second approach by Palaeologus and Ducas, Frederick tried once again to inject a little of his own spirit into his followers, but with no better success. Sadly, he had to confess to the envoys that there was nothing more he could do; they would have to launch their campaign alone. Manuel was not unduly worried by the news. Strategically, it might have been useful to have the German army fighting his battles for him; diplomatically, on the other hand, the situation would be very much simpler without, and it was plain from the reports he was receiving that there would be no shortage of allies. The revolt was now spreading all over South Italy under a new leader – the King's own first cousin, Count Robert of Loritello. In the late summer of 1155, Robert met Michael Palaeologus at Viesti. Each was able to provide just what the other lacked. Palaeologus had a fleet of ten ships, seemingly limitless funds and the power to call when necessary on further reinforcements from across the Adriatic. Robert could claim the support of the majority of the local barons, together with the effective control of a considerable length of coast – a vital requirement if the Byzantine lines of communication were to be adequately maintained. Agreement was quickly reached; then the two allies struck.

Their first objective was Bari. Until its capture by Robert Guiscard in 1071, this city had been the capital of Byzantine Italy and the last Greek stronghold in the peninsula. The majority of its citizens, being themselves Greek, resented the government of Palermo and looked gratefully towards any opportunity of breaking free from it. A group of them opened the gates to the attackers; and though the Sicilian garrison fought bravely from the old citadel and the church of St Nicholas, they were soon obliged to surrender and to watch while the Bariots themselves fell on the citadel – by now the symbol of Sicilian domination – and, despite Palaeologus's efforts to stop them, razed it flat.

News of the fall of Bari, coupled with a sudden spate of rumours of King William's death – he was indeed seriously ill – shattered the morale of the Apulian coastal towns. Trani yielded in its turn; then the neighbouring port of Giovinazzo. Further south, resistance was still fierce: William of Tyre reports that when the Patriarch of Jerusalem landed that autumn at Otranto on his way to visit the Pope, he found the entire region in such turmoil that he was forced to re-embark and make his way up the coast by sea as far as Ancona. Only at the beginning of September did King William's army make its appearance, under his Viceroy Asclettin. It consisted of some two thousand knights and a considerable force of infantry, but it was no match for the rebels and was largely destroyed outside the walls of Andria. The loyalist lord of that town, Count Richard of Andria, who had fought heroically for his King, was unhorsed during the battle and finished off by a priest of Trani who, we are told, ripped him open and tore out his entrails. Seeing him lying dead, the local population surrendered on the spot. For those still faithful to King William, the future looked grim.

From Tivoli first and later from Tusculum, Pope Adrian had followed these developments with satisfaction. Though he had no love for the Greeks, he greatly preferred them to the Sicilians; and it delighted him to see the detested William, having escaped the vengeance of Barbarossa, finally receiving his deserts. Whether it was he who now took the initiative to ally himself with the Byzantines, or whether the first approach came from Manuel Comnenus in Constantinople or Michael Palaeologus in Apulia, is not altogether clear. At all events, discussions were held in the late summer, in the course of which Adrian undertook to raise – almost certainly at Byzantine expense – a body of mercenary troops from Campania. On 29 September he marched south.

It may seem surprising, only a century after the great schism between the Eastern and Western Churches, to find an Emperor of Byzantium in military alliance with the Pope of Rome; but Adrian doubtless saw in the South Italian situation an opportunity that might never recur. He was encouraged, too, by the exiled Apulian vassals who, seeing the possibility of regaining their old fiefs, joyfully agreed to recognize him as their suzerain in return for his support. Already on 9 October Prince Robert of Capua and several other high-ranking Norman barons were reinvested with their hereditary possessions, and before the end of the year all Campania and most of Apulia was in Byzantine or papalist hands. Michael Palaeologus, mopping up the few pockets of resistance that remained, could congratulate himself on a success greater than he could have dared to hope. In barely six months he had restored Greek power to a point almost equal to that of a hundred and fifty years before. News had recently come to him that his Emperor, encouraged by such rapid progress, was sending out a full-scale expeditionary force to consolidate his gains. At this rate it might not be long before all South Italy acknowledged the dominion of Constantinople. King William would be annihilated; Pope Adrian, seeing the Greeks succeed where the Germans had failed, would acknowledge the superiority of Byzantine arms and would adjust his policies accordingly; and the great dream of the Comneni – the reunification of the Roman Empire under the aegis of Constantinople – would be realized at last.

*

King William was a man who found it hard ever to leave his palace; but once he was obliged to go forth, then – however disinclined to action he had been in the past – he would fling himself, not so much with courage as in a headstrong, even foolhardy spirit, in the face of all dangers.

So writes Hugo Falcandus, the most detailed – and by far the most readable – chronicler of Norman Sicily whose work has come down to us. He is also the most destructive and, even when paying tribute to his sovereign as here, nearly always allows his malice to show through. But there is truth in what he says. In this particular case, William's initial inertia was understandable. From September until Christmas he lay in Palermo desperately ill, leaving his Kingdom to be effectively governed by his 'Emir of Emirs', the Lombard Maio of Bari; next, in the opening weeks of 1156 while still convalescent, he was obliged to deal first with riots in the capital itself and then with a rebellion of Sicilian barons in the south of the island. He was, however, successful in both operations; and his victory over the barons provided him with just the moral encouragement he needed. The spring had come, his health was restored, his blood was up. He was ready to tackle the mainland.

Army and navy met at Messina; this was to be a combined operation, in which the Greeks, the papalists and the rebel barons were to be attacked simultaneously from land and sea. In the last days of April, the army crossed to the mainland and set off through Calabria, while the fleet sailed down through the straits and then turned north-east towards Brindisi. For the Byzantines and the rebel forces alike, it had been a bad winter. First, thanks to the increasing arrogance of Michael Palaeologus, there had been a split between them, Robert of Loritello having ridden off in disgust. Then Palaeologus himself had died, after a short illness, in Bari. For all his overbearing ways he had been a brilliant leader in the field, and his death had been a serious blow to his countrymen. John Ducas had eventually got the army moving again and had even achieved a reconciliation with the Count of Loritello; but the old confidence between the two was never quite restored, the momentum of 1155 never altogether regained.

For three weeks already Brindisi had been under siege. The royalist garrison in the citadel was putting up a heroic resistance, and had effectively brought Byzantine progress in the peninsula to a stop. And now, with the news of King William's advance, the Greeks saw their rebel allies begin to fall away. The mercenaries chose, as mercenaries will, the moment of supreme crisis to demand impossible increases in their pay; meeting with a refusal, they disappeared *en masse*. Robert of Loritello deserted for the second time, and many of his compatriots followed him. Ducas, left only with the few troops that he and Palaeologus had brought with them, plus those which had trickled over the Adriatic at various times during the past nine months, found himself hopelessly outnumbered. Of the Sicilian forces, it was the fleet that arrived first, and for another day or two he was able to hold his own. The entrance to Brindisi harbour is by a narrow channel, barely a hundred yards across. Twelve centuries before, Julius Caesar had blocked it to Pompey's ships; and now John Ducas, by drawing up the four vessels under his command in line abreast across its mouth and stationing detachments of infantry along each bank, employed similar tactics. But when William's army appeared on the western horizon, Byzantine hopes were at an end. Attacked simultaneously from the land, the sea and the inner citadel, Ducas could not hope to hold the walls; he and his men were caught, in the words of Cinnamus, as in a net.

The battle that followed was short and bloody, and the Greek defeat was total. The Sicilian navy, having occupied the little islands that circled the harbour entrance, effectively prevented any escape by sea. Ducas himself, the other Byzantine survivors and those Norman rebels who had not already fled, were taken prisoner. The four Greek ships, were seized, together with large sums of gold and silver which had been entrusted by Manuel to Michael Palaeologus, for the payment of mercenaries and for whatever bribes might be necessary. On that one day – it was 28 May 1156 – all that the Byzantines had achieved in Italy over the past year was wiped out as completely as if they had never come.

The King treated his Greek captives according to the recognized canons of war; but to his own rebellious subjects he showed no mercy. For him as for his father before him, treason remained the one crime that could not be forgiven. Of the erstwhile insurgents who fell into his hands, only the luckiest were imprisoned. The rest were hanged, blinded or tied about with heavy weights and thrown into the sea. Brindisi, which had resisted valiantly, was spared; Bari, which had readily capitulated to the invaders, paid the price. William gave the inhabitants two clear days in which to salvage their belongings; on the third day the city was destroyed, including the cathedral. Only the great church of St Nicholas and a few smaller religious buildings were left standing.

It was the same old lesson – a lesson that should by now have been self-evident, but one that the princes of medieval Europe seemed to find almost impossible to learn: that in distant lands, wherever there existed an organized native opposition, a temporary occupying force could never achieve permanent conquest. Whirlwind campaigns were easy, especially when backed by bribes and generous subsidies to the local malcontents; when, however, it became necessary to consolidate and maintain the advantage gained, no amount of gold was of any avail. The Normans had succeeded in establishing themselves in South Italy and Sicily only because they had arrived as mercenaries and remained as settlers; even then, the task had taken them the best part of a century. When they embarked on foreign adventures – such as the two invasions of the Byzantine Empire by Robert Guiscard and Bohemund – even they were doomed to failure. Manuel Comnenus had presumably trusted those communities of Apulia and Calabria who still spoke Greek and maintained, after a fashion, their Greek traditions to declare in his favour – as indeed the people of Bari had done. What he had not taken into account was, first, that such communities represented only a small minority of the total population and, second, that William of Sicily's forces were a good deal better placed than his own to deal with any trouble that might arise. The outcome of the recent campaign – however promisingly it had begun – had not been unlucky. It had been inevitable.

The news of the catastrophe was received with horror in Constantinople. Poor John Ducas, unable to defend himself from his Palermo prison, proved a convenient scapegoat; but everyone knew that the ultimate responsibility was the Emperor's, and Manuel felt his humiliation bitterly. It was made all the greater the following summer, when a Sicilian fleet of 164 ships, carrying nearly ten thousand men, swooped down on the prosperous island of Euboea, sacking and pillaging all the towns and villages along its coast. From there it continued to Almira on the Gulf of Volos, which received similar treatment; then – if we are to believe Nicetas Choniates – it sped up the Hellespont and through the Marmara to Constantinople, where a hail of silver-tipped arrows was loosed upon the imperial palace.[1]

The time had come, it was clear, for a radical change in the Empire's

---

1 Is Nicetas confusing this raid with that of George of Antioch in 1149, described on p. 103? Possibly, though there is no reason why the exploit should not have been repeated. Where he is almost certainly wrong is in identifying the palace as that of Blachernae, which would have been inaccessible unless the Sicilians had launched an expedition on terra firma the length of the Land Walls or had sailed up the Golden Horn. Their target is much more likely to have been the old imperial palace on the Marmara.

foreign policy. If Manuel could not recover the lost Italian provinces by force of arms, nor – at least in the long term – could his rival, Frederick Barbarossa; but Frederick, full of energy and ambition, would certainly lead another expedition into the peninsula as soon as he was free to do so, and might even succeed in toppling William from his throne. In such an event, dreaming (as he was known to dream) of uniting the two Empires under a single sceptre – his own – might he not make Byzantium his next objective? The conclusion was plain. William, upstart as he was, was a good deal preferable to Frederick. Some form of agreement with him would have to be reached – though it would have to be a less humiliating one than that which he had imposed upon Pope Adrian who, deserted by his allies, had already been forced to come to terms. The result had been the Treaty of Benevento, signed in June 1156, in which the Pope had recognized William's dominion not only over Sicily, Apulia, Calabria and the former Principality of Capua, but also over Naples, Amalfi, Salerno and the whole region of the Marches and the northern Abruzzi. It was addressed to

William, glorious King of Sicily and dearest son in Christ, most brilliant in wealth and achievement among all the Kings and eminent men of the age, the glory of whose name is borne to the uttermost limits of the earth by the firmness of your justice, the peace which you have restored to your subjects, and the fear which your great deeds have instilled into the hearts of all the enemies of Christ's name.

Manuel had no intention of putting his name to any document of this kind; he intended to deal with the King of Sicily from a position of at least relative strength. And so, some time during the summer of 1157, he sent a new emissary to Italy: Alexis, the brilliant young son of his Grand Domestic Axuch. Alexis's orders were ostensibly much the same as those given earlier to Michael Palaeologus – to make contact with such rebel barons as were still at liberty, to hire mercenaries for a new campaign along the coast, and generally to stir up as much disaffection as he could; but Manuel had also entrusted him with a second task – to establish secret contact with William and discuss terms for a peace. The two objectives were not as self-contradictory as might appear at first sight: the fiercer the preliminary fighting, the more favourable to Byzantium William's conditions were likely to be.

Alexis discharged both parts of his mission with equal success. Within a month or two of his arrival he had Robert of Loritello once again ravaging Sicilian territory in the north and another of the leading rebels,

Count Andrew of Rupecanina, driving down through the Capuan lands and seriously threatening Monte Cassino – beneath which, in January 1158, the Count even defeated a royalist army in pitched battle. Meanwhile, although Alexis's own support for these operations debarred him from undertaking peace talks in person, he was able to call on the services of the two most distinguished of the Greeks who were still held captive in Palermo, John Ducas and Alexius Bryennius; and through their mediation, some time in the early spring, a secret agreement was concluded. Alexis, having deceived his Apulian supporters into thinking that he was going to fetch more men and supplies, left them in the lurch and slipped away to Constantinople; William, though still understandably suspicious of Byzantine motives, returned all his Greek prisoners and dispatched a diplomatic mission to Manuel under his sometime tutor and close friend, Henry Aristippus.[1] A treaty of peace was duly signed, though its provisions are unknown; and the Norman barons, suddenly bereft of funds, had no course but to abandon their new conquests and seek another, more reliable champion.

---

1 Henry returned with a valuable present from the Emperor to the King – a Greek manuscript of Ptolemy's *Almagest*. This tremendous work, a synthesis of all the discoveries and conclusions of Greek astronomers since the science was born, was hitherto known in the West only through Arabic translations.

8

Manuel Comnenus –
The Later Years

[1158–80]

The People of Antioch were by no means pleased by the arrival of the Emperor. But when they saw that it was not in their power to prevent him they came before him like slaves, having adorned the streets with carpets and covered the pavements with flowers ... The Syrians who are gluttons, the Isaurians who are thieves, the Cilicians who are pirates, all were there with the rest. Even the Italian knights, who are so proud, put away their pride in order to be present, on foot, at the triumph.

Nicetas Choniates,
'Manuel Comnenus', III, iii

At the time of the signing of the Sicilian peace treaty, Manuel Comnenus had occupied the throne of Byzantium for fifteen years. No one could have accused him of inactivity. Quite apart from his remarkably success-ful handling of all the problems – military, diplomatic and administrative – presented by the Second Crusade, he had personally waged war against the Seljuks and the Danishmends in Anatolia, the Cumans in Thrace, the Sicilians at Corfu and the Serbs and Hungarians in the Danubian provinces; and had he not been fully occupied with these last, he would certainly have also been present during the recent campaign in South Italy. The one region to which he had been able to pay relatively little attention was that in which he had begun his reign – Cilicia, and the Crusader states of Outremer; and in the autumn of 1158 he set out from Constantinople at the head of a great army to make good the omission.

He was furious, and with good reason. The first object of his wrath was Thoros, the eldest surviving son of Leo the Rubenid. Thoros had escaped from prison in Constantinople in 1143 and had sought refuge with his cousin, Joscelin II of Edessa, while he collected his three younger brothers and a group of like-minded compatriots; with their help he had soon recaptured his family's castle of Vahka, high in the Taurus mountains. From there, in 1151, he had swept down on to the Cilician plain, defeating a small Byzantine force and killing the imperial governor at Mamistra. Manuel had immediately sent his cousin Andronicus with an army against him, but Thoros had taken Andronicus by surprise and put his army to flight. After seven years, this upstart prince was still unpunished.

Far more serious, however, than any number of Armenian adventurers was Reynald of Châtillon, Prince of Antioch. The younger son of a minor French nobleman, Reynald had joined the Second Crusade and then decided to stay on in the East. There he might have lived out his life in well-deserved obscurity but for the death of Raymond of Poitiers, who on 28 June 1149 had allowed himself and his army to be surrounded by the forces of the Emir Nur ed-Din. The consequence was a massacre, after which Raymond's skull, set in a silver case, was sent by Nur ed-Din as a present to the Caliph in Baghdad – there, presumably, to join that of his predecessor Bohemund. Fortunately, the Emir did not follow up his victory with a march on Antioch; it was nevertheless generally agreed that Raymond's widow, the Princess Constance, must find herself another husband as soon as possible. Constance – despite her four children she was still only twenty-one – asked nothing better; but she was difficult to please. She turned down three candidates proposed by her cousin King Baldwin III of Jerusalem – to say nothing of one who had been suggested (at her request) by Manuel Comnenus as her overlord[1] – and it was not until 1153 that her eye fell on Reynald, whom she married as soon as Baldwin, only too glad to give up his responsibility for Antioch, had given his permission.

She could hardly have made a more disastrous choice. Not only was the new Prince generally considered a parvenu adventurer; from the beginning he proved faithless and utterly irresponsible. Having promised Manuel, in return for his recognition as Prince, to attack Thoros and his brothers, after a single brief battle he allied himself with them; and while they moved, with his full connivance, against the few remaining Byzantine strongholds in Cilicia, he himself prepared an expedition against another, more important imperial possession, the peaceful and prosper-

---

1 Manuel's choice had been the Caesar John Roger, the widower of his sister Maria. He had presumably thought that the Caesar's Norman blood would recommend him to the Latins of Antioch. Perhaps it did; but Constance refused to consider a man well over twice her age and soon sent him packing.

ous island of Cyprus. Such an enterprise, however, needed finance; and Reynald now demanded the necessary funds from Aimery, Patriarch of Antioch, who was known to be rich and against whom he bore a grudge for having opposed his marriage. The Patriarch refused; whereupon he was seized, imprisoned and beaten about the head. His wounds were then smeared with honey and he was taken up on to the roof of the citadel, where he was made to spend a whole day in the grilling heat of an Antiochene summer, defenceless against the myriads of ravening insects that descended upon him. That evening, understandably, he paid up; and a few days later, in company with two envoys sent by a furious King Baldwin to demand his immediate release, left for Jerusalem.

In the spring of 1156 Reynald and his ally Thoros had launched their attack on Cyprus. The garrison – under John Comnenus, the Emperor's nephew, and a distinguished general named Michael Branas – fought bravely, but were hopelessly outnumbered. Both were imprisoned, while the Franks and Armenians together abandoned themselves to an orgy of devastation and desecration, of murder, rape and pillage such as the island had never before known. Only after three weeks did Reynald give the order to embark; and all the plunder for which there was no room on the ships was sold back to those from whom it had been stolen. The prisoners too were obliged to ransom themselves; and since by this time there was not sufficient money left on the island, most of the leading citizens and their families – including Comnenus and Branas – were carried off to Antioch and kept incarcerated there until their ransoms could be raised, while several captured Greek priests had their noses cut off and were sent mockingly to Constantinople. The island, we are told, never recovered.

The Emperor marched his army overland to Cilicia with vengeance in his heart. Then, leaving the main force to follow the narrow, rocky road along the coast, he hurried on ahead with five hundred cavalry. His aim was to take the Armenians by surprise, and he succeeded. Two weeks later all the Cilician cities as far as Anazarbus were back in Byzantine hands. There was only one disappointment: Thoros himself, alerted in Tarsus by a passing pilgrim, had managed to gather his family together just in time and to escape to a ruined castle high in the mountains. For weeks the army searched for him, but in vain. Manuel's temper had therefore not greatly improved by the time he drew up his army outside the walls of Mopsuestia.

But if Manuel was angry, Reynald was panic-stricken. It was plain from the reports he had received that the imperial army was far too strong to be resisted; his only hope lay in abject submission. He sent messengers to Manuel with an offer to surrender the citadel to an imperial garrison, and when this was rejected presented himself in sackcloth outside the Emperor's camp. Manuel was in no hurry to receive him. High-ranking envoys were by now arriving from the local potentates and even from the Caliph himself; the Prince of Antioch could wait his turn. When the summons came at last, Reynald and his suite were obliged to walk, barefoot and bareheaded, all through Mopsuestia and out to the camp beyond; they were then led, between ranks formed by the crack regiments of the imperial army, to a great tent in which they found the *basileus* enthroned, surrounded by his court and the foreign envoys. Reynald prostrated himself in the dust at his feet, his followers raising their hands in supplication. For some considerable time Manuel took no notice, unconcernedly continuing his conversation with those around him; when he finally deigned to hear the Prince's submission he made three conditions. The citadel of Antioch must be surrendered to an imperial garrison immediately on demand; the city must provide a contingent for his army; and a Greek Patriarch was to be installed in place of the Latin. Only when Reynald took his oath on all three was he pardoned and dismissed.

A few days later King Baldwin arrived from Jerusalem. Though he and Manuel had never met, there was a strong family connection since he had recently married the Emperor's niece Theodora, daughter of his elder brother Isaac. The bride, though still only thirteen, was plainly nubile and extremely beautiful, and Baldwin was delighted with her. He had not, however, attempted to conceal his dissatisfaction at the news of Reynald's pardon; and the Emperor, wrongly suspecting that he wanted Antioch for himself, had at first been reluctant to receive him. But he soon relented and the two took to each other the moment they met. Baldwin was now thirty, intelligent and cultivated and possessed of more than a little of Manuel's famous charm. He remained ten days in the camp, during which time he secured a pardon for Thoros, who was subjected to the same treatment as Reynald but was allowed to keep his possessions in the mountains. It was probably due to his intervention, also, that the change of Patriarch was indefinitely postponed. Aimery was restored to his patriarchal throne and was formally reconciled with Reynald – though it is unlikely, after what had happened, that the two ever became close friends.

On Easter Sunday, 12 April 1159, Manuel Comnenus made his ceremonial entry over the fortified bridge into Antioch. Twenty-one years before, he had accompanied his father in a similar procession; the present occasion was still more impressive. The local authorities had done their best to prevent it: there was, they claimed, a conspiracy to assassinate him and they could not guarantee his safety. Manuel demanded a number of hostages, and insisted that all the Franks taking part in the ceremony – including even the King of Jerusalem himself – should be unarmed; but he refused to cancel the procession. In the forefront marched the blond giants of the Varangian Guard, each with his battle-axe carried on a massive shoulder. Then came the Emperor himself, his imperial purple mantle all but concealing his coat of mail, the pearl-hung diadem on his head. At his side, 'busying himself', writes Cinnamus, 'with the stirrup-leather of the imperial saddle', walked the Prince of Antioch, the other Frankish vassals following; then Baldwin of Jerusalem, bare-headed; and finally the members of the imperial court. Just inside the gates Aimery stood waiting in his patriarchal robes, his clergy behind him; and it was he who led the procession through flower-strewn streets, first to Mass in St Peter's Cathedral and then on to the palace.

The celebrations continued for eight days. Apart from endless church services, there were banquets, receptions, investitures and parades of every kind. As a gesture to the Franks, Manuel even organized a knightly tournament – something unknown in the East – during which he himself, to the horror of most of his older subjects, took part in the jousting. Majestic where majesty was required, smiling and friendly on less formal occasions, he endeared himself to the Antiochenes, nobles and citizens alike. Meanwhile he and the King of Jerusalem took an ever greater liking to each other, and when Baldwin broke his arm in a hunting accident Manuel insisted on treating it himself, just as he had treated King Conrad a dozen years before.

By the time the Emperor left Antioch, relations between Byzantium and Outremer were better than they had ever been; and they might well have so continued had he now moved against Aleppo, as the Franks expected. As soon as he reached the frontier, however, he was met by Nur ed-Din's ambassadors with proposals for a truce. The Emir's offer was generous indeed: not only would he release all his six thousand Christian prisoners, he would also send a military expedition against the Seljuk Turks. Manuel – possibly with some relief – agreed to call off his campaign and immediately started back to Constantinople, his army behind him.

The reaction of the Franks can well be imagined. Why had the Emperor bothered to march all the way across Asia Minor with his huge army, only to march all the way back again without once engaging the Saracen enemy? For the six thousand returned prisoners they cared little. True, these included one or two distinguished Frenchmen like Bertrand of Blancfort, Grand Master of the Temple; but the vast majority were Germans captured during the Second Crusade, many of whom were by now broken in health and would constitute only an additional burden on the depleted treasury. Nothing could alter the fact that Manuel had been received with all the honour due to him, in the belief that he would rid the Crusader states of an enemy who threatened their very existence. Instead, he had made a shameful agreement with that enemy and was now leaving them to their fate. No wonder they felt betrayed.

In fact, Manuel had had little choice. However vital Syria might be to the Crusaders of Outremer, to him it was only one – and by no means the most important – of the many outlying provinces of his Empire. His throne was relatively secure, but not to the point where he could afford to spend many months several hundred miles from his capital, at the end of impossibly long lines of communication and supply which could be broken from one moment to the next by Arab or Turkish raiders. Already there were reports of conspiracy in Constantinople and trouble on the European frontier. It was time to return. Besides, was Nur ed-Din doing him any real harm? On the contrary, he was frightening the Franks, and Manuel was well aware that the Franks remained loyal to him only when they were afraid. The Seljuks of Anatolia were in any case an infinitely greater danger than the Atabeg of Aleppo, whose offer of what would effectively be an alliance against them was not one that he could afford to refuse.

Subsequent events proved him right. In the autumn of 1159, after only some three months in Constantinople, he was back again in Anatolia fighting the Seljuk Sultan, Kilij Arslan II. It was a four-pronged attack: the Emperor himself, with the main body of his army further strengthened by a detachment of troops sent by the Prince of Serbia, swept up the Meander valley; his general John Contostephanus, with levies provided according to their respective treaties by Reynald and Thoros and a contingent of Pechenegs, drove north-westwards through the Taurus passes; Nur ed-Din advanced from the middle Euphrates; and the Danishmends invaded from the north-east. Against such an onslaught the Sultan quickly gave up the struggle; by the terms of a treaty signed early in 1162 he returned all the Greek cities occupied by his subjects within recent years, promised to respect the frontiers, forbade all further raiding, and agreed to provide a regiment whenever called upon to do so, to fight alongside the imperial army. Finally, in the spring of that same year, he paid a state visit to Constantinople.

From the moment of Kilij Arslan's first arrival, the Emperor was determined to dazzle him. He first received his guest seated on a throne raised on a high daïs, covered in slabs of gold and set with carbuncles and sapphires surrounded with pearls. He himself wore on his head the imperial diadem, around his shoulders a great cloak of purple encrusted with still more pearls, together with huge cabochon jewels. From his neck, on a golden chain, hung a ruby the size of an apple. Invited to sit by his side, Cinnamus tells us that the Sultan at first hardly dared to obey. And this was only the beginning. Twice each day during his twelve-week stay in the capital, the Sultan's food and drink were brought to him in vessels of gold and silver, all of which immediately became his property; none were ever returned to the palace. After one banquet Manuel presented him with the entire table service. Meanwhile hardly a day passed without some new and ever more brilliant entertainment. There were banquets, tournaments, circuses, games in the Hippodrome – even a water pageant, at which the wonders of Greek fire were displayed to remarkable effect. Throughout the festivities, however, the Emperor made clear by a thousand little signs, negligible by themselves but unmistakable when taken together, that his honoured guest was not a foreign monarch but a vassal prince.

The only attempt from the Sultan's side to match these manifestations was unfortunately less successful, when a member of his suite announced that he would give a demonstration of flying. Swathed in a coat which appeared to consist entirely of immense and cavernous pockets, he explained that the air trapped in these pockets would support him as he flew. He then climbed up to a platform high above the Hippodrome, whence he launched himself into space. When the body was carried from the arena a moment later the assembled populace, we are told, could not contain its laughter; and for the remainder of their stay in the city the surviving members of the Sultan's suite had to endure constant taunts and catcalls as they walked through the streets.

John II had left the Byzantine position in Asia Minor stronger than it had been at any time since Manzikert; his son had now made it stronger still. The Seljuk Sultan had been brought low, the Atabeg of Mosul had been badly frightened. Manuel was now on the friendliest possible terms with both of them; but they had learned their lesson. The land route to the Holy Land was once again open to pilgrims from the West. Among Christians, only the Franks of Outremer continued to grumble. They were to have even greater reason for dissatisfaction before long.

At the end of 1159, while her husband was campaigning in Anatolia, the Empress Irene, née Bertha of Sulzbach, had died in Constantinople, leaving only two daughters. Manuel gave her a splendid funeral, and buried her in his father's monastery of the Pantocrator; but he still desperately needed a son. Accordingly, after a decent interval of mourning had elapsed, he sent an embassy to Jerusalem under his general John Contostephanus to ask King Baldwin to nominate as his second bride one of the princesses of Outremer.

There were two obvious candidates, both Baldwin's cousins and both, we are told, of exceptional beauty. Mélisende, and Mary, respectively the daughters of the late Count Raymond II of Tripoli and of Constance of Antioch by her first husband, Raymond of Poitiers. To Baldwin, the House of Antioch gave nothing but trouble; it was therefore not surprising that his choice should have fallen on Mélisende. Excitement spread quickly through the Crusader East. Count Raymond III spent a fortune on his sister's trousseau and preparations for the wedding, meanwhile making ready a fleet of no fewer than twelve galleys to escort her in suitable state to her new home. Only gradually was it realized that there had been no word from Constantinople. What had happened? Was there to be no marriage after all? Had the Byzantine ambassadors been so indelicate as to mention those persistent rumours of her illegitimacy, which were founded on nothing more than the strained relations known to have existed between her parents?

Perhaps they had; but the Emperor had other reasons to delay his decision. In November 1160 Reynald of Antioch had been captured by Nur ed-Din. His wife Constance had immediately assumed power; but she had never been popular, and a strong body of opinion had preferred the claims of her fifteen-year-old son Bohemund, known as the Stammerer. In theory, the question should have been referred to the Byzantine Emperor, as suzerain of Antioch, for a decision; in fact, however, the Antiochenes tended to look towards Jerusalem on such occasions, and it was to King Baldwin, rather than to Manuel, that they had turned. The King had declared for young Bohemund, with Patriarch Aimery acting as Regent until he came of age. Furious and humiliated, Constance had promptly appealed to the imperial court.

Manuel too was angered at Baldwin's presumption; and it was this incident, rather than any doubts about the paternity of Mélisende, that decided him. But he volunteered no statement. Only when, in the summer of 1161, the impatient Raymond sent an embassy to ask his intentions did he finally confirm that the marriage would not after all take place. In Tripoli there was consternation. Poor Mélisende went into a decline from which she never recovered;[1] her brother converted his twelve galleys into men-of-war and led them off to harass the coastal towns of Cyprus. King Baldwin, deeply concerned, rode up to Antioch, where to his astonishment he found another high-powered delegation from Constantinople, headed by Anna Comnena's son Alexius Bryennius, which had re-established Constance on the throne and was already in the process of drawing up a marriage contract between the Emperor and the ravishing young Princess Mary. In September 1161 she set sail from St Symeon and at Christmas, in the presence of the Patriarchs of Constantinople, Antioch and Alexandria, she was married to Manuel in St Sophia.

Baldwin could only accept the inevitable. He gave his young cousin his blessing and then started back, via Tripoli, to Jerusalem; but he never reached it. In Tripoli he fell gravely ill. After Christmas, still not recovered, he struggled on to Beirut but could go no further. He died there on 10 February 1162, aged just thirty-two.

Manuel Comnenus wept when he heard the news. Baldwin had been a good King; with his energy, his intelligence and his natural political flair he might even have proved a great one. Although the two had inevitably had their differences, on a personal level they had been firm friends who had genuinely enjoyed each other's company – no small consideration where ruling monarchs are concerned.

But the Emperor's thoughts were no longer in the East; it was the consequences of another royal death, occurring on 31 May 1161, which now preoccupied him – that of King Geza II of Hungary. The Hungarians had always been troublesome neighbours, sandwiched as they were between the two great Empires and with interests in Croatia and Dalmatia which could not but conflict with those of Byzantium. Geza had particularly mistrusted the alliance between Conrad and Manuel. In the early years he had not dared to take much serious action, but after Conrad's death he had grown bolder, and had waged intermittent

---

1 She was the origin of the *Princesse Lointaine*, made famous by the twelfth-century troubadour poet Jaufré Rudel and, more recently, by Edmond Rostand's play of that name. See also Petrarch's *Trionfo d'amore*, Swinburne's *Triumph of Time* and Browning's *Rudel and the Lady of Tripoli*.

warfare against Byzantium for the next four years until Manuel, anxious to free his hands for South Italy, negotiated a treaty of peace in 1156. Neither party, however, had any delusions about its duration: Geza was determined to build up a strong and independent nation, while Manuel's heart was set on nothing less than the elimination of Hungary as a separate state and its incorporation into his Empire.

Geza's death led to a disputed succession, in which Manuel did not hesitate to intervene. His own candidate was Geza's brother Stephen, to whom he sent money and weapons on a considerable scale; but Stephen was ultimately unsuccessful and the throne passed to his nephew and Geza's son, Stephen III. To him, in 1163, Manuel sent his ambassador George Palaeologus with an offer: if Stephen would recognize his younger brother Béla as heir to Croatia and Dalmatia, the Emperor would not only give Béla the hand of his daughter Maria but would make him heir to his own imperial throne. Stephen accepted, and Palaeologus escorted the young Prince back to Constantinople, where he was baptized into the Orthodox Church with the Byzantine name of Alexius and granted the title of Despot – one previously used only by the Emperor himself, and henceforth ranking immediately below him, taking precedence over the titles of both *sebastocrator* and Caesar.

All this, one might think, should have marked the end of the Hungarian hostilities; it did nothing of the sort. Already in 1164 Manuel and Béla crossed the Danube, on the dubious grounds that Stephen had not kept to his agreement of the previous year. Further campaigns followed – campaigns notable for the outstanding courage shown by the regiment of Seljuks provided by the Sultan under the terms of his treaty – and the fighting continued until 1167, when a major victory by the Byzantine army under Manuel's nephew Andronicus Contostephanus[1] left the Emperor in possession of Dalmatia, Bosnia, Sirmium[2] and the greater part of Croatia.

Béla and his betrothed played a major part in the ensuing celebrations. It was noted however that after four years their marriage seemed no nearer; and in 1169 the reason for the delay became clear when the Empress Mary bore her husband a son. Now it was Manuel's turn to go back on his undertakings. Breaking off Béla's engagement to his daughter, he married him instead to his wife's half-sister, Princess Anne of

---

1 He was the son of the Emperor's sister Anna, who had married Stephen Contostephanus.

2 The region of what is now northern Croatia and north-western Serbia, south of the Drava and Danube rivers.

Châtillon, simultaneously demoting him to the rank of Caesar. Three years later, he made his son – also named Alexius – co-Emperor. Such displeasure as Béla may have felt was quickly dissipated: the spring of that same year of 1172 saw the death of his brother Stephen and – with more than a little help from Manuel – his own accession to the Hungarian throne. Before leaving Constantinople he swore fealty to the *basileus*, promising that he would always pay due regard to the best interests of the Empire. He was to prove as good as his word.

The success of Manuel's Hungarian policy had another happy result for him: it deprived the constantly rebellious Serbs of their most valuable ally. The imperial army had always managed to quell their repeated insurrections, but had never succeeded in stopping them altogether. In 1167 the Grand Zhupan Stephen Nemanja won a notable victory, and for a time it looked as though Manuel had met his match; but the death of Stephen of Hungary and a major campaign in the summer of 1172 led by the Emperor himself put an end to all Nemanja's hopes. Like Reynald of Châtillon, he was obliged to humble himself before his conqueror, and later to take part in Manuel's triumphal entry into Constantinople as a defeated rebel.

Among the nations of the West, the principal sufferer from these developments was Venice. She too had claims over Dalmatia, where in the past she had been only too pleased to make common cause with the Byzantines against Hungarian rapaciousness; and the reaction on the Rialto to the Emperor's cool annexation of the entire coast can well be imagined. Not that the Venetians expected any better from him: for some time now they had been watching with increasing concern while he allowed Genoa, Pisa and Amalfi steadily to consolidate their positions in Constantinople – formerly, so far as foreign merchants were concerned, the exclusive preserve of the Most Serene Republic. Nearer to home, he was treating the city of Ancona – which still maintained a substantial Greek-speaking population – as if it were a Byzantine colony; there were even rumours that he might be planning to claim it for his Empire, with the obvious long-term objective of reviving the old Exarchate.

But Manuel also had a case. The number of Latins permanently resident in Constantinople at this time was probably not less than eighty thousand, all enjoying the special privileges that he and his predecessors, in moments of economic or political weakness, had been forced to grant. Of these, the Venetians were the most numerous, the most favoured and the most objectionable. Nicetas Choniates, chief of the palace secretariat, goes so far as to complain that their colony had become 'so insolent in its wealth and prosperity as to hold the imperial power in scorn'. It was therefore hardly surprising that the Emperor should wish to teach them a lesson; and before long he was given the perfect opportunity to do so. Some time early in 1171, the new Genoese settlement at Galata – the district of Constantinople on the further side of the Golden Horn – was attacked and largely destroyed. Those responsible for the devastation were never identified; for Manuel, however, here was just the opportunity that he had been looking for. Casting the blame squarely on the Venetians, on 12 March he decreed that all citizens of the Serenissima anywhere on Byzantine soil should be placed under immediate arrest, their ships and property confiscated. A few managed to escape in a Byzantine warship, put at their disposal by a Venetian-born captain in the imperial service; but the majority were less lucky. In the capital alone, ten thousand were seized; and when all the prisons had been filled to bursting, monasteries and convents were requisitioned to accommodate the overspill.

The reaction in Venice when the news reached the Rialto was first incredulity, then fury. The universal belief that the attack on the Genoese had been a pretext deliberately fabricated by the Byzantines was strengthened when the Genoese themselves declared that the Venetians had had nothing to do with it moreover the smoothness and efficiency with which the arrests had been carried out – on the same day throughout the Empire – showed that they must have been carefully planned weeks in advance. It was remembered also that only two years before, to stamp out rumours that he was contemplating an action of this kind, the Emperor had given Venetian ambassadors specific guarantees for the security of their countrymen – guarantees which had actually attracted further Venetian capital to the East and had thus further increased the spoils that he was now enjoying.

The last of the old ties that had bound Venice to Byzantium were forgotten. The Republic was bent on war. A forced loan was ordered, for which every citizen would be liable according to his means;[1] Venetians living abroad – such of them, at least, as were not languishing in Manuel's prisons – were recalled home and pressed into service; and in little over three months Doge Vitale Michiel had succeeded in raising a

---

1 It was to facilitate the collection of this loan that the city was divided into six districts, or *sestieri*, which still today form the basis of its postal system.

fleet of more than 120 sail which, the following September, he led out of the lagoon against the Empire of the East. Stopping at various points in Istria and Dalmatia to pick up such Venetian subjects as he might find, he continued round the Peloponnese as far as Euboea, where imperial ambassadors were awaiting him. They brought conciliatory messages from their master who, they emphasized, had no wish for war. The Doge had only to send a peace mission to Constantinople; he would then find that all differences could be resolved, on terms that he would not consider unfavourable.

Vitale Michiel accepted. It was the worst mistake of his life. While his emissaries continued their journey to the Bosphorus, he took his fleet on to Chios to await developments. It was there that disaster struck. Plague broke out in the overcrowded ships and spread with terrible speed. By early spring thousands were dead, the survivors so weakened and demoralized as to be unfit for war or anything else. At this point the ambassadors arrived from Constantinople. They had been abominably treated, and their mission had proved a total failure. The Emperor clearly had not the faintest intention of changing his attitude; his only purpose in inviting them had been to gain time while he improved his own defences. Shattered and humiliated, Michiel returned to face a general assembly of his subjects. He would have been better advised to remain in the East. In their eyes he had shown criminal gullibility in falling so completely into a typically Byzantine trap; and now, it appeared, he had brought the plague back to Venice. This last incompetence could not be forgiven. The whole assembly rose against him, while a mob gathered outside calling for his blood. Slipping out of a side door of the palace, the luckless Doge fled to seek asylum in the convent of S. Zaccaria. He never reached it. Before he had gone more than a few hundred yards he was set upon and stabbed to death.

It was to be fourteen years before diplomatic relations were restored between Byzantium and Venice, and thirty-two before the Venetians took their revenge; but only five years after the return of Vitale Michiel and his plague-stricken fleet to the lagoon, the Republic became the centre of attention of all Christendom. On 24 July 1177 Michiel's successor, Sebastiano Ziani, played host to the most important political ceremony of the twelfth century: the formal reconciliation of Pope Alexander III and the Western Emperor, Frederick Barbarossa.

Ever since his ill-fated coronation in the summer of 1155, Frederick's relations with the Papacy had grown worse and worse. From the outset he had been determined to assert his authority over North Italy; but the vast majority of the cities and towns of Lombardy were just as firmly resolved to break the old feudal fetters in favour of republican self-government, and Pope Adrian supported them. In August 1159, representatives of Milan, Crema, Brescia and Piacenza had met the Pope at Anagni and, in the presence of envoys from King William of Sicily, had sworn the initial pact that was to become the nucleus of the great Lombard League. The towns promised that they would have no dealings with the common enemy without papal consent, while the Pope undertook to excommunicate the Emperor after the usual period of forty days.

But he never did so. While still at Anagni he was stricken by a sudden angina, and on 1 September he died. His death gave Frederick Barbarossa an opportunity to sow yet more dissension. Recognizing that the next Pope, if freely elected, would continue along the lines set by his predecessor, he deliberately engineered a schism within the papal Curia. Thus it was that, just as Cardinal Roland of Siena – who, as Adrian's chancellor, had been the principal architect of his foreign policy – was being enthroned in St Peter's as Pope Alexander III, his colleague Cardinal Octavian of S. Cecilia suddenly seized the papal mantle and put it on himself. Alexander's supporters snatched it back; but Octavian had taken the precaution of bringing another, into which he somehow managed to struggle – getting it on back to front in the process. He then made a dash for the throne, sat on it, and proclaimed himself Pope Victor IV. It was hardly an edifying performance; but it worked. Frederick's ambassadors in Rome immediately recognized Victor as the rightful Pontiff. Virtually all the rest of Western Europe soon gave its allegiance to Alexander, but the damage was done and the chaotic Italian political scene was further bedevilled, for the next eighteen years, by a disputed papacy. Meanwhile Frederick – who had been finally excommunicated by Alexander in March 1160 – continued to do him all the harm he could, even going so far as to arrange for the 'election' – by two tame schismatic cardinals – of another anti-Pope when Victor died four years later.

To Manuel Comnenus, the quarrel between Barbarossa and the Pope seemed a perfect opportunity to re-establish the supremacy of Byzantium throughout Christendom. Since his rival was clearly unwilling to fulfil the Western Emperor's traditional role as protector, he would assume it himself; this new *rapprochement* might even achieve the reunion of the Eastern and Western Churches, in schism now for well over a century. When therefore two high-ranking papal legates arrived in Constantinople early in 1160, to request the Emperor's support for Alexander against the anti-Pope Victor, he received them warmly; and for the next five years he seems to have maintained secret negotiations with the Pope and the King of France – Louis having to some extent conquered his instinctive mistrust of Byzantium – in the hopes of forming a general alliance of the princes of Europe and the cities and towns of Italy which would eliminate Frederick once and for all.

But the results of these negotiations proved disappointing; and in 1166 Manuel decided to take the bull by the horns and to put to Pope Alexander a firm proposition. He would make a series of important concessions on theological and liturgical matters with the object of ending the schism, and would provide subsidies on a scale which would enable the Pope to buy not only Rome but the whole of Italy if he wanted to; in return, Alexander would award him the imperial crown, thus restoring the old unity of the Empire. The offer was well-timed: the Pope's principal champion, William of Sicily, had died on 7 May and his son and namesake was still a minor. Alexander would have to look elsewhere for support, and Constantinople was the obvious place. Soon afterwards two more cardinals were on their way to the Bosphorus to find out exactly what the Emperor had in mind.

It was, however, no use: the Churches were by now too far apart for any agreement to be possible. We know nothing of the discussions. John Cinnamus tells us that the Pope's first condition was that Manuel should remove his residence to Rome; if so, he must certainly have refused – such a suggestion could not be seriously contemplated. The cardinals returned, with the outstanding problems no nearer solution than before. A year or so later Manuel tried again, but with no greater success. What he had underestimated was the depth of his own unpopularity in the West where, particularly since the Second Crusade, he was generally believed to harbour sinister designs on Syria and the Holy Land, including the elimination of the Frankish princes and the reintroduction of the Eastern rite. He also failed to understand that in the eyes of Alexander he was demanding far too much for himself. The Pope's need for support in no way lessened his claim to supremacy: whether there were two Empires or one, the Vicar of Christ on Earth would always come first.

The first five years of the 1170s saw Manuel Comnenus at the pinnacle of his career. In the East, he had imposed his suzerainty over the Crusader states of Outremer, consolidated it with a dynastic marriage and brought the Seljuk Sultan to heel. In the West, he had seen his friend – some would have said his creature – Béla III become King of Hungary and had made huge territorial gains at Hungarian expense; he had humbled the Serbian Grand Zhupan, Stephen Nemanja; and he had broken the power of Venice within his Empire, to his own enormous profit. His only major failure had been his attempt to reconquer South Italy; with that single exception, he could hardly have played his hand better.

But the East and the West were well over a thousand miles apart; Manuel could not be everywhere at once, and after his treaty with Kilij Arslan he had turned his back on Asia Minor for more than a decade. During that time the Seljuk Sultan had not been idle. True, he had avoided any hostile act against the Empire. Gradually, however, he had managed to eliminate one after the other of his principal Muslim rivals until only Nur ed-Din himself was left; and in 1173 word reached Constantinople that the Sultan was intriguing with the Atabeg of Mosul and the two were on the point of forming a military alliance. (Did the Emperor but know it, Kilij Arslan was also in touch with Frederick Barbarossa.) Manuel crossed at once into Asia and at Philadelphia – the modern Alaşehir – confronted the Sultan, who blandly explained that Nur ed-Din had not forgiven him his Christian alliance and that he had had no choice but to respect his wishes. Byzantium, he assured Manuel, had nothing to fear; meanwhile he was only too happy to renew the earlier treaties.

For the moment, danger had been averted; but on 15 May 1174 the mighty Atabeg of Mosul died in his turn, leaving the Danishmends – whom he had long protected and championed – defenceless against Seljuk strength. Kilij Arslan unhesitatingly annexed their territories, and two refugee Danishmend princes appealed to Constantinople. The next two years were taken up with diplomatic negotiations – the Sultan prevaricating and procrastinating, always reiterating his desire for peace and still more treaties – and minor skirmishes, during which Manuel worked hard to strengthen his frontier fortresses; then, in the summer of 1176, the Emperor marched on Iconium, travelling through Laodicea (near the modern Denizli) and the valley of the upper Meander until he reached the mountainous region near the Seljuk frontier. Here he was met by envoys from the Sultan, with a final offer of peace on generous terms. Most of his senior officers favoured its acceptance, pointing out the hazards of a long journey with heavy equipment – for they had brought their siege engines with them – through the mountains in which the Seljuks occupied all the strategic high places. Unfortunately the army also contained a number of young noblemen eager for their first experience of battle. They pressed hard for a continuation of the campaign, and the Emperor foolishly heeded them.

Just beyond the ruined fortress of Myriocephalum, Manuel's route led through the long pass of Tzybritze, so narrow that when they entered it on 17 September the imperial troops and their baggage were strung out over a distance of some ten miles. Until that moment the Turks had restricted their activities to minor harassment by small bands of irregulars; now they struck, sweeping down on the army from the mountains to each side and deliberately concentrating their fire on the beasts of burden, whose dead bodies quickly rendered the road impassable. Baldwin of Antioch, brother of the Emperor's new wife, charged with his cavalry regiment up the hill and into the thick of the enemy; he and all his men were killed. Had Manuel shown something of the same spirit, the day might have been saved; but at this of all moments his courage deserted him. In a hasty council of war he horrified his senior officers by suddenly announcing his intention of taking flight. The commanding general Andronicus Contostephanus made a strong protest, his words being echoed by a common soldier who, having overheard the discussion, bitterly reproached the Emperor for wishing to abandon an army whose loss was due entirely to his own imprudence. Manuel reluctantly agreed to remain; but his reputation was badly injured and was never fully to recover.

As dawn broke the Seljuks resumed the attack, and for some time it looked as though a general massacre was inevitable. Then there was a sudden lull; and a Turkish emissary arrived at the imperial camp, leading a finely caparisoned horse which, he said, was a present from his master. The Sultan, he reported, had no desire for further bloodshed; if the Emperor would agree to destroy the fortifications of Dorylaeum and Sublaeum – two fortresses which he had strengthened only a year or two before – he for his part would be happy to conclude a treaty of peace. Hardly able to believe his good fortune, Manuel accepted; and the two armies withdrew.[1]

Nicetas Choniates tells us that on the homeward journey the Emperor

---

1 Michael the Syrian suggests that the Sultan also insisted on the payment of a considerable sum of money – something a good deal easier to believe than Manuel's own testimony, in a letter written to Henry II of England, to the effect that Kilij Arslan also offered to return his Christian captives and to assist the Empire against all its enemies (Roger of Hoveden, *Annals*, AD 1176).

had wished to follow an alternative route, but that his guides insisted on taking him back past the scene of the battle so that he could see for himself the full extent of the slaughter. It was a painful journey, with the remnants of the army still under intermittent attack from armed bands of Seljuk Turks who, cheated of what they considered their legitimate spoils by the unexpected peace, had quite simply refused to recognize it. When at last he reached Sublaeum, Manuel ordered the razing of the fortifications as he had promised. A few days later at Philadelphia he sent messengers to the capital with a full report of the disaster, comparing it to that of Manzikert – except, he pointed out, that he himself had not been captured like his predecessor Romanus, and that Kilij Arslan had agreed to make peace.

The question remains: why had the Sultan done so? He had been given a matchless opportunity to destroy the effective military power of the Byzantine Empire; why had he not taken it? We shall never know. Perhaps he was unaware of the extent of his victory. He himself had probably sustained quite heavy losses, and may have been less certain than Manuel of the battle's final outcome. Perhaps, too, he felt that he might well be in need of the Empire's diplomatic – and even military – support in the future. In any case, the dismantling of the two fortresses, enabling as it would his subjects to spread themselves without let or hindrance through the Sangarius and Meander valleys, would in itself be no small reward; nor could it be doubted that Myriocephalum had destroyed Manuel's hopes of reimposing his rule across Asia Minor. He was to make one or two more defensive and retaliatory sorties on a small scale; but never again would he lead a major campaign in the East. In future, it would be all that his shattered army could do to man the frontier.

This is not to say that there was no more serious fighting. It soon became plain that once back in Constantinople the Emperor, despite his solemn undertaking, had no intention of touching the fortifications of Dorylaeum, and in 1177 or thereabouts – the chronology is not entirely clear – the furious Kilij Arslan led his army deep into imperial territory and ravaged the whole Meander valley, sacking Tralles and Pisidian Antioch. But this operation, and others that were to follow, was in the nature of a raid rather than a permanent invasion and made no ultimate difference to the map of Anatolia.

What, ultimately, did Manuel Comnenus achieve in the East? Where the Saracens were concerned, absolutely nothing – owing to a single cardinal mistake. Trusting too much to the peace treaty signed with Kilij

Arslan in 1162, he had left him for the next eleven years to his own devices. This *détente* – assisted by the immense amount of gold and silver given to the Sultan during his twelve weeks in Constantinople – had allowed him to eliminate his Muslim rivals and establish himself as the only important force to be reckoned with in Eastern Anatolia. Thus Manuel, through a combination of wild generosity and a curious lack of political foresight, had succeeded only in replacing a number of small and mutually hostile rulers with a single determined one – by whom he was finally defeated.

In the spring of 1178 Philip, Count of Flanders, passed through Constantinople on his way back from the Holy Land. The Emperor received him with his usual generous hospitality, presented to him his little son Alexius and suggested that on his return to France the Count might like to sound out King Louis on the possibility of a marriage between the young Prince and one of the King's daughters. Philip agreed, and in due course Louis consented in his turn. So it came about that at Easter 1179 the Princess Agnes of France – Louis's daughter by his third wife Alix of Champagne – set out for Constantinople and a new life in the East; and on Sunday, 2 March 1180, in the Triclinium of the Great Palace, the Patriarch Theodosius celebrated her marriage to Alexius and laid the imperial diadem on her head. She was nine years old, her husband ten.

It was Manuel's last diplomatic success. Within a matter of weeks he fell seriously ill. Weakening both in mind and body – he had never been the same after Myriocephalum – he now gave himself up more and more to the attentions of his court astrologers, who comforted him by prophesying that he would live another fourteen years, during which time he would lead his armies to victory after victory. Such was his trust in them that until his very last days he refused to make any arrangements for the regency during Alexius's minority. Meanwhile the astrologers, in an attempt to divert attention from the inaccuracy of their previous predictions, spoke darkly of coming earthquakes and other natural cataclysms; and the Emperor, panic-stricken, ordered the excavation of deep subterranean shelters and even the demolition of certain parts of the palace.

The earthquakes failed to occur; but by mid-September Manuel could no longer doubt the approach of death. He spoke tearfully of his son, and of the difficulties that he would have to face on his succession; but he was no longer capable of planning any effective dispensations. At last he bowed to the entreaties of the Patriarch and made a formal renunciation of the astrologers and his belief in them; then he sighed deeply, took his pulse and asked for an ordinary monk's habit. His imperial insignia were removed, he struggled as best he could into the rough homespun, and shortly afterwards, on 24 September, aged about sixty, he died. He was buried in the church of the Pantocrator, near the entrance. Many years before, he had carried on his own shoulders from the Boucoleon port to the Great Palace the heavy stone, recently brought from Ephesus, on which Christ's body was said to have been laid after its deposition from the cross. This stone was now placed upon his tomb.

It is impossible not to feel sorry for Manuel. Of the five Comnenus Emperors, he was the most brilliant, the most imaginative; and these very qualities were perhaps his undoing. His father and grandfather had worked slowly and patiently to minimize the damage done by Manzikert, proceeding cautiously and step by step. Manuel's quicksilver mind saw possibilities everywhere; and once seen they were immediately pursued. Had he concentrated, as he should have done, on the situation in the East and the threat posed by Kilij Arslan, he might have re-established Byzantine power throughout Anatolia. But he remained fascinated by the West, and allowed his attention to be taken up in turn by Italy and Hungary, Serbia and Venice, the Western Emperor and the Pope. He gained many victories, military and diplomatic, but he consolidated none of them; by the time he died, nearly all his achievements had proved temporary and he left the Empire in a worse state than he found it.

And poorer too. Manuel's diplomacy was based, even more than that of most of his fellow-princes, on subsidies, sweeteners and bribes. He was extravagant in his own tastes and insanely generous not only to his friends but to virtually everyone with whom he came in contact. Finally, the scale and frequency of his campaigns drained his Empire dry, both of money and of men. He had continued his father's policy of settling war prisoners in various regions and making them liable for military service, thereby reviving the old system of smallholder-soldiers on which the Empire had relied in former centuries; but such measures remained quite inadequate to meet his demands. As a result he was obliged to hire ever-increasing numbers of mercenaries, who lived off the local populations – taking, as Nicetas Choniates tells us, 'not only their money but even the very shirts off their backs'.

All this is more than enough to account for Manuel's unpopularity in the provinces of the Empire; but even in Constantinople he seems to have had few real friends. The trouble here was, once again, the attraction that he always felt for Western Europe: its art, its customs, its institutions. His subjects were disgusted by the way Western visitors always received a warmer welcome than those from the East, and in particular by his preference for Western architects whenever there was a new house or palace to be built. They were shocked by the informality of his manners – by the light-hearted way, for example, in which he would enter a Western-style tournament (surely bad enough in itself) and compete on equal terms with Frankish knights. Finally, they resented the constant implication that they were old-fashioned, sticking to out-dated concepts and outmoded traditions. They were glad to see him go.

Fortunately for him, he went just in time, leaving his successors to reap the wild wind. He also missed the Third Crusade, the spectre of which – for he had known that it must come – had haunted him through the last years of his life. For that, admittedly, he cannot be blamed; but of the other misfortunes that were to descend upon Byzantium, many – perhaps most – were of his making. He left behind him a heavy heritage: one that would have defeated better men by far than those who were, alas, to succeed him.

9
Andronicus the Terrible

[1180–85]

In the life of this prince, so brilliant and yet so corrupt, at once an abominable tyrant and a superb statesman, one who could have saved the Empire but only precipitated its ruin, we find combined, as in a magnificent summary, all the essential characteristics, all the contrasts of Byzantine society: that strange mixture of good and evil – cruel, atrocious and decadent, yet also capable of grandeur, energy and effort; a society which, during so many centuries, in all the troublous times of its history, always succeeded in finding within itself the necessary resources for life and for survival, not without glory.

Charles Diehl,

Figures Byzantines, Vol. II

Alexius II Comnenus was an unimpressive child. Nicetas Choniates tells us that 'this young prince was so puffed up with vanity and pride, so destitute of inner light and ability as to be incapable of the simplest task ... He passed his entire life at play or the chase, and contracted several habits of pronounced viciousness.' Meanwhile his mother, Mary of Antioch, governed as Regent in his stead. As the first Latin ever to rule in Constantinople, she started off at a grave disadvantage. To the Byzantines, her husband's passion for all things Western had been quite bad enough; they now feared – and with good reason – still further extensions to the Italian and Frankish merchants of their trading rights and privileges; and they were more worried still when Mary took as her chief adviser another character of extreme pro-Western sympathies – Manuel's nephew, the *protosebastus* Alexius, uncle of the Queen of Jerusalem. Before long it was generally believed that her adviser was also her lover, though from Nicetas's description it is not easy to see what the Empress – whose beauty was famous throughout Christendom – saw in him:

He was accustomed to spend the greater part of the day in bed, keeping the curtains drawn lest he should ever see the sunlight ... Whenever the sun appeared he would seek the darkness, just as wild beasts do; also he took much pleasure in rubbing his decaying teeth, putting in new ones in the place of those that had fallen out through old age.

As dissatisfaction grew, various conspiracies began to be hatched; notably one by Mary's stepdaughter Maria. The plot was discovered; with her husband Rainier of Montferrat and her other associates, Maria barely had time to flee to St Sophia and barricade herself in. But the Empress Regent was not prepared to respect any rights of sanctuary. The imperial guard was dispatched with orders to seize the conspirators, and the Great Church was saved from desecration only through the mediation of the Patriarch himself. This incident deeply shocked the Byzantines, and the subsequent exile of His Beatitude to a monastery for his part in the affair made the regime more unpopular than ever. Such was the state of public indignation against her that Mary never dared to punish her stepdaughter. Nor, later, did she lift a finger when the people of Constantinople marched *en masse* to the Patriarch's monastery and carried him on their shoulders back to the capital. The whole affair could hardly have been handled more ineptly.

This first *coup* had failed; but there followed a threat from another of the Emperor's relatives – a man this time, and one of a very different calibre. Andronicus Comnenus, the Emperor's first cousin – he was the son of the *sebastocrator* Isaac – was a phenomenon. In 1182 he was already sixty-four years old, but looked nearer forty. Over six feet tall and in magnificent physical condition, he had preserved the good looks, the intellect, the conversational charm and wit, the elegance and the sheer panache that, together with the fame of his almost legendary exploits in the bed and on the battlefield, had won him an unrivalled reputation. The list of his conquests seemed endless, that of the scandals in which he had been involved very little shorter. Three in particular had roused Manuel to fury. The first was when Andronicus carried on a flagrant affair with his own cousin – and the Emperor's niece – the Princess Eudocia Comnena, effectively answering criticism by pointing out that 'subjects should always follow their master's example, and two pieces from the same factory normally prove equally acceptable' – a clear allusion to Manuel's association with Eudocia's sister Theodora, for whom he was well known to cherish an affection that went well beyond the avuncular. Some years later, Andronicus had deserted his military command in Cilicia with the deliberate intention of seducing the lovely Philippa of Antioch. Once again he must have known that there would be serious repercussions: Philippa was the sister not only of the reigning prince, Bohemund III, but of Manuel's own wife, the Empress Mary. This, however, as far as Andronicus was concerned, merely lent additional spice to the game. Though he was then forty-eight and his quarry just twenty, his serenades beneath her window proved irresistible. Within a few days he had added yet another name to his list.

The conquest once made, Andronicus did not remain long to enjoy it. Manuel, outraged, ordered his immediate recall; Bohemund also made it clear that he had no intention of tolerating such a scandal. Possibly, too, the young Princess's charms may have proved disappointing. In any case Andronicus left hurriedly for Palestine to put himself at the disposal of King Amalric of Jerusalem; and there, at Acre, he met for the first time another of his cousins – Queen Theodora, the twenty-one-year-old widow of Amalric's predecessor, King Baldwin III. She became the love of his life. Soon afterwards, when Andronicus moved to his new fief of Beirut – recently given him by Amalric as a reward for his services – Theodora joined him. Consanguinity forbade their marriage, but the two lived there together in open sin until Beirut in its turn grew too hot for them.

After a long spell of wandering through the Muslim East, Andronicus and Theodora finally settled down at Colonea, just beyond the eastern frontier of the Empire, subsisting happily on such money as they had been able to bring with them, supplemented by the proceeds of a little mild brigandage; but their idyll was brought to an end when Theodora and their two small sons were captured by the Duke of Trebizond and sent back to Constantinople. Andronicus, agonized by their loss, hurried back to the capital and immediately gave himself up, flinging himself histrionically at the Emperor's feet and promising anything if only his mistress and his children could be returned to him. Manuel showed his usual generosity; Theodora was, after all, his niece. Clearly a ménage at once so irregular and so prominent could not be allowed in Constantinople; but the couple were given a pleasant castle on the Black Sea coast where they might live in moderately honourable exile – and, it was hoped, peaceful retirement.

Alas, it was not to be. Andronicus had always had his eye on the imperial crown and when, after Manuel's death, reports reached him of the growing dissatisfaction with the Empress Regent he needed little persuading that his opportunity had come at last. Unlike Mary of Antioch – 'the foreigner', as her subjects scornfully called her – he was a true Comnenus.

He had energy, ability and determination; more important still at such a moment, his romantic past lent him a popular appeal unmatched in the Empire. In August 1182 he marched on the capital. The old magic was as strong as ever. The troops sent out to block his advance refused to fight; their general, Andronicus Angelus, surrendered and joined him[1] – an example soon afterwards followed by the admiral commanding the imperial fleet in the Bosphorus. As he progressed, the people flocked from their houses to cheer him on his way; soon the road was lined with his supporters. Even before he crossed the straits, rebellion had broken out in Constantinople, and with it exploded all the pent-up xenophobia that the events of the previous two years had done so much to increase. What followed was the massacre of virtually every Latin in the city: women and children, the old and infirm, even the sick from the hospitals, as the whole quarter in which they lived was burnt to the ground. The *protosebastos* was found cowering in the palace, too frightened even to try to escape; he was thrown into the dungeons and later, on Andronicus's orders, blinded;[2] the young Emperor and his mother were taken to the imperial villa of the Philopation, there to await their cousin's pleasure.

Their fate was worse than either of them could have feared. Andronicus's triumph had brought out the other side of his character – a degree of cruelty and brutality that few had even suspected, unredeemed by a shred of compassion, scruple or moral sense. Though all-powerful, he was not yet Emperor; and so, methodically and in cold blood, he set about eliminating everyone who stood between himself and the throne. Princess Maria and her husband were the first to go; their deaths were sudden and mysterious, but no one doubted poison. Then it was the turn of the Empress herself. Her thirteen-year-old son was forced to sign her death warrant with his own hand, and she was strangled in her cell. In September 1183 Andronicus was crowned co-Emperor; two months later the boy Alexius met his own death by the bowstring and his body was flung into the Bosphorus. 'Thus,' wrote Nicetas, 'in the imperial garden, all the trees were felled.' Only one more formality remained. For the last three and a half years of his short life, Alexius had been married

---

1 It was typical of Andronicus Comnenus that he should have had a joke ready when Angelus came over to his colours. 'See,' he is said to have remarked, 'it is just as the Gospel says: *I shall send my Angel, who shall prepare the way before thee.*' The Gospel in fact says no such thing; but Andronicus was not a man to quibble over niceties of that kind.

2 Though not before he had recovered his nerve and lodged a formal complaint that his English guards – presumably Varangians – were not allowing him enough sleep.

to Agnes of France, now re-baptized in the more seemly Byzantine name of Anna. Scarcely was her husband disposed of when the new Emperor, now sixty-four, had married the twelve-year-old Empress – and, if at least one modern authority is to be believed,[1] consummated the marriage.

No reign could have begun less auspiciously; in one way, however, Andronicus did more good to the Empire than Manuel had ever done. He attacked all administrative abuses, wherever he found them and in whatever form. The tragedy was that as he gradually eliminated corruption from the government machine, so he himself grew more and more corrupted by the exercise of his power. Violence and brute force seemed to be his only weapons; his legitimate campaign against the military aristocracy rapidly deteriorated into a succession of bloodbaths and indiscriminate slaughter. According to one report,

he left the vines of Brusa weighed down, not with grapes but with the corpses of those whom he had hanged; and he forbade any man to cut them down for burial, for he wished them to dry in the sun and then to sway and flutter as the wind took them, like the scarecrows that are hung in the orchards to frighten the birds.

Before long, however, it was Andronicus himself who had cause for fear. His popularity was gone: the saviour of the Empire was revealed a monster. Once again the air was thick with revolt and sedition; conspiracies sprang up, hydra-headed, in capital and provinces alike. Traitors were everywhere. Those who fell into the hands of the Emperor were tortured to death, often in his presence, occasionally by his own hand; but many others escaped to the West, where they could be sure of a ready welcome – for the West, as Andronicus was well aware, had not forgotten the massacre of 1182 and there also the storm-clouds were gathering. As early as 1181 King Béla III of Hungary – who had previously been kept in check only by his personal friendship with Manuel – had seized back Dalmatia, much of Croatia and the district of Sirmium, won by the Emperor at such cost only a few years before. In 1183, in alliance with the Serbian Grand Zhupan Stephen Nemanja, he invaded the Empire: Belgrade, Branichevo, Nish and Sardica were all

---

1 Diehl, *Figures Byzantines*, Vol. II, which includes scholarly but highly readable short biographies of both Andronicus and Agnes. What became of Theodora is unknown. She too may have come to an unpleasant end; but she was still relatively young, and it is more probable that she was packed off to end her days in a convent.

sacked, to the point where the soldiers of the Third Crusade, passing through these cities six years later, found them abandoned and in ruins.

There was trouble, too, in Asia – not from the Muslims but from the land-owning military aristocracy against which (despite being a part of it himself) Andronicus nurtured a particular hatred. Indeed, one of his distant cousins – Manuel's great-nephew Isaac Comnenus – went so far as formally to establish himself in the strategically vital island of Cyprus, declaring its political independence: the first step, it could be argued, towards the Empire's eventual disintegration.

The paramount threat, however, came from one of the oldest and most determined of all the enemies of Byzantium: Norman Sicily.

Early in January 1185 the Arab traveller Ibn Jubair was at the port of Trapani in western Sicily, having just taken passage on a Genoese ship to return to his native Spain. A day or two before he was due to depart, an order arrived from the government in Palermo: until further notice the harbour was to be closed to all outgoing traffic. A huge war fleet was being made ready. No other vessel might leave till it was safely on its way.

A similar order had been simultaneously circulated to every other port of Sicily: a security embargo on an unprecedented scale. Even within the island, few people seemed to know exactly what was happening. In Trapani, Ibn Jubair reports, everyone had his own idea about the fleet, its size, purpose and destination. Some said it was bound for Alexandria, where a Sicilian naval expedition had ended in disaster eleven years before; others suspected an attempt on Majorca, a favourite target for Sicilian raiders in recent years. There were also, inevitably, many who believed that it would sail against Constantinople. In the past year hardly a ship had arrived from the East without its quota of blood-curdling reports concerning Andronicus's latest atrocities; and it was now widely rumoured that among the increasing number of Byzantines taking refuge in Sicily was a mysterious youth claiming to be the rightful Emperor, Alexius II. If, as men said, this youth had actually been received by the King and had convinced him of the truth of his story, what could be more natural than that William the Good[1] should launch an expedition to replace him on his throne?

We shall never know whether such a claimant did in fact present

---

1 King William II (the Good) of Sicily had succeeded his father William I (the Bad) on the latter's death in 1166.

himself at the court in Palermo. There is nothing inherently improbable in the story. *Coups d'état* of the kind that Andronicus had achieved normally produce a pretender or two: Robert Guiscard had unearthed one to strengthen his hand before his own Byzantine adventure in 1081, and the Metropolitan Eustathius of Thessalonica – of whom we shall be hearing more before long – takes it for granted that a pseudo-Alexius was wandering through northern Greece shortly before the time of which Ibn Jubair was writing. But whether the rumour was true or false, we know for a fact that William did not lack encouragement for his enterprise: one of Manuel's nephews – irritatingly enough, also called Alexius – had recently escaped to Sicily and had been received at court, since when he had been urgently pressing the King to march on Constantinople and overthrow the usurper.

Throughout the winter of 1184–5 William was at Messina. He hated soldiering, and never went on campaign himself if he could avoid it; but on this occasion he had taken personal charge of the preparations. Though he admitted it to no one, his ultimate objective was nothing less than the crown of Byzantium; and he was determined that the force he sent out to attain it should be worthy of such a prize – stronger, both on land and sea, than any other ever to have sailed from Sicilian shores. And so it was. By the time it was ready to start, the fleet – commanded by his cousin Count Tancred of Lecce – is said to have comprised between two and three hundred vessels and to have carried some eighty thousand men, including five thousand knights and a special detachment of mounted archers. This huge land army was placed under the joint leadership of Tancred's brother-in-law Count Richard of Acerra and a certain Baldwin, of whom virtually nothing is known apart from an intriguing description by Nicetas:

Although of mediocre birth, he was much beloved of the King and was appointed general of the army by virtue of his long experience of military affairs. He liked to compare himself with Alexander the Great, not only because his stomach was covered – as was Alexander's – with so much hair that it seemed to sprout wings, but because he had done even greater deeds and in an even shorter time – and, moreover, without bloodshed.

The expedition sailed from Messina on 11 June 1185 and headed straight for Durazzo. Although William's attempt to seal all Sicilian ports had not been entirely successful – Ibn Jubair's Genoese captains had had little difficulty in bribing their way out of Trapani – his security precautions seem to have had some effect; it is hard to see how

Andronicus could otherwise have been caught so unprepared. As we know, he had long mistrusted Western intentions; and he must have been aware that Durazzo, as his Empire's largest Adriatic port and the starting point from which the main imperial road – the Via Egnatia – ran eastward across Macedonia and Thrace to Constantinople, was the obvious if not the only possible Sicilian bridgehead. Yet he had made little effort either to strengthen the city's fortifications or to provision it for a siege. When he did at last receive reports of the impending attack, he quickly sent one of his most experienced generals, John Branas, to take charge of the situation; but Branas arrived at Durazzo only a day or two before the Sicilian fleet, too late to accomplish anything of value.

Durazzo had already fallen once to the Normans, 103 years before. On that occasion, however, it had been after a long and glorious battle, fought heroically on both sides: a battle in which the Byzantine army had been led by the Emperor himself, the Norman by the two outstanding warriors of their age, Robert Guiscard and his son Bohemund; in which Robert's wife, the Lombard Sichelgaita, had proved herself the equal in courage of both her husband and stepson; in which the stalwart axe-swinging Englishmen of the Varangian Guard had perished to the last man. This time it was a very different story. Branas, knowing that he had no chance, surrendered without a struggle. By 24 June, less than a fortnight after the fleet had sailed out of Messina, Durazzo was in Sicilian hands.

The subsequent march across the Balkan peninsula was swift and uneventful. Not a single attempt was made to block the invaders' progress. On 6 August the entire land force was encamped outside the walls of Thessalonica; on the 15th the fleet, having sailed round the Peloponnese, took up its position in the roadstead; and the siege began.

Thessalonica was a thriving and prosperous city, with fifteen hundred years of history already behind it and a Christian tradition going back to St Paul. As a naval base it dominated the Aegean; as a commercial centre it vied with Constantinople itself, even surpassing it during the annual trade fair in October, when merchants from all over Europe gathered there to do business with their Arab, Jewish and Armenian colleagues from Africa and the Levant.[1] Thanks to this fair, the city also boasted a

---

1 The fair has continued, intermittently, until the present day. Thessalonica maintained its predominantly Jewish character throughout Ottoman times and up to the Second World War, when its entire Sephardic population of some fifty thousand was deported to Poland, never to return.

permanent Western mercantile community living in its own quarter just inside the walls. Largely composed of Italians, it was to prove of more than a little value to the besiegers during the days that followed.

Yet the principal blame for the disaster that overtook Thessalonica in the summer of 1185 must lie not with any foreigner but with its own military Governor, David Comnenus. Although he had strict instructions from the Emperor to attack the enemy at every opportunity and with all his strength,[1] and although – unlike Branas at Durazzo – he had had plenty of time to prepare his defences and lay in provisions, he had done neither. Within days of the beginning of the siege his archers had run out of arrows; soon there were not even any more rocks for the catapults. Worse still, it soon became clear that he had failed to check the water cisterns, several of which were found – too late – to be leaking. Yet at no time did he betray the slightest sign of shame or discomfiture. Nicetas Choniates, who seems to have known him personally, writes:

Weaker than a woman, more timid than a deer, he was content just to look at the enemy, rather than make any effort to repulse him. If ever the garrison showed itself eager to make a sortie he would forbid it, like a hunter who holds back his hounds. He was never seen to carry arms, or to wear a helmet or cuirass . . . And while the enemy battering-rams made the walls tremble so that the masonry was crashing everywhere to the ground, he would laugh at the noise and, seeking out the safest corner available, would say to those around him, 'Just listen to the old lady – how noisy she is!' Thus he would refer to the largest of their siege-machines.

Nicetas was not himself at Thessalonica during those dreadful days; his account of them, however, is based on the best possible authority – that of Eustathius, the city's Metropolitan Archbishop. Though a Homeric scholar of repute, Eustathius was no stylist; neither, as a good Greek patriot, did he ever attempt to conceal his own detestation of the Latins, whom – with good reason in his case – he considered no better than savages. But his *History of the Latin Capture of Thessalonica*, turgid and tendentious as it is, remains the only eye-witness account we have of the siege and its aftermath. The story it tells is not a pretty one.

---

1 'Andronicus's orders were "to see that the city was preserved and, far from being afraid of the Italians, to leap on them, bite them and prick them." Those were his own exact words, though I believe that only he knew precisely what he meant. Those who liked to joke about such things gave them a most unseemly interpretation, which I have no intention of repeating here' (Nicetas).

Even had it been adequately prepared and defended, it is unlikely that Thessalonica could have held out very long against so furious and many-sided an attack as that which the Sicilians now launched upon it. The garrison resisted as bravely as its commander permitted, but before long the eastern bastions began to crumble. Meanwhile, on the western side, a group of German mercenaries within the walls was being bribed to open the gates. Early on 24 August, from both sides simultaneously, the Sicilian troops poured into the second city of the Byzantine Empire.

So huge an army from Sicily must have contained hundreds of soldiers of Greek extraction; hundreds more, from Apulia and Calabria as well as from the island itself, must have grown up near Greek communities, been familiar with their customs and religious traditions, even spoken a few words of their language. It would have been pleasant to record that these men had exerted a moderating influence on their less enlightened comrades; but they did nothing of the kind – or, if they tried, they failed. The Sicilian soldiery gave itself up to an orgy of savagery and violence unparalleled in Thessalonica since Theodosius the Great had massacred seven thousand of its citizens in the Hippodrome eight centuries before.[1] It is perhaps more than coincidental that Eustathius puts the number of Greek civilian dead on this present occasion at the same figure; but even the Norman commanders estimated it at five thousand, so he may not be very far out. And murder was not all: women and children were seized and violated, houses fired and pillaged, churches desecrated and destroyed. This last series of outrages was surprising. In the whole history of Norman Sicily we find remarkably few cases of sacrilege and profanation, and none on such a scale as this. Even the Greeks, for all their poor opinion of Latin behaviour, were as astonished as they were horrified. Nicetas admits as much:

These barbarians carried their violence to the very foot of the altars, in the presence of the holy images . . . It was thought strange that they should wish to destroy our icons, using them as fuel for the fires on which they cooked. More criminal still, they would dance upon the altars, before which the angels themselves trembled, and sing profane songs. Then they would piss all over the church, flooding the floors with their urine.

Some degree of pillage had been expected; it was after all the recognized reward for an army after a successful siege, and one which the Greeks would not have hesitated to claim for themselves had the roles

1 See *Byzantium: The Early Centuries*, p. 112.

been reversed. But these atrocities were something different, and Baldwin took firm measures at once. The city had been entered during the early hours of the morning; by noon he had managed to restore a semblance of order. Then the logistical problems began. Thessalonica was not equipped to cope with a sudden influx of eighty thousand men. Such food as there was tended to disappear down Sicilian gullets, and the local population soon found itself half-starved. The disposal of the dead presented further difficulties. It was several days before the task was completed, and long before that the August heat had done its work. An epidemic ensued which, aggravated by the overcrowding – and, Eustath-ius maintains, the immoderate consumption of new wine – killed off some three thousand of the occupying army and an unknown number of the local inhabitants.

From the start, too, there were serious confessional troubles. The Latins took over many of the local churches for their own use, but this did not stop certain elements of the soldiery from bursting into those that had remained in Greek hands, interrupting the services and howling down the officiating priests. A still more dangerous incident occurred when a group of Sicilians, suddenly startled by the sound of urgent, rhythmic hammering, took it to be a signal for insurrection and rushed to arms. Only just in time was it explained to them that the noise was simply that of the *semantron*, the wooden plank by which the Orthodox faithful were normally summoned to their devotions.[1]

Within a week or two an uneasy *modus vivendi* had been established. Baldwin showed himself a tactful commander and Eustathius, though technically a prisoner, seems to have done much to prevent unnecessary friction. His flock, for their part, soon began to discover that there was money to be made out of these foreigners who had so little understanding of real prices and values. Before long we find him lamenting the ease with which the ladies of Thessalonica were wont to yield to the Sicilian soldiers. But the atmosphere in and around the city remained explosive, and to Greek and Sicilian alike it must have been a relief when the army drew itself up once more in line of battle and, leaving only a small garrison behind, headed off to the East.

---

1 The beating of the *semantron* is of considerable symbolic significance. The Church represents the ark of salvation; and the monk who balances the six-foot plank on his shoulders and raps his tattoo on it with a little wooden hammer is echoing the sound of Noah's tools, summoning the chosen to join him. In Ottoman times, when the ringing of church bells was forbidden, the *semantron* continued in regular use. It is seldom heard nowadays, except on Mount Athos – where it remains the rule – and in a few isolated rural monasteries.

By this time Andronicus had dispatched no less than five separate armies to Thessalonica to block the enemy advance. This fragmentation of his forces seems to have been yet another indication of the Emperor's growing instability: had they been united under a single able commander they might have saved the city. As it was, all five retreated to the hills to the north of the road whence, apparently hypnotized, they watched the Sicilian army march on their capital. Baldwin's vanguard had thus pressed as far as Mosynopolis, nearly half-way to Constantinople, when there occurred an event that changed the entire situation – completely and, so far as the invaders were concerned, disastrously. Driven now beyond endurance, his subjects rose up against Andronicus Comnenus and murdered him.

In Constantinople as elsewhere, the news from Thessalonica had brought the inhabitants to the verge of panic. Andronicus's reactions were typical of his contradictory nature. On the one hand he took firm action to repair and strengthen the city's defences. The state of the walls was carefully checked, houses built too closely against them were destroyed wherever it was considered that they might provide a means of entry for a besieging army; a fleet of a hundred ships was hastily mobilized and victualled. Though this was less than half the size of the Sicilian naval force – now reported to be fast approaching – in the confined waters of the Marmara and the Bosphorus it might yet serve its purpose.

But at other moments and in other respects the Emperor seemed totally indifferent to the emergency, drawing back further and further into his private world of pleasure. In the three years since his accession his life had grown steadily more depraved.

He would have liked to emulate Hercules, who lay with all the fifty daughters of Thyestes in a single night;[1] but he was nevertheless obliged to resort to artifice as a means of strengthening his nerves, rubbing himself with a certain balm to increase his vigour. He also ate regularly of a fish known as the *scincus*, which is caught in the river Nile and is not dissimilar to the crocodile; and which, though abhorred by many, is most effective in the quickening of lust.

By now, too, he was developing a persecution mania that led him to new extremes of cruelty. A day on which he ordered no one's death,

---

1 Nicetas nods here. Their father was not Thyestes but Thespius. This thirteenth labour of Hercules must have been the most arduous of the lot, but its success rate was remarkable: all the girls produced male children, in many cases twins.

writes Nicetas, was for him a day wasted: 'men and women lived only in anxiety and sorrow, and even the night afforded no rest, since their sleep was troubled with hideous dreams and by the ghastly phantoms of those whom he had massacred.' Constantinople was living through a reign of terror as fearful as any in its long, dark history – one which reached its culmination in September 1185, with the issue of a decree ordering the execution of all prisoners and exiles, together with their entire families, on charges of complicity with the invaders.

Fortunately for the Empire, revolution came just in time to avert tragedy. The spark was fired when the Emperor's cousin Isaac Angelus, a normally inoffensive nobleman who had incurred Andronicus's displeasure when a soothsayer had identified him as successor to the throne, leaped on the imperial henchman sent to arrest him and ran him through with his sword. Then, riding at full gallop to St Sophia, he proudly announced to all present what he had done. The news spread: crowds began to collect, among them Isaac's uncle John Ducas and many others who, though they had played no part in the crime, knew that in the existing atmosphere of suspicion they would be unable to dissociate themselves from it. Therefore, says Nicetas, 'seeing that they would be taken, and having the image of death graven on their souls, they appealed to all the people to rally to their aid'.

And the people responded. The next morning, having spent the night in the torchlit St Sophia, they hurried through the city calling every householder to arms. The prisons were broken open, the prisoners joined forces with their deliverers. Meanwhile, in the great church, Isaac Angelus was proclaimed *basileus*.

One of the vergers climbed on a ladder above the high altar and took down the crown of Constantine to place it on his head. Isaac showed reluctance to accept it – not for reasons of modesty nor because of any indifference towards the imperial diadem but because he feared that so audacious an enterprise might cost him his life. Ducas, on the other hand, stepped forward at once, and taking off his cap presented his own bald head, which shone like the full moon, to receive the crown. But the assembled people cried out loudly that they had suffered too much misery from the grizzled head of Andronicus, and that they would have no more senile or decrepit Emperors, least of all one with a long beard divided in two like a pitchfork.

When the news of the revolution reached Andronicus on his country estate of Meludion, he returned to the capital confident in his ability to reassert his control. Going straight to the Great Palace at the mouth of the Golden Horn he ordered his guard to loose its arrows on the mob and, finding the soldiers slow to obey, seized a bow and began furiously shooting on his own account. Then, suddenly, he understood. Throwing off his purple cloak and boots, he covered his head with a little pointed bonnet 'such as the barbarians wear' and, hastily embarking his child-wife and his favourite concubine Maraptica – 'an excellent flautist, with whom he was besottedly in love' – on to a waiting galley, he fled with them up the Bosphorus.

Simultaneously the mob broke into the palace, falling on everything of value that it contained. Twelve hundred pounds of gold bullion alone and three thousand of silver were carried off, and jewels and works of art without number. Not even the imperial chapel was spared: icons were stripped from the walls, chalices snatched from the altar. And the most venerable treasure of all – the reliquary containing the letter written by Jesus Christ in his own hand to King Abgar of Edessa – disappeared, never to be seen again.

The Emperor, the Empress and Maraptica were soon caught. The ladies, who behaved throughout with dignity and courage, were spared; but Andronicus, bound and fettered with a heavy chain about his neck, was brought before Isaac for punishment. His right hand was cut off and he was thrown into prison; then, after several days without food or water, he was blinded in one eye and brought forth on a scrawny camel to face the fury of his erstwhile subjects. They had suffered much from him, and were eager for their revenge. As Nicetas reports:

Everything that was lowest and most contemptible in the mob seemed to combine . . . They beat him, stoned him, goaded him with spikes, pelted him with filth. A woman of the streets poured a bucket of boiling water on his head . . . Then, dragging him from the camel, they hung him up by his feet. He endured all these torments and many others that I cannot describe, with incredible fortitude, speaking no other word among this demented crowd of his persecutors, but *O Lord, have pity on me; why dost thou trample on a poor reed that is already quite broken?* . . . At last, after much agony, he died, carrying his remaining hand to his mouth; which he did, in the opinion of some, that he might suck the blood that flowed from one of his wounds.

He had been, as Eustathius of Thessalonica observed, a man so full of contradictions that he can with equal justice be extravagantly praised or bitterly condemned; a colossus who possessed every gift save that of moderation and who died as dramatically as he had lived; a hero and a villain, a preserver and a destroyer, a paragon and a warning.

Isaac Angelus, when at last he accepted the crown, inherited a desperate situation. At Mosynopolis, the invaders' advance column was less than two hundred miles from Constantinople; their fleet, meanwhile, was already in the Marmara, awaiting the army's arrival before launching its attack. Immediately on his accession, he sent Baldwin an offer of peace; when it was refused, he did what Andronicus should have done months before – appointed the ablest of his generals, Alexius Branas, to the supreme command of all five armies, sending with him the most massive reinforcements that the Empire could provide. The effect was instantaneous: the Greeks were infused with a new spirit. They saw too their enemy grown overconfident; no longer expecting resistance, the Sicilian soldiers had dropped their guard and relaxed their discipline. Carefully selecting his place and his moment, Branas swooped down upon them, routed them completely and pursued them all the way back to the main camp at Amphipolis.

It was, wrote Nicetas, a visible manifestation of the Divine Power:

Those men who, but a short while before, had threatened to overturn the very mountains, were as astonished as if they had been struck by lightning. The Romans,[1] on the other hand, no longer having any commerce with fear, burned with the desire to fall upon them, as an eagle falls upon a feeble bird.

At Dimitriza,[2] just outside Amphipolis on the banks of the river Strymon – now the Struma – Baldwin at last consented to discuss peace. Why he did so remains a mystery. The defeat at Mosynopolis had not affected the main body of his army, encamped in good order around him. He still held Thessalonica. Though the new Emperor in Constantinople was not senile as his predecessor had been, he was not in his first youth; and his claim to the throne was certainly weaker than that of Andronicus or, arguably, of Manuel's nephew Alexius, who had accompanied the army all the way from Messina and was seldom far from Baldwin's side. But winter was approaching, and the autumn rains in Thrace fall heavy and chill. To an army that had counted on spending Christmas in Constantinople, Mosynopolis had probably proved more demoralizing than its strategic importance really warranted.

1 The Byzantines always so described themselves, seeing their Empire as the unbroken continuation of that of ancient Rome. The word *Romiòs* is still used, on occasion, by their descendants today. See Patrick Leigh Fermor's brilliant essay on the subject in *Roumeli* (London, 1966).

2 This place-name is something of a mystery, since there is no trace of it along the Strymon. Chalandon calls it Demetiza, then adds in brackets – without giving his authority – the obviously Turkish word Demechissar. If he is right, it is tempting to see this word as a corruption of Demir-Hisar, i.e. Iron Fort; in which case we may be talking about the modern Greek town of Siderokastron, which today stands just where Dimitriza might have been expected to be.

Alternatively, Baldwin may have had a darker purpose. The Greeks certainly claimed that he did. On the pretext that he intended to take advantage of the peace negotiations to catch them in their turn unprepared, they resolved to strike first; and on 7 November they did so – 'awaiting', Nicetas himself assures us, 'neither the sound of the trumpets nor the orders of their commander'. The Sicilian army was taken unawares. Its soldiers resisted as best they could, then turned and fled. Some were cut down as they ran; many more were drowned as they tried to cross the Strymon, now swift and swollen from recent rains; others still, including both Baldwin and Richard of Acerra, were taken prisoner – as was Alexius Comnenus, whom Isaac subsequently blinded for his treachery. Those who escaped found their way back to Thessalonica, where a few managed to pick up ships in which to return to Sicily. Since, however, the bulk of the Sicilian fleet was still lying off Constantinople waiting for the land army to arrive, the majority were not so lucky. The Thessalonians rose up against them, taking a full and bloody revenge for all that they had suffered three months before. Of the titanic army which had set out so confidently in the summer, it was a poor shadow that now plodded back through the icy mountain passes to Durazzo.

Byzantium was saved. Nevertheless, the Byzantines would have done well to take the Sicilian invasion as a warning. Other Western eyes were fixed covetously on their Empire. Only twenty years later Constantinople was again to face attack. Next time it would succeed.

10

The Fall of Jerusalem

[1185–98]

The date of the conquest of Jerusalem was the anniversary of the Prophet's ascension to Paradise . . . The Sultan held court to receive congratulations . . . His manner was at once humble and majestic as he sat among the lawyers and scholars, his pious courtiers. His countenance shone with joy, his door was wide open, his benevolence spread far and wide. There was free access to him, his words were heard, his actions prospered, his carpet was kissed, his face glowed, his perfume was sweet, his affection all-embracing . . . The back of his hand was the *qibla* of kisses, and the palm of his hand the *Ka'ba* of hope.

Imad ed-Din al-Isfahani, Secretary to Saladin

The house of Angelus, which had thus found greatness so suddenly and unexpectedly thrust upon it, was neither old nor particularly distinguished. Indeed, it would probably have remained virtually unknown outside the Lydian city of Philadelphia had not one of the daughters of Alexius I, the *porphyrogenita* Theodora, fallen in love with Isaac's grandfather Constantine Angelus and married him. Thenceforth the family's rise was swift. By the time of Manuel's accession it was one of the most prominent in Constantinople, providing the Emperor with several military commanders of varying quality; and when the time came for the feudal aristocracy to make a stand against the excesses of the last of the Comneni, men found it natural that an Angelus should take the lead.

Nevertheless, it was a sad day for the Empire when he did so; for of all the families who at one time or another wore the imperial crown of Byzantium, the Angeli were the worst. Their supremacy was mercifully short: the three Angelus Emperors – Isaac II, Alexius III and Alexius IV – reigned, from first to last, a mere nineteen years. But each was in his own way disastrous, and together they were responsible for the greatest catastrophe that Constantinople was ever to suffer until its final fall.

Isaac's reign started well enough. In their retreat, the Normans had evacuated not only Thessalonica but also Durazzo and Corfu. Admittedly they had managed to keep the neighbouring islands of Cephalonia – where the great Guiscard had died and Zacynthus, which were lost for ever to the Empire; but even these seemed a small price to pay for what many Byzantines saw as a miraculous deliverance. Meanwhile the second of the Empire's principal enemies, King Béla III of Hungary, proved only too happy to sign a peace treaty, sealing it by giving Isaac the hand in marriage of his ten-year-old daughter Margaret, who adopted the Byzantine name of Maria. Some of the new Emperor's more sensitive subjects may have regretted that he found it necessary to blind both the surviving sons of his predecessor – one of whom died almost immediately afterwards – but for the majority the beginning of his reign was, as Nicetas writes, like a gentle spring after a bitter winter, or a peaceful calm after a furious tempest.

They were soon to be disillusioned. Andronicus, for all his faults, had done much to stamp out corruption; Isaac, continues Nicetas, sold government offices like vegetables in a market. Bribery once again became the rule, the provincial tax-collectors reverted to their old extortionate ways, the army and navy fell into a demoralized decline as the funds which should have gone to their maintenance were used to buy off potential enemies or were frittered away on ever more elaborate court entertainments. Meanwhile the theme system, which had been the backbone of administration and defence, effectively disintegrated; and the feudal aristocracy, which Andronicus had held firmly in check, grew steadily more obstreperous.

Not that the Emperor was entirely inactive. Though he made no effort to recover the lost Ionian islands, Cyprus or even Cilicia (which had fallen to the Armenians), he did at least show considerable energy in the putting down of rebellions and the protection of his frontiers, leading expeditions in 1186–7 against insurgents in Bulgaria and Wallachia; but he was unable to prevent the formation by two local noblemen of the Second Bulgarian Empire, and a later campaign in 1190 was to end in catastrophe when his army was ambushed and he himself narrowly escaped with his life. Meanwhile the Serbian Grand Zhupan Stephen Nemanja had allied himself with the rebels, and had made full use of the hostilities to increase his own power. Eventually Stephen agreed to a treaty with Byzantium, by the terms of which his son married the Emperor's niece and was given the title of *sebastocrator*; but by now it was clear to everyone that Serbia was, like Bulgaria, an independent state. The days of Byzantine supremacy in the Balkans were over. They would not return.

And worse was to come; for Byzantium – and indeed all Europe – was now swept up in a new crisis. In the middle of October 1187 came dreadful news: the Saracens had taken Jerusalem.

To any dispassionate observer of affairs in the Levant, the Saracens' capture of Jerusalem must have seemed inevitable. On the Muslim side there had been the steady rise of Saladin, a leader of genius who had vowed to recover the Holy City for his faith; on the Christian, nothing but the sad spectacle of the three remaining Frankish states of Jerusalem, Tripoli and Antioch, all governed by mediocrities and torn apart by internal struggles for power. Jerusalem itself was further burdened, throughout the crucial period of Saladin's ascendancy, by the corresponding decline of its leper King, Baldwin IV. When he came to the throne at the age of thirteen in 1174, the disease was already upon him; eleven years later he was dead. Not surprisingly, he left no issue. At the one moment when wise and resolute leadership was essential if the Kingdom were to be saved, the crown of Jerusalem devolved upon his nephew – a child of eight.

The death of this new infant King, Baldwin V, in the following year might have been considered a blessing in disguise; but the opportunity of finding a true leader was thrown away and the throne passed to his stepfather, Guy of Lusignan, a weak, querulous figure with a record of incapacity which fully merited the scorn in which he was held by most of his compatriots. Jerusalem was thus in a state bordering on civil war when, in May 1187, Saladin declared his long-awaited *jihad* and crossed the Jordan into Frankish territory. Under the miserable Guy, the Christian defeat was assured. On 3 July he led the largest army his kingdom had ever assembled across the mountains of Galilee towards Tiberias, where Saladin was laying siege to the castle. After a long day's march in the most torrid season of the year, this army was obliged to camp on a waterless plateau; and the next day, exhausted by the heat and half-mad with thirst, beneath a little double-summited hill known as the Horns of Hattin, it was surrounded by the Muslim army and cut to pieces.

It remained only for the Saracens to mop up the isolated Christian fortresses one by one. Tiberias fell on the day after Hattin; Acre followed; Nablus, Jaffa, Sidon and Beirut capitulated in quick succession. Wheeling south, Saladin took Ascalon by storm and received the surrender of Gaza without a struggle. Now he was ready for Jerusalem. The defenders of the Holy City resisted heroically for twelve days; but on 2 October, with the walls already undermined by Muslim sappers, they knew that the end was near. Their leader, Balian of Ibelin – King Guy having been taken prisoner after Hattin – went personally to Saladin to discuss terms for surrender.

Saladin, who knew Balian well and liked him, was neither bloodthirsty nor vindictive: after some negotiation he agreed that every Christian in Jerusalem should be allowed to redeem himself by payment of a suitable ransom. Of the twenty thousand poor who had no means of raising the money, seven thousand would be freed on payment of a lump sum by the various Christian authorities. That same day the conqueror led his army into the city; and for the first time in eighty-eight years, on the anniversary of the day on which Mohammed was carried in his sleep from Jerusalem to Paradise, his green banners fluttered over the Temple area from which he had been gathered up, and the sacred imprint of his foot was once again exposed to the adoration of the Faithful.

Everywhere, order was preserved. There was no murder, no blood-shed, no looting. The thirteen thousand poor, for whom ransom money could not be raised, remained in the city; but Saladin's brother and lieutenant, al-Adil, asked for a thousand of them as a reward for his services and immediately set them free. Another seven hundred were given to the Patriarch, and five hundred to Balian of Ibelin; then Saladin himself spontaneously liberated all the old, all the husbands whose wives had been ransomed and finally all the widows and children. Few Christians ultimately found their way to slavery. This was not the first time that Saladin had shown the magnanimity for which he would soon be famous through East and West alike; but never before had he done so on such a scale. His restraint was the more remarkable in that he could not have forgotten the massacre that had followed the arrival of the Christians in 1099.[1] The Christians, for their part, had not forgotten it either; and they could not fail to be struck by the contrast. Saladin might be their arch-enemy; but he had set them an example of chivalry which was to remain ever before them in the months to come.

When the news of the fall of Jerusalem reached the West, Pope Urban III died of shock; but his successor Gregory VIII lost no time in calling upon Christendom to take up arms for its recovery; and, as the forces gathered, it became plain to Isaac that the coming Crusade would prove a more dangerous threat to his Empire than either of its predecessors. At its head would be Byzantium's old enemy, Frederick Barbarossa, who

1 See p. 42.

was known to be in communication with the Sultan of Iconium and was already building up support among the newly-independent principalities in the Balkan peninsula. Scarcely more friendly was King William of Sicily, who had also declared his intention of taking the Cross. Fortunately for Byzantium William died in November 1189, aged only thirty-six and leaving no issue; but the marriage nearly four years before of his aunt Constance, to whom his crown now passed, to Barbarossa's eldest son Henry was a clear enough indication that Sicilian foreign policy would remain unchanged. Of the two other Western sovereigns who had agreed to participate, Richard Coeur-de-Lion of England was William's brother-in-law,[1] while Philip Augustus of France, remembering the recent sufferings inflicted on his sister Agnes, was unlikely to be any better disposed.

Richard and Philip Augustus elected to travel to the Holy Land by sea, bypassing the Empire altogether. They consequently play little part in this narrative – though it should perhaps be recorded that in May 1191 Richard took the opportunity of an unscheduled stop in Cyprus to conquer the island from Isaac Comnenus (whom he sent off in silver chains to prison in Tripoli), handing it over first to the Templars and then in the following year to Guy of Lusignan, the deposed King of Jerusalem. Frederick Barbarossa on the other hand preferred the land route, setting out from Ratisbon in May 1189 with an army variously estimated at between a hundred and a hundred and fifty thousand – the largest ever yet to leave on a Crusade. He had naturally informed the Emperor of his intentions and had even signed an agreement with Byzantine emissaries at Nuremberg some months before; but Isaac was well aware of his intrigues with the Balkan princes – to say nothing of the Seljuk Sultan – and his misgivings were only strengthened when he heard of the magnificent reception granted to the Western Emperor by Stephen Nemanja on his arrival in Nish, in the course of which both the Serbs and the Bulgars had offered to take an oath of allegiance and to conclude an alliance against Byzantium. He next sent the two former ambassadors to the German court, Constantine Cantacuzenus and John Ducas, to await the great army at the frontier; but instead of greeting Barbarossa as instructed in their Emperor's name they unexpectedly turned their coats and encouraged him to attack their master. Frederick, greatly cheered, occupied Philippopolis as if it were a conquered city.

1 In 1177 William had married the twelve-year-old Joanna, third and youngest daughter of King Henry II of England.

By this time Isaac was close to panic; and when envoys arrived from Barbarossa – with no other object than to discuss the transport of his army to Asia – he lost his head completely and flung them into prison, presumably intending to hold them as security for Frederick's behaviour. It was a disastrous move. The enraged Emperor immediately ordered his eldest son Henry – who had remained in Germany – to secure papal blessing for a Crusade against the schismatic Greeks, to collect a fleet and to bring it with all speed to Constantinople. Meanwhile he sent his second son Frederick of Swabia to take the Thracian town of Didymotichum as a counter-hostage. Isaac, faced with the prospect of an amphibious attack on his capital, could only capitulate. Discussions continued spasmodically through the winter, as a final result of which he promised to provide the necessary transport and provisions for the journey across Anatolia in return for an undertaking by Frederick to cross by the Dardanelles rather than the Bosphorus, thereby avoiding Constantinople altogether.

Once over the straits, the imperial army marched via Philadelphia, Laodicea and Myriocephalum – where the whitened bones of Manuel's soldiers still littered the battlefield – to the Seljuk capital at Iconium Constant harassment by bands of mounted Turkish archers had already warned Frederick that the Sultan, despite their past communications, had no intention of allowing the army unimpeded passage through his territory; and it now emerged that he had sent an army of his own, under his son Qutb ed-Din, to protect the city. Only after a pitched battle before the walls was Frederick able to force an entry. Then, after a week's rest, he pressed on again through the Taurus towards the coastal city of Seleucia.

On 10 June 1190, after a long and exhausting journey through the mountains, Frederick Barbarossa led his troops out on to the flat coastal plain. The heat was savage, and the little river Calycadnus[1] that ran past Seleucia to the sea must have been a welcome sight. Frederick, who was riding alone a short distance ahead of the army, spurred his horse towards it. He was never seen alive again. Whether he dismounted to drink and was swept off his feet by the current, whether his horse slipped in the mud and threw him, whether the shock of falling into the icy mountain water was too much for his tired old body – he was nearing seventy – we shall never know. He was rescued, but too late. Most of his followers reached the river to find their Emperor lying dead on the bank.

---

1 In modern Turkish the Calycadnus is now less euphonically known as the Göksu.

Almost immediately, the army began to disintegrate. The Duke of Swabia assumed command, but he proved no substitute for his father. Many of the German princelings returned to Europe; others took ship for Tyre, the only major port of Outremer still in Christian hands; the rump of the army, carrying with it the Emperor's body not very successfully preserved in vinegar, marched grimly on, though it lost many more of its men in an ambush as it entered Syria. The survivors who finally limped in to Antioch had no more fight left in them. By this time, too, what was left of Frederick had gone the same way as his army; his rapidly decomposing remnants were hastily buried in the cathedral, where they remained for another seventy-eight years – until a Mameluke army under the Sultan Baibars burnt the whole building, together with most of the city, to the ground.

Fortunately for Outremer, Richard and Philip Augustus arrived with their armies essentially intact; and it was thanks to them that the Third Crusade – although, since it failed to recapture Jerusalem, it too must ultimately be accounted a failure – was at least somewhat less humiliating than the Second. Acre was retaken, to become capital of the Kingdom of Jerusalem for another century until the Mameluke conquest; but that Kingdom, henceforth reduced to the short coastal strip between Tyre and Jaffa, was a pale reflection of what Crusader Palestine had once been. It was to struggle on for another century, and when it finally fell to Baibars in 1291 the only surprise was that it had lasted so long.

On Christmas Day, 1194, by virtue of his marriage nine years before to the Princess Constance, Frederick Barbarossa's son Henry VI had received the royal crown of Sicily in Palermo Cathedral. His wife was not with him. Pregnant for the first time at the age of forty, she was determined on two things: first, that her child should be born safely; second, that it should be seen to be unquestionably hers. She did not put off her journey to Sicily, but travelled more slowly and in her own time; and she had got no further than the little town of Jesi, some twenty miles west of Ancona, when she felt the pains of childbirth upon her. There on the day after her husband's coronation, in a large tent erected in the main square to which free entrance was allowed to any matron of the town who wished to witness the birth, she brought forth her only son whom, a day or two later, she presented in the same square to the assembled inhabitants, proudly suckling him at her breast. Of that son, Frederick – later to be nicknamed *Stupor Mundi*, the Astonishment of the World – we shall hear more as our story continues.

At the time of Frederick's birth, his father was already contemplating a new Crusade. Not surprisingly, Henry saw the débâcle that had followed his own father's death as a humiliation for the Empire. Had Barbarossa lived, he had little doubt that Jerusalem would have been recovered; it was plainly his duty to retrieve the family honour. In doing so, he would also increase his prestige among the nobility of the Empire, both lay and ecclesiastical, and perhaps improve his own distinctly chilly relations with the Papacy, thereby indirectly facilitating his acceptance by his Sicilian subjects. In Easter week of 1195 he took the Cross; on Easter Day – 2 April – at Bari, he issued his public summons to the Crusade; and a few days later he wrote a firm letter to the Emperor Isaac, making it clear to him that he was expected to contribute to the coming expedition rather than to obstruct it – more specifically by the provision of a fleet. For good measure he added a demand that Isaac should return to him that part of the Balkan peninsula between Durazzo and Thessalonica formerly conquered by the Sicilian army, and finally that the *basileus* should pay compensation for the damages suffered by his father while crossing Byzantine territory.

The letter was a typical piece of imperial bluster; but it missed its target. On 8 April 1195 – quite possibly on the very day that his letter was written – Isaac Angelus fell victim to a *coup* engineered by his elder brother Alexius, who deposed and blinded him and had himself crowned Emperor in his stead. If Isaac had been a poor Emperor, it can only be said that Alexius III was a good deal worse. Given his weakness and cowardice, to say nothing of his lack of any semblance of administrative ability, it is difficult to understand why he should have coveted the throne as he did. Isaac had at least displayed some degree of energy where the Empire's external affairs were concerned; Alexius showed none. During the eight years of his reign the disintegration of the Empire became steadily more apparent, and he was to leave it, as we shall see, in a state of total collapse.

To Henry VI, these developments in Constantinople were of little interest; he had no intention of relaxing the pressure, and he soon discovered that Alexius was every bit as easily manipulated as his predecessor. Thus, when he demanded a heavy tribute to pay for his mercenary troops, the terrified Emperor immediately instituted a special tax known as the *Alamanikon*, or 'German levy', which made him more than ever unpopular with his subjects; and when even this proved inadequate, he supplemented it by stripping the precious ornaments from the imperial tombs in the church of the Holy Apostles. Two years later, in May 1197, Alexius was obliged to stand impotently by while his niece Irene, daughter of the blinded Isaac, was married off by Henry to his own younger brother, Philip of Swabia. This was a brilliant move on Henry's part. He had found Irene in Palermo, where she had formerly been married to the son of Tancred of Lecce, a bastard cousin of King William of Sicily who had seized the throne on William's death and had ruled, competently if illegitimately, over Sicily until his own death a little over four years later. Whether or not the rumours were true that Isaac had promised to accept the couple as his heirs, their marriage enabled Henry to pose as a defender of their rights; and it was to do much to strengthen Philip's position during the Fourth Crusade.

But the Fourth Crusade was not yet; and so what, it may be asked, became of the great expedition proclaimed by Henry in 1195? Many of the foremost names in Germany had responded to his call: the Archbishops of Mainz and of Bremen, no fewer than nine bishops – one of whom, the Bishop of Hildesheim, was Chancellor of the Empire – the Dukes Henry of Brabant (Count-Palatine of the Rhine), Henry of Brunswick, Frederick of Austria, Berthold of Dalmatia and Ulrich of Carinthia, and countless lesser nobles. They had sailed from Messina throughout the summer of 1197 and on their arrival had immediately advanced against the Saracen foe. During the first weeks of their campaign they were relatively successful, advancing north as far as Sidon and Beirut, which were abandoned and destroyed at their approach. By the end of October, however, the news reached them that on 28 September Henry, who had remained in Sicily to deal with a major insurrection, had died of a fever at Messina. Many of the greater nobles decided to return at once to protect their interests in the later power struggle, and when later reports told of the outbreak of civil war in Germany most of the others followed. Thus it was that when, at the beginning of February 1198, the German rank and file were preparing to confront an Egyptian army advancing up from Sinai, they suddenly realized that their leaders had deserted them and panicked. There followed a headlong flight northward to the safety of Tyre – where, fortunately, their ships were waiting. A week later they were gone. The second German expedition had been, if anything, a still greater fiasco than the first.

The Fourth Crusade

[1198–1205]

You took the Cross upon your shoulders; and on that Cross and on the Holy Gospels you swore that you would pass over Christian lands without violence, turning neither to right nor to left. You assured us that your only enemy was the Saracen, and that his blood only would be shed . . .

Far from carrying the Cross, you profane it and trample it underfoot. You claim to be in quest of a pearl beyond price, but in truth you fling that most precious of all pearls, which is the body of our Saviour, into the mud. The Saracens themselves show less impiety.

Nicetas Choniates,
'Alexius Ducas', IV, iv

The end of the twelfth century found Europe in confusion. The Empires of both East and West were rudderless; Norman Sicily was gone, never to return. Germany was torn apart by civil war over the imperial succession and both England and France were similarly – though less violently – occupied with inheritance problems following the death of Richard Coeur-de-Lion in 1199. Of the luminaries of Christendom, one only was firmly in control: Pope Innocent III, who had ascended the papal throne in 1198 and had immediately proclaimed yet another Crusade. The lack of crowned heads to lead it did not worry him; previous experience had shown that Kings and princes, stirring up as they invariably did national rivalries and endless questions of precedence and protocol, tended to be more trouble than they were worth. A few great nobles would suit his purpose admirably; and Innocent was still casting about for suitable candidates when he received a letter from Count Tibald of Champagne.

Tibald was the younger brother of Henry of Champagne, Count of Troyes, who had been ruler of the Kingdom of Jerusalem – though he was never crowned King – from the time of his marriage to Amalric I's daughter Isabella in 1192 until his accidental fall from a window of his palace at Acre in 1197. He had not accompanied Henry to Palestine; but as the grandson of Louis VII and the nephew of both Philip Augustus and Coeur-de-Lion, he had the Crusades in his blood. He was energetic and ambitious; and when, in the course of a tournament at his castle of Ecri on the Aisne, he and his friends were addressed by the celebrated preacher Fulk of Neuilly, who was travelling through France rallying support for a new expedition to the East, he responded immediately. Once he had sent a message to Pope Innocent that he had taken the Cross, there could be no other leader.

It was clear to everyone, however, that major problems lay ahead. Coeur-de-Lion, before leaving Palestine, had given it as his opinion that the weakest point of the Muslim East was Egypt, and that it was here that any future expeditions should be directed. It followed that the new army would have to travel by sea, and would need ships in a quantity that could be obtained from one source only: the Venetian Republic. Thus it was that during the first week of Lent in the year 1201, a party of six knights led by Geoffrey de Villehardouin, Marshal of Champagne, arrived in Venice. They made their request at a special meeting of the Great Council, and a week later they received their answer. The Republic would provide transport for four and a half thousand knights with their horses, nine thousand squires and twenty thousand foot-soldiers, with food for nine months. The cost would be 84,000 silver marks. In addition Venice would provide fifty fully-equipped galleys at her own expense, on condition that she received one-half of the territories conquered.

This reply was conveyed to Geoffrey and his colleagues by the Doge, Enrico Dandolo. In all Venetian history there is no more astonishing figure. We cannot be sure of his age when, on 1 January 1193, he was raised to the ducal throne; the story goes that he was eighty-five and already stone-blind, though this seems hardly credible when we read of his energy – indeed, his heroism – a decade later on the walls of Constantinople. But even if he was in only his middle seventies, he would still have been, at the time of the Fourth Crusade, an octogenarian of several years' standing. A dedicated, almost fanatical patriot, he had spent much of his life in the service of Venice, and in 1172 had been one of the Republic's ambassadors on the abortive peace mission to Manuel Comnenus.

Did his loss of sight date from this time? According to his later namesake, the historian Andrea Dandolo, his arrogance and stubbornness antagonized Manuel to such a point that he actually had him arrested and partially blinded; on the other hand a contemporary and so possibly more reliable source – an appendix to the *Altino Chronicle* – reports that the next Venetian embassy to Constantinople was sent only after the three previous ambassadors had returned safe and sound. This, combined with what we know of Manuel's character and the absence of any other references to what must have created a major outcry in Venice had it in fact occurred, suggests that imperial displeasure cannot be blamed on this occasion. Another theory[1] holds that while in Constantinople Dandolo had been involved in a brawl, in the course of which his eyes had been injured. This too seems improbable in view of the *Altino* testimony; besides, he was not even then in his first youth, but a mature diplomatist of fifty or so. Thirty years later, at any rate, the facts are no longer in doubt. Geoffrey de Villehardouin, who knew him well, assures us that 'although his eyes appeared normal, he could not see a hand in front of his face, having lost his sight after a head wound'.

Fortunately for posterity, Geoffrey has left a full record not only of the Crusade itself but also of these preliminary negotiations. No one was better placed to do so, and few men of his time could have done it better. His style has clarity and pace, and in his opening pages he gives us a vivid account of Venetian democracy in action. The Doge, he writes,

assembled at least ten thousand men in the church of St Mark, the most beautiful that there is, to hear the Mass and to pray God for His guidance. And after the Mass he summoned the envoys and besought them, that they themselves should ask of the people the services they required. Geoffrey de Villehardouin, Marshal of Champagne, spoke by consent for the others . . . Then the Doge and people raised their hands and cried aloud with a single voice, 'We grant it! We grant it!' And so great was the noise and tumult that the very earth seemed to tremble underfoot.

On the following day the contracts were concluded. Geoffrey notes in passing that the agreement did not mention Egypt as the immediate objective. He gives no explanation; but he and his colleagues were almost certainly afraid – and with good reason as it turned out – that the news would be unpopular with the rank and file, for whom Jerusalem was the only legitimate goal for a Crusade and who would see no reason to waste time anywhere else. Moreover an Egyptian expedition would necessitate a dangerous landing on a hostile shore, as opposed to a quiet

1 Runciman, *A History of the Crusades*, Vol. III, p. 114.

anchorage at Christian Acre and an opportunity to recover from the journey before going into battle. The Venetians for their part would have been only too happy to cooperate in the deception, for they too had a secret. At that very moment their own ambassadors were in Cairo, discussing a highly profitable trade agreement; and in the course of these discussions they are believed to have given a categorical undertaking not to be party to any attack on Egyptian territory.

Such considerations, however, could not be allowed to affect plans for the Crusade, by which still greater prizes might be won; and it was agreed that the Crusaders should all forgather in Venice on the feast of St John, 24 June 1202, when the fleet would be ready for them.

Just how Enrico Dandolo proposed to deflect the Frankish Crusaders from Egypt we shall never know. He and his agents may have been partly responsible for leaking the Egyptian plans through the countries of the West; certainly these became public knowledge in a remarkably short time. But if he hoped that the popular reaction to this news would induce the leaders to change their minds, he was mistaken. It was the followers who changed theirs. Many, on hearing of their proposed destination, renounced the Crusade altogether; many more decided to head for Palestine regardless, arranging their own transport from Marseille to one of the Apulian ports. On the day appointed for the rendezvous in Venice, the army that gathered on the Lido numbered less than one-third of what had been expected.

For those who had arrived as planned, the situation was embarrassing in the extreme. Venice had performed her share of the bargain: there lay the fleet, war galleys as well as transports – no Christian man, writes Geoffrey, had ever seen richer or finer – but sufficient for an army three times the size of that assembled. With their numbers so dramatically reduced, the Crusaders could not hope to pay the Venetians the money they had promised. When their leader, the Marquis Boniface of Montferrat – Tibald of Champagne having died shortly after Villehardouin's return the previous year – arrived in Venice rather late, he found the whole expedition in jeopardy. Not only were the Venetians refusing point-blank to allow a single ship to leave port till the money was forthcoming; they were even talking of cutting off provisions to the waiting army – a threat made more serious in that the bulk of that army was confined to the Lido and strictly forbidden to set foot in the city itself. This last measure was not intended to be deliberately offensive; it was a normal precaution on such occasions, designed to prevent disturbances of the peace or the spread of infection. But it scarcely improved the atmosphere. Boniface emptied his own coffers, many of the other knights and barons did likewise, and every man in the army was pressed to give all he could; but the total raised, including quantities of gold and silver plate, still fell short by 34,000 marks of what was owing.

For as long as the contributions continued to come in, old Dandolo kept the Crusaders in suspense. Then, as soon as he was sure that there was no more to be got, he came forward with an offer. The Venetian city of Zara,[1] he pointed out, had recently fallen into the hands of the King of Hungary. If, before embarking on the Crusade proper, the Franks would agree to assist Venice in its recapture, settlement of their debt might perhaps be postponed. It was a typically cynical proposal, and as soon as he heard of it Pope Innocent sent an urgent message forbidding its acceptance. But the Crusaders, as he later came to understand, had no choice.

There followed another of those ceremonies in St Mark's that Enrico Dandolo, despite his years, handled so beautifully. Before a congregation that included all the leading Franks, he addressed his subjects. Geoffrey de Villehardouin, who was there, reports his speech as follows:

'Signors, you are joined with the worthiest people in the world, for the highest enterprise ever undertaken. I myself am old and feeble; I need rest: my body is infirm. But I know that no man can lead you and govern you as I, your Lord, can do. If therefore you will allow me to direct and defend you by taking the Cross while my son remains in my place to guard the Republic, I am ready to live and to die with you and the pilgrims.'

And when they heard him, they cried with one voice, 'We pray God that you will do this thing, and come with us!'

So he came down from the pulpit and moved up to the altar, and knelt there, weeping; and he had the cross sewn on to his great cotton hat, so determined was he that all men should see it.

Thus it was that on 8 November 1202 the army of the Fourth Crusade set sail from Venice. Its 480 ships, led by the galley of the Doge himself, 'painted vermilion, with a silken vermilion awning spread above, cymbals clashing and four trumpeters sounding from the bows', were however bound neither for Egypt nor for Palestine. Just a week later, Zara was taken and sacked. The fighting that broke out almost immediately afterwards between the Franks and the Venetians over the division of the spoils scarcely augured well for the future, but peace was eventually

---

1 Now Zadar, on the Dalmatian coast.

restored and the two groups settled themselves in different parts of the city for the winter. Meanwhile the news of what had happened had reached the Pope. Outraged, he at once excommunicated the entire expedition. Though he was later to limit his ban to the Venetians alone, the Crusade could hardly be said to have got off to a good start.

But worse was to follow. Early in the new year a messenger arrived with a letter for Boniface from Philip of Swabia – not only Barbarossa's son and the brother of Emperor Henry VI, whose death five years before had left empty the imperial throne of the West, but also the son-in-law of the deposed and blinded *basileus* Isaac Angelus. Now it happened that in the previous year Isaac's young son, another Alexius, had escaped from the prison in which he and his father were being held; and Philip's court had been his obvious place of refuge. There he had met Boniface shortly before the latter's departure for Venice, and there the three of them may have roughed out the plan which Philip now formally proposed in his letter. If the Crusade would escort the young Alexius to Constantinople and enthrone him there in place of his usurper uncle, Alexius for his part would finance its subsequent conquest of Egypt, supplying in addition ten thousand soldiers of his own and afterwards maintaining five hundred knights in the Holy Land at his own expense. He would also submit the Church of Constantinople to the authority of Rome.

To Boniface the scheme had much to recommend it. Apart from what appeared to be the long-term advantages to the Crusade itself and the opportunity to pay off the still outstanding debt to Venice, he also smelt the possibility of considerable personal gain. When he put the idea to Dandolo – to whom, also, it probably came as a less than total surprise – the old Doge accepted it with enthusiasm. He had been in no way chastened by his excommunication; this was not the first time that Venice had defied papal wishes, and it would not be the last. His earlier military and diplomatic experiences had left him with little love for Byzantium; besides, the present Emperor had on his accession made intolerable difficulties over renewing the trading concessions granted by his predecessor. Genoese and Pisan competition was becoming ever more fierce; if Venice were to retain her former hold on the Eastern markets, decisive action would be required. Such action, finally, would involve a welcome postponement of the Egyptian expedition.

The Crusading army proved readier to accept the change of plan than might have been expected. A few of its members refused outright and set off for Palestine on their own; the majority, however, were only too happy to lend themselves to a scheme which promised to strengthen and enrich the Crusade while also restoring the unity of Christendom. Ever since the great schism – and even before – the Byzantines had been unpopular in the West. They had contributed little or nothing to previous Crusades, during which they were generally believed to have betrayed the Christian cause on several occasions. Young Alexius's offer of active assistance was a welcome change and not to be despised. Finally, there must have been many among the more materialistically inclined who shared their leader's hope of personal reward. The average Frank knew practically nothing about Byzantium, but all had been brought up on stories of its immense wealth. And to any medieval army, whether or not it bore the Cross of Christ on its standard, a fabulously rich city meant one thing only: loot.

Young Alexius himself arrived in Zara towards the end of April; and a few days later the fleet set sail, stopping at Durazzo and Corfu, in both of which he was acclaimed as the rightful Emperor of the East. On 24 June 1203, a year to the day after the rendezvous in Venice, it dropped anchor off Constantinople. The Crusaders were astounded. Geoffrey reports:

You may imagine how they gazed, all those who had never before seen Constantinople. For when they saw those high ramparts and the strong towers with which it was completely encircled, and the splendid palaces and soaring churches – so many that but for the evidence of their own eyes they would never have believed it – and the length and the breadth of that city which of all others is sovereign, they never thought that there could be so rich and powerful a place on earth. And mark you that there was not a man so bold that he did not tremble at the sight; nor was this any wonder, for never since the creation of the world was there so great an enterprise.

Alexius III had had plenty of warning of the arrival of the expedition, but had characteristically made no preparations for the city's defence; the dockyards had lain idle ever since his idiotic brother had entrusted the whole Byzantine shipbuilding programme to Venice sixteen years before; and according to Nicetas Choniates – who as a former imperial secretary was well placed to know what was going on – he had allowed his principal admiral (who was also his brother-in-law) to sell off the anchors, sails and rigging of his few remaining vessels, now reduced to useless hulks and rotting in the inner harbour. He and his subjects watched, half-stunned, from the walls as the massive war fleet passed beneath them, beating its way up to the mouth of the Bosphorus.

Being in no particular hurry to begin the siege, the invaders first landed on the Asiatic shore of the straits, near the imperial summer palace of Chalcedon, to replenish their stores. 'The surrounding land was fair and fertile,' writes Villehardouin; 'sheaves of new-reaped corn stood in the fields, so that any man might take of it as much as he needed.' There they easily repulsed a half-hearted attack by a small detachment of Greek cavalry – it fled at the first charge, but its purpose was probably only reconnaissance – and later, with similar lack of ceremony, dismissed an emissary from the Emperor. If, they told him, his master was willing to surrender the throne forthwith to his nephew, they would pray the latter to pardon him and make him a generous settlement. If not, let him send them no more messengers, but look to his defence.

Soon after sunrise on the morning of 5 July, they crossed the Bosphorus and landed below Galata, on the north-eastern side of the Golden Horn. Being a commercial settlement, largely occupied by foreign merchants, Galata was unwalled; its only major fortification was a single large round tower. This tower was however of vital importance, for in it stood the huge windlass for the raising and lowering of the chain that was used in emergencies to block the entrance to the Horn.[1] To defend it a considerable force was drawn up, with the Emperor himself rather surprisingly at its head. Perhaps – though given the general demoralization of the Byzantines since the coming of the Angeli, it is far from certain – the defenders might have done better under different leadership; everyone knew how Alexius had seized the throne, and his character was not one to inspire either love or loyalty. In any case the sight of well over a hundred ships, disembarking men, horses and equipment with speed and precision – for the Venetians were nothing if not efficient – filled them with terror, and scarcely had the first wave of Crusaders lowered their lances for the attack than they turned and fled, the Emperor once again in the lead.

Within the Galata Tower itself, the garrison fought more bravely, holding out for a full twenty-four hours; but by the following morning it had to surrender. The Venetian sailors unshackled the windlass, and the great iron chain that had stretched over five hundred yards across the mouth of the Golden Horn subsided thunderously into the water. The fleet swept in, destroying such few seaworthy Byzantine vessels as it found in the inner harbour. The naval victory was complete.

---

1 The tower no longer stands, having been demolished in 1261. The present Galata Tower is a fourteenth-century replacement on a different site.

Constantinople, however, did not surrender. The walls that ran along the shore of the Golden Horn could not compare in strength or splendour with the tremendous ramparts on the landward side, but they could still be staunchly defended. Gradually the Byzantines began to regain the courage and determination that they had heretofore so conspicuously lacked. In all the nine centuries of its existence, their city had not once fallen to a foreign invader. Perhaps, until now, they had never really thought it could. Awake at last to the full extent of the danger that threatened them, they prepared to resist.

The assault, when it came, was directed against the weakest point in the Byzantine defences: the sea frontage of the Palace of Blachernae, which occupied the angle formed by the Land Walls and those following the line of the Horn, at the extreme north-west corner of the city. It was launched on the morning of Thursday, 17 July, simultaneously from land and sea, with the Venetian ships riding low in the water under the weight of their siege machinery: catapults and mangonels on the fore-castles, covered gangplanks and scaling-ladders suspended by rope tackles between the yard-arms. The Frankish army, attacking from land, was initially beaten back by the axe-swinging Englishmen and Danes of the Varangian Guard; it was the Venetians who decided the day – and, to a considerable degree, Enrico Dandolo in person.

The story of the old Doge's courage is told not just by some biased latter-day panegyrist of the Republic, but by a Frankish eye-witness: Geoffrey de Villehardouin himself. He reports that although the Venetian assault craft had approached so close in-shore that those manning the ladders in the bows were fighting hand-to-hand with the defenders, the sailors were at first reluctant to beach the vessels and effect a proper landing.

And here was an extraordinary feat of boldness. For the Duke of Venice, who was an old man and stone-blind, stood fully armed on the prow of his galley, with the banner of St Mark before him, and cried out to his men to drive the ship ashore if they valued their skins. And so they did, and ran the galley ashore, and he and they leaped down and planted the banner before him in the ground. And when the other Venetians saw the standard of St Mark and the Doge's galley beached before their own, they were ashamed, and followed him ashore.

As the attack gathered momentum, it soon became clear to the defenders that they had no chance. Before many hours had passed, Dandolo was able to send word to his Frankish allies that no less than twenty-five towers along the wall were already in Venetian hands. By this time his men were pouring through breaches in the rampart into the city itself, setting fire to the wooden houses until the whole quarter of Blachernae was ablaze. That evening Alexius III Angelus fled secretly from the city, leaving his wife and all his children except a favourite daughter – whom he took with him, together with a few other women, ten thousand pounds of gold and a bag of jewels – to face the future as best they might.

Byzantium, at this gravest crisis in its history, was left without an Emperor; and it may seem surprising that a hastily-convened council of state should have fetched old Isaac Angelus out of his prison and replaced him on the imperial throne. Thanks to his brother's ministrations he was even blinder than Dandolo, and had moreover proved himself a hopelessly incompetent ruler; he was, however, the legitimate Emperor, and by restoring him the Byzantines doubtless believed that they had removed all grounds for further intervention by the Crusaders. So in a way they had; but there remained the undertakings made by young Alexius to Boniface and the Doge. These Isaac was now obliged to ratify, agreeing at the same time to make his son co-Emperor with him. Only then did the Franks and Venetians accord him their formal recognition, after which they withdrew to the Galata side of the Golden Horn to await their promised rewards.

On 1 August 1203, Alexius IV Angelus was crowned alongside his father and assumed effective power. Immediately he began to regret the offers he had made so rashly at Zara in the spring. The imperial treasury, after his uncle's extravagances, was empty; the new taxes that he was obliged to introduce were openly resented by his subjects, who knew all too well where their money was going. Meanwhile the clergy – always an important political force in Constantinople – were scandalized when he began to seize and melt down their church plate and perfectly furious when they heard of his plans to subordinate them to the hated Pope of Rome. As autumn gave way to winter the Emperor's unpopularity steadily grew; and the continued presence of the Franks, whose greed appeared insatiable, increased the tension still further. One night a group of them, wandering through the city, came upon a little mosque in the Saracen quarter behind the church of St Irene, pillaged it and burnt it to ashes. The flames spread, and for the next forty-eight hours Constantinople was engulfed in its worst fire since the days of Justinian, nearly seven centuries before.

When the Emperor returned from a brief and unsuccessful expedition against his fugitive uncle, it was to find most of his capital in ruins and his subjects in a state of almost open warfare against the foreigners. The situation had clearly reached breaking-point; but when, a few days later, a delegation of three Crusaders and three Venetians came to demand immediate payment of the sum owing to them, there was still nothing he could do. According to Villehardouin – who, predictably, was one of the delegates – the party narrowly escaped a lynching on its way to and from the palace. 'And thus,' he writes, 'the war began; and each side did to the other as much harm as it could, both by sea and by land.'

Ironically enough, neither the Crusaders nor the Greeks wanted such a war. The inhabitants of Constantinople had by now one object only in mind: to be rid, once and for all, of these uncivilized thugs who were destroying their beloved city and bleeding them white into the bargain. The Franks, for their part, had not forgotten the reason they had left their homes, and increasingly resented their enforced stay among what they considered an effete and effeminate people when they should have been getting to grips with the infidel. Even if the Greek debt were to be paid in full, they themselves would not benefit materially; it would only enable them to settle their own outstanding account with the Venetians.

The key to the whole impossible affair lay, in short, with Venice – or, more accurately, with Enrico Dandolo. It was open to him at any moment to give his fleet the order to sail. Had he done so, the Crusaders would have been relieved and the Byzantines overjoyed. Formerly, his refusal had been on the grounds that the Franks would never be able to pay him their debt until they in their turn received the money that Alexius and his father had promised them. In fact, however, that debt was now of relatively little interest to him – scarcely more than was the Crusade itself. His mind was on greater things: the overthrow of the Byzantine Empire and the establishment of a Venetian puppet on the throne of Constantinople.

And so, as prospects of a peaceful settlement receded, Dandolo's advice to his Frankish allies took on a different tone. Nothing more, he pointed out, could be expected of Isaac and Alexius, who had not scrupled to betray the friends to whom they owed their joint crown. If the Crusaders were ever to obtain their due, they would have to take it by force. Their moral justification was complete: the faithless Angeli had no further claim on their loyalties. Once inside the city, with one of their own leaders installed as Emperor, they could pay Venice what they owed her almost without noticing it and still have more than enough to finance the Crusade. This was their opportunity; they should seize it now, for it would not recur.

Within Constantinople too, it was generally agreed that Alexius IV must go; and on 25 January 1204 a great concourse of senators, clergy and people gathered in St Sophia to declare him deposed and elect a successor. It was during their deliberations – which dragged on inconclusively for three days before fixing on a reluctant nonentity named Nicholas Canabus – that the only really effective figure at that moment on the Byzantine stage took the law into his own hands.

Alexius Ducas – nicknamed Murzuphlus on account of his eyebrows, which were black and shaggy and met in the middle – was a nobleman whose family had already produced two Emperors and who now occupied the court position of *protovestarius*, with its rights of unrestricted access to the imperial apartments. Late at night he burst into where Alexius IV was sleeping, woke him with the news that his subjects had risen against him and offered him what he claimed was the only chance of escape. Muffling him in a long cloak, he led him by a side door out of the palace to where his fellow-conspirators were waiting. The unhappy youth was then clapped into irons and consigned to a dungeon where, having survived two attempts to poison him, he eventually succumbed to the bowstring. At about the same time his blind father also died; Villehardouin, with that impregnable *naïveté* that characterizes his whole chronicle, attributes his demise to a sudden sickness, brought on by the news of the fate of his son; it does not seem to have struck him that so convenient a malady might have been artificially induced.[1]

With his rivals eliminated – and Nicholas Canabus having retired once again into the obscurity he should never have left – Murzuphlus was crowned in St Sophia as Alexius V. Immediately he began to show those qualities of leadership that the Empire had lacked for so long. For the first time since the Crusaders' arrival the walls and towers were properly manned, while workmen sweated day and night strengthening them and raising them ever higher. To the Franks, one thing was plain: there was to be no more negotiation, far less any question of further payments on a debt for which the new Emperor in any case bore no responsibility.

---

1 A fellow Crusader, Robert of Clary, probably comes closer to the truth when he writes: '*Si li fist lachier une corde u col, si le fist estranler et sen pere Kyrsaac ausi.*' (He [Murzuphlus] had a cord put about his neck and had him strangled, together with his father Isaac.')

Their one chance was an all-out attempt on the city; and now that Murzuphlus had not only usurped the throne but had revealed himself as a murderer to boot, they were morally in an even stronger position than if they had moved against Alexius IV, a legitimate Emperor and their erstwhile ally.

An all-out attempt on the city: it was exactly what Enrico Dandolo had been advocating for months, and from the moment of Murzuphlus's *coup* the old Doge seems to have been recognized, by Venetians and Franks alike, as the leader of the entire expedition. Boniface of Montferrat strove to maintain his influence; with the imperial crown almost within his grasp, it was more than ever vital to him that he should. But his association with the deposed Emperor had been too close, and now that Alexius IV had gone he found himself in some degree discredited. Besides, he had links with the Genoese – and Dandolo knew it.

Early in March there began a series of council meetings in the camp at Galata. They were concerned less with the plan of attack – despite Murzuphlus's work on the defences, its success was apparently considered a foregone conclusion – than with the future administration of the Empire after its conquest. It was agreed that the Crusaders and the Venetians should each appoint six delegates to an electoral committee, and that this should choose the new Emperor. If, as was expected, they decided on a Frank, then the Patriarch should be a Venetian; otherwise vice versa. The Emperor would receive a quarter of the city and of the Empire, including the two chief palaces – Blachernae on the Golden Horn and the old palace on the Marmara. The remaining three-quarters should be divided equally, half going to Venice and half in fief to the Crusading knights. For the Venetian portion, the Doge was specifically absolved from the need to do the Emperor homage. All plunder taken was to be brought to an agreed spot and distributed in similar proportions. Finally, the parties were to undertake not to leave Constantinople for a full year – until March 1205 at the earliest.

The attack began on Friday morning, 9 April. It was directed against that same stretch of sea wall facing the Golden Horn where Dandolo and his men had distinguished themselves nine months before. This time, however, it failed. The new, higher walls and towers, no longer accessible from the Venetian mastheads, provided useful platforms from which the Greek catapults could wreak havoc among the besiegers below. By mid-afternoon the attackers had begun to re-embark their men, horses and equipment and beat their way back to Galata and safety. The next two days were spent in repairing the damage; then, on the

Monday following, the assault was renewed. This time the Venetians lashed their ships together in pairs, thus contriving to throw twice as much weight as before against each tower. Soon, too, a strong north wind blew up, driving the vessels far further up the beach below the walls than the oarsmen could ever have done and allowing the besiegers to work under cover of makeshift shelters stretched from one mast to another. Before long, two of the towers were overwhelmed and occupied. Almost simultaneously, the Crusaders broke open one of the gates in the wall and surged into the city.

Murzuphlus, who had been commanding the defenders with courage and determination, galloped through the streets in a last desperate attempt to rally his subjects. 'But', writes Nicetas,

they were all swept up in the whirlpool of despair, and had no ears either for his orders or his remonstrances ... Seeing that his efforts were in vain, and fearing to be served up to the Franks as a choice morsel for their table, he took flight, accompanied by Euphrosyne, wife of the Emperor Alexius [III] and her daughter Eudocia, whom he passionately adored; for he was a great lover of women and had already repudiated two wives in a manner not canonical.

The three sought refuge with the ex-Emperor in Thrace, where Murzuphlus duly married Eudocia and began to gather his forces for a counter-offensive.

Once the walls were breached, the carnage was dreadful; even Villehardouin was appalled. Only at nightfall, 'tired of battle and massacre', did the conquerors call a truce and withdraw to their camp in one of the great squares of the city.

That night, a party of Crusaders, fearing a counter-attack, set fire to the district which lay between themselves and the Greeks ... and the city began to blaze fiercely, and it burnt all that night and all the next day until evening. It was the third fire at Constantinople since the Franks arrived. And there were more houses burnt than there are to be found in the three greatest cities of the Kingdom of France.

After this, such few defenders as had not yet laid down their arms lost the spirit to continue. The next morning the Crusaders awoke to find all resistance in the city at an end.

But for the people of Constantinople the tragedy had scarcely begun. Not for nothing had the army waited so long outside the world's richest capital. Now that it was theirs and that the customary three days' looting was allowed them, they fell on it like locusts. Never, since the barbarian invasions some centuries before, had Europe witnessed such an orgy of brutality and vandalism; never in history had so much beauty, so much superb craftsmanship, been wantonly destroyed in so short a space of time. Among the witnesses – helpless, horrified, almost unable to believe that human beings who called themselves Christians could be capable of such enormities – was Nicetas Choniates:

I know not how to put any order into my account, how to begin, continue or end. They smashed the holy images and hurled the sacred relics of the Martyrs into places I am ashamed to mention, scattering everywhere the body and blood of the Saviour. These heralds of Anti-Christ seized the chalices and the patens, tore out the jewels and used them as drinking cups . . . As for their profanation of the Great Church, it cannot be thought of without horror. They destroyed the high altar, a work of art admired by the entire world, and shared out the pieces among themselves . . . And they brought horses and mules into the Church, the better to carry off the holy vessels and the engraved silver and gold that they had torn from the throne, and the pulpit, and the doors, and the furniture wherever it was to be found; and when some of these beasts slipped and fell, they ran them through with their swords, fouling the Church with their blood and ordure.

A common harlot was enthroned in the Patriarch's chair, to hurl insults at Jesus Christ; and she sang bawdy songs, and danced immodestly in the holy place . . . nor was there mercy shown to virtuous matrons, innocent maids or even virgins consecrated to God . . . In the streets, houses and churches there could be heard only cries and lamentations.

And these men, he continues, carried the Cross on their shoulders, the Cross upon which they had sworn to pass through Christian lands without bloodshed, to take arms only against the heathen and to abstain from the pleasures of the flesh until their holy task was done.

It was Constantinople's darkest hour – even darker, perhaps, than that, two and a half centuries later, which was to see the city's final fall to the Ottoman Sultan. But not all its treasures perished. While the Frenchmen and Flemings abandoned themselves to a frenzy of wholesale destruction, the Venetians kept their heads. They knew beauty when they saw it. They too looted and pillaged and plundered – but they did not destroy. Instead, all that they could lay their hands on they sent back to Venice – beginning with the four great bronze horses which had dominated the Hippodrome since the days of Constantine and which, from their platform above the main door of St Mark's, were to perform a similar function, for the best part of the next eight centuries, over the

179

Piazza below.[1] The north and south faces of the Basilica are studded with sculptures and reliefs shipped back at the same time; inside the building, in the north transept, hangs the miraculous icon of the Virgin Nicopoeia – the Bringer of Victory – which the Emperors were wont to carry before them into battle; while the Treasury to the south possesses one of the greatest collections of Byzantine works of art to be found anywhere – a further monument to Venetian rapacity.

After three days of terror, order was restored. As previously arranged, all the spoils – or that part of them that had not been successfully concealed – were gathered together in three churches and careful distribution made: a quarter for the Emperor when elected, the remainder to be split equally between the Franks and Venetians. As soon as it was done, the Crusaders paid their debt to Enrico Dandolo. These formalities satisfactorily concluded, both parties applied themselves to the next task: the election of the new Emperor of Byzantium.

Boniface of Montferrat, in a desperate attempt to recover his lost prestige and strengthen his own candidacy, had tracked down the Empress Maria, widow of Isaac Angelus, and married her. He need not have bothered. Dandolo refused outright to consider him and – since the Franks were divided while the Venetians voted as a single bloc – had no difficulty in steering the electors towards the easy-going and tractable Count Baldwin of Flanders and Hainault, who on 16 May received his coronation in St Sophia – the third Emperor to be crowned there in less than a year. Although the newly-appointed Patriarch, the Venetian Tommaso Morosini,[2] had not yet arrived in Constantinople and so could not officiate at the ceremony, there can have been few among those present who would have denied that the new Emperor owed his elevation entirely to the Venetian Republic.

In return, Venice appropriated the best for her own. By the terms of her treaty with the Crusaders she was entitled to three-eighths of the city and the Empire, together with free trade throughout the imperial dominions, from which both Genoa and Pisa were to be rigorously excluded. In Constantinople itself, the Doge demanded the entire district

1 Alas, no longer. Some years ago the Italian authorities, pleading atmospheric pollution, saw fit to incarcerate them in a small, dark room within the Basilica and to replace them on the gallery with lifeless replicas in fibreglass.

2 'Fat as a stuffed pig,' snorts Nicetas, 'and wearing a robe so tight that it seemed to have been sewn on to his skin'. Though already a monk, Morosini had not taken orders at the time he was selected for the Patriarchate. He was ordained deacon at once, priest a fortnight later and bishop the following morning.

surrounding St Sophia and the Patriarchate, reaching right down to the shore of the Golden Horn; for the rest, he took for Venice all those regions that promised to reinforce her mastery of the Mediterranean and to give her an unbroken chain of colonies and ports from the lagoon to the Black Sea. They included Ragusa and Durazzo; the western coast of the Greek mainland and the Ionian Islands; all the Peloponnese; Euboea, Naxos and Andros; the chief ports on the Hellespont and the Marmara – Gallipoli, Rhaedestum and Heraclea; the Thracian seaboard, the city of Adrianople and finally, after a brief negotiation with Boniface, the all-important island of Crete. The harbours and islands would belong to Venice absolutely; where mainland Greece was concerned, however, Dandolo made it clear that as a mercantile republic Venice had no interest in occupying more than the key ports. For the rest, she was only too pleased to have the responsibility taken off her hands.

Thus it emerges beyond all doubt that it was the Venetians, rather than the French or Flemings – or even the Emperor Baldwin himself, who remained little more than a figurehead – who were the real beneficiaries of the Fourth Crusade; and that their success was due, almost exclusively, to Enrico Dandolo. From that day, four years before, when the Frankish emissaries had arrived on the Rialto to ask the Republic's help in their holy enterprise, he had turned every new development to Venetian advantage. He had regained Zara; he had protected Egypt from attack and so preserved Venice's commercial interests with the Muslim world; he had subtly redirected the Frankish forces towards Constantinople, while leaving the ostensible responsibility for the decision with them. Once there, his courage had largely inspired the first attack; his capacity for intrigue had brought down the Angeli, making essential a second siege and the physical capture of the city; his diplomatic skill had shaped a treaty which gave Venice more than she had dared to hope and laid the foundations for her commercial Empire. Refusing the Byzantine crown for himself – to have accepted it would have created insuperable constitutional problems at home and might well have destroyed the Republic – and declining even to serve on the electoral commission, he nevertheless made sure that his influence over the election (which was held under his auspices, in the old imperial palace that he had temporarily appropriated for himself) would be tantamount to giving Venice a majority and would ensure the success of his own candidate. Finally, while encouraging the Franks to feudalize the Empire – a step which he knew could not fail to create fragmentation and disunity and would prevent its ever becoming strong enough to obstruct Venetian expansion – he had kept Venice outside the feudal framework, holding her new dominions not as an imperial fief but by her own right of conquest. For a blind man not far short of ninety it was a remarkable achievement.

Yet even now old Dandolo did not rest. Outside the capital, the Greek subjects of the Empire continued their resistance. Murzuphlus was to cause no further trouble: soon after his marriage he was blinded in his turn by his jealous father-in-law, and when in the following year he was captured by the Franks they brought him back to Constantinople and flung him to his death from the column of Theodosius in the centre of the city. But – as the next chapter will tell – another of Alexius III's sons-in-law set up an Empire in exile at Nicaea, two of the Comneni did the same at Trebizond and, in Epirus, a bastard Angelus proclaimed himself an autonomous Despot. On all sides the erstwhile Crusaders had to fight hard to establish themselves, nowhere more fiercely than in Venice's newly-acquired city of Adrianople where, just after Easter, 1205, the Emperor Baldwin fell into the hands of the Bulgars and the old Doge, who had fought determinedly at his side, was left to lead a shattered army back to Constantinople. He is not known to have been wounded; but six weeks later he was dead. His body, rather surprisingly, was not returned to Venice but was buried in St Sophia – where, in the gallery above the south aisle, his tombstone may still be seen.

He had deserved well of his city; it is a source of greater surprise that the Venetians never erected a monument to the greatest of all their Doges. But in the wider context of world events he was a disaster. Though it cannot be said of him that he gave the Crusades a bad name, that is only because the record of those successive forays over the previous century had already emerged as one of the blackest chapters in the history of Christendom. Yet the Fourth Crusade – if indeed it can be so described – surpassed even its predecessors in faithlessness and duplicity, in brutality and greed. Constantinople in the twelfth century had been not just the wealthiest metropolis of the world, but also the most intellectually and artistically cultivated and the chief repository of Europe's classical heritage, both Greek and Roman. By its sack, Western civilization suffered a loss greater than the sack of Rome by the barbarians in the fifth century or the burning of the library of Alexandria by the soldiers of the Prophet in the seventh – perhaps the most catastrophic single loss in all history.

Politically, too, the damage done was incalculable. Although Latin rule along the Bosphorus was to last less than sixty years, the Byzantine

Empire never recovered its strength, or any considerable part of its lost dominion. Under firm and forceful leadership – which would not be lacking in the century to come – a strong and prosperous Byzantium might have halted the Turkish advance while there was still time. Instead, the Empire was left economically crippled, territorially truncated, powerless to defend itself against the Ottoman tide. There are few greater ironies in history than the fact that the fate of Eastern Christendom should have been sealed – and half Europe condemned to some five hundred years of Muslim rule – by men who fought under the banner of the Cross. Those men were transported, inspired, encouraged and ultimately led by Enrico Dandolo in the name of the Venetian Republic; and, just as Venice derived the major advantage from the tragedy, so she and her magnificent old Doge must accept the major responsibility for the havoc that they wrought upon the world.

12
The Empire in Exile

[1205-53]

It is not so much a difference of dogma that turns the hearts of the Greeks against you as the hatred of the Latins which has entered into their spirit, in consequence of the many and great evils which the Greeks have suffered from the Latins at various times, and are still suffering day by day.

Barlaam of Calabria to Pope Benedict XII, c.1340

In contrast to Doge Dandolo, who now proudly styled himself 'Lord of a Quarter and Half a Quarter of the Roman Empire', the Emperor Baldwin I cut a sorry figure. When another three-eighths of the Empire had been parcelled out among the Frankish knights as imperial fiefs, he was left with just a quarter of the territory that had been ruled by his immediate predecessors. Essentially it comprised Thrace – though not of course Adrianople, which had gone to the Venetians – and the north-west region of Asia Minor, together with certain islands of the Aegean including Lesbos, Samos and Chios; but even this pathetically diminished patrimony was contested. Boniface of Montferrat in particular, who had been virtually certain of the throne and was furious at having been passed over, angrily refused the Anatolian lands he was offered and instead seized Thessalonica, where he established a kingdom extending over a large part of Macedonia and Thessaly. Somehow, too, he managed to assume the suzerainty over the lesser Frankish rulers springing up to the south, notably the Burgundian Otto de la Roche in Boeotia and Attica (the so-called Duchy of Athens) and the Frenchman William of Champlitte – soon to be succeeded by the house of Villehardouin – in the Peloponnese.

It comes as no surprise to learn that the new rulers were detested throughout these formerly Byzantine lands. Economically there were few major changes: apart from the fact that taxes were henceforth paid to a Latin landlord rather than to a Greek, provincial and country life probably continued much as it had always done. Morally and spiritually, however, the climate was entirely altered. Not only were the Franks overbearing and arrogant, making no effort to conceal their scorn for what they considered an inferior as well as a subject race; they were also staunch upholders of the Church of Rome, and unhesitatingly imposed the Latin rite wherever they could. For the local proletariat and the peasantry there was little to be done; sullenly, resentfully and with bitterness in their hearts, they accepted the inevitable. The aristocracy, on the other hand, was a good deal less submissive; many Greek nobles left their ancestral lands in disgust and moved to one of the Byzantine successor states in which the national spirit and the Orthodox faith were still preserved.

Of these states, the largest, the most powerful and by far the most important was the so-called Empire of Nicaea, of which Alexius III's son-in-law Theodore Lascaris was recognized as Emperor in 1206, being crowned there two years later. It occupied a broad strip of land at the western extremity of Anatolia, averaging some two hundred miles across and extending from the Aegean to the Black Sea coast. To the north and west lay the Latin Empire; to the south and east, the Seljuk Sultanate. Although the official capital remained Nicaea – which after 1208 was the seat of the Patriarch and where all the imperial coronations took place – Theodore's successor John III Vatatzes was to establish his chief residence in the Lydian city of Nymphaeum (now Kemalpaşa) which was far better placed from the strategic point of view; and for most of the fifty-seven-year period of exile from Constantinople it was from here rather than from Nicaea that the Empire was effectively governed.

The two other successor states were less important. Situated as they were, one on the Adriatic coast and the other at the south-eastern extremity of the Black Sea, they were too remote to exert much influence on the march of events; nor could they ever boast the special prestige which the presence of the Patriarchate conferred upon Nicaea. The Despotate of Epirus (to use its later title) was founded soon after the capture of Constantinople by a certain Michael Comnenus Ducas, the illegitimate son of the *sebastocrator* John Angelus Ducas (grandson of Alexius I Comnenus through his daughter Theodora) and thus a cousin of Isaac II and Alexius III, although – not altogether surprisingly – neither he nor his father ever used the name of Angelus themselves. From his capital at Arta he established control over the entire north-western coast of Greece and part of Thessaly – a domain which was soon to be substantially increased by his half-brother Theodore who, succeeding him in 1215, captured Thessalonica from the Latins nine

Family Trees

These family trees include only the names relevant to this chapter.
For fuller family trees, see p xxii–iii and xxvii.

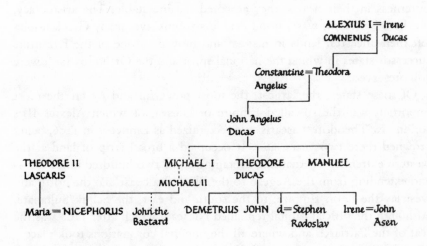

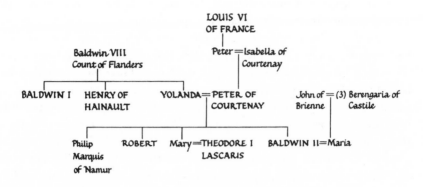

years later and promptly had himself crowned Emperor as a rival to John Vatatzes of Nicaea. This rivalry, however, did not last long: in 1242 Vatatzes obliged Theodore's son John to renounce the imperial title in favour of that of *despotes*, and four years later he appropriated Thessalonica for himself.

Unlike Nicaea and Epirus, the Empire of Trebizond was not the result of the fall of Constantinople. Indeed, it had been founded in April 1204 – within days of the disaster – by Alexius and David Comnenus, grandsons of the Emperor Andronicus through his son Manuel, who had married a Georgian princess. After the fall of Andronicus in 1185 the young brothers had been taken for safety to Georgia, where they had been brought up at the royal court. Determined to continue the Comnenus dynasty in opposition to the Angeli, they had captured Trebizond – with the help of the Georgian Queen Thamar – in April 1204. Later in the same year David had pushed west along the Black Sea coast with his army of Georgians and other mercenaries to occupy Paphlagonia as far as Heraclea; but much of this territory was lost soon afterwards, and for the greater part of its 257-year history – for it was to continue after the recovery of Constantinople and did not ultimately fall to the Turks until 1461 – the Trapezuntine Empire was confined to a narrow strip of coastline rather less than four hundred miles long between the Pontic mountains and the sea.

As ruler of what was generally accepted as Byzantium in exile, Theodore I Lascaris of Nicaea faced initial difficulties which to lesser men would have been insurmountable. Quite apart from his rivals in Epirus and Trebizond – where in the autumn of 1204 David Comnenus was already advancing westward with alarming speed – petty Greek principalities were springing up like mushrooms within his own borders: one in Philadelphia, another in the valley of the Meander, yet a third in the obscure little town of Sampson near Miletus. Then, as the terrible year drew to its close, a Frankish army led by Baldwin himself, with his brother Henry and Count Louis of Blois, crossed the straits and began to move across Asia Minor. Theodore – who had been obliged to build up a whole new administrative machine as well as an army – was still hopelessly unprepared; and on 6 December 1204 he suffered a calamitous defeat at Poimanenon, some forty miles south of the Marmara – probably the modern Eski Manyas – giving the Franks control of the whole coastal region of Bithynia as far as Brusa (Bursa). Had they been able to continue their advance another sixty miles to Nicaea itself, Theodore's

Empire might well have been annihilated almost at its birth; fortunately for him, however, they were recalled in the nick of time by a serious crisis in the Balkans.

For Baldwin's arrogance had caught up with him. The Greek landowners in Thrace, who had initially been prepared to accept their Frankish overlords, now found themselves treated as second-class citizens. They rebelled, summoning to their aid the Bulgarian Tsar Kalojan and offering him the imperial crown if he could drive the Latins from Constantinople. The Tsar asked nothing better. Earlier in 1204 he had already been crowned King (though not Emperor) by Innocent III's envoy and had accepted the jurisdiction of Rome; this, however, in no way diminished his alarm at the proliferation of Latin states throughout the peninsula, and he was as anxious as were the Byzantines themselves to rid the land of the Crusader blight. By the beginning of 1205 he was on the march; and on 14 April he virtually annihilated the Frankish army outside Adrianople, killing Louis of Blois and taking prisoner the Emperor himself, who never regained his freedom and died soon afterwards. Thus, just a year after the capture of Constantinople, the power of the Latins was broken. In all Asia Minor, only the little town of Pegae (now Karabiga) on the southern shore of the Marmara remained in Frankish hands.

Now at last Theodore Lascaris could settle down in earnest to the forging of his new state – following, however, the old Byzantine pattern in every detail, for he never for a moment doubted that his countrymen would be back, sooner or later, in their rightful capital. Such members of the imperial household, officers of state and civil servants as he was able to track down were restored to their former posts; exiled bishops and other distinguished ecclesiastics were summoned to Nicaea, and – after the death of the Patriarch, who had stubbornly refused to leave his own place of refuge in Didymotichum – it was they who were invited to elect his successor. Their choice fell on a certain Michael Autorianus who, some time during Holy Week in 1208, crowned and anointed Theodore as *basileus*.

There were now effectively two Eastern Emperors and two Patriarchs, the Latin in Constantinople and the Greek in Nicaea. Clearly there could never be peace between them: each was determined to destroy the other. Baldwin's brother and successor Henry of Hainault was for the first eighteen months of his reign fully occupied with Kalojan, who by the summer of 1206 had sacked Adrianople, mopped up most of Thrace and advanced to the very walls of the capital; but on 26 October 1207, while preparing to besiege Thessalonica, the Bulgar Tsar was murdered by a Cuman chieftain[1] and Henry was able to increase the pressure on his rival in Nicaea. He did not march at once – he too, like Theodore, had had to set up a proper government and administration – but in 1209, conquering with some difficulty his Crusader scruples, he concluded a military alliance with Kaikosru, the Seljuk Sultan of Iconium, who also saw the establishment of a new Greek state in western Asia Minor as a provocation and a threat.

The Sultan, his forces now supplemented by a contingent of Frankish troops, was already preparing an expedition against Nicaea when he received an unexpected visitor: the former Emperor Alexius III. Towards the end of 1204 Alexius had fallen into the hands of Boniface, in whose castle of Montferrat he had spent several years as a prisoner. In 1209 or 1210, however, he had been ransomed by his cousin Michael, Despot of Epirus, and had made his way to Iconium in the vague hope that the Sultan might help him recover his throne. Now Kaikosru, it need hardly be said, was not interested in replacing the Greek Emperor so much as in eliminating him altogether; on the other hand he immediately recognized Alexius as a useful pawn in the diplomatic game, enabling him to set himself up as champion of a legitimate ruler against a parvenu usurper. With the ostensible aim of overthrowing Theodore and installing Alexius in his place, in the spring of 1211 he invaded Nicaean territory. The two sides – each of which had a contingent of Latin mercenaries at its core – were evenly matched, and there were several hard-fought though indecisive battles; but during the last, near Antioch on the Meander, the Sultan was unhorsed and killed – if Greek sources are to be believed, by the Emperor Theodore himself in single combat. The Seljuk army took to its heels; Alexius III was taken prisoner once again and dispatched to a monastery, where he was to spend the rest of his life.

The victory brought Theodore little territorial gain; but it eliminated his last Greek rival and – since Kaikosru's successor Kaikawus immediately came to terms – freed him at least temporarily from the Seljuk threat, enabling him to concentrate his forces exclusively against the

---

1 In his last campaigns Kalojan had killed as many Greeks as he had Latins, to the point where he proudly styled himself *Romaioctonos* ('killer of the Romaioi', i.e., the Byzantines) on the analogy of Basil II *Bulgaroctonos*. Not surprisingly he was by now detested by the Greeks, who saw the date of his death – the feast-day of St Demetrius of Thessalonica – as a clear indication that he had really been killed by the saint himself. The fact remains that it was Kalojan alone who had saved the Nicaean Empire from destruction by Baldwin three years before, and who had thus made it possible for the Greeks to regain Constantinople half a century later.

Crusaders. Here, alas, he was less successful. On 15 October 1211 beside the Rhyndacus river his army suffered another defeat by Henry, who advanced to Pergamum and Nymphaeum; but the Latins, by now once again hard pressed by the Bulgars in their rear, proved unable to pursue their advantage. In late 1214 the rival Emperors concluded a treaty of peace at Nymphaeum: Henry would keep the north-west coast of Asia Minor as far south as Atramyttion (now Edremit); all the rest as far as the Seljuk frontier, including the territories recently conquered by the Latins, would go to Theodore.

This treaty marked the beginning of Nicaean prosperity. The young Empire had finally obtained formal recognition by the Crusaders of its right to exist; moreover, its western borders were now as secure as those on the east. Almost simultaneously, the Latin Empire began to decline. The widowed Emperor Henry, forced against his better judgement into a dynastic marriage with a Bulgar princess, found himself enmeshed in a hopeless tangle of Balkan politics; then, on 11 June 1216 at the age of only forty, he died suddenly at Thessalonica. By far the most capable of the Latin rulers of Constantinople, in barely a decade he had transformed a lost cause into a going concern. Unlike his insufferable brother Baldwin, he had respected the rights and the religion of his Greek subjects and had even achieved a balance of power with Nicaea. Had his successors possessed a fraction of his ability, there might never again have been a Greek Emperor on the throne of Byzantium.

Despite his two wives, Henry of Hainault had died childless; and to succeed him the Frankish barons in Constantinople elected his brother-in-law Peter of Courtenay, husband of his sister Yolanda. Peter, who was then in France, set out for the East in the first weeks of 1217. He had hoped to stop in Rome for a full-scale imperial coronation by Pope Honorius III; and he made no secret of his disappointment when the Pope, fearful that if the ceremony took place in St Peter's he might claim the crown of the Western Empire as well, insisted on holding it in the church of S. Lorenzo, outside the walls. A week or two later he set sail for Durazzo, accompanied by a Venetian fleet and an army of 5,500 men, with the object of recovering the city from the Despot of Epirus, Theodore Ducas; but the expedition ended in fiasco when the city proved impregnable and Peter was captured, together with a good many of his men, in the mountains of Albania. He was thrown into an Epirot prison and never heard of again.

The Empress Yolanda on the other hand, who had wisely decided to travel out with her children by sea, arrived without mishap in Constantinople, where she was almost immediately delivered of a son, Baldwin. Her first-born, the Marquis Philip of Namur, having categorically refused to accompany the rest of his family to the East, she then governed as Regent until her death in 1219, confirming her brother's conciliatory policy towards Nicaea by giving her daughter Mary to Theodore Lascaris as his third wife. News of this step, however, was received with horror in Epirus, where Theodore Ducas, not content with the capture – and quite possibly the murder – of Peter of Courtenay, was becoming less and less inclined to accept Lascaris as the lawful *basileus*.

Ducas's star was rising fast. Morally he was in a somewhat equivocal position, having spent the first five years after the fall of Constantinople in Nicaean territory with Theodore Lascaris to whom, after his imperial coronation, he had sworn an oath of fealty; he had eventually joined his brother Michael at Arta only on Michael's urgent summons. Since then, however, the situation had changed. Nicaea's treaty of 1214 with the Franks had been, to Theodore, an unpardonable betrayal; and the subsequent behaviour of its Emperor, who seemed to have spent much of his time fighting the distant Empire of Trebizond instead of preparing for the recapture of the capital, had strained his loyalty to near breaking point. Lascaris's marriage to a Latin princess was the last straw.

Such, at least, was his public position. The truth was a good deal simpler. Theodore could never be satisfied with the Despotate of Epirus. Unlike his bastard brother, he was the legitimate son of the *sebastocrator* John Angelus Ducas and thus the great-grandson of Alexius I Comnenus. With Comnenus, Angelus and Ducas blood in his veins – a fact which he emphasized by regularly styling himself with all three names – he could consequently boast a far stronger claim to the imperial throne than Theodore Lascaris.[1] His immediate ambitions were now focused on Thessalonica; but Thessalonica was, after all, only the second city in the Empire: in the eyes of Theodore Angelus Ducas Comnenus, it was little more than a stepping-stone to his ultimate goal, Constantinople itself.

Things had not gone well for Thessalonica since Boniface of Montferrat had established himself there after the Fourth Crusade. Boniface had been killed fighting the Bulgars in 1207, and the Kingdom

---

1 The genealogy becomes a little complicated here, largely because of the understandable reluctance of the *sebastocrator* John (father of Michael and Theodore) to assume his father's name of Angelus, preferring to adopt that of Ducas, to which his only claim was through his grandmother; but a glance at the Comnenus and Angelus family trees should make the position clear.

had since been governed by his widow, acting as Regent for her son Demetrius. It had been further weakened by the departure of many of his knights to their various homelands and – though it was still the Latin Empire's most important vassal – since the arrival of the Empress Yolanda it could no longer rely on the firm support from Constantinople that it had enjoyed in Henry's day. When Theodore marched into Thessaly and Macedonia in 1218 it was plain that its days as an independent Crusader state were numbered. In fact, the Despot met with spirited resistance; and it was only in the autumn of 1224, after a long and arduous siege, that Thessalonica finally fell. With it fell its Latin Kingdom. Theodore now ruled supreme from the Adriatic to the Aegean, over a dominion which included Epirus, Aetolia, Acarnania, Thessaly and most of Macedonia. Soon afterwards – though the precise date is uncertain – in open defiance of Theodore Lascaris, he was crowned by the Bishop of Ochrid (who had a running feud with the Patriarch of Nicaea) as Emperor of the Romans.

Thus it was that, in place of the single Empire that had existed little more than a generation before, there were now three – two Greek and one Latin. And not far away there loomed yet a fourth: for the second Bulgarian Empire also was steadily increasing in strength. Tsar Kalojan had taken full advantage of the Fourth Crusade and the general Balkan disarray that followed it to extend his rule over much of Thrace and Macedonia. His nephew Boril had been rather less successful; but in 1218 Boril had been overthrown and blinded by his cousin John II Asen, and John too coveted Constantinople. Of the four powers, by far the weakest was the Latin Empire itself, by 1225 reduced to the region immediately to the north and west of the capital and a small area of Asia Minor south of the Marmara. The Empress Yolanda had died in 1219, leaving the throne to her son Robert; but Robert was a weak and feckless youth – one authority, a certain Aubrey de Trois-Fontaines, describes him as being *quasi rudis et idiota* – and was totally outclassed by Theodore, John Asen and John Vatatzes, who had inherited the Empire of Nicaea from his father-in-law Theodore Lascaris in 1222.

Lascaris had been a great ruler, who had achieved more than most people in 1205 would have thought possible. Since he left no sons, the choice of Vatatzes, husband of his eldest daughter Irene, had seemed an obvious one; it failed, however, to find favour with his two surviving brothers, who promptly made their way to Constantinople and persuaded the young Emperor to make a military intervention on their behalf. Robert, with characteristic stupidity, agreed; he achieved nothing, and his army was cut to pieces by Vatatzes at Poimanenon, where Theodore Lascaris had suffered a similar – though ultimately less disastrous – defeat at the hands of the Latins, twenty-odd years before. He had still not recovered from the blow when, a few months later, came the news of the capture of Thessalonica. It was too much for him. From that moment on he gave himself up to a life of pleasure, seducing women – Greek and Frankish indiscriminately – robbing churches and monasteries of their remaining treasures, making scarcely any attempt to govern what was left of his Empire. He also became infatuated with the daughter of a comparatively low-born French knight killed at the battle of Adrianople, whom he secretly married and installed in the Palace of Blachernae. This time it was his barons who could bear it no longer. One night several of them burst into the imperial bedchamber, where they slashed the girl's nose and lips until she was almost unrecognizable, seized her mother and subsequently drowned her. Typically, Robert took no action against them but at once fled to Rome, where he lodged a formal complaint with Pope Gregory IX. Gregory showed him little sympathy and told him to return to Constantinople; but he had got no further than Clarenza in the Morea – the modern Killini – when he died, in January 1228.

The Emperor Robert left no legitimate children; and since his brother and successor Baldwin II was still only eleven, once again a Regent had to be found. The first choice of the barons of Constantinople fell on his sister Mary, widow of Theodore Lascaris, who had returned to the city after the death of her husband; but she died a few months later, and the search was renewed. A somewhat surprising applicant was John Asen of Bulgaria, who suggested a dynastic marriage between Baldwin and his daughter Helena, after which he proposed to take the Empire under his own protection and restore to it all its conquered territories, Thessalonica included. But the barons rejected him out of hand, and turned instead to the most distinguished of living Crusaders: the former King of Jerusalem, leader of the Fifth Crusade[1] and papal marshal John of Brienne.

There was only one drawback: John, having been born in about 1150, was now nearly eighty years old. But he was still remarkably spry – his daughter by his third wife, Berengaria of Castile, was still only four – and no one else could match his record. In 1210, at the age of sixty, he

---

1 Proclaimed by Innocent III at the Fourth Lateran Council of 1215, the Fifth Crusade was fought mostly in Egypt and has little direct relevance to our story.

had married the seventeen-year-old Queen Maria of Jerusalem. She had died in childbirth two years later, and John had ruled as effective King on behalf of his infant daughter Isabella until her marriage in 1225 to the Western Emperor Frederick II, *Stupor Mundi* – immediately after which he had been deposed by his new son-in-law on the grounds that, with his daughter now married, he no longer had any legal claim to the throne. Furious, he had fled to Rome, where he had appealed to Pope Honorius. Honorius had been sympathetic; he could not give him back his Kingdom, but he had appointed him Governor of his Tuscan patrimony. When two years later Gregory IX had succeeded to the papal throne and had been almost immediately attacked by imperial troops, John had rallied instantly to his defence.

Then, suddenly and unexpectedly, came the call to Constantinople. John was not at first over-eager to accept, but when Gregory insisted – here was, after all, an unrepeatable opportunity to increase papal influence over the Latin Empire – he finally allowed himself to be persuaded. He made, however, a number of conditions to protect his own future after Baldwin had reached his majority. The young Emperor must immediately marry Maria, his four-year-old daughter, who must in turn be given a suitable dowry in the form of land; he himself must be recognized as *basileus* in his own right for the rest of his life, with Baldwin succeeding him on his death; and at the age of twenty Baldwin, if not yet Emperor, should be invested with the Empire of Nicaea, together with all Frankish possessions in Asia Minor. Even then, John did not leave at once for Constantinople. It was early in 1229 before the barons gave their approval to his terms; and there was still a campaign to be fought against his hated son-in-law before he could leave Italy. Only in the autumn of 1231 did he finally appear off the Golden Horn. A few days later he was crowned Emperor in St Sophia.

During this three-year interregnum, the balance of power in the Balkans had suffered a radical change. To the Emperor Theodore, waiting in his capital at Thessalonica, Constantinople – now without even a Regent to provide leadership – appeared more vulnerable than ever it had been; on the other hand, he had the Bulgars to consider. Only a year or two before, he and John Asen had concluded a treaty of peace; scarcely had they done so, however, than the Tsar had offered to recover Thessalonica for the Latins. The man could clearly not be trusted. Besides, with so dangerous a threat to the north, how could he possibly regain his ancient heritage? There was but one solution: the Bulgar menace must be eliminated. In the early spring of 1230, Theodore led his army across the frontier. Asen made a great show of outraged innocence, marching out against the invaders with the text of the peace treaty emblazoned across his standard; and in April 1230, near the little village of Klokotnitsa on the Maritsa river between Adrianople and Philippopolis, the two armies joined in battle.

It was all over quite quickly. Despite his courage, his confidence and his unbroken record of victories, Theodore found that he had met his match at last. His army was shattered, he himself taken prisoner. To be sure, his brother Manuel was allowed to stay on in Thessalonica with the title of Despot; but this was only because he was married to Asen's daughter. Manuel continued – much to the amusement of John Vatatzes and his Nicaean subjects – to sign decrees in the crimson ink reserved for Emperors; apart from that, he was an obvious puppet of his father-in-law and made little pretence of being anything else.

The Latins had been saved from almost certain destruction – and by a nation that they had previously spurned. Any gratitude that they might have felt must however have been overshadowed by alarm, as they watched John Asen advance unopposed across Thrace, Macedonia and Albania, effortlessly appropriating Theodore's former domains until he could claim as Bulgar territory the whole of the northern Balkans, from the Adriatic to the Black Sea. In an inscription in the church of the Forty Martyrs at his capital of Trnovo he proudly recorded his conquests. He was now, he claimed, master of all the lands between Durazzo and Adrianople; only Constantinople with its immediately adjacent towns remained in Frankish hands – 'and these too are subject to my authority, for they have no Emperor but myself and they obey my will, for God has so ordained it'. Even in theoretically independent Serbia he was able to replace Stephen Radoslav, who was Theodore's son-in-law, with Stephen Vladislav, who was one of his own. Nor was the Bulgar Tsar the only beneficiary of Klokotnitsa. Away in his palace at Nymphaeum, John Vatatzes was also quietly rejoicing. For a moment it had seemed as if Theodore might become a serious rival, and that Constantinople might fall to Thessalonica rather than to Nicaea; that danger was now past, never to return.

The effective elimination of the fourth participant in the struggle for supremacy led inevitably to a radical realignment among the other three. No longer would John Asen make diplomatic overtures to the Latins on the Bosphorus; it now seemed to him that Vatatzes would be a far more useful ally, particularly since he was on the point of another decision, even more far-reaching: to abandon the Church of Rome.

Western Christianity, despite Kalojan's conversion, had never taken root among the Bulgars, among whom the old Byzantine traditions had always prevailed; besides, any future offensive against the Latin Empire would be a lot easier to justify if the Tsar were not seen to be attacking his co-religionists. A quarrel with Pope Gregory in 1232 gave him just the excuse he needed, and the break was made. With the ready consent of the Patriarch of Nicaea – together with those of Jerusalem, Alexandria and Antioch – a Bulgarian Orthodox Patriarchate was once again established, with its seat at Trnovo; and three years later in Gallipoli John Asen signed a treaty of alliance with Nicaea, which was subsequently sealed in Lampsacus by the marriage of his daughter Helena – rejected by young Baldwin seven years before – to the son of John Vatatzes, Theodore II Lascaris. In the late summer of 1235 the combined forces of Orthodoxy were outside the walls of Constantinople, besieging the city by land and sea.

Once again the Latins were under threat. Despite his age, John of Brienne fought like a tiger for the defence of his Empire, and Venetian ships provided invaluable support; when, however, the siege was resumed in the following year Constantinople would surely have been doomed but for a sudden change of heart on the part of John Asen, who awoke one morning to the realization that an energetic Greek Empire would constitute an infinitely more serious threat to Bulgaria than an exhausted Latin one and called off the attack, even going so far as to send ambassadors to Nicaea to retrieve the unfortunate Helena. In the summer of 1237 he went further still, allowing a large band of Cumans, fleeing from the Mongol invasion of the lower Danube basin, to cross his territory and take service with the new Emperor Baldwin – John of Brienne having died, aged nearly ninety, the previous March; and that autumn he himself led an army of Bulgars, Cumans and Latins against Tzurulum, one of the most important Nicaean strongholds in Thrace.

That siege was still in progress when disaster struck. Messengers arrived with the news that Trnovo was in the grip of a furious epidemic, which had already carried off the Tsar's wife, one of his sons and the recently-installed Patriarch. To John Asen, this could only be the judgement of heaven. He immediately withdrew from the siege (which was successfully continued by his Cuman and Latin allies) and made peace with Vatatzes, to whom he was to give no further trouble. Soon, however, he began to look for a new wife; and somehow his prisoner Theodore of Thessalonica – whom he had recently had blinded for plotting against him – managed to persuade him to marry his daughter

Irene. The diplomatic advantages to John Asen of such a marriage are not altogether clear; to Theodore, on the other hand, they were immediate. As the Tsar's father-in-law, he was at once released from his captivity and returned in disguise to Thessalonica, where he deposed his brother Manuel and enthroned instead his own son John, restoring to him the title of Emperor.

The year 1241 proved a watershed in the history of all the contesting Empires. Before it was over, three of the protagonists in the long drawn-out struggle for Constantinople were in their graves: John Asen of Bulgaria, Manuel of Thessalonica and Pope Gregory IX, one of the most redoubtable and consistent champions of the Latin Empire. More important still, that same year also saw the Mongol horde under its leader Batu Khan sweep through Moravia and Hungary into the Danube basin, leaving the Bulgars little opportunity to involve themselves in further adventures to the East. Thus another once formidable nation was effectively eliminated. The power of Thessalonica had already been broken at Klokotnitsa. The Latin Empire, which had been steadily cut down to the point where it amounted to little more than the city of Constantinople itself, had survived only thanks to dissension among its enemies. Of those enemies, there now remained but one: the Empire of Nicaea, whose ruler John Vatatzes continued to prepare, with steadily increasing confidence, for the reconquest of the ancient capital.

He still had the problem of Thessalonica to settle. Although the so-called Empire was no longer a threat from the military point of view, legally it remained a rival claimant to Constantinople – a position that clearly could not be tolerated. Its Emperor John he knew to be a weak and pious figurehead, who longed only to enter a monastery; the real power, such as it was, was back in the hands of Theodore, as ambitious – despite his blindness – as he had ever been. Thus it was Theodore whom, towards the end of 1241, John Vatatzes invited to Nicaea as his guest. The invitation was accepted, and the old man was received with every courtesy; only when he came to take his leave was it politely explained to him that his departure would unfortunately not be possible. He was in fact a prisoner, and a prisoner he remained until the following summer, when Vatatzes escorted him back to Thessalonica with a considerable army and then sent him as an envoy to his son to negotiate a treaty. The result was that John, like Manuel before him, agreed to exchange the title of Emperor for that of Despot, and acknowledged the supremacy of Nicaea.

While Vatatzes was still in Thessalonica, word was brought to him that the Mongols had invaded the Seljuk lands of Asia Minor and were already on the very threshold of his own dominions. For the next few years the situation looked grave indeed, especially after June 1243, when the invaders defeated the Sultan Kaikosru II at the battle of Kösedağ and forced him to pay tribute. The Emperor of Trebizond, who had been a vassal of the Sultan, suffered much the same fate and was obliged to transfer his allegiance to the Mongol Khan. In face of the common danger, Vatatzes concluded an alliance with Kaikosru, but the precaution proved unnecessary: the Mongols moved away again, leaving the Nicaean lands untouched and his own position *vis-à-vis* his neighbours stronger than ever.

In 1244 he was able to strengthen it still further. His first wife Irene, daughter of his predecessor Theodore Lascaris, had died; and John now married Constance, the illegitimate daughter of Frederick II. Frederick had no quarrel with the Emperor Baldwin, to whom he was distantly related; but having been brought up in the largely Greek court of Palermo he knew and understood the Greeks, spoke their language perfectly and sympathized with them in their long exile from their rightful capital. He was therefore delighted with the match – though the same could not be said for the twelve-year-old Constance, who found herself rechristened with the more Byzantine name of Anna and wedded to a man exactly forty years older than herself, a man moreover whom everyone knew to be engaged in a shameless affair with one of her own waiting-women. Pope Innocent IV was deeply shocked by the marriage, just as the Patriarch of Nicaea was horrified by Vatatzes's treatment of his luckless young wife; but the friendship between the two Emperors remained unaffected.

With the Mongols gone – leaving a broken Sultanate behind them – John Vatatzes could now turn his attention back again to the Balkans. The Bulgar Empire too had been crippled by this most recent of the barbarian invasions; while the death in 1246 of Tsar Coloman, John Asen's twelve-year-old son, and the succession of his still younger half-brother Michael, further troubled the waters in which Vatatzes cheerfully intended to fish. By the autumn of that year he had taken Serres, and from there had occupied all the territory between the Strymon and Maritsa rivers together with a good deal of western Macedonia. He was still encamped at Melnik on the Strymon when a group of Thessalonians arrived with a proposal. When the Despot John had died two years before, his father Theodore had replaced him with his younger brother

Demetrius; but Demetrius had proved dissolute and pleasure-loving, and a large number of his subjects had now had enough, of him and his entire family. If the Emperor would guarantee to the city the continuation of its ancient rights and privileges, it would be surrendered to him without a struggle. Vatatzes asked nothing better. In December he entered Thessalonica unopposed, exiled old Theodore to a country estate and took Demetrius back to Asia Minor as his prisoner, leaving as his European Viceroy his distant kinsman Andronicus Palaeologus.

One more enemy was left to conquer before he could concentrate on Constantinople. Some nine years before, the region of Epirus had separated from Thessalonica and set itself up once again as an independent despotate under Michael II, an illegitimate son of its original founder Michael I. It too had taken advantage of the Mongol occupation of Bulgaria, and had regained much of the territory conquered by John Asen in 1230; around Ochrid and Prilep, it now shared a common frontier with the Empire of Nicaea. John Vatatzes did not attack it: in such wild and mountainous terrain a war might go on for years. Instead, in 1249 he concluded a treaty of friendship with Michael, sealing it by betrothing his granddaughter Maria to Michael's son Nicephorus.

All would have been well if the aged Theodore, still making as much trouble as ever, had not persuaded his nephew to renounce the treaty and take up arms once again against the Nicaean Empire. In 1251 Michael obediently did so, capturing Prilep and advancing as far as the Axius river (now the Vardar). John Vatatzes was taking no more chances. He crossed to Europe with the largest army he could raise, and early in 1253 forced the Despot's surrender. Michael had good reason to regret his foolishness: he was obliged to cede not only the territory he had recently occupied but also all that region of western Macedonia that he had conquered from the Bulgars and part of Albania as well. His son Nicephorus was carried off to the court of his grandfather-in-law-to-be as a hostage for his future good behaviour. As for the old, blind, insufferable Theodore, he too was shipped across the Marmara, to end his days in the prison he so richly deserved.

13
The City Recovered

[1253–61]

If we have just retaken the city in spite of the resistance of its defenders ... it is only as a result of the Divine Power which on the one hand renders impregnable (when it so desires) those cities which seem the most feeble, and which on the other enfeebles those which appear the most invincible. We have undergone so many failures to take Constantinople (although we were greater in number than the defenders) because God wished us to know that the possession of the city was a grace dependent on his bounty. He has reserved for our reign this grace, which obliges us to eternal gratitude, and in according it to us he has given us the hope of retaking the provinces which we lost with it.

The Emperor Michael VIII Palaeologus
to his people, quoted by George Pachymeres

The Latin Empire was tottering. Already in 1236 young Baldwin, now nineteen, had left for Italy in a desperate attempt to raise men and money, and Pope Gregory IX had appealed to the conscience of Western Christendom to save Constantinople from the barbarous schismatics who threatened it; but the response had been half-hearted. Despite the death of John of Brienne in 1237, Baldwin had remained away for nearly four years, his return delayed – he claimed – by personal business in France and by the deliberate machinations of Frederick II; it was not until the first weeks of 1240 that he had returned to the Bosphorus, in time to receive his imperial coronation during Holy Week. Behind him had marched an army of some thirty thousand men; but when they discovered that he had no means of paying them they soon dispersed. This chronic shortage of money was also responsible for another decision that had a disastrous effect on morale within Constantinople, among Greeks and Latins alike: the pawning to Venice of the city's most hallowed possession, the Crown of Thorns that Christ had worn on the Cross. When the moment came to redeem it their Emperor was unable to do so: the opportunity was seized instead by St Louis of France, and the precious relic was shipped off to Paris, where Louis built the Sainte-Chapelle to receive it.[1]

Baldwin had obviously developed a taste for the West, and it is difficult to blame him; a tour of the courts of Europe, even cap in hand, must have been vastly preferable to life in gloomy, beleaguered Constantinople. In 1244 he was off again – to Frederick II (whom he begged to use his good offices to extend the current truce with John Vatatzes); to Count Raymond in Toulouse; to Innocent IV in Lyon (with whom he attended the Great Council in 1245 at which Frederick, already twice excommunicated, was declared deposed); to St Louis in Paris; and even to London, where King Henry III made a small and distinctly grudging contribution to his funds. But Constantinople was by now past saving; when the wretched Emperor returned in October 1248 it was to find himself in such financial straits that he was obliged to start selling off the lead from the roof of the imperial palace. Even then, he would probably have been surprised to learn that he was to reign for another thirteen years; nor, very probably, would he have done so if his enemy in Nicaea had survived much longer than he did. But on 3 November 1254, while still in his early sixties, John Vatatzes died in Nymphaeum; and with the succession of his son Theodore much of the momentum that he had generated was lost.

It is another of the ironies of history that John III Vatatzes, who was more responsible than any other single man for the eventual reconquest of Constantinople, did not live to enter it in triumph. During the last ten years of his life his health had been steadily deteriorating, the epileptic fits to which he had always been subject becoming increasingly frequent and at times tending seriously to unbalance him. There had, for example, been an extraordinary occasion in 1253 when the most brilliant of his younger generals, Michael Palaeologus, had been arraigned on a charge of conspiracy. George Acropolites – whose chronicle is our principal Greek source for this period of imperial exile – records that the accusation was based on nothing more than a conversation overheard between two private citizens, one of whom later claimed that he had been misinterpreted. The Emperor, however, had not only decided to pursue the matter but had ordered that, to prove his innocence, Michael should submit to ordeal by red-hot iron – a Western custom previously unheard-of in Byzantium. Fortunately for all con-

---

1 It is now kept in the Cathedral of Notre-Dame.

cerned, the case collapsed;[1] and within a matter of months John, in a dramatic change of mood, had actually promoted the young general to the rank of 'Grand Constable' (another Western innovation), with command over all the Latin mercenaries. But by now it was clear to everyone at court that their Emperor was rapidly losing his grip.

John Vatatzes had been a great ruler none the less – one of the greatest, perhaps, in the whole of this history. He had inherited from his predecessor Theodore Lascaris a small but viable state, patterned on Byzantium, efficiently administered and strongly defended; but he himself during his reign had more than doubled it in size. When thirty-two years later he left it to his son Theodore II, its dominions extended over most of the Balkan peninsula and much of the Aegean, its rivals were crippled or annihilated, and it stood poised to achieve at last the purpose for which it had been established.

The Emperor's domestic record was no less impressive. Dispossessed landowners who had joined him in Asia Minor were rewarded with lands expropriated from those who had thrown in their lot with the Latin Empire; and along his own frontiers – which he fortified until they were stronger than ever before – he reintroduced the traditional Byzantine practice of granting smallholdings to his soldiers in return for military service when required. The Cumans in particular, as recent refugees from the Mongols, were delighted to be offered homesteads in Thrace or Macedonia, Phrygia or the valley of the Meander, and only too pleased to rally to the colours at the Emperor's call. All his subjects without distinction were continually reminded that they lived in a state of emergency, and that sacrifices were required of them until Constantinople should be theirs. Foreign imports – especially those from Venice – were forbidden; self-sufficiency was now the watchword, in both industry and agriculture, and Vatatzes himself set an example by running a profitable farm of his own, using the profits from his sales of eggs to buy his first wife Irene what he referred to as her 'egg crown' – a jewelled coronet, which he publicly presented to her as proof of how much might be achieved by careful and efficient husbandry.

The coronet was well-deserved, for Irene had proved an ideal wife to him. Together they set up countless hospitals, orphanages and charitable

---

1 Michael Palaeologus had agreed to the ordeal on the condition that that he should receive the iron from the hands of the Metropolitan Phocas of Philadelphia (one of his principal accusers). When the Metropolitan declined on the grounds that the custom was barbarous, Michael had declared that as 'a Roman born of Romans' he too would submit only to Roman law.

foundations, endowed churches and monasteries, and worked indefatigably for the relief of the poor. Art and literature were encouraged, and the foundations laid for the spectacular cultural revival which was to occur in the reign of their son Theodore, under whom Nicaea would become, for the space of a generation, as active a centre for Byzantine culture as Constantinople had been in the previous century. In consequence John Vatatzes was deeply and genuinely loved by his subjects. His treatment of his second wife must be remembered against him; in all else he seems to have been in every way what his friend George Acropolites described as a 'kind and gentle soul'; and it is not altogether surprising to learn that he was canonized soon after his death and revered as a local saint. He was buried near Nymphaeum, at the monastery of Sosandra.

Although John Vatatzes did not live to see the recapture of Constantinople, he knew as he lay on his deathbed that the day towards which he had worked all his adult life could not be long delayed – despite some doubts that he must have entertained about the abilities of his only son and successor. Not that the young Theodore II Lascaris – he took his imperial name from his mother – was altogether unworthy of the throne. Educated by Nicephorus Blemmydes, who was perhaps the outstanding scholar of his day, he had grown up to be an intellectual who produced in the course of his short life a whole corpus of literary, theological and scientific works; but he never allowed these interests to deflect him from the business of government. For his gravest weakness he could not be held responsible: he had inherited his father's epilepsy in a far more serious form. What to Vatatzes had been – at least until his last years – little more than an occasional inconvenience became in his son a serious disability, which tended as he grew older to impair his judgement and drain him of energy, often leaving him physically prostrate. This was dangerous enough in Constantinople; when he was with his army in the field it was potentially disastrous. He nevertheless led a number of successful campaigns against the Bulgars – who had attempted something of a comeback after their losses of eight years before – showing much personal courage and a surprising degree of military skill.

Theodore ruled with a strong and ruthless hand. Instinctively distrustful of the aristocracy, he ignored it as far as possible and relied instead on a small group of humbly-born civil servants, chief among them being his *protovestiarius* George Muzalon and the latter's two brothers, Theodore and Andronicus; and he enraged the clergy by appointing as

Patriarch an unworldly and bigoted ascetic named Arsenius, thus an-
nihilating at a single stroke his father's old dream of union with Rome.
Where foreign policy was concerned, he seems to have been content to
play a waiting game. Trouble threatened, briefly, from the Seljuk Sultan;
but a new Mongol advance occurred just in time. The Sultan, instead of
attacking Theodore, was compelled to seek his support against the
invaders.

As for the Bulgars, a second campaign in 1255–6 obliged them to sign
a peace treaty; and relations were still further improved when the Tsar
Michael Asen was murdered in 1256, to be succeeded in the following
year by a boyar named Constantine Tich – who immediately repudiated
his wife to marry Theodore's daughter Irene. Another dynastic marriage,
planned in 1249 but celebrated only seven years later, was that of John
Vatatzes's daughter Maria to Nicephorus, son of the Despot Michael II
of Epirus. It should have cemented the bonds between Epirus and
Nicaea; unfortunately it had precisely the opposite effect, Theodore
having unwisely made a last-minute demand for Durazzo and the
Macedonian city of Servia as a condition of the marriage. The bridegroom's mother, who had accompanied her son to the imperial camp on
the Maritsa, was obliged to agree for fear of being taken prisoner; but
when she returned to tell her husband that she had given away two of
the most important cities in his dominions, the Despot understandably
flew into a rage and launched an immediate campaign against Thessalonica, encouraging the Serbs and the Albanians to support him. Within
days, Macedonia was up in arms.

The general best qualified to handle the situation was, without any
doubt, Michael Palaeologus; the Emperor, however, detested him. The
two had known each other since childhood, and Theodore had always
felt the jealousy of an introverted semi-invalid towards the brilliant,
handsome young aristocrat who seemed to possess all the gifts he
himself so conspicuously lacked. He had also inherited his father's
instinctive mistrust of Michael – which, in his more violent moods,
bordered on the pathological. Earlier that year he had accused him –
quite unjustifiably – of high treason, threatening him to the point where
the young general had been obliged to seek refuge with the Seljuks,
commanding the Sultan's Christian mercenaries against the Mongol
invaders. Michael had sworn fidelity to the Emperor, who with a similar
oath had guaranteed his future safety. None the less, it was only after
some hesitation that Theodore decided to entrust him with the new
command; and even then he was unable to overcome his suspicions

altogether. Fearing, presumably, that his general might turn against him, he gave him too small an army to be of any real use. Michael and his men fought bravely, penetrating as far as Durazzo; but they were unable to stem the Epirot tide. By early summer the Despot was at the gates of Thessalonica, and Michael Palaeologus, recalled in disgrace and shortly afterwards excommunicated, was languishing in a Nicaean prison.

Why, on this occasion, did Michael give in without a struggle? Probably because he was confident – correctly, as it turned out – of being able to persuade the Emperor that he was guiltless. He may also have realized that Theodore had but a short time to live; if there was to be any dispute over the succession, it was important that he should be in Nicaea rather than the Balkans. However that may be, this totally unmerited treatment of the Empire's outstanding general, at a time when his presence was desperately needed in Thessalonica, confirmed the leading families of Nicaea in their conviction that their *basileus* was no longer capable of responsible government. From the outset of his reign he had made no secret of his hostility to them, and his treatment of Michael Palaeologus was only the most recent example of his impulsiveness and unreliability. Although largely excluded from the administration, they were still strongly represented in the higher echelons of the army and navy; and there would almost certainly have been a military revolt had not Theodore Lascaris suddenly and most conveniently succumbed to his disease in August 1258, aged thirty-six.

His eldest son John being a child,[1] Theodore – with characteristic disregard for popular feeling – had appointed the hated George Muzalon as Regent. On his deathbed he had forced the leading members of the aristocracy to swear allegiance to John and George together, but their detestation for the *protovestiarius* and his cronies was too great: in the course of a memorial service for the late Emperor held at Sosandra monastery just nine days after his death they murdered Muzalon, together with one of his brothers, at the high altar and hacked the bodies to pieces. A palace revolution ensued, the result of which was to nominate the hastily liberated Michael Palaeologus – who had almost certainly been the chief instigator of the plot – in his stead.

Michael was now thirty-four. He was in many respects the obvious choice. His family was an old and distinguished one – a Nicephorus

---

1 Of our four principal sources, Acropolites gives his age as eight, Pachymeres nine, Gregoras and Sphrantzes (writing a good deal later) six.

Palaeologus had been Governor of Mesopotamia under Michael VII in the eleventh century – and he himself could claim kinship with the three imperial houses of Ducas, Angelus and Comnenus, while his wife Theodora was a great-niece of John Vatatzes.[1] To be sure, his record was not entirely without blemish: there had been his trial for treason and his flight to the Sultan, to say nothing of his recent brief imprisonment. But the circumstances in which these had occurred were well known, and no one took them too seriously. His complicity – to put it no higher – in the murder of Muzalon should have been seen as a darker stain on his character; but the *protovestiarius* had been so universally hated that few seem to have been disposed to hold it against him. He remained immensely popular with the army – particularly the Latin mercenaries whom he commanded – and was well thought of by the clergy; even the ambiguous attitude of Theodore Lascaris towards him was now considered a point in his favour. He was instantly awarded the title of Grand Duke (*megas dux*) and soon afterwards – at the insistence of the clergy – that of Despot. Finally in November 1258 he was raised on a shield and proclaimed co-Emperor, his coronation taking place at Nicaea on Christmas Day. He and Theodora were crowned first, with imperial diadems heavy with precious stones; only afterwards was a narrow string of pearls laid upon the head of his young colleague, John IV.

Few of those present at the joint coronation had any serious doubt that it was Michael VIII Palaeologus who would lead his subjects back into their ancient capital. Before he could do so, however, there was one more enemy to be faced. Early in 1258 young Manfred of Sicily, the bastard son of Frederick II, had invaded Epirus, occupied Corfu and captured several coastal towns, including Durazzo, Avlona and Butrinto. The Despot Michael, reluctant to give up his Macedonian campaign when Thessalonica seemed on the point of falling, had decided instead to form an alliance with him against Nicaea, giving him the hand of his eldest daughter Helena and suggesting that the conquered territories might be considered as her dowry. Manfred had accepted with alacrity, and as a token of his good intentions had sent his new father-in-law four hundred mounted knights from Germany. Soon afterwards the new alliance was joined by William of Villehardouin, the Latin Prince of Achaia in the northern Peloponnese, who married Michael's second

---

1 There is little evidence for the theory according to which Michael was also descended from an old Italian family in Viterbo. See D. J. Geanakoplos, *Emperor Michael Palaeologus and the West*, p. 18n.

daughter Anna. The ultimate object of the expedition was of course Constantinople, but this would clearly involve the capture of Thessalonica – as the European capital of the Nicene Empire – on the way.

Thus, at the time of the accession of Michael Palaeologus, it seemed that virtually the whole of the Greek mainland was ranged against him. Before the year 1258 was ended he had sent ambassadors to the three allies, in the hopes of persuading them to abandon their hostile plans, and a further embassy to Rome – always implacably hostile to the Hohenstaufen – with the usual hints of union of the Eastern and Western Churches; but the hour was too late for diplomacy, and the envoys returned empty-handed, as he had feared they would. Fortunately he had made alternative arrangements, having dispatched that same autumn a large expeditionary force to the Balkans, containing important contingents from Hungary and Serbia as well as the usual regiments of Cuman and Turkish mercenaries. It was commanded by his brother, the *sebastocrator* John Palaeologus, and the Grand Domestic Alexius Strategopulus; and early in 1259 he ordered them to advance against the enemy.

Michael of Epirus and his army were still in their winter quarters at Castoria. Taken by surprise, they fled to Avlona – still under the control of Manfred – where the Despot appealed to his allies for urgent assistance. He did not call in vain: Manfred at once sent a further detachment of cavalry and Prince William personally brought a large army up from Achaia. Numbers are notoriously hard to assess; but if we put the total strength of the forces of the Western alliance at forty-five thousand we shall probably not be very far wrong. They almost certainly outnumbered those at the disposal of John Palaeologus, who marched northward to meet them at Pelagonia (now Bitolj, or Monastir); and there, some weeks later – the precise date is unknown, but it was probably in the early summer – the two armies met.

Almost immediately, the coalition fell apart. The *sebastocrator* John had had orders from his brother to exploit the lack of unity between the three armies, and did so to remarkable effect. His brilliant guerrilla tactics did the rest. The Despot Michael and his son Nicephorus, persuaded – without the slightest justification – that their allies were planning to betray them to the enemy, deserted the camp under cover of darkness and fled with most of their men, finally taking refuge in Cephalonia. Another son, John the Bastard, taunted by Villehardouin over his illegitimacy, joined the Nicene forces out of pique. By the time the battle began John Palaeologus, at the head of a united and well-disciplined army, found only the French and German cavalry of Villehardouin and Manfred ranged against him; and they proved defenceless in the face of his Cuman archers. Manfred's knights surrendered and were taken prisoner, as – subsequently – was Villehardouin himself, who was found hiding in a haystack near Castoria and was recognized only by his protruding front teeth. John then advanced through Thessaly, while his principal lieutenant, Alexius Strategopulus, marched straight to Epirus and captured its capital, Arta. The victory was complete.

Determined to keep up his momentum, early in 1260 the Emperor – now commanding his troops in person – marched on Constantinople itself. Unfortunately we know little about this campaign, our principal sources (Acropolites on the one hand, Pachymeres and Gregoras on the other) giving two such different versions of what occurred that it is sometimes hard to believe that they are describing the same expedition. Michael had apparently succeeded in suborning a prominent Latin in the city, who on an agreed signal was to open one of the gates; when at the critical moment this man proved unable to do so, he switched to an alternative plan and launched an attack on Galata, immediately opposite the city across the Golden Horn. But here too disappointment awaited him. Without a fighting navy[1] he was unable to make any impact on the great iron chain that barred the Horn; meanwhile the Latins of Galata, assisted by many others who rowed over each morning from Constantinople, put up a far tougher resistance than he had expected. After a short time he decided to waste no more time on an operation which even if ultimately successful would yield him only limited advantage, and gave the order to retire.

To poor Baldwin, trembling in Constantinople, the departure of Michael Palaeologus and his army gave little comfort: since Pelagonia it was plain that the recapture of the city could only be a question of time, and a short time at that. Of all the allies to whom he had once looked for succour, there now remained only the Papacy and the Republic of Venice. Pope Alexander IV was deaf to his appeals; that left the Venetians, who had been more responsible than anyone else for the Latin Empire, and whose fleet of thirty ships still diligently patrolled the approaches to the Golden Horn and the Bosphorus. In his frantic search for money with which to strengthen his defences, Baldwin managed to raise a further loan from the merchants of the Rialto, putting up his own son Philip as security. But soon the value of even Venetian support

---

1 The Nicaean Empire had never possessed much of a navy, despite the efforts of both John Vatatzes and Theodore II to create one.

began to appear problematical; for Michael Palaeologus, desperate for a navy, had entered negotiations with Venice's arch-rival Genoa,[1] and on 13 March 1261 a treaty was signed at Nymphaeum by the terms of which, in return for their help in the struggle to come, the Genoese were promised all the concessions hitherto enjoyed by Venice, with their own quarter in Constantinople and the other principal ports of the Empire and free access to those of the Black Sea. For Genoa this was a historic agreement, laying as it did the foundations for her commercial empire in the East; for Byzantium it was ultimately to prove a disaster, since the two sea-republics would gradually usurp all that remained of her naval power and pursue their centuries-old rivalry over her helpless body. But that was in the future. In the spring of 1261, the Genoese alliance must have seemed to Michael and his subjects like a gift from heaven.

After all the treaties and alliances, all the discord and the bloodshed, all the heroic dreams and the disappointed hopes of the previous threescore years, the recovery of Constantinople eventually came about almost by accident. In the high summer of 1261, Michael VIII had sent the Caesar Alexius Strategopulus[2] to Thrace with a small army, to check that the Bulgarian frontier was quiet and to indulge in a little mild sabre-rattling outside Constantinople, sounding out the city's defences at the same time. When he reached Selymbria, Alexius learned from the local Greek inhabitants that the Latin garrison was absent, having been carried off by the Venetian fleet to attack the Nicaean island of Daphnusia, a useful harbour which controlled the entrance to the Bosphorus from the Black Sea.[3] They also told him of a postern gate in the Land Walls through which armed men could easily pass into the city. The year's truce with the Latin Empire that had been arranged at the time of Michael's withdrawal from Galata in September 1260 was theoretically still in

---

1 Contrary to what is implied in most modern accounts, the initial overtures seem almost certainly to have been made by the Genoese. See Geanakoplos, op. cit., pp. 83-5.

2 He had been granted the title after his capture of Arta in 1259. Until the eleventh century the caesar had been the highest dignity in the Empire, reserved for senior members of the imperial family. Alexius I had however lowered it slightly; it was now one degree below *sebastocrator*.

3 Was the Daphnusia expedition somehow inspired by Michael Palaeologus, to empty Constantinople of its defenders at the moment of Strategopulus's attack? If not, it certainly seems a remarkably fortunate coincidence. But Geanakoplos (op. cit., pp. 97–104), after careful consideration of the evidence on both sides, concludes that 'one must ... abandon, however reluctantly, the hypothesis of premeditation so compatible with the characteristic resourcefulness exhibited by Michael throughout his entire career'.

force; but the Latins were already breaking it by their attack on Daphnusia, and anyway to Alexius Strategopulus the opportunity seemed too good to miss. That night a small detachment of his best men slipped unobserved into the city, took the few guards by surprise and threw them from the ramparts. They then quietly opened one of the gates. At dawn on 25 July 1261 the rest of the army poured in after them, meeting scarcely any resistance.[1]

Baldwin, asleep at Blachernae, was awakened by the tumult and fled for his life, leaving the imperial crown and sceptre behind him. Making his way on foot from one end of the city to the other, he narrowly escaped capture and was wounded in the arm; but somehow he reached the Great Palace, and found a Venetian merchantman in the little harbour of the Bucoleon. On this he escaped, together with the Venetian *podestà* and a few others, to the Latin-held island of Euboea.[2] Meanwhile Alexius Strategopulus and his men set fire to the entire Venetian quarter of the city, so that the sailors on their return from Daphnusia, finding their houses destroyed and their terrified families huddled on the quay-side, would have no spirit for a counter-attack or any real choice but to sail back to their lagoon. Among the remaining Franks there was widespread panic, joyfully described by the Greek chroniclers. Some fled to monasteries, frequently disguising themselves as monks to escape the vengeance of the Caesar's soldiers; others hid wherever they could find a place of concealment; a few, we are told, even resorted to the sewers.

They need not have worried. There was no massacre. Gradually they emerged from their various refuges and made their way – many of them staggering under the weight of their most valuable possessions – down to the harbour where the thirty Venetian ships were waiting, together with a large vessel which had recently put in from Sicily. No mention is made of their numbers; there may have been about a thousand all told. The moment they were all aboard, this fleet also left for Euboea – not, apparently, even pausing to load up with provisions, since it is recorded that many of the refugees died of hunger before reaching their destination.

---

1 Such, at least, is the version of the story told by George Acropolites. Gregoras, who follows him in the most essential details, mentions a subterranean passage with its entrance near the monastery of the Fountain. Pachymeres talks of scaling-ladders set up at the Fountain Gate. We can take our choice.

2 Euboea was known to the Latins – and to many later historians – as Negropont, or Negroponte. Since, however, this name is used indiscriminately for the island, its capital Chalkis, the Frankish lordship and the Venetian political unit, it seems advisable to retain the Greek version here.

The Emperor Michael was two hundred miles away, asleep in his camp at Meteorium in Asia Minor, when the imperial messengers arrived. His sister Eulogia[1] woke him – according to Acropolites, by tickling his toes – and told him the news. At first he refused to believe her; only when he was handed Baldwin's abandoned regalia could he be convinced of the truth of the report. Immediately he began to make his preparations; and three weeks later, on 15 August 1261, 'the new Constantine' (as he called himself, being the second 'founder' of Constantinople) made his formal entry into the capital. It was not in any sense a triumph: aware of the immense historical and symbolic significance of the event, he had resolved to make it rather an act of thanksgiving. Entering by the Golden Gate, he first stopped to hear special prayers composed by his Grand Logothete, the chronicler George Acropolites; then, preceded by the great icon of the Hodegetria – 'She who points the way' – that had been painted, as everyone knew, by St Luke himself, he proceeded on foot along the traditional route down the Mesē and through the whole city as far as St Sophia, where a second coronation ceremony was performed by Patriarch Arsenius. This time, however, he and his wife were crowned alone, while their baby son Andronicus was proclaimed as heir presumptive.

And what, we may ask, of John Lascaris, Michael's ten-year-old co-Emperor? He had been left behind in Nicaea, neglected and forgotten. A little over four months later, on Christmas Day, his eyes were put out. It happened to be his eleventh birthday.[2]

From the start, the Latin Empire of Constantinople was a monstrosity. The miserable offspring of treachery and greed, in the fifty-seven years of its existence it achieved nothing, contributed nothing, enjoyed not a single moment of distinction or glory. After 1204 it made no territorial conquests, and before long had shrunk to the immediate surroundings of the city that had been ruined and ravaged in giving it birth. The wonder is that it lasted as long as it did. Of its seven rulers, only Henry of Hainault – if we leave aside the octogenarian John of Brienne – rose

---

1 Pachymeres records that Eulogia, who was several years older than her brother, used to lull him to sleep as a child by singing of how he would one day become Emperor and enter Constantinople through the Golden Gate.

2 He was confined in the fortress of Dakibyze, on the southern shore of the Marmara, where he remained until his death nearly half a century later, in 1305.

above the mediocre; not one seems to have made the slightest attempt to understand his Greek subjects, let alone to learn their language. Meanwhile its Frankish knights trickled back to the West, its allies turned away, its treasury lay empty. And its fall was, if anything, even more ignominious than its beginning – overpowered in a single night by a handful of soldiers, while its defenders were engaged on an exercise of almost unimaginable pointlessness and futility.

If this pathetic travesty of an Empire could only have confined its misdeeds to itself, it might have been passed over with little more than a pitying glance; and the reader would have been spared a long and unedifying chapter of this book. Alas, it did not. The dark legacy that it left behind affected not only Byzantium but all Christendom – perhaps all the world. For the Greek Empire never recovered from the damage that it had sustained during those fateful years, danger that was spiritual as well as material. Nor, bereft of much of the territory that remained to it after the disaster of Manzikert, with many of its loveliest buildings reduced to rubble and its finest works of art destroyed or carried off to the West, did it ever succeed in recovering its former morale. Henceforth the Byzantines might continue to look back with pride on the glories of their past; but they would contemplate their future with trepidation and fear.

They had been robbed of something else too. Before the Latin conquest their Empire had been one and indivisible, under a single *basileus* who stood above them, half-way to heaven, Equal of the Apostles. Now, that unity was gone. So magnificent a conception was no longer tenable. There were the Emperors of Trebizond, still stubbornly independent in their tiny Byzantine microcosm on the Black Sea shore. There were the Despots of Epirus, for ever struggling to recapture their early days of power, always ready to welcome the enemies of Constantinople and to provide a focus of opposition. How, fragmented as it was, could the Greek Empire continue to perform the function that it had fulfilled for so long – that of the last grand eastern bulwark of Christendom against the Islamic tide?

But Christendom too had been changed by the Fourth Crusade. Long divided, it was now polarized. For centuries before and after the Great Schism of 1054, relations between the Eastern and the Western Churches had fluctuated between the politely distant and the bitterly acrimonious; their differences, however, had been essentially theological. After the sack of Constantinople by the Western Crusaders, this was no longer true. In the eyes of the Byzantines, those barbarians who had desecrated their altars, plundered their homes and violated their women could no longer be considered, in any real sense of the word, Christians at all. On more than one occasion in the future, attempts would be made to force the Orthodox Church back into union with Rome; some, like that of Michael Palaeologus himself in 1274, would even be briefly successful. But such attempts could never succeed for long, simply because in the end the eventualities that they were designed to avoid always appeared to the Greeks preferable to the idea of submission to Rome. 'Better the Sultan's turban than the cardinal's hat,' they were to say; and they meant it.

14
The Angevin Threat

[1261–70]

Michael Palaeologus, the schismatic, having usurped the name of Emperor . . .
has seized the imperial city of Constantinople and the whole Empire, and has
expelled the Emperor Baldwin and the Latins residing there . . . We therefore
are ready with God's help to undertake the pious task of restoring the noble
limb severed by the schismatics from the body of our common mother, the
Holy Roman Church.

Second Viterbo Treaty, 27 May 1267

The *basileus* was back in his capital; and among the small Greek population who had remained in occupied Constantinople the rejoicings
continued far into the night, with all the bells of the city pealing in
jubilation and little groups of monks and nuns hurrying from one
church or monastery to the next, decorating each in turn as if for some
great religious feast. Michael Palaeologus, however, took no part in
these festivities. His first sight of the city from which he was to rule had
affected him profoundly. Everywhere was desolation: churches in ruins,
palaces razed, once-prosperous residential areas now reduced to piles of
blackened timber. Even among those houses that had escaped the
conflagration of 1204, many had subsequently been demolished and used
for firewood. There had been no attempt at rebuilding; much of the
debris still lay where it had fallen more than half a century before. After
his coronation Michael had quietly withdrawn to the Great Palace on the
Bosphorus – that of Blachernae, though newer and a good deal more
comfortable, he felt to be tainted by the presence of the Latin Emperors[1]
– to ponder the formidable problems that faced him.

The most immediate was the defence of the capital. The larger part of

---

1 Pachymeres tells us that 'it was filled with thick smoke and Italian fire, which the servants of
the uncouth Baldwin had allowed to permeate it'.

Greece, after all, was still under Frankish domination; Epirus and Thessaly, though Greek, remained implacably hostile, as did Serbia and Bulgaria. Venice and Genoa controlled Byzantine waters and much of the eastern Mediterranean. Pope Urban IV – a certain Jacques Pantaléon, the son of a leather-merchant in Troyes and former Latin Patriarch of Jerusalem who had been raised to the Papacy a fortnight after the recovery of Constantinople – could not be expected to accept without a struggle the collapse of the Latin Empire of the East; and Manfred, now back in Sicily, would be only too glad of an excuse to return to the offensive. An alliance of some or all of these Western and Balkan powers, efficiently organized and properly led, could kill the newly-restored Empire at its birth. Among the Emperor's first priorities, therefore, was to make a thorough examination of the land and sea walls, improving and strengthening them wherever necessary. The weakest section, as he well knew, was that running along the banks of the Golden Horn; it was this that the Crusaders had breached in both 1203 and 1204. Eventually he was to give it a whole new inner rampart, thus presenting any attacking fleet with a double range of fortifications; for the moment, however, he contented himself with raising a giant wooden screen, seven feet high, the entire five-mile length of the wall, covered with hides to make it at least partially fireproof.

Ideally, of course, no enemy should be able to enter the Horn in the first place. The Emperor accordingly renewed the great iron chain that had formerly extended across the entrance to provide a barrier against all hostile shipping. But this chain could never be entirely impregnable and was certainly no substitute for a strong and effective fleet; hence the intensive programme of shipbuilding which Michael inaugurated during the first months after the reconquest. Meanwhile he had no alternative but to put his faith in the Genoese – his only Western allies – transferring to them the former palace of the Venetians[1] and taking every opportunity to remind them of their obligations under the Treaty of Nymphaeum, signed only a few months before.

Next, there was the transfer of the government to be effected – and this was no easy matter. The Byzantine bureaucratic machine was complex and often unwieldy; to rehouse all its various departments – to say nothing of all the officials who administered them – in a largely

---

1 Formerly the Byzantine monastery of the Pantocrator. The Genoese immediately demolished it to the sound of triumphant musical fanfares, sending several of its stones back to Genoa, where they were incorporated into the famous Bank of St George.

devastated city was an awesome task. It was made possible only by the
fact that Constantinople had also suffered a dramatic reduction of its
population. Many Greeks had left when the Crusaders arrived, and many
more had trickled away during the intervening years. A considerable
number had inevitably been replaced by Latins, but now most of these
had also disappeared, leaving whole sections of the city silent and
abandoned. One of the new Emperor's first actions was to summon all
former refugees back to the capital, and in 1262 to introduce a
whole new community of *tsakones* – Greeks from the region around
Monemvasia in the south-eastern Peloponnese, which was formally
ceded to him in that year by the Prince of Achaia.

Meanwhile the imperial army was set to work on an ambitious
programme of rebuilding. Living accommodation was a primary need,
but Michael concentrated also on the ravaged churches and monasteries,
realizing as he did their vital importance to popular morale. The
Latins, seeing these as monuments of a detested heresy, had shown
them scant respect – stripping the lead from their roofs, defacing their
mosaics and frescos, robbing them of their treasures and sacred vessels.
For the Byzantines, on the other hand, the reawakening of their religious life simultaneously revived their feelings of patriotism and
national pride – while ensuring the greatest possible degree of ecclesiastical support for Michael's policies. Nor did the Emperor forget the
public buildings of the capital: law-courts and theatres, market-places
and forums. Finally, to symbolize all that he had done, he erected
before the church of the Holy Apostles a tall column bearing a statue
of his patron St Michael. At its foot stood another statue representing
the Emperor himself, holding in his hands a model of Constantinople
and offering it in the traditional manner to the Archangel. He had
deserved well of his city and his people; and he was determined that
they should not forget it.

Michael Palaeologus had been right in his assessment of Pope Urban;
but he had no wish to antagonize him unnecessarily. After his first
coronation at Nicaea he had punctiliously sent an embassy to the Holy
See, giving it official notice of his accession to the throne; now, after his
second, he did so again, loading his two envoys – though Greeks, both
had been members of Baldwin's secretariat – with rich presents for the
Pope. But if he had hoped thus to turn away the worst of the papal
wrath, he was to be disappointed. However difficult it may be to believe
Pachymeres when he tells us that one of the envoys was flayed alive

while the other barely escaped with his life, there can be no doubt that they were given a distinctly hostile reception.

Urban, meanwhile – urged on by Baldwin – was pressing for a new Crusade to recover Constantinople for the West, and had already excommunicated the Genoese for casting in their lot with the Eastern Empire. The Venetians on the other hand were predictably giving him their fullest support, even going so far as to offer free passage to all who were prepared to take up arms against the Emperor. Elsewhere, to the Pope's disappointment, there was little enthusiasm. The crusading zeal that had been such a feature of the previous century was gone. In France, St Louis sensibly maintained that the purpose of Crusades was to fight the infidel and not one's fellow-Christians, however schismatic they might be. Germany had been in a state of confusion ever since the death of Frederick II in 1250. The Kingdom of Aragon was keeping a covetous eye on Sicily, but was little interested in anything further afield. As for England, despite its distinguished crusading record, the Pope seems simply not to have bothered about it. That left Frederick's son Manfred, who would have asked nothing better; apart from the rich territories to be gained, an alliance with Rome would almost certainly have achieved the papal recognition of his throne that he had so long desired. He and Baldwin did everything they could think of to effect a reconciliation with the Pope, but in vain. To Urban, who had inherited in full measure his predecessors' hatred of the Hohenstaufen, such an alliance would have been anathema. The King of Sicily, as he well knew, had ambitions of his own where Constantinople was concerned; and even if Baldwin were to be reinstated, the prospect of owing his return to Manfred was one too ghastly to be contemplated.

Michael Palaeologus – who had already built up for himself a formidable intelligence service – was well aware of these approaches to the Pope, which he looked upon with grave concern. He had long tried, without success, to reach some accommodation with Manfred; in the summer of 1262 he made another attempt. It happened that Manfred's half-sister Anna, widow of John Vatatzes, was still living at the imperial court; Michael now proposed to divorce his wife Theodora and marry her. Historians, ancient and modern alike, seem uncertain as to how to interpret this curious offer. Such a marriage could indeed hardly have failed to bring the two rulers closer together; on the other hand it would have provoked a major scandal at court and would almost certainly have resulted in the Emperor's excommunication by Patriarch Arsenius, who had already publicly censured his treatment of little John Lascaris.

Istanbul: St Sophia (with minarets added after the Turkish conquest)

Venice: the Bronze Horses of St Mark, (*above*) in their previous position on
the west front of St Mark's Basilica; (*below*) in their present sad repository

Istanbul, St Sophia (south gallery): the Virgin and Child,
flanked by John II Comnenus and the Empress Irene

Istanbul, The Church of St Saviour in Chora (Kariye Camii): a mosaic portrait of
Theodore Metochites, presenting the Church to Christ, c.1320

Manuel I Comnenus and the Empress Mary of Antioch

Cefalù Cathedral, Sicily: apse mosaic of Christ Pantocrator, *c.*1150

Mistra: the monastery of the Peribleptos, late fourteenth century

Syria: the Crusader castle of Krak des Chevaliers, c.1140

Seljuk architecture: the bridge at Batman, Anatolia, thirteenth century

John VI Cantacuzenus, portrayed as both Emperor and monk (Paris, Bibliothèque Nationale)

Marshal de Boucicaut, with St Catherine, from the Boucicaut Hours (Paris, Musée Jacquemart-André)

The Emperor Frederick Barbarossa
(Rome, Vatican Library)

Ηκωστ την ταρίστε την θησωνόμως,
βλεπωμακαι δακρύω, ουτίνα φρουταφ
τα σαυτον άλ στερκράτηπωτ ηλάτου μ
όσον χρέσα άλ ιεδω, ωφοίοντι μοι
ου λάσαι πάσαν άσου άλθορεσ άμα,

Εικαί ττοσαυτον την συν παν των εβης
ημαεδσαυτω και προσου φιλτα τεμοι
αλλα και κοσμήσω σε ταισ ε φημιαισ
γαρ καττα ξίαν σοι, ου κρο τον ηγοσσ
σω σα λεγ ετ καλοίων λα ιην ηπ όλως:

Ηκω των μυθησου,
και στε μεν ταν τ
αρίστε εκαι ττρος
στ εκ εδε λλη εικ
ηφισαι φηρ, ου λ
λω ωσινα δακρεπ
τω γ ταφ ου θε αλ
στω ημαεδ αυτω
και ττροσου, ου σ
σ φιρ λε τίου υ ωλ
έφαμεν αφ ηρη
και του του δε ου
λ του καττοισ τα
ν οισ κοσμηστω
φ χρέσα αλφα σι
ωσσται τογαρ
και λξίαν, ου ελ
ου λλη ττου ιερε
θρομτησου γου
ττραν άλωσαι
δε ιαυτου λκρισ
σω λλ λε, σωφα
συ εικ ηλ όλωσ
ει χτι:-

Ηλύθου κλ λωφ ερ τα άδ, του θησου θρεωκα
ουτοι εδρι δα φησι εσο ρωρ τα πον ταφον,
εις δ ι σωρφ λ λεω, όστε θ δοσ λεμή τω,
μτρ, ά τσι λ λωφ λω, και σ προσ μεν εα άλα
ττω δε κα τω σα ττ ιοιατ ιε ος, χ ροστου δον
τ αφο τη ταυ ξ λ σ ημ δολ εσ, ουκα εσ άμ,

και σε μεν, σκα τταρ μερ τι όρ ττ θρ ήδλ
ιει καττω δακρυεσ άμ, ττοτε μ μωοι ομε αυτω
τω θ ορ δε με αυτ αν η, το κλ λιση νε όντασ
κοσ μ ημ, και σ μηρ ος λ τ ροισ ημ λ τεμ εασ ι
δ ήρ και μ στω π τε προς προς πετ ικ ηχ τα
ιτι ει εττη
τω συ τ α ο χρι σσοισ α λαξ ίατ τ όσα :-

The Emperor Manuel II Palaeologus (1391–1425)
(Paris, Bibliothèque Nationale)

John VIII Palaeologus, a medal by Pisanello, 1438 (Florence, Bargello)

The Emperor Andronicus II (?) Palaeologus (Athens, Byzantine Museum)

A Turkish Janissary, by Gentile Bellini, late fourteenth century (London, British Museum)

Istanbul: the Fortress of Rumeli Hisar on the Bosphorus,
built by the Sultan Mehmet II in 1452, photographed *c.*1914

Istanbul: the Land Walls of Constantinople, with the ruins of
the Imperial Palace of Blachernae (Tekfur Saray)

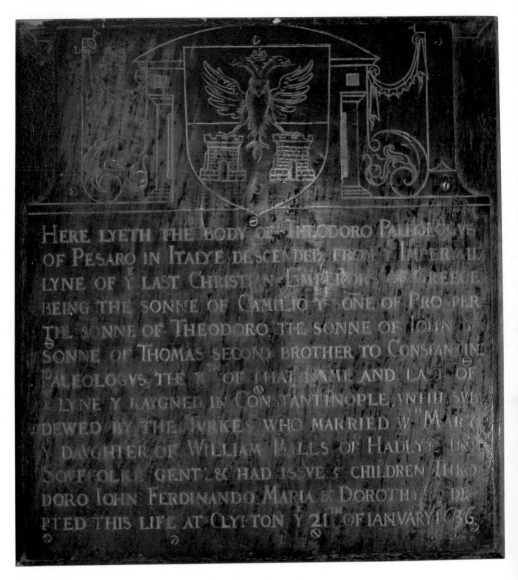

HERE LYETH THE BODY OF THEODORO PALIOLOGVS
OF PESARO IN ITALYE DESCENDED FROM Ỹ IMPERIALL
LYNE OF Ỹ LAST CHRISTIAN EMPERORS OF GREECE
BEING THE SONNE OF CAMILIO Ỹ SONNE OF PROSPER
THE SONNE OF THEODORO THE SONNE OF IOHN Ỹ
SONNE OF THOMAS SECOND BROTHER TO CONSTANTINE
PALEOLOGVS THE 8 OF THAT NAME AND LAST OF
Ỹ LYNE Ỹ RAYGNED IN CONSTANTINOPLE VNTILL SVB
DEWED BY THE TVRKES WHO MARRIED WᵗH MARY
Ỹ DAVGHTER OF WILLIAM BALLS OF HADLYE IN
SOVFFOLKE GENT & HAD ISSVE 5 CHILDREN THEO
DORO IOHN FERDINANDO MARIA & DOROTHY & DE
PTED THIS LIFE AT CLYFTON Ỹ 21ᵗH OF IANVARY 1636

St Leonard's Church, Landulph, Cornwall:
an inscribed plaque in memory of Theodore Palaeologus,
descendant of the last Emperor of Byzantium, 1636

George Pachymeres claims that Michael's real motive was 'burning love' for Anna. There is nothing inherently improbable in the idea; Michael (who had already sired two illegitimate daughters) might easily have succumbed to the charms of a woman who was still only thirty and – as far as we can judge – a good deal more attractive than her late husband's behaviour towards her might have suggested. But none of our other sources provide any corroboration for the theory, any more than does Michael's own subsequent decision to return her to her brother when he was persuaded to abandon the project under pressure from the Patriarch, Anna herself and his wife Theodora – who had no desire to end her days in a convent. In exchange, Manfred sent back the Caesar Alexius Strategopulus, who had been captured by the Despot of Epirus and handed over to him at his request; but Michael's long-desired political alliance remained a dream.

He was not unduly discouraged. There was plenty of work to be done nearer home, where he was determined to restore to the Empire the frontiers that had existed before 1204. He began in the Peloponnese, in 1262 releasing Prince William of Achaia from the prison in which he had languished during the three years since his captivity after the battle of Pelagonia, and receiving in return the all-important fortresses of Monemvasia, Mistra, Maina, Geraki and the district of Kinsterna – a significant first step in the re-establishment of imperial power in the peninsula. He and William then took solemn oaths never again to go to war against one another, the agreement being sealed by William's becoming godfather to the Emperor's son Constantine and being accorded the rank and title of Grand Domestic of the Empire.

The oaths, it need hardly be said, were broken almost as soon as they were made. In May 1262 at Thebes, William entered into an alliance with the Venetians against the Empire; and only two months later, at Viterbo,[1] he was party to a further agreement between Pope Urban, Baldwin, Venice and all the Latin barons of the Peloponnese, by the terms of which the Pope formally released him from his pledges to the 'Greek schismatics'. For Michael Palaeologus, this was provocation enough. In the first months of 1263 an imperial fleet of newly-built ships sacked the Frankish-held islands of Cos, Naxos and Paros, attacked the cities of Oreos and Karystos at the opposite ends of Euboea and finally

---

1 Viterbo, some sixty miles from Rome, had been chosen by Pope Alexander IV in 1257 as his principal place of residence. It was to continue in papal favour for the next twenty-eight years, until the death of Martin IV in 1285.

descended on the south-eastern Morea, where it seized much of the coast of Laconia; meanwhile an army of some fifteen thousand men – a third of whom were Seljuk mercenaries – under the command of the Emperor's brother, the *sebastocrator* Constantine, was carried by Genoese ships directly to Monemvasia, whence it advanced north-west to besiege Lacedaemon, the ancient Sparta. William of Achaia – now seriously alarmed – hurried to Corinth in an attempt to mobilize his fellow-princes, whereupon Constantine abandoned his siege and led the army in a series of forced marches across the Peloponnese to William's capital at Andravida.

For a moment it looked as though all Achaia was doomed; the situation was saved only by the courage of the *bailli* whom William had left in charge, a local Greek named John Katavas. Despite his advanced age and a bad attack of gout, Katavas hastily assembled the three-hundred-man garrison and led it out to a narrow defile near the imperial camp. When a quick reconnaissance revealed that the invaders were still resting after their long journey, he immediately gave the order to attack. Constantine and his men, taken off their guard, could offer little resistance. Many of them were slaughtered; the remainder sought refuge in the neighbouring forests. The *sebastocrator* himself, narrowly escaping with his life, fled back across the peninsula to Mistra.

Only a month or two later, off the little island of Spetsai, a mixed fleet of forty-eight imperial and Genoese ships sailing southward to Monemvasia encountered a substantially smaller Venetian force of thirty-two galleys. Precise details of the engagement that followed are unclear, but it ended in a crushing defeat for the Genoese, whose fleet – more than half of which had refused to fight – was ignominiously scattered. They lost one of their admirals and, we are told, up to a thousand of their men.[1] It was to be several years before they were once again a significant force in the eastern Mediterranean; more important still, they surrendered the respect of Michael Palaeologus, who paid for their naval patrols and demanded better returns for his money.

The Emperor had other reasons, too, for dissatisfaction. Since the Nymphaeum pact and the expulsion of the Venetians, the Genoese had been flooding into Constantinople, where they were now settling in such numbers – and trading so aggressively – as to constitute a serious threat to the native merchant community. Fully conscious of the extent to

---

1 For the figures we have to rely on Martino da Canale, a Venetian. He puts the casualties for his own side at 420.

which the Byzantines depended on their shipping, they were constantly increasing their handling charges on Greek goods; and the growing hostility that they aroused was rapidly assuming dangerous proportions. It was surely with these considerations in mind as well as his understandable disgust with their performance at Spetsai that, in the autumn of 1263, Michael abruptly dismissed their remaining fleet of some sixty galleys and ordered it to return home. This was not the end of the Nymphaeum agreement; before long Genoa sent him a number of replacements which, with rather bad grace, he accepted. But this half-hearted reconciliation proved short-lived: in the following year a conspiracy was discovered on the part of the Genoese *podestà* in Constantinople, Guglielmo Guercio, to betray Constantinople to King Manfred of Sicily. Confronted by the Emperor in person with incontrovertible evidence of the plot, Guercio immediately confessed his guilt, whereupon he and his countrymen were banished altogether from the city. Just three years after the Treaty of Nymphaeum, the Genoese alliance had ended in disaster.

More than ever now, Michael Palaeologus needed friends. Manfred had ignored his overtures; King Louis was too fully occupied with his own crusading campaigns to give much thought to Byzantium. There remained Pope Urban. He was no less hostile than before; but his hostility sprang, not from any personal animosity to Michael of the kind that he felt towards Manfred, but simply from a natural desire to see Constantinople once again subject to Rome. On the other hand, his relations with the Hohenstaufen faction were steadily worsening, he was fully aware of Manfred's long-term ambitions and would, as Michael well knew, infinitely prefer a heretic Greek Emperor on the Bosphorus to the King of Sicily. It looked as if he might be ready to strike a bargain.

Now it so happened that in Constantinople at the time was a certain Nicholas, the Latin Bishop of Crotone in Calabria. He was, like most of his fellow-Calabrians, a Greek; and for many years he had maintained regular contacts with the Empire, having formerly corresponded with both John Vatatzes and Theodore Lascaris. Michael could wish for no better intermediary; and the Bishop accordingly left for Rome in the spring of 1263 with a letter to the Pope, hinting at the possibility of a union of the two Churches. Whether this letter also suggested a joint alliance against the King of Sicily we shall never know; but it certainly had the desired effect. Replying on 18 July, the Pope announced his intention of sending to Constantinople four Franciscan nuncios, armed with full powers to seal a union in his name. Meanwhile, in the expectation that the Emperor and the Prince of Achaia would soon be co-religionists, he adjured them both to cease hostilities forthwith.

Here, however, Urban asked too much. If Michael were to subject the Eastern Church to Roman authority, he would do so on his own terms; he remained as determined as ever he had been to drive the Latins out of Greece. In early October, therefore, he resumed the war against William, claiming that the non-appearance of the promised nuncios could only mean that the Pope had changed his mind. At the time it must have seemed a fairly unconvincing excuse, given that the journey from Rome to Constantinople could easily take three months or more. By the following spring, when the Franciscans had still not arrived, the Emperor's case was admittedly stronger; as things turned out, however, it mattered little.

Once again the *sebastocrator* Constantine led his army across the Peloponnese against the Achaian capital of Andravida; once again the Latins rode out to meet him; and about ten miles from the city, just outside the little town of Sergiana, the two armies met. Hardly had the battle begun when the Grand Constable Michael Cantacuzenus – Constantine's second-in-command, but by far his superior in ability and courage – fell from his horse and was cut to pieces. The sight was too much for the *sebastocrator*, who immediately withdrew from the field and led his army back to besiege the relatively inconsequential fortress of Nikli in northern Laconia. Here, however, a further catastrophe awaited him. The five thousand Seljuk mercenaries, who had not been paid for the past six months, suddenly demanded their wages and, when they still did not receive them, deserted *en masse* to the enemy.

At this point the wretched Constantine, somewhat unconvincingly pleading sickness, abandoned what was left of his army and returned to well-deserved obscurity in the capital. William of Achaia, on the other hand, seized the offensive and invaded the Byzantine lands of the southern Peloponnese where, thanks largely to the renegade Turks, he scored a crushing victory over the Greek forces and advanced to Mistra. Here at last the Greeks managed to put up a successful resistance. They could not, however, prevent William's army from ravaging the neighbourhood as far as the walls of Monemvasia before it retired once again to Nikli.

Fortunately for Michael Palaeologus, William now decided to call a halt. For all his military successes, the war had brought devastation to much of his territory and ruin to many of his subjects; the loss of life, too, had been considerable.[1] So anxious was he for a period of peace that for some time he seriously entertained a Byzantine proposal for the marriage of his daughter and heir Isabella to Andronicus Palaeologus, Michael's eldest surviving son, despite the fact that his whole principality would then have passed to the Empire after his death. It was only under pressure from his Latin vassals – who had no wish to see their estates swallowed up, quite possibly in their own lifetimes – that he finally broke off negotiations.

To the Emperor, who had been within an ace of acquiring the entire Morea without sacrificing another man or loosing a single arrow, this decision must have come as yet another bitter blow. Frustrated, humiliated and friendless as ever, he had no choice but to turn again to Rome. After his recent quite unfounded accusations of bad faith – to which the Pope had replied by giving the Achaian war the status of a Crusade – he knew that he had no right to expect a favourable reception to any new overtures; his only hope lay in making Urban an offer that he could not refuse:

To the venerable father of fathers, most blessed Pope of old Rome, father of our Majesty, Lord Urban, supreme and sacrosanct Pontiff of the Apostolic See . . .

In the past, legates and nuncios were often sent back and forth, but they could not speak to each other and, since they conversed through ignorant interpreters, they seldom arrived at the real truth. This gave birth to a constantly increasing hatred between brothers, an extinction of love and a veiling of the True Faith . . .

But a voice from the West touched our heart, and there came to our Empire Nicholas, the venerable Bishop of Crotone. And he revealed to us all things, one after another, and so we find the holy Roman Church of God to be not different from ours in the divine dogma of its Faith, but feeling and chanting these things almost with us. We therefore venerate, believe in, and uphold the sacraments of this Roman Church. To the Mother of our Church in all things, all peoples, all patriarchal sees and all nations, in devotion, obedience and love of this Church shall be subjected by the power of our Serene Highness.

Even this necessarily abbreviated version of the letter is enough to explain why the Pope rose at once to the bait. Not only would the Byzantine Emperor be a faithful and obedient member of the Church of Rome; Manfred would have to renounce his dreams of Constantinople. Moreover, Michael had not even confined himself to the question of

---

1 Sanudo tells us that one unfortunate lady lost seven successive husbands on the field of battle – though whether she was Greek or Latin he does not reveal.

ecclesiastical union; he went on to offer active support in the Crusade to the Holy Land on which Urban still set his heart. The papal reply, dated 23 May 1264 and addressed 'to Palaeologus, Illustrious Emperor of the Greeks', was drafted in the same fulsome – occasionally almost unctuous – terms. Once again it was entrusted to Nicholas of Crotone, whom it named leader of a plenipotentiary papal legation that included two more Franciscans, Gerard of Prato and Raynerius of Sens.[1]

It arrived in the high summer, and negotiations began immediately; but if the Pope had expected to dictate terms, he was quickly disappointed. The Emperor's representatives explained at the outset that they could not settle matters by themselves; they insisted on the contrary that all the questions at issue, both political and ecclesiastical, must first be discussed by a full council. The papal legates had no choice but to agree – a major concession in itself, and as it turned out a fatal one, since before such a council could be convened Urban died suddenly at Perugia, on 2 October 1264.

Even more than the return of Byzantium to the Latin fold, the chief preoccupation of Pope Urban during the last year of his life had been his arch-enemy, Manfred of Sicily. Their quarrel was not just a personal one: by now the age-old rivalry between the Papacy and the Western Empire had cut a great rift across the Italian political scene, polarizing itself into two opposite camps: the Guelfs – who were, roughly speaking, the papal party – and the Ghibellines, who supported and were supported by the Hohenstaufen. Nevertheless, Urban detested Manfred. In particular, he still bitterly resented the latter's seizure in 1258 of the Kingdom of Sicily (which included much of South Italy and now had its capital at Naples) from Manfred's six-year-old nephew Conradin, an action which had brought his dominions right up against the southern frontier of the Papal State. The Regno – as that Kingdom was generally called – was, by tradition, under papal suzerainty; and from the moment of Manfred's *coup d'état* the Papacy had been looking for another, friendlier prince with whom to replace him. Several had been considered, including Edmund of Lancaster, son of Henry III of England; but the choice had finally fallen on Charles, Count of Anjou and Provence, the younger brother of King Louis of France.

---

1 What, we may ask, of the four Franciscans who had been dispatched to Constantinople the previous year? Urban asked that they too should be included in the legation if they were still in the city; but they seem to have vanished without trace.

No two brothers could have been more different. Unlike the saintly Louis, Charles was the very archetype of the younger son who cannot forgive fate for the accident of his birth. Cold and cruel, self-seeking and consumed with ambition, he asked nothing better than to take over Manfred's Kingdom in the papal name. The new Pope, Clement IV – another Frenchman – completed the arrangements that Urban had begun; Charles formally accepted the offer; his wife (who fully shared his ambitions) pawned her jewels to pay for the expedition; Louis gave his reluctant consent; and at Whitsun 1265 the new King arrived in Rome. It was typical of Charles's megalomania that he should immediately have installed himself at the Lateran Palace. He was a natural autocrat, with an unshakeable belief in himself as the chosen instrument of the Almighty. Against his army of thirty thousand Crusaders – for Pope Clement had by now declared the war a Crusade – Manfred stood little chance. On 26 February 1266, outside Benevento, he went down fighting. Only after three days was his body discovered; denied by Charles a Christian burial, it was laid beneath the bridge at Benevento, with every soldier in the French army casting a stone on the cairn as he passed. Manfred's wife, Helena of Epirus, and his three young children were imprisoned at Nocera. Of the four, three never appeared again; one son was still there forty-three years later. Charles was not a man to take chances.

In 1268 he proved it more conclusively still. Manfred's nephew Conradin marched south from Germany in a last desperate attempt to save his family's inheritance. On 23 August Charles shattered his army at Tagliacozzo; Conradin himself was captured, subjected to a travesty of a trial, found guilty of treason and beheaded in the market square of Naples. He was just sixteen, and the last of the Hohenstaufen.

Tagliacozzo marked the supplanting of the Germans by the French as the rulers of South Italy. Now it was Charles and the Guelfs who were everywhere supreme, just as it had been Manfred and the Ghibellines a decade before. To Michael Palaeologus, closely watching developments from Constantinople, the change was distinctly unwelcome. Manfred had been trouble enough; Charles, he strongly suspected, would be far, far worse – and events were soon to prove him right. For the next sixteen years his struggle with the King of Sicily was to continue, a duel between titans that was to dominate the rest of his life.

Charles started as he meant to continue. He had not been a year on the throne before, by dint of some distinctly shady diplomatic business, he had acquired the island of Corfu and part of the coast of Epirus, a perfect springboard for any invasion of imperial territories in Greece or Macedonia; and in May 1267, after a month of discussions at the papal court in Viterbo with Pope Clement, Prince William of Achaia and the deposed Emperor Baldwin – who had never given up hope of regaining his throne – he put his seal on two treaties which made his long-term intentions clearer still. The first provided for the marriage of William's daughter Isabella – who had been formerly intended for Andronicus Palaeologus – to Charles's son Philip of Anjou, and their inheritance of the principality on William's death. The second, amounting as it did to nothing less than a detailed exposition of Charles's plans for a restoration of the Latin Empire on the Bosphorus, deserves a short summary here.

The King of Sicily undertook that, within six or at the most seven years, he or his heirs would provide two thousand cavalry to fight for Baldwin. In return, Baldwin would cede to him suzerainty over the principality of Achaia; all the Aegean islands except Lesbos, Samos, Chios and Cos; one-third of the expected conquests, to exclude Constantinople and the four islands above-named but including Epirus, Albania and Serbia; the Kingdom of Thessalonica if Hugh, Duke of Burgundy (to whom Baldwin had given it in fief the previous year) failed to fulfil his obligations; and, finally, the imperial throne itself in the event of Baldwin and his son Philip of Courtenay dying without legal heirs. Meanwhile Venice would regain all her former rights in the Empire and, to seal the new alliance, Philip of Courtenay would marry Charles's daughter Beatrice as soon as she reached marriageable age.

It was, by any standards, an astonishing document. True, the King of Sicily did not succeed in laying direct claim to the imperial throne; Baldwin and Pope Clement (who was already becoming a little uneasy at the speed with which Charles was building up his position) would have seen to that. But it did immediately secure for him – in return for the vague promise of scarcely significant reinforcements, a long time in the future – what was in effect a small empire in the eastern Mediterranean, and one which would allow him to move against Constantinople equally easily by land and sea. No wonder Michael Palaeologus felt anxious when he heard the news. He too was now seriously threatened. He too, like Baldwin before him, might well find himself – if Charles of Anjou had his way – Emperor in a beleaguered city.

Although the death of Pope Urban had inevitably led to a suspension of negotiations on the union of the Churches, it was plain to Michael that after Benevento an improvement in his relations with the Papacy was more necessary than ever; and he took the earliest opportunity of reopening his correspondence with Rome. Clement IV, however, immediately showed himself to be a good deal less tractable than his predecessor, categorically rejecting a council of the kind the Greeks had proposed since, as he put it, 'the purity of the faith could not be cast into doubt'. Thus there could be no discussion of the *filioque*[1] clause, nor of the use of leavened bread, nor of the all-important question of ecclesiastical jurisdiction – nor, in short, of any of the theological and liturgical differences that had separated the Eastern and the Western Churches for centuries past. Instead, Clement sent the Emperor the text of a 'confession of faith', which he insisted must be accepted unconditionally before any further progress could be made. His letter ended:

... With the opportunity afforded by this missive, we proclaim that neither are we wanting in justice (as we should not be) towards those who complain that they are oppressed by your Magnificence, nor shall we desist from pursuing this matter in other ways which the Lord may provide for the salvation of souls.

Whether or not the final clause accurately reflected the divine purpose of the Angevin army, the implied threat was clear enough.

Equally clear was the fact that if the Pope maintained this position there could be no question of Church union. The overwhelming majority of the Orthodox clergy were opposed to it in any case; if they were to be persuaded to accept it at all, it would certainly not be on the terms now proposed. Sensibly, Michael chose in his reply to ignore these altogether, and to concentrate instead on his promise to participate in a Crusade to the Holy Land – in which he also undertook to enlist the invaluable support of the King of Armenia. But Clement would not be mollified, and when he died in November 1268 the two sides were still as far apart as ever they had been.

Even an uncooperative Pope, however, was better than no Pope at all. Charles's influence was strong in the Curia, and for the next three years he succeeded in keeping the pontifical throne without an occupant, thus enabling himself to act as he liked towards the Byzantines – or, indeed, anyone else – without any restraint from Rome. By now, fortunately, Michael had acquired two allies. At the end of 1267 he had signed a new agreement with Genoa, by the terms of which he had welcomed back

1 The word – literally meaning 'and from the Son' – used to signify the Western belief that the Holy Ghost proceeded from the Father *and the Son* rather than directly and exclusively from God the Father. See *Byzantium: The Apogee*, p. 85.

those Genoese who had been expelled after the Guercio incident, ceding to them the whole district of Galata on the further side of the Golden Horn.[1] Then, in the first weeks of the following year, he signed another – with Genoa's arch-rival, Venice.

As early as 1264 Michael had sent ambassadors to the Rialto, and in 1265 he had approved a compact offering to Venice privileges which, if they did not quite equal those which she had formerly enjoyed, represented at least an immense improvement on the existing state of affairs. At the time the Venetians had refused to ratify; the Byzantine East was still in turmoil, the future of the Empire still uncertain, and they saw no point in committing themselves. Four years later, however, the situation had changed. During the interim, not only had the lack of a proper base in the Levant left them dangerously vulnerable to attacks by the Turkish and Albanian corsairs who infested the eastern Mediterranean; they were also gravely concerned at Charles's acquisition of Corfu and part of the Epirot coast, from which vital strong-points he was perfectly capable of blockading the entire Adriatic if he chose. Against these considerations, the vague undertakings of the second Treaty of Viterbo carried little weight. In November 1267 Doge Renier Zeno sent two of his most experienced diplomats to the Bosphorus with full powers to conclude a treaty, and on 4 April 1268 that treaty was signed – to be ratified in Venice less than three months later.

It was, admittedly, to remain in force for a mere five years; but during that time the Venetians promised non-aggression, the withholding of all help to the enemies of the Empire and the liberation of their Greek prisoners in Crete, Modone and Corone, the three principal bases remaining to them in Greek waters. In return, the Emperor undertook to respect Venetian settlements both there and elsewhere, and once more to allow Venetian merchants freedom to reside, travel and trade, without let or hindrance or the payment of duties, throughout his dominions. Two concessions only were missing: Venice's three-eighths share of city and Empire – though it had gradually become in practice more of a titular claim than a genuine economic benefit – and the exclusivity that she had previously enjoyed. For, Michael insisted, the Genoese would retain all their existing rights. The dangers of the old policy, by which

---

1 It has been suggested that Michael put the Genoese in Galata to avoid any repetition of the Guercio conspiracy. In fact, however, the district had been favoured by them throughout the days of the Latin Empire and even before. They certainly showed no dissatisfaction with the arrangement, and Galata continued to be predominantly Genoese until the Turkish conquest.

one of the republics was given full imperial preference at the expense of the other, had now been conclusively demonstrated. Henceforward there would be free competition between them – though they were specifically enjoined not to attack each other in the straits or the Black Sea – and Byzantium could profit by their rivalry without driving the less favoured party into the arms of its enemies.

But if Michael's military and diplomatic position was stronger than it had been at any time since the reconquest, that of his enemy was rapidly growing stronger still; for Charles of Anjou, now freed of all papal constraints, was openly preparing for war against the Greek Empire. Dockyards throughout the Regno were working overtime; food, money, troops, supplies of provisions of every kind were sent urgently to the Morea, which Charles intended to make the principal bridgehead of his expedition. To prevent leaks of strategic information, all commercial traffic was banned between Italy and Greece. Charles was also busy building up a network of alliances with the princes of central Europe: Béla IV of Hungary, Stephen Urosh I of Serbia and Constantine Tich of Bulgaria – whose wife Irene, sister of the blinded and captive John Lascaris, never allowed him to forget Michael's treatment of her brother.[1] In his determination to leave nothing to chance, he even sent ambassadors to the Seljuk Sultan, the King of Armenia and the Mongol Khan; and in August 1269 he succeeded in concluding a commercial treaty with the imperial ally Genoa, thus confirming the furious Michael in his frequently-expressed opinion that the Genoese were not to be trusted. (A similar approach to Venice came to nothing.) Meanwhile the ex-Emperor Baldwin had signed a treaty with Theobald of Champagne, King of Navarre, promising him a quarter of all future conquests – though without prejudice to the agreements already made with Charles, the Duke of Burgundy or the Venetians. With virtually the whole of western and central Europe now ranged against him, the future of Michael Palaeologus and his Empire looked bleak indeed.

It was no use looking for other potential allies; there were none available. Henceforth the Emperor would have to rely on diplomacy alone. One last hope remained – in the improbable person of King Louis

---

1 Angevin documents suggest that John Lascaris somehow escaped from his place of captivity and took refuge at Charles's court in Naples; but this is implicitly contradicted by both Pachymeres and Gregoras and seems highly improbable. Charles may of course have welcomed a pretender to give his enterprise more legal credibility, just as Robert Guiscard had in 1080 (see p. 16); but he had after all firmly committed himself to Baldwin, and could hardly espouse John's claim as well.

of France. As a devout Catholic and the elder brother of Charles of Anjou, Louis would not normally have seemed a probable source of salvation; but, as Michael well knew, he was on the point of completing preparations for another Crusade and, as always when Crusades were in question, could think of nothing else. Byzantine envoys hastened to Paris with a letter from their master. The *basileus*, it explained, would have been happy to join the King's forthcoming expedition against the Saracens of North Africa, and indeed to provide a strong military contingent; unfortunately, however, he was in danger of imminent attack by His Majesty's brother – an eventuality which, if it were allowed to occur, would obviously prevent both parties from lending the Crusade the assistance it deserved. A second embassy in the spring of 1270 announced that the Emperor was ready, with his clergy and people, to return to the Roman obedience and, so far as his conflict with Charles was concerned, would submit himself unconditionally to Louis's personal decision.

The King replied at once. In the absence of a Pope he would immediately inform the Curia of this proposal, recommending its early consideration and the dispatch of a senior prelate to Constantinople. Soon afterwards the Bishop of Albano arrived on the Bosphorus. He had been carefully and thoroughly briefed: the 'confession of faith' enclosed in Pope Clement's earlier letter, with its clear statement of papal primacy, was to be circulated to every Greek church and monastery for signature by all the leading churchmen of the Empire, the signed documents being returned to Rome for safekeeping. Meanwhile a council was to be held in Constantinople at which that same confession would be read out and publicly accepted by Emperor, Patriarch, clergy and people.

For the second time, Michael decided to ignore this condition. He thanked the Bishop of Albano for his trouble and allowed him to return to the West, meanwhile dispatching a third embassy to King Louis. It included two senior churchmen, the Chartophylax of St Sophia John Beccus and the Archdeacon of the Imperial Clergy Constantine Meliteniotes, both laden with lavish presents. They had, however, got no further than Cape Passero at the south-eastern tip of Sicily when they discovered that the Crusade had already departed for Tunis. There they arrived in early August, to find Louis gravely ill with typhoid fever. More than two weeks passed before he felt able to receive them – and then he could only whisper of his desire for peace between his brother and the Emperor. On the following day, 25 August, he died. 'Their hands empty except for promises', the Greek envoys returned home – just as Charles of Anjou was arriving in Tunis with his navy.

Why, finding his brother dead and personally assuming overall command of the army, did Charles not immediately give up the Crusade and set off there and then for Constantinople? It may have been out of loyalty to Louis – though from what we know of his character this does not seem very likely. More probably he found the campaign already so far advanced and with such excellent prospects of success that it would have been foolish not to have seen it through to the end – a supposition strengthened by the fact that soon afterwards he inflicted an overwhelming defeat on the Emir of Tunis; then, in November, he sailed to the Sicilian port of Trapani for the winter. His army and navy in full readiness, his morale and that of his men boosted by a triumphant victory, freed by his brother's death of the last force that might conceivably have restrained him, Charles of Anjou had never been more dangerous, Michael Palaeologus never more threatened. Only a miracle, it seemed, could save him now.

And then that miracle happened. Scarcely had Charles's fleet reached Trapani than, on 22 November, there arose one of the worst storms ever to have struck western Sicily. All eighteen of his largest men-of-war were reduced to matchwood, together with innumerable smaller vessels; men and horses, most of whom were still on board, perished by the thousand; vast quantities of stores and provisions went irretrievably to the bottom. Within a few hours, both army and navy were effectively destroyed. Michael Palaeologus wept when he heard the news. Once again the Blessed Virgin, Protectress of Constantinople, had saved the city. The King of Sicily would not be a serious menace to his Empire for several years to come.

15
The Uncertain Unity
[1270–82]

For having so adroitly avoided the dangers that beset us, we shall incur no
blame ... rather shall we earn the praise of all men of prudence and wisdom.
One consideration only has persuaded me to seek union: the overriding need to
avert the perils by which we are threatened ... But for that I should never have
embarked on this affair.

Michael Palaeologus, quoted by George Pachymeres

By the last week of August of the year 1271, Western Christendom had
– thanks to the intrigues of Charles of Anjou – been without a Pope for
two years and nine months, the longest interregnum in the history of the
Papacy; and there is no telling how much longer it might have continued
had not the *podestà* at Viterbo, where the conclave was being held, gone
to the somewhat extreme length of removing the roof from the palace in
which the cardinals were assembled. This step had the desired effect; and
on 1 September Teobaldo (or Tedaldo) Visconti, Archdeacon of Liège,
was elected Supreme Pontiff. The news was brought to him in Palestine,
whither he had accompanied Prince Edward of England, soon to become
King Edward I. He embarked on the first available ship, and on arrival
in Rome took the name of Gregory X.

Gregory's journey to the East had left an indelible impression on him.
He never lost his interest in the Holy Land and made the recovery of
Jerusalem the primary objective of his papacy. He genuinely doubted,
however, whether this end could ever be achieved without the help of
the Greek Empire; and the healing of the rift between the two Churches
therefore assumed still greater importance in his eyes than it had to
either of his two immediate predecessors. Even before his departure
from Palestine he had written in the most cordial terms to Michael
Palaeologus, emphasizing his desire for union; and in October 1272 he
followed this up with a personal invitation to the Emperor to attend a
General Council of the Church, which he proposed to hold at Lyon in

two years' time. Meanwhile, he suggested, informal discussions between the two parties might begin at once, to settle as many questions as possible before the council began. He enclosed with his letter a copy of Clement IV's 'confession of faith'; but, unlike his predecessor, he was a realist. Understanding, far better than Clement ever did, the difficulties with which Michael would have to contend and fully conscious of the shortage of time available, he did not demand complete and unequivocal submission on the part of clergy, monasteries and people. Recognition of papal primacy on the part of the bishops would, he implied, be quite enough. His instructions to his ambassadors regarding the possible formulas to be adopted are even more revealing:

'We, coming voluntarily to obedience of this Church, will recognize and accept the Roman primacy' ... or, if the words 'we recognize' cannot be secured, there may be accepted in their place the following words or their equivalent: 'We therefore, the Emperor, agree with the truth of the Catholic faith' ... But if the words 'we agree' also cannot be secured, in their place may be substituted the following words or their equivalent: 'We desire to recognize this faith, to assume it, profess it, and to be united with ... the Holy Roman Church, our mother ... in the profession of faith, and to come to obedience of this Roman Church, [and] to recognize its primacy.'[1]

Realizing that any prevarications or delay on his part would inevitably risk driving Gregory into Charles's camp, Michael replied in kind. He assured the Pope that negotiations with his legates were already under way, and that he himself was putting the question of union before all other affairs of state. His representatives would certainly attend the forthcoming council; he asked only for a papal safe-conduct for them lest Charles, 'moved by his hatred of peace, may try to bring this divine work to nothing so that it may remain unfinished'. It was a wise precaution: the King of Sicily was, he knew, perfectly capable of arranging for the disappearance of the Byzantine delegation as it passed through his dominions, and then accusing him of bad faith in not having sent one at all.

The Pope may well have shared his misgivings. He immediately granted the request, instructing the Abbot of Monte Cassino to meet the imperial envoys on their arrival in the Regno and to escort them as far as Rome. Meanwhile he continued, in his dealings with Charles,

---

1 The full text of Gregory's letter is given in J. Guiraud, *Les registres de Grégoire X*. For the translation – and for much else in this section – I am indebted to D. J. Geanakoplos, op. cit.

to impress upon him his moral duty to work towards the proposed union rather than to frustrate it. The King objected that he had a moral duty of his own: by the terms of the second Treaty of Viterbo of 1267, he had committed himself to launch his campaign within seven years, in other words before May 1274. Gregory begged him, however, to accept a year's postponement; and Charles, who had still not finished rebuilding his fleet after the disaster at Trapani, none too reluctantly agreed.

Despite the good offices of the Abbot of Monte Cassino and the self-restraint of the King of Sicily, the journey of the Greek envoys to the Council of Lyon was not a pleasant one. Leaving the Golden Horn in March 1274, they ran into an equinoctial storm off Cape Malea, in the course of which one of their two vessels was wrecked and all on board perished, including the Minister of the Treasury Nicholas Panaretos and the Grand Interpreter George Berrhoiotes. Lost too were all the lavish presents from the Emperor to the Pope, including several priceless gold icons and a sumptuous altar-cloth of gold and pearls which Michael Palaeologus had presented to St Sophia seven years before.

By the time the three remaining envoys – the former Patriarch Germanos,[1] the Metropolitan of Nicaea Theophanes and the Grand Logothete George Acropolites – reached Lyon towards the end of June, the council had already been in session for seven weeks. The cathedral of St Jean (which still looks much as it did in 1274) was thronged with all the leading ecclesiastics of Western Christendom, including the entire College of Cardinals and the former Latin Patriarch of Constantinople, the Venetian Pantaleone Giustinian – a total congregation of some fifteen hundred. Though all the Catholic reigning monarchs had been invited, one only – James I of Aragon – actually came; Charles of Anjou was conspicuous by his absence. On 24 June the three envoys were escorted in ceremonial procession to the papal palace, where the Pope received them and gave them the kiss of peace. They in return presented him with letters from the Emperor, his son Andronicus and the Ortho-dox bishops. There were no negotiations, no discussions. Five days later however, on 29 June, Gregory himself presided at a special bilingual Mass to celebrate the forthcoming union, with the ecclesiastical envoys

---

1 Germanos had been obliged to resign the Patriarchate in 1266 – after a single year in office – when he failed to revoke the anathema pronounced against Michael by his predecessor Arsenius for the blinding of John Lascaris.

playing an active part in the liturgy: gospel, epistle and creed were chanted in both Latin and Greek, including three somewhat pointed repetitions of the *filioque*. It was the one word that, more than any other, could normally be trusted to stick in Byzantine throats; if it did so on this occasion, the envoys somehow managed to conceal their discomfiture.

Finally, on 6 July, the union was formally enacted. After a sermon by the Cardinal Bishop of Ostia – the future Pope Innocent V – and a few words of welcome from Gregory, the Emperor's letter was read in Latin translation. It included the 'confession of faith' in full – with of course the *filioque* – and acknowledged papal primacy, asking only that the Byzantine Church should be allowed to retain its creed (which dated from before the schism) and such Eastern rites as did not conflict with the findings of the Ecumenical Councils. The other two letters followed, the Greek bishops also signifying their acceptance of the union but giving notification that if it came to pass the existing Patriarch would resign his office, while they themselves would accord to the Papacy 'all rights to which it had been entitled before the schism' – a somewhat nebulous concession, given that most of the papal claims had been formulated only as a result of the events of 1054. Finally the Grand Logothete George Acropolites took the oath in the Emperor's name, in terms similar to those set out in his letter; the Pope chanted the Te Deum and preached a sermon expressing his joy at the reconciliation; the creed was chanted again in Latin and Greek; and the ceremony was over. For the first time in 220 years, the Eastern and Western Churches were in communion one with the other.

Or so at least it seemed.

Throughout that summer of 1274, all remained quiet on the Bosphorus; it was only with the return of the imperial envoys in the late autumn that clergy and people began to understand the full significance of what had occurred. The acknowledgement of papal primacy was bad enough, even though – as the Emperor constantly reminded them – the length and difficulty of the journey between Rome and Constantinople was enough to ensure that the Patriarchs would lose virtually nothing of their effective independence. When, he asked, would the Pope appear in Constantinople to take precedence over the Greek bishops, and how often would anyone cross so vast a sea to carry an appeal to Rome? But the betrayal – and in the eyes of many Byzantines, both clerical and secular, it was nothing less – went far deeper than that. Their Empire was, and had always been, a theocracy, their Emperor the Vice-Gerent of God on earth, Equal of the Apostles. Far more than the Patriarch, he symbolized the religious faith of his people. But he was not all-powerful. By what right, they demanded, had he consented to an alteration to the very cornerstone of their religion, the Orthodox creed itself? That creed had been slowly and painstakingly evolved by the seven great Ecumenical Councils of the Church; it could be properly amended only by another such council, at which all five Patriarchs must be present. Thus the Emperor had effectively ridden roughshod over the canon law, uncanonically adopting a Western version of the creed which was itself uncanonical. In doing so, moreover, he had most surely given mortal offence to the Blessed Virgin, under whose special protection their city lay. Just seventy years earlier the people of Constantinople had forfeited that protection, with results that were still remembered by the entire adult population. What new tribulations must they now expect?

The Emperor's submission was also a bitter blow to their national pride. For centuries they had looked down on the West as being not only heretical but also crude and unsophisticated, barbaric and boorish; and the fifty-seven-year occupation of their city, during which they had been alternately bullied and patronized by a succession of semi-literate thugs, had given them no reason to change their opinions. Now, after only thirteen years of freedom, they saw themselves being harnessed once again to the Frankish yoke; and they were not prepared to submit without protest.

It seems to have been after a special service on 16 January 1275, at which the ceremony at Lyon was re-enacted in the chapel of the imperial palace, that the demonstrators first took to the streets; and feeling ran yet higher when the well-known unionist John Beccus – last encountered four years before when, as Chartophylax of St Sophia, he was one of his Emperor's chief emissaries to St Louis of France – was raised to the patriarchal throne. The Church was now more bitterly divided than at any time since the days of Photius over four centuries before; and the bitterness spread even as far as the imperial family itself, where the Emperor's sister Eulogia – who had by now taken the veil – showed herself so determined an opponent of her brother's policies that he was obliged to put her under arrest. Escaping soon afterwards, she fled to Bulgaria where she and her daughter Maria – who had married the Bulgar Tsar Constantine Tich as his second wife in 1272 – busied themselves planning an alliance with the Mamelukes of Egypt which, they hoped, would ultimately drive her brother from his throne.

This plan fortunately came to nothing; more worrying for the Emperor was the reaction of Nicephorus, ruler of Epirus – who had succeeded his father Michael a few years before – and his brother John the Bastard of Thessaly. These two, largely if not wholly for political reasons, made their territories the principal refuge of all those who continued to oppose the union. John indeed went further, setting himself up as a champion of Orthodoxy and later, on 1 May 1277, even summoning a 'synod' of fugitive monks to pronounce formal sentence of anathema on Emperor, Patriarch and Pope.

Had Michael Palaeologus for once misjudged the temper of his subjects? Perhaps he had, to some degree. Utterly convinced as he was that the action he had taken had been the only way to save the Empire from another potentially catastrophic Latin invasion, he had certainly hoped to induce them to take a similarly realistic view. But he had always known that he might fail to do so, in which case the consequences would simply have to be faced. As he saw the situation, he could not have acted otherwise than he did. For some weeks after the protests began in earnest, he was reluctant to inflict punishment upon the agitators; only when every attempt at persuasion failed did he reluctantly resort to force. Once his decision was taken, however, there were no half measures. Anti-unionists who refused to remain silent were imprisoned, exiled or blinded; others were tortured, yet others suffered confiscation of all their property. The monasteries, who headed the opposition, were treated with particular harshness: one dangerously voluble monk, Meletios by name, had his tongue cut out.

Union with Rome, by depriving the King of Sicily and the titular Latin Emperor, Philip of Courtenay – whose father Baldwin had died in 1273 – of any moral justification for their intended invasion, had temporarily saved the Greek Empire; it legitimized Michael's claim to Constantinople in the eyes of the West; it even eliminated papal opposition to his programme for finishing off the work he had started and clearing the last remnants of Latin occupation from the Balkan peninsula. But the cost, both to the Emperor and to his people, had been heavy indeed.

Long before the imperial envoys had even reached Lyon for the ceremony of union, their master's latest campaign in the Balkans was already under way; his troops had occupied the strategic port of Butrinto in Albania and the inland fortress of Berat, driving the Angevin army back to Durazzo and Avlona on the Adriatic. King Charles, seriously alarmed, dispatched what reinforcements he could; but he was too fully occupied in Italy and Sicily fighting off the Genoese and their Ghibelline allies – who were making incessant raids on the Sicilian coastal towns, as well as those of Apulia and Calabria – to take any real offensive on his own account, and was obliged to accept severe losses in both men and territory. The following year the Emperor kept up the pressure, simultaneously launching a major attack on John the Bastard in Thessaly under the command of his brother, the Despot John Palaeologus, and sending a fleet of seventy-three ships to harass the Latins and intercept any aid that might be sent.

The Bastard, taken by surprise, found himself under siege in his castle of Neopatras; but he had been in tight corners before. One dark night he lowered himself by rope down the walls and, in the guise of a groom seeking a runaway horse, managed to pass unsuspected through the Greek camp. Three days later he reached Thebes, where the local ruler, Duke Jean I de la Roche, lent him three hundred horsemen. With these, hurrying back to Neopatras, he attacked the Greek army from behind. The Despot John did everything he could to rally his men, but panic seized them and they fled.

The effect of this victory – much enhanced by the courage and resourcefulness shown by the Bastard, who had not only beaten the imperial army but had also made it look extremely silly – was to put new heart into the Latin lords. Quickly collecting a number of Venetian vessels from Euboea and Crete and supplementing these with any others that they could find, they attacked the Greek fleet at Demetrias on the Gulf of Volos. At first the advantage seemed to be with the assailants: many of the Greek sailors were wounded, others were flung into the sea. Just in time, however, John the Despot arrived from Thessaly with a locally-gathered army;[1] and slowly the tide of battle turned. By evening nearly all the leaders of the Franks had been captured, and all but two of the Latin ships. Michael Palaeologus, when he heard the news of the two battles, made no secret of the fact that in his eyes the victory far outweighed the defeat. His brother the Despot John, however, took the opposite view. For him, not even his recent triumph could atone for the

---

1 It is hard to know exactly what happened at Demetrias. Gregoras insists that it was fought not on sea but on the shore, which would certainly make better sense of what follows. Another problem is that John is said to have heard of the battle while still at Neopatras – i.e., within a day of that engagement – which would have given the Latins only a few hours in which to have got their navy together and launched their attack. But there is no doubt of the Greek victory, nor of its importance.

conduct of his army at Neopatras. No sooner was he back in Constantinople than he resigned his command and returned to civilian life, a sad
and broken man. His natural successor would have been the *protostrator*[1]
Alexius Philanthropenus, who had commanded the fleet at Demetrias;
but Alexius was still recovering from wounds sustained in the course of
the battle, and the Emperor's choice fell instead on a renegade Italian
whom we know only as Licario.

This man was, so far as we can gather, a member of a prominent
Veronese family long resident on the island of Euboea – where, however,
he had incurred the displeasure of the Latin rulers by an unseemly
liaison with Felisa dalle Carceri, widow of one of them. In 1271 he had
offered his services to the Empire. His first victory – the capture of the
fortress of Karystos – had been rewarded by the grant of the whole of
Euboea as an imperial fief, in return for a pledge of continued service
with two hundred knights. In succeeding years he mopped up the entire
island except the city of Chalkis, and also recovered a number of others:
Skyros, Skopelos, Skiathos and Amorgos were captured from their
Venetian lord Filippo Ghisi, who was sent back to Constantinople in
chains; Ceos, Seriphos and Astipalaia followed soon after, as did San-
torini and Therasia. Lemnos, thanks to the determination of its lord
Paolo Navagaioso and his wife, surrendered only after a three-year siege.

The way now seemed clear for the final conquest of Euboea – of
which only the capital, Chalkis, remained in Latin hands. A battle
outside the walls resulted in the capture of one of the island's rulers,
Felisa's brother Giberto da Verona, and of Jean de la Roche, Duke of
Athens-Thebes; but before Licario could follow up his victory Jean's
brother, Jacques de la Roche, Governor of Nauplia, arrived with a large
army, while almost simultaneously came the news that the Byzantine
army had suffered another serious defeat at the hands of John the
Bastard. Chalkis, Licario decided, would have to wait. Returning to
Constantinople with his prisoners, he was promoted by the Emperor to
the rank of Grand Constable, commander of all the Latin mercenaries of
the Empire – a post previously held by Michael himself. For Giberto da
Verona, the shock proved too great: seeing one of the humblest of his
erstwhile vassals arrayed in his sumptuous official robes and even
whispering confidentially into the imperial ear, he died of apoplexy on
the spot. Jean de la Roche was luckier; he was ransomed for 30,000
soldi, though he too died soon afterwards.

---

1 Technically, the commander of the vanguard and light cavalry.

As for Licario himself, his name vanishes from the chronicles as suddenly as it appears. There is no mention of his death – as there surely would have been had he been killed in battle – or of any disgrace; we can only assume that he too died of natural causes, probably in Constantinople. He never lived to capture Chalkis, or to assume over his native island the dominion that was rightly his; he deserves mention in these pages, however, as the most brilliant naval commander of his day and as one of the protagonists in the long struggle of Michael Palaeologus to regain his Balkan Empire.

This continuing warfare in the Balkans and the Aegean was a source of genuine sorrow to Pope Gregory; but he was enough of a realist to know that he could not prevent it, and in 1275 he did at least succeed in arranging a year's truce between Michael Palaeologus and Charles of Anjou, thereby – as he hoped – allowing both of them time in which to consider the only military operation to which he would give his blessing: a new Crusade. It comes as something of a surprise to read that at this point Michael proposed that the Crusading armies, instead of coming by sea, should follow the route of the First Crusade – across the Balkans to Constantinople and then, once over the Bosphorus, through Asia Minor into Syria and Palestine. Such a plan sounds dangerous indeed. It would, apart from anything else, have involved a serious risk that the Latins might attempt another attack on Constantinople. True, it might also have led to the reconquest of Anatolia from the Turks and Mongols; but even if this proved possible, who was to guarantee that the recovered lands would be returned to their rightful suzerain? The thought of still more Latin princelings strutting about on imperial territory can have given Michael no pleasure at all.

On the other hand, if the Crusaders were coming in any event, was it not better that they should be put to good use? Here at least was a chance of ridding Anatolia once and for all of the infidel; when would there ever be another? And had not his great-great-great-great-grandfather Alexius Comnenus used the armies of the First Crusade in a similar way, with considerable success? Michael must have thought long and hard before making his proposal. Pope Gregory, however, was immediately interested. The idea of recovering the great Christian cities – even Antioch itself – could not have failed to appeal to him; this way, too, the armies would be spared the dangers of a long and uncomfortable sea voyage. Such was his enthusiasm that he even suggested a personal meeting with the Emperor as soon as possible after Easter 1276 in

Brindisi – or, if Michael hesitated (as well he might) to set foot in the Regno, across the Adriatic at Avlona.

But on 10 January – just three months before the appointed meeting – the Pope died at Arezzo; and though his gentle and peace-loving successor Innocent V was to maintain close contacts with the Greek ambassadors he was a good deal less eager for a Crusade, and proved interested neither in the idea of the land expedition nor in that of a meeting with the Emperor. Both plans were accordingly abandoned. This was the last time in history that a united Christendom might – just possibly – have expelled the Turks from Anatolia and returned it, after two hundred years, to Byzantium. The opportunity, for reasons that will become all too clear by the end of this chapter, would never recur.

Innocent – Pierre de Tarentaise – was another Frenchman; and his election had naturally raised the spirits of Charles of Anjou, who had intrigued shamelessly on his behalf and who at once hurried to the papal court. Charles could not forgive Michael for having outwitted him at Lyon; nor had he ever concealed his disgust at Pope Gregory's policy of good relations with Byzantium. His designs on Constantinople were as determined as ever they had been, and when he found that the new Pope was no more sympathetic to them than his predecessor, we have it on the authority of both Pachymeres and of a contemporary Sicilian chronicler, Bartolomeo of Neocastro, that he chewed his sceptre in his rage. But Innocent died in his turn after a pontificate of five months; his successor, Adrian V, after only five weeks; while Adrian's successor John XXI lasted just seven months before the ceiling of his new study in the palace at Viterbo fell on him and crushed him to death.[1] Only in November 1277 did the College of Cardinals, after sitting for six months in their fourth conclave in a year and a half, finally succeed in defying the endless machinations of Charles of Anjou by electing a Pope who was to reign long enough to make a lasting mark on papal policy.

Giovanni Gaetani Orsini, who took the name of Nicholas III, was a member of one of Rome's oldest and most powerful families. As such he

---

1 John was the only Portuguese ever to reach the papal throne, and the only Pope to achieve Dante's Paradise. He may also have been the only doctor: his *Book of the Eye* enjoyed much popularity, although according to Mgr. Mann (*The Lives of the Popes in the Middle Ages*, Vol. XVI) 'some of his remedies we should even now consider disgusting, and others are too curious to be set down here'. In fact he was only the twentieth pontiff to bear the name of John, but certain misguided chroniclers had unfortunately counted John XV twice.

had little patience with Charles's constant interference in papal affairs, and still less with his openly imperialist claims. For years the King of Sicily had used his title of Senator of Rome to sway – or attempt to sway – papal elections, bribing French and Italian cardinals alike to vote for his own candidates, just as he had taken advantage of the Imperial Vicariate of Tuscany to further his political ambitions in the peninsula. Within weeks of his election, the new Pope had stripped him of both positions. He also absolutely forbade Charles to pursue his plans for an attack on Constantinople. This last prohibition was not prompted by any particular sympathy for Michael Palaeologus, nor indeed for the Byzantine Empire as a whole; Nicholas simply saw the East and the West as two opposing forces, with the Papacy holding the balance between them and ensuring that neither became too powerful. But Michael cared little what Nicholas thought; for him it was enough to see his enemy humbled, his Empire free at last of the menace that had hung over it for so long.

In one respect the Pope remained every bit as firm as his predecessors: he was determined that the Byzantine Empire, having accepted ecclesiastical union at Lyon, should give proof that that union was now complete and that the Greek Church was prepared to obey in every detail, in liturgy as well as in doctrine, the dictates of Rome. Michael Palaeologus had already gone a long way in this direction. Apart from the ceremony at Lyon, he had agreed to that of January 1275 in Constantinople which had caused the first riots; and in April 1277, in the Palace of Blachernae and in the presence of the Patriarch, the senior clergy and the papal nuncios, he and his son Andronicus – co-Emperor since 1272 – had taken further oral oaths in ratification of those sworn on their behalf at Lyon by George Acropolites, after which they had signed various documents in Latin confirming the points covered. These included the *filioque*, the doctrine of purgatory, the seven sacraments as maintained in Rome, the use of unleavened bread in the Mass and of course papal supremacy, with the right of appeal to the Holy See. After this, all should have been well; unfortunately the Greek clerics had refused to make similar personal avowals, while the collective letter drafted on their behalf by Patriarch John Beccus had been transparently ambiguous on several major issues. A few months later, a synod at St Sophia had tried to show its sincerity by anathematizing Nicephorus of Epirus and John the Bastard for maintaining the old Orthodoxy – in answer to which, as we have already seen, John had had a similar sentence pronounced against Michael, John Beccus and Pope Nicholas in return; but to the Roman Curia the sincerity of the Greek Church in Constantinople continued to be deeply suspect.

Nicholas III was determined to settle the matter once and for all. He possessed little of the patience of Gregory X, and none of his diplomatic finesse. In the spring of 1279 he sent Bishop Bartholomew of Grosseto at the head of a new embassy to the Emperor, with a whole series of categorical demands. First, 'the Patriarch and the rest of the clergy of every fortress, village or any other place, individually and collectively, must recognize, accept and confess with a sworn oath the truth of the faith and primacy of the Roman Church ... without any condition or addition'. A full text of the required oath was appended. Secondly, 'those who exercise the office of preachers must publicly and carefully instruct their congregations in the true faith, and chant the Creed with the addition of the *filioque*'. In order to ensure that this was done, the papal legates were personally to visit all the chief cities of the Empire and collect, from everyone they found in cathedrals, churches and monasteries, duly witnessed individual professions of faith and acceptances of papal supremacy. Signed copies of these were to be sent to Rome. Only then could the Greek clergy apply for confirmation of the offices they held; meanwhile all such offices would be considered uncanonical and would not be recognized in Rome. Nicholas specifically refused the Emperor's earlier requests – which had been repeated in the Patriarch's letter – that the Greeks should be allowed to preserve their ancient rites dating from before the schism: 'unity of faith,' he wrote, 'does not permit diversity in its confessors or in confession.' Finally, the Pope announced his intention of appointing a cardinal-legate, with his official residence in Constantinople.

To Michael, who had continually reassured his subjects that their capital would remain free of permanent papal representatives, this last demand must have been particularly irksome; but his whole position where Rome was concerned was rapidly becoming intolerable. His own Church – most of whose members had never wanted unity in the first place – made no secret of its anger at this continuing harassment by successive Popes, and he knew that he could press it no further. To make matters worse he had recently had a serious difference of opinion with John Beccus, as a result of which the latter had tendered his resignation and withdrawn to the monastery of the Mangana. This awkward fact he was able to conceal from the nuncios, by telling them that the Patriarch had merely retired for a well-earned rest and somehow persuading Beccus to maintain this fiction by receiving them in his retreat; but there was no way, as he well knew, of satisfying their demands. He could only do his utmost not to offend them more than necessary and try once again to temporize; and for this he needed ecclesiastical support. Summoning all the senior churchmen to the palace, he spoke to them more frankly than ever before:

You well know with what difficulty the present agreement was achieved . . . I am aware that I have used force against many of you and have offended many friends, including members of my own family . . . I believed that the affair would be ended and that the Latins would demand nothing more . . . but thanks to certain people who are determined to create discord they are now demanding further proof of union. That is the purpose of the present mission. I wished to inform you of this in advance so that when you hear the envoys you will not be unduly disturbed or, observing my own conduct towards them, suspect me of bad faith.

As God is my witness, I shall not alter one accent, one iota of our faith. I promise to uphold the divine Creed of our fathers, and to oppose not only the Latins but anyone who would call it in question. If I receive the envoys cordially it will do you no harm. I believe that we should treat them kindly, lest we create new problems for ourselves. For this new Pope is not so well-disposed towards us as was Gregory.

His words had their effect. The Greek prelates listened to Bishop Bartholomew in silence and managed somehow to remain polite. But they refused adamantly to swear the required oaths. The best the Emperor could do was to secure another written declaration similar to that of two years before; but many of those who had signed on the first occasion refused to do so again, and he was obliged to invent a number of fictional bishops and forge their signatures before the document looked even moderately impressive. Meanwhile, to convince the nuncios of his sincerity, Michael had them taken to the imperial prisons, where they could see for themselves the treatment accorded to those – including members of the imperial family – who had opposed the union. Finally on 1 September, in their presence, he and Andronicus repeated their former oaths both orally and in writing.

There was no more to be done. Bartholomew and his fellow-envoys may or may not have been persuaded of the good faith of Michael and his son; but with regard to the body of the Greek Church they can have only been confirmed in their previous suspicions. Whatever the documents they carried back with them might suggest, true ecclesiastical unity remained a chimera. In Byzantine hearts, the schism still ruled as strongly as ever.

*

If Pope Nicholas III had failed to bring the Empire back whole-heartedly into the Roman fold, he had been no more successful in reconciling it with Charles of Anjou. True, he had forbidden Charles to launch his threatened invasion; but his repeated efforts to achieve a treaty of peace between the two rivals had been ignored by both of them – Charles because he still harboured dark designs on Constantinople, and Michael because a treaty might have tied his hands in the Balkans, where his undeclared war against the princes of Achaia, Epirus and Thessaly was now yielding rich rewards.

William of Achaia had died on 1 May 1278, a year after the death of his son-in-law and heir Philip of Anjou. Thus, by the terms of the Treaty of Viterbo in 1267, Charles himself had inherited the principality and with it the overlordship of all Eastern Europe still in Latin hands. To Michael Palaeologus, this development caused little concern: henceforth Achaia, instead of having a prince of its own who could be a focus for its people's loyalty, was to be just one of many territories under a foreign, absentee ruler for whom – preoccupied as he was with Constantinople – it was relatively unimportant. The rapacity and corruption of the successive *baillis* whom Charles sent out as governors in his name soon brought the local populations, Latin and Greek alike, into a state of open revolt: and the imperial troops, working out of their two chief bases at Monemvasia and Mistra, were able to continue the reconquest of the Morea even faster than before.

Charles hardly bothered. The Peloponnesian ports and harbours would have been useful to him had he been planning a naval expedition against the Empire; but his lack of sufficient naval transport and his failure to reach an agreement with Venice – which had in fact made a new treaty with Michael in 1277 – ruled out any such possibility. The attack would therefore have to be made by land. True, the Pope had forbidden it; but the Pope was already in his sixties and would not last for ever. In any case Charles was quite prepared to defy him if necessary. When the moment finally came, the Angevin armies would have to take the Via Egnatia, the time-honoured route across the neck of the Balkan peninsula, which would in turn necessitate a bridgehead in Albania or northern Epirus. This region too was now coming under increasing Byzantine pressure; and on 10 April 1279 Charles concluded a formal treaty with Prince Nicephorus whereby, in return for military assistance against the Empire, Nicephorus declared himself a vassal of the King of Sicily and ceded to him a number of important strongholds.

For the next eighteen months a steady stream of men and horses poured across the Adriatic, where they were assembled into a fighting force by Hugh the Red of Sully, one of Charles's most trusted generals. With them came immense quantities of arms and siege engines and another small army of sappers, engineers and carpenters to provide technical support. The death of Nicholas III – which had occurred, most conveniently, in August 1280 – meant the end of the papal ban; and in the late autumn of that year the army of some eight thousand, including two thousand cavalry and a large force of Saracen archers, moved eastwards across Albania to the Byzantine fortress-town of Berat. Standing as it did on a high rock dominating the western end of the Via Egnatia, Berat represented the first link in the chain of strongholds that Sully planned to forge across the whole breadth of the peninsula, and he at once gave orders for a siege. As befitted its importance, the town possessed a strong and well-equipped garrison; but the size of the Angevin army suggested that it would not easily be discouraged, and the local commander very understandably sent messengers to Constantinople with an urgent appeal for reinforcements.

They found Michael Palaeologus in a state of considerable anxiety. Tempers were still running high over the issue of ecclesiastical unity, by whose opponents he had not been forgiven; many of them, he feared, might see in the Angevin expedition a means of getting rid of him once and for all. Nor did he have much confidence in the Venetians, who had returned to the city after the treaty of 1277 and whose numbers continued to increase, despite the Republic's abrogation of the agreement two years later. If Berat were to fall, Charles would be in Thessalonica in a matter of weeks; and what then would be the prospects for Constantinople? Entrusting his nephew Michael Tarchaneiotes – son of his sister Maria – with the command of all the finest troops he could muster, the Emperor ordered a night-long vigil throughout the city. For that night at least, Church unity was forgotten: it was the old Byzantine liturgy that echoed from a thousand churches as the people prayed for the salvation of their Empire.

The siege continued throughout the winter, while Charles sent a constant flow of messages to his commander, encouraging him to ever greater efforts and even, in December, commanding him to take the town by storm. But Berat's superb defensive position made such a task virtually impossible to fulfil; Sully could only ravage the surrounding countryside and hope to starve the Greek garrison into surrender. Meanwhile the garrison put up a stout defence, and was at last rewarded in March

1281 by the sight of the relief army approaching over the horizon. Still more welcome – since by this time they were seriously short of food – were the rafts loaded with provisions which, under cover of darkness, began to float down the Asounes river – now the Lium – into the city. Meanwhile Tarchaneiotes, who had been instructed by the Emperor to avoid pitched battles, dug his army in among the surrounding hills and awaited his opportunity.

It was not long in coming. A day or two later, Sully – who was easily recognizable by his flaming red hair – decided to make a personal reconnaissance of the Greek positions and had just ridden out of his camp, accompanied by an escort of twenty-five men, when his horse was suddenly shot from under him and he found himself surrounded by a band of Turkish mercenaries. Some of the escort escaped, and galloped back to the camp with the news; whereupon the Angevin army believing their leader dead, panicked and took to their heels, the Greeks – including those from the garrison within the town – following them in hot pursuit. The Latin cavalry, heavily armed as always, were well protected from the imperial archers; but their huge, slow horses were brought down one after the other, and by evening the greater part of the Angevin army, including nearly all its commanders, was in Byzantine hands. The prisoners, including Sully himself, were brought back to Constantinople and forced to participate in an imperial triumph through the streets of the city.

Michael Palaeologus later had a fresco of the victory painted on the wall of his palace, and no wonder: it was the greatest that he had scored over the Latins since Pelagonia and the recovery of Constantinople. As a direct result of it, moreover, he now found himself in control of the whole interior of Albania and northern Epirus as far south as Ioannina. To Charles of Anjou, on the other hand, the events of those few fateful hours brought utter humiliation before friends and enemies alike, the complete loss of two years' hard work – to say nothing of vast expenditure – on his expeditionary force and the indefinite postponement of his long-held dream of an empire in the East.

But though the dream might be postponed, it was by no means abandoned. The disaster at Berat seems if anything to have strengthened Charles's determination to destroy Michael Palaeologus. Despite his losses his situation was by no means hopeless, and had been greatly improved by the election to the papal throne in February 1281, six months after the death of Pope Nicholas, of the Frenchman Simon de

Brie.[1] Simon, who took the name of Martin IV, had served at the court of St Louis; later, as papal legate, he had been instrumental in preparing Charles's candidature for the throne of Sicily. A fervent patriot who deeply distrusted all Italians, he was totally devoted to the French royal house and made no secret of his readiness to submit the Papacy to the interests of France. Charles could henceforth pursue his expansionist policies without fear of any trouble from Rome.

The first object of these policies was Venice. Since Berat there could no longer be any question of sending another land expedition against Constantinople. Any new army would have to go by sea, and that would in turn be possible only with the help of the Venetian fleet. Recent attempts by Charles to woo the Serenissima had always come to nothing, owing to the Veneto-Byzantine treaty of 1277; but the intervening four years had brought a significant change in the Venetian attitude. On the Rialto the treaty was quickly seen to be almost worthless. Venice's trade had steadily decreased, her merchants had been treated as second-class citizens, their rights under the treaty ignored. Worst of all from their point of view, the Genoese were thriving, and enjoying to the full the privileges which were being withheld from the Venetians. In 1279 the Doge had abrogated the treaty, since when Venice's relations with the Empire had deteriorated still further; and by 1281 she was ready to make her volte-face. The treaty that was signed on 3 July at Orvieto by Charles, the Latin 'Emperor' Philip of Courtenay and the accredited representatives of the Republic provided for a sea-borne expedition against Constantinople, in which all three sovereigns – Charles (or his eldest son), Philip and Doge Giovanni Dandolo – would participate in person, to set out in the spring of 1283. A Venetian fleet of at least forty armed galleys would leave the lagoon not later than 1 April, to make contact with the transports to be provided by Charles and Philip at Brindisi a fortnight later.

Pope Martin was not a signatory to the treaty; but the fact that it was signed in the papal palace at Orvieto is proof enough that it had his enthusiastic support. Moreover, just three months later on 18 October, the Pope suddenly – and apparently spontaneously – pronounced sentence of excommunication on the Byzantine Emperor:

We declare that Michael Palaeologus, who is called Emperor of the Greeks, has

---

1 Charles had not been exclusively responsible for the choice of Simon as Pope. By that time the Orsini family had made themselves so unpopular in Viterbo that the mob had burst into the conclave and carried off the two Orsini cardinals until the election was over.

incurred excommunication as supporter of the Greek schismatics and consequent heretics ... We absolutely forbid all individual kings, princes, dukes, marquises, counts, barons and all others of whatever eminence, condition or status, all cities, fortresses and other places from contracting with this Michael Palaeologus any alliance or association of any sort or nature that may be proposed while he is excommunicate ... Furthermore his lands shall undergo ecclesiastical inter-dict, and he shall be deprived of all property that he holds from any churches whatever, and he shall suffer other spiritual penalties as we think best; and any such alliances contracted ... we declare to be null and void.

Twice in the following year this sentence was to be renewed; but for Michael the first was enough. No *basileus* had ever done so much as he had for the Papacy. He and his son had twice sworn fidelity to the Church of Rome and had accepted every single item of its Creed, the *filioque* not excepted. He had done his utmost to persuade his own ecclesiastics to do likewise – risking civil war and even his own throne in the process – and had even achieved a fair measure of success. And now, instead of rewarding him, that same Latin Church had put him under its ban, in one irresponsible moment undoing the work of twenty years – not only on his part but on that of at least six previous Popes – and leaving him alone to face his enemies. Surprisingly, he did not even now renounce the union: he still considered himself bound by his oath, and there was always the possibility that Martin's successor might revoke the ban. But he ordered the Pope's name struck from the diptychs – the lists of those whose names were regularly remembered during public prayers – and simultaneously suspended all the measures that he had previously taken to impose the Latin rite on his subjects. Meanwhile he made every effort to restore good relations with the Greek Church. It looked as though he would be needing its support more than ever in the trials to come.

Charles of Anjou was now the most powerful sovereign in Europe. Quite apart from his own Kingdoms of Sicily (which included all South Italy) and Albania, he was ruler of Achaia, Provence, Forcalquier, Anjou and Maine, overlord of Tunis and Senator of Rome. The King of France was his nephew, the King of Hungary and the titular Emperor of Constantinople his sons-in-law. In the diplomatic field, too, he had taken every possible precaution. He had treaties of alliance with Serbia, Bulgaria, the Greek Princes of Epirus and – most important of all because of her naval supremacy in the Mediterranean – the Republic of Venice. The Pope was his puppet, who had moreover obligingly elevated what was essentially to be a war of conquest to the status of a Crusade.

He had learnt his lesson from the reverse of the previous year, and was now preparing a naval expedition on a far grander scale than anything that he had hitherto contemplated. To achieve this he had imposed crippling taxes throughout the Regno, with an additional tithe for the Crusade which brought many of his subjects to the brink of destitution. The money raised allowed him comfortably to exceed the levels foreseen in the Orvieto treaty: he was now building three hundred ships in Naples, Provence and his Adriatic ports, while another hundred had been ordered from Sicily – a fleet massive enough to carry some twenty-seven thousand mounted knights, to say nothing of siege machinery, sledge-hammers, axes, ropes, cauldrons for boiling pitch, several thousand iron stakes and mattocks, and all the other equipment necessary for the success of the most ambitious campaign of his career.

Against him stood Michael Palaeologus, the Republic of Genoa and a newcomer to this story, King Peter III of Aragon. Peter, whose wife Constance was the daughter of King Manfred, believed himself to be the legitimate heir of the Hohenstaufen and naturally detested the Angevins, whom he considered usurpers of a Kingdom that was rightfully his. Ever since his succession in 1276 he and his brilliant Italian Chancellor John of Procida had been working for Charles's overthrow. An Aragonese envoy had twice secretly visited Michael in Constantinople, continuing on each occasion to Sicily with generous quantities of Byzantine gold which he had used to fan the flames of discontent;[1] and by the end of 1280 Peter was making little attempt to conceal his aggressive intentions. He and Michael might be prompted by very different motives, but in their attitude to Charles of Anjou they were as one.

Peter of Aragon and John of Procida did their work well. Charles had never been unpopular in South Italy, where he had proved on the whole an able and conscientious ruler; but in Sicily he had always been hated, and the crippling taxation that he had imposed in recent years, in a cause for which his Sicilian subjects had little sympathy – many of them indeed, being of Greek origin, strongly favoured the Byzantines – made the island a fertile field for subversion. By Easter 1282, with the King's vast armada lying at anchor in the harbour at Messina while his bailiffs

---

1 According to Sicilian legend – and of course Verdi's opera *Les Vêpres Siciliennes*, in which John plays a major part in the consequent rising – this envoy was in fact John of Procida himself; but John was already in his late sixties, and throughout the period of his reported travels his signature appears regularly on Aragonese documents. Sir Steven Runciman (*The Sicilian Vespers*, pp. 208–9) suggests that the secret envoy may have been one of his sons.

toured the farms and homesteads, requisitioning – without compensation – grain, fodder, horses and even whole herds of cattle and pigs to sustain the army on its long journey, anti-Angevin feeling was near flash-point.

The fatal spark was lit on Easter Monday, 30 March, outside the church of Santo Spirito, which stands to this day in Palermo. The usual crowd thronged the square, enjoying the spring sunshine and waiting for the bell that was to call them for the evening Mass. Suddenly a group of Angevin soldiers appeared, obviously drunk; and one of them – a sergeant named Drouet – began importuning a young Sicilian woman. Unfortunately for him, her husband was standing nearby, and when he saw what was happening he fell upon Drouet in true Sicilian style and stabbed him to death. The other soldiers dashed forward to avenge him – and found themselves surrounded. They too were quickly dispatched. And so, as the church bells pealed out for vespers, the people of Palermo ran through the city, calling on their fellow-citizens to rise against their oppressor. *'Moranu li Franchiski!'* they cried in their heavy Sicilian dialect. 'Death to the French!' Nor did they call in vain. All night long the massacre continued. Dominican and Franciscan friars were dragged from their convents and told to say the word *ciciri* – unpronounceable, it was maintained, by any but Italians. Those who failed were cut down where they stood. The victims, men and women, amounted to well over two thousand. By the following morning not a Frenchman was left alive in Palermo.

And the revolt was already spreading across the island. By the end of April it had reached Messina, where the seventy Angevin vessels lying in the harbour were set on fire. Once again Charles was obliged to postpone his Greek expedition; ordering to Messina all the two hundred ships still lying in the mainland ports, he immediately flung the whole force that he had gathered for the conquest of Constantinople against the rebels. Meanwhile he set to work to raise yet another army, and on 25 July led it in person across the straits and laid siege to Messina. Throughout the summer this siege continued; but it was of no avail. On 30 August Peter of Aragon landed at Trapani at the head of an immense host and on 2 September entered Palermo, where he was proclaimed King of Sicily. (He would doubtless have preferred a proper coronation, but the French Archbishop of Palermo had been massacred and his colleague of Monreale had fled.) A fortnight later his ambassadors presented themselves before Charles of Anjou in his camp outside Messina.

For Charles the situation was now desperate. The speed of Peter's unopposed advance was a clear enough indication of his popularity in the island. It was also plain that the forces of the Aragonese, both on land and at sea, were more than a match for his own. If he remained where he was and attempted to resist them, there was a serious danger that their navy might institute a blockade; he would then be caught between their advancing army and the still unconquered Messina, with no possibility of retreat across the straits. The only sensible course was to return to the mainland while he could, reassemble his troops at leisure and make plans for a new invasion – perhaps at some more vulnerable point along the coast – the following year. Summoning what dignity he could, he told Peter's ambassadors that, while he naturally repudiated all their master's claims to the island, he was prepared to make a temporary withdrawal. The evacuation began at once, and continued at ever-increasing speed as the Aragonese army approached; but vast quantities of baggage and stores were left behind, together with a number of unfortunate soldiers whom the triumphant Messinans were only too happy to massacre before opening their gates to Peter on 2 October.

For Michael Palaeologus and his subjects, the war of the Sicilian Vespers and the consequent elimination of Charles of Anjou as a serious threat to Byzantium was, if not another miracle, at least a further proof that the Almighty was on their side. The Emperor himself had been in no way responsible for the incident at the church of Santo Spirito, nor for the events which followed. He had, however, by his diplomatic intrigues and his generous financial contributions to the Sicilian rebels, done much to prepare the ground; and in the short autobiographical note that he composed at the end of his life for the benefit of his son Andronicus he saw no reason to be over-modest about it:

The Sicilians, having nothing but contempt for the forces remaining to the barbarian King, had the courage to take up arms and deliver themselves from servitude; and were I now to dare to claim that God planned their liberation, and that he achieved it through my own hands, I should be speaking no more than the truth.

Even now, his anxieties were not over. The moment he realized that his Empire was no longer under immediate threat from the King of Sicily he set off on a campaign against the Turks, who had taken full advantage of his preoccupations in the West to increase their pressure along his eastern frontier; and no sooner had he returned from Anatolia than he was obliged to launch another expedition against John the

Bastard of Thessaly – of which, owing to the death of his brother the *sebastocrator* and several other of his principal generals, he took personal command. Determined to destroy John once and for all, he did not hesitate to appeal to his son-in-law,[1] the Mongol Nogay, Khan of the Golden Horde, who immediately dispatched four thousand Tartar tribesmen to his aid.

But Michael was now in his fifty-ninth year, and his exertions had taken their toll. By the time he left his capital he was obviously far from well. The Empress Theodora did her utmost to persuade him to stay in Constantinople, at least until the following spring; but he refused to listen to her and in late November embarked at Selymbria, on the northern shore of the Marmara, just in time to encounter a violent storm which seems to have done some damage to his ship: he was obliged to land again at Rhaedestum (now Tekirdağ), only some twenty miles further along the coast. Thence he continued his journey on horseback, but when he reached the little Thracian village of Pachomios he could go no further. He took to his bed, and on Friday, 11 December 1282 he died, proclaiming Andronicus, his son and co-Emperor, as his successor.

Andronicus's first decisive act as sole Emperor was also one of his wisest. Unhesitatingly he gave his orders, which were carried out the same night. His father's body was taken, under cover of darkness, to a distant place, where it was covered with earth to protect it from wild animals. There was no grave, no ceremony. According to Gregoras, Andronicus acted as he did out of disgust for Michael's betrayal of the Church – although, he adds, no son was ever more dutiful; but his real motive was almost certainly to save the body from insult. He had no delusions as to the late Emperor's unpopularity in the capital. Moreover, since Michael had never formally renounced the Roman faith, in Orthodox eyes – despite his papal excommunication – he had died a heretic; there could therefore be no question of a state funeral. If, as seemed likely, the Church were to show its disapproval by refusing him a Christian burial, it would surely be better to deny it the opportunity. For

---

1 Michael had given Nogay the hand of one of his illegitimate daughters, Euphrosyne, in about 1272. Another, Maria, had been betrothed to the Mongol Ilkhan, Hulagu, in 1265. He had died before the marriage and she had married his son Abagu instead. After Abagu's assassination by his brother Ahmet in 1281, she returned to Constantinople, where she retired to the convent whose church was thereafter known, in her honour, as St Mary of the Mongols. Most of it still stands today, the only Byzantine church that has been continuously in Greek hands since before the Turkish conquest.

some years the body lay where it had been buried; much later, Androni-cus had the remains transferred to the nearby monastery at Selymbria. But the Emperor in whose reign Constantinople had been reconquered, and who had saved his Empire from almost certain annihilation by the combined forces of Western Europe, was rewarded by what can only be described as a posthumous sentence of exile and never returned, in life or in death, to his capital.

Michael Palaeologus is principally remembered today for the recovery of Constantinople. For this, as we have seen, he deserves little of the credit. The Latins were already at their last gasp and could not in any event have held out much longer, while he himself was not even present when his troops first entered the city. But then he was never really a soldier-Emperor: nearly all the most important battles of his reign were fought without him. Though an outstanding general in his youth, after his accession he tended to leave the actual fighting to others, taking the field in person only when he felt it absolutely necessary to do so. This was not due to any lack of courage. It was simply because, in the circum-stances then prevailing, military operations took second place to diplo-macy – and in this field he was a master, perhaps the most brilliant that Byzantium ever produced. With virtually the whole European continent ranged against him, no one knew better than he when to act and when to prevaricate, when to stand firm and when to concede, when to conclude an alliance and when to arrange a marriage, when to threaten, when to cajole and when to bribe. To preserve the security of his Empire he was ready to make any sacrifice – even the independence of the Orthodox Church; yet when he died he left not only the Empire safer than at any time for the previous century, but the Church as free as it had ever been.

It could be argued that he was lucky; but so are most great men, and Michael Palaeologus was a great Emperor. Like all great men, he also had his faults. He was devious and duplicitous; though he would doubtless have argued that when his back was to the wall he had little choice in the matter, the fact remains that neither before nor after his accession did anyone really seem to trust him. Though temperamentally slow to anger, when finally roused he could be cruel and utterly without mercy. The reign of terror that he instituted in Constantinople in his determination to enforce Church unity was fearsome even by Byzantine standards. There was a vein of callousness too: quite apart from the murder of George Muzalon and his brother, his treatment of the child-

Emperor John Lascaris shocked all his contemporaries including his own family, and continues to sicken us today. Yet the more we read about him, the more the conviction grows that few if any of his predecessors could have guided the Empire with so sure a hand through one of the most dangerous periods in all its history. Lucky he may have been; but his people, in having him when they needed him most, were luckier still.

Their immediate posterity were less fortunate. Economically, thanks to his policies of bribery and appeasement, Michael left the Empire on the verge of bankruptcy. Militarily, his return to Constantinople and his continued preoccupation with Europe thereafter allowed the Turks and Mongols a virtually free rein in Anatolia, enabling them to consolidate and even to increase their conquests. He himself would once again have maintained that he had no alternative, that he possessed neither the manpower nor the resources to fight simultaneously on two fronts and that, of the two, the Western represented the more immediate danger. In the short term he would have been right. But to most thinking Byzantines it was clear that the paramount threat to their Empire came from the East, where the forces of Islam were a more formidable enemy, even if a less immediate one, than the King of Anjou could ever have been. If the capital had remained at Nicaea, Byzantine power in western Asia Minor would have held the balance well enough, particularly since the Seljuk Sultanate had never really recovered from its defeat by the Mongols at Kösedağ in 1243; the transfer of the government back to Constantinople proved, in this respect, little short of disastrous.

There was nothing new in all this. Standing as it did at the juncture of two continents, Byzantium had always had to look to both East and West, and every *basileus* worthy of his salt had found himself obliged to concentrate on one or the other. Thus, in the circumstances, it is difficult to see how Michael could have acted otherwise than he did. If there is blame to be apportioned, we must surely look elsewhere: to the nations of the West – and in particular to the Orthodox Greek princelings of the Balkan peninsula – who were so blinded by their own ambition that they could not see the looming threat, not just to themselves but to all Christendom, from which a strong and united Byzantium might yet have saved them.

16

The Catalan Vengeance

[1282–1311]

In a warfare of twenty years a ship or a camp was become their country; arms were their sole profession and property; valour was the only virtue which they knew; their women had imbibed the fearless temper of their lovers and husbands; it was reported that with a stroke of their broad-sword the Catalans could cleave a horseman and a horse; and the report itself was a powerful weapon.

Gibbon (on the Catalans),
The Decline and Fall of the Roman Empire,
Chapter LXII

The Emperor Andronicus II returned to Constantinople with one thought uppermost in his mind: to abrogate the Union of Lyon and to proclaim once again the full independence of the Orthodox Church. Although as co-Emperor he had been obliged to support his father's policies, in his heart he had always hated them. Deeply devout by nature and imbued with the traditional Byzantine passion for theology – his constant preoccupation with ecclesiastical affairs was to be one of his chief weaknesses as a ruler – he could never forget that his father had died under the ban of the Church and was consequently doomed, as he believed, to eternal damnation. He himself was determined not to suffer the same fate; and no sooner was he back in the capital than he made formal recantation of his earlier oaths of loyalty to Rome. The Patriarch John Beccus, who had been the principal champion of unity after the late Emperor himself, was stripped of his office and confined to a monastic cell; meanwhile the former Patriarch Joseph, now an old man in the last stages of decrepitude, was brought back to the Patriarchate on a stretcher and ceremonially reinstated. Those – monks and laymen alike – whom Michael had imprisoned and mutilated for their faith were paraded through the streets and hailed as martyrs. In St Sophia there was a special service of purification and rededication, just as there had been after the departure of the Latins twenty-one years before.

All too soon, however, the mood of celebration changed to one of anger: calls were heard for revenge, for the trial and conviction of those who had betrayed their Church. Of these, the loudest and most insistent came from a group of schismatics known as the Arsenites. They took their name from the former Patriarch Arsenius who, having excommunicated Michael VIII for his treatment of John Lascaris, had been finally deposed in 1267. Though Arsenius himself had by now been many years in his grave, they had steadfastly refused to recognize his later successors Joseph and John Beccus. Indeed, in the eyes of the more extreme members of the sect, Lascaris was still the rightful Emperor. Michael had been a usurper under the ban of the Church, and his son, having been crowned by Joseph, had no better claim.

Andronicus did his best to placate the Arsenites, giving them a special church in Constantinople and even going so far as to appoint one of them, the Bishop of Sardis, as his personal confessor. When, however, on the death of Patriarch Joseph early in 1283, there was chosen to succeed him a scholarly layman from Cyprus – who took the name of Gregory II – rather than one of their own number as they had expected, Arsenite tempers flared up again; and it was in a further effort to assuage them that Gregory immediately convened a synod in the church of Blachernae. Here two of his fellow-Patriarchs, those of Alexandria and Antioch, were called upon to make formal recantation of their past pro-unionist statements – the latter actually resigned and fled to Syria – while from Michael's widow, the Empress Theodora, was required a profession of her Greek faith and a solemn undertaking that she would never request for her husband a proper Christian burial.

These measures did much to mollify the Orthodox; but they cut little ice with the Arsenites. In 1284 therefore we find the Emperor actually permitting the body of Arsenius, who had died in exile, to be returned to the capital, where it was buried in a specially-constructed shrine in the monastery of St Andrew. Six years later in 1290 he was to make a still more memorable gesture, when he personally paid a visit to the blind John Lascaris, in the prison at Dakibyze on the Marmara where he had languished for the past twenty-nine years. George Pachymeres' account of their interview is tantalizingly short, mentioning only that the Emperor begged John's forgiveness for Michael's ill-treatment of him, inquired whether there was anything he could do to make his life more comfortable, and finally asked for his recognition as the rightful Emperor of Byzantium. Perhaps wisely in the circumstances, Pachymeres does not record the prisoner's reply.

By this time Patriarch Gregory had been tried for heresy and obliged to resign, and after a longish interregnum Andronicus had managed to secure the election of a former hermit from Mount Athos named Athanasius. To the pious Emperor, the new Patriarch's undoubted asceticism seemed just what was needed to divert the Church from the undesirable political issues that had occupied it for so long; to his ecclesiastics, on the other hand, the man was little more than an unwashed fanatic who went about in a hair shirt and sandals and devoted his time to castigating them for their worldliness and wealth. When he began to institute measures to deprive the richer churches and monasteries of their valuables, they made no secret of their hostility: Athanasius was attacked and even occasionally stoned in the street, to the point where he never ventured forth without a bodyguard. In the summer of 1293 the Emperor returned from several months in Asia Minor – where he had been looking into the administration and defences of the rapidly dwindling Byzantine territories – to be met by a delegation of leading churchmen demanding the Patriarch's removal. He resisted it as best he could; but the opposition was too strong, and in October Athanasius resigned in his turn – though not before drawing up a patriarchal bull in his own handwriting, in which he anathematized his enemies and all those who had been involved in the conspiracy against him. This document he characteristically concealed in the capital of a column in the north gallery of St Sophia. It was discovered only some years later – when, it need hardly be said, it caused a considerable commotion.

Meanwhile, the political situation of the Empire was growing ever more desperate. There had admittedly been a bright spot in 1284, when the widowed Emperor[1] had taken as his second wife the eleven-year-old Yolanda, daughter of William V, Marquis of Montferrat. William still styled himself 'King of Thessalonica', a title that dated back to the Fourth Crusade; this claim he now surrendered to his new son-in-law, ostensibly as part of Yolanda's dowry. It had not been pressed for a number of years, but Andronicus – who in fact had paid him handsomely for it – clearly considered it important that there should be no ambiguity about the position of the second city in the Empire. He knew moreover

---

1 Andronicus's first wife Anne, the daughter of Stephen V of Hungary, had died in 1281, the year before his accession.

that if by any chance Thessalonica were attacked, he would find it hard indeed to come to its rescue; for he had already decided, in view of the state of the imperial finances, to pare his armed forces to the bone.

Economies were indeed necessary, in the military field as everywhere else; and yet, even with his Asiatic dominions shrinking almost daily, it seems hard to believe that the Emperor could have acted as irresponsibly as he did. The loss of Anatolia had long since deprived Byzantium of its traditional source of manpower; for many years already it had had to rely on foreign mercenaries. Andronicus's mistake was not only to reduce the numbers of these to almost suicidally low levels; it was also to disband the seasoned mercenary regiments, taking on instead motley groups of footloose wanderers and refugees whose comparative cheapness was no substitute for discipline or experience. As for the navy, he abolished it altogether – to the obvious delight of the Genoese, who could now demand a far higher price for their support and could meanwhile devote their energies to developing their own interests in Constantinople, the Black Sea and the Aegean without interference from Byzantium. They benefited too – as did the Turks, who having at last reached the shores of the Mediterranean, had begun to establish a navy of their own and welcomed the expert guidance in shipbuilding and seamanship which they received from the thousands of penniless sailors who now in desperation applied to them for employment.

The Turks were no longer the unified fighting force that they had been during the heyday of the Seljuk Sultanate. The Sultan's defeat by the Mongols at Kösedağ in 1243 had effectively put an end to his power in Anatolia; and since Hulagu's capture of Baghdad in 1258 and the consequent destruction of the Abbasid Caliphate, the Seljuks had been no more than Mongol vassals. Meanwhile a number of Turkish tribes – together with countless families of Turkoman nomads from Persia and Mesopotamia – having fled westward before the Mongol advance, had finally settled in the no man's land along the Byzantine frontier; and with the collapse of the Sultanate they had taken to making regular destructive incursions into imperial territory – incursions which the Empire, whose position in Asia Minor had never recovered from the restoration of 1261, was virtually powerless to resist. These raids they soon began to consider – and indeed to justify – as a branch of the traditional Islamic *jihad*, or Holy War against the infidel; and from there it was but a short step to see themselves as Ghazis, or Warriors for the Faith. All through the second half of the thirteenth century their numbers had steadily increased. By the first years of the fourteenth only a few major strongholds – Nicaea and Nicomedia, Sardis and Brusa, Philadelphia, Lopadium[1] and Magnesia – and a few isolated ports like Ania (now Kuşadasi) and Heraclea on the Black Sea still held out; apart from these beleaguered enclaves, all Anatolia had been engulfed in the Turkish tide.

In the West, too, the situation was deteriorating fast. There had been some rejoicing in Constantinople when Charles of Anjou had died in 1285, leaving his throne to his son Charles II, who was at that time a prisoner of Peter of Aragon; but the young King was freed four years later, and soon showed himself just as hostile to Byzantium – and just as dangerous – as his father had been before him. In 1291 – the year of the fall of Acre, the last Crusader Kingdom of Outremer – he proposed an alliance with Nicephorus, Despot of Epirus, to be cemented by the marriage of the latter's daughter Thamar with his own son Philip.[2] For once Andronicus was quick to react, sending what was left of his army, supported by the Genoese fleet, to attack the Epirot capital of Arta. The expedition at first proved surprisingly successful,. regaining not only Ioannina but also Durazzo before it was forced to withdraw; but it could not prevent the projected alliance. On Philip's marriage in 1294 he was made overlord of all his father's Greek possessions, with the title of Prince of Taranto. Henceforth Epirus was to be held as a fief of Naples. This second Angevin threat to Constantinople was still no bigger than a man's hand, but it was already unmistakable.

Meanwhile in Serbia a new ruler, Stephen Miliutin, had come to the throne in 1282[3] under the name of Stephen Urosh II, and before the year was out had declared his support for Charles of Anjou, allied himself with Epirus, declared war on the Empire and captured Skoplje, which he made his capital. Here, for Andronicus, was another anxiety. Skoplje was a strategic strong-point on the Axius river, commanding the road south to Thessalonica and northern Greece. Moreover, Miliutin was known to have gone through a form of marriage with a daughter of John Ducas of Thessaly. A Serbian–Thessalian alliance would constitute

---

1 Now Ulubad.

2 This marriage would have been the more galling for the Emperor in that Thamar had been formerly proposed by her parents as a bride for his son Michael, the later co-Emperor: an arrangement that would have brought Epirus back into the Empire. Alas, the Patriarch had objected to the marriage on canonical grounds and the opportunity had been lost.

3 His reigning elder brother, Stephen Dragutin (Stephen Urosh I), had been injured in that year after a fall from his horse and had decided to divide the Kingdom with Miliutin. Technically the two were co-rulers until Dragutin's death in 1316, but from 1282 Miliutin was effectively in control.

a serious threat not only to Thessalonica itself but to the whole westward route across the Balkan peninsula to the Adriatic.

At length in 1297 Andronicus, all too conscious of his military weakness, decided on a diplomatic solution. Hearing that Miliutin's only legal wife (though he kept two full-time concubines, to say nothing of the Thessalian princess) had recently died, he proposed that she should be replaced by his own sister Eudocia, the widow of John II of Trebizond. To a Serbian ruler the prospect of being brother-in-law to the Emperor of Byzantium was irresistible, and Miliutin accepted with delight; difficulties arose only when Andronicus broached the matter with Eudocia, who would have none of it. If, she objected, her brother thought that she would be prepared to go and live with a lecherous barbarian who had at least one wife already, he was very much mistaken; besides, it was common knowledge that her intended husband was now involved in a torrid relationship with his sister-in-law – who was, incidentally, a nun.

The Emperor knew his sister too well to think that he could persuade her; at the same time he could not lose face with Miliutin. There was only one solution: Simonis, his daughter by Yolanda-Irene. True, she was five years old, and her husband-to-be about forty; none the less, she must be sacrificed. At Easter 1299 he personally escorted Simonis to Thessalonica, where her bridegroom was waiting; and there, in his presence, the wedding took place, the Archbishop of Ochrid officiating. Miliutin, we are told, was enchanted with his bride – particularly since she brought as her dowry all the Macedonian territory that he had already conquered; he agreed, however, that she should remain in the Serbian royal nursery for a few more years, until she was old enough to live with him as his wife. In Constantinople, the Patriarch John XII resigned in protest; but even he could not find anything strictly uncanonical about the marriage, and after a few months' indecision he was finally persuaded to resume his office.

In Constantinople itself, the end of the thirteenth century was a time of unrelieved trouble, the beginning of the fourteenth if anything worse. Michael Palaeologus, for all his unpopularity, had at least been a strong and decisive Emperor; his son, quite apart from his morbid religiosity, was proving himself ever weaker and more feckless, incapable of halting the Empire's accelerating decline. As early as 1292, while he was in Asia Minor, a conspiracy had been discovered, the ringleader of which proved to be his own brother Constantine. The rebel prince was thrown into prison, where he was to remain until his death twelve years later; but the plots continued, and in the autumn of 1295 the Empire's foremost general, Alexius Philanthropenus – hero of the battle of Demetrias twenty years before – emboldened by a series of victories against the Turks, rose in open revolt. It too came to nothing: betrayed by certain of his soldiers, he was captured and blinded. But the Emperor, who had liked and trusted him, had been deeply shaken by his treachery and never entirely regained his nerve.

Moreover, as if Constantinople did not have enough troubles of its own, it had also become one of the principal battlefields on which Genoa and Venice settled their differences. In July 1296 – a few weeks after the column erected by Michael VIII had been ominously toppled by an earthquake – a fleet of seventy-five Venetian ships sailed up to the mouth of the Bosphorus and launched a vicious attack on the Genoese colony at Galata, setting fire to the harbour buildings and warehouses along the shore. The imperial garrison hastened to the rescue, whereupon the Venetians turned their fire on the city itself, burning all the Greek houses within range as they passed by the sea walls along the Marmara. Andronicus immediately sent ambassadors to Venice with a strong protest; but the Genoese of Galata had no time for diplomatic niceties. In December they launched their own counter-attack, destroyed the principal Venetian buildings and massacred all the leading Venetians in the city.

Now it was Venice's turn. The following summer another fleet appeared, bearing a personal dispatch from the Doge. In it he accused the Emperor of having encouraged the Genoese in their behaviour, held him responsible for the damage done and demanded full compensation. Given time, Andronicus would probably have paid up, to prevent any further incident; but before he could do so – and apparently before the great chain could be raised to bar their way – the Venetians swept into the Golden Horn and, dropping anchor beneath the Palace of Blachernae, set fire to one of the Emperor's galleys beached on the shore. They then returned, with a host of Genoese prisoners, to Venice. At about the same time yet another Venetian fleet burst through the Genoese blockade of the Bosphorus and into the Black Sea, where it seized the Crimean port of Caffa – now Feodosia – and held it against furious attack from the local Tartars until, with the coming of winter, it was forced to withdraw.

In 1299, to the fury of the Byzantines, Venice and Genoa signed a separate peace; the Venetians, however, were still insisting on their compensation and in the summer of 1302 raided Constantinople for the third time in seven years. Once again they made their way into the Golden Horn; once again they set fire to such Byzantine buildings as were in range; once again the Emperor, bereft of his navy, was unable to stop them. This time, however, when they had done all the damage they could, they occupied the island of Prinkipo – now Büyükada – in the Marmara. It was then being used as a vast refugee camp for Anatolian Greeks rendered homeless by the Turkish advance; and these refugees the Venetians now threatened to massacre or to carry off into slavery if the Emperor did not pay them what he owed. Powerless against such barefaced blackmail, Andronicus gave in – agreeing also to a ten-year treaty by which Venice was confirmed in all her privileges in Constantinople.

The year 1302 was, in many respects, an *annus horribilis* for Byzantium. In the early spring the Emperor's son Michael IX – he had for the past eight years been co-Emperor with his father – suffered a humiliating defeat at the hands of the Turks near Magnesia[1] in Caria. Deserting what was left of his army (most of whom, it is only fair to state, had already slipped away themselves) he narrowly escaped with his life. Next there had been the Venetian raid; and then, only a few weeks later on 27 July, a Byzantine force – largely composed of Alan tribesmen who had fled to the Empire, as the Cumans had done before them, when the Mongols overran the Danube valley – encountered just outside the city of Nicomedia a Turkish army more than twice its size, commanded by a local Ghazi Emir named Othman. The battle that followed was not particularly bloody; most of the retreating Greeks and Alans managed to make their way back into Nicomedia. But Othman's way was now clear, his advance irresistible. He and his men surged southwestward along the southern shore of the Marmara, laying waste virtually the entire province of Bithynia, sweeping through the Troad and continuing until they reached the Aegean coast at Adramyttium. They did not waste time at the great fortified cities of Nicomedia, Nicaea, Brusa and Lopadium; these remained intact, and provided a refuge for much of the local peasantry whose lands had been devastated. Pachymeres paints a tragic – and nowadays all-too-familiar – picture of the scene:

---

1 Not Magnesia ad Sipylum, the modern town of Manisa near Izmir, but Magnesia on the Meander, some thirty kilometres east of Kuşadasi. Apart from the ruins of the temple to Artemis, little remains today of what was once the seventh city of the Roman Province of Asia.

The road was covered with men and animals, running confusedly hither and thither, like ants. Not a soul was there, in that vast crowd, who did not mourn the loss of at least one of his parents. Here was a woman who wept for her husband, here a mother who grieved for her daughter, here a brother who sought his brother, everywhere men and women bereft of those who were dearest to them. It was pitiful to see among that teeming multitude some who had taken refuge within the walls, some still outside, others dragging behind them the miserable remnants of their lives and possessions. No one, however callous he might be, could listen without tears to the tales of the sickly children, the despairing women, the old and the crippled, strung out along the roads . . . The violence of these horrors can be ascribed to no other cause than the wrath of heaven, their cessation to its mercy.

Such is the first appearance in history of the name of Othman who, having begun his career at the end of the thirteenth century as ruler of one of the smallest of all the Ghazi Emirates of Anatolia, lived to establish that extraordinary dynasty which was to give its name to the Ottoman Empire.

And it was in that same year of 1302 that Andronicus Palaeologus received a communication from Roger de Flor, leader of the Grand Company of Catalans.

The Grand Company was, in essence, a band of professional Spanish mercenaries – most but by no means all of them from Catalonia – who had been recruited in 1281 by King Peter of Aragon for use in his campaigns in North Africa and Sicily. More recently they had been fighting for Peter's son Frederick against his brother, King James of Aragon,[1] and Charles II of Anjou; but on 31 August 1302 Frederick and Charles signed a peace treaty at Caltabellotta in Sicily, by which the island's independence was finally recognized; and the Catalans, unable to return to Spain – where King James understandably looked upon them as traitors – had to find new employment for their swords.

Roger de Flor was an adventurer cast in the Guiscard mould – one of those figures, distinctly larger than life, around whom legends tend all too easily to grow up. He is said to have been the son of Richard von der Blume, the outstandingly handsome German falconer of Frederick

---

1 When King Peter III died in 1285 he was succeeded in Aragon by his eldest son Alfonso and in Sicily by his second son James. On Alfonso's death in 1291 James also took over the throne of Aragon, but under pressure from the Pope agreed to cede Sicily to Charles II in exchange for Corsica and Sardinia; the Sicilians, however, refused outright to return to Angevin rule and invited a third brother, Frederick, to be their King.

II, who after the Emperor's death had given faithful service both to his son Manfred and his grandson Conradin. Richard, however, had been killed in 1268 at Tagliacozzo,[1] after which the victorious Charles of Anjou had not only had Conradin beheaded but had confiscated the possessions of all who had supported him; and Richard's widow had been left destitute in Palermo. Somehow she found a ship to take her and her two young sons to Brindisi, where – so the story goes – their hunger was such that she fainted outside a brothel. The girls took her in and fed her; and soon afterwards – perhaps as much out of gratitude as anything else – she joined the staff.

Of the elder of her sons we know nothing; the younger, though still only eight years old, managed to get himself taken on the strength of a Templar galley. When we next hear of him in 1291, after nearly twenty years' sailing the Mediterranean and fighting the Barbary pirates, he had latinized his name from Rutger von der Blume to Roger de Flor and was master of a ship of his own, named – appropriately enough – the *Falcon*. In that year, however, the city of Acre – the last bastion of the Crusader states of Outremer – faced its final siege by the Mamelukes.[2] Roger, as a Serving Brother of the Temple, at first fought valiantly in its defence; then, when he saw the situation to be hopeless, he returned to his ship – to find himself surrounded by a crowd of panic-stricken women and children, all desperate to escape the unsavoury fate that awaited them were they to fall into infidel hands. To them Roger represented last-minute salvation; but with so many clamouring to be taken on board he could afford to be selective. He accepted only those who had managed to bring their gold and jewels with them; and even then he drove a hard bargain. The *Falcon* was quickly filled to capacity; by the time its captain had landed his passengers in Cyprus and set sail for his home port of Marseille he was a rich man.

Retribution, however, quickly followed. When news of his conduct reached the Grand Master of the Temple, Roger was expelled from the Order and denounced to Pope Boniface VIII as a thief and an apostate. Fleeing by land to Genoa, he persuaded the Doria family to fit him out with a new vessel, the *Olivetta*, and embarked on a career of out-and-out

1 See p. 225.

2 The Mamelukes were a dynasty of Sultans that reigned over Egypt and Syria from the middle of the thirteenth to the beginning of the sixteenth centuries. Originally the Turkish slave bodyguard of the last Ayoubid Sultan in Cairo, they murdered him in 1250 and seized control; ten years later, their leader Baibars defeated the invading Mongols under Hulagu at 'Ain Jalut near Nazareth, and extended their rule over Palestine and Syria.

piracy – which, in the space of the next few years, was to multiply his wealth many times over. Only then did he offer his services to Frederick of Sicily, who immediately appointed him admiral. Roger soon proved as courageous a fighter on land as at sea, and quickly acquired a loyal following. So the Catalan Company was born.

Such was the man who, towards the end of 1302, sent two envoys to Andronicus Palaeologus, offering his Company's services for nine months. Despite the obvious advantages of such an engagement to him personally – putting him as it did effectively out of reach of both the Templars and the Pope, neither of whom had forgotten his treachery – he demanded, as usual, a high price. His men were to be given four months' wages in advance, at double the rate normally payable by the Empire to its mercenaries; he himself was to be granted the rank of *megas dux* – at that time fifth in the whole hierarchy of Byzantium – and to receive the hand in marriage of the Emperor's niece Maria, the daughter of his sister Irene and her husband, John III Asen of Bulgaria. To his chief of staff, Corberán d'Alet, would go the title of Seneschal of the Empire.

Andronicus, knowing full well that he had his back to the wall, accepted these conditions without demur; and in September 1302 a fleet of thirty-nine galleys and transports sailed into the Golden Horn, carrying not only some two and a half thousand fighting men – more than half of them cavalry – but also (to the Emperor's mild consternation) their wives, mistresses and children: a total of some six and a half thousand. Shortly afterwards, with full Byzantine ceremony, Roger married his bride in Constantinople; his men, however, behaved with less decorum. Fighting broke out between them and the local Genoese; and on the wedding night itself – if the Spanish chroniclers are to be believed – Roger was obliged to leave the bed of his sixteen-year-old bride to restore order in the streets. An estimate from the same source of three thousand Genoese dead is clearly an exaggeration; but enough damage had been done for the Emperor to insist on the Catalans' early departure from the capital. A few days later the entire Company, together with its womenfolk, crossed the Marmara to Cyzicus, at that very moment under siege by the Turks.

Now at last the Catalans proved their worth. Thanks to them, by the spring of 1303 the Turkish army was everywhere in retreat. On the other hand, Andronicus began to realize that he had unleashed forces which he could not begin to control. Hitherto all imperial mercenaries had been under Greek command, subject to the orders of the Emperor or one of his generals. The Catalans, by contrast, showed scant respect for their

Byzantine employers. They took their own decisions and followed their own battle-plans; when there was any plunder to be taken, they kept it for themselves. Moreover their overbearing arrogance caused constant disaffection among their allies, and it was not long before the five hundred Alan mercenaries who were theoretically fighting at their side discovered that every Catalan was receiving double pay. The result was mutiny, followed by mass desertions; and by the time the Catalans reached the headquarters of the co-Emperor Michael IX at Pegae they had aroused such hostility among the Greeks that he closed the gates against them. But for Pegae they cared little; their eyes were on Philadelphia.

Philadelphia – now the relatively insignificant town of Alaşehir, but then an important frontier city and military base – was also under siege, not by the Ottoman Turks but by another tribe, the Karamans, who were at that time and in that area more powerful still. After their arrival the Catalans lost no time. Despite a forced march of some 120 miles, they attacked at dawn on the following day. The Turks fought hard, but their arrows had next to no effect on the mail-clad Europeans. By noon, according to the Spanish chroniclers, some eighteen thousand of them lay dead on the field; the remainder, including the Emir himself, had fled. For Roger de Flor this was the perfect opportunity to follow up his victory. By pursuing his enemy, driving deep into Karaman territory, he might have inflicted upon the Emir a still more decisive defeat and opened the way for the Byzantine reconquest of Anatolia; but he did nothing of the sort. Instead, he led his men back to the coast to make contact with his fleet – which, he was pleased to discover, had filled in the time by occupying Chios, Lemnos and Lesbos.

In less than two years the former pirate had become a member of the imperial family, had scored decisive victories over both the Ottoman and the Karaman Turks and had secured much of south-western Asia Minor. After such triumphs there was little thought in his mind – if indeed there ever had been – of fighting selflessly for Byzantium. He was of course delighted to go on taking the Emperor's money; but the experience of the past few months had awoken new hopes – hopes of an independent Kingdom of his own in Anatolia where the country was fertile, the climate as benign as anywhere on earth, the only enemies weak and disunited. Henceforth, wherever he went, he exerted absolute authority – even going so far as to punish (if necessary by death) any Byzantines, civil, military or monastic, who offended him.

*

At the beginning of 1304 Roger de Flor embarked on an ambitious expedition to the East. Why he did so is not altogether clear, since he must have known full well that he would thus be allowing both the Ottomans and the Karamans to regroup and rearm as best they might; but he and his Company set out in the early spring, and by the middle of August they had reached the 'Iron Gates' of the Taurus. A pass so narrow that the pack-mules had to be unloaded before they could be taken through it in single file, there could have been no more perfect place for an ambush; and Roger wisely decided to send out mounted scouts to reconnoitre. It was as well for him that he did, for there indeed a Turkish army lay waiting for him. Another desperate battle followed; once again the Catalans carried all before them. There, however, they halted. Several of Roger's junior commanders urged a further advance, across the Euphrates into Syria; but their leader would have none of it and gave the order to return.

Why did he do so? According to the chronicler Ramón Muntaner – who was with him on the campaign – messengers had arrived from the Emperor, recalling him to the West. By now Roger de Flor had long passed the stage at which imperial orders were to be unquestioningly obeyed. What concerned him was the fact that the expedition was taking him further and further out of touch: if there were a crisis in Constantinople, he must be in a position to take advantage of it. Besides, he had left vast quantities of treasure at Magnesia and was beginning to worry about its safety. And what about pay, for himself and his men? Despite their behaviour and their overbearing attitude to the Byzantines, they were still technically mercenaries and the Emperor now owed them nearly a year's wages. Finally, unprincipled adventurer as he was, Roger never liked unnecessary risks: again and again during this period of his career we find him taking the side of caution, restraining his more impulsive followers from their daredevil plans. On the high Anatolian plateau across which they would have to march, he explained, the onset of winter was only a few weeks away. They must retrace their steps while it was still safe to do so.

And so they did – but only to find that in their absence a Greek knight named Attaliotes had seized Magnesia, and with it all their accumulated treasure. At once they put the town under siege; but before it could be taken another, more urgent message reached them from the Emperor: that Theodore Svetoslav, the usurper who had driven the Mongols from Bulgaria and united most of it – including the Byzantine ports on the Black Sea – under his rule, had invaded Thrace and was already threatening Constantinople. Alone, Andronicus could do nothing; only with Catalan assistance could he hope to save his capital. Here was an appeal that could not be ignored: Roger immediately saw that Theodore presented a dangerous new complication, and that if not effectively dealt with he might prove a grave obstacle to his own long-term plans. Magnesia – which was stoutly defended – must be left till later. Marching through the Troad to the Hellespont, he led his men across the straits and pitched his camp in Gallipoli.

At this point the precise chronology becomes uncertain: Greek and Spanish sources give conflicting – and extremely one-sided – accounts of what took place, and it is impossible to reconcile them altogether. It seems, however, that some time during the winter of 1304–5 word came from the co-Emperor Michael that the services of Roger de Flor and his men would not after all be necessary; and soon afterwards Roger learned that Michael had promulgated an edict to the Byzantine forces that the Grand Duke was no longer to be obeyed. No explanation was offered, no indication of how the Bulgar crisis had been settled so suddenly and with such apparent ease. Could it have been – one cannot help wondering – that there had in fact been no Bulgar crisis at all, that the whole thing had been nothing more than a fabrication designed to bring Roger and his men back from the East to where the Byzantines could keep a proper eye on them?

However that may be, it was fortunate for Roger de Flor that he should have been within reach of Constantinople when, early in 1305, a fleet of nine Spanish galleys appeared in the Golden Horn, commanded by a certain Berenguer d'Entença, an old comrade-in-arms from the Sicilian campaign whom James II of Aragon had now appointed his special envoy to the Emperor. The purpose of Berenguer's visit, apart from the bringing of reinforcements – which had not been asked for, though they were none the less welcome for that – remains something of a mystery: the rumour, assiduously spread by the Genoese, that he was connected with a secret conspiracy to restore the Latin Empire was not to be borne out by subsequent events, while Gregoras's claim that he had been invited by Andronicus in the hopes of playing him off against Roger seems little short of absurd. At all events the envoy was received with every honour and was soon afterwards himself awarded the title of *megas dux*, Roger being simultaneously promoted to the rank of Caesar.

This latter honour was admittedly in some degree deserved: the Catalan Company had fought at least three decisive battles against the Turks in Anatolia, to say nothing of innumerable minor skirmishes from which they had almost always emerged victorious. But it was also intended as a palliative. Michael doubtless realized that his action at the time of the Bulgar scare had antagonized Roger both dangerously and unnecessarily. Moreover the Company had by now been a full year without pay, and its two commanders, in their heated negotiations with the Emperor, were adopting an increasingly threatening tone. Unfortunately there was little – as usual – that Andronicus could do. The imperial coffers were empty. Recently he had been obliged to debase the coinage yet again: the gold content of the *hyperpyron* – the name, ironically enough, meant 'highly refined' – was now down to less than twenty per cent, and Roger angrily refused to be fobbed off with what he understandably described as base metal. Berenguer d'Entença showed his indignation more forcibly still: he returned the gold and silver dinner service on which his meals had been provided – although, if Pachymeres is to be believed, not before he had put them to the most ignoble uses – boarded his flagship and set sail for the Company's camp at Gallipoli. As he left Blachernae, he ostentatiously hurled his ducal regalia overboard in full sight of the palace.

At last agreement was reached – though only after Andronicus had granted Roger's demand for the whole of Byzantine Anatolia in fief; and in the spring of 1305 the Catalans began their return to Asia. Before leaving for his new domains, however, Roger decided to make a formal visit to Michael IX, whom he had never met and who was then at Adrianople. The co-Emperor, he knew, had no love for himself and his men, whom he mistrusted even more than did his father; Roger's real purpose may well have been to try to improve relations between them, or at least to reach some sort of understanding – as he had so signally failed to achieve with Andronicus.[1] His pregnant wife Maria and her mother both implored him not to venture among his openly avowed enemies, but he ignored them both and on 23 March 1305 set off, with an escort of three hundred cavalry and a thousand infantry, for Michael's headquarters.

Roger was received in Adrianople with full honours and remained there over a week – a clear enough sign, surely, that he saw this as something more than a courtesy visit. Was Michael deliberately playing

---

1 Of the several theories that have been put forward as to Roger's real reason for his visit to Michael IX, the most interesting is that of Alfonso Lowe, in *The Catalan Vengeance*, who speculates that he was deliberately lured to his death by Andronicus and Michael together, on the pretext of discussing the elimination of Theodore Svetoslav and his replacement by the rightful ruler of Bulgaria, Roger's own brother-in-law. But it is only speculation; we shall never know.

for time, so as to summon enough reinforcements to deal with the Catalans as necessary? Perhaps he was. All we can say for certain is that on 5 April, the eve of his departure for Gallipoli, Roger de Flor was assassinated. Pachymeres – who was over a hundred miles away in Constantinople – identifies the assassin as George Gircon, the Alan chieftain whose son had been killed by the Catalans at Cyzicus and who had long nurtured a particular hatred for their leader; he goes on to report that the murder took place on the threshold of the private apartments of the co-Empress, Rita-Maria of Armenia, though precisely what Roger was doing there he does not explain. Western sources on the other hand – which may in the circumstances be more reliable – while also attributing the crime to Gircon, claim that the scene was a farewell banquet, given by Michael in his honour. Towards the end of the feast the latter withdrew according to normal custom, leaving his guests to continue their drinking at their leisure; then, suddenly, the doors were flung open and a fully-armed company of Alan mercenaries burst into the hall. The Catalans – surrounded, outnumbered and almost certainly drunk – stood no chance. Roger was killed with the rest.

No longer was there any question of an alliance between the Greeks and the Catalan Company. Henceforth it was open war.

As soon as the news reached the Catalan camp at Gallipoli, the move to Asia stopped; those who had already crossed the straits were summoned back, and the peninsula on which the town stood was declared Spanish territory. The Company then drove across Thrace taking, as it marched, a terrible vengeance. It had of course been seriously depleted at Adrianople; but an active programme of recruitment had attracted companies of Turks and Bulgars and before long it was as numerous as ever. Michael IX, now seriously alarmed by a turn of events for which he had been at least partially responsible, did his utmost to halt its advance; but his army was smashed by the Catalans near the castle of Aprus near Rhaedestum (Tekirdağ) and he himself, after fighting with conspicuous courage, narrowly escaped with his life.

The province of Thrace, lying as it did across the direct road to Constantinople from the West, had suffered much hardship over the centuries. It had been ravaged by Avars and Huns, by Gepids and Bulgars, by Scythians and Slavs and Christian Crusaders. But the Catalans were the worst. So savage were their massacres, so unspeakable their atrocities, that it sometimes seemed as though they were determined to leave no single Thracian alive. Farms and villages – sometimes whole towns –

were abandoned, as thousands of panic-stricken refugees streamed into Constantinople, leaving their cornfields ablaze behind them. Adrianople and Didymotichum remained impregnable, but their garrisons no longer dared to take any initiative. Once one of the richest and most fertile territories of the Byzantine Empire, Thrace was now a desert.

But deserts are little more rewarding to their conquerors than to their inhabitants, and in the summer of 1308 the Catalans turned west towards Thessalonica. They failed to capture the city, but they destroyed several smaller towns and plundered and pillaged the monasteries of Mount Athos before descending first into Thessaly and then, in 1310, yet further south into Boeotia where they took service with Walter of Brienne, the French Duke of Athens and Thebes. Walter had long had his eye on Thessaly, and with Catalan help he effortlessly brought the young and ailing John II Ducas[1] to his knees. Before long, however, Walter discovered in his turn that the Catalans were dangerous employees, easier to hire than to dismiss. On 15 March 1311 they annihilated his army on the banks of the Cephissus river; he himself was killed, together with most of his knights. The victors then advanced to Athens, where they set up their own Duchy. It was to last another seventy-seven years.

And so the Catalans pass out of our story. In less than a single decade they had inflicted almost as much damage on the Byzantine Empire as the Turks had done in a century. And they had been paid by the Emperor to do it. In order to find their wages, Andronicus Palaeologus had been obliged to debase his coinage and to impose still heavier taxes on his already desperate subjects. The damage they had done in Thrace was to take generations to repair; the flood of refugees they had driven from their homes was to create near-famine in Constantinople. Had they kept to the terms of their agreement with Andronicus, concentrating on pushing back the Turks and renouncing all territorial ambitions for themselves, they might have turned back the Islamic tide and the whole future history of the Levant might have been changed. Alas, they did not; instead, almost exactly a century after the Fourth Crusade, they dealt the Empire that they had come to save yet another paralysing blow, from which it would not recover.

---

1 Grandson of John I Ducas through his son Constantine.

17
The Two Andronici

[1307–41]

The Devil has still the same inclination to injure men that he has had since the beginning of the world; and although he does not always do them all the harm he intends, yet he succeeds in doing them a great part of it.

Andronicus II, to his grandson Andronicus III
after the capture of Constantinople

Although the first decade of the fourteenth century was overshadowed, as far as Byzantium was concerned, by the Company of Catalans, this was by no means the only problem with which the unfortunate Andronicus Palaeologus was called upon to deal. To the west, Theodore Svetoslav continued to threaten – at least until 1307, when Andronicus conceded to him the Black Sea ports that he had already occupied, together with the hand in marriage of Michael IX's daughter Theodora. Then Charles II's son Philip of Taranto joined forces with the Catholic Albanians and captured Durazzo. Meanwhile another Western European prince had entered the fray: Charles of Valois, brother of the French King Philip the Fair. In 1301 he had married Catharine of Courtenay, granddaughter of the Emperor Baldwin; now he in his turn was determined to restore the Latin Empire. To that end he had enlisted the help of Pope Clement V – who had obligingly pronounced sentence of anathema on Andronicus – as well as concluding agreements with Venice, with Miliutin of Serbia (by this time somewhat disenchanted with his father-in-law) and even, in 1308, with the Catalan Company. In that same year, however, his wife died; the right of succession passed to their daughter Catharine of Valois and Charles found himself without a claim after all – particularly after Philip of Taranto, having divorced his first wife Thamar, married Catharine in 1313. But although his machinations eventually came to nothing, during the first years of the century he too had caused the Emperor considerable anxiety.

To the east, once the Catalans had left Anatolia in 1304, the Turks

273

continued to advance. In that very year the tribe of Aydin took Ephesus; in 1307 Othman seized the fortress of Trikokkia, thereby destroying communications between Nicomedia and Nicaea; and in 1308, by their capture of Iconium, the Karamans finally put an end – after over two centuries – to the long-moribund Seljuk Sultanate. In 1309 Byzantium suffered a further loss, when the island of Rhodes (which had for some time been effectively controlled by the Genoese) fell to the Knights of St John.[1] With every day that passed, it seemed, the Empire diminished, its Emperor having long ago given up any hope of stemming the Turkish tide.

In Constantinople, the Arsenites became ever more troublesome. What little comfort they might have derived from the departure of the puritanical firebrand Athanasius in 1293 was taken from them when, at the Emperor's insistence, he was reinstated ten years later;[2] and by 1304 their behaviour had become such that Andronicus – all his attempts to appeal to their better natures having failed – put an armed guard on their monastery at Mosele. When, in the year following, another plot against his life was discovered just in time and its chief instigator, a certain John Drimys, was found to have close Arsenite connections, Andronicus ordered the monastery to be closed for good and many of its members put under arrest. By now, however, the movement was rapidly losing impetus. John Lascaris, blind and imprisoned, no longer seemed so desirable a candidate for the throne as he had twenty years before; besides, most of the old Empire of Nicaea had already fallen to the Turks. In 1309 Patriarch Athanasius – who was said to have looked upon Byzantium as one vast monastery – retired to his own smaller one, this time for good; and his successor Niphon immediately set to work to heal the Arsenite schism once and for all. He achieved his object within a year: on 14 September 1310, in the course of a dramatically impressive ceremony at St Sophia, the Orthodox Church was formally reunited.

To Andronicus, the relief must have been immense; but in the same year he was faced with a new enemy – his own wife Irene, the former

---

1 The Knights Hospitaller of St John of Jerusalem were, like the Templars, a military Order which had been obliged to leave Palestine after the fall of Acre in 1291. They were to make their headquarters in Rhodes (where their splendid Hospital still survives) until the island's capture by Süleyman the Magnificent in 1522, soon after which they moved to Malta.

2 Athanasius had enjoyed a remarkable stroke of good luck. On 15 January 1303 he had proclaimed from his monastic refuge that the divine wrath would shortly fall upon the people of Constantinople; that same night there was a minor earthquake, which was followed by a considerably more serious one two days afterwards.

Yolanda of Montferrat. The eleven-year-old girl he had married had turned into a formidably ambitious and self-willed woman, and for some time relations between the two had been growing ever more tense. Matters came to a head when Irene proposed that on her husband's death the Empire should not pass to Michael IX alone but should be divided among all four sons – the younger three being of course her own. Predictably – and rightly – Andronicus rejected the idea out of hand; whereupon the Empress accused him of favouritism towards his first-born and left Constantinople with her three boys for Thessalonica which, besides being her childhood home, had the additional advantage of relative proximity to her daughter Simonis, now sixteen, at the Bulgar court. There she remained for the next seven years until her death, constantly intriguing against her husband with anyone who would listen to her.

Another resident of Thessalonica – he must have arrived shortly after his stepmother – was the co-Emperor Michael. Though still only in his middle thirties, he was already disappointed and disillusioned. A brave but disastrously untalented soldier, he had spent much of his adult life on campaign without ever winning a major battle. Apart from a few insignificant victories over the Bulgars in 1304, his career had been marked by defeat after defeat, first in Asia Minor and later in the Balkans. His most recent débâcle had been at the hands of an army of some two thousand Turks who, after having joined the Catalans, had remained in Thrace when the latter moved into Greece and were to terrorize the region for the next two years, helping themselves to what little there was left to pillage and seriously disrupting communications. Early in 1311 Michael had led an army against them, with the usual catastrophic result. After this he had been relieved of his military command and had retired into private life.

By his Armenian wife Maria (her original name, Rita, having been replaced as was customary by a more respectable-sounding Byzantine one) Michael had four children – the eldest of whom, Andronicus, an intelligent and outstandingly good-looking boy, was in turn crowned co-Emperor at the age of nineteen in February 1316. There were now three Emperors sharing the throne, and the succession should have been assured for at least two more generations to come. Young Andronicus, however, soon began to show signs of dangerous instability. He drank, he gambled, he caroused, he ran up hideous debts with the Genoese in Galata; and he was notoriously fond of women. The year after his coronation he was married off to a noble German lady of stultifying tedium named Adelaide of Brunswick-Grubenhagen; but after the birth of one child (who died in infancy) he took little interest in her and reverted to his old ways – if indeed he had ever abandoned them.

By now the young man's behaviour was beginning to cause his father and grandfather serious anxiety; but matters were brought to a head only in 1320 when, suspecting one of his mistresses of infidelity, he carefully laid an ambush for his unknown rival near her house. Whether that rival really was his own brother Manuel or whether Manuel just chanced to be passing at the wrong moment is not altogether certain; in any case he was set upon and killed. Michael IX, when the news was brought to him, was still mourning the death of his daughter Anna;[1] he was already a sick man, and this second shock was more than he could bear. He went into a decline and died on 12 October at Thessalonica. Andronicus II furiously disowned his grandson and named his own younger son Constantine as heir to the throne of Byzantium.

The result was civil war.

The old Emperor was now sixty years old – a considerable age in Byzantine times – and during the nearly forty years that he had been on the throne the situation in the Empire had gone from bad to worse. He was fortunate to have as his chief adviser (and later Grand Logothete) the writer and scholar Theodore Metochites, who served him devotedly from 1290 until the end of his reign; but even Theodore was powerless to stop the decline. Thrace was devastated, Asia Minor virtually lost. In the absence of a navy or merchant fleet, trade – and food supplies – were in the hands of the perpetually squabbling Venetians and Genoese. Taxes were being increased year by year; the revenue was spent, however, not on rearmament but on tribute – protection money to the Catalans and Turks, paid in the hopes that they would thereby be persuaded to leave imperial territory alone. No wonder that, when the young Andronicus refused to accept his grandfather's decree and raised the flag of rebellion in Adrianople, there were many in the capital – particularly among the younger generation of the nobility and landowning classes – who rallied enthusiastically to his support.

At the young Emperor's right hand was John Cantacuzenus, one of

---

1 Anna's first husband had been Thomas, Despot of Epirus; but in 1318 Thomas had been murdered by his nephew Nicholas Orsini, the Italian Count of Cephalonia, who had immediately adopted the Orthodox faith, established himself in Epirus as his uncle's successor and married his widow. Anna herself had died two years later.

the leading members of the military aristocracy: his father had been Governor of the Morea, and he himself was an important landowner in the Empire, possessing huge estates in Macedonia, Thrace and Thessaly. Though he was a year or two older than Andronicus, they had been close friends since childhood; and John, whether as *éminence grise*, Grand Domestic, reluctant rebel or Emperor, was to dominate the Byzantine political scene for much of the century. Equally important for posterity, he was to write a long and detailed history of the Empire between 1320 and 1356, drawing largely on his own memories of people and events and frequently quoting from original documents. Inevitably, it is to some extent biased in his own favour; but since he was the most outstanding soldier and statesman of his day it is certainly not to be dismissed on that account.

Second only to John Cantacuzenus in importance among the supporters of Andronicus III was a certain Syrgiannes Palaeologus. He was in fact a minor member of the imperial family only through his mother, his father having been of Cuman descent; and, as we shall see, he was to prove an unreliable ally. He and John, however, had both bought governorships for themselves in Thrace – the sale of offices was not the least of the abuses that had grown up under the Palaeologi – where they had immediately set to work fanning the flames of dissatisfaction among the local populace, already crushed under the ever-increasing weight of imperial taxation. At Easter 1321 the young Emperor joined them. If Gregoras is to be believed, one of his first acts was to exempt the entire province from paying any taxes at all; and by means of this and other extravagant promises he quickly won the support he needed. Syrgiannes then marched on the capital where old Andronicus, terrified lest the revolt should spread, hastily came to terms. By 6 June the two sides had agreed on a partition of the Empire. Andronicus II was to rule on the Bosphorus as before, Andronicus III in Adrianople.

Only a few years previously, when the Empress Irene had made a similar proposal, it had been received with horror; the fact that it was now so readily agreed shows all too clearly how far the Emperor's position had deteriorated in the past decade. To preserve some semblance of unity, old Andronicus insisted that responsibility for foreign policy should be his alone; but almost from the first his grandson showed himself determined to follow his own diplomatic path, and before long there were effectively two separate Empires pursuing completely different policies, more often than not in active opposition to each other.

In such circumstances peace could not endure for long, and early in

1322 hostilities were resumed. They seem to have been caused, strangely enough, by Syrgiannes himself. He had always been jealous of John Cantacuzenus, whom he rightly believed to enjoy the special favour of the young Emperor; and this jealousy now led him to change sides. Returning to Constantinople, he went straight to old Andronicus and encouraged him to teach his grandson a lesson. But it was no use. In both Thrace and Macedonia the rebels were too popular, and it soon became clear that if the old man continued to oppose them he might very probably lose such territories that remained in his control. In July 1322 the two Emperors reached a settlement for the second time. There was no longer to be any question of partition; both were now to rule jointly over the whole Empire, while Andronicus III was reconfirmed as sole heir. Andronicus II however would remain the senior, with the right of veto over any of his grandson's policies.

This time the peace lasted a full five years: years in the course of which, on 2 February 1325, Andronicus III was crowned for the second time in St Sophia and, on 6 April 1326, the Ottoman Turks captured Brusa after a seven-year siege and made it their capital.[1] More alarming even than this latter disaster was the news that Andronicus II's own nephew, the Governor of Thessalonica John Palaeologus, had announced his secession from the Empire. John was also the son-in-law of the Grand Logothete Theodore Metochites; and although Theodore himself remained as always loyal to his master, his two sons – who commanded the important military bases of Melnik and Strumica – immediately identified themselves with the rebellion. John then appealed for support to the Serbian King Stephen Dechanski (to whom he had given his daughter in marriage) and set off in person for the Serbian court.

Had he succeeded in forging an alliance with King Stephen, the Empire might well have been faced with a new and serious danger; in such an event grandfather and grandson might even have temporarily forgotten their rivalry and made common cause against the enemy. But John Palaeologus died, suddenly and unexpectedly, soon after his arrival in Skoplje; the immediate danger receded; and in the autumn of 1327 civil war broke out for the third time in less than seven years. On this occasion the two Emperors did not fight alone. Stephen Dechanski (whose young wife was, after all, the Emperor's great-niece) declared his

---

1 · Brusa was actually taken by Orhan, the son of Othman. The latter died in the same year and did not live to see the new capital; but Orhan had his body brought there for burial in the citadel. Brusa thus became something of a shrine, and the burial-place of all the early Ottoman Sultans.

support for Andronicus II, while the Bulgar Tsar Michael Sisman – who had divorced his first wife, Stephen's sister, in order to marry Theodora, widow of Theodore Svetoslav and sister of Andronicus III – was only too happy to conclude an alliance with his new brother-in-law. As before, there was little serious fighting; it proved scarcely necessary, since young Andronicus – making more and more of those extravagant promises and donations that had served him so well in the past – was hailed wherever he appeared. In January 1328 he went with John Cantacuzenus to Thessalonica, where he was given a magnificent reception as *basileus*. Nearly all the other principal cities and castles in Thrace and Macedonia sent messages of support.

Meanwhile, quietly and unhurriedly, he was making his preparations to march on the capital as soon as the spring rains were over. Before he could do so, however, disturbing news was brought to him: Tsar Michael had unaccountably decided to change sides, and had sent three thousand Bulgarian cavalry for the defence of Constantinople. Andronicus hesitated no longer. Hurrying eastward with an advance guard, he managed to intercept the Bulgars before they had taken up their positions and persuaded their commander to order an immediate withdrawal, pointing out to him that he was acting in direct violation of the alliance entered into by his master less than a year before. Then, after sending the Tsar an angry message reminding him of his treaty obligations, he settled down to await the rest of his army.

The departure of the Bulgars was not the only blow sustained by the old Andronicus in the spring of 1328. Venice and Genoa were back once more at their usual tricks and, heedless of the sufferings of the Greek population, were using Constantinople and its surrounding waterways as their principal battleground. Throughout April a Venetian fleet of forty ships had been blockading Galata and the entrance to the Bosphorus, bringing the inhabitants of the city to the brink of famine. The years of civil war, during which opposing armies had trampled backwards and forwards across the fertile fields of Thrace, had made local agriculture impossible and interrupted their normal overland supply of food from the western provinces; now they could not even bring it in by sea. What little was available fetched huge prices, far beyond the reach of a people bled white by taxation, whose economy had long since been brought to a standstill. The old Emperor's popularity was diminishing day by day, his authority growing ever more insecure.

In such circumstances, the capture of the city by his grandson met with scant resistance. On the evening of 23 May 1328 Andronicus and John Cantacuzenus, at the head of a party of twenty-four men with siege ladders, crept up to the section of the great bastion opposite the Romanus Gate. Ropes were lowered by accomplices within the city, the ladders were hoisted up, and within minutes the first of the young Emperor's men were over the wall, opening the gate for their comrades. There was no killing, little looting; no one was hurt. Old Andronicus, awoken from a deep sleep, was initially terrified; but his fears were quickly allayed. All that was asked of him was to sign a deed of abdication; once that was done he was allowed to keep his imperial title and insignia and to continue, if he wished, to live in the Palace of Blachernae. Meanwhile a delegation was sent to free the Patriarch, Esaias by name, who in the previous year had refused to obey Andronicus II's order to excommunicate his grandson and had been confined to the monastery of the Mangana. On his way back to his palace he was escorted not, Gregoras tells us, by the procession of distinguished ecclesiastics that might have been expected, but by a troupe of musicians, comedians and dancing girls, one of whom soon had him so helpless with laughter that he almost fell off his horse.

Apart from the old Emperor – who may well have been relieved to be spared a continuation of responsibilities for which he was manifestly unsuited – the only serious sufferer was his Grand Logothete, Theodore Metochites. In the absence of any other convenient scapegoat, this gentle scholar was now universally blamed for all his master's misfortunes and failures. Much of his property was confiscated; his house was plundered and burnt; he himself was initially exiled, but was then permitted to return to the monastery of St Saviour in Chora, which he had restored and embellished at his own expense some years before.[1] There – near the point where the Land Walls run down to the Golden Horn, only a stone's throw from Blachernae – he lived out the years remaining to him, dying at last in March 1332.

He outlived Andronicus II by a month. The old Emperor remained in Constantinople for two years after his abdication; then he too was packed off to a monastery, where he took the name of Antonius. On 13 February 1332 he dined with his daughter Simonis, the widow of

---

[1] The church of the Chora – more generally known today as Kariye Camii – still stands. Thanks to its dazzling mosaics and superb frescos, a visit there is one of the most memorable experiences that even Istanbul has to offer. The mosaics include a splendid representation of Theodore himself, offering his church to Christ, while the fresco of the *Anastasis*, or Harrowing of Hell, in the apse of the side chapel to the south is perhaps the supreme masterpiece of all Christian art.

Stephen Miliutin of Serbia, and died within hours of rising from the table. He was seventy-three years old, and had reigned for almost exactly half a century. Seldom in all its thousand-year history had Byzantium been more in need of a strong and determined ruler; seldom had it suffered a weaker one. Had Andronicus II been less of a pietist and more of a statesman; had he made things happen instead of waiting until they happened to him; had he possessed half the diplomatic skills of his father, the courage of his son or the energy of his grandson he might have turned both the coming of the Catalans and the fall of the Seljuks to his advantage and possibly even arrested the Empire's decline. Instead, lacking as he was in any long-term vision or any clear political objective, he allowed it to drift rudderless from one catastrophe to the next until Andronicus III – who, with all his faults, at least knew what he wanted and was ready to fight for it – removed him, gently but firmly, from the helm. As for his unfortunate subjects – beleaguered, half-starving and crippled by senseless taxation – they were glad to see the last of him.

Andronicus III was now thirty-one. The past decade had brought him at last to something like maturity. True, with his thousand huntsmen, thousand hounds and thousand falcons, he may have given rather too much attention to the pleasures of the chase; and not all his subjects approved of his love of jousting, a sport that had been re-introduced[1] into Byzantine court circles by the Italian entourage of his second wife Anne, the daughter of Count Amadeus V of Savoy. Still, he had put the worst excesses of his youth behind him; and though he would always be capable of sudden bouts of irresponsibility and recklessness – and never lost his dangerous weakness for making promises that he was unable to fulfil – he was to prove himself a fearless soldier and, on the whole, a conscientious ruler. He was certainly an immense improvement on his grandfather.

Above all he was fortunate: fortunate in having at his side, throughout his thirteen-year reign, a man of quite outstanding ability in both the political and military fields and – more important still – unwavering loyalty to himself. John Cantacuzenus was more than the Emperor's friend and counsellor; he was, in a very real sense, his inspiration. Just as it was he who had been the guiding force behind the recent rebellion, so it was he, after the success of that rebellion, who now directed the

---

1 It may be remembered that Manuel Comnenus had also shown a certain enthusiasm for this most un-Byzantine of sports. See p. 123.

affairs of the Empire. He refused all titles – even those of Regent and co-Emperor, both of which were offered him by a grateful Andronicus – and held no titular office of state except that of Grand Domestic, or commander-in-chief; but few people in Constantinople had any doubts as to where the effective power really lay.

Yet it was probably Andronicus himself, rather than his Grand Domestic, who took the initiative for one of the first and most important decisions of his reign. He was fully aware – as, to their cost, were his subjects – that the imperial legal system was by now deeply corrupt. We have seen how easily John Cantacuzenus and Syrgiannes Palaeologus had bought governorships for themselves in Thrace; even the Grand Logothete Theodore Metochites, a man everywhere respected for his integrity and deeply versed in moral philosophy, unhesitatingly bought and sold high offices of state. Andronicus II had attempted to tackle the problem some thirty years before, with his usual lack of success; his grandson, less than a year after his accession as sole Emperor, now returned to the charge by instituting, in 1329, a new board of judges whom he designated 'Universal Justices of the Romans'. They were four in number – two ecclesiastics and two laymen – and effectively constituted a Supreme Court of Appeal, empowered to supervise the administration of the law throughout the Empire, with a special brief to watch for cases of corruption and tax evasion in high places. Local justices were appointed in outlying regions with similar responsibilities. The system was not, it must be admitted, entirely successful. Corruption, once it has taken root, is notoriously hard to eradicate: as early as 1337, at a special court held in St Sophia under the joint presidency of Emperor and Patriarch, three of the four Universal Justices were themselves found guilty of accepting bribes, deprived of their office and sent into exile. But successors were immediately appointed, and the institution was to continue for as long as the Empire itself.

On the international stage, Andronicus's new policy of non-appeasement quickly began to show results. Within a month of his *coup*, Tsar Michael Sisman of Bulgaria invaded Thrace as he had done several times in the past. On this occasion, however, Andronicus retaliated by launching an immediate invasion of his own and capturing a Bulgarian stronghold; and when, two months later, Michael tried the same thing again he found a Byzantine army drawn up against him. The result was a treaty of peace, which prevented any further violations for the next two years and might well have lasted a good deal longer had not the Bulgarian army been totally destroyed on 28 July 1330 at Velbuzd – now Kjustendil – by the Serbs under Stephen Dechanski. The Tsar himself was mortally wounded in the battle, and died in captivity soon afterwards. Stephen installed his nephew John Stephen[1] on the Bulgarian throne, and poor Theodora had to flee for her life.

For Andronicus his sister's misfortune proved something of a blessing, giving him as it did a convenient pretext for interference in Bulgarian affairs. Ostensibly to avenge her honour, he seized the Black Sea ports of Mesembria and Anchialus which his grandfather had ceded to the Bulgars nearly a quarter of a century before, together with several fortresses that lined the imperial frontier. He did not, however, keep them long, for the following year was to bring palace revolutions to both the Slav states. In Bulgaria John Stephen and his mother Anna were thrown out in favour of Sisman's nephew John Alexander, while in Serbia Dechanski – who, it was considered, had failed to follow up his victory in the approved manner – was murdered by a group of nobles and replaced by his son Stephen Dushan. The two new rulers then formed an alliance, which they cemented by a marriage between Stephen Dushan and John Alexander's sister Helena; together they then began to work, the Serbs in Macedonia and the Bulgars in Thrace, towards the realization of their common dream – the overthrow of the *basileus* and the establishment of a great Slav Empire in Constantinople. John Alexander easily won back the disputed Black Sea ports, while Stephen pushed steadily southward into Byzantine territory – much helped, it must be said, by the Empire's own internal troubles, not the least of which was the desertion in 1334 of Syrgiannes Palaeologus to the Serbian camp.

Syrgiannes is a difficult character to understand. An aristocrat on his mother's side – though a half-breed on his father's – he had been one of the closest and most intimate friends both of the Emperor and of his Grand Domestic. He was extremely intelligent and seems to have been possessed of unusual charm; but he knew the meaning neither of faith nor of loyalty. Once already he had betrayed his master – during the civil war, when he had shamelessly gone over to Andronicus II. Soon afterwards he had been implicated in a plot to murder the old Emperor, and had been sentenced to life imprisonment; but he had been released by Andronicus III after his assumption of power, formally pardoned – at

---

1 John Stephen was the son of Dechanski's sister Anna, the first wife of Michael Sisman, whom he had divorced to marry Andronicus's sister Theodora. See p. 279.

the insistent demand, we are told, of John Cantacuzenus – and, somewhat surprisingly, appointed Governor of Thessalonica. On his arrival there, he immediately began to make trouble, intriguing against Cantacuzenus and ingratiating himself with the Emperor's mother Rita-Maria – who had settled in the city after her husband's death – to the point where she adopted him as her son. In 1333 she died in her turn, and it soon became clear that Syrgiannes was once again hatching a conspiracy, this time against the Emperor himself and presumably with a view to replacing him on the throne. Whether or not he was already in touch with Stephen Dushan is not certain; but Thessalonica was too close to the Serbian frontier for comfort, and Andronicus was taking no chances. Syrgiannes was put under close arrest and taken to the capital for trial; before proceedings could begin, however, he escaped across the Golden Horn to Galata and thence, via Euboea and Thessaly, to Serbia. There Stephen Dushan welcomed him warmly and gave him command of an army, which in the spring of 1334 captured Kastoria and a number of neighbouring strongholds.

The Emperor and John Cantacuzenus hurried to Macedonia, determined to eliminate Syrgiannes once and for all. Uncertain, however, whether their hastily-gathered army was sufficient for the task, they decided on a more devious method. Selecting one of the senior officers on the staff, a certain Sphrantzes Palaeologus,[1] they proposed to him a plan whereby he would be appointed a local governor of several small towns around Thessalonica. This, they believed, would be the perfect bait for Syrgiannes, who would immediately try to subvert him. Sphrantzes in turn would accept these overtures, and quickly gain his confidence; it would then be an easy matter for him to arrest Syrgiannes and deliver him up for punishment.

All went as arranged – except that at the critical moment Sphrantzes exceeded his brief and, instead of seizing the traitor, killed him outright. He was reprimanded for his disobedience, but was soon afterwards promoted to the rank of Grand Stratopedarch[2] with a considerable increase of salary. It was a small price for the Emperor to pay: only a month or two later, in August 1334, he and Stephen Dushan met on the

---

1 The surname is uncertain. John Cantacuzenus – who should know – refers to him simply as Sphrantzes, and adds that although he was a senior member of the Senate, he was of undistinguished birth.

2 According to a fourteenth-century book of ceremonial, the holder of this rank was responsible for the provisioning of the army; in most cases, however, the title seems to have been purely honorific.

frontier near Thessalonica where, in return for the promise of Byzantine help against Hungary, it was agreed that those places taken by Syrgiannes should revert to the Empire.

Andronicus needed them, for Stephen made it abundantly clear that all his other conquests of the past two years – and they included Ochrid, Prilep, Strumica and even Vodena (the modern Edhessa) – were to remain in Serbian hands. A large part of Macedonia was now lost for ever. The final collapse had begun.

In Asia Minor it was proceeding apace. When, at the end of May 1329, reports reached Constantinople that the Ottoman Turks under Orhan were blockading Nicaea, the Emperor and John Cantacuzenus crossed the straits to Chalcedon with an army of some four thousand and advanced south-eastwards along the shore of the Marmara. On the third morning of their march they spied the Turkish army encamped in the hills above the little village of Pelekanos (now Manyas). As well as being far more strategically placed, it appeared to be about twice the size of their own; but after a brief council of war they decided that if Orhan came down on to the plain to meet them they would stand and fight. He did so; and on 10 June the battle began. It raged all that day, under a sweltering sun, and by evening it seemed that the Byzantines – who had by that time beaten off two major Turkish attacks – had the advantage. Their own casualties, however, were already severe; they knew moreover that Orhan, who had deliberately held back part of his army, would almost certainly fling it against them the next day. Cantacuzenus therefore advised that, as soon as possible after dawn, they should begin a discreet and dignified withdrawal.

So indeed they did; unfortunately some of the younger and less experienced soldiers, driven to distraction by constant harassment from the Turkish archers, broke ranks in order to drive them away. Knowing full well the dangers of such an action, Cantacuzenus wheeled his horse and galloped off in their pursuit; and a moment or two later Andronicus, who had not seen him, did the same. It was just as they had feared. They found the young hotheads surrounded, and in the bitter fighting that followed the Emperor was struck in the thigh. He only just managed to regain the body of the army – his horse, streaming with blood, expired on arrival – and the next day he was returned on a stretcher to Constantinople. The wound proved to be quite superficial; and all would have been well had not some of the soldiers, seeing him carried away, assumed that he had been killed. They panicked, and it was with the greatest difficulty that John Cantacuzenus – who had also had an extremely narrow escape – managed to restore a semblance of order, just in time to fight another engagement against the pursuing Turks outside the walls of Philocrene.

The battle of Pelekanos was the first personal encounter between an Emperor of Byzantium and an Ottoman Emir. It had not been a disaster on the scale of Manzikert, but it had shown beyond any reasonable doubt that the Turkish advance in Asia Minor was unstoppable. If any proof were needed, it was soon forthcoming: Nicaea – the imperial capital just seventy years before – fell on 2 March 1331, Nicomedia six years later. All that remained of the Empire in Asia – apart from one or two Aegean islands – was the occasional isolated town that the Turks had not yet bothered to conquer: Philadelphia for example, and Heraclea on the Black Sea. But none of these had any strategic value and their collapse, as everybody knew, was merely a matter of time. Meanwhile his possession of the entire Asiatic shore of the Marmara enabled Orhan to build up his sea power, with which he now began to subject the European shore to almost continuous attack.

For Andronicus, where the situation to the south and east was concerned, only three small shreds of comfort remained. First, diplomatic relations had been opened with the Turks. In August 1333 he himself had crossed over to Nicomedia. His pretext had been to give encouragement to the besieged city; in fact he had attended a secret meeting with Orhan to discuss a possible treaty of peace, during which he had agreed to pay the Emir an annual tribute in return for leaving the last Byzantine possessions in Asia undisturbed. Second, all the evidence suggested that Orhan, far from being the half-crazed and fanatical barbarian of the popular imagination, was – like his father Othman before him – a reasonable and civilized man. He had made no attempt to impose Islam on the Christians whose lands he had occupied, ordered no reprisals on those who had offered him resistance. After his capture of Nicaea he had allowed all the inhabitants who wished to do so to leave the city, together with their icons and holy relics. (Remarkably few had taken advantage of the offer.) His principal objective was to build a state, as his dying father had enjoined him to do, dedicated to justice, learning and the Muslim faith but embracing people of all races and creeds. Conversion and conquest were secondary concerns; they came in their own good time – and time, he knew, was on his side.

The last circumstance from which some consolation could be drawn was a distinct strengthening of Byzantine power in the Aegean. From the moment of his accession Andronicus had begun to rebuild his navy, and within a few years Byzantine ships were once again making the Empire's presence felt among the islands. It was probably thanks to them that Chios rebelled in 1329 against the Genoese family of Zaccaria – who had ruled it for the past quarter of a century – and returned to the imperial fold. Almost equally important was the mainland city of New Phocaea[1] at the northern entrance to the bay of Smyrna (Izmir), to which the Emperor sailed from Chios at the end of the same year to accept an oath of allegiance. Unfortunately Genoa was not the only Western power involved in the eastern Mediterranean. The Knights of St John from their castle in Rhodes, the Venetians, the Lusignans of Cyprus[2] and other families like the Zaccaria – several of whom had ruled in individual islands since the Fourth Crusade – were all pursuing their own interests. One interest, however, they had in common: that of delivering the area from the depredations of the Turkish emirates along the coast.

Not surprisingly, therefore, the idea was put forward – and fervently espoused by Pope John XXII in Avignon[3] – of a great Christian League which would deal first of all with the Muslim pirates and then advance through Asia Minor to the Holy Land in a full-blown Crusade. But here was another problem: what part would Byzantium play? On this point, though Venice and the Knights – the two most enthusiastic proponents of the expedition – welcomed imperial participation, the Pope remained firm. For as long as the Empire was determined to remain schismatic, he insisted, it could on no account be a member of the League.

It was the same old story: even after the débâcle following the Council of Lyon, the Papacy was still unable to accept the fact that the schism could not be ended by a stroke of the imperial pen. Andronicus III himself would have had no insuperable objections to reunion; but he was certainly not going to repeat the mistake of his great-grandfather by attempting to impose it from above. In any case, the Pope's attitude did not really interest him. He did not believe in Crusades; his people never

1 Phocaea (now Foça) had been tragically looted by the Catalans in 1307 or 1308. They stole, *inter alia*, a piece of the Holy Cross, a shirt made by the Virgin for St John, and the latter's own manuscript of the Book of Revelation.

2 Cyprus had fallen to Richard Coeur-de-Lion on his way to the Third Crusade. He had passed it first to the Templars and then, in 1192, to the French house of Lusignan.

3 The Papacy had moved its seat to Avignon in 1307. It was to remain there for the next seventy years.

had, and history had proved them right. His own preoccupations were domestic: the defence of his capital and his Empire – objectives for which, as he knew all too well, the nations of the West would have little sympathy. For him, in any case, the Genoese were far more troublesome than the Turks; only six years after their loss of Chios, in the late autumn of 1335, they evened the score with the capture of Lesbos. Andronicus retaliated by ordering the immediate destruction of the defences of Galata, across the Horn from Constantinople. Then he and John Cantacuzenus sailed for the Aegean to negotiate a new alliance – with Umur Pasha, Emir of Aydin.

Umur, known as 'the Lion of God' and subject of one of the great epic poems of Turkish literature,[1] was a typical Ghazi, a 'Warrior for the Faith' who spent his life harassing the Christians – principally the Genoese, the Venetians and the Knights of St John – around the islands of the Aegean and even, in 1332 and 1333, as far as Euboea and the Greek mainland. He particularly disliked the Genoese and warmly welcomed the Byzantine proposals, as a result of which a combined Byzantine and Turkish fleet was to reconquer Lesbos in 1336. Later, as we shall see, he was also to contribute considerable numbers of trained fighting men for the Emperor's European campaigns. But the negotiations led to more than just an alliance: they resulted in a life-long friendship between the Emir and John Cantacuzenus. And the importance of that friendship was to prove, in the years to come, infinitely greater than either could have suspected.

The only major territorial success that Andronicus and Cantacuzenus could record – though that too was to prove sadly fleeting – was in Thessaly and Epirus. As long ago as 1318, the last representatives of the ruling dynasties of these two Greek states had died within a few months of each other: John II of Thessaly unremarkably enough, Thomas of Epirus murdered – as we have seen[2] – by his nephew Nicholas Orsini, who succeeded him both on the throne and in the bed of his widow, Andronicus III's sister Anna. After John's death Thessaly disintegrated. Most of it was torn apart by Catalans, Venetians and various local barons, all out for what they could get; only a relatively small corner, in the north-west between Trikkala and Kastoria, was peaceably governed by a certain Stephen Gabrielopulus Melissenus – who, since he

---

1 The *Destan*, written in the 1460s by the poet Enver.
2 See p. 276n.

bore the title of *sebastocrator*, had presumably been empowered by the Emperor to do so. But in 1333 he died in his turn, and this region too was faced with anarchy. The situation was saved by the Emperor himself – who was fortunately in Macedonia at the time – and the Governor of Thessalonica, Michael Monomachus. Both hurried with their armies to the threatened area, where they drove off the Despot of Epirus – John Orsini, who had murdered his brother Nicholas in 1323 – and rapidly re-established imperial rule as far south as the Catalan border.

With Thessaly back within the Empire, it was clearly only a matter of time before Epirus followed. The family of Orsini had never been generally accepted as legitimate rulers; and the consequent internal struggles, combined with incessant attacks from outside, had brought the once-prosperous despotate to the point of collapse. The already powerful pro-Byzantine party in Arta numbered among its leaders the Despot's wife Anna;[1] and in 1335, encouraged by recent events in Thessaly, she poisoned her husband – it was the third murder of an Orsini by an Orsini in seventeen years – and herself assumed the regency on behalf of her seven-year-old son Nicephorus. Two years later, when the Emperor returned to the region to put down an Albanian revolt, Anna sent a deputation to him at Berat proposing an arrangement whereby she and Nicephorus would continue to reign in Epirus in return for recognizing him as their suzerain; but Andronicus would have none of it. Epirus had now been an independent Despotate for over 130 years; henceforth, he insisted, it must be administered by an imperial Governor, responsible directly to himself. Then and there he appointed to the new post one of his closest friends and companions-in-arms, the *protostrator* Theodore Synadenus, who had been one of the leaders of the *coup* against his grandfather nine years before. Anna, her son and her two little daughters were given a property in Thessalonica, there to live out their lives in comfortable exile.

As so often in Byzantine history, however, things did not go altogether according to plan. Suddenly young Nicephorus disappeared – and was found to have been abducted by certain members of the Epirot nobility, almost certainly with the collusion of those Western powers who had an interest in the continuation of the independent Despotate. Carried off to Italy, he was finally delivered to the court of Catharine of Valois,

---

1 She was herself a Greek, the daughter of another Andronicus Palaeologus – not the Emperor but one of the Byzantine commanders in the area.

Princess of Taranto and titular Latin Empress of Constantinople.[1] There he remained until the autumn of 1338, when Catharine accompanied him to her house in Achaia – of which her husband Philip was also ruler – and, using him as a figurehead, settled down to promote an anti-Byzantine rising in Epirus. It was not long before she succeeded. In Arta, the Governor Theodore Synadenus was arrested and imprisoned; and early in 1339 young Nicephorus himself returned in state to Epirus, where he was installed in the coastal stronghold of Thomocastrum.

But the revolt was short-lived. Outside Arta, Ioannina and one or two other towns it failed to spark. The Emperor himself was back in 1340, as usual with John Cantacuzenus at his side; Arta was successfully besieged; and well before the end of the year a general amnesty had been announced and Synadenus restored to liberty. The Grand Domestic then rode off to Thomocastrum where, despite the presence of the Angevin fleet off the coast, Nicephorus was easily persuaded to abandon his claims and return to Thessalonica. There, in a somewhat vague gesture of compensation, he was granted the title of *panhypersebastos* and promised the hand of Cantacuzenus's daughter Maria in marriage. For a boy not quite thirteen, it had been an eventful year.

In the early spring of 1341, while still at Thessalonica, the Emperor celebrated the wedding of his cousin Irene to John Cantacuzenus's eldest son Matthew, thus binding the two families still more closely together. Soon afterwards he and his Grand Domestic returned together to Constantinople – into the thick of a new crisis. This time, however, it was a crisis of a very different kind: a crisis that could have arisen only in Byzantium. It concerned a small group of Orthodox hermits, mostly on Mount Athos, known as the hesychasts.

Hesychasm – the Greek word means 'holy silence' – was nothing new. From the earliest days of Christianity, the Orthodox Church had maintained a strong tradition of mystical asceticism whose adherents had spent their lives in silent and solitary meditation. Then, in the 1330s, a monk named Gregory of Sinai had wandered through the eastern Mediterranean spreading the word that by following certain physical techniques it was possible to obtain a vision of the divine, uncreated Light that had surrounded Jesus Christ at his Transfiguration on Mt Tabor. Gregory's

---

1 Catharine, it will be remembered, was the daughter of Charles of Valois by his wife Catharine of Courtenay, granddaughter of the Emperor Baldwin; her husband, Philip of Taranto, was the son of Charles II of Anjou. See p. 273.

teachings had found particular favour on the Holy Mountain, which quickly became the centre of the hesychast movement. Unfortunately, however, they also aroused the age-old Byzantine passion for religious disputation; particularly since the recommended techniques – which included the lowering of the chin to the chest, the fixing of the eyes on the navel, the regulation of breathing and the unceasing repetition of the Jesus Prayer[1] – were all too obviously open to criticism and even to ridicule.

The spearhead of the opposition to the hesychasts was an Orthodox monk from Calabria by the name of Barlaam. His remarkable learning and erudition had soon caught the attention of John Cantacuzenus, who had found him a teaching post at the University of Constantinople; and in 1339 he had even been sent on a secret embassy to the Pope at Avignon to explain the Byzantine position on Church union. On his return, however, he had been rash enough to enter into a public debate with Nicephorus Gregoras, the greatest scholar of his day, by whom he had been thoroughly trounced; and it may partly have been in an effort to cover his shame that he now launched a violent campaign against practices which he considered to be nothing more than superstition, and heretical superstition at that. But the hesychasts too had their champion – one of their own number, the theologian Gregory Paıamas, who produced a vast manifesto, *Triads in Defence of the Holy Hesychasts*. This document, subsequently endorsed by all Gregory's colleagues on the Mountain, constituted a formidable piece of evidence and was largely responsible – with Cantacuzenus himself, whose own sympathies were strongly pro-hesychast – for persuading the Emperor to call a council of the Church and so to settle the matter.

That council was held in St Sophia on 10 June 1341, under the presidency of the Emperor himself. It was over in a single day, and resulted in an overwhelming victory for the hesychasts. Barlaam and all his works were condemned. Gregory Palamas and his friends behaved with commendable generosity, embracing him and complimenting him on the presentation of his case. He himself however, having first admitted his errors, then took the decision in extremely bad part, loudly complaining that the inquiry had been rigged against him before returning, chastened and discredited, to Calabria. There, according to Cantacuzenus, in his deep disillusionment he renounced Orthodoxy altogether and adopted the Church of Rome, ending a somewhat chequered career as Bishop of Gerace.

---

1 'Lord Jesus Christ, Son of God, have mercy on me.'

After the members of the council had returned to their homes, the Emperor complained of exhaustion and retired to rest at the monastery of the Hodegon[1] – where, on the following day, he was stricken with a violent fever. For the next four days it grew steadily worse, and on 15 June 1341 he died. He had ruled wisely and well – better far than the grandfather who had done his utmost to keep him from the throne. For all the waywardness of his early youth, he had matured into an energetic, hardworking and – except when the pleasures of the chase got the better of him – conscientious Emperor. His legal reforms and the measures he took against corruption earned him the gratitude of his subjects, not only for introducing them in the first place but for the determination with which he carried them out. Always more of a soldier and man of action than a diplomat or statesman, he was fortunate enough to have John Cantacuzenus at his right hand throughout his reign, and intelligent enough to take his advice.

His tragedy, and that of his successors, was to have come to the throne at a time when his Empire was already doomed: his gains in the Balkans – which were due not so much to Byzantine military prowess as to the internal disintegration of the states concerned – were to prove transitory, and were in any case insignificant compared with the effective loss of Anatolia, which had brought the Ottoman Turks to within sight of Constantinople. This decline was no fault of his, and he had been powerless to prevent it. None the less, he had achieved more than most people would have thought possible; and the partnership (for such it was) of himself and his Grand Domestic did much to raise the spirits of a sad and demoralized people – and to prepare them for the still greater tribulations that lay ahead.

1 The monastery stood just to the east of St Sophia, down by the sea walls.

18
Civil War

[1341–7]

There is nothing more conducive to the destruction of a nation, whether it be republic or monarchy, than the lack of men of wisdom or intellect. When a republic has many citizens, or a monarchy many ministers, of high quality it quickly recovers from those losses that are brought about by misfortune. When such men are lacking, it falls into the very depths of disgrace. That is why I deplore the present state of the Empire which, having produced so many excellent men in the past, has now been reduced to such a level of sterility that today's governors possess nothing to elevate them above those whom they govern.

John Cantacuzenus,
to ambassadors from the Empress Anne

Even before the body of Andronicus III Palaeologus had been laid in its grave, it was plain that he had made one disastrous mistake: he had given no clear instructions regarding his successor. There could be no doubt that John, the elder of his two sons, who had celebrated his ninth birthday three days after his father's death, was the heir-presumptive; but the Byzantine monarchy was not in theory hereditary – even though it usually proved to be so in practice – and his father had, surprisingly enough, taken no steps to proclaim or crown him co-Emperor. The Grand Domestic John Cantacuzenus cherished no imperial ambitions; he had been invited more than once by Andronicus to share the throne, but had always refused. His loyalty to the little prince and to his mother, the Empress Anne of Savoy, was unquestioned. On the other hand he had effectively directed the affairs of the Empire for thirteen years, and in the circumstances it never struck him that he would not continue to do so. Almost without thinking he moved into the imperial palace, devoting his energies to the maintenance of law and order and the ensuring of a smooth transfer of power.

The task, however, proved harder than he had expected. His closeness

293

to the late Emperor had aroused bitter jealousies. During Andronicus's life these had remained largely hidden; now they emerged for the world to see. Perhaps the most resentful of all was the Empress Anne herself, conscious as she was that her husband had always preferred the company of his Grand Domestic to her own. Then there was the Patriarch, John Calecas. Having begun his career most unpromisingly as a married priest,[1] he owed his promotion entirely to Cantacuzenus who, having first arranged his pro forma election as Metropolitan of Thessalonica, had then prepared his way to the Patriarchal throne. But in John Calecas ambition outweighed gratitude. Had not Andronicus, he demanded, twice already appointed him Regent, before leaving Constantinople on campaign? And did not this clearly indicate that he should be Regent on this occasion also?

The Grand Domestic could easily have pointed out that since he had himself always accompanied the Emperor on his campaigns he would not in the past have been eligible for the regency, and that the present situation was thus in no sense a parallel; he was far more concerned, however, by the behaviour of another of his former protégés, Alexius Apocaucus. An upstart adventurer of obscure origin, making no pretence to noble birth or gentle breeding, Apocaucus had been – with Cantacuzenus himself, Theodore Synadenus and Syrgiannes Palaeologus – one of the leading supporters of Andronicus III in his struggle with his grandfather. Since then he had attached himself to the Grand Domestic, who had helped and befriended him and thanks to whom he had acquired considerable power and immense wealth. Indeed it was Cantacuzenus who, only a short while before, had obtained for him his present position – the equivalent to High Admiral – which carried with it the command of a newly-built fleet guarding the Hellespont against Turkish marauders. On the death of Andronicus his first thought had been to profit by this association, and he had persistently urged his patron to accept the crown – which, as he rightly pointed out, was his for the asking. He, Apocaucus, might then have enjoyed the same position in relation to the new Emperor as the latter had to the old.

John Cantacuzenus, however, was adamant. His duty was to the reigning house of Palaeologus which, after eighty years and three Emperors – four if the unfortunate Michael IX is included – he believed to have established its legitimacy. In his eyes, to accept the throne would

---

[1] In the Orthodox Church married priests are normally ineligible for promotion, candidates for bishoprics and all other high offices being chosen from among celibate monks.

be nothing less than an act of usurpation, and he refused to consider it. And so Apocaucus turned against his old friend and began working for his downfall, while Empress, Patriarch and Grand Domestic together evolved a somewhat uneasy *modus vivendi* for the conduct of state affairs.

How long this would have lasted is open to question; after only a month, however, the third member of the triumvirate was called once again to the defence of the Empire. The death of a *basileus* was nearly always seen by neighbouring states as an invitation to make trouble, while an interregnum was more promising still; and before long Byzantium's three main enemies were all back on the offensive – the Serbs advancing on Thessalonica, the Bulgars massing on the northern frontier and the Turks plundering the coast of Thrace. To meet this triple threat John Cantacuzenus was obliged to recruit troops at his own expense, and in mid-July he left Constantinople. He met with quite astonishing success: by the time he returned to the capital in September, order had been restored and treaties signed with Stephen Dushan, John Alexander and the Emir Orhan. As bonus, a delegation had arrived from the Morea offering the surrender to the Empire of the Principality of Achaia, where the local barons had been deeply incensed by the decision of Catharine of Valois to turn over the government to the Florentine banking house of Acciajuoli.

To John Cantacuzenus, this last development was the most welcome of all. With Achaia back in imperial hands, the Catalans in southern Greece would almost certainly be obliged to come to terms and the Empire's position in the Balkan peninsula would be immeasurably strengthened. And yet, as things turned out, it would have been better for him had the offer never been made; for the ensuing negotiations obliged him on 23 September to return with his army to Thrace, and during this second enforced absence from the capital his enemies struck. Led by Alexius Apocaucus, a group of the highest personages in the Empire – they included the Empress Anne (who had by now been persuaded that John had been plotting against her and her son), the Patriarch, and even Cantacuzenus's own father-in-law, the Bulgar Andronicus Asen – declared the Grand Domestic to be a public enemy. A mob was quickly collected – never a serious difficulty in Constantinople – which marched on his palace, pillaged it and burnt it to the ground. His country estates were destroyed or confiscated. The Patriarch was at last able to proclaim himself Regent, while Apocaucus, promoted to the rank of *megas dux*, was appointed Prefect of the City. Meanwhile John's mother and other members of his family were placed under house arrest; all those of his known associates who had not already escaped were hunted down; and an order, signed personally by the Empress, was sent to him at his camp at Didymotichum, some twenty-five miles to the south of Adrianople, relieving him of his command and disbanding the army.

But the conspirators had gone too far. What they had perpetrated was an outrage – and a cowardly one at that, taking advantage as they had of their victim's absence on the Empire's behalf, for what were quite obviously their own selfish ends; and when the imperial messengers reached Didymotichum the army supported John Cantacuzenus to a man. Then and there, on 26 October 1341, they proclaimed him *basileus*. He himself maintained his old reluctance, insisting that the young John V – though still uncrowned – remained the rightful Emperor; and there is no reason to to doubt his sincerity. After all, had he had any desire for the throne, he could easily have assumed it on the death of Andronicus; and among the several pages of his chronicle intended – needlessly – to justify his acceptance of it there is a curious and disarming passage in which, describing the ceremony of his investiture (when he ordered the names of the Empress Anne and John V to be proclaimed before those of himself and his wife Irene) he tells of how the hastily-prepared ceremonial robes failed to fit him, the inner one being impossibly tight, the outer several sizes too big.

But whatever his feelings in the matter, John Cantacuzenus was now Emperor, acclaimed in the traditional manner – though for the first time in centuries – by the army; and since there could clearly be no question of his recognition by the present regime in Constantinople, that could mean one thing only: the resumption of civil war. Within days of his investiture came news of his excommunication by the Patriarch; and on 19 November, John V was duly crowned in St Sophia. The lines of battle were drawn.

Not, however, in favour of John Cantacuzenus. For years, both in Constantinople and in the provinces, the rift had been widening between proletariat and aristocracy. As the enemies of Byzantium had continued their remorseless advance and increasing numbers of refugees from the conquered lands had come flooding into the capital, so the condition of the poor had become more and more desperate; the rich landowners on the other hand, who seldom paid their taxes and were in a position to take full advantage of the corruption which – at least till very recently – had been endemic, had remained relatively untouched.

Such wealth as existed in the impoverished Empire had thus become concentrated in the hands of the aristocratic few, while the majority of the population could feel only indignation and resentment. In most Western societies, the cities and towns had gradually produced a flourishing bourgeoisie of merchants and craftsmen, who provided a useful cushion between the wealthy and the proletariat; in the Byzantine Empire this had never occurred, and there was nothing to prevent the economic polarization which now became evident in all its ugliness. Alexius Apocaucus, in directing the mob against the property of the Grand Domestic, had unleashed dangerous forces indeed. The sack of John's palace had doubtless revealed riches such as the poor had never seen; his mother's, and those of his fellow-noblemen which had received similar treatment, had disgorged – by his own admission – prodigious quantities of food of all kinds, to say nothing of gold, silver and jewels. All this Apocaucus – who must for the first time have been grateful for his own humble origins – was able to turn to his own good use, setting himself up as the champion of the down-trodden and dispossessed against the forces of wealth and privilege personified by John Cantacuzenus.

The contagion spread with alarming rapidity. When, on the day following John's investiture, the news was announced in Adrianople, it provided a spark sufficient to ignite a revolt similar to that which had occurred in the capital. The local aristocracy, as might have been expected, sided with Cantacuzenus; but the populace immediately rose up against them, surging through the streets in an orgy of pillage and destruction. Those nobles who were not immediately seized fled for their lives; meanwhile a people's commune took over the city in the name of the regency and was duly recognized by Apocaucus, who sent his own son Manuel to Adrianople as his official representative. Within a few weeks all Thrace was up in arms, the landowning classes either hiding or in headlong flight. Events in Thessalonica were still more dramatic. The Governor, John's old friend Theodore Synadenus, at one moment secretly offered to open the gates; but he was driven out before he could do so. A political party known as the Zealots seized control in his place, setting up their own government and instituting a reign of terror against all who opposed them. Once again Apocaucus tried to impose his authority, sending his other son John as titular Governor; but the Zealots largely ignored him, and for the next seven years ran Thessalonica as a virtually independent republic.

By now John Cantacuzenus must have been close to despair. Little more than a month before, he had still enjoyed a unique position in

Constantinople, where he had exercised almost limitless power and was – a few political enemies apart – universally respected. He had a series of remarkable military and diplomatic victories behind him and was looking forward to the early surrender of the Morea – a development that might have brought Greece back into the Imperial fold and have proved a turning-point in the fortunes of Byzantium. Now he was outlawed, excommunicated and condemned as a public enemy of the Empire, to the service of which he had devoted his life. His house had been destroyed, his property looted, his estates confiscated. His mother had been driven from her home, dispossessed, and so ill-treated that she was to die a few weeks later. His closest friends had deserted him – including, as he now heard, Theodore Synadenus himself – aware that all those suspected of association with him risked the confiscation of their property and, very probably, imprisonment and death. His very name was being used as a symbol of the exploitation of the poor by the rich – an abuse against which he had struggled throughout his adult life. True, he was now an Emperor, by investiture if not by formal coronation; but he had never sought the imperial throne, and his enforced acceptance of it had served only to blacken him still further in the eyes of the legitimate Emperor, to whom his loyalty had even then never wavered.

More than anything, he needed allies. He sent an urgent message to his old friend Umur, Emir of Aydin; but Umur was far away, and for John Cantacuzenus time was now running dangerously short. And so he turned, after long hesitation, to Stephen Dushan. Knowing that Stephen had always been an enemy of the Empire and that such a step might consequently prove unpopular, before leaving for Serbia John gave his men the option of following him or not: he was not altogether surprised when only about two thousand agreed to do so. In his present position, on the other hand, he could not afford to be particular; he remembered also that, when he had briefly met the Serbian King on the frontier eight years before, the two had got on together remarkably well. On their second meeting in July 1342, at Prishtina near Skoplje, they fared even better. Stephen was only too ready to take advantage of the Empire's troubles. Had John Cantacuzenus been prepared to grant his request for the greater part of Byzantine Macedonia, he might have been yet more forthcoming; but he willingly agreed to give his new friend his protection and support, and as an earnest of his good intentions provided him with a detachment of mercenaries to assist him on his way back to Didymotichum. It was as well that he did: for John Cantacuzenus had advanced no further than Serres when he found the road blocked against him. He was obliged to lay siege to the city itself, and while he was doing so his army fell victim to a hideous epidemic. Some fifteen hundred of his best men perished in a matter of weeks, and only with the greatest difficulty did he succeed in fighting his way back to the Serbian frontier. Now, in addition to his other anxieties, he found himself cut off from Didymotichum, his wife and his family.

Thanks to Stephen Dushan, Cantacuzenus was able to survive through the remainder of 1342. Then, shortly before Christmas, there came the news for which he had been hoping. Umur was on his way. The moment the Emir had received John's appeal he had begun to prepare his fleet. As soon as it was ready, he sailed northward up the Aegean to the mouth of the Maritsa river; thence he led his men to Didymotichum – which, despite its position, had remained loyal to Cantacuzenus – reinforced its defences and left a garrison. Owing to the appalling winter weather he was obliged to give up his plans to march across Thrace to join his old friend; but the help that he had afforded was invaluable, while the generosity, willingness and speed of his response gave John all the moral encouragement of which he was in such desperate need.

The tide was beginning to turn. In that same winter of 1342–3 the province of Thessaly declared in John's favour, and the coming of spring saw a similar voluntary submission on the part of several important towns of Macedonia. Apocaucus, seriously alarmed, arrived in Thessalonica with a naval squadron, but left quickly enough a week or two later when Umur's flagship appeared on the horizon, followed by a fleet of some two hundred ships. This time the two friends were able to make contact, and together they laid siege to Thessalonica. The city proved too strong for them, but with the help of the Emir's six thousand men Cantacuzenus was able to break through to Didymotichum, there to embrace his wife again after almost a year's separation.

In Constantinople – where food was now shorter than ever – morale was sinking fast. John Cantacuzenus's recent successes were bad enough; almost more terrible, however, to the Empress Anne and her entourage was the thought that the Turks were now on the loose in her European provinces. Umur's troops had wrought havoc wherever they had passed; the luckless populations of Thrace and Macedonia had had all too much experience of invading armies in the past, but even they had seldom suffered such brutality as this. It was by no means the first time that Turkish soldiers had been brought to these regions: the

Catalans had introduced them thirty-five years before, as had Anne's own husband Andronicus during his long struggle with his grandfather. More recently still, the Empress herself had been in contact with the Emir Orhan, who had rejected her approaches only because he expected better things from her rival. Nevertheless she was terrified by the idea of these pagan barbarians, no longer confined to Asia but now, it seemed, at the very gates of the capital; and in the summer of 1343 she sent one of her Savoyard knights to Avignon with a despairing appeal to Pope Clement VI, announcing not only her own submission – she had after all been brought up in the Latin faith – but that of her son John, of Alexius Apocaucus and, most surprising by far, of the Patriarch of Constantinople, John Calecas himself.

At least where the last two were concerned, Anne was certainly lying; and fearing perhaps that the Pope would suspect as much, she shortly afterwards dispatched two more appeals, to Venice and Genoa respectively. She was well aware, however, that neither of these republics would ever give anything for nothing; and she knew also that her imperial treasury, drained by two civil wars in swift succession, had no funds to pay the subsidies that they would unquestionably demand. And so she took the dreadful step for which she is remembered more than for anything else: in August 1343, for the sum of 30,000 Venetian ducats, she pawned the Byzantine crown jewels to the Most Serene Republic. They were never to be redeemed; and the Empress's action somehow symbolizes, more dramatically than any other could possibly have done, the depths to which the once-great Empire of the Romans had sunk.

It did her no good. No help came – from Avignon, Genoa or Venice. Now too, as her enemy steadily consolidated his position, several of her most trusted adherents began to desert her. In 1344 John Vatatzes, one of the leading generals in Thrace, went over to Cantacuzenus; so, a month or two afterwards, did the Governor of Adrianople, Alexius's son Manuel Apocaucus, while Adrianople itself surrendered early the following year. As for Alexius himself, his own behaviour gave proof of his growing desperation. He never left his house without a numerous bodyguard; and he kept a ship, fully manned and provisioned, in the Golden Horn in case he needed to make a quick escape. All those Byzantines of whose loyalties he cherished the slightest suspicion – and they included virtually all the rich – were arrested. Part of the Great Palace of Constantine – long abandoned and in ruins – was converted into a prison in order to accommodate them.

It was here that Apocaucus met his death. On 11 June 1345, during one of his regular tours of inspection of the building work, a number of prisoners taking their exercise in the main courtyard suddenly noticed that, wishing apparently to have a short private conversation with one of his aides, he had separated a little from his bodyguard. Immediately they saw their opportunity. A small group of them – including, we are told, his own nephew – fell upon him. At first their only weapons were stones; then they found a heavy wooden club; finally they seized an axe from one of the workmen and struck off their victim's head, which they proudly exhibited, impaled on a spike, above the prison walls. Meanwhile the bodyguard, seeing what had happened, panicked and fled. The prisoners who had done the deed remained in the building, which they knew they could stoutly defend against any punitive expedition; but they did not actually expect anything of the kind. Had they not after all performed a public service, in ridding the Empire of a universally hated tyrant? Were they not likelier to be acclaimed as saviours, loaded with congratulations and rewards?

The course of action favoured by the Empress when she heard the news fell somewhere between the two. Her instructions to the *panhyperse-bastos* Isaac Asen were to order all the prisoners to return to their homes, with a guarantee that no measures would then be taken against them. Unfortunately, however, Asen – crushed, as John Cantacuzenus charita-bly explains, by the weight of his workload – failed to carry out the order; and the next morning a former member of Apocaucus's staff persuaded a party of sailors to avenge their master's death. The sailors were armed; the prisoners were not. Though some – including the murderers themselves – managed to take refuge in the neighbouring church of the Nea[1] and subsequently escaped, about two hundred were massacred, many of them on the church's very threshold.

The death of Alexius Apocaucus was, for all his faults, a serious blow to the regency; but it was by no means the end. For John Cantacuzenus there was still plenty of work to be done before he could enter Constantinople in triumph. Besides, he had a new problem on his hands: Stephen Dushan had turned against him. Determined to conquer all Macedonia, the Serbian ruler was even now laying siege to Serres; John was thus being forced to fight two enemies on two fronts simultane-ously. There had also been a major disappointment at Thessalonica where the titular Governor John Apocaucus, determined to assert his

1 See *Byzantium: The Apogee*, pp. 96–7.

authority, had had the leader of the Zealots murdered, taken control of the government and, on hearing of his father's death, had publicly announced his support for Cantacuzenus, to whom he had offered to surrender the city. Unfortunately his enemies had moved too fast: long before John or his son Manuel – who was commanding in Berrhoea (now Verria) – could reach the city, Apocaucus and a hundred or more of his followers had been seized. One after another they were thrown from the walls of the citadel and hacked to pieces by the mob below, who then went rampaging through the streets, beating to death every noble they could find. Soon the Zealots were as firmly in control of Thessalonica as ever they had been.

Once again, John was in desperate need of an ally. Stephen Dushan had betrayed him; the Emir Umur, whose loyalty remained unshaken, had suffered a serious disaster in 1344 when the Pope's long-delayed League had finally sailed against him, captured his harbour at Smyrna and destroyed his fleet. Somehow, the following year, he had managed a brief campaign in Thrace on behalf of his old friend; but his support could no longer be what it had been in the past. His neighbour the Emir of Saruchan, now settled in Lydia, was admittedly well-disposed; he had provided troops before and would probably do so again. But John Cantacuzenus, if he were to fight his way back to the capital, needed help on a larger scale than this; and in the first weeks of 1345 he made contact with Orhan himself.

Although from the political and religious point of view John deplored the Turks as much as did the rest of his countrymen, on the personal level he had always got on with them remarkably well. We have it on his own authority that he had studied Turkish; and the results, however halting, would certainly have given them pleasure – particularly as few noble Greeks of the period would have condescended even to try. With Orhan he quickly established a friendship as close as that he had enjoyed with Umur – even closer perhaps, since the Emir soon fell besottedly in love with Theodora, the second of John's three daughters. All three, Enver records, were lovely as houris; while Gregoras claims that in return for Theodora's hand Orhan promised to serve her father faithfully as a vassal, with his entire army. He and Theodora were married in 1346 at Selymbria. The bride was permitted to keep her Christian faith, and was later to work indefatigably on behalf of the Christian residents, both free and enslaved, of her husband's emirate.

But that same year was marked by other, more sinister, developments. On Easter Sunday, in the Cathedral of Skoplje, Stephen Dushan was crowned by the Serbian Archbishop – whom he had recently raised to the rank of Patriarch – with the title of Emperor of the Serbs and Greeks. He could hardly have made his ambitions clearer; and it was almost certainly as a deliberate response to this act of bravado that, at Adrianople only five weeks later on 21 May, the Feast of SS. Constantine and Helena, John had imperial crowns – hastily manufactured by a local goldsmith – laid on his own head and that of his wife by the Patriarch Lazarus of Jerusalem. His investiture and proclamation of five years before were now confirmed. He refused, however, all suggestions that his eldest son Matthew should be crowned co-Emperor; that position was reserved for John Palaeologus, now fourteen years old and still, so far as he was concerned, the senior legitimate monarch.

Just two days before Cantacuzenus's coronation, on 19 May, a tragedy had occurred in Constantinople: part of the east end of St Sophia, having stood for a little over eight hundred years, had suddenly collapsed into a pile of rubble. To the Byzantines, superstitious as always, it was the most dreadful of omens; God Himself was now forsaking them. The popularity of the Patriarch – which had never been high – sank lower than ever, and by the end of the year it would have been hard to find anybody in Constantinople, the Empress alone excepted, who was not praying for the return of John Cantacuzenus.

At last John was ready, and his accomplices within the city had their plans prepared. The date chosen for his arrival was 1 February 1347; even now, however, the operation almost ended in failure. For his march on the capital – he was coming from Selymbria with a thousand picked men – he had deliberately selected a devious and obscure route in order not to attract attention; the journey consequently took longer than he had expected, with the result that he eventually arrived outside the walls twenty-four hours later than had been arranged. In his *History*, he himself confesses to appalling anxiety that his friends might not be there; by a singular stroke of luck, however, they too had been prevented from reaching the gate on the previous evening and had consequently suffered a similar delay. And so it was that, late at night on 2 February, the Emperor John Cantacuzenus slipped through a narrow gap in the bricked-up Golden Gate and entered Constantinople for the first time in five and a half years, his thousand men behind him.

Early the following morning he drew up his troops before the Palace of Blachernae and, with the courtesy that he had never failed to show her, requested an audience with the Empress. The request was refused.

*

Anne of Savoy knew that she was beaten and had hastily done all she could to ingratiate herself with her conqueror; on the previous day she had even succeeded, with the help of a synod of bishops, in deposing the Patriarch. But five years of daily brainwashing by Apocaucus had convinced her that Cantacuzenus was determined to kill her and her four children, and she obstinately refused to allow him admission to the palace. Only after certain of his followers, many of whom had suffered imprisonment and torture under the regency, finally lost patience and laid storm to the building did the guard – who, whatever fate might befall their Empress, had no wish to share it – dare to disobey her orders and open the gates.

Five days later, on 8 February, agreement was reached between the parties. For the next ten years the two Emperors would reign jointly, with John Cantacuzenus occupying the senior position. After that time they would enjoy equal status. All political prisoners were to be released. There were to be no reprisals on either side, and the possessions of each were to be as they had been before the civil war. The whole compact, in short, was eminently reasonable – so reasonable that one wonders why it could not have been agreed half a dozen years before.

There was only one exception to the general amnesty. The ex-Patriarch John Calecas, the senior Emperor's bitterest surviving enemy, who had excommunicated him in 1341, continued to reject all his attempts at reconciliation. It was not only that he had been Regent for John Palaeologus, and thus titular head of the defeated regime; his pride had been further wounded by his deposition on the eve of John Cantacuzenus's return. This was, however, no fault of the latter; nor had the reasons for it been entirely, or perhaps even primarily, political. Rather were they the direct result of the Patriarch's continued opposition to the monk Gregory Palamas, and the disputed doctrine of hesychasm.

For, despite the council in St Sophia, the argument still raged. Almost as soon as Barlaam had disappeared from the scene in 1341, a new figure had entered the lists: the monk Gregory Acindynus, who was deeply versed in Western scholasticism and now replaced the discredited Calabrian as the chief scourge of the hesychasts. So eloquent was he, and so persuasive, that within two months of the first council in 1341 it had been found necessary to hold a second – again presided over by John Cantacuzenus – which had reached the same conclusion as its predecessor, vindicating Palamas for the second time while Acindynus was condemned once more. This second council had however been held in August, at precisely the time when the Patriarch was intriguing for the regency; and he had firmly refused to uphold the findings of a council chaired by his arch-rival. Instead he had made common cause with Acindynus and others, and had had little difficulty in bringing the Empress herself over to his side.

From this moment onwards, the twists and turns of the hesychast controversy provide a typically Byzantine counterpoint to those of the civil war. Because John Cantacuzenus favours the hesychasts, John Calecas opposes them; because Gregory Palamas supports Cantacuzenus as Regent, Gregory Acindynus champions the Patriarch. While the regency in Constantinople is still relatively secure, the hesychasts are under constant attack; in 1343 Palamas is arrested and imprisoned, in 1344 he is excommunicated. Then, when the victory of Cantacuzenus begins to seem imminent, the religious pendulum also swings: Palamas is released, the Patriarch becomes a liability and is deposed. Such an analysis is inevitably over-simplified: Nicephorus Gregoras for example, though politically a Cantacuzenist, was violently – even fanatically – opposed to hesychasm, and there were doubtless many pro-hesychasts among those whose political loyalties rested exclusively with the Palae-ologi. Yet the general lines of the dispute remain clear enough, providing the perfect illustration of the manner in which, in Byzantine history, political and religious issues never run parallel but are always inextricably entangled.

It was of course this very tendency that had enabled the Patriarch to manipulate the hesychast issue for his own political ends. With his own downfall and the arrival of John Cantacuzenus, however, he could do so no longer, and so the end of his story can be quickly told. A synod, at which Cantacuzenus and the Empress jointly presided towards the end of February – and which Calecas predictably refused to attend – con-firmed his deposition *in absentia* and upheld the orthodoxy of Gregory Palamas. As for Acindynus, he was obliged to flee from Constantinople and died shortly afterwards in exile. The new Patriarch Isidore Boucharis, who had himself been a hesychast monk, appointed his old friend Palamas Archbishop of Thessalonica (though the city was still in the hands of the Zealots), formally lifted the sentence of excommunica-tion on John Cantacuzenus and finally – on 21 May 1347, precisely a year after his first coronation at Adrianople – officiated at his second coronation in the church of the Virgin at Blachernae. A week later the Princess Helena, the youngest of John's beautiful daughters, was married in the same church to his co-Emperor, the fifteen-year-old John V.[1]

Coronations and marriages should be joyful occasions; about these two ceremonies, however, there was more than a touch of sadness. By tradition they should have been held at St Sophia; but, after its collapse in the previous year, the Great Church was no longer usable. They should also have made use of the Byzantine crown jewels; but these, thanks to the Dowager Empress, were now in pawn. Those present noted to their sorrow that the replacements were made of glass, while at the banquets that followed the wine was served in pewter vessels and the food from plates of cheap earthenware. All the gold and silver that had so dazzled the eyes of visitors in former times was gone – sold to finance a civil war that need never have occurred.

[1] There has in the past been some confusion over the numeration, but it is nowadays customary to describe John Palaeologus and John Cantacuzenus as John V and VI respectively. While John VI remained the senior Emperor, he always insisted that John V, as a Palaeologus, should take precedence over him.

19

The Reluctant Emperor

[1347–54]

For we are fallen into so lamentable a weakness, that far from being able to impose the yoke on others, we are hard put to avoid it ourselves ... Let us therefore earn once again the esteem of our friends, and the fear of our enemies. If on the other hand we fall through despair into a contemptible idleness, we shall soon be reduced to servitude. There is no middle way. Either we save the Empire, by keeping our ancient virtues; or we lose it, and live under the domination of our conquerors. Take, therefore, a noble resolution, and act in the interests of your glory, your security, your liberty and your lives.

John Cantacuzenus,
appealing to his subjects for funds, 1347

'If,' wrote Nicephorus Gregoras, 'John Cantacuzenus had not lapsed into the heresy of Palamas, he would have been one of the greatest of Byzantine Emperors.' Nicephorus may have been wrong about the heresy; none the less, one can see what he means. John VI was a man of integrity, courage, high intelligence and a rare degree of political vision. Had he firmly asserted his claim to the throne on the death of Andronicus III in 1341, he might well have checked the Empire's decline and even put it back on the road to prosperity; but six years later too much damage had been done for any real recovery to be possible. It was John's misfortune to inherit a divided and bankrupt Empire, deeply demoralized and under attack from every side; and when at last he found himself in undisputed possession of the supreme power, although he had thought long and hard about the Empire's political and economic collapse and was fully aware of the steps necessary to launch its recovery, he seems to have lacked that last ounce of steel necessary to impose his will.

He had other misfortunes too, and one of them was to be a contemporary of Stephen Dushan, the self-styled Emperor of the Serbs and the Greeks. It was Stephen who had been the real beneficiary of the civil war, brilliantly playing one side against the other and taking every advantage of the weakness of the regency and the Cantacuzenists alike. After his capture of Serres in September 1345 he was master of virtually all Macedonia except Thessalonica itself; only a month later we find him describing himself – in a document addressed to the Doge of Venice – as *fere totius imperii romani dominus*, 'Lord of almost the whole Roman Empire'; and, as this title implies, he had no intention of stopping at Macedonia. In the years that followed he was also to conquer Albania and Epirus, Acarnania and Aetolia, and finally Thessaly – all of them at the cost of only a few short sieges and without fighting a single major battle. By the time of his death in 1355 his Empire extended from the Adriatic to the Aegean and from the Danube to the Gulf of Corinth, a territory many times larger than that which now remained to Byzantium.

By then, too, he was almost a Greek himself. His people had long since cast off their barbarian image. Andronicus II's Logothete Theodore Metochites, visiting the Serbian capital on diplomatic business as early as 1298, had been deeply impressed not only by the luxury of the court but by its strong Byzantine flavour; and during the intervening half-century the hellenizing process had continued apace. Dushan ruled the southern part of his Empire from Greece, leaving his son – the later Stephen Urosh V, but still only a child – in nominal charge of the Serbian lands in the north; he himself spoke fluent Greek, integrated Greek officials into his administration and gave them Greek titles. Nor, when necessary, did he hesitate to adopt Greek institutions: the *Syntagma*, or manual of law, by the Byzantine canonist Matthew Blastares formed the basis for a considerable part of the new legislative code which he first promulgated in 1349 to put his new Empire on a sound legal footing.

There can be no question but that the ambitions of Stephen Dushan were fixed on the throne of Constantinople, and little doubt that he would have achieved them but for a single weakness: Serbia had always been a land-locked Kingdom, and even after his maritime conquests he had no effective navy. The more parlous the situation of the Empire, the more essential was the maintenance of the Land Walls of the capital; and despite the ravages of the civil war this tremendous bastion was still as impregnable as ever it had been. It followed that Constantinople could be successfully attacked only from the seaward side; and without a fleet Dushan was as powerless to conquer the city as his great predecessor Symeon had been more than four centuries before. Again and again he tried to ally himself with Venice for the final onslaught, but the Venetians always rejected his advances; they had no wish to replace the weak Byzantine Empire with a powerful Serbian one.

Yet Stephen Dushan represented neither the beginning nor the end of the misfortunes of John VI – who, in the very first year of his reign, was called upon to face an enemy more implacable by far than any number of Balkan rivals. In the spring of 1347 Constantinople was stricken by the Black Death, brought almost certainly by ships escaping from the already plague-ridden Genoese colony of Caffa in the Crimea, which was then under siege by the Mongols. The city had suffered similar visitations in plenty over the centuries, but never one so virulent or on such a scale. We need not necessarily believe – though our local sources give no statistics to contradict him – the anonymous contemporary chronicler from the Italian town of Este, who claims that in Constantinople it accounted for eight-ninths of the entire population; to the Byzantines, however, already broken in spirit by two civil wars in a single generation, it must have seemed the final proof of what they had suspected for so long: that the Holy Virgin, their patron and protectress, had, more than a thousand years, at last deserted them.

Less dramatic than the progress of the Serbian Emperor or the spread of the Black Death, but equally disturbing for John Cantacuzenus, was the general situation of the Empire. Once upon a time it had extended from the Straits of Gibraltar to Mesopotamia; now it was limited to the former province of Thrace – with the two vital cities of Adrianople and Didymotichum – and a few islands in the northern Aegean (though not Chios, which had been retaken by the Genoese in 1346). To this pathetic rump could be added, after 1350, the city of Thessalonica, which finally rid itself of the Zealots in that year; but Thessalonica was now a tiny Byzantine enclave within the dominions of Stephen Dushan, accessible only by sea.

Economically, the position was still more catastrophic: the civil war had reduced the Thracian countryside to a desert in which no farming was possible and which was moreover under constant harassment by marauding bands of Turks, while the coast was under continual attack by pirates from the Emirates of Asia Minor. Such food as was available was brought in from the Black Sea by the Genoese, who could cut off supplies whenever they liked. Trade, too, was at a standstill: Gregoras tells us that whereas the Genoese customs in Galata were collecting

200,000 *hyperpyra* a year, across the Golden Horn in Constantinople the corresponding figure was a mere 30,000 – and the *hyperpyron* itself was losing value with every day that passed. Any major expenditure by the government was made possible only by appeals for gifts or loans, which were all too often directed away from their stated purpose. When around 1350 Symeon, Grand Duke of Muscovy, sent a large quantity of gold for the restoration of St Sophia after its recent collapse, this magnificent contribution to a Christian cause found its way almost immediately into Muslim pockets: it was spent on the recruitment of Turkish mercenaries.

John's first care was to consolidate those parts of the Empire that still remained. His youngest son, Andronicus, had been carried off by the Black Death; of the two remaining, the elder, Matthew, was made responsible for an extensive area of Thrace between Didymotichum and Christopolis, along the Serbian frontier; the younger, Manuel, was a little later given charge of the Morea, henceforth to be considered as an autonomous despotate. It has been suggested that in making these appointments John was simply finding a useful occupation for two potentially headstrong princes, but such an interpretation seems to do him – and them – less than justice. Stephen Dushan, he well knew, would not rest until he had brought both these areas under his own control; and he knew too how easy it was for imperial territories to break away when under pressure. Since the civil war, there were few personal loyalties left among the leading Byzantines; in conferring these posts on his sons he was very sensibly putting the two key areas of his diminished Empire into the hands of men he could trust.

Next he looked towards Galata and the Genoese, who were simultaneously holding the Empire up to ransom and draining its economy dry. But nothing could be done against them without a fleet – of merchantmen as well as war galleys – and there was no money to build one. The rich – and the word can henceforth be used only in its comparative sense – were appealed to for funds, but largely in vain: by now they had all lost the bulk of their fortunes, and they were too despondent and generally apathetic to make further sacrifices. Only with enormous difficulty did the Emperor manage to raise a hopelessly inadequate 50,000 *hyperpyra* with which to launch his programme. Then there was the problem of the customs dues. It was clearly intolerable that the annual receipts in Galata should be nearly seven times those in Constantinople, and to remedy the situation John decreed a dramatic reduction of import tariffs to the point where foreign vessels were once again attracted to the western, rather than the eastern bank of the Golden Horn.

Not surprisingly, the Genoese lodged a strong protest; and when this was ignored they had no hesitation in resorting to force. In August 1348 a flotilla of their ships sailed across the Horn, burning the few Byzantine vessels they could find. John Cantacuzenus was away in Thrace; his wife Irene, however, with her younger son Manuel and her son-in-law Nicephorus – husband of their daughter Maria[1] – inspired a spirited resistance on the part of the entire population of Constantinople. The Genoese warehouses along the shore were set on fire; huge rocks and flaming bales were catapulted into Galata. The fighting continued sporadically for weeks – long enough for the Genoese to send for additional ships and equipment from Chios and to install vast catapults of their own on two of their largest warships. More sinister still, on another vessel they constructed a huge siege tower, higher than the sea walls of the capital. When it was ready, nine smaller ships towed it across the Horn and a fierce battle took place against the walls; at one stage it looked as if the city were about to suffer a major invasion.

But the Genoese had underestimated their opponents. The people of Constantinople fought like tigers for their city; even the slaves, writes Gregoras, were given weapons by their masters and taught themselves the use of bows and arrows. Finally the whole tower collapsed and the would-be invaders were forced to withdraw with heavy casualties to Galata, whence on the following day they sent ambassadors to Irene to sue for peace. But the Byzantines' blood was up; and when the Emperor returned on 1 October he gave orders for the stepping-up of the shipbuilding programme, the money to be provided – compulsorily if necessary – from the citizens not only of Constantinople but from all over Thrace. The timber from the Thracian forests had, we are told, to be transported overland in huge ox-wagons; the Empire possessed no vessels capable of carrying them, and the sea routes were anyway controlled by the Genoese.

In Galata, meanwhile, major defensive works were in progress. The walls along the Horn – they covered that stretch of the eastern shore running between the present Galata and Atatürk bridges – were raised and strengthened, and two more converging walls were added, running up the hillside behind to form a fortified triangle. At the apex of this was built a large cylindrical tower known as the Tower of Christ,

1 See p. 290.

which – better known as the Galata Tower – survives today.[1] From time to time while the work was in progress, the Genoese would repeat their suggestions for peace talks, but the Emperor still refused to listen: his fleet was now rapidly taking shape, and he was determined to use it.

By the early spring of 1349 it was ready – nine fair-sized ships and about a hundred smaller ones, several of which had been built and equipped by wealthier citizens at their own expense. At the beginning of March the first detachment left its dockyard on the Marmara and sailed to the mouth of the Golden Horn – where, on the evening of the 5th, it managed to capture and set fire to one of the largest of the Genoese vessels. On the evidence of subsequent events, however, it looks as though this initial triumph may have been more a matter of luck than anything else; for when the rest of the Byzantine ships arrived on the following day they suffered disaster – from which it became evident that their commanders and crews were ignorant of the most fundamental rules of seamanship. Precisely what occurred remains something of a mystery. Did a sudden gale strike the fleet just as it was rounding what is now Seraglio Point into the Golden Horn? Such, certainly, is the testimony of John Cantacuzenus himself and of another eye-witness, an intensely patriotic Byzantine named Alexius Macrembolites; but it hardly explains what happened next. All our contemporary sources, Greek though they are, assert that the whole fleet was suddenly and simultaneously seized with panic, and that soldiers and sailors together hurled themselves lemming-like into the sea before they had even engaged with the enemy. The astonished Genoese first suspected a trick; as they approached, however, they saw that the Byzantine ships were indeed abandoned; all they had to do was to tow them across to Galata.

Can it, one wonders, have been quite as simple as that? Is there really no other explanation for so extraordinary an outbreak of mass hysteria, for cowardice on so gigantic a scale? But if there was a better reason, what could it have been? And even if there was not, if the cause of the whole débâcle was indeed nothing but a sudden squall taking inexperienced seamen by surprise, why did the captains not order their crews to lower the sails and ride it out? We shall never know. Of the result, on the other hand, there can be no question. From one moment to the next

---

1 The guides – and postcards – which claim that the Tower was built by Justinian are not to be believed. The building is now used as a restaurant and nightclub. By day and by night, the balcony running round the outside affords one of the most spectacular views in all Istanbul, both across the Golden Horn and up the Bosphorus.

the sea was full of floundering men, some sinking under the weight of their armour, others being carried over by the current to the Galata side, where the Genoese made short work of them. Relatively few managed to reach their home shore in safety.

And even that was not the end of the story. Somehow, the terror spread to those watching the proceedings from the city:

Every spot both inside and outside the walls and gates was packed with people. A trumpeter or a drummer might have inspired them with a little fighting spirit; instead, they stood like corpses, until suddenly they turned and stampeded in flight, trampling over each other while the enemy watched in wonder and amazement, commiserating with the disaster rather than exulting in their victory; for they felt that some evil genius must have been at work, to cause men so freely to sacrifice their lives when there was no one in pursuit.[1]

It was the same with the soldiers who had been sent round to the east of Galata with orders to attack it from behind. Seeing what had occurred, they hurled away their weapons and fled. In its long history, Byzantium had suffered many defeats more serious than that of 6 March 1349; but none, perhaps, more shameful.

And yet, when a week or two later plenipotentiaries arrived from Genoa to conclude a formal treaty of peace, they proved remarkably accommodating. The Republic readily agreed to pay the Empire a war indemnity of more than 100,000 *hyperpyra*; it undertook to evacuate the land behind Galata which it had illegally occupied; finally, it promised never again to attack Constantinople. In return, Byzantium surrendered virtually nothing. No wonder the ambassadors were loaded with presents and given an elaborate ceremonial farewell: John and his subjects had obtained far more than they had expected – or deserved.

Encouraged by the success of these negotiations, John Cantacuzenus quickly put all memories of the recent disaster behind him. Determined to restore his Empire's reputation in the eyes of the world and heedless of the unpopularity that he knew he was incurring, he imposed new taxes on his subjects and began once again to rebuild the fleet – taking care, this time, to ensure proper training for the officers and men to whom it was to be entrusted. Soon, too, his luck began to change. Later in the year he actually persuaded the Genoese – who seem at last to have understood that the continued prosperity of Galata largely depended on

---

1 For this translation from Gregoras (II, 864–5), as for so much else in these final chapters, I am indebted to Professor D. M. Nicol, *The Last Centuries of Byzantium, 1261–1453*.

Byzantine goodwill – to restore to the Empire the island of Chios, which they had reoccupied during the recent civil war; and in September he renewed the peace treaty with Venice – concluded in 1342 by John V and the Empress Anne – for a further five years.

Next, it was the turn of Thessalonica to return to the fold. After the bloodbath of 1345 the Zealots had if anything tightened their grip, paying lip-service (though no more than that) to the imperial claims of John V but firmly denying those of Cantacuzenus, and refusing outright to allow Gregory Palamas, who had been appointed Metropolitan Archbishop in 1347, to take up his See. They went too far, however, when they talked openly of surrendering the city to Stephen Dushan. Stephen, taking them (perhaps rather rashly) at their word, appeared at the gates with an army, and early in 1350 the Zealot leaders – now hopelessly divided – were deposed by their own people in favour of Alexius, son of old Theodore Metochites, who made no secret of his support for the legitimate government. John Cantacuzenus saw his opportunity. Immediately he dispatched his eldest son Matthew to Thessalonica at the head of a formidable army – it included twenty thousand Turkish cavalry put at his disposal by his son-in-law Orhan – while he himself, with his co-Emperor John V, followed by sea. The sudden recall of Orhan's troops to Asia Minor almost put paid to the whole expedition, but on reaching the mouth of the Strymon river Matthew was lucky enough to find a fleet of Turkish pirates, who willingly agreed to join him. With their help the two Emperors made a ceremonial entry into Thessalonica in the autumn of 1350, where the overwhelming majority of the population gave them a warm welcome. Gregory Palamas followed them soon afterwards. The remaining Zealots were either exiled or sent for trial in Constantinople.

Leaving John V in Thessalonica, Cantacuzenus spent several weeks on campaign in Macedonia and Thrace, regaining Berrhoea, Edessa and a number of smaller fortresses. Only at the beginning of 1351 did he return definitively to the capital – to find that the dispute over the hesychasts had flared up yet again. The absence of Palamas – their leader and principal spokesman – in Thessalonica, far from allowing the issue to be forgotten, had encouraged their opponents to return to the attack. With John Calecas and Gregory Acindynus both dead, their place at the head of the anti-hesychast movement had been taken by the historian Nicephorus Gregoras, supported by Bishop Matthew of Ephesus and other prominent ecclesiastics; and it was clear that, in characteristic Byzantine fashion, the controversy was now colouring, distorting and occasionally poisoning any number of quite unrelated issues, infecting the entire body politic and the machinery of the state.

To settle the question once and for all, a third council – presided over, like its two predecessors, by John Cantacuzenus in person – was convened on 28 May 1351 in the Palace of Blachernae. Both Gregory Palamas, arriving hotfoot from Thessalonica, and Nicephorus Gregoras spoke emotionally and at considerable length in defence of their convictions; but the discussions ended, as everyone had known that they would, in a total vindication of the hesychasts. At a fourth and final council in July its findings were confirmed; and on 15 August, in the course of a solemn ceremony in St Sophia, John presented to the Patriarch Callistus a formal *tomos* in which they were set forth in detail, together with a call for the excommunication of all who opposed them. This document was counter-signed – unwillingly, if Gregoras is to be believed – by John Palaeologus on his return from Thessalonica in the following year.

Poor Gregoras never got over his defeat, and never forgave his old friend Cantacuzenus for what he insisted on considering a betrayal. The excommunication in particular came as a bitter blow, since he had taken monastic vows only a short time before the sentence was pronounced. In the monastery of the Chora – where he was confined for the next three years – he spent his days churning out pamphlets and denunciations of Palamas, the hesychasts and everything they stood for. He was released in 1354, but by then his sense of injustice had become too much for him: once the foremost historian and theologian of his time, he had degenerated into a hopeless obsessive, losing the sympathy of all his former friends and supporters – though he certainly did not deserve the fate that befell him after his death some five years later when, we are told, his body was dragged through the streets of the capital. We can only be grateful that he did not live long enough to learn of the very different treatment that was reserved for his arch-enemy Gregory Palamas, who was canonized in 1368 and is now venerated among the saints of the Eastern Church.

At the end of 1349, with the ink on his treaties with Venice and Genoa still scarcely dry, John Cantacuzenus might have been forgiven for thinking that his difficulties with the two mighty sea republics were over. Alas, for both of them the rewards offered by commerce around the Black Sea proved too great to resist. Their rivalry soon turned once again to open war, and the proximity of Galata to Constantinople made it impossible for Byzantium not to support one republic or the other – almost invariably emerging the loser. When, for example, in May 1351 a Venetian fleet sailed into the Golden Horn to attack Galata, and the Genoese – furious that the Byzantines did not immediately come to their assistance – brought their catapults into position and began lobbing huge rocks over the walls, John reluctantly sided with Venice; almost immediately, however, the Venetians withdrew and he was left alone to face the Genoese wrath. The result was another sea battle on 28 July, with Genoa victorious as usual. Only three months later a Genoese fleet on its way to Galata captured and sacked the port of Heraclea on the northern shore of the Marmara. Its subsequent journey past Constantinople and up the Bosphorus was uneventful – the Emperor having prudently put all the other cities and towns on the alert – but once in the Black Sea it turned north-west and wrought similar havoc on the unoffending city of Sozopolis.

By now Venice, too, was growing seriously alarmed. The previous November the Genoese had seized Euboea, one of her most valuable colonies: the initiative was clearly theirs, and they seemed determined to keep it. Fortunately she had another potential ally at hand: King Peter of Aragon, eager to lessen Genoa's influence in the western Mediterranean, had agreed to provide the Venetians with a fleet of twenty-six fully-armed men-of-war, provided only that they agreed to pay two-thirds of its upkeep. John Cantacuzenus now offered another twelve vessels on the same conditions, with the further proviso that, in the event of victory, Galata should be razed and the various islands seized by Genoa restored to him – together with the imperial crown jewels, which had already been seven years in pawn to Venice.

The diplomatic negotiations that preceded these agreements and the military preparations that followed them were prolonged. The Aragonese treaty was signed only in July 1351; and at just about the same time a report was received by John Cantacuzenus to the effect that the Venetians – assisted by Stephen Dushan – were trying to subvert his son-in-law John V, who was still in Thessalonica. They had, it appeared, offered him a 'loan' of 20,000 ducats in return for the cession of Tenedos, an island of considerable strategic importance to them since it controlled the entrance to the Hellespont.[1] Cantacuzenus, unable to leave the capital himself, sent the Empress Anne at once to Thessalonica to stiffen

1 According to Virgil (*Aeneid*, II, 21ff.) the Greeks had hidden there, watching and waiting, while the Wooden Horse was sent into Troy.

her son's resolve and to try to dissuade Stephen from so dangerous a policy. Fortunately she was successful on both counts and another civil war was averted; but the incident hardly improved the prospects of the new Venetian alliance.

It was consequently not until the beginning of 1352 that the rival fleets met in the Marmara. Each side had entrusted its fortunes to an admiral of outstanding ability – the allies to the Venetian Nicolò Pisani, Genoa to a member of that brilliant family whose name was to blaze across the republic's history for five centuries and more, Paganino Doria; and on 13 February the two faced each other at the mouth of the Bosphorus, beneath the walls of Galata. Paganino, guarding his home waters, had the advantage of position and had drawn up his ships in such a way that the attackers could not approach him without danger-ously constricting their own line. Pisani saw the trap at once. The sea was rough, the days were short; it was clear that any attack would be folly. But the Aragonese commander refused to listen. Before Pisani could stop him, he cut his cables and bore down upon the Genoese; and the Venetians and Byzantines had no course but to follow.

The ensuing battle quickly resolved itself into a straight contest between Venice and Genoa. The Byzantines retired almost at once, without engaging the enemy; the Aragonese, after their initial heroics, lasted very little longer. It was left to the two most formidable naval powers of the time to fight it out by themselves, and so they did – savagely, with no quarter given on either side. Soon fire broke out, which the high winds quickly spread through both fleets; but they fought on, far into the night, by the light of their own blazing ships. Finally it was the Venetians, with the wind and current both against them, who had to yield. They had lost most of their galleys and some fifteen hundred of their best fighting men, an appallingly high figure at any time; coming as it did less than four years after the Black Death – which had destroyed six out of every ten of their population – it was more catastrophic still. But when the dawn came, to reveal the surface of the water almost invisible beneath the wrecks and the multitude of human corpses, Doria found that his own losses had been almost as heavy, to the point where he was obliged to conceal them from his fellow-citizens in Galata for fear of provoking a general panic. His, certainly, was the victory in the technical sense; but it was a victory that had cost him more dearly than many a defeat.

For John Cantacuzenus it was defeat pure and simple. Neither the

Venetians nor the Aragonese had the stomach to continue the fight; the survivors, after repairing as best they could the battered hulks that remained to them, sailed back to the West. John, however, had no choice but to negotiate yet another peace with the Genoese. It was concluded in May – at just about the time that John V Palaeologus returned to the capital after his protracted stay in Thessalonica. The young Emperor was now twenty years old, no longer content to submit unquestioningly, as he had in the past, to his father-in-law's bidding. For some time the two surviving Cantacuzenus sons had been entrusted with the government of important areas of the Empire. His own mother, the Empress Anne, had recently been given control over Macedonia, with her capital at Salonica. It was time for him also to claim his due.

John VI was well aware of his son-in-law's ambitions, and of the danger of civil war if they were not satisfied. He therefore offered the co-Emperor – who accepted it with alacrity – the greater part of Thrace, strategically of vital importance since it controlled the approaches to Constantinople itself. There was only one problem: the area in question comprised the large city of Didymotichum and most of the appanage that John had already granted to his son Matthew. In an attempt at solution Matthew was allotted Adrianople and its surroundings, but he was left feeling ill-used and resentful of his brother-in-law – who, to make matters worse, was now his immediate neighbour.

The first to break the uneasy peace was, surprisingly enough, John Palaeologus. Possibly in order to pre-empt an attack by Matthew, he crossed the latter's frontier in the summer of 1352 and laid siege to Adrianople. Matthew immediately appealed to his father, who hastened to his relief at the head of a considerable force of Turkish troops, put at his disposal by the Emir Orhan and commanded by the latter's son Süleyman Pasha. John for his part summoned help from the Serbs and Bulgars, an appeal to which Stephen Dushan responded with four thousand cavalry. In the event the city was saved, but this proved to be of comparatively little importance. Far more significant was the fact that the Empire was once again at war with itself, and – more ominous still – that John VI had thrown an army of infidels against his own Christian subjects. After the relief of Adrianople Süleyman's Turks had been allowed to pillage, plunder and terrorize the neighbouring towns and villages; and, at least so far as the victims and public opinion at large were concerned, they had done so in the senior Emperor's name.

It scarcely mattered when, a few months later, the same Turks destroyed a joint Serbian–Bulgarian army on the frozen Maritsa river;

they were then fighting, ostensibly at least, as perfectly legitimate mercenaries against a foreign enemy. But those earlier atrocities were something altogether different; and from his association with them, whether deliberate or accidental, the reputation of John Cantacuzenus never recovered. Even in Constantinople it was now in rapid decline. After all, the people reminded themselves, he was not of the true imperial family: even if he had not actually usurped the throne, he was in a sense only a caretaker Emperor. Now that young John Palaeologus had grown to manhood, was it right that he should still be obliged to share his authority – and to share it with a man who, in recent years, had brought the Empire little but disaster?

By this time John VI had probably lost all appetite for power. Already in 1341 he had bought himself a plot of land from the monastery of Vatopedi on Mount Athos, and in 1350 he had made a handsome endowment to the monastery of St George at Mangana; since then he had often spoken wistfully of the attractions of the monastic life. From the first, too, he had supported the legitimate claims of John Palaeologus, whom he could easily have overthrown – as many of his friends had advised – after the death of Andronicus III. But had young John not now proved that he could not be trusted? And had he not, moreover, shown himself to be a serious threat to the survival of the Empire itself – a ready tool of the Venetians, the Bulgars and of Stephen Dushan, one who possessed neither the judgement to perceive the dangers they represented nor the strength to resist their blandishments? In April 1353, on the advice of a body of his supporters in Constantinople, John Cantacuzenus performed an act which, six years before at his coronation, would have been to him unthinkable. At a public ceremony in the Palace of Blachernae, he declared John V formally deposed and named his son Matthew co-Emperor in his stead – making it clear, however, that the Palaeologi had been in no sense disinherited and that John's son Andronicus (who was of course a Cantacuzenus on his mother's side) remained as heir apparent. He then exiled his unfortunate son-in-law, with his family, to Tenedos.

Not for the first time, however, he had underestimated the strength of the opposition. Patriarch Callistus, a firm adherent of John V, flatly refused to perform Matthew's coronation. Instead, he pronounced sentence of excommunication on Cantacuzenus, then resigned his office and retired to a monastery. A few days later he slipped across to Galata and with Genoese help soon found his way to Tenedos, where the deposed Emperor gave him a warm welcome. Meanwhile a certain Philotheus, formerly Bishop of Heraclea, was elected as his successor. He, predictably enough, proved to be an enthusiastic Cantacuzenist; but it was not until February 1354 that Matthew and his wife Irene were finally crowned, and even then the ceremony took place not in St Sophia, as might have been expected, but in the church of the Virgin at Blachernae.

Less than a month later, on 2 March, a large part of Thrace was ravaged by a violent earthquake. Hundreds of towns and villages were destroyed; during the blizzards and deluges of rain which followed, many of the survivors died of cold and exposure. In the once-great city of Gallipoli – from which, fortunately, most of the population had managed to escape by sea – scarcely a house was left standing. The disaster would have been terrible enough by any standards; it was however made still more catastrophic by the conduct of the Turks – both the marauding bands of irregulars who had made Thrace their home and the more disciplined troops of Süleyman Pasha across the straits in Asia Minor. For Süleyman himself, it provided precisely the opportunity for which he had been waiting. When the news was brought to him at Pegae he set off at once for the stricken lands, taking with him as many Turkish families as he could find to install in the abandoned towns. The majority headed for the ruins of Gallipoli itself, whither many more of their compatriots were shortly afterwards brought to join them; and within a few months the city had been repaired, with its walls rebuilt and an exclusively Turkish population resident where a Greek one had been before.

For the Empire, this first settlement by the Turks on the European continent was a calamity greater even than the earthquake itself. The devastated areas would sooner or later recover; Gallipoli – the principal crossing-point for travellers bound from Thrace to Asia Minor – seemed permanently lost. To John VI's formal demand for its restitution, Süleyman replied that the city had fallen to him through the will of Allah; to return it would be an act of impious ingratitude. He had not after all taken it by force; his men had simply occupied a place that had been abandoned by its former inhabitants. Such was the Emperor's anxiety to regain Gallipoli that he quadrupled the amount of compensation he had first suggested, but the Pasha remained obdurate. John then appealed to Orhan, who agreed to meet him near Nicomedia to discuss the matter; John arrived, however, to find only a message awaiting him to the effect that the Emir had suddenly been taken ill and was unable to make the journey.

By now John Cantacuzenus must have felt that his own God had forsaken him. More than ever he must have longed to put his worldly cares behind him and retire, before it was too late, to the life of prayer and contemplation for which he longed, enabling him to make his peace with his Creator and pass his remaining years in tranquillity. Some time during the summer, with a faint hope in his heart that he might be able to come to some arrangement with his Christian son-in-law, he sailed to Tenedos; but the islanders would not even service his ships, and John Palaeologus – knowing that time was on his side – refused point-blank to receive him. Sadly he returned to Constantinople, there to await the developments that he was powerless now to control.

They were not long in coming. On 21 November 1354 John Palaeologus slipped out of Tenedos. It was a dark, moonless night with occasional bursts of heavy rain, but there was a good following wind that drove him quickly up the Hellespont and into the Marmara. In the early hours of the 22nd he reached Constantinople which, still under cover of darkness, he succeeded in entering unobserved. Once inside the city, however, he immediately made his presence known, and by dawn the crowds were already gathering in the streets and calling his name. Before long, inevitably, they went on the rampage. Again the family mansion of John Cantacuzenus was plundered and set on fire; the houses of many of his supporters suffered a similar fate. Some of the rioters seized control of the arsenal; others marched on Blachernae. John V, meanwhile, temporarily installed himself in the old Palace of the Emperors opposite St Sophia.

It was from there, on 24 November, that he sent a messenger to his father-in-law suggesting a meeting; and in the negotiations that followed he showed himself surprisingly understanding of the latter's position. He did not insist on his abdication; rather he proposed that the two should rule jointly as before, with Matthew Cantacuzenus continuing to reign from Adrianople over his own territory until his death. John VI would be obliged to surrender the fortress at the Golden Gate which he had recently rebuilt and strengthened, and which he had garrisoned with a regiment of Catalan mercenaries; but he would remain the senior Emperor and would continue to live at Blachernae, while John V would occupy the private palace of Theodore Metochites, one of the largest and grandest in the city.

The immediate crisis was over, and the two Emperors swore a solemn oath to observe the agreement that they had made. Many problems, however, remained unsolved. One was the continued presence of Süleyman's Turks in Thrace; another was the increasing unpopularity of John

Cantacuzenus, of which he himself was fully aware. He knew too that such supporters as he had, discouraged by the open hostility shown them throughout the capital, were rapidly falling away. For about a week he bore the situation as best he could; then, after a particularly violent demonstration against him, he finally took the decision that he had been considering for so long. On 4 December, at a ceremony in Blachernae, he solemnly laid aside the diadem, divesting himself too of the dalmatic and the purple buskins, embroidered with golden eagles, which only Emperors might wear. In their place he adopted the simple black robe of an Orthodox monk. His wife Irene similarly put off her imperial pomp to become a nun at the convent of Kyria Martha, which had been founded in the 1270s by Maria Palaeologina, sister of Michael VIII, and in which her mother-in-law Theodora Cantacuzena lay buried. He himself retired first to the monastery of St George at Mangana, later moving to another, smaller foundation which had recently been established by his old friend and supporter John Charsianeites, from whom it took its name.

John Cantacuzenus – known henceforth as the monk Joasaph – had been Emperor only seven years; but he had effectively governed the Empire for a quarter of a century, and guided it for ten years longer still. He was to live for another twenty-nine, until 1383. The first years after his retirement were largely devoted to the completion of his *Histories*, which continue until 1356. When this work was done he turned to theology, and to a long and closely-reasoned defence of the hesychast doctrine. As we shall soon see, however, he did not altogether withdraw from political life, much as he may have wished to do so.

Many historians – Edward Gibbon among them – have cast doubts on John's sincerity. Was his abdication, they ask, really as voluntary as he pretends? Was he not in fact driven from the throne by his ambitious young son-in-law? There is no reason to think so. All his life John had been a deeply religious man. For fifteen years at least he had been dreaming of just such a withdrawal; and the humiliations and disappointments that he had recently suffered were surely more than enough to persuade him to take the step he had contemplated for so long. His subjects, all too clearly, had no further use for him. He had made his peace with his son-in-law John V, whose right to the throne was far greater than his own and who had by now made at least some demonstration of his ability to rule the Empire. If he were ever to abdicate, this surely was the moment to go.

It is hard not to feel sorry for John Cantacuzenus. Few Emperors had worked harder for the imperial good; few had possessed less personal ambition. He might, had he so wished, have been co-Emperor with Andronicus III in the 1330s, and certainly on Andronicus's death the throne had been his for the asking; but he had always refused. Only after the Empire had been torn apart by civil war had he assumed the diadem, and even then with genuine reluctance; and he would never have deposed John Palaeologus, nominating his own son in his place, had he not been genuinely convinced that John, by resuming that war, was throwing the whole future of Byzantium into jeopardy. Unfortunately, this moment of self-assertion had come too late. Had he shown it in 1341, he might well have held the Empire together and spared its citizens thirteen years of misery. By 1353 the damage had been done.

Luck, too, was against him. The foolhardiness of John Palaeologus, the hesychast controversy, the Black Death, the aggression of the Turks, the ambitions of the Genoese and the Venetians: without any of these afflictions, he might conceivably have won through. Together, they made his task impossible. The greatest burden of all, however, was the bankruptcy of the Empire itself – a bankruptcy as much moral as financial. Not only was the treasury empty; the Byzantines themselves had lost heart. Their old self-confidence was gone, and with it the will to recover their past greatness. A truly charismatic personality might perhaps have been able to galvanize them into action; but John Cantacuzenus, wise statesman and excellent general as he had been, was primarily a scholar and an intellectual; he was not ultimately an inspired leader of men. Instead of enthusing his subjects with determination and courage, he had succeeded only in alienating their affection and their trust. Thirty-five years of dedicated service to the Empire had been ill repaid. As he and his wife exchanged the trappings of Empire for their coarse monastic habits, it is hard to believe that they can have done so with anything but relief.

20

The Sultan's Vassal

[1354–91]

The Tsar chose a heavenly kingdom
And not an earthly kingdom.
He built a church on Kosovo.
He built it not with floor of marble
But laid down silk and scarlet on the ground.
There he summoned the Patriarch of Serbia
And twelve great bishops.
Then he gave the soldiers the Eucharist and their battle orders.
In that same hour that the Prince gave orders to his soldiers
The Turks attacked Kosovo . . .

Then the Turks overwhelmed Lazar,
And the Tsar Lazar was destroyed,
And his army was destroyed with him,
Of seven and seventy thousand soldiers.
All was holy, all was honourable,
And the goodness of God was fulfilled.

The Kosovo Cycle

With the departure of John VI Cantacuzenus, it was generally acknowledged by all the princes of Christendom that Byzantium was on the
verge of collapse. To what power, however, was it to fall? Already four
months before the abdication, the Venetian *bailo* in Constantinople had
reported to his government that the Byzantines were ready to make their
submission to anyone who asked them to; four months after it, we find
the Doge of Venice proposing the immediate annexation of the Empire,
if only to save it from the Ottoman tide.

As it happened, however, there was at that moment another power in
eastern Europe more powerful than either Venice or the Turks: Stephen
Dushan, whose dominions encompassed – as well as Serbia, Macedonia
and much of Bulgaria – the entire Greek mainland as far as the Gulf of

Corinth, excepting only Attica, Boeotia and the Peloponnese. Throughout his life, Stephen had been inspired by a single dream – to rule his own Serbian Empire from the imperial throne in Constantinople. To this end he had negotiated at one time or another with every ruler in Europe who might have proved useful to him, including the Turkish Emirs and even the Pope, over whom he had dangled the usual bait of ecclesiastical union; and he might well have achieved his ambition – and even, conceivably, changed the history of Europe – had he not been stricken by sudden illness while still in his prime. He died in December 1355, aged only forty-six, having made no proper arrangements for the succession.

Immediately his Empire began to disintegrate. His son Stephen Urosh V, who had been left in charge of the old Serbian region to the north while Stephen Dushan had governed the Greek lands of 'Romania', had neither the ability nor the authority to prevent various other members of his family – and even quite humble members of his court[1] – from declaring themselves independent princes. Within a year, the 'Empire of the Serbs and Greeks' was as if it had never been. To the Byzantines it seemed an almost miraculous deliverance. In fact, however – as they well knew – they were themselves too weak to draw any positive advantage. John V made no effort to recapture the former Byzantine dominions, and although Nicephorus II, the deposed Despot of Epirus, made a determined attempt to do so he had achieved little before being killed in battle in 1358. The truth was that the death of Dushan meant nothing more than the substitution of one threat by another: for the collapse of the Serbian Empire presented the Turks with just the opportunity that they had been waiting for. No longer was there any power in Europe capable of resisting their advance.

Although John V had already been co-Emperor for fourteen years, he was still only twenty-three – and a very different person from his father-in-law. Where John Cantacuzenus had pursued a policy of unashamed appeasement with the Ottoman Turks, even going so far as to marry his daughter to the Emir Orhan, John Palaeologus had little patience with diplomacy. He believed – rightly – that the world was not ultimately large enough to contain Byzantines and Turks together. It followed that the latter must be eliminated. This meant war, and war – given the

---

1 One of them, Vukashin, who ruled as Despot between Prilep and Lake Ochrid, had been Stephen Dushan's cupbearer; his brother John Uglesha, Despot of Serres, had been the Tsar's *hippokomos*, or groom.

present state of the Empire – meant a grand Christian alliance against the infidel. The age of the Crusades might be over, and attempts at such alliances in more recent years had not proved conspicuously successful; but Pope Clement VI, despite his exile in Avignon, had managed to form a league against Umur of Aydin in 1344, and now that the Turks had acquired a permanent foothold in Europe the nations of the West must surely see the necessity, both political and religious, of taking decisive action while there was still time.

Just a year after his accession, on 15 December 1355, John sent envoys to Avignon bearing a letter addressed to Clement's successor, Innocent VI. It contained a long and detailed proposal, according to which the Pope would immediately dispatch to Constantinople five hundred knights, a thousand infantry, fifteen transport ships and five galleys. These would serve under the Emperor's personal command, against not only the Turks but also his own Greek enemies in the Balkans, for a period of six months. Throughout that time a papal legate would reside in the capital, where he would oversee the appointments of distinguished ecclesiastics favourable to the cause of Church union. Mass conversions would almost certainly follow, and there would be no longer any obstacle to imperial submission to the Holy See. As a further guarantee of his good faith, the Emperor would send his second son Manuel – then aged five – to Avignon; should he himself for whatever reason fail to honour his commitments to the letter, His Holiness would be free to bring up the boy as he wished, educating him in the Catholic faith and eventually marrying him to whomsoever he chose. Meanwhile Manuel's elder brother Andronicus, the heir-presumptive to the throne, would receive intensive instruction in Latin language and literature, and three Latin colleges would be founded to ensure that the sons of the imperial nobility should enjoy a similar degree of enlightenment. If by any chance the Emperor proved unable to bring about the mass conversions for which he hoped, he would at least make a personal submission himself; if on the other hand he was successful, he would request further, more ambitious assistance: nothing less than a great Christian army that would drive the Turks back into Central Asia. This too would be commanded by the Emperor, who would take the title of 'Captain-General and Standard-Bearer of the Holy Mother Church'.

This extraordinary missive reached Avignon in June 1356; Innocent VI, a sensible down-to-earth Frenchman, does not seem to have taken it too seriously. He returned a polite reply, expressing his gratification that John was willing to lead his people back into the Roman fold but making no reference to any of his detailed proposals. Clearly he expected no conversions *en bloc*, and had no intention of sending any Christian armies; what did interest him, however, was the possibility of the Emperor's own personal conversion. He therefore expressed his readiness to dispatch to him two special legates, through whose agency he looked forward to receiving John into the Holy Church as his faithful son in Christ.

These legates were both bishops. One was a Carmelite named Peter Thomas; the other was William Conti, a Dominican. They arrived in Constantinople in April 1357, and were warmly welcomed by the Emperor; but they achieved little. The assertion by Peter Thomas's hagiographer[1] that he succeeded in converting the Emperor is amply disproved by later events; in fact both bishops, seeing that the situation bore no resemblance to what John had suggested in his letter, soon gave up the struggle. Conti returned to his flock, while Peter Thomas travelled on to Cyprus, where he was subsequently appointed Apostolic Legate in the East. As for the Emperor, he was lucky to get off so lightly. Had the Pope taken his letter at its face value, sent an army as requested and then demanded the fulfilment of his promises, his position would have been difficult indeed. There was, it is true, a fairly substantial party in Constantinople that was not averse to ecclesiastical union; it included Demetrius Cydones, the distinguished scholar and translator of St Thomas Aquinas, who at about this time was actually received into the Roman Church. But the overwhelming majority of influential Byzantines, both lay and clerical, still upheld the old beliefs; indeed, Patriarch Callistus – who had resumed his office after the abdication of his enemy John VI – had recently obtained from both the Bulgarian and the Serbian Patriarchates the recognition of the supremacy of Constantinople. In such circumstances it is difficult to believe that John V could have entertained any serious hopes of ecclesiastical union; even if he did, by the summer of 1357 they must certainly have been swept away.

The story of John Palaeologus's letter to the Pope remains worth telling, however, for one reason only: as an example of the Emperor's basic unreliability, his tendency to act on a sudden impulse without any but the most cursory consideration of its possible consequences. As his father-in-law John Cantacuzenus had always known, his were not the hands into which to confide the fate of an Empire threatened on the

---

1 Philippe de Mézières, Chancellor of the French Kingdom of Cyprus, *The Life of St Peter Thomas*.

outside with imminent destruction, and on the inside with disintegration and collapse.

Meanwhile, the Ottomans were spreading across Thrace. Süleyman's capture of Gallipoli in 1354 had given them the bridgehead they needed, and their advance had begun almost at once. Before long, too, those other bands of freebooting Turks who had come over in answer to appeals by John Cantacuzenus to the Emirs of Aydin or Saruchan – together with others who had arrived independently as corsairs – rallied to their standard. As early as 1359 an advance guard had reached the walls of Constantinople. Fortunately it was not large enough to constitute any immediate threat to the city; but the rest of Thrace, less well protected and exhausted by civil war, proved an easy victim. In 1361 Didymotichum fell; in 1362, Adrianople. In every city and village that was captured, a large part of the native population was transported to slavery in Asia Minor, its place being taken by Turkish colonists. That same year, 1362, saw the death of Orhan. He was succeeded as Emir – Süleyman having died two years before – by his son Murad, who soon proved himself a more energetic and determined leader than either his father or his elder brother, campaigning not only in Thrace but also in Bulgaria, capturing Philippopolis in 1363 and putting considerable pressure on the Bulgar Tsar John Alexander to collaborate with him against Byzantium.

When reports of their discussions reached Constantinople, John Palaeologus lost no time: with what few ships and fighting men he had available, in 1364 he personally led a punitive attack on the Bulgarian Black Sea ports and occupied Anchialus. It did him little strategic good, but was probably worth it for the psychological effect it had on his subjects. Doomed the Empire might be, but it had shown itself to be still capable of an occasional victory. On the Emperor's return his hopes were briefly raised by a report that Pope Urban V was at last making arrangements for a Crusade, to be led by the Catholic Kings Louis I of Hungary and Peter I of Cyprus, with the active and enthusiastic participation of his own cousin Count Amadeus VI of Savoy;[1] but instead of marching against the Turks this expedition eventually headed for Egypt, where in October 1365 it suffered an ignominious defeat. Once again John had to look for allies.

He had already tried Serbia – or what was left of it – sending

---

1 The father of Amadeus had been a half-brother of John's mother, the Empress Anne.

Patriarch Callistus as his personal envoy. The Patriarch had seen the widow of Stephen Dushan, but had unfortunately died almost immediately afterwards without having reached any substantive agreement; and the inevitable rumours of poison, though certainly unfounded, scarcely improved the atmosphere. Genoa and Venice were friendly but similarly ineffectual. Pope Urban and Peter of Cyprus had shot their bolts, and had succeeded only in making themselves look ridiculous. There remained Louis the Great, King of Hungary. He had been prudent enough to withdraw in time from the Egyptian expedition; instead – abhorring, like so many of his co-religionists, schismatics far more than infidels – he had decided to wage a holy war of his own, against not the Turks but the Christian Bulgars. In 1365 the frontier province of Vidin was occupied by a Hungarian army – an occupation which brought in its wake vast numbers of Franciscan missionaries, who immediately set about the more or less forcible conversion of the local inhabitants.

It was hardly the best background against which to conduct diplomatic negotiations. John seems to have thought, however, that Louis might still – in the right circumstances – be persuaded to help him; and he decided to go himself to Hungary. Such a step was absolutely without precedent. Emperors had frequently travelled outside their own frontiers at the head of a conquering army; but never, in all Byzantine history, had a *basileus* left his capital in the role of petitioner to the Christian West. On the other hand, John might have argued, the situation had never been so desperate. Leaving the Empire in the hands of his eldest son Andronicus, in the first bitter weeks of 1366 he sailed northward along the Black Sea coast and thence up the Danube to Buda, his two younger sons Manuel and Michael accompanying him. King Louis gave him an appropriate welcome; but he had already been in consultation with the Pope, and as soon as discussions began he made his position clear. Conversion must be the first priority. Only after Emperor and Empire had made their submission to Rome could there be any question of military assistance. This time John knew that he could make no definite commitments; even if he had, Louis would probably not have believed him. Leaving both his sons as hostages (though precisely for what is not clear)[1] he set off sadly homewards – only to find his way blocked and himself an effective prisoner of the Bulgars, who had been

---

1 There is no record of how long the two young princes were forced to remain in Buda; we know, however, that both were back in Constantinople in time for the negotiations on Church union which began in June 1367.

not unnaturally alarmed at the prospect of a Byzantine–Hungarian alliance.

Once only in imperial history had an Emperor been captured by a foreign power: Romanus Diogenes, after the battle of Manzikert, almost three centuries before. Romanus, however, had been taken by his Seljuk enemies, treated with consideration and courtesy and freed after a week. John was held by his Christian neighbours, utterly ignored by the Bulgar Tsar John Alexander – who was the father-in-law of his captive's own first-born son Andronicus – and left in a small frontier town for some six months. Such treatment of the one true Emperor of the Romans, Vice-Gerent of God on earth, would have been unthinkable in former days. There could be no more forcible illustration of the depths to which the Empire had sunk. Even when John's release came at last, he owed it not to the Tsar but, surprisingly enough, to his cousin Amadeus of Savoy.

After the failure of the 1365 expedition Amadeus had decided to do a little crusading of his own. In May 1366, with fifteen ships and some 1,700 men, he had sailed from Venice for Constantinople, determined to help his cousin against the Turks. On his arrival at the mouth of the Hellespont he had been joined by the Emperor's brother-in-law Francesco Gattilusio, the Genoese ruler of Lesbos who had married John's sister Maria; and the two immediately launched an attack on Gallipoli – which, after two days' furious fighting, they recaptured. The effect of this victory on Byzantine morale can be easily imagined. For the past twelve years Gallipoli had been the Turkish bridgehead, the first Muslim outpost on the European continent, from which all further advances had begun. Henceforth it would be much more difficult for Murad to send reinforcements to his army in Thrace. Even now, there was much agonized discussion in Constantinople as to whether this Roman Catholic army should be allowed entry into the city; thanks largely to the persuasive powers of Demetrius Cydones, however, on 2 September the gates were finally opened.

It was probably at this point only – unless he had previously heard the news from Gattilusio – that Amadeus learned of his cousin's captivity. He spent a month in preparation, then sailed up the Black Sea coast, occupying the ports of Mesembria and Sozopolis in the name of the Empire and laying siege to Varna, whence he sent an ultimatum to the Tsar at Trnovo. Possessing as he did so valuable a hostage, we may wonder why John Alexander did not demand the restitution of the captured ports as the Emperor's ransom; but Bulgaria's military and economic position was by now so weak that Amadeus would almost certainly have called his bluff. Finally the Tsar gave his authority for the Emperor to cross his territory, and John reached the camp of the Count of Savoy at Mesembria just before Christmas. The two remained together on the coast throughout the winter; not until the spring of 1367 did they return to Constantinople.

Why, it may be asked, did they delay so long? Above all, because they had serious business to discuss. The Count of Savoy was by now desperately short of funds. Gallipoli, Mesembria and Sozopolis needed substantial garrisons if they were to remain in Byzantine hands; and such garrisons were expensive, in men as well as money. It seemed to Amadeus only reasonable that the Empire should make at least some contribution to their upkeep, as well as providing soldiers for another Bulgarian campaign. And there was another matter, still more important, to be raised. In return for the Pope's blessing on his expedition, Amadeus had sworn to take up once again the cause of Church union and had actually brought with him a papal envoy in the person of Paul, the former Bishop of Smyrna who had recently been elevated to the titular rank of Latin Patriarch of Constantinople. Preliminary discussions on so delicate an issue were obviously far better held away from the hothouse atmosphere of the capital.

By the time he reached the Bosphorus, John's mind was made up. He could not commit his subjects – and still less his Church – to union: were he even to attempt to do so, they would almost certainly depose him. But he could himself make a personal submission to Rome; and at the same time he could arrange for high-level discussions between Paul and the Orthodox leaders, in the hopes that they too would eventually come to see the desirability of healing the breach which had cut them off for so long. Even this was to prove difficult enough, Patriarch Philotheus[1] categorically refusing to have any dealings with a man who pretended to his own title. He raised no objection, however, when John appointed his father-in-law, the monk Joasaph – formerly the Emperor John Cantacuzenus, of whom the Patriarch had always been

---

1 To avoid confusion it should be explained that the Patriarchs Callistus I and Philotheus (Coccinus) alternated between 1350 and 1376, each holding office for two separate periods. Callistus, an adherent of John V first appointed in 1350, resigned in 1353 (see p. 319). Philotheus, who supported John VI, succeeded him and continued until John's abdication in 1354. Callistus then took over once again and ruled over the Church until he died in 1363, after which Philotheus returned early the following year and remained in power until his own death in 1376.

an enthusiastic champion – to represent the Orthodox Church in his stead.

This appointment is not so surprising as might appear. For centuries it was assumed that John Cantacuzenus spent the years after his abdication in strict monastic seclusion, immersed in his theological studies and emerging only at rare intervals when an imperial summons had to be obeyed. In fact, however – and particularly after the restoration of his old friend Philotheus to the Patriarchal throne in 1364 – he seems to have played an increasingly important role in state affairs. Philotheus himself describes him as being 'a pillar of the government, its greatest counsellor, and a virtual father to the imperial family',[1] suggesting that by this time he may well have possessed power – or at least influence – not far short of that which he had enjoyed during his years as Emperor.

The discussions began in June 1367. From the Byzantine point of view, they were remarkably successful. John Cantacuzenus pointed out that unity was the devout wish of the Eastern Church just as much as it was of the Western; but the existing differences could be settled only by means of a truly ecumenical council, to be attended by Pope, Patriarchs, Archbishops and Bishops from both sides – and this had never been acceptable to Rome. There was, he emphasized, no other way. As Michael VIII had so tragically demonstrated nearly a hundred years before, union could not be unilaterally imposed from above; the Emperor had no control over the souls of his subjects. Paul, it appears, took some persuading; but in the end he agreed to a council such as had been proposed, to be held at Constantinople within two years. Meanwhile he himself would return to the West, together with Count Amadeus and representatives of the Orthodox clergy, both pastoral and monastic, who would constitute a sort of advance guard in expectation of the Emperor's own arrival at a somewhat later date.

Earlier that same year Pope Urban had attempted to move the Papacy back to Rome. The transfer was not a success – soon afterwards, at the insistence of the French cardinals, he was obliged to return to Avignon, where the papal court was to remain until 1377 – but it was to Italy, not France, that the Byzantine delegation travelled that summer, being received by Urban in Viterbo, where they were given a warm welcome. Thence they accompanied him to Rome – sad, impoverished and half-ruined as it was – and were present at his formal entry into the

---

1 *Antirrhetici libri XII contra Gregoram*, ed. J. P. Migne, M.P.G., Vol. cli, quoted by J. W. Barker, *Manuel II Palaeologus*, p. 37.

city on 16 October. From that moment on, however, they grew more and more depressed. The Patriarch Paul, it soon became clear, had been speaking in Constantinople without instructions. Urban had no intention whatever of calling, let alone personally attending, an ecumenical council: what, he asked, could be the purpose of debating matters of faith which had already been established beyond question by the authority of the Holy See? On 6 November he signed twenty-three separate letters, addressed to all those in high authority who might be interested in Church union, stressing the importance of the Byzantines' return to the fold and of the Emperor's promised visit to Rome in person. Not one of the letters mentioned a council, even as a remote possibility. Still less was there any question of an international Crusade of the kind for which John Palaeologus had hoped.

But John kept his promise. Once again leaving his eldest son – now crowned co-Emperor as Andronicus IV – as Regent in Constantinople, he set off in the early summer of 1369, accompanied by a suite consisting of his brother-in-law Francesco Gattilusio, Demetrius Cydones and a few other of his subjects whose sympathies were openly pro-Western – but including not a single member of the Orthodox hierarchy, which had refused to a man to have anything to do with a visit that it could hardly bear to contemplate. Landing in Naples, he spent a few days as guest of the Queen of Sicily, recovering from the voyage and preparing for whatever discussions might lie in store; he then sailed on to Rome, where Urban joined him shortly afterwards. There, on Thursday, 18 October, he formally signed a document declaring his acceptance of the Catholic faith and his submission to the Holy Roman Church and its father the Pope, sealing it with his imperial golden seal; and the following Sunday, in the presence of the entire Curia, he did obeisance to the Supreme Pontiff on the steps of St Peter's, kneeling before him and kissing him on the feet, hands and finally the lips. High Mass followed in the Basilica.

The deed was done. It remained, however, an individual act – personally binding on the Emperor but on no one else. There was no question of any union of the two Churches, which remained as far apart as ever they had been; nor of any ecumenical council, nor of any military assistance against the Turks. Apart from a dangerous weakening of his own position in Constantinople, the public self-abasement of the one true Emperor of the Romans had achieved nothing. And – had John Palaeologus but known it – there was a further and infinitely greater humiliation ahead.

*

For some time now the Emperor had been in correspondence with Andrea Contarini, Doge of Venice. The Most Serene Republic, wrote the Doge, was fully aware of the Empire's present financial embarrassments; he felt it however only proper to mention the imperial crown jewels, pawned by the Empress Anne in 1343 against a loan of 30,000 ducats, the interest on which was rapidly increasing. If they were not redeemed in the near future, the Republic would have no choice but to sell them. There was also the matter of compensation for the damage done to Venetian property in Constantinople: 25,663 *hyperpyra*, of which only 4,500 had so far been paid. In his reply John had again explained the nature of his difficulties and pleaded for understanding – not altogether unsuccessfully, since he was rewarded while in Rome by a letter renewing the Venetian–Byzantine treaty, which had expired two years before, for another five years from February 1370, allowing the damages claim to be paid in annual instalments and agreeing to retain the crown jewels for a further period in the Treasury of St Mark's. Contarini did however suggest that the Emperor might like to call at Venice on his homeward journey, in order that the two of them might discuss the outstanding problems in a friendly manner.

Leaving Rome in March 1370 and making another brief stop in Naples, the imperial squadron was in Venice by early May. In normal circumstances this first-ever visit by a Byzantine Emperor to the Serenissima would have been celebrated with a degree of magnificence of which no other state was capable; but Byzantium's reputation was gone. Although John put on as good a show as he could, there was no concealing the fact that he and his Empire were heavily in debt; and the Venetians had little respect for poverty. He was received coolly, and with the minimum of ceremony. When Emperor and Doge settled down to talk, however, the atmosphere improved; for John immediately made the Venetians an offer which he knew that they could not refuse. For many years they had had their eye on the island of Tenedos at the entrance to the Hellespont. This he now proposed to cede, in return for a Venetian undertaking not only to return the crown jewels but to provide him with six war galleys and 25,000 ducats in cash – 4,000 payable at once, since by this time he had revealed that he did not actually have enough money to get home.

The Doge was happy to agree; but then came disaster. The Genoese colony in Constantinople, appalled at the prospect of so valuable a prize falling into the hands of their arch-rivals, put pressure on the Regent

Andronicus; and Andronicus refused outright to give up the island. With the agreement that he had so recently made now null and void, John found himself in an impossible position. Lacking sufficient funds to enable him to leave the lagoon, he was effectively a prisoner in Venice. He sent a desperate appeal to his son, suggesting that he might sell some ecclesiastical property or even Church treasures to secure his release; but Andronicus professed himself shocked by so impious a suggestion and raised not a finger to help him. Deliverance finally came through John's second son Manuel, whom he had recently appointed Governor of Thessalonica. Leaving the city in the depths of winter, Manuel hastened along the snow-covered Via Egnatia with gold and treasure enough to secure his father's release, as well as to provide collateral for a further loan. Thanks to him and to him alone, John was able to leave Venice in March 1371 with 30,000 ducats, together with provisions for his homeward journey. It took him seven months. He reached his capital only at the end of October, after a two-year absence during which, despite his conversion to the Roman Catholic faith, he had achieved precisely nothing.

There was more bad news awaiting him. The Turks in Europe, realizing that they were not yet ready to attack Constantinople, had wheeled about and advanced into Macedonia. King Vukashin – the most powerful of the Serbian rulers among whom the Empire of Stephen Dushan was now divided – and his brother John Uglesha, Despot of Serres, had hurriedly mobilized a joint force and marched to meet them; and on 26 September 1371 the two armies had met at Chernomen on the river Maritsa, some twenty miles west of Adrianople. It was the first pitched battle since the Turkish invasion of Europe; and it ended in the total destruction of the Serbian army. Both Vukashin and John Uglesha were killed, and the river ran red with the blood of their slaughtered followers.

Here was a disaster not only for the Serbs, but for Byzantium and indeed for the whole of Christendom. No longer was there any barrier to keep the invaders from overrunning Serbia, Macedonia and Greece. The few surviving members of the Serbian nobility were not altogether dispossessed; henceforth, however, they would be mere vassals of their Turkish overlords, bound to recognize the suzerainty of the Ottoman Sultan (as Murad now styled himself), to pay him tribute and – the ultimate humiliation – to lend him military assistance on demand. Curiously enough, one of these vassals – Vukashin's son Marko

Kralyevich[1] – was to become the greatest of Serbian folk heroes, whose name is still remembered and regularly invoked during his people's all-too-frequent periods of military crisis.[2]

Where Byzantium itself was concerned, there was one small consolation: Manuel Palaeologus had taken advantage of the situation by riding out from his base at Thessalonica and occupying the territories of Uglesha, including the city of Serres itself. But he was not to hold them for long, and meanwhile his father had been obliged by the steadily worsening financial situation to appropriate one half of the monastic property in what was left of the Empire. It was made clear to the monasteries that their lands would be returned to them if the situation improved; but the situation did not improve. On the contrary, the government was soon afterwards forced to take still more stringent measures, while John himself became progressively more defeatist. By 1373 he had become a Turkish vassal, as had the Bulgarian Tsar; thus it was that within twenty years of the first permanent Ottoman settlement on European soil, the three chief powers in the Balkan peninsula were all dependencies of the Sultan.

Since contemporary sources, such as they are, are silent on the subject, the terms of John V's compact with Murad are not altogether clear. Negotiations between them seem to have begun towards the end of 1372, about a year after the Emperor's return, and to have reached fruition two or three months later. John's motive was probably sheer despair. With the Turks in control of both Serbia and Bulgaria, any effective Crusade – always unlikely – was impossible. Byzantium, now completely cut off by land from the West, could no longer put up even a show of resistance. Only by joining forces with the Sultan could John perhaps hope to save something from the wreckage of his Empire. Murad might at least bring the wandering bands of Turkish marauders in Macedonia and Thrace under some sort of control; he might also

---

1 The Serbian language is unique among those using the Cyrillic script in having a recognized letter-for-letter system of transliteration, since Croatian – which is essentially the same tongue, as close as American is to English – uses the Latin alphabet. It might therefore be more scholarly to use this system for Serbian proper names; but this would mean writing Dušan, Uglješa, Kraljević, etc., which the average reader would find a lot more bewildering.

2 'Prodigiously strong, he carried for weapon a mace weighing sixty pounds of iron, thirty pounds of silver and nine pounds of gold. His horse, Piebald, was the fleetest in the world and understood the human tongue; and from one side of its saddle swung the mace and from the other a counterweight of red wine in a skin, for Marko was a hard drinker though he was never drunk.' Rebecca West, *Black Lamb and Grey Falcon*, Vol. ii, pp. 167–8.

strengthen John's own hand against his son Andronicus, who was causing him increasing anxiety.

But vassalage also involved disagreeable duties; and in May 1373 – within a few months of the signing of the agreement – John found himself in Anatolia, campaigning at the Sultan's side. This in itself must have been humiliation enough; but soon word reached him from the capital that Andronicus (who probably resented his father's growing attachment to Manuel) had taken advantage of his absence to come out in open revolt – allying himself, curiously enough, with Murad's own discontented son Sauji, who had also taken up arms against his father. Fortunately the insurrection was unsuccessful: the rebels were both quickly brought to heel. The furious Sultan had Sauji blinded – the wretched youth died soon after – and demanded that the Emperor insist on a similar penalty, both for Andronicus and his young son, who had taken no part in the revolt. John, much as he hated the brutality, knew that he could not refuse; he did, however, secretly arrange for some mercy to be shown to the victims. They did not entirely lose their sight but were imprisoned in Constantinople, Andronicus being formally deprived of his right to the succession. His position as heir-apparent was taken by Manuel, now twenty-three years old, who was hastily summoned from Thessalonica and, on 25 September, crowned co-Emperor.

Only three years later, John had cause to regret his forbearance. In March 1376, a squadron of ten Venetian ships arrived in Constantinople, carrying ambassadors from the Doge. With Andronicus out of the way, they pointed out, there was no reason why the agreement reached in Venice six years before should not now be implemented. In return for the cession of Tenedos, the Venetians were willing to make a further payment of 30,000 ducats and to return the crown jewels. They would also guarantee freedom of worship to the population of the island, whose Greek element would remain under the authority of the Patriarch of Constantinople. Finally, they promised, the imperial standard would continue to fly over the island, alongside the banner of St Mark.

John Palaeologus was only too happy to agree; as was to be expected, however, the Genoese colony in Constantinople felt very differently. Once again, they were determined to prevent the passing of Tenedos into Venetian hands; once again, their thoughts turned to their ally Andronicus. In July 1376 they somehow contrived to engineer his escape from prison. Ferried secretly across to Galata, he made contact with Murad, who – perhaps surprisingly in the circumstances – provided him with a mixed force of cavalry and infantry; then, after a month's siege, he bludgeoned his way into the capital. John and the rest of his family were able to hold out for a few days in the fortress of the Golden Gate, but they were soon forced to surrender; Andronicus had the pleasure of consigning them to the dungeons in the Tower of Anemas[1] that he himself had so recently left. One of his first actions after his assumption of power – it had probably been a condition of his escape – was to make a formal grant of Tenedos to Genoa. A year later, on 18 October 1377, he had himself crowned as Andronicus IV and his little son as his co-Emperor, John VII.

But the Genoese never received their reward. The Byzantine Governor of Tenedos refused to surrender the island to them – though he was happy to yield it shortly afterwards to the Venetians, who immediately sent a fleet to claim what they understandably believed was their due. To show his good faith, Andronicus was obliged to support a Genoese attempt to recover it by force – 'for which purpose', wrote Demetrius Cydones, 'he is preparing munitions and ships and is compelled to hire soldiers, a thing which is for him more difficult than flying'[2] – but the attempt was predictably unsuccessful. Sultan Murad was more fortunate. He had no love for Andronicus, for whom he had only recently recommended blinding; and he had supported him in his later insurrection on one condition, which was immediately fulfilled – the restitution of Gallipoli, captured by Amadeus of Savoy ten years before. By the end of 1377 this all-important bridgehead was once again in his possession; once again his dominions in Europe were united with those in Asia Minor, immeasurably strengthening his position for the next stage of his advance.

The captive Emperors, father and son, languished for three years in the Tower of Anemas. How they regained their liberty is not entirely clear. The initiative seems to have been their own, although it is possible that the Venetians were implicated in much the same way as the Genoese had assisted the escape of Andronicus. In any case they somehow managed to escape across the Bosphorus to the only refuge available to them, Murad's camp near Chrysopolis. Once there, Manuel – who seems to have done the negotiating – promised the Sultan, in return for the reinstatement of himself and his father, an increased tribute, additional

---

1 The ruins of this building, which had been one of the city's darkest and most dreaded prisons since the days of Alexius Comnenus three hundred years before, still survive at the northern end of the Land Walls, where it adjoined the Palace of Blachernae.

2 *Letters*, No. 167. Quoted (as is the epigraph to this chapter, which is taken from the same letter) by Professor Nicol, op. cit., pp. 290–91.

military assistance as necessary and, most humiliating of all, the city of Philadelphia, the last remaining Byzantine outpost in Asia Minor. Agreement was quickly reached. The Turks provided an army; the Venetians, only too happy to be rid of the incurably pro-Genoese Andronicus, sent a small fleet; and on 1 July 1379 John V and Manuel II re-entered their capital by the Charisius Gate. Andronicus fled in his turn – to his Genoese friends in Galata, taking with him as hostages his mother the Empress Helena and her father the monk Joasaph, the former John VI, both of whom he suspected of complicity in arranging for John's and Manuel's escape.

For the next year there was civil war between John and Andronicus, Constantinople and Galata – supported respectively by the Venetians and the Genoese. The Sultan's position was more doubtful: ostensibly he too backed the legitimate Emperors, but it was greatly in his own interest to see the Byzantines divided among themselves, and he may well have given covert help to Andronicus from time to time, if only to keep the hostilities going. The fortress of Galata suffered a long and painful siege, and the fighting continued for nearly two years: not until April 1381 did the warring factions reach an agreement. By its terms Andronicus was reinstated as heir to the throne, with his son John to succeed him, and meanwhile granted a small appanage on the northern coast of the Marmara with its capital at Selymbria and including the cities of Panidus, Rhaedestum and Heraclea.

Manuel was away on campaign with Murad at the time that this agreement was reached, and his reaction to it is not recorded. He more than anyone had deserved well of his father: he had bought him – and brought him – back from Venice, shared his captivity in Constantinople and, in marked contrast to his brother, had always fought loyally at his side. Having been formally granted the right of succession eight years previously, he had good reason to resent its withdrawal, particularly in such circumstances. But he was anyway angry, unable to forgive his father's craven defeatism. He was perfectly prepared to fight, if he had to, for the Sultan against Murad's Muslim enemies in Anatolia; but he refused absolutely to accept the Turkish claim to the Balkan peninsula, which he still believed it was possible to defend. In the autumn of 1382 he returned to Thessalonica – no longer, however, as Governor in John's name but defiantly, as an Emperor in his own right, determined to have no more truck with this constant family bickering which served only to waste men, money and materials that should have been employed against the infidel invaders. It was fortunate indeed for him when – after one last insurrection against his father – the insufferable Andronicus IV died in June 1385, leaving him once again the legitimate co-inheritor of what was left of Byzantium.

The year 1381, that had seen the end of this most recent outbreak of internecine strife, also brought to a close another, longer conflict – that between Venice and Genoa. Starting with the dispute over Tenedos, this contest had soon become generalized; and its last round had been fought on Italian soil and in Italian waters – the Tyrrhenian, the Adriatic and even in the Venetian lagoon itself. By now, however, the heat had gone out of the war, and the two exhausted republics gratefully accepted the offer of Count Amadeus of Savoy to mediate. Neither had won; after four years of devastation and bloodshed, both found themselves politically very much where they had been before – a situation confirmed by the Treaty of Turin, signed on 23 August, which provided for the continuation of trade in the Mediterranean and the Levant by both republics side by side. As for Tenedos, it would be neutral ground, its fortifications razed, its population transferred to Crete and Euboea, its neutrality guaranteed by Amadeus himself. Finally, as an earnest of their good intentions, both Venice and Genoa promised to do everything in their power to bring about the conversion of the Roman Empire to the Catholic Faith.

But what was this Empire? If the truth be told, it was in fact no longer an Empire at all. Rather was it a group of four small states, ruled by four so-called Emperors and a Despot. After 1383 each of these was a member of the house of Palaeologus, but each remained effectively independent of the other three, if not of his Turkish overlords. John V continued to reign in Constantinople, though now as a vassal of the Ottoman Sultan and as little more than a plaything of Venice and Genoa; Andronicus IV – until his death – with his son and co-Emperor John VII, both of them still more dependent on Turkish favour, ruled over the north shore of the Marmara; Manuel II governed Thessalonica; while Theodore I, John V's fourth son, held sway over the Despotate of the Morea, with his capital at Mistra.

This last appointment needs a little explanation. For over thirty years southern Greece had been administered, with signal success, by John VI's son Manuel Cantacuzenus; but when Manuel had died without issue in 1380 John V had decided to appoint his son Theodore in his place. The old ex-Emperor, who was still recovering from the privations he had suffered as a hostage during the long and arduous siege of Galata, had raised no objection, and had even decided to settle at Mistra himself;[1] but one of his grandsons, who regarded the Despotate as his family's legal appanage, had enlisted the help of both the Turks and the local Latin princes to fight for it on his behalf. Eventually Theodore had managed to establish himself as ruler, though he too was obliged to accept Turkish vassalage; and from that time forward he was to make the Morea the strongest and most prosperous bastion of a tottering Byzantium.

On all other fronts, that Empire was disintegrating fast. From his base at Thessalonica Manuel Palaeologus, still in pursuit of his dream of re-establishing Byzantine authority over Macedonia and Thessaly, was fighting a determined rearguard action, and in the summer and autumn of 1383 scored several encouraging victories against the invaders – so encouraging indeed as to cause his terrified father serious embarrassment in his diplomatic dealings with the Sultan. But such triumphs were of little real value against the Ottoman flood. Advancing up the Vardar river, a formidable force of Turks – swelled now by many regiments from the conquered Christian lands – had already captured Ochrid and Prilep in 1380 before pushing north-west into Albania. Further to the east, another of Murad's armies overran Bulgaria, taking Sardica in 1385 and advancing in the following year as far as Nish. In 1386 the monasteries of Mount Athos also made their joint submission to the Sultan. There remained only Thessalonica, and Thessalonica itself was now in grave danger. Serres, a mere seventy miles away, had fallen in September 1383, and as soon as its conquerors had had enough of the rapine and plunder that followed their conquest it was inevitable that they should have turned their attention to the last great Christian city that stood between themselves and Constantinople. In mid-October the Turkish general Khaireddin – 'Torch of the Faith' – who was also the Sultan's Grand Vizier, issued an ultimatum to the Thessalonians: surrender or massacre. Manuel Palaeologus acted at once. Summoning his subjects to an assembly in the main square he exhorted them, in a long and moving speech, to resist the infidel with all the strength at their command; then he began work on the defences.

Thessalonica had survived so long only because Murad's lack of naval power had made it impossible for him to set up an effective blockade. Nothing, therefore, would have been easier for the princes of Christian Europe than to have sent the beleaguered city reinforcements and

---

1 It was there that he was to die, aged seventy-eight, on 15 June 1383.

supplies by sea. Had they done so it could have survived almost indefinitely, and Manuel and Theodore together might even have united northern Greece and saved it from the Sultan. But no help came, and as the months went by the Emperor saw that he was gradually losing the support of his own people, more and more of whom began openly advocating surrender. Despite this widespread defeatism he managed to hold out for three and a half years; but with the coming of spring in 1387 the general morale had sunk to the point where it was plain that continued resistance was impossible. He himself however still refused to submit; and on 6 April, cursing the Thessalonians for their fecklessness and pusillanimity, he sailed away to Lesbos and left them to their fate. Three days later they opened the gates, thereby escaping the bloodshed and pillage which they would inevitably have suffered had they fought on to the end.

The three years that followed the fall of Thessalonica were perhaps the saddest of Manuel's life. His great campaign had failed; he had been betrayed by his Thessalonian subjects; his father's policy of appeasement had been proved right. A further humiliation awaited him at Lesbos, where Francesco Gattilusio refused to allow him entrance to the city of Mitylene and he and his followers were obliged to pitch their camp in the fields, under the scorching summer sun. From there he moved on to another scarcely more hospitable island – probably Tenedos – and thence, at the instigation of a Turkish embassy sent specially to him with messages of friendship, to the Ottoman court at Brusa. His first encounter with the Sultan since the failure of his campaign in Serbia and Macedonia and the loss of Thessalonica must have been painful indeed, marking as it did his own admission of defeat and the end of all his hopes for a successful Christian counter-offensive in the Balkans. But Murad gave him a warm welcome and showed him every courtesy, pressing him insistently to return to Constantinople and make his peace with his father.

Now that Manuel had given up the struggle, there was indeed no reason why the two Emperors should not settle their differences; but John V – whose only aim was to keep the Sultan well-disposed towards Byzantium in general and himself in particular – had been badly frightened by his son's disobedience and was determined that he must do some sort of penance before there could be any formal reconciliation. He therefore banished Manuel to the island of Lemnos; and Manuel – who was exhausted, deeply demoralized and anyway had nowhere else to go – seems to have accepted the sentence without complaint.

*

Manuel Palaeologus was still in exile on Lemnos when, in the summer of
1389, the Serbs made their last heroic attempt to shake off the Ottoman
yoke. After the disaster on the Maritsa it had seemed impossible that
they should ever fight as a nation again; and yet, weakened and divided
as they now were, with the glorious if short-lived Empire of Stephen
Dushan no more than a distant memory, a league of Serbian boyars
gathered together under the leadership of a certain Prince Lazar Hrebe-
lianovich, who had seized control of northern Serbia after the death of
Stephen Urosh V in 1371, to resist the Turkish advance. It included Vuk
Brankovich, ruler of the southern district of Kosovo, and was later also
joined by Tvrtko, Prince of Bosnia. Between 1386 and 1388, after the
Sultan had been obliged to return to Anatolia, this league had proved
remarkably successful, defeating the Turks in a number of skirmishes
and even in one or two pitched battles. But in 1389 Murad was back in
the Balkans, with several new regiments brought with him from Asia;
and in the early summer he advanced on the plain of Kosovo, 'the field
of blackbirds'.

The battle that followed on 15 June has entered Serbian folklore, and
has inspired, in The Kosovo Cycle, one of the greatest of all medieval
epics; Tsar Lazar – as he is always known – has joined Marko
Kralyevich as a hero of national legend. The true story, however, in so far
as it can be disentangled from that legend, is not particularly edifying.
Serbian morale was low. The princes were in disagreement among
themselves, and treason was widely hinted at: Lazar himself, in a speech
on the eve of the battle, openly accused his own son-in-law, Milosh
Obravich, of working for the enemy. Murad, on the other hand, though
he spent much of the night in prayer, was so confident of victory that he
had ordered that all castles, towns and villages in the region should be
spared; the castles he would need later, and he had no wish to antagonize
his future subjects unnecessarily.

Next morning, the Sultan drew up his army in its usual order. He
himself commanded the centre, with his crack regiment of Janissaries
and his personal guard of cavalry; on the right was his elder son Bayezit
with the European troops, on the left his younger son Yakub with the
regiments from Asia. To begin with, fortune was against them. Ignoring
an initial advance by two thousand Turkish archers, the Serbian cavalry
launched a massive charge that broke through the Turkish left flank.
But Bayezit immediately swung round and urged his men at full gallop
to the rescue, laying about him to left and right with his heavy iron
mace. After this counter-attack, the Turks gradually gained the upper

hand – though it was only after Vuk Brankovich fled the field towards the end of the day, taking with him twelve thousand of his men, that the surviving Serbs finally broke up in disorder and fled.

Whether or not Brankovich's treachery was the result of a secret compact with the Sultan will never be known; if there was one, Murad never lived to reveal it. Just how he met his death is also uncertain; it seems, however, to have been the work of Milosh Obravich, furious at the aspersions which had been publicly cast upon him by his father-in-law and determined to prove his loyalty. According to the most probable version of the story, he pretended to desert to the enemy and was brought before Murad; he made his formal obeisance and then, before the guard could prevent him, plunged a long dagger twice into the Sultan's breast – with such force, we are told, that the blade emerged at the back. He was immediately set upon and dispatched in his turn, but the deed was done. Murad's last act was to summon Lazar – who had been taken prisoner at an earlier stage in the battle – and condemn him to execution.

The report of the Sultan's murder spread to the West, where the battle was consequently at first thought to have ended in a major victory for Christendom; in Paris, a week or two later, King Charles VI went so far as to order a service of thanksgiving in Notre-Dame. Gradually, however, as more reports filtered through, the tragic truth became known. The Turks, under the brilliant leadership of their new Sultan, had carried the day; the Serbian army had been utterly destroyed. Of the few Serbian nobles who survived – they included Lazar's son Stephen Lazarevich – each was obliged to swear a personal oath of fealty to Bayezit. But the Serbian nation, even in its fragmented form, was no more. It was to be over four hundred years before it arose again.

Had Tsar Lazar and his fellow-boyars been able to unite seven years earlier, had they appealed to Manuel Palaeologus for assistance and had Manuel decided to throw in everything he had on one last heroic bid to stop the infidel once and for all, might the battle of Kosovo have ended differently? It is possible, but unlikely – and unlikelier still that even a victory for Christendom at that time and that place would have had any lasting effect on the future of the Balkan peninsula. In a year or two at the most the Turks would have been back, better armed, better provisioned and in greater numbers than before. Their manpower was virtually limitless: new regiments could be summoned from Anatolia in a matter of weeks, and even in Europe there were plenty of Christian mercenaries ready and willing to march against their co-religionists for good pay and a chance of plunder. The harsh truth was that, in the fourteenth and fifteenth centuries, the Ottoman armies were virtually unconquerable by anything less than a concerted European Crusade; and that such a Crusade, though frequently proposed and discussed, was never to come into being. Against so formidable a force, the Christian East had no hope; we can only wonder that it lasted as long as it did.

Bayezit's very first action, after his proclamation as Sultan on the field of Kosovo, had been to order the death of his brother and fellow-commander Yakub. Sentence was immediately carried out; the young Prince was garrotted with a bowstring. He had shown great courage in the battle and was much loved by his men, but for Bayezit these qualities only increased the likelihood of his one day stirring up sedition. Thus was instituted the terrible tradition of imperial fratricide – to be codified into law by Bayezit's great-grandson Mehmet II – which for the next three centuries was indelibly to stain the history of the Ottoman ruling house.[1]

The Sultan had started as he meant to go on. A man of almost superhuman energy, impetuous and unpredictable, as quick in taking decisions as he was in implementing them and utterly merciless to all who stood in his way, it was not for nothing that he was known by his subjects as *Yildirim*, the Thunderbolt. During his thirteen-year reign he was to prove himself an astute diplomat, as his father had been before him; but for Bayezit, unlike Murad, diplomacy had little instinctive appeal. He thought in terms of conquest, and of Empire. The simple title of Sultan was not enough; he now styled himself Sultan of Rum, the ancient formula that had been adopted by the Seljuk emirs three hundred years before to assert their dominion over 'Roman' Anatolia. To Bayezit however 'Rum' signified something more than it had to Alp Arslan and his successors. No longer did it mean simply the former Byzantine territories in Asia Minor; it now included the Second Rome itself – the city of Constantinople.

And – fortunately for the new Sultan – Constantinople was still torn between rival factions within the imperial family. The senior Emperor John V was still reigning from the Palace of Blachernae, and the

---

[1] To give but one example: Sultan Mehmet III, on his accession in 1595, had no fewer than nineteen of his brothers strangled, together with six pregnant slaves, their favourites from the harem. (Later he also killed his mother and his son, but that was not part of the tradition.)

unspeakable Andronicus IV was in his grave; but Andronicus's detestation of his father was fully shared by his own son John VII – who, having been careful to maintain the dynastic claims he had inherited, was at the time of the Kosovo battle actually in Genoa drumming up support for another insurrection. Returning shortly afterwards to the capital, he found messengers awaiting him from Bayezit; and on the night of 13 April 1390, with the aid of a small force put at his disposal by the Sultan, he succeeded in overturning John V for the second time, making his triumphal entry into the city the following morning. Once again the Emperor – together with Manuel, whom he had summoned back from Lemnos just a fortnight before, and a number of loyal followers – barricaded himself into the fortress of the Golden Gate[1] and, in an unwonted display of courage, settled down to withstand a siege.

Manuel, however, slipped away to seek assistance. His first two attempts to rescue his father were unsuccessful, but on 25 August he appeared with two galleys lent by the Knights of St John from their base in Rhodes, one each from Lemnos, Christopolis and (somewhat surprisingly) Constantinople, and four other smaller vessels of unknown provenance. Fortunately the Golden Gate stronghold was only a few yards from the Marmara, and possessed its own harbour into which the little fleet had no difficulty in forcing its way. Fighting continued for the next three weeks, but on Saturday, 17 September the old Emperor and his men made a sudden sally, taking his grandson completely off his guard and driving him out of the city.

Fully reconciled at last, John and Manuel returned triumphantly to the Palace of Blachernae. There was, however, a price to be paid for their success. The Sultan, away in Anatolia, looked upon the failure of his attempt to install John VII on the throne as not so much a political reverse as a personal insult. Furious, he demanded that Manuel should immediately join him on campaign, bringing with him all the tribute that was by now owing. A similar summons was sent to John VII, with whom he was almost as angry. In the circumstances the two men, despite their mutual detestation, could only obey; nor, that same autumn, could they refuse the Sultan's orders to take part in the siege of Philadelphia. And so it was that not one but two Emperors of the Romans found themselves directly instrumental in enforcing the

---

1 This probably formed the nucleus of the Fortress of the Seven Towers (Yediküle), which was much enlarged by Mehmet II after the conquest of the city and of which the ruins still stand today.

Bursa: the Green Tomb (Yeşil Türbe), the mausoleum of Sultan Mehmet I, d. 1421

Mistra, monastery of the Peribleptos: The Baptism of Christ, late fourteenth century

The Emperor Manuel II Palaeologus and his family, from the manuscript of St Denis

The Battle of Dorylaeum, 1097 (Paris, Bibliothèque Nationale)

Charles VI of France and Manuel II Palaeologus, 1400 (London, British Library)

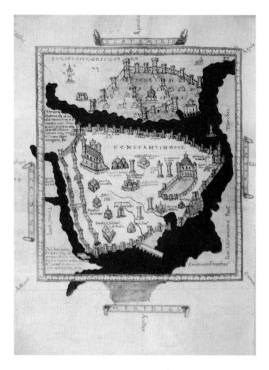

Map of Contantinople, sixteenth century (Chantilly, Musée Condé)

The Ottoman army at the siege of Constantinople, 1453,
fresco in the Moldovita Monastery, Romania, c.1537

The siege of Constantinople, 1453.
On the left, the Sultan's ships are being rolled down to the Golden Horn

Mehmet II, by Gentile Bellini
(London, National Gallery)

The Vatican, Borgia Apartments: The Dispute of St Catherine of Alexandria with
the Philosophers before the Emperor Maximinus, by Pinturicchio.
The white-turbanned figure to the right of the Emperor is
a portrait of Andrew Palaeologus, Despot of the Morea

capitulation of the last surviving Byzantine stronghold in Asia Minor.[1] Of all the many humiliations inflicted on the dying Empire, this was surely the most ironical.

Soon afterwards Bayezit sent John V another still more peremptory ultimatum. The fortress of the Golden Gate – which, in the previous year, had saved his crown if not his life – was to be demolished. Failure to obey would result in the immediate imprisonment and blinding of Manuel, who was still being held at the Sultan's camp. Once again the poor Emperor had no choice but to comply; it was, however, the last indignity that he was called upon to suffer. With the coming of winter he retired to his private apartments, where he took to his bed and turned his face to the wall. He died on 16 February 1391, aged fifty-eight.

He had reigned as *basileus* – if we date that reign from his coronation in November 1341 – just a few months short of half a century, the longest reign of any Emperor in the eleven-hundred-year history of Byzantium. Even if we consider it to have begun only after the abdication of John Cantacuzenus in 1354, it had lasted nearly thirty-seven years, a period matched by Alexius I and Manuel I Comnenus but exceeded only by his great-grandfather Andronicus II and by Constantine VII Porphyrogenitus in the tenth century. It was, by any standards, too long. At one of the most desperate moments of its history, the Empire was governed by a ruler who was neither intelligent nor far-sighted, and who possessed virtually none of those qualities necessary to a successful statesman. Already as early as 1355, when he had made his extraordinary proposals to Pope Innocent, he had shown a barely credible lack of political understanding; thereafter, again and again, we find him giving way to the sudden impulse, almost always with disastrous results. Would any of his predecessors, one wonders, have decided to embark on a vitally important diplomatic mission to Hungary – involving a long and arduous journey in mid-winter – without taking any advance soundings as to how he would be received or what were his chances of success? Would any but he have sailed so impetuously off to Venice, fully aware that he was heavily in debt to the Republic but apparently oblivious of the fact that if the negotiations failed he would not even have enough money to return home? Did any other have to be rescued on four separate occasions – once on the Bulgarian border, once in Venice and twice in his own capital of Constantinople? Such humiliations as these,

1 See p. 339. Had John V and Manuel retracted their promise of 1378? Or had the people of Philadelphia simply refused to submit to the Sultan? We shall never know.

largely self-inflicted as they were, brought John not so much pity as ridicule – and did his reputation far more harm in the eyes of Western Europe than those which he suffered at the hands of the Ottoman Sultan.

John V's passive obedience to his Turkish suzerains forms a dramatic contrast, too, to the aggressive policies of his early years. By the end, admittedly, he was powerless: unable even to protest against the treatment accorded to him, far less to resist it. And yet – the issue cannot be altogether avoided – did his record have to be quite so unedifying? Could he not have sent a regiment or two to support those gallant Serbs who fought, so bravely and against such odds, at the Maritsa and on the plains of Kosovo? Of course not, he might have replied, and anyway look what happened to them; was this really the time for suicidal heroics? And was he not in any case the sworn vassal of the Sultan? The argument is unanswerable, but the questions persist: how would Basil the Macedonian have dealt with the situation, or his namesake the Bulgar-Slayer? What would Alexius Comnenus have done in similar circumstances, or his son John II, or even Michael Palaeologus? Would they all have been as craven as John V?

Somehow, one feels, they would not. Would they, on the other hand, have left the Empire in any better state? It seems improbable. By the last decade of the fourteenth century the Ottoman conquest of eastern Europe and Asia Minor had acquired a momentum that it was no longer possible to check. Of the Sultan's Christian enemies, Serbia and Bulgaria had been effectively annihilated. Only Byzantium remained; but it was a Byzantium so reduced, so impoverished, so humiliated and demoralized as to be scarcely identifiable as the glorious Empire of the Romans that it had once been. And yet, doomed as it was, it was never to give up the struggle. Three more Christian Emperors were to reign in Constantinople, all three of them men of determination and spirit. Thanks to them, it was to last another six decades – and, at the end, to go down fighting.

21

The Appeal to Europe

[1391–1402]

Shut the gates of the city and govern within it, for everything beyond the walls is mine.

Sultan Bayezit to Manuel II

Within days of his accession, Manuel II showed his mettle. There was, he knew, a serious danger that Bayezit, as Byzantium's suzerain, might appoint his nephew John VII as *basileus*; and this was a risk that he could not possibly accept. When the news of his father's death reached him he was still a hostage of the Sultan, who had returned to his capital at Brusa. At once he began to make his plans, and on the night of 7 March 1391 he slipped out of the camp and made his way secretly to the coast, where a ship was waiting to take him across the Marmara to Constantinople.

He was welcomed in the capital with enthusiasm. For the late Emperor there was little mourning. If John V had ever enjoyed the respect of his subjects – he had certainly never known their love – that respect had long since been forfeited. Unimpressive both as a ruler and as a man, he had for the past quarter-century adopted an increasingly subservient attitude to the Sultan. In the West, he had made the Empire an object of ridicule and contempt. Worst of all, he had betrayed the Orthodox Church, of which he should have been the mainstay. To all this Manuel II presented a refreshing contrast. Now in the prime of life – at the time of his accession he was not quite forty-one – in appearance he was every inch an Emperor: Bayezit himself had once observed that his imperial blood was recognizable from his bearing alone, even to those seeing him for the first time. He enjoyed perfect health and possessed apparently boundless energy; in short, he seemed to be far less the offspring of his father than of his grandfather. Though not, alas, a chronicler like John Cantacuzenus – would that he had been, since our sources for this desperate period of Byzantine history are once again lamentably few – he

349

shared with him both a deep love of literature and the traditional Byzantine passion for theology; Demetrius Cydones regularly hails him in his letters as 'the philosopher Emperor'. Nothing gave him greater pleasure than the composition of essays and dissertations on matters of Christian doctrine, the more abstruse the better. He remained, however, a man of action. Twice, in 1371 and again in 1390, he had come to the rescue of his increasingly incapable father, on both occasions with complete success. In happier times he might have been a great ruler.

But the existing situation left little scope for greatness. The Emperor was now but a weak and virtually helpless vassal of the Ottoman Sultan; and the Sultan, who would probably have preferred to see the far more amenable John VII on the throne of Constantinople, had been outraged by the quiet deliberation with which Manuel had assumed it without his authority. His reaction was to inflict two more humiliations on the hapless Byzantines. The first was to set aside a whole area of the city for Turkish merchants, who would be no longer subject to imperial law but whose affairs would be regulated by a *qadi*, or judge, appointed by himself. The second – in May 1391, only two months after Manuel's accession as sole Emperor – was to summon him once again to Anatolia to take part in yet another of his campaigns, this time to the Black Sea coast – a feudal obligation distasteful enough in itself, but made considerably more so by the company of John VII (to whom he could still hardly bring himself to speak) and by the sadness and devastation of the country through which they marched. He wrote to his friend Cydones:

The plain [where we are encamped] is deserted, as a result of the flight of its inhabitants to the woods and the caves and the mountain-tops as they tried to flee from what they are unable to escape: a slaughter that is inhuman and savage and without any formality of justice. No one is spared – neither women nor children, nor the sick, nor the aged . . .

There are many cities in these regions, but they lack the one thing without which they can never be true cities; they have no people . . . And when I ask the names of the cities, the answer is always 'we have destroyed these places and time has destroyed their names' . . .

What is indeed unbearable for me is that I am fighting beside these people when to add to their strength is to diminish our own.[1]

---

1 The letters are quoted at length by J. W. Barker (op. cit., pp. 88–96). The translations are basically his, but shortened and simplified in order to spare the reader the infuriating convolutions of Manuel's literary style.

The Emperor was back in Constantinople by the middle of January 1392, and on Saturday, 10 February he took to himself a bride. She was Helena, daughter of Constantine Dragash, the Serbian Prince of Serres – like himself, a vassal of the Sultan. The marriage was followed the next day by a joint coronation. For Manuel this was not strictly necessary – he had already been crowned nineteen years before – but he believed with good reason that such a ceremony, performed with the full Orthodox ritual and as much pomp and display as could be managed, would provide the best possible tonic to his subjects' morale. It would remind them, too, of what Byzantium stood for: of that astonishing continuity with which Emperor had succeeded Emperor without a break – even though occasionally in exile – for thirteen centuries since the days of ancient Rome; of the fact that, whatever dangers he himself might be facing, whatever occasional indignities he might be called upon to suffer, he remained supreme among the princes of Christendom, Equal of the Apostles, God's own anointed Vice-Gerent on earth.

This was the message that went out to the vast congregation on that cold February day in St Sophia, as Patriarch Antonius slowly lowered the imperial diadem on to the head of the *basileus* and Manuel himself then crowned his consort in her turn. At that moment, as the mosaics glinted gold in the candlelight, the clouds of incense curled up to the spreading dome above and the coronation anthem echoed through the Great Church, it hardly seemed to matter that the true regalia were still in pawn to the Venetians; or that the Emperor whose semi-divinity was being so loftily extolled had in fact returned only a month before from a campaign on behalf of the infidel Sultan; or that that Sultan, already the master of nearly all eastern Europe, was even now at the gates of the capital. Such ignoble considerations certainly did not occur to the Archimandrite Ignatius of Smolensk, who has left an ecstatic account of the proceedings he was fortunate enough to witness; still less do they appear to have troubled the anonymous Byzantine eye-witness who describes with almost equal enthusiasm the solemn state with which the newly-crowned pair returned to the palace, their horses' bridles held by the caesars, despots and *sebastocrators*, before showing themselves enthroned to their cheering subjects.

For a year and a half after his coronation Manuel was left in comparative peace; but in July 1393 a serious insurrection in Bulgaria against the Sultan brought swift retribution, and the following winter Bayezit called his principal Christian vassals to his camp at Serres. Apart from the

Emperor himself, they included his brother Theodore, Despot of the Morea, his father-in-law Constantine Dragash, his nephew John VII and the Serbian Stephen Lazarevich. None of them knew, however, that the others had been summoned also: only when they were all assembled did they realize how completely they had put themselves in the Sultan's power. Manuel himself was convinced that a general massacre had been intended, and that Bayezit had countermanded his own orders only after the eunuch entrusted with the executions – who may well have been Ali Pasha, the son of Khaireddin, conqueror of Thessalonica – had refused or somehow prevaricated. Here, in short, was yet another example of his suzerain's mercurial changes of mood, when he would instantaneously switch from blind and savage fury to displays of almost exaggerated kindness and courtesy:

First he showed his anger by the outrages he committed against our followers, gouging out their eyes and cutting off their hands . . . and when in this fashion he had assuaged his unreasonable spirit, thereafter he very simple-mindedly attempted to make his peace with me – whom he was injuring and had dishonoured with myriad injustices – greeting me with gifts and then sending me home, just as children who weep after being punished are soothed with sweetmeats.

What better proof was there that the Sultan was by now emotionally unstable, and consequently more dangerous than ever? Eventually, after giving his vassals further grim warnings of the consequences of any future disobedience, he let them go – apart from Theodore, who was obliged to accompany him on campaign to Thessaly and was there put under severe pressure to yield Monemvasia, Argos and several other fortresses in the Peloponnese. The luckless Despot undertook to comply; fortunately, however, he escaped soon afterwards to his own territory, where he immediately rescinded his promises. Manuel meanwhile, still shaken by what he believed till the end of his life to have been a narrow escape from death, returned with all speed to Constantinople.

Soon afterwards he received yet another summons from Bayezit. This time he flatly refused. His experience at Serres had driven him to an inescapable conclusion: the days of appeasement were over. Such a policy might have succeeded with Murad – who, despite occasional bouts of savagery, had been an essentially reasonable man with whom civilized discussions were possible. Bayezit, on the other hand, had shown himself to be unbalanced and deeply untrustworthy. Manuel's first instincts had been right after all. The sole chance of survival was in resistance. Meanwhile, however, he had no delusions as to the momentousness of the decision he had taken. His refusal of the Sultan's summons would be interpreted as an act of open defiance, a casting-off of his former vassalage – in effect, a declaration of war.

One consideration only enabled him to contemplate such a step: however determined Bayezit might be to annihilate him, however great the Turkish army or formidable their siege engines, he still believed in the impregnability of Constantinople. On both occasions that the city had fallen to armed force – in 1203 and again in 1204, during the Fourth Crusade – the attacks had been launched from the sea, against the relatively inferior fortifications which ran along the shore of the Golden Horn. Such an operation would be impossible for Bayezit, who was still without an effective navy. He could attack only by land, from the west, and despite the recent demolition of the fortress by the Golden Gate the Land Walls were as strong as ever they had been. They had stood for almost a thousand years; the Byzantines had long since lost count of the number of would-be conquerors who had turned away from them, furious and frustrated at their own impotence and often without loosing a single arrow.

Manuel was soon able to put his theory to the test. In the spring of 1394 an immense Turkish army marched against Constantinople, and by the beginning of autumn the siege had begun in earnest. The Sultan had ordered a complete blockade, and although an occasional vessel managed to run the gauntlet – notably a Venetian merchantman which arrived early in 1395 with a much-needed shipment of grain – for some time essential supplies ran desperately short. All the land outside the walls – anyway inaccessible to the inhabitants – had been laid waste; the only areas available for cultivation were the plots and gardens within the city itself. Many a cottage was demolished for the sake of the resulting firewood, so that the bakers could bake their bread. Fortunately for the citizens, however, the situation gradually eased. The blockade was not lifted – it was to continue in one form or another for eight years, during which spasmodic attacks continued to be made on the walls – but gradually, as the ever-unpredictable Bayezit lost interest in the siege and involved himself in other operations that offered more immediate rewards, the pressure in some degree relaxed. At last Manuel was able to devote some of his time to diplomacy – for, he was well aware, without foreign alliances his Empire could have no long-term prospects of survival.

John VI had not been the only *basileus* in the past century to have discovered, to his cost, just how difficult it was to persuade the princes of the West of what should have been a self-evident truth: that the dangers now faced by Byzantium constituted an almost equal threat to themselves. In the last decade of the fourteenth century, however, the advances of the Turks across the Balkans had begun to cause them genuine anxiety. Bulgaria finally fell with the capture of its capital, Trnovo, in July 1393; so, over the next two years, did Thessaly. Further south, in Attica and the Morea, the already confused situation had been still further complicated by the irruption, some twenty years before, of a company of adventurers from Navarre. They had made themselves sworn enemies of the Despot Theodore, as well as of the Acciajuoli family who had recently captured Athens from the Catalans; before long the whole area was up in arms, and the veteran Turkish general Evrenos-Beg saw his chance. Defeating Theodore below the walls of Corinth, with the enthusiastic help of the Navarrese he smashed his way into the Morea and seized two Byzantine fortresses in the very heart of the Despotate. Then on 17 May 1395 Prince Mircea the Elder of Wallachia, supported by Louis the Great's son-in-law King Sigismund of Hungary, did battle against the Turks at Rovine. Several Serbian princes fought as vassals on the side of the Sultan, among them Stephen Lazarevich, the legendary hero Marko Kralyevich and Manuel's own father-in-law, Constantine Dragash; and though the struggle was inconclusive it resulted in Mircea's being obliged in his turn to accept Turkish suzerainty.

All these events made a deep impression in the West. Sigismund, whose Kingdom was the most immediately affected, made a general appeal to the princes of Christendom; and this time the princes responded. So also did the two rival Popes, Boniface IX in Rome and Benedict XIII in Avignon. The knighthood of France was particularly inspired by the prospect of what had now, thanks to the Popes, become a Crusade; no fewer than ten thousand, together with another six thousand from Germany, joined Sigismund's sixty thousand Hungarians and the ten thousand Wallachians raised by Mircea. Another fifteen thousand came from Italy, Spain, England, Poland and Bohemia. Manuel himself – though he had concluded a formal agreement with Sigismund in February 1396 and had promised to arm ten galleys – was prevented by the blockade from making any strategic contribution; but the Genoese in Lesbos and Chios took responsibility for the mouth of the Danube and the Black Sea coast, as did the Knights of Rhodes. Even Venice –

after long hesitation, waiting as always to see how her own best interests were most likely to be served – sent a small fleet to patrol the Hellespont and keep open the vital lines of communication between the crusading army and Constantinople.

This immense force – it almost certainly numbered over a hundred thousand men – gathered in Buda and set off in August 1396 down the valley of the Danube. By definition, Crusades are hampered from the outset by an excess of religious enthusiasm: the ardent young knights saw themselves as heroes of an earlier age of chivalry, driving all before them to the very doors of the Holy Sepulchre. Were heaven itself to fall, they boasted, they could support it on the points of their lances. Sigismund's continued efforts to impose discipline and caution were in vain. The expedition began well enough, when the Bulgar Prince Stracimir, ignoring his oath of vassalage to the Sultan, opened the gates of Vidin; but further downstream at Rahova a pointless massacre of the local inhabitants boded ill for the future. A month or so after their departure the Crusaders reached Nicopolis, to which they immediately laid siege; and it was there that the Sultan – living up once again to his nickname of the Thunderbolt – caught up with them.

On the morning of Monday, 25 September a group of French knights, spotting what appeared to be a small detachment of Turkish cavalry at the top of a nearby hill, galloped forward to the attack. Unfortunately for them, Bayezit's army was drawn up out of sight in the valley behind. Suddenly the Frenchmen saw that they were surrounded. The Turks made short work of them, then charged down the hill and fell upon the rest of the Crusader army, which was taken completely by surprise. What followed was a massacre. Among those captured the French leader, Count John of Nevers, was spared because of his rank: being the son of the Duke of Burgundy, he could be trusted to fetch a good ransom. A number of other prisoners were equally lucky. The rest – some ten thousand of them – were beheaded in the Sultan's presence. Those who escaped – they included Sigismund himself and Philibert de Naillac, Grand Master elect of the Knights of St John – managed to find Venetian ships to take them back to the West; a German eye-witness, who had been taken captive but whose extreme youth had somehow saved him from execution, tells of how, as these vessels passed through the Dardanelles, he and three hundred other surviving prisoners were drawn up on the banks and made to jeer at the conquered King.[1]

1 Johann Schiltberger, Hakluyt Society, Vol. lviii, 1879.

In its own curious way, the depressing expedition known to history as the Crusade of Nicopolis proved to be something of a milestone. Not only was it the last of the great international Crusades;[1] it was the first trial of strength between the Catholic nations of the West and the Ottoman Sultan. As such, it hardly augured well for the future.

The years 1395 and 1396 had provided the people of Constantinople with a period of relief. Bayezit had had other things on his mind; his blockade had been distinctly half-hearted, and it had been possible to bring substantial quantities of food and other supplies into the beleaguered city. By the first weeks of 1397, however, he was back – determined, if it refused to surrender, to take it by assault. Fortunately Manuel's faith in the Land Walls proved fully justified – so much so indeed that at one moment the Sultan seems to have cast an appraising eye on the far less impressive fortifications to the east of Galata; but here the Genoese and the Byzantines together, for once putting up a united front, successfully held the battlements against every attack. Refusing to give up his enterprise, Bayezit then turned his attention to the Bosphorus; and the defenders of Galata watched with consternation as a great castle rose on the opposite side – a castle that still in part survives and is nowadays known as Anadolu Hisar.[2]

More worrying for Manuel than any considerations of physical defence, however, was the state of morale within Constantinople. The city was once again sealed; supplies were fast diminishing, and reports of deaths from starvation increasingly common. Many of the poorer citizens in their desperation were slipping out of the city at night and making their way across the Bosphorus to the Asian shore, where they could expect food, shelter and a warm welcome from the Turks. It was an open secret, too, that the Sultan had repeatedly offered to raise both siege and blockade together if the people would agree to accept John VII as their rightful ruler. John had always had a body of supporters within the city, and there were probably many others too who felt, after nearly three years of hardship and deprivation, that the substitution of the nephew for the uncle would be a small price to pay for peace.

By the spring, the Emperor was becoming seriously alarmed. King

---

1 Unless we count the equally unsuccessful 'Crusade of Varna' of 1444; but that was on a far smaller scale. See pp. 404-6.

2 The ruined fortress that we see today includes extensions added by Mehmet II in 1452, when he was building the castle of Rumeli Hisar opposite.

Sigismund had promised another expedition, but it seemed increasingly unlikely that he would keep his word; and by March Manuel was making arrangements to entrust Constantinople to Venice if he were obliged to leave in a hurry. The Venetians for their part, on 7 April, dispatched three galleys to the city 'for the comfort of the Lord Emperor and' – a rare expression of consideration – 'of the Genoese of Pera [Galata]', indicating that they would be sending several more as soon as these could be prepared. In fact, however, such emergency measures were to prove unnecessary: the Emperor kept his nerve, and not long afterwards Bayezit, obliged at last to face the fact that the defences of Constantinople were indeed too strong for him, once again lost interest in the siege. But he did not abandon it altogether; though food supplies became a little easier, the people continued to suffer. A year and a half later, moreover, in September 1398, we find the Venetian Senate ordering its Captain of the Gulf to be ready to defend the city from a possible Turkish attack by sea from Gallipoli. As for Manuel himself, he remained under heavy pressure. Every hour of every day, Ducas tells us, he would murmur the same prayer:

O Lord Jesus Christ, let it not come about that the great multitude of Christian peoples should hear it said that it was during the days of the Emperor Manuel that the City, with all its holy and venerable monuments of the Faith, was delivered to the infidel.

Meanwhile, following the constantly-repeated advice of the Venetians, the Emperor redoubled his efforts to obtain aid from abroad. It was not an easy task; whatever Crusading flame might once have flickered among the rulers of Western Europe had been effectively snuffed out at Nicopolis. Manuel, however, saw things in a different light. For him the recent expedition, disastrous as it had been, had shown just what Christendom could achieve if only it was prepared to make the effort. Any new Crusade would obviously learn from past mistakes, and might well succeed where its predecessor had failed. In that event the Turks would be driven back into Asia, and the shadow that had hung for so long over eastern Europe might be lifted for ever. And so, in 1397 and 1398, imperial embassies set forth once again – to the Pope, to the Kings of England, France and Aragon and to to the Grand Duke of Muscovy, while similar delegations were sent by Patriarch Antonius to the King of Poland and the Metropolitan of Kiev.

In Rome Pope Boniface IX, still smarting from the humiliation of Nicopolis, was only too ready to do anything he could to eradicate what he saw as a serious stain on his reputation. With the possibility of Church union also ever-present in his mind, he promulgated two bulls – in April 1398 and March 1399 – calling upon the nations of the West to participate in a new Crusade or, failing that, to send financial contributions for the defence of Constantinople. Full indulgences were offered to those who answered the call; collecting boxes would be set up in all the churches. The response of King Charles VI of France, when an embassy led by the Emperor's uncle, Theodore Palaeologus Cantacuzenus, reached him in October 1397, was even more satisfactory. Only the year before, Charles had become overlord of Genoa[1] and its colonies – John VII had even tried to sell him his title to the Byzantine crown in return for 25,000 gold florins and a château in France – and he was consequently far from indifferent to the fate of the threatened city. Though unable to provide any immediate military assistance, he promised Theodore that he would do so at the earliest possible moment, giving him as an earnest of his good intentions the sum of 12,000 gold francs to take back to the Emperor.

The Byzantine delegation, reaching England in the summer of 1399, could hardly have arrived at a worse moment. Richard II was in Ireland through most of June and July, and returned to England to find the country up in arms against him. He was captured by Henry Bolingbroke (the future Henry IV) in August, formally deposed in September and almost certainly murdered – though it is just possible that he died of grief – the following February. His predicament was consequently a good deal graver even than Manuel's; yet somehow he found time to receive the Byzantine emissaries and to express his concern, giving his full approval for the proposed collection of funds – a contribution box was placed in St Paul's Cathedral – and ordering the immediate payment on account of 3,000 marks, or £2,000 sterling. (The entire sum was subsequently embezzled by a Genoese broker, but Richard can scarcely be blamed for that.)

Charles VI, on the other hand, proved as good as his word: he had undertaken to send a military force to the East, and in 1399 he did. It was led by the greatest French soldier of his day, Jean le Maingre, better known as Marshal Boucicault. The Marshal had fought three years

---

1 Soon after the peace of Turin, the governmental system of Genoa had begun to crumble. Torn asunder by factional strife, the Republic was to elect and depose ten Doges in five years, until in 1396 the Genoese voluntarily surrendered to a French domination which was to continue until 1409.

before at Nicopolis, where he had been captured and – nearly a year later – ransomed; and he longed for vengeance. Leaving Aigues-Mortes at the end of June with six vessels carrying some twelve hundred men, he made many stops along the way to do further recruiting and eventually, having smashed his way through the Turkish blockade of the Hellespont, reached Constantinople in September. Manuel gave him an enthusiastic welcome and named him Grand Constable, and together they took part in several minor operations on both sides of the Bosphorus. But Boucicault saw at once that none of this was of any real importance. An army that was to achieve anything worth while against the Turks would have to be on a far larger scale and could be obtained in one way only: the Emperor must himself make the journey to Paris and plead his cause in person before the French King.

Manuel asked nothing better, but there was a problem: who would look after the Empire in his absence? The obvious candidate was John VII, if only because if he selected anyone else John would be sure to reassert his claim to the throne; but uncle and nephew had not been on speaking terms for years. At this point Boucicault came into his own. He went straight to John at Selymbria and persuaded him to agree to a reconciliation. The two then returned together to Constantinople, where the family quarrel which had poisoned relations between the Palaeologi for twenty-five years was quickly healed. According to the terms of their agreement, John would act as Regent in Manuel's absence, and on his return would be granted Thessalonica. True, the city was then under Turkish occupation; but this state of affairs, it was confidently hoped, would prove to be only temporary.

And so, on 10 December 1399, the Emperor left Constantinople for the West, accompanied by Boucicault, the Empress Helena and their two small sons, the seven-year-old John and his brother Theodore, who was probably not more than four or five. The fact that he did not take them with him to France but settled them with his own brother in the Morea is a clear enough indication of his true feelings towards John VII; the reconciliation was all very well, but if the Regent did decide to make trouble there was at least no risk of his taking the imperial family hostage. And even then Manuel's mind was not entirely at rest: what if Bayezit should launch a sudden attack on the Peloponnese? The first weeks of 1400 were taken up with planning for the possible escape of his wife and children and their refuge in the Venetian ports of Modone and Corone. Only after their future was absolutely assured did he set sail for Venice, where he and Boucicault arrived in April.

There the two separated, the Marshal travelling straight on to Paris to prepare for the Emperor's arrival. Manuel remained a few days in Venice before continuing his journey via Padua, Vicenza, Pavia and Milan, where Duke Gian Galeazzo Visconti, its ruler, gave a great banquet in his honour and loaded him with presents, promising to travel himself to Constantinople if the other rulers proved cooperative. It was all a far cry from the sort of treatment that John V had received in Venice in 1370; now, as Manuel moved through Italy, he was cheered and fêted in every town through which he passed. The contrast was not altogether surprising. John had visited Venice as a beggar and a discredited debtor; his son was seen as a hero. Italy had at last woken up to the Turkish danger, and in Italian eyes this tall, distinguished figure – having come, as it were, straight from the front line – was the principal defender of Christendom, the potential saviour of Europe.

Something else had happened, too, in the past few years: the Italians had discovered Greek literature and learning, and had taken it to their hearts. Until the last decade of the fourteenth century, Greek had been effectively a dead language in Italy. Petrarch had possessed a Greek manuscript of Homer, on which he would regularly plant a reverent kiss but of which he understood scarcely a word.[1] The study of Greek achieved no real impetus until 1396, when a pupil of Demetrius Cydones named Manuel Chrysoloras was installed in the newly-founded chair of Greek in Florence. Thenceforth the spark travelled quickly. Early in 1400 Chrysoloras had moved on to Milan – leaving behind him a small but enthusiastic body of Greek-speaking scholars and the first Greek grammar ever to appear in Italy – and was there to greet the Emperor on his arrival. In Milan as elsewhere, Manuel thus found all the educated citizens passionately eager for Greek culture and hanging on his every word. Scholar and intellectual as he was, he did not disappoint them.

On 3 June 1400 – just three weeks short of his fiftieth birthday – Manuel Palaeologus arrived in Paris. King Charles VI was waiting for him at the suburb of Charenton with the snow-white horse on which he

---

1 He and his pupil Boccaccio had finally and with much difficulty unearthed an old and extremely dirty monk from a remote Basilian monastery in the depths of Calabria and in 1360 had brought him to Florence. Despite his villainous appearance and unpleasant personal habits – Petrarch described him as 'the concierge of the Cretan labyrinth' – Boccaccio had lodged him in his house and set him down to translate the *Iliad*; but before the monk could get very far he was struck by lightning.

was to enter the city. A monk from Saint-Denis, who was an eye-witness of all that took place, was particularly struck by the way Manuel transferred himself directly from one mount to another:

... Then the Emperor, dressed in his imperial robe of white silk, seated himself on the white horse presented to him by the King during his journey, mounting it nimbly without even deigning to set a foot upon the ground. And those who – while marking his moderate stature, distinguished by a manly chest and by yet firmer limbs, though under a long beard and showing white hair everywhere – yet took heed of the grace of his countenance, and adjudged him indeed to be worthy of imperial rule.[1]

Riding in the centre of a magnificent procession, Manuel was escorted to the old Louvre, where an entire wing had been redecorated to receive him. Lavish entertainments were prepared in his honour; the King himself took him hunting; he was invited to the Sorbonne to meet the country's most distinguished scholars. On every side he was revered and venerated as the Emperor he was. No amount of celebration and festivity could however conceal the fact that he failed to achieve his main object. He had several meetings with the King and his council, in the course of which they agreed to provide him with another force of twelve hundred men for a year, commanded once again by Boucicault; but this, as he and the Marshal well knew, was useless. Nothing would succeed against the Turks but a full-blown international Crusade; and this, apparently, King Charles refused to contemplate.

The situation was not improved by the fact that, within a few weeks of the Emperor's arrival, Charles gave way to one of his periodic fits of insanity, after which all negotiations had to be suspended. Manuel, however, was by this time in correspondence with the Kings of Castile and Aragon, both of whom spoke encouragingly of aid – while remaining somewhat vague about the scale on which it was envisaged. He also made contact with a certain Peter Holt, a prior of the Order of St John, about the possibility of a visit to England. This, Holt pointed out, would not be without its problems: Richard II, with whom he had formerly corresponded, had been deposed in the previous year by the present ruler, King Henry IV; Henry was at present occupied in putting down a rebellion in Scotland; moreover, although England and France were at present temporarily at peace, relations between them were as usual severely strained, and it was far from certain that His Majesty

---

1 Religieux de Saint-Denis, *Chronica Karoli sexti*, quoted by J. W. Barker, op. cit.

would wish to receive any ruler, however distinguished, who had so recently enjoyed the hospitality of the French King.

Fortunately, the prior's misgivings proved unfounded; he and Manuel were obliged to spend two frustrating months in Calais, waiting until King Henry had returned from Scotland and was ready to receive them, but in December they finally made the crossing. Stopping for a few days at Canterbury, they reached London four days before Christmas. The King met them at Blackheath and escorted them into the city. Far from showing any coolness towards his guest, he too treated him with the utmost reverence and respect: his own position in the Kingdom was still uncertain – many of his subjects rightly considered him a usurper of the throne, and a probable murderer to boot – and he believed with good reason that to be seen playing host to the Emperor of Byzantium would do much to enhance his prestige. On Christmas Day he entertained his guest to a banquet in his royal palace at Eltham.[1] As in Paris, everyone was deeply impressed by Manuel's dignity, as by the spotless white robes that he and his entourage all wore. Among those present was the lawyer Adam of Usk. 'I reflected,' he wrote, 'how grievous it was that this great Christian prince should be driven by the Saracens from the furthest East to these furthest western islands to seek aid against them . . . O God, what dost thou now, ancient glory of Rome?'[2]

The Emperor himself seems to have been equally impressed by King Henry:

There is the ruler with whom we are staying at present, the King of Great Britain [sic] which is, one may say, a second universe. He overflows with merits and is bedecked with manifold virtues . . . He is most illustrious both in form and in judgement; with his might he astonishes all, and with his sagacity he wins himself friends. He extends a hand to everyone, and furnishes every sort of assistance to those who are in need of aid. He has established a virtual haven for us in the midst of a twofold tempest, both of the season and of fortune . . . and he appears most pleasant in conversation, gladdening us, honouring us and loving us no less . . . He is to furnish us with military assistance in the shape of men-at-arms, archers, money and ships which will convey the army wherever necessary.

Not all those who knew the King shared his guest's enthusiasm; but

---

1 The old moated palace of Eltham – a mile or two south-east of Greenwich – still stands. Although a royal palace since the days of Edward III (1327–77) it was largely rebuilt by Edward IV in the 1470s; from this period dates the Great Hall with its tremendous hammerbeam roof. Of the building in which Manuel Palaeologus was regally entertained, little or nothing now remains.

2 *Chronicon*, p.57. Quoted by Runciman, *The Fall of Constantinople*, p. 1.

Henry, powerless as he was to provide the military aid that he so cheerfully promised, seems at least to have shown genuine sympathy with the Byzantine cause. Told of the disappearance of the 3,000 marks contributed by his predecessor, he at once ordered a formal inquiry; and when the peculation was revealed he immediately made good the loss, at the same time presenting Manuel with a further £4,000 said to have been contributed to the church collection boxes – astonishing testimony to the generosity of the people of England towards a nation which few had ever seen, and of which the vast majority can never even have heard.

After some seven weeks in England, Manuel was back in Paris towards the end of February 1401. He was to stay there for more than a year, continuing his negotiations with the Kings of Aragon and Portugal, the Pope in Rome and the anti-Pope in Avignon; he also seems to have joined with Charles – who had by now temporarily recovered his sanity – in an attempt to contact the Mongol leader Tamburlaine and to encourage him to lead his immense and apparently invincible horde against Bayezit. Throughout the summer he continued optimistic; several of his surviving letters written from Paris at this time make it clear that he still believed a great international expedition to be in preparation. With the coming of autumn, however, his correspondence grew steadily more discouraging. For the King of Aragon, the season was too far advanced; Henry of England was fully occupied with another rebellion, this time on the part of the Welsh; the Florentines, to whom Manuel had sent his own kinsman Demetrius Palaeologus with a request for aid, sent many expressions of sympathy but pointed out that they had an 'Italian Bayezit' (the Milanese Gian Galeazzo Visconti) of their own to deal with.

Most disappointing of all were the French. They, ideally, should have masterminded the new Crusade, organized it, orchestrated it, given it shape and purpose. But Charles VI was largely incapacitated – no one knew when madness would once again overcome him – and his disease had led to power struggles between various members of his family which paralyzed the government still further. In the autumn of 1401 Marshal Boucicault – who was to have led the new French expedition – was nominated instead as Governor of Genoa,[1] where he arrived at the end of October. Yet even now the Emperor refused to give up hope. A few months later he wrote to Venice, suggesting that Doge Michele Steno might take over the leadership where Charles had failed; but the

1 See p.358n.

Doge prevaricated. Venice, he pointed out, had already gone to considerable expense to help 'the Christians of Romania'. Any further aid must be contingent on similar contributions being made by other nations of the West.

After such reverses, why did the sad and disillusioned Emperor remain in Europe as long as he did? Certainly not, as has been suggested, because he dreaded returning to his capital with the news of his failure. A deeply conscientious man with an unassailable sense of duty, he had not seen his wife and children for nearly two years and would not have wished to stay away from his home and capital for a day longer than he thought necessary. But he was also determined. His father's policy of appeasement had failed; resistance was the only alternative. Somehow it must be made to work; thus, for as long as there seemed the slightest possibility of persuading all or any of the princes of the West to change their minds, he himself must remain among them.

How long he would have done so we shall never know; because in September 1402 the Seigneur Jean de Chateaumorand – whom Boucicault had left in Constantinople with a token force of some three hundred French troops – arrived in Paris with news that instantly changed the entire situation. The Mongols under Tamburlaine had destroyed the Ottoman army. Bayezit himself had been taken prisoner. For Manuel Palaeologus, there was no longer any reason to remain in the West. He began to prepare for his journey home.

22

The Legacy of Tamburlaine

[1402–25]

I shall be as a son to you if you will be my father. From henceforth let there be no rivalry or differences between us.

> Prince Süleyman to the Emperor John VII

For most of the time that Manuel Palaeologus had been absent from Constantinople, the capital had remained in a state of siege. His nephew John VII had done his best, and was throughout valiantly supported by Chateaumorand and his French troops, who would make periodic foraging sorties outside the walls under cover of night or while the besiegers were otherwise off their guard. Without them, the city might well have fallen half a century earlier than it did, for Bayezit was in arrogant mood. We read in one anonymous account of how, gazing covetously across at the great churches and palaces, he mentally decided on a use or an occupant for each: for himself, he proposed to take over St Sophia as his official residence. Meanwhile he had kept up the pressure and at one moment – probably in the summer or autumn of 1401 – had sent John an ultimatum:

If I have indeed driven the Basileus Manuel from the city, I have done so not for your sake but for my own . . . If then you wish to be our friend, withdraw from thence and I will give you whatever province you may choose. But if you do not, then, with God and his great Prophet as my witnesses, I will spare no one, but all will I utterly destroy . . .

Byzantium still had strength enough for a spirited reply to the Turkish envoys:

Go, report to your Lord: we are in poverty and distress and there is no great power to whom we may have recourse, except to God Himself, who gives succour to the powerless and who overcomes the powerful. And so, if you wish to do anything, do it.

But the city could not hold out for ever. By the summer of 1402, when John heard from his uncle that no appreciable help could be expected from the West, he knew that he would have to come to terms. According to Ruy González de Clavijo, Spanish ambassador to the Mongol court at Samarkand, he actually reached an agreement with the Sultan by the terms of which he undertook to surrender the city once the latter had overcome the Mongol invaders; a Greek chronicle in the Vatican Library goes even further, maintaining that ambassadors from Constantinople bearing the keys to the city were already on their way to the Ottoman camp. Be that as it may, it seems clear that Bayezit's defeat came, for Byzantium, not a moment too soon; and that the deliverer of the city was not Manuel, or John, or even Boucicault or Chateaumorand. It was Tamburlaine himself.

Timur-lenk, or Timur the Lame, otherwise known as Tamerlane or Tamburlaine, had been born in 1336. Claiming descent from Genghis Khan, he had seized the throne at Samarkand in 1369, and thirty years later his dominions extended from Afghanistan and northern India to the borders of Anatolia. His name was feared the length and breadth of Asia – the Mongol army was known to destroy everything in its path and to leave nothing but death and devastation in its wake – and though now in his middle sixties he had lost none of his energy or his ambition. A campaign in 1400 culminating in the capture of Sebasteia – which he predictably levelled to the ground, massacring the entire population – was not immediately followed up, since he had work to do in Mesopotamia; but in the spring of 1402 he was back once more in Asia Minor, ready for the ultimate trial of strength with the Ottoman Sultan.

It occurred on Friday, 28 July, on the Chubuk plain just to the north of Ancyra. The immense Turkish army was commanded by the Sultan in person, who took his place in the centre with his crack regiment of ten thousand Janissaries. The left wing he entrusted to one of his sons, Süleyman; the right, which was composed largely of European contingents, to his Serbian vassal Stephen Lazarevich. The Christians fought heroically, the Muslims less so. Bayezit had made the cardinal mistake of placing his Anatolian Tartar cavalry in the front line. Unwilling to fight men of their own race, they deserted almost at once and went over to the enemy. An hour or two later, fifteen thousand of the Ottoman army, Christian and Muslim alike, lay dead on the battlefield. But Bayezit refused to surrender; he was not used to losing battles. Withdrawing to a small hill-top, he and his sons, together with his bodyguard and the remaining Janissaries, fought on late into the night until at last they too recognized that the situation was hopeless. The fate of the eldest of the Princes, Mustafa, is uncertain; he disappeared and was presumed dead. Another, Musa, was captured. The others managed to escape, but their father could not move so fast: overtaken by the Mongol archers, he too was taken prisoner and led in chains to Tamburlaine's tent, where the great conqueror was playing chess with his son.

Tamburlaine at first accorded Bayezit all the honour due to a captive sovereign; soon, however, his attitude changed. Thenceforth, as he advanced through Anatolia, he is said to have had the Sultan carried before him in an iron cage.[1] Occasionally he imposed still greater humiliations upon his captive, using him as a footstool and a mounting-block. Soon he took over Bayezit's harem for his own personal use and forced the Sultan's Serbian wife Despina to serve, naked, at his table. After eight months of such treatment, even Bayezit's spirit was broken. In March 1403 he suffered a sudden apoplexy, and a few days later he was dead – probably as a direct consequence of the stroke, but quite possibly by his own hand.[2]

Tamburlaine, on the other hand, was in his element. Descending on Brusa, the Ottoman capital, his hordes burned, pillaged and raped their way through the city; they then turned against Smyrna, which had been in Latin hands – principally those of the Knights of St John – since 1344. The Knights fought valiantly, but the walls finally gave way and in December 1402 the last Christian enclave in Asia Minor was left a smouldering, deserted ruin. Meanwhile all the non-Ottoman Emirs – of Aydin, Karaman, Saruchan and the rest – who had been driven out by Orhan and Murad and many of whom had taken refuge with the Mongols – were returned to their former territories. Tamburlaine was now well on the way to achieving his long-term object, the total elimination of Ottoman power in Anatolia. The four sons of Bayezit admittedly constituted something of an obstacle; but they were already at loggerheads over the succession, and by judiciously encouraging one against the other he was able to ensure that none became a serious threat.

Had he lingered in the region for very much longer, he might well

---

1 'And what wouldst thou have done to me (said Tamerlane) had it been my fortune to have fallen into thy Hands, as thou art now in mine? I would (said Bajazet) have inclosed thee in a Cage of Iron, and so in triumph have carried thee up and down my Kingdom. Even so (said Tamerlane) shalt thou be served.' (Richard Knolles, *Turkish History*, London, 1687–1700.)

2 Christopher Marlowe, in *Tamburlaine the Great*, has him dash out his brains against the bars of the cage.

have dealt a fatal blow to the house of Othman. But Tamburlaine, like all his race, was a nomad: he could never stay in the same place for long. In the spring of 1403, looking once again for new worlds to conquer, he left Asia Minor and led his horde back to Samarkand. Two years later he set off across the steppe to attack China, but fortunately for the Chinese he died on the journey – the victim, so Gibbon informs us, of a fever accelerated by 'the indiscreet use of iced water'. He left behind him no Empire, no properly constituted system of government; nothing but devastation and chaos. It would be some years before the sons of Bayezit were able to re-establish themselves in their Anatolian heartland.

In Europe, however, it was a very different story. Tamburlaine never crossed the straits, and Rumelia – the Sultan's European dominions – remained as firmly as ever in the Ottoman grip. To make matters worse, the vast numbers of Turkish soldiers already there were now joined by many thousands more, fleeing from the Mongol menace. For the first few months, these refugees were not unwelcome, even to the Byzantines. Since the battle of Ancyra it was the Mongols, not the Turks, before whom Europe trembled; if, as seemed more than likely, they were suddenly to stream across the Hellespont, then the more men available to resist them the better. Only when it became clear that there would be no such invasion did the Christian peoples of eastern Europe look around them and wonder whether they were not, if anything, worse off than before.

In fact, as they soon realized, the great battle had altered the situation very much for the better. First, it had divided the Ottoman Empire into two; no longer was there any regular communication between the European and the Asiatic provinces. Secondly – and of far greater immediate importance to the average Byzantine – the blockade of Constantinople was lifted: after eight years, normal food supplies were restored and the people could go about their lawful occasions without wondering where they might find their next meal. Finally there was the effect on the national morale. Byzantium might still be in desperate danger; but the Sultan had shown that he too was human, and by no means invincible. His army had been beaten once. It could be beaten again.

Even after the news of Bayezit's defeat had been brought to him in France, Manuel Palaeologus seemed to be in no particular hurry to return to Constantinople. He did not leave Paris until 21 November. Then, with an escort of two hundred men under Chateaumorand, he travelled by easy stages to Genoa – where his old friend Marshal Boucicault awaited him and, on 22 January 1403, gave a magnificent banquet in his honour. Having left the city on 10 February, he reached Venice only on 14 March. Where he was in the interval is not recorded; we know, however, that while in Genoa he had tried – albeit unsuccessfully – to arrange for tripartite talks with the Genoese and the Venetians, and it seems likely that he had decided to take advantage of his passage through Italy to hold discussions with as many as possible of the Italian states on the subject of assistance against the Turks. His attempts to date had been admittedly disappointing; but the defeat of Bayezit had convinced him that there would never be a more appropriate time for a concerted onslaught by the European powers, and he had no intention of giving up his efforts to bring this about.

Venice also gave Manuel a warm welcome, tempered only by her eagerness to get him back to Constantinople as soon as possible. The changed situation in the East would obviously have important diplomatic consequences, in which the Serenissima was determined to play her full part; and she greatly preferred to negotiate with Manuel than with John VII, who made no secret of his pro-Genoese sympathies. She therefore fitted out three warships for the Emperor and his suite of forty, and eventually persuaded him to sail on 5 April. Even then he insisted on stopping in the Morea, to pick up his wife and family and to hold discussions with his brother Theodore.[1] Only on 9 June 1403 did he finally step ashore in his capital, accompanied by John VII, who had ridden out to Gallipoli to meet him. He had been absent almost exactly three and a half years.

There was more good news awaiting him. In August of the previous year Prince Süleyman, Bayezit's eldest surviving son, had appeared in Gallipoli with the intention of taking over the European provinces. His was a character very different from that of his father. Tolerant and easygoing, his instinct was always towards compromise; he preferred the conference table to the battlefield, and a life of luxurious self-indulgence to either of them. After some weeks of preliminary discussions, formal negotiations had been opened towards the end of the year, attended by Süleyman himself and a Christian League represented by envoys from

1 Theodore had sold Corinth to the Knights of St John in 1396, after which the Knights had made a determined attempt to establish themselves throughout the Peloponnese. This had however aroused the fury of the local inhabitants, and the Despotate was rapidly relapsing into chaos. The hard-pressed Despot was now engaged in negotiations to buy the Knights out again – which in 1404 he finally managed to do.

Venice, Genoa and the Knights of Rhodes, Stephen Lazarevich and the Latin Duke of Naxos. These had soon led to a treaty, which had been signed early in 1403.

When the terms of this treaty were reported to Manuel on his arrival in Venice, he was scarcely able to believe what he heard. The Byzantines were released alike from their vassalage to the Sultan and from all obligation of paying him tribute. Instead, Süleyman had freely undertaken to accept the Byzantine Emperor as his suzerain. In token of his good faith he had returned to the Empire the city of Thessalonica and its surrounding district, including the Thracian Chalcidice with Mount Athos; a considerable length of the Black Sea coast, from the mouth of the Bosphorus up as far as Mesembria or even Varna; and the Aegean islands of Skyros, Skiathos and Skopelos. All Byzantine prisoners, and those of the other signatories, were to be released. Finally – and still more incredibly – Süleyman undertook that Turkish vessels would not enter either the Hellespont or the Bosphorus without prior permission of the Emperor and the rest of the League. In return he asked only that he should be allowed to rule over Thrace from the palace at Adrianople.

Manuel's first action on his return to the capital was to confirm the treaty with his own signature. Almost immediately, however, his old antipathy to his nephew flared up again: he banished him to Lemnos and quite possibly – though we cannot be sure – also deprived him of the appanage of Thessalonica, which he had formally promised him before his departure. Whatever its reason, John VII did not take kindly to his new exile. Within a few weeks of his arrival in Lemnos he made contact with his Genoese father-in-law Francesco II Gattilusio, lord of the neighbouring island of Lesbos, some fifty miles away to the north-west; and in mid-September the two set out with a small flotilla of seven ships with the apparent intention of seizing Thessalonica by force. Whether they ever reached the city we do not know; perhaps the news of their departure was alone enough to bring Manuel to his senses. Some time in October agreement was reached between the two Emperors, and John was installed in Thessalonica with the title of 'Basileus of all Thessaly'.

What were Manuel's motives in exiling his nephew? Throughout his absence in the West, John VII's behaviour had been exemplary. He had ruled conscientiously and well without, so far as we know, the slightest attempt to assert his own claims at the expense of his uncle's; he had concluded an extraordinarily favourable treaty with Süleyman which had immeasurably strengthened the imperial position; and on Manuel's return he had surrendered the supreme power unhesitatingly and with good grace. Yet Manuel was by nature neither unjust nor vindictive; he would surely not have acted as he did without good cause. Was it just a clash of personalities? Did he simply find his nephew unbearable and decide that Constantinople was not big enough for them both? Was he perhaps angry with John for having agreed to surrender the city to Bayezit – assuming that he had indeed done so – after the Sultan had dealt successfully with Tamburlaine? Or was he, even after his experience in the West, still bent on military action against the Turks and frankly disgusted by the terms of the recent agreement, however favourable it might in the short term have appeared? But if so, why had he himself signed it immediately on his return?

Several other theories have been put forward, none of them entirely convincing. One suggests that John's exile was a mere pretence – nothing more than an attempt by the Emperor to appease Tamburlaine, who was angry about what he considered the pro-Turkish policy of Byzantium after the battle of Ancyra. Another adduces two little-known contemporary texts referring to the death, at the age of seven, of the young Emperor ('*basileus*') Andronicus Palaeologus, presumably the son of John VII and his wife Irene Gattilusio. (Until recently, the existence of this small and shadowy figure was not even suspected; nowadays, however, it is more or less generally agreed.[1]) If, the theory goes, little Andronicus was born after Manuel's departure to the West – and it seems unlikely that, had John already produced an heir, the Empire would have been entrusted to him for so long – and if his father had had him crowned co-Emperor before Manuel's return, it is hardly surprising that the latter acted as he did. The principal objection to all this is that although the texts refer to Andronicus as *basileus* they give no indication of when he received his coronation. If such a ceremony had indeed occurred during the senior Emperor's absence it is hard to believe that it would not have been mentioned by any other source; it is thus a good deal more likely that John had crowned his son not in Constantinople at all but as '*basileus* of Thessaly' during his later years in Thessalonica – in which case the entire theory falls to the ground.

The truth will never be known. Fortunately, John seems to have settled with every appearance of contentment in Thessalonica, showing no regrets for his days of power in the capital, causing his uncle no

---

1 One other piece of evidence for the existence of Andronicus V is an ivory at Dumbarton Oaks in Washington DC, almost certainly depicting John and Andronicus together at Thessalonica in 1403/4.

further trouble and spending much of his time in establishing and endowing various religious and charitable foundations for the salvation of his soul. He died in September 1408, having first donned the monastic habit and adopted – like his great-grandfather John Cantacuzenus – the monkish name of Joasaph. His presumed heir, the *basileus* Andronicus V, having predeceased him, the senior line of the Palaeologus was now extinct.

Manuel once again took up the reins of government in Constantinople, to find that there had occurred an extraordinary reversal of roles. Only a few years before, rival Byzantine Emperors had been contending for power, while the Turkish Sultan had amused himself by playing one off against the other to his own considerable advantage. Now it was the Turkish lands that were in chaos, for the Turks had no law of primogeniture and no less than four of the sons of Bayezit were fighting for the Ottoman crown; and the Emperor, who after the recent treaty was compelled to show at least a degree of friendship to his erstwhile enemies, found himself ineluctably drawn into the struggle.

The first round of that struggle was already over by the time Manuel returned to Constantinople. One of the four warring Princes, Isa, who had managed to establish himself in Brusa after the departure of Tamburlaine, was driven out by his brother Mehmet. He had fled to Constantinople, where he had been given temporary refuge by John VII; but he had soon returned to Anatolia, only to suffer another defeat by Mehmet, who had immediately had him murdered. Then in 1404 another of the princes, Musa, who had shared his father's captivity but had been released after Bayezit's death to escort his body back to his capital for burial, declared war on his brother Süleyman in Adrianople. After three years of inconsequential skirmishing Süleyman, with uncharacteristic spirit, crossed into Asia Minor and, in Mehmet's absence, seized Brusa in the spring of 1407. His supremacy, however, did not last long: Musa, encouraged by Mehmet, invaded Thrace and began whipping up support from the neighbouring Christian states, and in 1409 Süleyman was obliged to hurry back to Europe to save his own territory.

All this merely confirmed Manuel in his view that, whatever the immediate advantages of the 1403 treaty, he could not indefinitely rely on Turkish friendship even in Adrianople, let alone in Anatolia. Still less could he relax his efforts to alert the Christian nations of Europe and to obtain their active assistance. Already in 1404 he had sent new embassies to France and Aragon; two years later he renewed his agreement with Venice, and in 1407 he wrote once again to Doge Steno, imploring him to settle his differences with the Genoese and launch a joint campaign against the Turks. Now after all was the ideal time to act, while the Ottoman Sultanate was torn by fratricidal strife; such a chance might never recur. But the Venetians remained unmoved. In the same year he sent one of his closest friends, the scholar Manuel Chrysoloras who had recently enjoyed such success in Florence and Milan, as his personal ambassador to King Charles VI in Paris. Chrysoloras carried with him, as a present for the King, a priceless manuscript of the works of Dionysius the Areopagite, bound in gold and ivory and containing a superb miniature of the Emperor, his wife and their three eldest sons.[1] Charles was delighted with it, but made no further offers of help; nor did the Kings of England and Aragon, to whom Chrysoloras presented himself at later stages of his journey.

The year 1407 saw the death after a long illness of Manuel's brother Theodore, Despot of the Morea. He had been an excellent ruler who, despite constant difficulties with both the Turks and his Frankish neighbours – and more recently with the Knights of St John – had somehow managed to maintain both the integrity of his dominion and the imperial prestige. The Emperor, who had loved and admired him, wrote a long funeral oration in his honour; then in the summer of 1408, he travelled himself to Mistra to pay his respects at his tomb and – since the Despot had left no legitimate male issue – to enthrone his own second son, another Theodore, in his place. He was still there in September, when the news came of the death of John VII. This he was able to receive with rather more equanimity; none the less, John had also left no heir and the succession had to be provided for. The Emperor accordingly hurried to Thessalonica, where he installed his third son, the eight-year-old Andronicus.

It was obviously Manuel's hope, when he returned to Constantinople early in 1409, to bring these two provinces, Thessaly and the Morea, directly under his own control, thereby strengthening both the power and the prestige of the Empire in the Greek peninsula; but before he could do very much more in this direction he found himself swept up once again in the struggle for the Ottoman Sultanate. That autumn a

---

1 See illustration. Though now in the Louvre, this manuscript was intended for the library of the Abbey of Saint-Denis – the patron saint of France having been wrongly identified with the Areopagite throughout the Middle Ages.

desperate Süleyman appeared in Constantinople. He had, it appeared, returned to Adrianople only to find himself under attack by his brother Musa, who had invaded Thrace from beyond the Danube and was even now preparing to march on the city. Addressing the Emperor as his beloved father, he explained that without Byzantine help he could not hope to survive the coming onslaught – doubtless reminding Manuel that Musa, if victorious, would prove an infinitely less agreeable neighbour than himself. As an earnest of his good intentions he offered two young members of his family, a boy and a girl, as hostages, and took a niece of Manuel's – an illegitimate daughter of his late brother the Despot Theodore – as his own bride.

Alas, the marriage was not long to endure. In the first two battles between the brothers, in June and July 1410, Süleyman was victorious; but, though he was never lacking in physical courage, there was a fundamental weakness in his character which somehow deprived him of staying power. The winter following, while Musa concentrated on building up his military strength, Süleyman locked himself up in his palace and surrendered himself to his favourite pastimes of drinking and debauch. Early in 1411 his contemptuous troops deserted him – many were also disgusted by his pro-Christian policy – and Adrianople fell almost without a struggle. Taken prisoner, he was brought on 17 February before his brother, who instantly had him strangled.

For Byzantium, this was serious news indeed. The Emperor, certainly, had no delusions about Musa, who had inherited all the violence and savagery of his father Bayezit, all his energy and efficiency, all his hatred of the Christians. One of his first actions on assuming power in Adrianople was to abrogate the treaty of 1403 and to declare his brother's various concessions null and void. He then sent a number of his regiments down into Thessaly to besiege Thessalonica, while he himself led the main body of the army directly against Constantinople, leaving the usual trail of devastation behind him. By this time, too, he had apparently been able to assemble a small naval squadron, which sailed unimpeded through the Hellespont and the Sea of Marmara to renew the old blockade.

The dismay of the people of Constantinople, finding themselves facing a siege by land and sea for the second time in ten years, can well be imagined. Fortunately, however, they were not called upon to undergo the tribulations that they had suffered in the days of Bayezit. The Byzantine navy, weak as it was, proved sufficient to drive the Turkish ships back into the Mediterranean, allowing supplies to be brought in;

meanwhile, despite everything that the Turks could hurl against them, the Land Walls proved as impregnable as ever. But Musa, powerless as he was to take the city by storm, showed no inclination to depart; and there is no telling how long the stalemate might have continued had the Emperor not resorted to the undercover diplomacy that he so well understood. There was, he knew, one chance only of eliminating Musa from the political scene: his brother Mehmet. Early in 1412 he dispatched a secret embassy to Mehmet's court at Brusa.

The fight for power among the sons of Bayezit had now polarized: two contenders only were left, Musa and Mehmet. To Mehmet, a far more sensible and balanced character than his brother, a Byzantine alliance seemed a small price to pay for the undisputed throne of the Ottomans. He rode at once to Chrysopolis, where Manuel met him and escorted him over to Constantinople. There he entertained him lavishly for three days while a Turkish army of fifteen thousand was being ferried across the Bosphorus. On the fourth day Mehmet led his men against his brother, still encamped beneath the walls of the city. The first attack was unsuccessful, though not disastrous; seeing that Musa's army was stronger than he had expected, Mehmet retired before much damage was done and returned to Asia Minor for reinforcements. His second attack, in which he was supported by Byzantine troops and a small army provided by Stephen Lazarevich, also ended in failure; but Mehmet was not easily discouraged. On 15 June 1413 a whole new army was transported on Byzantine vessels across the straits for a third attempt. By now Musa in his turn had alienated many of his men – not, like Süleyman, by his fecklessness, but by his cruelty and brutality – and had suffered many desertions; one look at the size of Mehmet's force was enough for him to order an immediate retreat. He and his men were driven back to Adrianople and beyond, and were finally defeated in pitched battle at Camurlu in Serbia on 5 July. He himself fought to the end, when he too was brought before his brother and strangled.

Go and say to my father the Emperor of the Romans that, with the help of God and the support of my father the Emperor, I have recovered my hereditary dominions. From this day forth I am and shall be his subject, as a son to his father. He will find me neither unheeding nor ungrateful. Let him but command me to do his bidding, and I shall with the greatest of pleasure execute his wishes as his servant.

This, according to the historian Michael Ducas, was the message that

Mehmet, now undisputed Sultan of Rumelia and Rum,[1] sent to Manuel Palaeologus after his victory. Mehmet was well aware – and freely admitted – that he owed that victory largely to the Emperor, and lost no time in confirming all the concessions made by Süleyman and abrogated by Musa. He knew too that after a decade of civil war the Sultanate desperately needed peace – an opportunity to restore law and order and to re-establish the machinery of government; and that the best way to ensure that peace was to maintain cordial relations, not only with Byzantium but with all the other Christian states, however tenuously constituted they might be, of the Balkan peninsula: Serbia, Bulgaria, Wallachia and Greece. Manuel for his part obviously asked nothing better. He had no delusions about long-term Turkish intentions, but there could be no doubt that the situation was better now than at any moment in the twenty-two years since his accession; moreover, for the first time in history, an Emperor of the Romans had established a close personal relationship with an intelligent and peace-loving Sultan. The future was still in God's hands; but perhaps there might be some hope for Byzantium after all.

Manuel Palaeologus was now sixty-three: an old man by the standards of the time, but still healthy and energetic, and determined to leave to his son John an Empire which, though plainly crumbling, remained as firmly based as he could make it. Its frontiers, admittedly, no longer extended much beyond the suburbs of Constantinople; but there remained Thessalonica and the Morea, at that time in the hands of his sons Andronicus and Theodore respectively. To the preservation of these two outposts of the Empire he had always attached supreme importance, knowing them to represent possible sources of succour for Constantinople in its hour of need and even – at the worst – places of refuge from which, were the capital to fall, the struggle could be continued; and he was anxious to visit them both once again before he died.

Leaving his son John to act as Regent in Constantinople, Manuel set sail for Thessalonica on 25 July 1414 with a fleet consisting of four galleys and two other vessels carrying contingents of infantry and cavalry. The purpose of this force soon became clear when he made an unannounced stop at Thasos, a normally inconsequential island

---

1 Rumelia was the name normally applied to all the European territory held by the Turks. Rum – i.e. Rome – was that which had originally been given to the Seljuk Sultanate after the battle of Manzikert, and was still used to describe Turkish Anatolia.

which was then under threat from Giorgio, a bastard son of Francesco Gattilusio of Lesbos. It took Manuel some three months to reassert his authority; only then did he continue his journey to Thessalonica, where he was warmly received by young Andronicus, now about fourteen, and where he spent some time attending to the affairs of Mount Athos. In the spring of 1415, his work done, he and his escort left by way of Euboea for the Peloponnese, arriving at the little port of Kenchreai – a mile or two from Isthmia on the Saronic Gulf – on Good Friday, 29 March.

The choice of landfall was deliberate, for the primary purpose of the Emperor's visit was not to confer with his son Theodore but to realize a project which had been in his mind ever since his previous visit in 1408: the creation of a strong defensive fortification running six miles across the Isthmus of Corinth – roughly along the route of the present Corinth Canal. This was in no sense a new idea: the first such bulwark had been erected in 480 BC, against the Persian Xerxes; and a second had followed in 369. In AD 253 the Roman Emperor Valerian had been responsible for another, and early in the sixth century yet another – far stronger and more impressive than its predecessors, with 153 towers and a great fortress at each end – had been built, predictably enough, by Justinian. The task facing Manuel was therefore essentially one of restoration rather than of original construction; nevertheless it says much for his workers – presumably those same soldiers who had accompanied him from Constantinople – that the entire work was completed in twenty-five days.[1] The result was known, from its length, as the Hexamilion, or 'Six-miler'; henceforth, in theory at any rate, the Peloponnese – which was by now largely in Greek hands – would be in effect a huge Byzantine island, impregnable by land and, it was hoped, with its own permanent navy to defend it from the sea. The work was financed by a special tax levied on the local populations, which caused such opposition that many came out in armed rebellion; but once again Manuel was prepared. His little army sprang into action, and the rebels were defeated near Kalamata in July. Then and only then did the Emperor travel on to Mistra, where his son Theodore awaited him. Not until March 1416 did he return to Constantinople.

The Hexamilion had been constructed as a defence against the Turks: a clear indication that, despite his friendship with Mehmet, Manuel

---

1 The remains can still be seen, to the south-west of the modern canal. Though its course is very roughly parallel, owing to the irregularities of the land the distance between the two varies from some 500 yards to a mile and a half.

remained fully alive to the long-term threat. For the time being, however, the Empire was safe. Mehmet was still restoring order in Anatolia, where he was having trouble with the Emirs of Aydin and Karaman, and in 1416 he had to face a new crisis: a rebellion in the name of a pretender claiming to be Bayezit's eldest son Mustafa, who had not been seen since his presumed death at the battle of Ancyra. The rising itself was quickly dealt with but the pretender's cause had been taken up – most ill-advisedly – by the Venetians, who engineered his escape to Europe. He eventually reached Thessalonica, where he flung himself upon the mercy of the young Despot Andronicus and was somewhat surprisingly offered refuge. The news was reported to Mehmet, who immediately appealed to the Emperor over so flagrant a breach of his treaty obligations; but Manuel prevaricated. The laws of asylum, he pointed out, did not permit him to surrender Mustafa; he was however perfectly prepared to hold him prisoner for the rest of his natural life, provided only that the Sultan undertook responsibility for his maintenance. To this Mehmet readily agreed, and the pretender was confined on the island of Lemnos. Both sides professing themselves satisfied with this arrangement, relations between Emperor and Sultan were scarcely ruffled; but Manuel had in fact achieved something of a *coup*, and Mehmet knew it. Whether Mustafa were genuine or not – and he almost certainly was not – the Byzantines now had in their hands a claimant to the Ottoman throne. If properly handled, he might prove extremely useful in the future.

Towards the end of the year 1414, a great council was called in the city of Constance to settle the schism that, for nearly forty years, had racked the Roman Church. It had begun in 1377, when Pope Gregory XI had brought the Papacy back to Rome from Avignon. Gregory had died a year later, and the ensuing election had been tumultuous in the extreme. The Roman populace was well aware that if the French cardinals and their supporters had their way, they and their successful candidate would return to Avignon, probably for good. In their determination to prevent such a disaster – from which their city might never have recovered – they had invaded the conclave itself. Its terrified members, in fear of their lives, had elected an Italian, Urban VI, who had announced his intention of remaining in Rome; unfortunately, within weeks of his coronation, he had so antagonized the cardinals of both the French and Italian parties that in desperation they had declared his election null and void and had elected a rival Pope, Clement VII, in his place. Urban, firmly entrenched in Rome, had refused to yield; and so the dispute had dragged on, with new Popes being elected on both sides as necessary. It was still as acrimonious as ever when on 19 December 1406 Urban's third successor, an eighty-year-old Venetian named Angelo Correr, assumed the throne of St Peter as Gregory XII.

Less than a week later Gregory wrote to the anti-Pope, Clement's successor Benedict XIII, in Marseille, proposing a meeting. If Benedict would resign, he added, he would be glad to do the same. The cardinals could then proceed to a single, undisputed election. Benedict accepted, and proposed a meeting at Savona. Almost immediately, however, difficulties began to arise. Savona was in French territory, and thus within Benedict's sphere of obedience. The journey there from Rome would be long, costly, and for an octogenarian distinctly dangerous. King Ladislas of Naples, who had reasons of his own for wishing the schism to continue, tried to seize Rome and forcibly prevent the Pope from leaving; though the attempt failed, it persuaded Gregory that the Holy City would not be safe in his absence. Finally, the strains of office were rapidly telling on the old man's strength and, as he drifted towards senility, he grew less and less able to resist pressures from his family – in particular two of his nephews, who were already digging deep into the papal coffers – which was doing everything in its power to prevent his resignation.

For all these reasons, the meeting at Savona never took place. In August 1407 Gregory did at last leave on his journey north, but by 1 November, the day appointed, he had got no further than Siena. The following April, when he had advanced as far as Lucca, his earlier fears were realized: Ladislas marched on Rome. The city, leaderless, impoverished and demoralized, surrendered with scarcely a struggle. The situation was now worse than ever. Both papal contenders were in exile, each was accusing the other of bad faith and, as the stalemate continued, the chances of conciliation seemed to be fast diminishing. Clearly there was nothing further to be hoped from either of the protagonists. On 25 March 1409 a General Council of the Church some five hundred strong met at Pisa, and on 5 June it repudiated both Gregory and Benedict as contumacious heretical and schismatics. Christians throughout the world were absolved from obedience to either, and ordered to observe a universal holiday; the council then went on to elect their single successor. Its choice fell on the Cardinal Archbishop of Milan, a certain Peter Philarges who, having started life as an orphaned beggar-boy in Crete, was to end it as Pope Alexander V.

Now, one is tempted to reflect, would have been the time for the two rivals to retire gracefully from the scene. Yet they did not do so, and for that the council itself was largely to blame. It had been summoned by neither of them, and by calling them to appear before it – and declaring them contumacious when they refused – it implied its superiority over the Papacy, a principle which neither could have been expected to endorse. A little more diplomacy, a little more tact and understanding for two old men who, in their very different ways, were both honest and upright and had neither of them asked to occupy their impossible positions, and the schism could have been healed. In the circumstances they had no choice but to declare the council's proceedings uncanonical and fight on. Before long it became clear that the only real effect of the Council of Pisa had been to saddle Christendom with three Popes instead of two. But the cardinals were unrepentant; and when Pope Alexander – the only contender unable, apparently, to stand the strain – died suddenly in May 1410 they lost no time in electing another.

Baldassare Cossa, who now joined the papal throng under the name of John XXIII,[1] was widely believed at the time to have poisoned his predecessor. Whether he actually did so is open to doubt. He had, however, unquestionably begun life as a pirate; and a pirate, essentially, he remained. Able, energetic and utterly without scruple, he owed his meteoric rise through the hierarchy to a genius for intrigue and extortion; morally and spiritually, he reduced the Papacy to a level of depravity unknown since the days of the 'pornocracy' in the tenth century.[2] A contemporary chronicler, Theodoric of Niem, records in shocked amazement the rumour current in Bologna – where Cossa had been Papal Governor – that during the first year of his pontificate he had debauched no fewer than two hundred matrons, widows and virgins, to say nothing of a prodigious number of nuns. His score over the three following years is regrettably not recorded; he seems, however, to have maintained a high average, for on 29 May 1415 he was arraigned before another General Council, which had been in session since the previous November at Constance. As Gibbon summed up: 'The most scandalous charges were suppressed: the Vicar of Christ on earth was only accused of piracy, murder, rape, sodomy and incest.' Predictably, he was found guilty on all counts – the council, benefiting from the lesson learnt at Pisa, requiring him to ratify the sentence himself.

---

1 The circumstances of his election and subsequent deposition have denied him a place on the canonical list of Popes. It was none the less somewhat surprising that Cardinal Angelo Roncalli should have adopted the same name on his election to the Papacy in 1958.

2 See *Byzantium: The Apogee*, p. 168.

Next, in early July, Gregory XII was prevailed upon to abdicate with honour, and with the promise that he would rank second in the hierarchy, immediately after the future Pope – a privilege that was accorded the more easily in view of the fact that, since he was by now approaching ninety and looked a good deal older, it was not thought likely that he would enjoy it for long. Indeed, two years later he was dead. By then, the anti-Pope Benedict had been deposed in his turn; and with the election of the new, legitimate Pope Martin V in 1417, the schism was effectively at an end.

Manuel Palaeologus, dreaming as always of the great Crusade that would for ever deliver Byzantium from the Ottoman menace, had followed these developments with interest. For the past few years there had obviously been no possibility of a major papal initiative; at the same time the Council of Constance – which had been instigated by Manuel's old ally King Sigismund of Hungary (since 1410 Emperor of the West) and which, at Sigismund's insistence, had been thrown open to representatives of both the Eastern and the Western Churches – seemed to present an ideal opportunity of making known his anxiety. It was unfortunate that his roving ambassador Manuel Chrysoloras – who had played a major part in the organization of the council – had died at Constance in April 1415, just six weeks before John's deposition; but Manuel had immediately sent new envoys to the council to raise, once again, the old question of Church union and to propose, as a gesture of good will, that Catholic princesses should be found for his two eldest sons, John and Theodore.

The new discussions on union proved as inconclusive as their predecessors; but the marriages of the two Princes came about just as their father had intended. In 1420 Theodore, Despot of the Morea – at the age of twenty-five still a bachelor – took as his bride Cleope Malatesta, daughter of the Count of Rimini;[1] and on 19 January 1421 Manuel's eldest son John married – with extreme reluctance – Sophia of Montferrat. John's first wife Anna, daughter of the Grand Duke Basil I of Moscow, had died of the plague just three years before, after four years of marriage and at the age of only fifteen; his second attempt at matrimony was even more ill-starred. The unfortunate Sophia was, according to Michael

---

1 The betrothal was celebrated by the twenty-year-old Guillaume Dufay – one of the greatest composers of the fifteenth century – with a motet '*Vasilissa ergo gaude*'. Despite the beauty of the bride and (we are told) her exemplary moral qualities, the marriage was not a success. Theodore developed a deep dislike for her, to the point that at one moment he seriously considered abdicating and entering a monastery in order to be rid of her once and for all.

Ducas, quite shatteringly plain: her figure, it was unkindly said, looked like Lent in front and Easter behind. John quite literally could not bear the sight of her. Respect for his father's wishes prevented him from sending the poor girl straight home again, but he relegated her to a remote corner of the palace and made, we are told, no attempt to consummate the marriage. She eventually escaped in 1426 – with the aid of the Genoese colony in Galata – and returned to her parents, entering a nunnery soon afterwards.

The importance for John Palaeologus of his second wedding was not that it afforded him a bride whom he would have been far better off without, but that it provided a fitting occasion for his coronation as co-Emperor. Remembering his own early difficulties as the result of a disputed succession, Manuel had left no doubt in anyone's mind that he intended his eldest son to succeed him. He had also given John a relentlessly thorough training in the art of good government, going so far as to compose whole treatises on the qualities, both spiritual and moral, necessary for a ruling prince. In 1414 he had left the regency in his hands and in 1416, to give him further administrative experience, he had sent him to join his brother Theodore in the Morea. When after nearly two years in Greece John had returned to Constantinople at the age of twenty-six, he was as well prepared for the imperial throne as either he or his father could have wished.

From the time of his coronation onward, we find John VIII taking an increasingly prominent part in the conduct of affairs and his influence becoming steadily stronger. Nowhere was this influence more evident than in the Empire's relations with the Ottoman Sultan. Since Mehmet's accession in 1413, both sides had enjoyed a welcome period of peace; there could be little doubt, however, that the Turks had derived far more benefit from this *détente* – during which Mehmet had done much to repair the damage done by the civil war – than had the Byzantines; and many of the younger generation in Constantinople, including John himself, believed that if the Empire were to have any chance of survival a more aggressive policy would have to be adopted. For as long as Manuel and Mehmet lived, it is unlikely that there would have been much change in the status quo: when in 1421 Mehmet asked leave to cross from Europe to Asia by way of Constantinople, Manuel refused to listen to those of his advisers who recommended that he should be seized and murdered. Not only did he grant the permission instantly but escorted the Sultan personally across the straits and dined with him at

Chrysopolis before returning. Shortly afterwards, however – on 21 May 1421 – Mehmet suddenly died. There are conflicting reports as to the cause of his death. One source speaks of a hunting accident; one of dysentery; another, more darkly, of poison. But no serious attempt was made to accuse the Byzantines. For some weeks the death was kept secret, to reduce the inevitable problems of the succession to a minimum; when the announcement was finally made, Mehmet's eldest son and designated heir was already firmly in control as Murad II.[1]

The war faction in Constantinople was meanwhile becoming ever more vocal, openly blaming Manuel – who had retired to the monastery of the Peribleptos to escape a serious epidemic of plague that was then raging through the city – for not having murdered the Sultan when he had the opportunity. Its leaders, who included the co-Emperor John, now demanded that recognition for Murad should be withheld, and that the pretender Mustafa – still captive on Lemnos – should be played off against him. Manuel seems to have been genuinely horrified by the suggestion; but he was old and tired, and when he saw that John could not be shaken he allowed him to carry the day. All too soon he was proved to have been right. Mustafa was released, and with Byzantine help he soon established himself in most of Rumelia; but he refused to surrender Gallipoli to the Empire as he had promised, citing a Muslim tradition which forbade the restoration of conquests to unbelievers. It was not long before John and his friends understood the mistake they had made in putting their trust in an adventurer.

And that was only the beginning. In January 1422 Mustafa and his supporters crossed the straits on Genoese ships, only to be decisively beaten by Murad and obliged to flee back to Europe. A week or two later Murad arrived from Asia Minor with a huge army, and rapidly put an end to all the pretender's hopes. But Mustafa's capture and immediate execution did little to assuage the Sultan's wrath. He was now bent on war. Refusing to listen to the Byzantine ambassadors who were sent to pacify him, he dispatched a section of his army to blockade Thessalonica; he himself had decided to lead the main body against Constantinople – not as a punitive raid but as a determined effort to take the city by storm.

---

1 Mehmet's greatest monument is the Green Mosque in Brusa. It was incomplete at the time of his death, and has remained so; but its loveliness is undiminished. The Sultan's tomb, set with turquoise tiles – replacements after the destruction of the originals in the great earthquake of 1855 – stands beside it and is, inside, every bit as beautiful.

The siege of 1422 was of a very different order from that instituted by Bayezit. His had been a war of attrition, intended to reduce the inhabitants to near-starvation; but Murad had none of his grandfather's patience. According to an eye-witness, John Cananus, he built a huge rampart of earth just outside the Land Walls and parallel to them, running all the way from the Marmara to the Golden Horn and enabling his catapults and siege engines to hurl their missiles over the walls on to the defenders within. The defenders, however, men and women working together, showed courage and determination – as the people of Constantinople always did when their city was in peril. John VIII himself was in supreme command and an example to all; he seemed to be everywhere at once, in every section of the walls, working ceaselessly, constantly shouting encouragement to those around him, impressing everyone with his energy and efficiency.

Fortunately for the Byzantines, the Sultan was superstitious. He had with him a holy man, allegedly descended from the Prophet himself, who had foretold that the city would fall on Monday, 24 August; and as that day dawned Murad launched a massive assault on the walls. The fight was long and hard, but somehow the defences held and finally the Turks fell back. They had concentrated all their efforts on that one great onslaught, and it had failed. Less than two weeks later, disappointed and discouraged, the Sultan ordered the siege to be abandoned. The watchers on the walls could hardly believe their eyes as they saw their would-be conquerors striking camp and slowly withdrawing westward across the plain. Few of them were aware that old Manuel, who had been prevented by age and increasing infirmity from taking any active part in the defence, had been secretly intriguing to place the late Sultan's youngest son – the thirteen-year-old Mustafa, of whom Mehmet in his will had designated him the guardian – on the Ottoman throne during his brother's absence; and that Murad, learning of this, had been obliged to leave when he did in order to avoid a new outbreak of civil war. There was, as far as they were concerned, only one explanation: the city's traditional patron and protectress, the Mother of God, had saved it yet again.

The secret backing of Mustafa was Manuel's last great service to Byzantium. The young Prince, having somehow avoided his brother's clutches, arrived in Constantinople on 30 September with a body of adherents to make formal acceptance of the alliance; but on the very next day, before he could even receive him, the old Emperor suffered a severe stroke which left him partially paralyzed. Fortunately his mind was unaffected; but the immediate after-effects were such that his son was obliged to take over all the negotiations with Mustafa – as also with a papal embassy led by Antonio da Massa, Provincial of the Franciscans, which had arrived three weeks before with a nine-point plan for Church union.

As things turned out, neither of these issues was to cause John too much trouble. Early in 1423 young Mustafa was betrayed to his brother and succumbed in his turn to the bowstring; while the papal proposals showed no advance on their countless predecessors, insisting that the Greek Church should 'return' to the Roman fold as the essential preliminary before any military expedition could be considered. In all other fields, however, the situation continued to deteriorate. True, Constantinople had secured a temporary respite; but Thessalonica was still under siege and, although a few supplies continued to come in by sea, trade had virtually ceased. By the approach of spring, serious famine threatened. Manuel's son Andronicus was, at only twenty-three, crippled with elephantiasis[1] and manifestly unable to cope. In the early summer he took an extraordinary and utterly unexpected step: with the full knowledge and approval of his father and brother, he sent an envoy to the Venetian authorities in Euboea offering the city to Venice.

Thessalonica was not sold, nor was it surrendered. Andronicus stated his reasons with the greatest possible frankness. The Empire could no longer afford to defend the city as it deserved, he himself was too ill to bear the responsibility for it in its present crisis. If Venice were prepared to assume the burden, he asked one thing only: that she should preserve all its political and religious institutions. The Venetians took their time in coming to a decision, but finally agreed to accept the offer; two representatives of the Doge sailed for Thessalonica, escorted by six transports laden with food and provisions, to take formal possession; and on 14 September the besieging Turks watched, powerless, as the banner of St Mark was proudly raised above the ramparts. After a decent interval, Andronicus left with his wife and young son for the Morea, where he became a monk and died four years later. The Venetians for their part sent emissaries to the Sultan, giving him formal notice of the transfer, but he refused to receive them.

As the year drew to its close and Murad remained implacable, John Palaeologus decided on one last appeal to the West. By now, it seemed

---

1 According, at least, to Chalcocondylas. Other sources speak of leprosy, or epilepsy. We can take our choice.

to him, everyone in Europe must see the magnitude of the danger. At any moment the Turkish army might return to the siege of Constantinople. In its present state the city could not hold out for ever; and once it had fallen, what was there to stop the Sultan continuing his westward advance? Leaving the regency to his nineteen-year-old brother Constantine – whom he simultaneously honoured with the title of Despot – on 15 November he sailed for Venice. He stayed there for over a month – the Senate having agreed to pay him a daily allowance to cover his expenses – but it was no use. The Venetians were prepared to defend their own interests wherever these existed – in Euboea and Thessalonica, in the Morea and the Greek islands. Where Byzantium was concerned, however, their old attitude remained unchanged: if John were able to persuade other nations of the West to contribute to an expedition, the Most Serene Republic would willingly add its share. Otherwise, not.

Leaving Venice towards the end of January 1424, the Emperor travelled on to Milan and Mantua for conversations with their respective Dukes, Filippo Maria Visconti and Gianfrancesco Gonzaga. The early summer found him in Hungary, but there again he was due for disappointment: as he had feared, Sigismund saw no possibility of effective aid while the Eastern and Western Churches remained in schism. Nor did he take particularly kindly to John's suggestion of mediating between Hungary and its old enemy Venice. It was a sad and bitterly disillusioned Emperor who took ship down the Danube, eventually reaching Constantinople on 1 November.

He found the situation slightly easier than when he had left it almost a year before. Peace had at last been made with the Sultan. The cost had been heavy – a sizeable annual tribute and the return of those parts of the Marmara and Black Sea coasts that had been previously granted by Süleyman and Mehmet – but at least the people of Constantinople could sleep securely in their beds without fearing the imminent reappearance of the Turkish siege engines. It was, perhaps, with some surprise that John found his father still alive. Old Manuel had never properly recovered from his stroke; by now he was permanently bed-ridden and sinking fast. His mind, however, remained clear, and he continued to worry over what he considered his son's excessive ambitions, summoning him to his chamber for long conversations about the dangers of antagonizing the Sultan unnecessarily and of going too far in the direction of Church union. After one of these talks, which had ended with John leaving the room tight-lipped and silent, Manuel turned to his old friend, the historian George Sphrantzes, and said:

At other times in our history, my son might have been a great *basileus*; but he is not for the present time, for he sees and thinks on a grand scale, in a manner which would have been appropriate in the prosperous days of our forefathers. But today, with our troubles closing in upon us from every side, our Empire needs not a great *basileus* but a good manager. And I fear that his grandiose schemes and endeavours may bring ruin upon this house.

Soon afterwards, following the time-honoured tradition, the old Emperor took monastic vows and donned a monk's habit, taking the name of Matthew. It was in this guise that he celebrated his seventy-fifth birthday on 27 June 1425. Just twenty-five days later the end came. He was buried the same day in the monastery church of the Pantocrator, the funeral oration being delivered by the twenty-five-year-old monk Bessarion, of whom we shall be hearing more before this story is done. Sphrantzes tells us that he was mourned more deeply and by more people than any of his predecessors. If so, it was no more than he deserved.

23
Laetentur Coeli!

As the metropolitans disembarked from the ships the citizens greeted them as was customary, asking 'What of our business? What of the Council? Did we prevail?' And they answered: 'We have sold our faith; we have exchanged true piety for impiety; we have betrayed the pure sacrifice and become upholders of unleavened bread.'

Michael Ducas

The Empire of which, on 21 July 1425, the thirty-two-year-old John Palaeologus became sole *basileus* was effectively bounded by the walls of Constantinople; and Constantinople now presented a dismal picture indeed. Already in 1403, Ruy González de Clavijo had remarked on its strange emptiness:

Despite its size and the huge circuit of its walls, it is poorly populated; for in the midst of it are a number of hills and valleys on which there are fields of corn and vineyards and many orchards; and in these cultivated areas the houses are clustered together like villages; and this is in the midst of the city.

Nearly a quarter of a century later, after three sieges – each of which resulted in the flight of many hundreds of citizens, the majority of whom never returned – and several visitations of the plague, the population must have declined still more dramatically. Precise figures are hard to estimate, but by 1425 the inhabitants are unlikely to have numbered more than fifty thousand, and may well have been considerably less.

Economically, too, the Empire was in desperate straits. Once the richest and busiest commercial centre in the civilized world, Constantinople had seen her trade taken over lock, stock and barrel by the Venetians and the Genoese; now they too had suffered from the constant warfare and political instability, and a few paltry customs dues were all that ever trickled into the Byzantine exchequer. The coinage, already debased, was

388

devalued again and again. Thanks to the successive sieges and the depopulation, the system of food distribution was on the point of collapse and frequently broke down altogether. The people were thus chronically undernourished, and their low resistance to disease caused one epidemic after another to rage unchecked through the city.

The simultaneous lack of manpower and of money made it impossible to keep the buildings in repair. Nearly all were by now seriously dilapidated. Many of the churches were little more than empty shells. Constantine's great Hippodrome, rapidly falling into ruin, was used as a polo ground. The Patriarch had long since deserted his palace in favour of somewhere warmer and drier. Even the imperial Palace of Blachernae was crumbling. Later in John's reign another Castilian traveller, Pero Tafur, was to report that

The Emperor's palace must have been very magnificent, but now it is in such state that both it and the city show well the evils which the people have suffered, and which they still endure . . . Inside, the building is badly maintained, except for those parts where the Emperor, the Empress and their attendants can live, although these are sorely cramped for space. The Emperor's state is as splendid as ever, for nothing is omitted from the ancient ceremonies; but, properly regarded, he is as a bishop without a see . . .

The city is sparsely populated. It is divided into districts, that by the sea-shore having the greatest population. The inhabitants are not well clad but are poor and shabby, showing all too well the hardship of their lot – which is however less bad than they deserve, for they are a vicious people, steeped in sin.

It was not an inspiring inheritance; and John must often have thought with envy of his younger brothers. One, the Despot Constantine, was admittedly not much better off: since his father's death he had governed a relatively small area covering the northern approaches to Constantinople, which the Turks had recently allowed the Empire to retain in fief; it included the port of Selymbria and the cities of Mesembria and Anchialus on the Black Sea coast. Strategically it was not without importance; but the Emperor held it only as the vassal of the Sultan, and it is hard to see what he or Constantine could have done if Murad had decided to take it back, or even to advance through it on his way to launch another attack on the capital. The other four of Manuel's sons were all in the Morea – an unmistakable indication of the importance which the southern Despotate had by now assumed in the thinking of the Palaeologi. Their reasons are equally clear. The Morea could be defended; Constantinople could not. The latter, admittedly, still had its Land Walls, which had never yet been breached and which had stood fast against three major sieges in the past quarter-century alone. But during that time the process of depopulation had continued remorse-lessly; every day saw a further decrease in the number of able-bodied men and women able to rally to the city's defence. Worse still was the failure of morale. Few intelligent people any longer cherished a real hope of deliverance. Western Europe had proved itself a broken reed. The Turks – after a brief setback – were now, under the determined and implacable Murad II, as strong as they had ever been. It was all too likely that when (as he surely would) he decided on yet another siege of the city, its inhabitants might make a voluntary surrender – if only to spare themselves the massacre and rapine which would inevitably follow if they did not.

The Morea, on the other hand, was relatively secure. True, it had suffered considerable devastation as recently as 1423, when an army of Turks had invaded Albania and then swept down through Thessaly, seeming almost to ignore Manuel's much-vaunted Hexamilion. But they had not remained for long, the wall had since been heightened and strengthened, and Venice – understandably alarmed at the prospect of a Turkish presence on the Adriatic shore – had promised to come to the rescue if the incident were ever repeated. Already Venetian ships patrolled the coasts, where they were more than a match for the still rudimentary Turkish navy. There remained a few French and Italian princelings ruling their little enclaves amid the mountain valleys; but they had lost much of their former power, and no longer threatened any serious trouble.

Inevitably, there were a few problems. The Peloponnesians, Manuel had complained ten years before, seemed to love fighting for its own sake. The Despots spent most of their time trying to reconcile one faction against another – a task which was not made easier by the fact that the local Greek nobility felt no loyalty to Byzantium and openly resented what they saw as a foreign ascendancy, foisted on them from distant Constantinople. Compared to those in the capital, however, conditions in the Morea were pleasant indeed; and by 1425 few people, offered the alternatives of living in Constantinople or in Mistra, would have hesitated at the choice.

The city of Mistra, lying on the slopes of the Taygetus range in the southern Peloponnese, had been founded by William of Villehardouin, great-nephew of the chronicler of the Fourth Crusade, in 1249. Just twelve years later, after the reconquest of Constantinople by Michael

Palaeologus, William had been obliged to surrender it – together with Monemvasia and the fortress of Maina on Cape Matapan – to Byzantium. For much of the next half-century it had remained little more than a small and remote Greek enclave, set deep in Frankish territory; not surprisingly, the Byzantine Governor preferred to reside at Monemvasia, from which he could keep in regular touch with the capital. As time went on, however, the Greek province steadily grew in size, the Latins retreated, and Monemvasia itself became an outpost. By 1289 we find the Kephale, as he was called, settled more centrally in Mistra; and thus it was to Mistra that the Emperor John VI Cantacuzenus had sent his son Manuel, first Despot of the Morea, in 1349 – exactly a hundred years after the city's foundation.

Manuel had been succeeded by Theodore Palaeologus, fourth son of John V, on whose death in 1407 the Despotate had passed to his nephew and namesake, Theodore II. By this time Mistra had developed into something far more than a mere provincial capital. It was now an artistic, intellectual and religious centre comparable with what Constantinople had been a century before. Its first important church had been built shortly before 1300; and a few years later this was incorporated into a large monastery, the Brontochion – which in turn gave rise to a second church, dedicated to the Virgin Hodegetria, 'she who points the way'. By this time the Metropolitan Church of St Demetrius was already almost completed; two other great churches, the Pantanassa and the Peribleptos, followed soon afterwards, possibly at the instigation of the Despot Manuel. He was certainly responsible for the church of St Sophia, which was used as the palace chapel. Alas, all these buildings have been wholly or partly ruined; but many of their frescoes – particularly those of the Peribleptos – still have the power to catch the breath.

These churches alone are enough to show the extent to which Mistra attracted the greatest artists in the Byzantine world; it was equally active in the field of scholarship. Manuel Cantacuzenus and his brother Matthew – who was technically co-Despot with him after 1361, although he left the business of government in Manuel's hands – were both highly cultivated men, while their father John, the ex-Emperor and one of the greatest scholars of his time, was a regular visitor to Mistra and had indeed died there in 1383. Small wonder was it that others followed. Among them were the famous Metropolitan Bessarion of Nicaea and the future Metropolitan Isidore of Kiev – both of whom were later to become cardinals in the Church of Rome – and the philosopher and theologian

George Scholarius, who under the name of Gennadius II would be the first Patriarch of Constantinople after the fall of the city. The greatest moment, however, in the intellectual life of Mistra was unquestionably that of the arrival in the city of the most original of all Byzantine thinkers, George Gemistos Plethon.

Unlike the rest, Plethon did not come to Mistra of his own free will. At an early age he had fallen foul of the Orthodox establishment. They had been shocked by his stay of several years in Turkish-held Adrianople – where he had studied Aristotle, Zoroastrianism and Jewish cabbalistic philosophy – and seriously alarmed when he gave a course of what they considered to be highly subversive lectures on Platonism at the university; he might well have been arraigned on charges of heresy had not the Emperor Manuel, his friend and admirer, suggested that he might find Mistra a more congenial environment. Plethon asked nothing better. He was acutely aware that Byzantium was the inheritor, not only of the Roman Empire, but of the literature and civilization of classical Greece; and he was happier living and teaching where the ancient Greeks had lived and taught than in what to them had been a barbarian land. Moreover, as a good Platonist he shared his master's frequently-expressed disapproval of Athenian democracy, infinitely preferring the discipline of Sparta; at Mistra, only some five miles away from the ruins of the ancient city, he could almost feel that he was there.

Apart from his year in Italy – to be described later in this chapter – Plethon remained for the rest of his life at Mistra. There he was a member of the Senate and a senior magistrate; but he saw himself primarily as the official court philosopher of the Despotate, in the old tradition of Plato at Syracuse or even of Socrates himself, strolling up and down the local *agora* with his disciples and – always inspired by the Spartan ethos – endlessly developing an elaborate scheme for the reform, the defence and ultimately the salvation of the Morea. This involved reliance on a standing army of citizen Greeks rather than on foreign mercenaries, on strict sumptuary laws and on rigorous standards of temperance and dedication. Land would be held in common; the import and export trades would be closely regulated; monks would be forced to work and make a proper contribution to society. All these reforms were formally proposed by Plethon in a whole series of memoranda, addressed to the Emperor Manuel and his son the Despot Theodore between 1415 and 1418, but it was no use: even at this critical moment in their history, the regime he advocated was too authoritarian, too socialist – in a word, too Spartan – for the Byzantines. They preferred, as they always had, to put their trust in God and the Holy Virgin; if any reforms were necessary, they must be achieved not in the political or social fields but in the hearts of men.

They would have been even more wary of Plethon had they known the directions his thought was taking him. His last work, *On the Laws*, completed only towards the end of his life – he was not to die till 1452, when he was ninety – seems to have proposed a new and extremely idiosyncratic religion, based partly on Persian Zoroastrianism and partly on the old Greek pantheon, where the ancient deities were revived – though more as symbols than anything else – and subordinated to an almighty Zeus. Sad to say, we know this curious composition only from its table of contents; virtually all the rest was destroyed after the author's death by his horrified friend George Scholarius, the future Patriarch. But though George Gemistos Plethon may have died a prophet with relatively little honour in his own country, in Europe – and above all in Renaissance Italy – he was deeply venerated. Not only was Cosimo de' Medici to found the Academy at Florence in his honour; in 1465, when that most cultivated of *condottieri*, Sigismondo Pandolfo Malatesta of Rimini, entered Mistra at the head of a Venetian army, he removed Plethon's body from its simple grave and took it back with him to his native city. There it still lies, in the magnificent tomb he built for it in the cathedral church of S. Francesco, a proud inscription paying tribute to 'the greatest Philosopher of his time'.

During the first five years of the new reign, things went well for the Despotate of the Morea. In 1427 John VIII, accompanied by his brother Constantine and George Sphrantzes, personally led a campaign which destroyed the fleet of Carlo Tocco, Lord of Cephalonia and Epirus, at the mouth of the Gulf of Patras. By the terms of the resulting treaty Tocco gave his niece Maddalena in marriage to Constantine, together with the region of Elis and the port of Clarenza (the modern Killini) in the north-western Peloponnese. Two years later Constantine wrested Patras itself from the control of its Latin Archbishop, even gaining recognition from Sultan Murad of its return to the Despotate; and by 1430 most of the Morea – with the important exceptions of the Venetian-held harbours of Corone, Modone and Nauplia – was back in Greek hands.

Progress in the south, however, was outweighed by disaster further north; for in March 1430 the city of Thessalonica fell once again to the Sultan. Its seven years under the banner of St Mark had not been a success. The Turks had maintained their blockade; meanwhile, as the Venetian governors persisted in ignoring the formal undertakings made at the time of the transfer of power, local resentment had steadily increased to the point where many of the inhabitants were shamelessly in favour of opening the gates to the infidel. Before long the Venetians, far from turning Thessalonica into a second Venice as they had promised, were heartily regretting that they had ever accepted the Despot's offer which, they complained – since the Sultan was forcing them to pay an annual tribute – was costing them some 60,000 ducats a year. On the other hand, they still had their pride; and when Murad himself arrived on 26 March with an army estimated – surely with wild exaggeration – at one hundred and ninety thousand men to demand the immediate surrender of the city, he was answered with a hail of arrows.

On the following day the monks of the monastery of the Vlataion (which still stands just inside the northern walls) are said to have sent a message to the Sultan advising him to cut the pipes that brought water into the city. Whether or not they were actually guilty of such treachery we shall never know, though it seems extremely unlikely – and unlikelier still that he acted upon their advice. This time he was putting his trust in brute strength; he had collected and equipped a huge army, and he was determined to use it. The attack began at dawn on 29 March, Murad himself taking command of the units drawn up along the eastern section of the walls which seemed to him to be the weakest. For some three hours his catapults, mangonels and battering rams did their worst, while his archers loosed further volleys of arrows every time a defender showed himself above the bastion. Gradually the Thessalonians, realizing that the situation was hopeless, grew more and more discouraged; many of them deserted their posts; and soon after nine o'clock in the morning the Sultan's men managed to bring the first scaling-ladder into place against the wall. A moment later a Turkish soldier was up and over the parapet, triumphantly throwing the severed head of a Venetian guard down to his comrades below as a sign that they should follow.

The people of Thessalonica were only too well aware of the fate that a-waited any city that resisted conquest, and that the Turks were conse-quently obliged to take by storm; but for many of them the events of the next seventy-two hours must have exceeded their worst fears. A Greek eye-witness, John Anagnostes, describes how the streets were loud with the war-cries of the Turks as they charged through the city in a frenzy of murder and pillage, and how these dreadful sounds mingled with the screams of children torn from their mothers and wives from their husbands. All the churches were looted, and many of them destroyed; the palaces of the nobility were ransacked, then either requisitioned or put to the torch. The number of victims of the massacre is unknown, but Anagnostes estimates that not less than seven thousand – mostly women and children – were carried off into slavery.

After the statutory three days, Murad called a halt. Thessalonica was the second city of the Byzantine Empire; he had no wish to reduce it to a smoking ruin. Its inhabitants had been taught the traditional lesson; those who had survived it had been punished enough. A general amnesty was declared; a number of distinguished citizens who had been imprisoned were immediately released; rich and poor alike were invited to return to their homes, with a guarantee that they would suffer no more ill-treatment. The Christian religion would everywhere be respected, apart from the conversion of certain churches into mosques – including the most venerable Panaghia Acheiropoietos ('not made with hands'), which had stood for almost a thousand years.[1]

And what, it may be asked, of the Venetian governors of the city – those who had boasted that they would turn it into a second Venice and whose determined resistance had been the cause of all the misery and bloodshed? Somehow, in the general chaos, they had managed to make their way down to the harbour, where a ship was waiting to bear them off to the nearest Venetian soil, the colony of Euboea. When they finally returned to their lagoon, it was to find the Doge and Senate extremely displeased with their performance: accused of having neglected the protection of the city that they had been charged to defend, they were thrown into prison. They were lucky to have escaped so lightly; their crimes were greater than their masters ever knew.

Away in the West, the Roman Catholic Church was still in confusion. The Council of Constance had failed to effect any real reforms; indeed, in at least one respect it had done more harm than good, since it had declared itself to be a General Council, with an authority that derived directly from God and was consequently superior to that of the Pope himself. This had dangerously intensified the already existing dispute between those who supported such a view and those who believed in

---

1 The church took its name from a celebrated icon it once contained, which was said to have been miraculously painted. It remained under Muslim control until early this century (the city was Turkish until 1913) and has unfortunately suffered more damage since – in 1923 when it was occupied by Greek refugees from Asia Minor, and more recently as a result of the severe earthquake of June 1978.

absolute papal supremacy, to a point where it began to present a serious threat to Church discipline; and it was largely in an attempt to settle the matter once and for all that Pope Martin V summoned a new council, to meet at Basel in 1431.

To John Palaeologus, this council seemed to offer a ray of hope. Once again as at Constance, representatives of all the Christian nations of the West would be present; and although their reactions on the previous occasion had been disappointing to say the least, much had happened in the past fifteen years to make them change their minds. Venice in particular had been brought face to face with Turkish arms at Thessalonica, and had suffered serious damage not only to her financial and strategic interests but – far more important – to her international prestige. Sigismund of Hungary, too, had watched powerless during the previous summer as the Sultan marched from Thessalonica right across the Balkan peninsula to Epirus, accepted the surrender of Ioannina without a struggle and then pressed on through Albania, pushing the frontiers of his Empire further and further back towards Sigismund's own. This time, perhaps, a Byzantine appeal might fall on more receptive ears; and where Venice and Hungary led, others would surely follow. John was also intrigued by the conflict over the authority of General Councils. Virtually all recent attempts at Church union had foundered on a similar issue, the Byzantines insisting on a council to be held at Constantinople, the Latins refusing to consider such a proposal; might there not be potential allies among the conciliarists, capable at last of swinging opinion in his favour?

The imperial ambassadors, arriving at the papal court in the late summer of 1431, found tensions running high. Pope Martin had died in February and his successor, Eugenius IV, in a desperate attempt to assert his authority, had ordered the council to leave Basel and to hold all future sessions in Italy where he could exercise a firmer control; the delegates, however, had announced that they were staying where they were. On 18 December Eugenius issued a bull dissolving the entire gathering and declaring its deliberations null and void; this time the delegates simply reaffirmed the decrees issued at Constance, pointing out that they too constituted a General Council – although at that time they numbered only fourteen of the senior clergy – and that their own authority was consequently paramount. For the next two years the dispute continued, and as it did so John found himself wooed ever more assiduously by both parties: the council pressing him to send an official delegation to Basel, the Pope equally anxious that he should do nothing of the kind. Finally in 1433 the Emperor took his decision, nominating three ambassadors to represent him at the council; when a papal legation arrived to remonstrate he sent another delegation, this time to Eugenius; and so he continued, playing one side off against the other, until in the summer of 1437 matters came finally to a head.

By this time the Pope had been obliged to revoke his former decision and to recognize the council after all; more important for John VIII, he had also reluctantly accepted what the Byzantines had never ceased to maintain: that true union could be achieved only by means of a council of the whole Church, to be attended by representatives of both East and West. To the vast majority of those concerned, however, it was now obvious that Basel was not the place. The past six years had seen too much ill feeling and bitterness; if the proposed council were to have any chance of success, a fresh start was essential. The more hidebound of the conciliarists objected – in 1439 going so far as to declare the Pope deposed and to elect an anti-Pope in his stead – but this arbitrary renewal of the papal schism cost them what little prestige they had left, and one by one the Christian nations submitted to the authority of Eugenius.

Ideally, the Emperor would have wished the new council to be held in Constantinople; but he was obliged to admit that in the circumstances now prevailing this was no longer practicable. He therefore willingly accepted the Pope's choice of Ferrara, confirming that he personally, together with his Patriarch, would head the imperial delegation. Eugenius, hearing this welcome news, lost no time. By September his legates were already in Constantinople to work out the details, while others were negotiating with the Venetians for the hiring of a fleet to bring the Byzantine delegation in proper state to Ferrara. Thus it was that John Palaeologus once again left his brother Constantine as Regent in Constantinople and on Wednesday, 27 November 1437 embarked on his historic journey, taking with him a party some seven hundred strong, among them the most distinguished group of Eastern churchmen ever to visit the West. There was the Patriarch himself, Joseph II – nearly eighty years old, crippled by heart disease but beloved of all who met him; eighteen Metropolitans, some of them representing his fellow-Patriarchs of Alexandria, Antioch and Jerusalem, and also including the brilliant young Metropolitan Bessarion of Nicaea; Isidore, Abbot of the monastery of St Demetrius in Constantinople, who had attended the Council of Basel and had been promoted in the previous year to be Bishop of Kiev and All Russia; and some twelve other bishops. Among the laymen were

George Scholarius, whose knowledge of Latin theology and, more particularly, of the thinking of St Thomas Aquinas would, it was hoped, confound the scholars of the West; and, most revered of all, George Gemistos Plethon himself from Mistra. All these were pro-Western, to a greater or lesser degree. The leading light of the ultra-Orthodox camp was Mark Eugenicus, Metropolitan of Ephesus. One of his Church's leading theologians and an implacable opponent of the *filioque*, he was to cause John much irritation and anxiety in the months that followed.

The Emperor also took with him his brother Demetrius, to whom in 1429 he had given the title of Despot. He did not delude himself that Demetrius would make any effective contribution to the coming debate; but he already knew him for a dangerous intriguer, and thought it safer to have him where he could keep an eye on him. Subsequent events were to prove him right.

The party reached Venice on 8 February 1438, and anchored off the Lido. This time the Republic was determined to spare no expense in giving the Emperor the most splendid reception it could devise. Early the following morning, Doge Francesco Foscari came out to greet him, and according to George Sphrantzes – who was not himself an eye-witness but claims the Despot Demetrius as his authority – showed him every mark of respect, making a deep obeisance and standing bareheaded while John remained seated before him. Only after a decent interval did the Doge take a chair, specially set for him at a slightly lower level on the Emperor's left, while the two discussed the details of John's cere-monial entrance into the city. Foscari then returned to prepare for the official reception.

At noon the Doge, attended as always by his six-man *Signoria*, sailed out in his state barge, the *Bucintoro*, its sides hung with scarlet damask, the golden lion of St Mark glinting from the poop, the oarsmen's jackets stitched with golden thread; as it advanced, other smaller vessels took up their positions around it, pennants streaming from their mastheads, bands of musicians playing on their decks. Coming alongside the Em-peror's flagship, Foscari went aboard and once again made his obeisances. He had originally assumed that the two rulers would then be rowed into the city in the *Bucintoro*, but John demurred. His imperial dignity, he considered, made it necessary that he should disembark in Venice from his own vessel; orders were accordingly given that this should be towed from the Lido to the foot of the Piazzetta, where what appeared to be the entire population of the city was waiting to greet its exalted guest, cheering him to the echo. From there the procession slowly wound its way up the Grand Canal, beneath the wooden Rialto Bridge where more crowds waited with banners and trumpets, and so finally at sunset to the great palace of the Marquis of Ferrara,[1] which had been put at the disposal of the imperial party for the duration of their visit. There the Emperor stayed for three weeks, writing letters to all the princes of Europe, urging them to attend the council or at least to send representatives. It was the end of the month before he himself left on the final stage of his journey.

Compared to his Venetian reception, John's arrival at Ferrara was a lacklustre affair, not improved by pouring rain. Pope Eugenius gave him a warm welcome, but even this was somewhat clouded when the Emperor was informed that his Patriarch, on his arrival a few days later, would be expected to prostrate himself and kiss the Pontiff's foot. Old Joseph was the mildest and gentlest of men, but even for him this was too much. When he received John's warning message he refused to come ashore until the demand was retracted. At last Eugenius was obliged to yield; had he not done so, it is doubtful whether the Council of Ferrara would ever have taken place. This was only the first of many painful problems of protocol and precedence to arise; both Emperor and Pope were extremely sensitive on all matters affecting their dignity. The relative positions of their two thrones in the cathedral, for example, raised difficulties which at one moment seemed almost insuperable. Later, when the venue had been shifted to the papal palace, John was to insist on proceeding on horseback to his throne itself; when this proved impossible, he demanded that a hole should be broken through a wall in order that he should not be seen dismounting, and that he could be carried to the throne without his foot touching the ground. This was done – and the sessions were suspended till the work was completed.

Such extraordinary punctilio may seem excessive, even ridiculous. To some extent it was part of the elaborate protocol which had always existed at the Byzantine court; but in Ferrara, as later in Florence, it also had a deliberate purpose. If John's mission to the West were to succeed, it was essential that he should be seen not as a suppliant but as the monarch of a great – if not the only – Christian Empire, a vital element

---

[1] This thirteenth-century palace, restored with marvellous insensitivity in the 1860s and – in consequence of its later history – better known today as the Fondaco dei Turchi, still stands on the upper reaches of the Grand Canal, opposite the S. Marcuola *vaporetto* station.

in the whole polity of Christendom which must be preserved at all costs from the cupidity of the Turk. The Patriarchal official Sylvester Syropulus, from whose invaluable if somewhat tendentious behind-the-scenes record of the council the above anecdotes have been taken, also records a remark made by the Emperor to the Patriarch before their departure from Constantinople, about the appearance of the Greek ecclesiastics: 'If the Church makes a dignified showing, it will be honoured by them and will be a credit to us. But if it is seen to be dirty and unkempt, it will be despised by them and counted for nothing.'

Quite apart from the vexatious questions of etiquette, the council got off to a bad start. John had stipulated that four months should elapse before the formal discussions on doctrine were begun; one of his principal reasons for attending was to seek help from the other European princes, and he was determined that no important decisions should be taken before their arrival. But spring turned to summer, and no princes appeared. The Latins grew more and more impatient, the Pope – who was responsible for the board and lodging of the entire Greek delegation – more and more concerned as his financial reserves fell ever lower. In June and July – to give themselves something to do – limited numbers of Greeks and Latins opened discussions on the question of Purgatory, which was doubtless where many of them felt themselves to be; but they reached no conclusions.

With August came the plague. Strangely enough, the Greeks appeared immune – the Emperor was in any case away from Ferrara for most of the time, indulging in his favourite sport of hunting – but there was heavy mortality both among the Latin delegates and in the city as a whole. Meanwhile the Latins grew even more irritated with their guests. Fortunately for them, however, the Greeks too were losing patience. They had been away from home for the best part of a year at a time of great anxiety and uncertainty, and had so far achieved nothing. Many of them too were short of money, for the papal subsidies were becoming increasingly irregular. Finally it was by now plain that none of the European princes had any intention of attending the council at all, so that there was no point in waiting for them any longer. It was to everyone's relief when deliberations began in earnest on 8 October.

For the first three months they were concerned almost exclusively with the *filioque* clause – and not even the question of whether the Holy Ghost did in fact proceed from the Father *and the Son* (rather than from the Father only) so much as that of whether the act of introducing it into the Nicene Creed was legitimate or no. The principal spokesman on the Greek side was the Metropolitan Mark Eugenicus, who rested his case on a specific regulation agreed in 451 by the Council of Ephesus: 'To no one is it allowed to recite, write or compose a faith other than that defined by the Holy Fathers in Nicaea.' The Latins argued that the disputed word was a clarification rather than an addition, and pointed out that the Creed as recited in the Greek Church already incorporated various changes from the Nicene original; but the Metropolitan would have none of it. It was anyway, they suggested, a profoundly insignificant point; in that case, he testily replied, why were they so determined to keep it in? The issue was further clouded by linguistic problems. Few of the delegates spoke any language other than their own, and there were no qualified interpreters. Additional difficulties arose when it was discovered, at a fairly early stage in the proceedings, that various Latin and Greek words at first believed to be precise equivalents were in fact nothing of the sort: to take but one example the Greek word *ousia*, meaning 'substance', carried with it various shades of meaning quite alien to the Latin *substantia*. The sessions ended on 13 December with agreement as far away as ever.

At this point the Pope managed to persuade the delegates to move to Florence. He gave as his reason the continued presence of the plague in Ferrara, but his true motives were almost certainly financial: the council had been sitting for eight months, it showed every sign of going on indefinitely, and it had already made alarming inroads on the papal treasury. In Florence, on the other hand, the Medici could be trusted to help out. But the move also proved beneficial in other ways. When the sessions were resumed towards the end of February 1439 the Greeks – tired, anxious, homesick and (if Syropulus is to be believed) hungry – seemed distinctly readier to compromise than they had been in the previous year. By the end of March they had agreed that the Latin formula according to which the Holy Spirit proceeded from the Father *and* the Son meant the same as a recently-accepted Greek formula whereby it proceeded from the Father *through* the Son. It was soon after this breakthrough that Patriarch Joseph finally expired; but then, as an observer rather unkindly remarked, after muddling his prepositions what else could he decently do?

With the *filioque* at last out of the way, the other outstanding questions were quickly settled. The Greeks disapproved of the Roman dogma on Purgatory (for which they could find no justification) and of the use of unleavened bread at the Sacrament (which, they thought, not only smacked of Judaism but was disrespectful of the Holy Ghost, symbolized by the leaven); they also deplored the Latin practice of giving communion in both kinds to the laity, and of forbidding the marriage of secular priests. But on all these issues they put up only a token opposition. When, on the other hand, the Latins violently attacked the recently-defined Eastern doctrine concerning the uncreated Energies of God, they declined to press the point. The question of papal supremacy might at other times have caused difficulties, but since the Council of Basel this had been a delicate subject and was consequently glossed over as far as possible.[1] Thanks largely to the Emperor himself – who employed persuasion and threats in equal measure to ensure the amenability of his subjects – by mid-summer agreement had been reached on every major issue, and on Sunday, 5 July the official Decree of Union – little more than a statement of the Latin position, apart from one or two concessions permitting Greek usages – was signed by all the Orthodox bishops and abbots except the Metropolitan of Ephesus, who had given in on absolutely nothing but was forbidden by John to exercise a veto. The Latins then added their own signatures; and on the following day the decree was publicly proclaimed in Florence cathedral, being recited first in Latin by Cardinal Giuliano Cesarini (who from the beginning had been the principal Latin spokesman) and then in Greek by the Metropolitan Bessarion of Nicaea. The Latin version began with the words *Laetentur Coeli* – 'let the heavens rejoice'. But the heavens, as it soon became clear, had precious little reason to do so.

It was February 1440 before John Palaeologus returned, via Venice, to Constantinople. He had a sad homecoming. After the departure of his luckless second wife Sophia of Montferrat, who had fled back to Italy fourteen years before, he had married Maria, the daughter of the Emperor Alexius IV of Trebizond. She had proved the love of his life, and he was broken-hearted to learn as he stepped from his ship that she had died a few weeks before. More serious for the Empire was the fact that the Council of Florence was already almost universally condemned. The Patriarchs of Jerusalem, Alexandria and Antioch disowned the delegates who had signed on their behalf. Mark Eugenicus, Metropolitan of Ephesus, was the hero of the hour. The signatories to the hated

---

1 It was during discussions on this subject that the Donation of Constantine – according to which Constantine the Great, on transferring his capital to Constantinople, was said to have left the imperial crown to the Pope to bestow on whomever he wished – was used as evidence for the last time. Only a year later the Renaissance humanist Lorenzo Valla proved it a forgery. (See *Byzantium: The Early Centuries*, p. 379.)

Laetentur Coeli were condemned as outcasts and traitors to the Faith, castigated throughout the capital and in several cases physically attacked – to the point where in 1441 a large number of them issued a public manifesto, regretting that they had ever put their names to the decree and formally retracting their support for it.

Such general revulsion could not but have a dangerous effect on the Emperor's own position. In the summer of 1442 his ever-ambitious brother Demetrius – who had accompanied him to Florence but had left early, together with George Scholarius and Plethon, and returned his minor Despotate at Mesembria – tried to seize the throne for himself in the name of Orthodoxy. Despite assistance from the Turks, he was quickly captured and put under house arrest; but his attempted *coup* was only a symptom of a greater dissatisfaction, which continued to grow – especially after the return to Constantinople of the Metropolitan of Ephesus the following year. Mark Eugenicus proved a far more dangerous opponent than Demetrius. In other circumstances he might have been dismissed as an incorrigible reactionary, but now he stood out as the most fearless and determined champion of the Faith. After all the practice that he had gained in Ferrara and Florence, he was a superb debater; and such was the genuine piety and the blamelessness of his life that there could be no question of trumping up charges against him and sending him into exile.

True, there were other distinguished pro-unionists who might have given John their support; but Bessarion of Nicaea, who had been converted to Catholicism in 1439 and almost immediately made a cardinal, had left Constantinople in disgust within a few months of his return and taken the first available ship back to Italy, never again to set foot on Byzantine soil.[1] His friend Isidore of Kiev, who had also been admitted to the Cardinalate, was less lucky: on his return to Moscow he was deposed and arrested – though later he too managed to escape to Italy and, as we shall see, was back in Constantinople soon afterwards as a papal representative. As for George Scholarius, that distinguished Latin scholar, he was to reveal feet of clay; before long he too renounced the *Laetentur Coeli* and retired to a monastery. After the death of Mark Eugenicus in 1444 he was to become the generally accepted leader of the anti-unionists.

---

1 In Rome Bessarion was to found an academy for the translation and publication of ancient Greek authors. By his death in 1472 he had amassed an important library of Greek manuscripts, all of which he left to Venice – where they became the nucleus of the Biblioteca Marciana.

The papal nuncio in Constantinople naturally kept his master fully informed of these developments, for which he tended to hold the Emperor responsible. Pope Eugenius, however, chose at least temporarily to overlook them. Church union now existed, at least on paper; and it was now incumbent on him to raise a Crusade against Byzantium's enemies. Were he to refuse to do so on the grounds of spiritual insubordination, he would not only be going back on his word to the Emperor; he would be proclaiming to all that the Council of Florence had been a failure, the *Laetentur Coeli* worthless. Besides, the Crusade was becoming more obviously necessary every day; for the Ottoman advance was relentless. Smederevo, the great Danubian fortress built by George Brankovich in 1420 some twenty-five miles south-east of Belgrade,[1] had surrendered in 1439 after a three-month siege; Brankovich himself had sought refuge in Hungary. Though Belgrade itself still held out, virtually all the rest of northern Serbia was under Turkish control. In 1441 the Sultan's army crossed into Transylvania; there could be no doubt that Hungary would be next.

It was thus the Hungarians – together with the Serbs under George Brankovich – who formed the bulk of the Pope's Crusade, the Hungarian King Ladislas (also King of Poland, the two Kingdoms having been temporarily united) whom he named its leader and a Hungarian general – the brilliant John Hunyadi, Voyevod of Transylvania – to whom he entrusted the supreme military command. The organization he placed in the hands of Cardinal Giuliano Cesarini, the principal Latin spokesman at Florence who had long been Eugenius's right-hand man, particularly where foreign relations were concerned. The necessary fleet was to be provided by the Venetians, the Duke of Burgundy and the Pope himself. It was to sail through the Hellespont, the Marmara and the Bosphorus to the Black Sea, thence if necessary proceeding up the Danube to meet the army, which would advance simultaneously from the north-west.

The Crusade set off some twenty-five thousand strong in the late summer of 1443, and within weeks succeeded in destroying the forces of the Turkish Governor of Rumelia just outside the Serbian city of Nish. Unopposed, it now marched onward into Bulgaria where Sofia surrendered, after only a token resistance, shortly before Christmas. January 1444 saw another major victory; and by late spring the Sultan was growing seriously alarmed. Suddenly, his Empire was threatened on

1 Its ruins still stand today, and very impressive they are.

every side. In Anatolia he was struggling to put down a dangerous rising of the Karamans. In Albania a certain George Kastriotes, the famous Scanderbeg, had raised the banner of revolt from his castle at Croia. In the Morea, Constantine Palaeologus – who, having exchanged his Black Sea appanage with his brother Theodore, had been ruling as Despot since the previous October – had rebuilt the Hexamilion and pushed on across the Gulf of Corinth, where before long he had occupied both Athens and Thebes and forced the local Duke Nerio II Acciajuoli to pay him the tribute that the Duke had previously owed to the Sultan as his vassal. Clearly, if Turkish power were to be maintained, Murad would have to make some sort of accommodation with his enemies.

In June, ambassadors from King Ladislas, George Brankovich and John Hunyadi were received at the Sultan's court in Adrianople. The result of the ensuing negotiations was a ten-year truce, by the terms of which, among other concessions, Murad promised to loosen his grip on Wallachia, and Brankovich had his Serbian territories restored to him. A month later the treaty was ratified by Ladislas at Szegedin. Freed at last – as he thought – from his problems in Europe, the Sultan left for Anatolia to deal with the Karaman rebels once and for all. When the news reached Rome, however, Pope Eugenius and his Curia were horrified. Hunyadi's victories and the recent promise of additional help from the Venetians had called up visions of the Turks being expelled altogether from Europe; were all the gains that the Crusade had so far achieved to be thrown away? Cardinal Cesarini was particularly incensed: refusing to see his careful organization brought to nothing, he hastened to Szegedin, immediately absolved King Ladislas from the oath he had sworn to the Sultan and virtually ordered the Crusade on its way again.

Ladislas should have refused. Not only was he breaking his solemn word – absolution or no absolution – to the Sultan; his forces were dangerously diminished. Many of the erstwhile Crusaders had already left for home and George Brankovich, who had in any case been delighted with the terms of the truce, was determined to observe it. But a few reinforcements had recently arrived from Wallachia, and the young King decided to do as he was bidden. In September he was back with the army – accompanied now by the cardinal himself. The Crusade started off once again, and despite sporadic resistance somehow managed to make its way across Bulgaria to the Black Sea near Varna, where Ladislas confidently expected to find his fleet awaiting him. The fleet, however, was otherwise engaged. Murad, on hearing of his betrayal, had rushed back from Anatolia with an army of eighty thousand men, and the allied ships – mostly Venetian – were desperately trying to prevent him from crossing the Bosphorus. They failed. Forcing his way across the strait, the furious Sultan hurried up the Black Sea coast and on 10 November 1444, with the broken treaty pinned to his standard, tore into the Crusading army. The Christians stood their ground and fought with desperate courage; outnumbered, however, by more than three to one, they had no chance. Ladislas fell; so, shortly afterwards, did Cesarini. The army was annihilated; of its leaders, only John Hunyadi managed to escape with a few of his men. The last Crusade ever to be launched against the Turks in Europe had ended in catastrophe. It was a devastating blow, from which Christian morale would never recover.

For the Emperor John Palaeologus, the disaster at Varna meant the negation of all his work, the frustration of all his diplomacy, the end of all his hopes. For this, he now realized, and for this alone he had risked the dangers of foreign travel, endured the barely concealed scorn of his fellow-princes, betrayed his Church and incurred the hatred and contempt of the vast majority of his own subjects. And the final humiliation was yet to come. When the victorious Sultan returned it was John, as his loyal and faithful vassal, who was obliged to bid him welcome and congratulate him on his triumph.

The Emperor's brother Constantine, on the other hand, was undismayed. He had found a new ally in the shape of the Duke of Burgundy, Philip V. Philip, a fervent believer in the fight against the infidel, had already provided – or at any rate offered to provide – ships for the recent disastrous Crusade, but like Constantine he had been in no way deterred by its failure. In the summer of 1445 he sent a company of several hundred of his own men to the Morea, thus enabling the Despot to embark on another raiding expedition through central Greece as far as the Pindus mountains and into Albania. He was welcomed everywhere he went, and at least one local Venetian governor was obliged to beat a hasty retreat. Meanwhile Constantine's own Governor of Achaia left his base at Vostitsa with a small company of cavalry and foot soldiers, crossed to the north shore of the Gulf of Corinth and drove the Turks out of western Phocis – the region around Delphi.

This last insult was too much for the Sultan. Only a few months before, he had abdicated his throne in favour of his son Mehmet; now he furiously resumed his old authority to take vengeance against these upstart Greeks. In November 1446, accompanied by the recently evicted

Duke of Athens and Thebes, he swept down into the Morea at the head of an army of some fifty thousand. Phocis was once again overrun; Constantine and his brother-Despot Thomas hurried back to the rebuilt Hexamilion, determined to hold it at all costs. But they had not reckoned on Murad's weaponry. He had brought with him not only the usual siege engines and scaling-ladders, but something that the Greeks had never seen before – heavy artillery. For five days his long cannons pounded away at the great wall; then, on 10 December, he gave the order for the final assault. Most of the defenders were taken prisoner or massacred; the Despots themselves barely managed to make their way back to Mistra.

But the Sultan was not yet ready for a war of conquest. That would come in its own time; meanwhile he was in no hurry. His purpose on this occasion was simply to chastise the Greeks, to teach them a lesson and to leave them in no doubt as to who was master, in the Morea just as everywhere else. Sending half his army under his General Turachan southwards towards Mistra, he himself set off with his regiment of Janissaries along the southern shore of the Gulf of Corinth, leaving a trail of devastation behind him. The city of Patras – though most of its population had fled across the Gulf to Naupactus – had prepared itself for a siege and refused to surrender; ignoring it, Murad marched on to Clarenza, where Turachan joined him. The general had failed to reach Mistra; it was by now mid-winter, and the mountain passes were blocked by snow. But he too had laid waste the countryside, burning and pillaging every town and village through which he had passed. The historian Laonicus Chalcocondylas – whose father had been briefly imprisoned after delivering a message from Constantine to the Sultan at an earlier stage of the campaign, after which he had been an eye-witness of the battle for the Hexamilion – reports that when Murad and his general returned to Adrianople they took with them no less than sixty thousand prisoners; a later account estimates the number of dead at twenty-two thousand.

In one respect the Despots were lucky: their capital was spared. The Italian traveller and antiquarian Ciriaco of Ancona, arriving at Mistra in July 1447, seems to have noticed few changes since his previous visit ten years before. He had an audience with the Despot Thomas, he met the ageing Plethon, and he was delighted to be taken by Laonicus Chalcocondylas to inspect the ruins of ancient Sparta on the plain below the city. Admittedly these interested the father of modern archaeology far more than contemporary Mistra, but he noted that the land was fertile and the recent harvest plentiful, and it is clear that – at least to the average visitor – life in the southern Peloponnese appeared normal enough. Things could, however, have been very different. Mistra had been saved by one thing only: an unusually early and severe winter. Had the Sultan launched his campaign in May or June rather than in November, Turachan would have had no difficulty in reaching the remotest corners of the Peloponnese; and Mistra, with all its churches and glorious frescos, would almost certainly have been reduced to ashes.

Constantine was able to spend most of the two years following the Turkish invasion doing his best to repair the damage it had caused; the Sultan, on the other hand, was still bent on extending his Empire. In the summer of 1448 he turned his attention to John Hunyadi, now Regent of Hungary. Hunyadi was ready for him. He had already gathered an army of Hungarians, Wallachians and assorted mercenaries, and marched south in the expectation of joining forces with the Albanian Scanderbeg. But Scanderbeg was fully occupied with the Venetians; and Hunyadi was without an ally when, on 17 October, he faced the Sultan on that same plain of Kosovo that had seen the destruction of the Serbian nation less than sixty years before. For three long days the battle raged; but by the 20th the Hungarians could fight no longer. John Hunyadi escaped, but was almost immediately captured by his former ally George Brankovich – now a faithful vassal of the Sultan – who held him until he had agreed to pay compensation for damage caused by his army in Serbia.

Eleven days later, on 31 October 1448, John VIII died in Constantinople. Though he was still only fifty-six, the disappointments of the past few years had aged him prematurely and left him a sad and broken man. After Varna and Kosovo there could be no more Crusades; few people anywhere in Europe now believed that the Empire could be saved from the infidel, and there were by now a good many, at least in the Latin world, who seriously doubted whether it was worth saving. Of all the Byzantine Emperors John is the best known in appearance, thanks to his portrait in the famous fresco of the Magi by Benozzo Gozzoli that adorns the chapel of the Palazzo Medici-Riccardi in Florence.[1] But he hardly merited his posthumous celebrity. Manuel II had remarked on his deathbed that the Empire needed not a great *basileus* but a good manager; it has been rightly observed[2] that John was neither.

---

1 See cover illustration.
2 By Professor Nicol, op. cit., p. 386.

He possessed neither the ability of his father nor the charismatic qualities of his brother. Much of his reign was spent, in defiance of Manuel's wise advice, in the pursuance of a policy which could never conceivably have succeeded; as a result he sacrificed his Church's independence, forfeited his own popularity and ultimately brought about only a miserable campaign that did far more harm than good.

Yet we must not be too hard on John VIII. He did his best, and worked diligently for what he believed to be right. Besides, the situation that he inherited was already past all hope; in such circumstances, virtually anything that he had attempted would have been doomed to failure. And perhaps it was just as well. Byzantium, devoured from within, threatened from without, scarcely capable any longer of independent action, reduced now to an almost invisible dot on the map of Europe, needed – more, probably, than any once-great nation has ever needed – the *coup de grâce*. It had been a long time coming. Now, finally, it was at hand.

24

The Fall

[1448–53]

Have ye heard of a city of which one side is land and the two others sea? The
Hour of Judgement shall not sound until seventy thousand sons of Isaac shall
capture it.

The Prophet Mohammed,
according to ancient Islamic tradition

John VIII Palaeologus had died childless. His first wife had succumbed
to the plague at the age of fifteen; his second he had refused even to
look at; his third he had dearly loved, but she too had failed to present
him with an heir. Admittedly he had five brothers – too many, as it
turned out, since they were endlessly squabbling among themselves and
he had proved totally incapable of keeping them in order – of whom the
first, Theodore, had predeceased him by four months and the second,
Andronicus, had died young in Thessalonica. Of the three survivors –
Constantine, Demetrius and Thomas – John had formally nominated
Constantine as his heir; but Demetrius, who was consumed by ambition
and had already made one unsuccessful bid for the throne after his
brother's return from Florence six years before, immediately hurried
from Selymbria to Constantinople to claim the succession. As self-
proclaimed leader of the anti-unionists – and recognized as such by
George Scholarius – he enjoyed a certain popularity in the capital and
might well have achieved his objective had it not been for his mother,
the Empress Helena; but she at once declared Constantine the rightful
Emperor, simultaneously asserting her right to act as Regent until he
should arrive from the Morea. Thomas, the youngest of the brothers,
who had reached Constantinople in mid-November, gave her his full
support; and Demetrius, seeing that he was beaten, finally did likewise.
Early in December the Empress sent George Sphrantzes to the Sultan's
court to obtain his approval for the new *basileus*.

Meanwhile two envoys had sailed for the Morea with powers to

invest Constantine as Emperor. Clearly they could not perform a coronation, nor was there any Patriarch at Mistra; the ceremony which was
held there on 6 January 1449 was almost certainly a purely civil one,
consisting of a public acclamation followed by a simple investiture. Such
a procedure had at least one perfectly valid historical precedent: Manuel
Comnenus had been similarly invested by his father John II in the wilds
of Cilicia. But on that occasion, and even when – as with John
Cantacuzenus in 1341 – a coronation had taken place outside the capital,
it had been thought proper to have the Emperor crowned by the
Patriarch of Constantinople in St Sophia as soon as this was practicable.
With Constantine XI Dragases – he always preferred to use this Greek
form of his Serbian mother's name – no such full ecclesiastical coronation
ever occurred. How could it have? The Orthodox Church, since the
Council of Florence, was in schism. The Patriarch Gregory III, a fervent
unionist, was not recognized – and was indeed execrated as a traitor – by
well over half his flock. Constantine himself, though he played down the
issue as much as he could, had never condemned the union; if by
upholding it he could increase even infinitesimally the chances of Western
aid it was, he felt, his duty to do so. But the price was high. The anti-
unionists, who continued vehemently to proclaim the folly of seeking
salvation from Western heretics rather than from the Almighty, refused to
pray for him in their churches. Without a coronation in St Sophia he
had no moral claim on their loyalties, or on those of any of his subjects;
yet any such coronation would have caused widespread riots and might
even have triggered off a full-scale civil war.

When Constantine Dragases first set foot as Emperor in his capital on
12 March 1449 – it is a sad reflection on the state of the Empire that he
had been obliged to travel from Greece in a Venetian ship, there being
no Byzantine vessels available – this whole impossible situation was
immediately clear to him; yet Pope Nicholas V, who had succeeded
Eugenius in 1447, was either unwilling or unable to accept it. Ever since
ecclesiastical union had first been mooted, the Papacy had insistently
refused to see the difficulties involved on the Byzantine side; and
Nicholas was no less blind than his predecessors. When in April 1451, in
yet another attempt to convince him, Constantine sent to Rome a long
and detailed statement by the anti-unionist leaders, he only urged the
Emperor to be firm with his opponents: if they spoke against the union
or showed any disrespect for the Church of Rome of which they were
now members they must be properly punished. Meanwhile, he continued,
Patriarch Gregory – who had resigned in despair a short time before –

must be reinstated; and the decree of the Council of Florence must be properly proclaimed in St Sophia and celebrated with a Mass of Thanksgiving. In May 1452 he finally lost patience and dispatched Cardinal Isidore of Kiev as Apostolic Legate to settle the matter once and for all.

The Emperor, meanwhile, had had other problems to consider, among the most pressing of which was that of the succession. He was now in his middle forties, and twice widowed. Both his marriages had been happy, but neither had proved fruitful. His first wife, Maddalena Tocco, had died in November 1429, after little more than a year of marriage; his second, Caterina Gattilusio – daughter of the Genoese lord of Lesbos – whom he had married in 1441, had survived for only a few months before dying at Palaiokastro on Lemnos, where she and Constantine together had been temporarily cut off by a Turkish fleet. Clearly he must now find a third. Various possibilities were explored. In the West there was a Portuguese princess, who happened also to be the niece of King Alfonso of Aragon and Naples; Isabella Orsini, daughter of the Prince of Taranto, was also considered. In the East, it seemed that either the ruling family of Trebizond or that of Georgia might be able to furnish a suitable bride. The Emperor's old friend George Sphrantzes was accordingly sent off to these last two courts to take diplomatic soundings.

It was while Sphrantzes was in Trebizond, in February 1451, that he heard of the death of Murad II. Immediately, a new idea came to him. The Sultan's widow Maria – in Turkish, Mara – was the daughter of old George Brankovich; although she and Murad had been married for ʾifteen years she had borne him no children, and it was generally believed that the marriage had never been consummated. She was, however, the stepmother of her husband's son and successor, the nineteen-year-old Mehmet, who was known to be energetic and ambitious and a sworn foe of Byzantium. If she were now to become its Empress, what better way could there be of keeping the boy under proper control? When the idea was put to the Emperor he was distinctly intrigued. The Palaeologi were already connected with the house of Brankovich, Constantine's niece Helena – daughter of his brother Thomas – having married Maria's brother Lazar. An ambassador at once sped off to Serbia to consult the parents of the intended bride. George and his wife were delighted, and readily gave their consent; the only opposition came from Maria herself, but her refusal was absolute. Years before, she explained, she had sworn an oath that if ever she escaped from the infidel she would devote the rest of her life to celibacy, chastity and charitable works. No amount of argument would induce her to change her mind – and subsequent events, it must be admitted, were fully to justify her decision. Poor Sphrantzes was sent back to Georgia to continue negotiations there, and these were soon successfully completed; but the proposed marriage never took place, and Constantine was to remain single for the rest of his short life.

Surprisingly little was known in Constantinople – and even less among the Christian peoples of the West – about the inscrutable young prince who had recently succeeded to the Ottoman throne at Adrianople. Born in 1433, Mehmet was the third of Murad's sons. He had had an unhappy childhood. His father had made no secret of his preference for his two elder half-brothers Ahmet and Ali, both children of well-born mothers, whereas Mehmet's own mother had been merely a slave-girl in the harem, and probably (though we cannot be sure) a Christian to boot. At the age of two he had been taken to Amasa, a province of northern Anatolia of which his fourteen-year-old brother was Governor; but Ahmet had died only four years later and the six-year-old Mehmet had succeeded him. Then, in 1444, Ali had been found strangled in his bed, in circumstances still mysterious. Mehmet, now heir to the throne, was summoned back urgently to Adrianople. Hitherto his education had been largely neglected; suddenly he found himself in the care of the greatest scholars that could be found and with them, over the next few years, laid the foundations of the learning and culture for which he was soon to be famous. At the time of his accession he is said to have been fluent not only in his native Turkish but in Arabic, Greek, Latin, Persian and Hebrew.

Twice, in the last six years of his life, Sultan Murad had abdicated the throne in favour of his son; twice his Grand Vizier Halil Pasha had prevailed upon him to resume the reins of government. Young Mehmet, he reported, was arrogant and self-willed, ever bent on going his own way and apparently determined to ignore the Vizier's advice. On one occasion he had adopted the cause of a fanatical Persian dervish, and had been enraged when the fellow was finally apprehended and burnt at the stake; on another he had ignored dangerous disturbances on the Greek and Albanian frontiers in favour of some crack-brained scheme to attack Constantinople. After Murad's second reluctant return to power he gave up all thoughts of retirement and settled down once again in Adrianople, banishing his unsatisfactory son to Magnesia in Anatolia; and it was there that news was brought to Mehmet that his father had died, on 13 February 1451, of an apoplectic seizure.

It took the new Sultan just five days to travel from Magnesia to Adrianople, where he held a formal reception at which he confirmed his father's ministers in their places or, in certain cases, appointed them elsewhere. In the course of these ceremonies Murad's widow arrived to congratulate him on his succession. Mehmet received her warmly and engaged her for some time in conversation; when she returned to the harem she found that her infant son had been murdered in his bath. The young Sultan, it seemed, was not one to take chances.

But he was only nineteen, and in the Western world there was a general feeling that he was still too young and immature to constitute a serious threat as his father had done – a delusion that Mehmet did everything he could to encourage. Within months of his succession he had concluded treaties with John Hunyadi of Hungary, George Branko-vich of Serbia and the Doge of Venice, Francesco Foscari; messages of good will had been sent to the Prince of Wallachia, the Knights of St John in Rhodes and the Genoese lords of Lesbos and Chios. To the ambassadors dispatched by Constantine Dragases to congratulate him on his accession he is said to have replied almost too fulsomely, swearing by Allah and the Prophet to live at peace with the Emperor and his people, and to maintain with him those same bonds of friendship that his father had maintained with John VIII. Perhaps it was this last promise that put Constantine on his guard; he seems at any rate to have been one of the first to sense that the young Sultan was not all he seemed, but was potentially very dangerous indeed.

Such a degree of perception was certainly not granted to the leaders of the Karamans of Asia Minor, who in the autumn of 1451 thought to take advantage of Mehmet's youth and inexperience – and of his absence in Europe – by mounting an insurrection against him to restore the local Emirates that they had enjoyed in former times. Within weeks he was in their midst with his army; and they soon had good cause to regret their temerity. For all but those directly concerned, this was a relatively unimportant interlude; but for Byzantium it had important consequences. On his return to Europe Mehmet would normally have taken ship across the Dardanelles; but when it was reported to him that an Italian squadron was patrolling the strait he crossed instead by the Bosphorus, a few miles up from Constantinople at the point where Bayezit had built his castle at Anadolu Hisar. Here the great channel was at its narrowest, and Mehmet decided to build another fortress, immediately opposite his great-grandfather's, on the European side. This would give him complete control of the Bosphorus; moreover it would provide a superb base from which Constantinople could be attacked from the north-east, where the Golden Horn constituted virtually its only line of defence.

There was one small technical objection to the plan: the land on which Mehmet proposed to build his castle was theoretically Byzantine. He ignored it. All the following winter he spent collecting his workforce: a thousand professional stonemasons and as many unskilled labourers as they could employ. In the early spring all the churches and monasteries in the immediate neighbourhood were demolished to provide additional materials, and on Saturday, 15 April 1452 the building operations began.

The reaction in Constantinople can well be imagined. In vain did the Emperor send the Sultan an indignant embassy, to remind him that he was breaking a solemn treaty on which the ink was scarcely dry and to point out that, when Bayezit had wished to build his castle on the Asiatic side, he had had the courtesy to ask the permission of Manuel II even though such permission had not been strictly necessary. The imperial ambassadors were sent back to their master unheard. After a brief interval a second embassy, weighed down with presents, followed the first: would the Sultan not at least spare the neighbouring Byzantine villages? Again the envoys were dismissed without an audience. A week or two later Constantine made one last effort: would the Sultan give his word that the building of his castle did not herald an attack on Constantinople? This time Mehmet had had enough. The ambassadors were seized and executed, the Emperor left to draw his own conclusions.

The vast castle of Rumeli Hisar still stands, essentially unchanged since the day it was completed – Thursday, 31 August – a little beyond the village of Bebek on the Bosphorus shore. Even now it is difficult to believe that its building took, from start to finish, only nineteen and a half weeks. When it was ready the Sultan mounted three huge cannon on the tower nearest the shore and issued a proclamation that every passing ship, whatever its nationality or provenance, must stop for examination. It soon became clear that he meant what he said. Early in November two Venetian vessels coming from the Black Sea ignored the instruction. They managed to escape the consequent cannonade, but a fortnight later a third ship, laden with food and provisions for Constantinople, was less lucky. When it too failed to stop it was blasted out of the water; the crew were executed, the captain – one Antonio Rizzo – impaled on a stake and his body publicly exposed as a warning to anyone else who might think of following his example.

In the West, opinions were hastily revised. The Sultan Mehmet II, it seemed, meant business.

The Sultan's treatment of the luckless Rizzo caused consternation throughout Christendom. Pope Nicholas in particular was horrified. By now he was genuinely eager to help; but he was also powerless, and he knew it. Already the previous March he had instructed the new Western Emperor – Frederick III of Hapsburg, who had come to Rome for his imperial coronation – to send the Sultan a threatening ultimatum. No one, least of all Mehmet, had paid any attention. France was still reeling after the damage suffered in the Hundred Years' War; the crusading enthusiasm of Philip the Good, Duke of Burgundy, had been considerably dampened by the memory of how his father John the Fearless had been taken prisoner at Nicopolis; England, rudderless under the holy but half-witted Henry VI, was also recovering from the damage wrought by the conflict with France and rapidly falling into the chaos that would lead, only three years later, to the Wars of the Roses; the Kings of Portugal and Castile were engaged in Crusades of their own; the Kings of Scotland and Scandinavia neither knew nor cared. That left Alfonso of Aragon, since 1443 enthroned in Naples, who asked nothing better; but as Alfonso's avowed motive was to seize the Byzantine throne he was not encouraged.

In the summer of 1452, as the towers of Rumeli Hisar rose ever higher above the narrow strait, the former Metropolitan Isidore of Kiev, now a Roman cardinal and official Papal Legate to the court of Constantinople, sailed for his new post. He was delayed for some time at Naples, while he recruited two hundred archers at the Pope's expense, and eventually arrived with his Genoese colleague Leonard, Archbishop of Mitylene, at the end of October. His instructions were simple; to see that the union of the Eastern and Western Churches, agreed at Florence thirteen years before, was properly implemented at last. The Emperor, he knew, was in full – if cautious – agreement. Even public opinion in the capital, though still divided, seemed to Isidore more favourable than before. The anti-unionists remained strong; but the chief minister and High Admiral, the *megas dux* Lucas Notaras, was working ceaselessly to extract concessions from them and it was not impossible that a compromise might be reached. A week or two later, the Cardinal was less optimistic: the former George Scholarius – now the monk Gennadius and leader of the dissidents – published a manifesto emphasizing the folly of apostasy at a moment when the Almighty alone could save the Empire, and agreement seemed as remote as ever. But then, in the nick of time, there came the news of the sinking of the Venetian vessel and the fate of its captain; and the pendulum swung yet again.

On Tuesday, 12 December 1452 the Emperor and his entire court, accompanied by Cardinal Isidore and the Archbishop of Chios, attended high mass in St Sophia. The *Laetentur Coeli* was formally read out, just as it had been at Florence; the Pope and the absent Patriarch Gregory were properly commemorated; and, in theory at any rate, the union was complete. And yet for Isidore, Leonard and their friends it was an empty victory. The service, despite the cardinal's somewhat overdone assurances to the contrary, had been poorly attended; according to Leonard – who was apparently a good deal readier to face facts – even the Emperor had seemed half-hearted and listless, while Notaras had been actively hostile. Afterwards there was no rejoicing; the dissidents too held their peace. Not a word was heard from Gennadius, back in his monastic cell. It was noticed, however, that the churches whose priests had espoused the union – including of course St Sophia itself – were henceforth almost empty; the people might have accepted the inevitable, but they worshipped only where the old liturgy remained unchanged, that the God of the Orthodox Church might still hear their prayers.

In January 1453 Mehmet II summoned his ministers to his presence in Adrianople. Byzantium, he told them, was still dangerous. Weak it might be, but its people were natural intriguers who could yet do the House of Othman much harm if they chose. Moreover they had potential allies far more formidable than they; if they decided that they were no longer capable of defending Constantinople, what was to prevent their entrusting it to the Italians or the Franks, who would do so for them? His own Empire, in short, could never be safe while the city remained in Christian hands, nor in such circumstances would he himself wish to be its Sultan. It must consequently be taken; and now – while its inhabitants were deeply demoralized and hopelessly divided among themselves – was the time to take it. Admittedly it was well defended; but it was by no means impregnable, and previous attempts had failed largely because its besiegers had been unable to prevent the arrival of food and supplies by sea. Now, for the first time, the Turks had naval superiority. If Constantinople could not be taken by storm, it could – and must – be starved into submission.

Mehmet spoke no more than the truth. Byzantine estimates of enemy forces are notoriously untrustworthy; but from the evidence of the

Italian sailors present in Constantinople over the weeks that followed, the Turkish fleet seems to have comprised not less than six triremes[1] and ten biremes, fifteen oared galleys, some seventy-five fast longboats, twenty heavy sailing-barges for transport and a number of light sloops and cutters. Even many of the Sultan's closest advisers were astonished at the size of this vast armada, which assembled off Gallipoli in March 1453; but their reactions can have been as nothing compared with those of the Byzantines, when they saw it a week or two later, making its way slowly across the Marmara, to drop anchor beneath the walls of their city.

The Ottoman army, meanwhile, was gathering in Thrace. As with the navy, Mehmet had given it his personal attention throughout the previous winter, making sure that it was properly equipped with armour, weapons and siege engines. He had mobilized every regiment, stopped all leave and recruited hordes of irregulars and mercenaries, making exceptions only for the garrisons needed for the protection of the frontiers and the policing of the larger towns. Once again, it is impossible to give more than approximations of their numbers; the Greek estimate of three to four hundred thousand is plainly ridiculous. Our Turkish sources – presumably fairly reliable – suggest some eighty thousand regular troops and up to twenty thousand irregulars, or *bashi-bazouks*. Included in the former category were about twelve thousand Janissaries. These élite troops of the Sultan had been recruited as children from Christian families, forcibly converted to Islam and subjected for many years to rigorous military and religious training; some had been additionally trained as sappers and engineers. Legally they were slaves, in that they enjoyed no personal rights outside their regimental life; but they received regular salaries and were anything but servile: as recently as 1451 they had staged a near-mutiny for higher pay, and Janissary revolts were to be a regular feature of Ottoman history until well into the nineteenth century.

Mehmet was proud of his army, and prouder still of his navy; but he took the greatest pride of all in his cannon. These weapons, in a very primitive form, had already been in use for well over a hundred years: Edward III had employed one at the siege of Calais in 1347, and they had been known in North Italy for a good quarter-century before that.

---

1 Unlike the ancient vessels of the same name, Turkish triremes and biremes possessed a single bank of oars only. In the triremes there were three rowers to each oar, in the biremes they sat in pairs.

But although useful against light barricades they were in those days powerless against solid masonry. By 1446 – a whole century later – they were effective enough, as we have seen, to demolish the Hexamilion; but it was not until 1452 that a German engineer named Urban presented himself before the Sultan and offered to construct for him a cannon that would blast the walls of Babylon itself.[1] This was precisely what Mehmet had been waiting for. He gave Urban everything he needed – together with four times his requested salary – and was rewarded only three months later by the fearsome weapon which, installed at Rumeli Hisar, sank Antonio Rizzo's ship. He then demanded another, twice the size of the first. This was completed in January 1453. It is said to have been nearly twenty-seven feet long, with a barrel two and a half feet in diameter at the front end. The bronze was eight inches thick. When it was tested, a ball weighing some 1,340 pounds hurtled through the air for well over a mile before burying itself six feet deep in the ground. Two hundred men were sent out to prepare for the journey to Constantinople of this fearsome machine, smoothing the road and reinforcing the bridges; and at the beginning of March it set off, drawn by thirty pairs of oxen, with another two hundred men to hold it steady.

The Sultan himself remained at Adrianople until the last detachments of his army had arrived from Anatolia; then on 23 March he left with them for the march across Thrace. Medieval armies – particularly if they were carrying siege equipment – moved slowly; but on 5 April Mehmet pitched his tent before the walls of Constantinople, where the bulk of his huge host had already arrived three days before. Determined to lose no time, he at once sent under a flag of truce the message to the Emperor that was required by Islamic law, undertaking that all his subjects would be spared, with their families and property, if they made immediate and voluntary surrender. If on the other hand they refused, they would be given no quarter.

As expected, he received no reply. Early in the morning of Friday, 6 April his cannon opened fire.

Long before the first Turkish soldier was sighted, the people of Constantinople had known that the siege was inevitable. Throughout the previous

---

1 Urban had previously approached the Byzantine Emperor with the same offer, but Constantine, unable to provide either the money or the raw materials for which he asked, had been obliged to refuse. Had he accepted, we can speculate endlessly on how the course of the next two years might have been altered; but it seems impossible that the fate of Byzantium could have been changed.

winter they had been working – men, women and children, the Emperor at their head – on the city's defences: repairing and reinforcing the walls, clearing out the moats, laying in stores of food, arrows, tools, heavy rocks, Greek fire[1] and everything else that they might need to repel the enemy. Although the main attack was clearly to be expected from the west, the sea walls along the Marmara shore and the Golden Horn had also been strengthened; everyone knew that it was from the Blachernae quarter that the Franks and Venetians had smashed their way into the city during the Fourth Crusade. By the coming of spring preparations were complete. Easter fell on 1 April. Even on that day of Christian rejoicing the Great Church of St Sophia was avoided by most Byzantines; but all of them, wherever they worshipped and whatever the outcome of the next few weeks or months, could pray for their deliverance in the knowledge that they had done everything they could to prepare for the coming onslaught.

Constantine too had done his best. The previous autumn he had sent further embassies to the West, but as usual to little avail. Three months after the death of Antonio Rizzo, in February 1453, the Venetian Senate had finally woken up to the seriousness of the situation and had voted to send two transports, each carrying four hundred men, to Constantinople, with fifteen galleys following as soon as they were ready; but on 2 March they were still discussing the flotilla's organization, on 9 March they passed a further resolution urging the greatest possible speed, and on 10 April they wrote to Rome pointing out somewhat self-righteously that all relief cargoes should reach the Dardanelles by the end of March, after which the prevailing north wind made it difficult for captains to beat their way up the straits. Their own vessels finally left the lagoon on 20 April, by which time three Genoese ships, chartered by Pope Nicholas and filled with food and war provisions at his own personal expense, had – as we shall soon see – already reached Constantinople.

Fortunately for the honour of the Serenissima, the Venetian colony in the city – who had given, it must be said, more than enough trouble in the past – responded nobly to the present challenge. The *bailo*, Girolamo Minotto, had written to his government as early as 26 January begging for a relief expedition, and regularly assured the Emperor that it would arrive before long. Meanwhile he promised every support, and further

---

1 See *Byzantium: The Early Centuries*, p. 323 and *passim*. Greek fire had been Byzantium's secret weapon for eight hundred years, and seems to have been as effective in the fifteenth century as it was in the seventh.

undertook that none of the Republic's vessels would leave the harbour without his express permission. Two Venetian merchant-captains, whose ships chanced to have anchored in Constantinople on their way home from the Black Sea, also agreed to remain to give what assistance they could. In all, the Venetians were able to provide nine merchantmen, including three from their colony of Crete. How many men they managed to put at the Emperor's disposal is uncertain. In his vivid eye-witness account of the siege the Venetian naval surgeon Nicolò Barbaro specifically lists sixty-seven 'noble'[1] compatriots who were present, but there was presumably a fair number of commoners as well.

The defenders also included a Genoese contingent. Many of them came, as might have been expected, from the colony at Galata – which, in the event of a Turkish victory, seemed to have little hope of survival; but in addition there was an honorable group from Genoa itself, consisting of young men who, appalled by the pusillanimity of its government – which had promised Constantine just one ship – had determined to fight for Christendom. Their leader, Giovanni Giustiniani Longo, was a member of one of the Republic's leading families and a renowned expert in siege warfare. He arrived on 29 January with a private army of seven hundred, including a mysterious engineer whose name, Johannes Grant, strongly suggests Scottish origins. Finally there was a single elderly Spanish grandee – Don Francisco de Toledo, who claimed descent from the Comneni – and a small party of Catalans, mostly permanent residents in the city but also including a few sailors who had voluntarily joined their ranks. These signs, such as they were, of international solidarity must have given the Emperor some encouragement, but another severe blow was in store for him: on the night of 26 February seven Venetian ships – all but one of them from Crete – slipped secretly out of the Golden Horn and down the Hellespont to the island of Tenedos, carrying with them some seven hundred Italians. Only a few days before their captains had sworn a solemn oath to remain in the city. To Constantine, the loss of so many potential defenders – effectively offsetting Longo's contribution of just a month before – was little short of catastrophic; but the faithlessness of those whom he had believed to be his friends was, perhaps, more wounding still.

---

1 The word 'noble' needs some explanation here. The Venetian nobility was based (for obvious reasons) not on feudal land tenure but on the antiquity of the individual families. Towards the end of the Republic's history it was occasionally possible for *nouveau-riche* families to buy their way into this nobility; but in the fifteenth century it was strictly limited to members of those families listed in the 'Golden Book', published some hundred and fifty years before.

Now and only now was it possible for the Emperor to make a precise assessment of the resources available to him for the defence of his capital. Moored in the Golden Horn were eight more Venetian vessels (including three Cretan), five Genoese and one each from Ancona, Catalonia and Provence, together with the ten which were all that remained of the Byzantine navy – a total of twenty-six, pitiable in comparison to the armada of the Sultan. But it was only when he came to assess his available manpower that Constantine realized the full gravity of his situation. Towards the end of March he ordered his secretary Sphrantzes to make a census of all able-bodied men in the city, including monks and clerics, who could be called upon to man the walls. The final figure was worse than he could have imagined: 4,983 Greeks and rather less than two thousand foreigners. To defend fourteen miles of walls against Mehmet's army of a hundred thousand, he could muster less than seven thousand men. These figures, he told Sphrantzes must on no account be revealed: only God could save the city now.

On Monday, 2 April, when the look-outs reported the first advance parties of Turks on the western horizon, the Emperor ordered the gates of the city to be closed, the bridges over the moats destroyed and the great chain stretched across the entrance to the Golden Horn from a tower just below the Acropolis (on what is now Seraglio Point) to another on the sea walls of Galata. There was nothing more to be done but to pray – and to await the final onslaught.

The walls in which Byzantium put its trust during that fateful spring of 1453 ran from the shores of the Marmara to the upper reaches of the Golden Horn, forming the western boundary of the city. They were already more than a thousand years old. Known as the Theodosian Walls after the Emperor Theodosius II in whose reign they were built, they were in fact completed in 413 when he was still a child; their true creator was his Praetorian Prefect Anthemius, who for the first six years of his reign was his guardian and Regent of the Eastern Empire. Unfortunately, only thirty-four years later in 447, no fewer than fifty-seven of Anthemius's towers were toppled by a violent earthquake – at the very moment moreover when Attila the Hun was advancing on the capital. Reconstruction had begun at once, and within two months the fortifications had been completely rebuilt, with an outer wall and moat added. Attila turned back when he saw them – as countless other enemies of Byzantium were to do over the centuries that followed – and no wonder; for in terms of medieval siege warfare the Land Walls of

Constantinople were indeed impregnable. Any attacking army had first to negotiate a deep ditch some sixty feet across, much of which could be flooded to a depth of about thirty feet in an emergency. Beyond this was a low crenellated breastwork with a terrace behind it about thirty feet wide; then the outer wall, seven feet thick and nearly thirty feet high, with ninety-six towers at regular intervals along it. Within this wall came another broad terrace, and then the principal element of the defence, the great inner wall, about sixteen feet thick at the base and rising to a height of forty feet above the city. It too had ninety-six towers, alternating in position with those of the outer wall. The result was probably the most elaborate bastion ever constructed in the Middle Ages. Only at the northern end, where the walls ran up against the imperial Palace of Blachernae, did a single bulwark replace the triple, but this was itself considerably strengthened by the enormously thick wall of the palace itself and was further protected by a moat, first constructed by John Cantacuzenus and recently redug by some of the galley crews.

By the morning of Friday, 6 April most of the defenders were deployed along the walls, the Emperor and Giustiniani in command of the most vulnerable section, the so-called *mesoteichion*, which crossed the valley of the little river Lycus about a mile from the northern end and which was clearly the point at which the Sultan intended to concentrate his attack. The sea walls along the Marmara and the Horn were less heavily manned, but their garrisons served the additional purpose of look-outs, keeping a close watch on Turkish ship movements. They reported to the Emperor that the Turkish admiral, a Bulgarian renegade named Süleyman Baltoğlu, was not only maintaining a continuous patrol of the Marmara shore – thus effectively sealing the small harbours dotted along it – but was also massing his fleet at the mouth of the Bosphorus opposite the quay known as the Double Columns.[1] Some three days after the siege began he led a number of his heaviest ships to ram the great chain in an attempt to break it; but the chain held.

The Sultan, meanwhile, had subjected the Land Walls to a bombardment unprecedented in the history of siege warfare. By the evening of the first day he had reduced to rubble a section near the Charisius Gate, whence the Mesē, Constantinople's central thoroughfare, ran the whole length of the city to St Sophia. His soldiers made repeated attempts to smash their way through, but again and again were forced to retreat

---

1 The site of the present Dolmabahce Palace.

under a hail of missiles until nightfall sent them back to their camp. By morning the wall had been completely rebuilt, and Mehmet decided to hold his fire until he could bring up more cannon to the spot. To fill in the time he ordered attacks on two small fortresses outside the walls – one at Therapia, a village just beyond his great new castle on the Bosphorus, and one at the little village of Studius. Both fought gallantly, but were ultimately obliged to surrender. The survivors were all impaled – those from Studius within sight of the Land Walls, as a lesson to those watching. Further orders were sent to Baltoglu to capture the Princes' Islands in the Marmara. Only the largest of these, Prinkipo, offered any resistance; the admiral finally put the fortress to the torch, adding sulphur and pitch as fuel to the fire. Those of the garrison who escaped being burned alive were immediately put to death; the civilian population were sold into slavery. The lessons to be drawn from such brutality were plain, as they were meant to be: the Sultan was not to be trifled with.

By 11 April all his cannon were in place and the bombardment resumed, to continue uninterruptedly for the next forty-eight days. Although some of the larger pieces could be fired only once every two or three hours, the damage they did was enormous; within a week the outer wall across the Lycus had collapsed in several places, and although the defenders worked ceaselessly to repair the damage behind makeshift wooden stockades it was already clear that they could not do so indefinitely. None the less, a surprise attack on the night of the 18th was courageously beaten off; after four hours' heavy fighting the Turks had lost two hundred men, at the cost – according to Barbaro – of not a single Christian life. At sea, too, the Emperor's ships scored a notable success: a second attempt by Baltoğlu on the chain – using this time a number of heavy galleys recently arrived from the Black Sea – proved no more effective than the first. These were also armed with cannon, but they could not achieve sufficient elevation to harm the tall Christian ships – while the Greek, Genoese and Venetian archers, loosing a hail of arrows from their crow's nests, inflicted huge damage on the Turkish vessels and forced them to retreat whence they had come.

Shortly afterwards that same stretch of water saw another, far more fateful engagement. The three Genoese galleys hired and provisioned by the Pope, having been delayed by the weather in Chios, finally arrived off the Hellespont. There they were joined by a heavy Byzantine transport with a cargo of corn from Sicily, made available by Alfonso of Aragon. In his anxiety to mass the strongest possible naval force outside Constantinople, Mehmet had ill-advisedly left the straits unguarded, and the ships were able to make their way without hindrance into the Marmara. The moment they appeared on the horizon – it was early in the morning of Friday, 20 April – the Sultan rode around the head of the Golden Horn to give his orders personally to his admiral. On no account were they to reach the city. The must be captured or, if capture proved impossible, sunk.

Baltoğlu prepared at once to attack. His sailing ships were powerless against the fresh southerly breeze; but the biremes and the triremes – several of which were armed with light cannon – were immediately mobilized and in the early afternoon the great fleet bore down upon the four approaching ships. Overwhelmingly outnumbered, to the casual onlooker these would have seemed to have little chance; but the steadily strengthening wind was in their favour, and the growing swell made the heavy Turkish vessels hard to manage. The others, moreover, had the advantage of height. Once again the Turkish captains, finding themselves virtually defenceless against the unremitting deluge of arrows, javelins and other projectiles that rained down upon them whenever they came within range, were forced to watch in impotence while the four galleys advanced serenely towards the Golden Horn. But then, just as they reached the entrance, the wind dropped. Acropolis Point, where the Horn, the Bosphorus and the Sea of Marmara meet, has been known since the days of antiquity for the strength and variety of its currents; and as the sails of the Christian ships flapped desultorily in the sudden calm, the crews felt themselves swept northward towards the Galata shore.

The advantage was now with the Turks. Baltoğlu, still wary of coming in too close, brought his heavier armed vessels as near as he dared and opened fire with his cannon. But it was no use. His guns lacked the necessary elevation; the balls all fell short. A few flaming missiles landed on the Christian decks, but the fires were extinguished before they did any serious damage. Desperate now – for he knew that with the Sultan in his present mood failure could be fatal – he gave the order to advance and board. His own flagship bore down upon the imperial transport, ramming it in the stern. The Genoese in their turn were quickly surrounded; the crews continued to loose their showers of arrows, but with thirty or forty Turkish vessels milling around each of theirs there was a limit to what they could achieve. It was, once again, the superior height of their ships that saved the day. Grappling and boarding an enemy ship can never have been easy; to do so when that ship stood substantially higher in the water than that of her attackers, making it necessary for them to climb up the side in the face of heavy resistance from above, was almost impossible; and the Genoese sailors were equipped with huge axes with which to lop off the heads and hands of all who made the attempt. Inevitably, too, the Turkish oars became increasingly entangled, making the ships themselves an easy prey.

The imperial transport, meanwhile, was still in difficulties. Fortunately she was well provided with Greek fire, and consequently able to give a good account of herself; but though she managed to repel boarders she could not shake herself free of the Turkish flagship, and was moreover running short of arrows and other weapons. Seeing her trouble, the Genoese captains somehow manoeuvred their ships alongside and lashed all four vessels together, till they stood like a great sea-girt castle amid the chaos and confusion that surrounded them. The crews, now united in a single body, fought like heroes; but it was clear that they could not do so for ever against an enemy that had an apparently limitless number of vessels to throw against them, and the courage that they showed seemed more and more to be the courage of despair. Then, just as the sun was setting, the wind got up again. The Christian sails billowed out, and the great floating fortress began to move again, slowly but inexorably, towards the entrance to the Horn, splintering any Turkish ship in its path. Baltoğlu, who had been severely wounded in the eye by a projectile – hurled, it was said, from one of his own ships – realized that he was beaten; in the gathering darkness he could only order his fleet back to its anchorage. A few hours later in the dead of night, the boom was opened and the four ships slipped quietly into the Golden Horn.

The Sultan had watched every moment of the battle from the shore, occasionally in his excitement riding his horse out into the sea until his robes were trailing in the water. He was famous for the violence of his rages; such was his fury when he saw the humiliation of his fleet that those around him began to fear for his health, and indeed his sanity. The next day he summoned Baltoğlu, publicly vilified him as a fool and a coward and ordered his immediate execution. The unfortunate admiral gained a reprieve after a deputation of his subordinate officers had testified to his courage; but he was bastinadoed and deprived both of his public offices and his private possessions – which Mehmet distributed among his beloved Janissaries. He was never heard of again.

The Byzantines, that fateful Friday, had been luckier than they knew. The arrival of the Genoese ships had brought the Sultan round to the

Double Columns. He was still there on the following day, when his cannon brought down a huge tower, the Bactatinian, on the Land Walls above the Lycus valley, and reduced to rubble much of the outer rampart at that point. Had the besiegers mounted an immediate assault, Constantinople might have fallen more than five weeks earlier than it did; but Mehmet was not there to give the order, and the opportunity was missed. That night the Greek engineers rebuilt the damaged section of the wall, and by the following morning it stood as firm – or almost as firm – as ever.

The Sultan, however, had other preoccupations. The fiasco he had recently witnessed had focused his attention on a single objective: somehow, he must gain control of the Golden Horn. The idea had been in his mind since the beginning of the siege, when he had set his engineers to work on a road running behind Galata, from a point near the Double Columns on the Marmara shore over the hill near what is now Taksim Square and down to the Golden Horn at Kasimpaşa. Iron wheels had been cast, and metal tracks; his carpenters, meanwhile, had been busy fashioning wooden cradles large enough to accommodate the keels of moderate-sized vessels. It was a herculean undertaking; but Mehmet had enough men and materials to make it a possible one. On 21 April the work was complete; and on Sunday morning, the 22nd, the Genoese colony in Galata watched dumbfounded as some seventy Turkish ships were slowly hauled, by innumerable teams of oxen, over a two-hundred-foot hill and then lowered gently down into the Horn.

Their consternation was, however, nothing to that of the Byzantines, who had known nothing of the Sultan's plan and found it hard to believe the evidence of their own eyes. Not only was their only major harbour no longer secure; they now had three and a half more miles of wall to defend, including the section breached by the Crusaders in 1204. A week later they made a determined effort to destroy the Turkish ships; but the Turks, forewarned by one of their agents in Galata, were ready for them. In the ensuing battle only one Turkish vessel was sunk, while fifty of the Christians' best sailors were killed; another forty who had swum ashore were executed on the spot, within sight of the city. The Greeks, in revenge, brought their own 260 Turkish prisoners down to the shore and beheaded them before the eyes of their compatriots across the Horn. Thenceforth, no quarter was given or expected.

Even then, it was some time before the Emperor recognized the full significance of Mehmet's achievement. Encouraged by the *bailo* Minotto, he still had hopes of the long-awaited relief expedition from Venice; but now, even if such an expedition were to arrive, how could it be received in safety? Gradually, too, he came to see the full extent of the treachery shown by the Genoese of Galata. A few of them, admittedly, had rallied to their compatriot Giovanni Giustiniani Longo and were doing heroic work along the walls; but the majority had not lifted a finger to assist – far less to save – their Christian brethren. It might have been impossible for them to sabotage the Sultan's preparations to move his ships overland into the Golden Horn; but could not at least some warning have been sent or signalled? The truth of the matter was, as Constantine well knew, that the Genoese had never liked the Greeks and felt absolutely no loyalty towards them. The Christian religion should have been a bond, particularly since the two Churches had been theoretically reunited; but to most Genoese (as to most Venetians) trade remained paramount. The important thing was to end up on the winning side, and there was no doubt in anyone's mind which that side was to be.

As if to prove the completeness of his control over Galata, Mehmet now threw a pontoon bridge over the Golden Horn, only a few hundred yards north-west of the Palace of Blachernae. Previously all messengers between his army beyond the walls and his fleet at the Double Columns had been obliged to make a long detour around the top of the Horn; henceforth they would be able to complete the journey in less than an hour. And the bridge had other uses too: broad enough for a regiment marching five abreast, it could also accommodate heavy carts and – on special rafts attached at intervals to the sides – cannon which could be used either to cover the soldiers' advance or to bombard the sea walls of the city.

By the beginning of May the Emperor knew that he could not hold out much longer. Food was running seriously short; fishing, long impossible in the Marmara, was since the arrival of the Turkish ships almost as dangerous in the Golden Horn; more and more of the defenders along the walls were taking time off to find food for their families. Only one hope – and that a faint one – remained: a relief expedition from Venice. It was now more than three months since Minotto had sent his appeal, and no word had come from the lagoons. Was there a fleet on its way, or not? If so, how big was it, and what was its cargo? Most important of all, when would it arrive? On the answers to these questions the whole fate of Constantinople now depended. And so it was that just before midnight on Thursday, 3 May a Venetian brigantine from the flotilla in the Horn, flying a Turkish standard and carrying a crew of twelve volunteers all disguised as Turks, slipped out under the boom.

On the night of Wednesday the 23rd it returned, tacking backwards and forwards up the Marmara against a sharp north wind, with a Turkish squadron in hot pursuit. Fortunately, however, Venetian seamanship was still a good deal better than Turkish, and soon after nightfall it succeeded in entering the Horn. The captain immediately sought an audience with the Emperor and Minotto. His news was as bad as it could be. For three weeks he had cruised through the Aegean, but nowhere had he seen a trace of the promised expedition, or indeed of any Venetian shipping. When he realized that it was useless to continue the search, he had called a meeting of the sailors and asked them what they should do. One had advocated sailing back to Venice, arguing that Constantinople was probably already in Turkish hands; but he had been shouted down. To all the rest, their duty was clear: they must report to the Emperor, as they had promised to do. And so they had returned, knowing full well that they would probably never leave the city alive. Constantine thanked each one personally, his voice choked with tears.

By now, too, the omens had begun. For months already pessimists had been pointing out that just as the first Emperor of Byzantinum had been a Constantine born of a Helena, so would the last; but shortly before the full moon on 24 May the portents took a more sinister turn. On the 22nd there was a lunar eclipse; a day or two later, as the holiest and most precious icon of the Virgin was being carried through the streets in one last appeal for her intercession, it slipped from the platform on which it was being carried. With immense difficulty – for it suddenly seemed preternaturally heavy – it was replaced, and the bearers continued on their way; but they had gone no more than a few hundred yards further when a thunderstorm burst over the city, the most violent and dramatic that anyone could remember. Such was the force of the rain and hail that whole streets were flooded and the procession had to be abandoned. The next morning the people of Constantinople awoke to find their city shrouded in thick fog, something quite unprecedented at the end of May; the same night the dome of St Sophia seemed suffused with an unearthly red glow that crept slowly up from the base to the summit and then went out. This last phenomenon was also seen by the Turks in Galata and at the Double Columns; Mehmet himself was greatly disturbed by it, and was reassured only after his astrologers had interpreted it as a sign that the building would soon be illuminated by the True Faith. For the Byzantines there could be only one explanation: the Spirit of God itself had departed from their city.

Once again, as they had done so often in the past, George Sphrantzes and his fellow-ministers implored the Emperor to leave Constantinople while there was still time, to escape to the Morea and head a Byzantine government in exile until he could lead an army to recover the city, just as his great predecessor Michael Palaeologus had done nearly two centuries before. Such was Constantine's exhaustion that he fainted as they spoke; but when he recovered he was as determined as ever. This was his city; these were his people. He could not desert them now.

On Saturday, 26 May Mehmet II held a council of war. The siege, he told those around him, had continued long enough. His Grand Vizier, old Halil Pasha, who had never approved of the campaign – or indeed of the headstrong young Sultan himself – enthusiastically agreed, and pressed his master to retreat before the arrival of the expected relief fleet or the army of John Hunyadi – long rumoured to be on the march – made retreat impossible; but Mehmet would have none of it. The Greeks, he maintained, were half-starving and utterly demoralized. The time had come for the final assault. His younger generals agreed with him, Halil was overruled and the decision was taken. The following day would be given over to preparations, the day after that to rest and prayer. The attack would begin in the early hours of Tuesday, 29 May.

No attempt was made to conceal the plan from the defenders within the city. Some of the Christians in the Turkish camp even shot arrows over the walls informing them of the Sultan's intentions, but such measures were hardly necessary. For the next thirty-six hours the preparatory work continued without interruption – filling the ditches, positioning the cannon, drawing up the catapults and siege engines, laying in stores of arrows, gunpowder, food, bandages, water for extinguishing fires and all the other innumerable needs of a great army in action. At night huge flares were lit to help the men at their labours, while drums and trumpets encouraged them to still greater efforts. Then, at dawn on the 28th, a sudden silence fell. Work ceased. While his men prepared themselves, physically and spiritually, for the morrow Mehmet set off on a day-long tour of inspection, returning only late in the evening to take his own rest.

Within the city, the anxiety of the past few weeks had strained tempers to breaking point. Relations between Greeks, Venetians and Genoese – never easy at the best of times – had now reached a point where the three communities were barely on speaking terms. Even on vital matters of defence, every order was questioned, every suggestion argued, every motive suspected. Then, it seemed from one moment to the next, on that last Monday of the Empire's history, the mood changed. As the hour approached for the final reckoning, all quarrels and differences were forgotten. Work on the walls continued as always – though the Turks might enjoy their day of rest, there could be no respite for the defenders – but elsewhere throughout the city the people of Constantinople left their houses and gathered for one last collective intercession. As the bells pealed out from the churches, the most sacred icons and the most precious of relics were carried out to join the long, spontaneous procession of Greeks and Italians, Orthodox and Catholic alike, that wound its way through the streets and along the whole length of the walls, pausing for special prayers at every point where the damage had been particularly severe, or where the Sultan's artillery might be expected to concentrate its fire on the following day.

The procession was soon joined by the Emperor himself; and when it was finished he summoned his commanders to address them for the last time. Two versions of his speech have come down to us, one by his secretary Sphrantzes and one by Archbishop Leonard of Mitylene; and though they differ in detail and phraseology they are sufficiently similar to give us the substance of Constantine's words. He spoke first to his Greek subjects, telling them that there were four great causes for which a man should be ready to die: his faith, his country, his family and his sovereign. They must now be prepared to give their lives for all four. He for his part would willingly sacrifice his own for his faith, his city and his people. They were a great and noble people, the descendants of the heroes of ancient Greece and Rome, and he had no doubt that they would prove themselves worthy of their forefathers in the defence of their city, in which the infidel Sultan wished to seat his false prophet on the throne of Jesus Christ. Turning to the Italians, he thanked them for all that they had done and assured them of his love and trust in the dangers that lay ahead. They and the Greeks were now one people, united in God; with His help they would be victorious. Finally he walked slowly round the room, speaking to each man in turn and begging forgiveness if he had ever caused him any offence.

Dusk was falling. From all over the city, as if by instinct, the people were making their way to the church of the Holy Wisdom. For the past five months the building had been generally avoided by the Greeks, defiled as they believed it to be by the Latin usages that no pious

Byzantine could possibly accept. Now, for the first and last time, liturgical differences were forgotten. St Sophia was, as no other church could ever be, the spiritual centre of Byzantium. For eleven centuries, since the days of the son of Constantine the Great, the cathedral church of the city had stood on that spot; for over nine of those centuries the great gilded cross surmounting Justinian's vast dome had symbolized the faith of city and Empire. In this moment of supreme crisis, there could be nowhere else to go.

That last service of vespers ever to be held in the Great Church was also, surely, the most inspiring. Once again, the defenders on the walls were unable to desert their posts; but virtually every other able-bodied man, woman and child in the city crowded into St Sophia to take the Eucharist and to pray together, under the great golden mosaics that they knew so well, for their deliverance. The Patriarchal Chair was still vacant; but Orthodox bishops and priests, monks and nuns – many of whom had sworn never to cross the threshold of the building until it had been formally cleansed of the last traces of Roman pollution – were present in their hundreds. Present too was Cardinal Isidore, formerly Metropolitan of Kiev, long execrated as a renegade and traitor to his former faith, but now heard with a new respect as he dispensed the Holy Sacrament and intoned once again the old liturgies.

The service was still in progress when the Emperor arrived with his commanders. He first asked forgiveness of his sins from every bishop present, Catholic and Orthodox alike; then he too took communion with the rest. Much later, when all but the few permanent candles had been put out and the Great Church was in darkness, he returned alone and spent some time in prayer; then he returned to Blachernae for a last farewell to his household. Towards midnight, accompanied by George Sphrantzes, he rode for the last time the length of the Land Walls to assure himself that everything possible had been done for their defence. On their return, he took his faithful secretary to the top of a tower near the Palace of Blachernae, where for an hour they watched together and listened. Then he dismissed him. The two never met again.

Constantine Dragases can have had little sleep that night, for Mehmet did not wait till dawn to launch his assault. At half-past one in the morning he gave the signal. Suddenly, the silence of the night was shattered – the blasts of trumpets and the hammering of drums combining with the blood-curdling Turkish war-cries to produce a clamour fit to waken the dead. At once the church bells began to peal, a sign to the whole city that the final battle had begun. The old people and children flocked to their local churches, or down to the Golden Horn where the church of St Theodosia,[1] decked with roses, was celebrating its patron's feast-day; the men – those who were not already there – and many of the women sped to the walls, where there was work to be done.

The Sultan never underestimated his opponents. He knew that if he were to take the city he must first wear down its defenders, attacking in wave after wave, allowing them no rest. He first sent forward the *bashi-bazouks*, Christian and Muslim alike, from every corner of Europe and western Asia. His army included many thousands of these irregulars. Largely untrained and armed with whatever weapons they happened to possess, they had little staying power, but their initial onslaught could be terrifying indeed. To Mehmet they also possessed a further advantage: they were expendable, ideal for demoralizing the enemy and making it an easy victim for the more sophisticated regiments that he would send in after them. For two hours they hurled themselves against the walls, and particularly against the most strategic section across the Lycus valley; yet somehow, thanks in large measure to the heroic efforts of Giovanni Giustiniani Longo and his men, the great bastion held firm. Shortly before four in the morning, the Sultan called them back. They had failed to breach the walls, but they had served their purpose well, keeping the defenders busy and draining them of energy.

The second wave of the attack followed hot on the first. It was provided by several regiments of Anatolian Turks, all – unlike the irregulars – fully trained and superbly disciplined. Pious Muslims to a man, each was determined to win eternal rewards in Paradise by being the first to enter the greatest city of Christendom. They fought with outstanding courage and on one occasion – after one of the largest cannon had pulverized a great stretch of the wall – came within an ace of forcing an entry; but the Christians, led by the Emperor himself, closed round them, killed as many as they could and drove the rest back across the ditch. When he heard the news, the Sultan flew into his usual rage; but he was not unduly disturbed. Fine soldiers as they were, he would not have wished the laurels of battle won by the Anatolians. That honour must be kept for his own favourite regiment of Janissaries; and it was these whom he now threw into the fray.

---

1 Under its Turkish name of Gül Camii, the Mosque of the Roses, the curiously tall church of St Theodosia – now islamicized and to some extent reconstructed – still stands today. There is a legend that it was the last resting-place of Constantine XI: see p. 439.

The Christians had no time to regroup or recover themselves before this third attack began. It opened with a hail of missiles – arrows, javelins, stones, even the occasional bullet – and hardly had this ceased when, in that steady, remorseless rhythm that had long struck terror into the hearts of all who heard it, the crack troops of the Ottoman army advanced across the plain at the double, their ranks unbroken and dead straight despite all the missiles that the defenders could hurl against them. The military music that kept them in perfect step was almost a weapon in itself, so deafening that it could be heard at the furthest end of the city and even across the Bosphorus. In wave after wave they came, flinging themselves furiously against the stockades, hacking away at the supports, throwing up scaling-ladders wherever the opportunity arose and then, at a given command, making way without fuss for the following wave, while they themselves waited and rested until their turn came round again. But for the Christians on the walls there could be no such alternation. The fighting had already lasted for well over five hours, and was now frequently hand-to-hand; and although they had so far been remarkably successful in keeping the besiegers at bay they knew that they could not last much longer.

Then disaster struck. Soon after dawn a bolt from a culverin struck Giovanni Giustiniani Longo, pierced his breastplate and smashed through his chest. The wound was not mortal, but Giustiniani – who had been holding the line where the pressure was at its greatest since the fighting began – was already exhausted and unable to continue. Collapsing on the ground and obviously in excruciating pain, he refused all the Emperor's entreaties to stay at his post and insisted on being carried down to a Genoese ship lying in the harbour. Constantine's attitude to a gravely wounded man may sound unreasonable; but he was well aware of the effect that Giustiniani's departure would have on his compatriots. Before the gate leading from the walls out into the city could be relocked, the Genoese streamed through it.

The Sultan, watching closely from across the ditch, may or may not have seen Giustiniani fall; but he knew at once that something was amiss, and immediately launched yet another wave of Janissaries. They were headed by a giant named Hassan, who smashed his way through to the broken stockade and was over it before the defenders could stop him. He was killed a moment later; but by now more and more of his companions were following where he had led, and soon the Greeks were retreating back to the inner wall. Caught between the two rows of fortifications, they were easy prey to the advancing Turks and many of them were slaughtered where they stood.

At this point those Janissaries who, having reached the inner wall, were congratulating themselves on being the first into the city, saw to their astonishment a Turkish flag flying from a tower a short distance away to the north. An hour or so before, a group of about fifty Turkish irregulars on patrol had found a small door in the wall, half-hidden at the foot of the tower and insecurely bolted. It was in fact a sally-port known as the Kerkoporta, through which the commanders of that particular stretch of the wall – three Genoese brothers called Bocchiardi – had organized several effective raids on the Turkish camp. The *bashi-bazouks* had managed to force the door open, and had made their way up a narrow stair to the top of the tower. Such an action, with no army to give them support, was virtually suicidal; but in the confusion after the wounding of Giustiniani they encountered no resistance and were able soon afterwards to hoist a Turkish standard, leaving the door open for others to follow. It was almost certainly they, and not the Janissaries, who were the first of the besiegers to enter the city.

By now, however, the Turks were pouring through the open breaches. Constantine himself, having seen that the situation at the Kerkoporta was hopeless, had returned to his old post above the Lycus valley. There, with Don Francisco de Toledo – who, despite his age, had shown superb gallantry throughout the campaign – his cousin Theophilus Palaeologus and his friend John Dalmata, he fought desperately for as long as he could to hold the gate through which Giustiniani had been carried. Finally, seeing that all was lost, he flung off his imperial regalia and, still accompanied by his friends, plunged into the fray where the fighting was thickest. He was never seen again.

It was early morning, with the waning moon high in the sky. The siege of Constantinople was over. The walls were strewn with the dead and dying, but of living, able-bodied defenders there was scarcely a trace. The surviving Greeks had hurried home to their families, in a desperate attempt to save them from the rape and pillage that was already beginning; the Venetians were making for their ships, the Genoese for the comparative security of Galata. They found the Golden Horn surprisingly quiet: most of the Turkish sailors had already left their ships, terrified lest the army should get the best of the plunder. The Venetian commander, Alvise Diedo, encountered no resistance when he set his sailors to cut through the thongs attaching the boom to the walls of Galata; his little fleet, accompanied by seven Genoese vessels and half a dozen Byzantine galleys, then swung out into the Marmara and thence down the Hellespont to the open sea. All were packed to the gunwales with refugees, many of whom had swum out to them from the shore to escape the fate that awaited those who remained.

They were well-advised to do so, for that fate was horrible indeed. By noon the streets were running red with blood. Houses were ransacked, women and children raped or impaled, churches razed, icons wrenched from their golden frames, books ripped from their silver bindings. The Imperial Palace at Blachernae was left an empty shell. In the church of St Saviour in Chora the mosaics and frescos were miraculously spared, but the Empire's holiest icon, the Virgin Hodegetria, said to have been painted by St Luke himself,[1] was hacked into four pieces and destroyed. The most hideous scenes of all, however, were enacted in the church of the Holy Wisdom. Matins were already in progress when the berserk conquerors were heard approaching. Immediately the great bronze doors were closed; but the Turks soon smashed their way in. The poorer and more unattractive of the congregation were massacred on the spot; the remainder were lashed together and led off to the Turkish camps, for their captors to do with as they liked. As for the officiating priests, they continued with the Mass as long as they could before being killed at the high altar; but there are among the Orthodox faithful those who still believe that at the last moment one or two of them gathered up the most precious of the patens and chalices and mysteriously disappeared into the southern wall of the sanctuary. There they will remain until the day Constantinople becomes a Christian city once again, when they will resume the liturgy at the point at which it was interrupted.

Sultan Mehmet had promised his men the three days of looting to which by Islamic tradition they were entitled; but after an orgy of violence on such a scale, there were no protests when he brought it to a close on the same day as it had begun. There was by then little left to plunder, and his soldiers had more than enough to do sharing out the loot and enjoying their captives. He himself waited until the worst excesses were over before entering the city. Then, in the late afternoon, accompanied by his chief ministers, his imams and his bodyguard of Janissaries, he rode slowly down the principal thoroughfare, the Mesē, to St Sophia. Dismounting outside the central doors, he stooped to pick

---

1 Its normal home was the church of St Mary at Blachernae, next to the palace; but it had been transferred to a church even nearer the walls, the better to inspire the defenders.

up a handful of earth which, in a gesture of humility, he sprinkled over his turban; then he entered the Great Church. As he walked towards the altar, he stopped one of his soldiers whom he saw hacking at the marble pavement; looting, he told him, did not include the destruction of public buildings. He had in any case already decided that the church of the Holy Wisdom should be converted into the chief mosque of the city. At his command the senior imam mounted the pulpit and proclaimed the name of Allah, the All-Merciful and Compassionate: there was no God but God and Mohammed was his Prophet. The Sultan touched his turbaned head to the ground in prayer and thanksgiving.

Leaving the Great Church, he crossed the square to the old, ruined Palace of the Emperors, founded by Constantine the Great eleven and a half centuries before; and as he wandered through its ancient halls, his slippers brushing the dust from the pebbled floor-mosaics – some of which have survived to this day – he is said to have murmured the lines of a Persian poet:

> The spider weaves the curtains in the palace of the Caesars;
> The owl calls the watches in the towers of Afrasiab.[1]

He had achieved his ambition. Constantinople was his. He was just twenty-one years old.

---

1 The author is unknown.

Epilogue

The news of the conquest of Constantinople was received with horror throughout Christendom. As the refugees spread westward they carried the epic story with them; and the story lost nothing in the telling. The one point on which few could agree was the fate of the last Emperor of Byzantium. Inevitably, there were rumours that he had escaped; but the vast majority of sources – including Sphrantzes, who was his closest friend and with whom he would certainly have communicated had he survived – record with apparent certainty that he was killed during the conquest of the city. According to Cardinal Isidore, who had escaped disguised as a beggar and found his way to Crete, Constantine's body had been identified after his death and his head had been presented as a trophy to the Sultan, who had heaped insults on it and carried it back in triumph to Adrianople; and various versions of the cardinal's story were widely disseminated.

One of the most interesting accounts of the fall, written almost immediately after the events it describes, is that of a Venetian from Euboea named Nicolò Sagundino. He had been taken prisoner by the Turks after their capture of Thessalonica in 1430, and had subsequently served as interpreter at the Councils of Ferrara and Florence; later still he had represented the Serenissima on several diplomatic missions, so he should be a fairly reliable witness – though his version, like all the others, can be based only on hearsay. On 25 January 1454 in Naples, in the course of a formal oration to King Alfonso V of Aragon, he gave a detailed account of Constantine's death because, he said, it deserved to be remembered for all time. According to his account, after Giovanni Giustiniani Longo had been wounded he told the Emperor that Byzantium was lost and urged him to escape while he could; Constantine refused to hear of such a suggestion and accused him of cowardice; he himself insisted on dying in the defence of his Empire. Advancing to the breach in the wall, he found that the enemy were already through it and, determined not to be taken alive, asked his companions to kill him; but none of them had the courage to do so. Only then did he throw off everything that might have identified him as Emperor and plunge forward, sword in hand, into the mêlée. He was cut down almost at once. After the fighting was over the Sultan, who had wanted him captured alive, ordered a search to be made for the body. When it was finally found he ordered the head to be impaled on a stake and paraded round the camp. Later he had it sent, together with twenty handsome youths and twenty beautiful virgins, to the Sultan of Egypt.

There is also a story, told by a certain Makarios Melissenos, a sixteenth-century Metropolitan of Monemvasia, who compiled the extended version of the chronicle of George Sphrantzes, according to which the Turkish soldiers searching for the Emperor's body eventually recognized it by the imperial eagles engraved, or possibly embroidered, on his greaves and boots. This is slightly at variance with the reports of Constantine having divested himself of all identifiable clothing, but such clothing may have been limited to the garments he could easily dispense with; he is unlikely to have had any alternative footwear immediately available, and he could hardly have fought barefoot. Melissenos adds that the Sultan ordered that the body should be given a Christian burial, a detail suggested by no other authority; but his work dates from over a century after the conquest and must be treated with caution. Would Mehmet, one wonders, really have allowed the Emperor a tomb, or even a simple grave, which would inevitably have become a place of pilgrimage and a focus for pro-Byzantine feeling in the city?

Such considerations notwithstanding, there is still perhaps the faintest possibility that the Emperor's body – or one believed to be his – might have been concealed by the faithful and buried secretly some time afterwards. We can dismiss Melissenos's claim that it found its final resting-place in St Sophia. Nor is it true that in the nineteenth century the Ottoman government provided the oil for the last Emperor's tomb near what is now Vefa Meydani; this story – totally without foundation but zealously propagated among the tourists of the time – almost certainly originated with the proprietor of the local coffee-shop. In the extremely improbable event that such a tomb exists at all, the most likely location for it is the church of St Theodosia – now a mosque and better known as Gül Camii – where, according to an old tradition, Constantine was buried in a small chamber concealed in the south-east pier. There is indeed such a chamber there, accessible by a narrow stair that leads up inside the pier itself. Within it is a coffin, and on the lintel of the doorway is a Turkish inscription reading 'Tomb of the Apostle, Disciple of Christ – Peace be unto him'. But the tradition, old as it is, comfortably postdates the conquest; the coffin is covered, as is usual in the Islamic world, with a green cloth; and there is another equally persistent tradition among the local people that it belongs to a Muslim holy man named Gül Baba. Of all the countless stories relating the fate of Constantine XI Dragases, by far the most probable is also the simplest: that the corpse was never identified, and the last Emperor was buried anonymously with his fellow-soldiers in a common grave.

The mystery that surrounds his body is almost equalled by that which concerns his sword. There is, in the Royal Armoury of Turin, a magnificent weapon engraved with Christian symbols and bearing a Greek dedication to an Emperor Constantine. Presented to the Armoury as part of a collection by a nineteenth-century ambassador to the Sublime Porte, it was examined in 1857 by the French scholar Victor Langlois, who identified it[1] as being unquestionably the sword of Constantine, which had come from Sultan Mehmet's tomb. He does not explain, however, how the sword was extracted from the tomb, nor why there should have been another sword, said to have been presented to the Emperor by Cardinal Isidore in 1452, preserved throughout the nineteenth century in Constantinople. There was, moreover, a third sword, very similar to the other two, which was presented by the Greek community of Constantinople to Prince Constantine, heir to the Greek throne, for his coming of age in 1886. This too seems to have been considered by some to have been the Emperor's, although an Athenian newspaper of the time emphasizes that the claim cannot be proved.[2]

Thanks to his position and the dramatic circumstances in which he met his end, Constantine Dragases was the sort of man around whom legends inevitably arise, to the point where he himself becomes a legendary figure. It is right and proper that he should be so; besides, after nearly five and a half centuries, we can no longer hope to separate the man from the myth. All the historian can do is record such facts as are known, and indicate the broad areas of speculation. He can point the way to the labyrinth; but he knows that it can never be penetrated.

*

1 'Mémoire sur le sabre de Constantin XI Dracosès, dernier empereur grec de Constantinople', *Revue de l'Orient et de l'Algérie et des Colonies*, Paris 1858; also 'Notice sur le sabre de Constantin XI, dernier empereur de Constantinople, conservé à l'Armeria Reale de Turin', *Revue archéologique*, 14:1, 1857.

2 All this information – and much else – I have taken from *The Immortal Emperor*, by Professor D. M. Nicol, which gives by far the fullest account of the aftermath of the fall of Constantinople available in English.

Not all the nobility of Byzantium suffered the fate of their Emperor. The passenger-list of one of the Genoese ships that escaped from the Golden Horn on 29 May bears the names of six members of the house of Palaeologus, John and Demetrius Cantacuzenus, two Lascaris, two Comneni, two Notaras and many members of other families only slightly less distinguished. They were taken to Chios, where some of them settled; others found their way by various routes to the Morea, Corfu, the Ionian Islands or Italy, where Venice soon became the chief city of the Byzantine diaspora. For some years already it had been the home of Anna Palaeologina Notaras, daughter of the *megas dux* (or Grand Duke) Lucas Notaras, and her niece Eudocia Cantacuzena; thirty years after the fall these two ladies were the centre of a numerous Greek refugee community.

All those members of Byzantine noble families who had neither perished in the siege and its aftermath nor managed to escape to the West were brought before the Sultan on the day after the conquest. Most of the noble ladies he freed at once; only the loveliest of their daughters – and a number of their sons – did he keep for his own delectation. Among the men he found Notaras himself and nine other former ministers, all of whom he personally redeemed from their captors and released. But his benevolence did not last long. Only five days later, in the course of a banquet, it was whispered in his ear that Notaras's third son, then aged fourteen, was a boy of striking beauty. Mehmet at once ordered one of his eunuchs to fetch him from his home and, when the eunuch returned to report that the furious *megas dux* was refusing to let him go, sent a group of soldiers to arrest both father and son, together with a son-in-law, the son of the Grand Domestic Andronicus Cantacuzenus. Brought into the Sultan's presence, Notaras still stood firm, whereupon Mehmet commanded that all three should be beheaded on the spot. The *megas dux* asked only that the two boys should meet their fate first, lest the sight of his own death should weaken their resolution. A moment later, as they lay dead before him, he bared his own neck.

As for those ordinary Greeks who had escaped the massacre, the Sultan had decided that they should comprise a self-governing community within his Empire under a leader, elected by themselves, who would be responsible to him for their behaviour; and with the elimination of virtually the entire Byzantine aristocracy this leader could only be the Patriarch. The last incumbent, Gregory III, had resigned three years before and had fled to Rome. Since, however, he was a unionist this was just as well: Mehmet instinctively mistrusted any Byzantine who had links with the West. His choice now fell – wisely – on the monk Gennadius, the former George Scholarius who, having attended the Councils of Ferrara and Florence, had renounced his earlier unionist views and become leader of the pro-Orthodox party. Together with his fellow-monks, he had been sold off into slavery; but he was eventually run to earth as a menial in the household of a rich Turk of Adrianople and almost immediately appointed Patriarch. In January 1454 he was enthroned – not in St Sophia (which was now a mosque) but in the church of the Holy Apostles. His insignia of office – robe, staff and pectoral cross – being formally handed to him by the Sultan, just as former Patriarchs had received it from the *basileus*.

In this way Mehmet declared himself protector of his Greek subjects, granting them an accepted place within his Empire and guaranteeing them freedom of Christian worship. They might no longer have an Emperor; but at least they retained their Patriarch, to provide a focus not only for their religion but also for their national feelings.[1] Gennadius was to serve three separate terms in the Patriarchal Chair, during which he strove successfully to establish a *modus vivendi* with the Turkish conquerors. He made only one serious mistake: a few months after his installation he voluntarily abandoned the church of the Holy Apostles in favour of that of the Theotokos Pammakaristos, thereby giving the Sultan the excuse to demolish it, replacing it on the summit of the fourth of the city's seven hills with the present Fatih (Conqueror) Mosque.[2] The Pammakaristos remained the Patriarchal church until 1568; five years later it too became a mosque, and is now known under the name of Fethiye Camii.[3]

Not until 1601 did the Patriarchate settle in its present site in the Fener quarter on the Golden Horn. And yet, to the Orthodox faithful,

1 This act of the Sultan's set the pattern for the Greek Orthodox Church that is illustrated by such relatively recent ecclesiastics as the Archbishops Damaskinos, Regent of Greece 1945–6, and Makarios, President of Cyprus 1959–74 and 1975–7. For nearly five hundred years the Church fulfilled this dual religious and nationalistic function, and the tradition is still very much alive.

2 The church was originally erected by Constantine the Great as a burial-place for himself and his successors (see *Byzantium: The Early Centuries*, pp. 78–9). Rebuilt by Justinian, it was later restored by Basil I and decorated with a cycle of mosaics. The Fatih Mosque, with the vast complex of buildings around it, was built between 1463 and 1470, and is the earliest major Ottoman monument in the city.

3 The Pammakaristos is still well worth visiting. The early fourteenth-century *parecclesion* on the south side contains a fine series of mosaics, roughly contemporary with those of Kariye Camii and recently restored by the Byzantine Institute of America.

far more important than its precise location is the fact that the Patriarch, now the Ecumenical Patriarch of the whole Greek Church, remains firmly based in modern Istanbul. His local congregation is minute: although until the end of the Balkan War in 1913 the Greeks living within the Ottoman Empire were far more numerous – and on the whole a good deal richer – than those in the Kingdom of Greece, they have now almost all departed. Today the principal responsibility of the Patriarch of Constantinople is to minister to the Orthodox communities in Western Europe, America and Australia. For this his place of residence is something less than ideal; but its symbolic value to every Greek is immense, being as it is a constant reminder of his Byzantine heritage. Though the imperial line ended with the death of Constantine Dragases, the line of Patriarchs stretches back over sixteen hundred years, in virtually unbroken succession to the fourth century. It was in Constantinople that the Orthodox Church was born; its heart is still there today.

Western Europe, for all its deep and genuine dismay, was not profoundly changed by the fall of the Byzantine Empire. The two states most immediately affected, Venice and Genoa, lost no time in making the best terms they could with the Sultan. The Venetian relief fleet – equipped largely by Pope Nicholas – was anchored off Chios, waiting for a favourable wind to continue its journey to Constantinople, when some of the Genoese ships that had escaped from Galata drew alongside with news of the disaster. Its captain, Giacomo Loredan, promptly withdrew to Euboea until such time as he should receive further orders. Not till 3 July did Alvise Diedo and the Venetian ships from Constantinople reach the lagoons. On the day following Diedo made a full report to the Senate. Now, perhaps for the first time, the Venetians began to appreciate the full significance of what had occurred. It was not just the fall of the capital of Eastern Christendom; that may have been an emotional shock, but Byzantium had long since ceased to have any real political importance. Nor was it the annihilation of a valuable trading post, although Venice could now estimate her casualties at some 550 Venetians and Cretans, killed during or immediately after the siege, and her financial losses at 300,000 ducats. There was a third consideration more serious still than these: the fact that the victorious Sultan could henceforth undertake any new conquests that he might choose. Everything now depended on securing his good will.

On 5 July further orders were sent to Loredan and to the selected Venetian ambassador, Bartolomeo Marcello. The former was to take whatever steps he thought necessary for the protection of Euboea ensuring that any merchandise passing through it bound for Constantinople would be diverted to Modone in the Peloponnese until further notice. As for Marcello, his orders were to emphasize to Mehmet the Republic's firm intention to respect the peace treaty concluded with his father and confirmed by himself, and to request the restitution of all Venetian ships remaining in Turkish hands, pointing out that these were not warships but merchantmen. If the Sultan agreed to renew the treaty, Marcello was to ask that Venice should be allowed to maintain her trading colony in the city, with the same rights and privileges that she had enjoyed under Greek rule, and was to press for the return of all Venetians still in captivity. If he refused, or sought to impose new conditions, the ambassador should refer back to the Senate. Meanwhile he was given authority to spend up to 1,200 ducats on presents for Mehmet and his court officials, to help the negotiations along.

Marcello soon found, as many another ambassador was to find after him, that Mehmet was a hard bargainer. It was only the following spring, after the best part of a year's negotiation, that an agreement was concluded. The remaining ships and prisoners were released and the Venetian colony allowed back under a new *bailo*; Girolamo Minotto had been put to death after the siege. No longer, however, would it enjoy those territorial and commercial concessions on which its former power and prosperity had depended. For two years Marcello stayed in Constantinople, trying to persuade the Sultan to change his mind. He failed. The Latin presence in the East had already begun its decline.

The Genoese had even more at stake than the Venetians, and had continued to play their double game. In Galata, their *podestà* – equivalent to the Venetian *bailo* – had opened the gates the moment the Turks had appeared, and had done everything he could to prevent his countrymen's unseemly exodus. At the earliest opportunity he had sent two envoys to Mehmet to congratulate him on his victory and to express the hope that the conditions governing the existence of the colony should remain unchanged; but the Sultan had driven them angrily away. Two days later, a second embassy found him in a more charitable mood. The Genoese of Galata would remain inviolate and in possession of their property, and might practise their religion unhindered so long as they rang no bells and built no new churches. They were free to travel and trade by land and sea throughout the Ottoman dominions; but they must surrender their arms and destroy their Land Walls and citadel. Every

444

male citizen must pay a capitation tax; there would be no more special privileges as in the past. Galata would in future be in precisely the same position as any other Christian community which had made voluntary submission to its Turkish conquerors. Theoretically the Genoese trading colonies along the northern shore of the Black Sea – including the prosperous port of Caffa in the Crimea – would be allowed to continue; but since the death of Antonio Rizzo few sailors ventured through the straits and few merchants were prepared to pay the immense tolls demanded. With the exception of the island of Chios – which remained Genoese till 1566 – by the end of the century Genoa's commercial Empire was gone.

In Rome, Pope Nicholas showed none of the cynicism and self-interest of the merchant republics. He did his utmost to galvanize the West for a Crusade, a cause which was enthusiastically supported not only by the two Greek cardinals, Isidore and Bessarion, but also by the Papal Legate in Germany Aeneas Sylvius Piccolomini, the future Pope Pius II. But it was no use. The Western Emperor Frederick III had neither the means nor the authority to do more than write a few pious letters, France and England were exhausted after the Hundred Years' War, while Philip the Good, Duke of Burgundy – the richest prince in Europe – made an impressive outward show of zeal but failed, when the moment came, to lift a finger. Only Ladislas of Hungary longed passionately for action; but he could do nothing without allies – and least of all without John Hunyadi, with whom he was unfortunately not on speaking terms.

From the point of view of Byzantium it hardly mattered. With the Turkish army at its present strength Constantinople could not conceivably be recaptured, nor was it possible to resurrect the Empire. The time for action was past. A century before, concerted action by the powers of Western Christendom against the Ottoman threat might have saved the situation – or, at least, have postponed the inevitable. Such action, though endlessly discussed, was not taken; and while Europe dithered, Byzantium died.

Among the Christians of the East there could obviously be no question of a Crusade; they could only strive to give what help they could to their defeated brethren and to obtain what terms they could for themselves. Their ambassadors arrived thick and fast at the Sultan's court – from George Brankovich in Serbia, from the Despots Demetrius and Thomas in the Morea, from the Emperor John Comnenus of Trebizond, from the Gattilusio lord of Lesbos and Thasos, from the Grand Master of the Knights of St John. To all, Mehmet's reply was the same: he had no quarrel with them, provided only that they recognized him as their suzerain and paid him increased tribute. All agreed except the Knights; they refused to do either on the grounds that they needed papal authority, which would obviously never be given. Mehmet let them go; there would be plenty of time to deal with them later.

In fact the Knights lasted longer than any of their fellow-Christians. Mehmet eventually moved against Rhodes in 1480 but failed to capture it and died the next year; it was left to his great-grandson Süleyman the Magnificent to take the island by storm in 1520.[1] Brankovich and Hunyadi both died in 1456. The Despotate of the Morea, already torn apart by the constant squabbling of the two brothers, was finally annihilated in 1460 and in the following year, on 15 August – two hundred years to the day since Michael VIII had regained Constantinople – David Comnenus, last Emperor of Trebizond, surrendered to the Sultan the last throne of the Byzantine world. Two years later he, his older children and his nephew were executed in Constantinople; their remains were thrown to the dogs outside the walls.

The house of Palaeologus, however, lived on a little longer. The Despot Demetrius died a monk in Constantinople; his only known child, a daughter named Helena, was taken with her mother into the Sultan's harem. His brother Thomas fled to Rome, bringing with him the head of St Andrew as a present to Pope Pius II.[2] His baby sons were brought up by Cardinal Bessarion. The elder, Andrew, born in the year of the fall, proved something of a disappointment. While continuing to style himself *imperator Constantinopolitanus*, he married a Roman prostitute and died a pauper in 1502, having sold all his titles to Ferdinand and Isabella of Spain. The younger, Manuel, returned to Constantinople, where he married, had two sons – John and another Andrew (who adopted Islam) – and lived quietly on a small pension provided by the Sultan. Thomas's younger daughter Zoe-Sophia was married to Ivan III, Grand Prince of Muscovy, in 1472. As niece of the last Emperor of Constantinople she brought her husband as part of her dowry the emblem of the double-

---

1 Even this marked no more than the end of a chapter in the Knights' long history. After a few years' wandering they settled in Malta until their expulsion by Napoleon. They are now based in Rome, where they still enjoy all the privileges of an independent state, maintaining diplomatic relations with many Roman Catholic countries.

2 The presentation is depicted in relief on Pius's tomb in the church of St Andrea della Valle – better known, perhaps, as the scene of the first act of *Tosca*.

headed eagle and, it was thought, the spiritual heritage of Byzantium – thereby doing much to foster the image of Moscow as the 'Third Rome'. Ivan the Terrible was her grandson.

As we have seen, there had been Palaeologi in the Empire since at least the eleventh century, and long before the Turkish conquest there were many bearers of the name whose connections with the imperial line were so tenuous as to be virtually non-existent. After the diaspora many of them settled in the West; there were numerous Palaeologi in Italy, particularly in the three cities of Venice, Pesaro and Viterbo. Later the name came to be found in Malta, France and Cephalonia, as well as in many places within the Ottoman Empire, including Athens, Romania and the island of Syros in the Cyclades. It has even turned up in England; and it is difficult to read without a thrill of excitement the words inscribed on a brass plaque in St Leonard's church at Landulph, Cornwall, which run:

> Here lyeth the body of Theodore Paleologvs
> of Pesaro in Italye descended from ye imperyall
> lyne of ye last Christian Emperors of Greece
> being the sonne of Camilio ye sonne of Prosper
> the sonne of Theodoro the sonne of John ye
> sonne of Thomas second brother to Constantine
> Paleologvs the 8th of that name and last of
> yt line yt raygned in Constantinople untill sub
> dewed by the Tvrkes, who married with Mary
> ye daughter of William Balls of Hadlye in
> Sovffolke gent: and had issue 5 children Theo
> doro, John, Ferdinando, Maria and Dorothy, & de
> parted this life at Clyfton ye 21th of Janvary 1636.

How one would love to believe it; alas, there is no very persuasive evidence to suggest that the Despot Thomas ever had a son named John. George Sphrantzes, who took care to record the names of all the family members, mentions only the Andrew and Manuel referred to above. Interestingly enough, however, a certain Leo Allatius, admittedly writing as late as 1648, refers quite clearly to '*Andrea, Manuele et Ioanne Thomae Palaeologi Despotae filiis*'.[1] Clearly, his authority is not to be compared with that of Sphrantzes, but there remains a slender possibility that Thomas might have had a bastard son John, or even that the inscription is slightly inaccurate and that the John referred to was the

---

1 Leo Allatius, *De ecclesiae occidentalis atque orientalis perpetua consensione*, col. 956.

son of Thomas's younger son Manuel, whom we know to have existed and to have borne that name.

In either of these cases, Theodore would be the direct descendant of Manuel II Palaeologus, and it is of some interest to read[1] that he and his two uncles were convicted in Pesaro – where they were subjects of the Medici Grand Dukes – of attempted murder. Theodore was exiled and found his way to England, where he took employment as a soldier and hired assassin in the service of the Earl of Lincoln. His marriage to Mary Balls was solemnized at Cottingham in Yorkshire – perhaps to avoid the Suffolk gossips, since their first child, Theodore, was born only ten weeks later. 'The register in Exeter Cathedral', writes Professor Nicol, 'gives the date of [the elder] Theodore's burial as 20 October 1636 and not, as in the inscription, 21 January. In 1795 his grave was accidentally opened revealing an oak coffin. When the lid was lifted the body was found to be in perfect condition; and it was possible to see that Theodore Palaeologus had been a very tall man with a strong aquiline nose and a very long white beard.'

One of Theodore's sons, Ferdinand, emigrated shortly before the Civil War to Barbados, where he married a lady called Rebecca Pomfret. He died in 1678 and was buried in St John's churchyard, where a tablet carved with Doric columns and the cross of Constantine bears the inscription: 'Here lyeth ye body of Ferdinando Palaeologus, descended from ye Imperial lyne of ye last Christian Emperor of Greece. Church-warden of this parish 1655–1656. Vestryman twentye years. Died Oct 3. 1679.' His son Theodorious [sic] married Martha Bradbury of Barbados, returned with her to England, settled in Stepney and died at Corunna in 1693, leaving a posthumous daughter eccentrically named Godscall Palaeologus. What happened to her is unknown; unless and until more is discovered, this fatherless little girl in Stepney remains – given only the existence of the shadowy John Palaeologus – the last known descendant of the Emperors of Byzantium.

The Roman Empire of the East was founded by Constantine the Great on Monday, 11 May 330; it came to an end on Tuesday, 29 May 1453. During those one thousand, one hundred and twenty-three years and eighteen days, eighty-eight men and women occupied the imperial

---

1 In Professor Nicol's *The Immortal Emperor*, from which this information is taken. In his final chapter he discusses the claims not only of Theodore but of several other pretenders, providing full references. See also Patrick Leigh Fermor, *The Traveller's Tree*, pp. 145–9.

throne – excluding the seven who usurped it during the Latin occupation. Of those eighty-eight, a few – Constantine himself, Justinian, Heraclius, the two Basils, Alexius Comnenus – possessed true greatness; a few – Phocas, Michael III, Zoe and the Angeli – were contemptible; the vast majority were brave, upright, God-fearing, unimaginative men who did their best, with greater or lesser degrees of success. Byzantium may not have lived up to its highest ideals – what does? – but it certainly did not deserve the reputation which, thanks largely to Edward Gibbon, it acquired in eighteenth- and nineteenth-century England: that of an Empire constituting, 'without a single exception, the most thoroughly base and despicable form that civilization has yet assumed'.[1] So grotesque a view ignores the fact that the Byzantines were a deeply religious society in which illiteracy – at least among the middle and upper classes – was virtually unknown, and in which one Emperor after another was renowned for his scholarship; a society which had with difficulty concealed its scorn for the leaders of the Crusades, who called themselves noblemen but could hardly write their own names. It ignores, too, the immeasurable cultural debt that the Western world owes to a civilization which alone preserved much of the heritage of Greek and Latin antiquity, during these dark centuries when the lights of learning in the West were almost extinguished.

Finally, it ignores the astonishing phenomenon of Byzantine art. Narrow this art may have been in its range, restricted as it essentially was to the great mystery of the Christian faith; within this limitation, however, it achieved a degree of intensity and exaltation unparalleled before or since, qualities which entitle the masterpieces – the *deesis* in the south gallery of St Sophia, the great Pantocrator in the apse of the cathedral of Cefalù in Sicily, the *Anastasis* in the *parecclesion* of St Saviour in Chora in Constantinople – to a place among the most sublime creations of the human spirit. The instructions given to the painters and mosaicists of Byzantium were simple enough: 'to represent the spirit of God'. It was a formidable challenge, and one which Western artists seldom even attempted; again and again, however, in the churches and monasteries of the Christian East, we see the task unmistakably – indeed, triumphantly – accomplished.

One of the first and most brilliant of twentieth-century Philhellenes, Robert Byron, maintained that the greatness of Byzantium lay in what he described as 'the Triple Fusion': that of a Roman body, a Greek mind

---

1 W. E. H. Lecky, *A History of European Morals*, 1869.

and an oriental, mystical soul. Certainly these three strands were always present, and were largely responsible for the Empire's unique character: indeed, the personality of every Emperor and Empress can be seen as a subtly different combination of the three elements. For this reason as for many others, the outlook of the Byzantines was radically different from ours; at bottom, however, they were human like the rest of us, victims of the same weaknesses and subject to the same temptations, deserving of praise and of blame as we are ourselves, and in roughly equal measure. What they do not deserve is the obscurity to which for centuries we have condemned them. Their follies were many, as were their sins; but much should surely be forgiven for the heroism with which they and their last brave Emperor met their end, in one of those glorious epics of world history that has passed into legend and is remembered with equal pride by victors and vanquished alike. That is why five and a half centuries later, throughout the Greek world, Tuesday is still believed to be the unluckiest day of the week; why the Turkish flag still depicts not a crescent but a waning moon, reminding us that the moon was in its last quarter when Constantinople finally fell; and why, excepting only the Great Church of St Sophia itself, it is the Land Walls – broken, battered, but still marching from sea to sea – that stand as the city's grandest and most tragic monument.

List of Emperors

(1081–1453)

The Byzantine Emperors

1081–1118 Alexius I Comnenus	1254–1258 Theodore II Lascaris
1118–1143 John II Comnenus	1258–1261 John IV Lascaris
1143–1180 Manuel I Comnenus	1259–1282 Michael VIII Palaeologus
1180–1183 Alexius II Comnenus	1282–1328 Andronicus II Palaeologus
1183–1185 Andronicus I Comnenus	1328–1341 Andronicus III Palaeologus
1185–1195 Isaac II Angelus	1341–1391 John V Palaeologus
1195–1203 Alexius III Angelus	1347–1354 John VI Cantacuzenus
1203–1204 Isaac II Angelus *and* Alexius	1376–1379 Andronicus IV Palaeologus
IV Angelus	1390 John VII Palaeologus
1204 Alexius V Murzuphlus	1391–1425 Manuel II Palaeologus
1204–1222 Theodore I Lascaris	1425–1448 John VIII Palaeologus
1222–1254 John III Ducas Vatatzes	1449–1453 Constantine XI Palaeologus

The Latin Emperors of Constantinople

1204–1205 Baldwin I of Flanders	1221–1228 Robert of Courtenay
1206–1216 Henry of Hainault	1228–1261 Baldwin II
1217 Peter of Courtenay	(1231–1237 John of Brienne)
1217–1219 Yolanda	

The Despotate of Epirus

1204–*c*. 1215 Michael I
c.1215–1224 Theodore

Emperors, then Despots
of Thessalonica
1224–1230 Theodore
1230–*c*.1240 Manuel
c.1240–1244 John
1244–1246 Demetrius

Despots of Epirus
c.1237–1271 Michael II
1271–1296 Nicephorus
1296–1318 Thomas
1318–1323 Nicholas Orsini
1323–1355 John Orsini
1335–1340 Nicephorus II

Sebastocrators of Thessaly
1271–1296 John I
1296–1303 Constantine
1303–1318 John II

List of Muslim Sultans

The Seljuk Sultans of Rum

1077/8–1086	Süleyman I	1220–1237	Kaikubad I
1092–1107	Kilij Arslan I	1237–1245	Kaikosru II
1107–1116	Malik-Shah	1246–1257	Kaikawus II
1116–1156	Masud I	1248–1265	Kilij Arslan IV
1156–1192	Kilij Arslan II	1249–1257	Kaikubad II
1192–1196	Kaikosru I	1265–1282	Kaikosru III
1196–1204	Süleyman II	1282–1304	Masud II
1204	Kilij Arslan III	1284–1307	Kaikubad III
1204–1210	Kaikosru I	1307–1308	Masud III
1210–1220	Kaikawus I		

The Ottoman Sultans to the Fall of Constantinople

1288–1326	Othman	[1402–1410	Süleyman]
1326–1362	Orhan	[1411–1413	Musa]
1362–1389	Murad I	1421–1451	Murad II
1389–1402	Bayezit I	1451–1481	Mehmet II
1402–1421	Mehmet I		

List of Popes

(1073–1455)

(Italicized names are anti-Popes)

1073–1085	Gregory VII		1261–1264	Urban IV
1080–1100	*Clement III*		1265–1268	Clement IV
1086–1087	Victor III		1268–1271	[vacancy]
1088–1099	Urban II		1271–1276	Gregory X
1099–1118	Paschal II		1276	Innocent V
1100–1102	*Theodoric*		1276	Adrian V
1102	*Albert*		1276–1277	John XXI
1105	*Sylvester IV*		1277–1280	Nicholas III
1118–1119	Gelasius II		1281–1285	Martin IV
1118–1121	*Gregory VIII*		1285–1287	Honorius IV
1119–1124	Calixtus II		1288–1292	Nicholas IV
1124–1130	Honorius II		1294	Celestine V
1124	*Celestine II*		1294–1303	Boniface VIII
1130–1143	Innocent II		1303–1304	Benedict XI
1130–1138	Anacletus II		1305–1314	Clement V
1138	*Victor IV*		1316–1334	John XXII
1143–1144	Celestine II		*1328–1330*	*Nicholas V*
1144–1145	Lucius II		1334–1342	Benedict XII
1145–1153	Eugene III		1342–1352	Clement VI
1153–1154	Anastasius IV		1352–1362	Innocent VI
1154–1159	Adrian IV		1362–1370	Urban V
1159–1181	Alexander III		1370–1378	Gregory XI
1159–1164	*Victor IV*		1378–1389	Urban VI
1164–1168	*Paschal III*		*1378–1394*	*Clement VII*
1168–1178	*Calixtus III*		1389–1404	Boniface IX
1179–1180	*Innocent III*		*1394–1423*	*Benedict XIII*
1181–1185	Lucius III		1404–1406	Innocent VII
1185–1187	Urban III		1406–1415	Gregory XII
1187	Gregory VIII		*1409–1410*	*Alexander V*
1187–1191	Clement III		*1410–1415*	*John XXIII*
1191–1198	Celestine III		1415–1417	[vacancy]
1198–1216	Innocent III		1417–1431	Martin V
1216–1227	Honorius III		*1423–1429*	*Clement VIII*
1227–1241	Gregory IX		*1424*	*Benedict XIV*
1241	Celestine IV		1431–1447	Eugenius IV
1243–1254	Innocent IV		*1439–1449*	*Felix V*
1254–1261	Alexander IV		1447–1455	Nicholas V

Bibliography

I. Original Sources

COLLECTIONS OF SOURCES

Archivio Storico Italiano. 1st ser. Florence, various dates. (A.S.I.)

Byzantinische Zeitschrift. (B.Z.)

Byzantion. Revue Internationale des Etudes Byzantines. Paris and Liège 1924–9; Paris and Brussels 1930; Brussels etc. 1931– . (B.)

Corpus Scriptorum Historiae Byzantinae. Bonn 1828– (incomplete). (C.S.H.B.)

COUSIN, L. *Histoire de Constantinople.* Fr. trans. 8 vols. Paris 1685. (C.H.C.)

DE BOOR, C. (Ed.) *Opuscula Historica.* Leipzig 1880. (B.O.H.)

Dumbarton Oaks Papers. Cambridge, Mass. 1941– . (D.O.P.)

GUIZOT, F. *Collection des Mémoires Relatifs à l'Histoire de France.* 29 vols. Paris 1823–7. (G.M.H.F.)

HAGENMEYER, H. *Die Kreuzzugsbriefe aus den Jahren 1088–1100.* Innsbruck 1902.

MAI, Cardinal A. (Ed.) *Novae Patrum Bibliothecae.* 10 vols. Rome 1844–1905. (M.N.P.B.)

MIGNE, J. P. *Patrologia Graeca.* 161 vols. Paris 1857–66. (M.P.G.)

— *Patrologia Latina.* 221 vols. Paris 1844–55. (M.P.L.)

Monumenta Germaniae Historica. Eds. G. H. Pertz, T. Mommsen *et al.* Hanover 1826– (in progress). (M.G.H.)

MULLER, C. I. T. *Fragmenta Historicorum Graecorum.* 5 vols. Paris 1841–83. (M.F.H.G.)

MURATORI, L. A. *Rerum Italicarum Scriptores.* 25 vols. Milan 1723–51. (M.R.I.S.)

Recueil des Historiens des Croisades. Académie des Inscriptions et Belles Lettres. Paris 1841–1906.

— Historiens Grecs, 2 vols. 1875–81. (R.H.C.G.)

— Historiens Occidentaux, 5 vols. 1844–95. (R.H.C.Occ.)

Revue des Etudes Byzantines. Bucharest and Paris, 1946– . (R.E.B.)

Revue des Etudes Grecques. Paris 1888– . (R.E.G.)

Revue Historique. (R.H.)

SANSOVINO, F. *Historia universale dell' origine et imperio de' Turchi.* 3 vols. Venice 1646.

Studies in Church History. (S.C.H.)

INDIVIDUAL SOURCES

ACROPOLITES, George. *Opera*. Ed. A. Heisenberg. Leipzig 1903.

ADAM of Usk. *Chronicon*. Ed. E. M. Thompson. London 1904.

Altino Chronicle. A.S.I. Vol. 8.

ALBERT of Aix (Albertus Aquensis). *Liber Christianae Expeditionis pro Ereptione Emundatione et Restitutione Sanctae Hierosolymitanae Ecclesiae*. R.H.C.Occ., Vol. 4.

ANAGNOSTES, John. See SPHRANTZES

ANNA COMNENA. *The Alexiad*. Ed. Ducange, R.H.C.G. Vol. 1. Eng. trans. by E. A. S. Dawes, London 1928; another by E. R. A. Sewter. London 1969.

Arab Historians of the Crusades. Select. and trans. from the Arabic sources by F. Gabrieli. Eng. trans. by E. J. Costello. London 1969.

ATTALEIATES, Michael. *Historia*. C.S.H.B. Vol. 50. Partial Fr. trans. by H. Grégoire, *Byzantinische Zeitschrift*. Vol. 28 (1958) and E. Janssens. *Annuaire de l'Institut de Philologie et d'Histoire Orientales et Slaves*. Vol. 20. 1968–72.

BARBARO, N. *Giornale dell' Assedio di Costantinopoli*. Ed. E. Cornet. Vienna 1856. Eng. trans. by J. R. Jones. New York 1969.

BRYENNIUS, Nicephorus. *Histories*. C.S.H.B. Vol. 26. Fr. trans. by H. Grégoire. B. Vol. 23. 1953.

CANANUS, John. *De Constantinopoli oppugnata*. Ed. I. Bekker. C.S.H.B. 1838 (with Sphrantzes, q.v.).

CANTACUZENUS, John. *Historiae*. Ed. L. Schopen. 3 vols. C.S.H.B. 1838 (Fr. trans. in C.H.C. Vols. 7, 8. Ger. trans. by G. Fatouros and T. Krischer, Stuttgart 1982).

CHALCOCONDYLAS, Laonicus. *De origine ac rebus gestis Turcorum*. C.S.H.B.

Chronicle of the Morea. Fr. version by J. Longnon. *Livre de la Conqueste de la Princée de l'Amorée*. Paris 1911.

CINNAMUS, John. *Epitome Historiarum*. C.S.H.B. Eng. trans. by C. M. Brand. New York 1976.

CLAVIJO, Ruy González de. *Embajada a Tamorlan*. Ed. F. López Estrada. Madrid 1943. Eng. trans. by G. Le Strange. London 1928.

CYDONES, Demetrius. *Letters*. Ed. with Fr. trans. by G. Cammelli. *Démétrius Cydonès, Correspondance*. Paris 1930.

DUCAS, Michael(?). *Historia Turco-Byzantina*. C.S.H.B. New edn ed. V. Grecu. Bucharest 1948.

EUSTATHIUS of Thessalonica. *De Thessalonica a Latinis capta, a. 1185*. Ed. I. Bekker. C.S.H.B. German trans. by H. Hunger. Vienna 1955.

GLYCAS, M. *Chronicon*. Ed. I. Bekker. C.S.H.B.

GREGORAS, Nicephorus. *Byzantina Historia*. Ed. L. Schopen and I. Bekker. In C.S.H.B. Ger. trans. by J. L. van Dieten. *Nikephoros Gregoras, Rhomäische Geschichte*, 3 vols. Stuttgart 1973–88.

— *Letters*. See Guilland, R.

GREGORY of Cyprus. *Laudatio*. M.P.G. Vol. 142.

IBN AL-ATHIR. *Sum of World History* (selection, with Fr. trans.) in R.H.C.Occ. Vol. 1.

IBN JUBAIR. *The Travels of Ibn Jubair*. Trans. R. J. C. Broadhurst. London 1952.

IGNATIUS of Smolensk. *Pélérinage d'Ignace de Smolensk*. Ed. G. P. Majeska, *Russian Travelers to Constantinople in the 14th & 15th C*, Washington, DC 1984.

LEONARD of Chios, Archbishop of Mitylene. *Epistola ad Papam Nicolaum V*. M.P.G. Vol. 159. 1866 (Italian version in Sansovino, *Historia Universale*, III).

Liber Pontificalis. De Gestis Romanorum Pontificum. Text, intro. and comm. by L. Duchesne. 2 vols. Paris 1886–92. (Reprint, Paris 1955.)

MALATERRA, Geoffrey. *Historia Sicula*. M.P.L. Vol. 149. M.R.I.S. Vol. 5.

MATTHEW of Edessa. *Chronicle*. Fr. trans. by E. Delaurier. Paris 1858.

MICHAEL the Syrian (Patriarch). *Chronicle*. Ed. with Fr. trans. by J. B. Chabot. Paris 1905–6.

MOUSKES, Philip, *Chronique rimée de Philippe Mouskès*. Ed. F. A. de Reiffenberg. *Collection de Chroniques Belges inédites*. II. Brussels 1838.

MUNTANER, Ramón. *Crónica*. Barcelona 1886. (Eng. trans. by Lady Goodenough in Hakluyt Society edition, London 1920.)

NICETAS CHONIATES. *Historia*. C.S.H.B. (Fr. trans. in C.H.C.)

ORDERICUS VITALIS. *Historia Ecclesiastica*. (Ed. A. Le Prevost and L. Delisle.) In *Société de l'Histoire de France*. 5 vols. Paris 1838–55. Eng. trans. with notes by T. Forester. 4 vols. London 1854.

OTTO of Freising. *Chronica, sive Historia de Duabus Civitatibus*. M.G.H. *Scriptores*. Vol. 20. Eng. trans. by C. C. Mierow. New York 1953.

— *Gesta Friderici Imperatoris, cum continuatione Rahewini*. Ed. Wilmans. M.G.H. *Scriptores*. Vol. 20. Eng. trans. by C. C. Mierow. New York 1953.

PACHYMERES, George. *De Michaele et Andronico Palaeologis*. 2 vols. Ed. I. Bekker. C.S.H.B. (French trans. in C.H.C., Vol.6.)

— *Georges Pachymérès: Relations historiques*. Ed. A. Failler. Vol. 1 (with Fr. trans. by V. Laurent). Paris 1984.

PRODROMUS, Theodore. *Poemata*. Selections in M.P.G. Vol. 133. R.H.C.G. Vol.2.

PSELLUS, Michael. *Chronographia*. Eng. trans. by E. R. A. Sewter. London 1953. Fr. trans. by E. Renauld. 2 vols. Paris 1926.

ROBERT of Clary. *La Conquête de Constantinople*. Ed. Lauer. Paris 1924.

ROGER of Hoveden. *Annals*. Eng. trans. by H. T. Riley. London 1853.

SANUDO, Marino. *Istoria del regno di Romania*. Ed. C. Hopf. In *Chroniques gréco-romanes*. Berlin 1873.

SPHRANTZES, George. *Chronicon Maius*. Ed I. Bekker. C.S.H.B. (includes Anagnostes).

STEPHEN, Count of Blois. Letters Nos. IV and X, in Hagenmeyer, *Die Kreuzzugsbriefe*.

SYROPULUS, Silvester. *Memoirs*. Ed. R. Creyghton, *Vera historia unionis non verae inter Graecos et Latinos*. The Hague 1660. (See also Laurent, V. below.)

THEOPHYLACT, Archbishop of Ochrid. *Letters*. M.P.G. Vol. 126.

VILLEHARDOUIN, Geoffrey of, *La Conquête de Constantinople*. Ed. E. Faral. 2 vols. Paris 1938–9.

WILLIAM of Tyre. *Belli Sacri Historia* and *Historia Rerum in Partibus Transmarinis Gestarum*. R.H.C.Occ. Vol.1. Also with French trans. G.M.H.F. Vols. 16–18.

ZONARAS, Joannes. *Annales*. Ed. L. Dindorf. 6 vols. Leipzig 1868–75. Also in M.P.G., Vols. 134–5.

II. Modern Works

AHRWEILER, H. *L'Expérience Nicéenne*. D.O.P. Vol. xxix. (1975) pp. 23–40.

ANGOLD, M. *The Byzantine Empire, 1025–1204: A Political History*. London 1984.

— *A Byzantine Government in Exile*. Oxford 1975.

BARKER, J. W. *Manuel II Palaeologus (1391–1425): A Study in Late Byzantine Statesmanship*. New Brunswick, N.J. 1969.

BERGER de XIVREY, J. *Mémoire sur la Vie et les Ouvrages de l'Empereur Manuel Paléologue*. Paris 1853.

BERTELÈ, T. 'I gioielli della corona byzantina dati in pegno alla repubblica bveneta nel sec. XIV e Mastino della Scalla'. In *Studi in Onore di A. Fanfani, II: Medioevo*. Milan 1962, pp. 90–177.

BIBICOU, H. *Une Page d'Histoire Diplomatique de Byzance au XIe. Siècle: Michel VII Doukas, Robert Guiscard et la pension des dignitaires*. B. Vols. 29–30. 1959/60.

The Blue Guide to Istanbul. Ed. J. Freely. 2nd edn. London and New York 1987.

The Blue Guide to Turkey (The Aegean and Mediterranean Coasts). Ed. B. McDonagh. London and New York 1989.

BRÉHIER, L. *Le Monde Byzantin, I: Vie et Mort de Byzance*. Paris 1947.

BUCKLER, G. *Anna Comnena*. London 1929.

BURY, J. B. *History of the Later Roman Empire*. 2 vols. London 1889.

— *History of the Eastern Roman Empire*. London 1912.

— *The Roman Emperors from Basil II to Isaac Komnenos*. *English Historical Review*. Vol. 4. 1889.

CAHEN, C. 'Notes sur l'histoire des croisades et de l'orient latin'. *Bulletin de la Faculté des Lettres de l'Université de Strasbourg*. Vol. 29. 1950–51.

— *Pre-Ottoman Turkey*. Trans. J. Jones-Williams. New York 1968.

Cambridge Medieval History. Esp. Vol. 4 (in two vols.). *The Byzantine Empire, 717–1453*. New edn, ed. J. M. Hussey. Cambridge 1966–7.

CHALANDON, F. *Les Comnène: Etudes sur l'Empire Byzantin aux XIe and XIIe Siècles.* Vol. 1: *Essai sur le Règne d'Alexis Ier Comnène.* Paris 1900. Vol. 2: *Jean II Comnène et Manuel Comnène.* Paris 1913. (Both volumes reproduced New York 1960.)

— *Histoire de la Première Croisade.* Paris 1925.

CHAPMAN, C. *Michel Paléologue, restaurateur de l'empire byzantin (1261–1282).* Paris 1926.

COBHAM, C. D. *The Patriarchs of Constantinople.* Cambridge 1911.

DÉCARREAUX, J. 'L'arrivée des Grecs en Italie pour le Concile de l'Union, d'après les Mémoires de Syropoulos'. *Revue des études italiennes* 7. 1960. pp. 27–58.

Dictionnaire d'Histoire et de Géographie Ecclésiastiques. Eds. A. Baudrillart, R. Aubert *et al.* Paris 1912– (in progress).

Dictionnaire de Théologie Catholique. 15 vols. in 30. Paris 1909–50 (with supplements).

DIEHL, C. *Etudes Byzantines.* Paris 1905.

— *Figures Byzantines.* 1st ser. Paris 1906; 2nd ser., Paris 1913. ·

— *Histoire de l'Empire Byzantin.* Paris 1918.

— *Choses et Gens de Byzance.* Paris 1926.

EBERSOLT, J. *Le Grand Palais de Constantinople et le Livre des Cérémonies.* Paris 1910.

Enciclopedia Italiana. 36 vols. Rome 1929–39 (with later appendices).

Encyclopaedia Britannica. 11th edn. 29 vols. Cambridge 1910–11.

— 15th edn. 30 vols. Chicago 1974.

Encyclopaedia of Islam. 4 vols. Leiden, London 1913–34. (New edn in progress, 1960–).

FINLAY, G. *History of the Byzantine and Greek Empires from 716 to 1453.* Vol. 2. London 1854.

FLICHE, A. and MARTIN, V. *Histoire de l'Eglise, depuis les Origines jusqu'à nos Jours.* Paris 1934.

FRENCH, R. M. *The Eastern Orthodox Church.* London and New York 1951.

GAY, J. *Le Pape Clément VI et les affaires d'Orient (1342–1352).* Paris 1904.

GEANAKOPLOS, D. J. *Emperor Michael Palaeologus and the West, 1258–1282: A Study in Byzantine–Latin Relations.* Cambridge, Mass. 1959.

GIBBON, E. *The History of the Decline and Fall of the Roman Empire.* 7 vols. Ed. J. B. Bury. London 1896.

GILL, J. *The Council of Florence.* Cambridge 1959.

— *John VIII Palaeologus: A Character Study.* Originally published in *Studi byzantini e neoellenici*, Vol. 9. 1957. Reprinted in author's collection, *Personalities of the Council of Florence, and Other Essays*, New York 1964.

GODFREY, J. *The Unholy Crusade.* Oxford 1980.

GRUMEL, V. *La Chronologie.* Vol. 1 of *Traité des Etudes Byzantines*, ed. P. Lemerie. Paris 1958.

GUILLAND, R. *Correspondance de Nicéphore Grégoras.* Paris 1927.

GUIRAUD, J. *Les registres de Grégoire X*. Paris 1892–1906.

HAUSSIG, H. W. *History of Byzantine Civilisation*. Trans. J. M. Hussey. London 1971.

HEYD, W. *Geschichte des Levantehandels im Mittelalter*. Stuttgart 1879. (Fr. trans. by F. Raynaud, *Histoire du commerce du Levant au moyen âge*, 2 vols. Leipzig 1936.)

HITTI, P. K. *History of the Arabs*. 3rd edn. New York 1951.

HOOKHAM, H. *Tamburlaine the Conqueror*. London 1962.

JANIN, R. *Constantinople Byzantine*. Paris 1950.

JENKINS, R. *The Byzantine Empire on the Eve of the Crusades*. London 1953.

KEEGAN, J. *A History of Warfare*. London 1993.

KINROSS, Lord. *The Ottoman Centuries*. London 1977.

KNOLLES, R. *Turkish History*. 3 vols. London 1687–1700.

LAURENT, V. Les *'Mémoires' du grand ecclésiarque de l'Église de Constantinople Sylvestre Syropoulos sur le Concile de Florence (1438–1439)*. Rome 1971.

LOENERTZ, R. J. *Jean V Paléologue à Venise (1370–71)*. R.E.B. Vol. 16. 1958.

— *Byzantina et Franco-Graeca (Articles parus de 1935 à 1966, réédités avec la collaboration de Peter Schreiner)* [Storia e Letteratura: Raccolta di Studi e Testi 118]. Rome 1970.

LOWE, A. *The Catalan Vengeance*. London 1972.

MAGDALINO, P. *The Empire of Manuel I Komnenos, 1143–1180*. Cambridge 1993.

MANGO, C. *The Mosaics of St Sophia at Istanbul*. Washington (Dumbarton Oaks) 1962.

MANN, H. K. *The Lives of the Popes in the Middle Ages*. 18 vols. London 1902–32.

MANZANO, R. *Los Grandes Capitanes Españoles*. Barcelona 1960.

MILLER, W. *The Latins in the Levant: A History of Frankish Greece, 1204–1566*. London 1908.

— *Essays on the Latin Orient*. Cambridge 1921.

NEANDER, A. *General History of the Christian Religion and Church*. 9 vols. Eng. trans. London 1876.

New Catholic Encyclopedia. Washington, DC 1967.

NICOL, D. M. *The Despotate of Epirus*. Oxford 1957.

— *The Byzantine Family of Kantakouzenos (Cantacuzenus) ca. 1100–1460. A genealogical and prosopographical study*. Dumbarton Oaks Studies, 11. Washington, DC 1968.

— 'The Byzantine Reaction to the Second Council of Lyons, 1274'. S.C.H. Vol. 7. 1971.

— *The Last Centuries of Byzantium, 1261–1453*. London 1972.

— *The Immortal Emperor*. Cambridge 1992.

NORWICH, J. J. *The Normans in the South*. London 1967.

— *The Kingdom in the Sun*. London 1970.

(The above two volumes published in one, under the title *The Normans in Sicily*, London 1992.)

— *A History of Venice: Vol. I, The Rise to Empire*. London 1977.

— *A History of Venice: Vol. II, The Greatness and the Fall*. London 1981.

(The above two volumes published in one, under the title *A History of Venice*, London 1982.)

— *Byzantium: The Early Centuries (330–800)*. London 1988.

— *Byzantium: The Apogee (800–1081)*. London 1991.

OBOLENSKY, D. *The Byzantine Commonwealth*. London 1971.

— *The Bogomils*. Oxford 1948.

OCKLEY, S. *History of the Saracens*. 4th edn. London 1847.

OSTROGORSKY, G. *History of the Byzantine State*. Trans. J. M. Hussey. 2nd edn. Oxford 1968.

Oxford Dictionary of Byzantium. Ed. A. P. Kazhdan *et al.* 3 vols. Oxford and New York 1991.

RAMSAY, Sir William. *The Historical Geography of Asia Minor*. Royal Geographical Society, Supplementary Papers. Vol. 4. London 1890.

ROWE, J. G. *Paschal II, Bohemund of Antioch and the Byzantine Empire*. Bulletin of the John Rylands Library. Vol. 49 (1966–7), pp. 165–202.

RUNCIMAN, Sir Steven. *A History of the Crusades*. 3 vols. Cambridge 1954.

— *The Medieval Manichee*. Cambridge 1946.

— *The Sicilian Vespers*. Cambridge 1958.

— *The Great Church in Captivity*. Cambridge 1968.

— *Mistra: Byzantine Capital of the Peloponnese*. London 1980.

SCHLUMBERGER, G. *Expédition des Almugavares ou routiers catalans en orient de l'an 1302 à l'an 1311*. Paris 1902.

— *Un Empereur de Byzance à Paris et Londres*. In *Byzance et les Croisades: Pages médiévales*. Paris 1927.

— *Le siège, la prise et le sac de Constantinople en 1453*. Paris 1926.

SETTON, K. M. (Editor-in-chief). *A History of the Crusades*. 2 vols. University of Wisconsin Press, Madison, Milwaukee and London 1969.

— *Catalan Domination of Athens, 1311–1388*. Cambridge, Mass. 1948.

SKOULATOS, B. *Les Personages Byzantins de l'Alexiade*. Louvain 1980.

SMITH, W. and WACE, H. *Dictionary of Christian Biography*. 4 vols. London 1877–87.

TAYLOR, J. *Imperial Istanbul: Iznik – Bursa – Edirne*. London 1989.

TEMPERLEY, H. W. V. *History of Serbia*. London 1919.

VASILIEV, A. A. *History of the Byzantine Empire, 324–1453*. Madison, Wisconsin 1952.

— *Manuel Comnenus and Henry Plantagenet*. B.Z. Vol.29. 1929–30. pp. 238–44.

VRYONIS, S. *Byzantium and Europe*. London 1967.

— *The Decline of Medieval Hellenism in Asia Minor and the Process of Islamization from the Seventh through the Fifteenth Century*. Los Angeles 1971.

WEST, Rebecca. *Black Lamb and Grey Falcon*. 2 vols. London 1944.

ZAKYNTHOS, D. *Le Despotat grec de Morée, 1262–1460*. Vol. 1. Paris 1932.

ZIEGLER, P. *The Black Death*. London 1969.

Index